WHAT THE PAPERS SAID

'Love him or hate him, the Kerry Packer story is the stuff of a television mini-series.'

Sunday Mail, Brisbane

'An armchair psychologist's feast.'

Good Weekend magazine

'Reporter Paul Barry comes to this book with no mean reputation. He pulled no punches in a biography of Alan Bond, nor does he hold any in this account of Packer . . . His thorough account of an enduring dynasty paints a picture of how individuals can have the levers of power pulled to suit their interests.'

The Courier Mail, Brisbane

'*The Rise and Rise* is a riveting read. It is a brilliant synthesis of all that is known and has been published about Kerry Packer and his family . . . a tribute to Barry's wide and deep journalistic skills.'

The Advertiser, Adelaide

'It is distinguished . . . by its effortless grasp of the material, its judicious choice of anecdote and detail, and its wry apprehension of the way the world works . . . a readable, professional narrative of a large man and his sprawling times.'

The Age, Melbourne

'Paul Barry's totally unauthorised biography of K. F. B. Packer is a detailed, fair, absorbing and generally comprehensive account of the life of a significant Australian to the age of 55.'

The Sydney Morning Herald

'Few have the brute strength, wealth and force of character to match the media baron portrayed in Paul Barry's engrossing *The Rise and Rise of Kerry Packer*'

Sunday Mail, Brisbane

T0363014

'The ABC journalist in his *The Rise and Rise of Kerry Packer* has taken a knife and cut through the layers of insulation Packer has built up around himself over the years.'

WHAT THE JUDGES SAID

'A well-written and extremely readable account of the career of one of Australia's leading media and business magnates, *The Rise and Rise of Kerry Packer* combines the highest standards of investigative journalism with admirable professional balance and a refusal to be intimidated by perceptions of power.'

Suzanne Falkiner and Roger Milliss, judges of the 1994 C.U.B. Banjo Award for Non-fiction.

THE RISE AND RISE OF KERRY PACKER

UNCUT

PAUL BARRY

BANTAM

SYDNEY AUCKLAND TORONTO NEW YORK LONDON

A Bantam book
Published by Random House Australia Pty Ltd
Level 3, 100 Pacific Highway, North Sydney NSW 2060
www.randomhouse.com.au

First published in hardback in Australia and New Zealand in 1993 by Bantam
in association with ABC Books for the Australian Broadcasting Corporation,
700 Harris Street, Ultimo, NSW 2007
This edition first published in Australia and New Zealand in 2007 by Bantam
This paperback edition published in Australia and New Zealand in 2008 by Bantam

Addresses for companies within the Random House Group can be found at
www.randomhouse.com.au/offices

National Library of Australia
Cataloguing-in-Publication Entry

Barry, Paul, 1952–.
Rise & rise of Kerry Packer uncut.

ISBN 978 1 86325 606 3 (pbk.)

Packer, Kerry, 1937–2005
Packer family.
Broadcasting – Australia.
Mass media – Australia.
Publishers and publishing – Australia – Biography.
Millionaires – Australia – Biography.

070.5092

Typeset by Midland Typesetters, Australia
Printed and bound by Griffin Press

CONTENTS

CONTENTS

For Jane, Alex, Amy and Josh,
Lisa, Leo, Lottie and Daniel

AUTHOR'S NOTE

A few days before this book was published in 1993 my then wife phoned me at work. She was in tears. A death threat had been left on the answering machine at home, telling me I was 'dead meat, burger meat at best' and I would know why. I had already been warned that writing about Kerry Packer might not be the safest thing to do. He was rich, he was powerful, he was intimidating, he had scared off other biographers with the threat of legal action. He might also be dangerous.

As it turned out, the threat was a hoax. Fortunately, Australia is not a country where the rich and famous have their critics rubbed out. But writing books about people like Packer is not without its risks: the main one being that you will spend the rest of your life in court, defending yourself against a defamation action that could cost hundreds of thousands of dollars in legal fees and damages. Billionaires like Packer can afford to sue without worrying whether their case is strong enough to win. They can do it just to punish you. And even in 1993 Kerry had a history of suing journalists personally, to teach them a lesson.

Kerry Packer did threaten to sue me while I was writing this book and his threats were particularly unpleasant. When I wrote to him early in the research to ask whether he would talk to me (he declined), his minions left me in no doubt that I would be taking my life in my hands if I didn't back off. I received a letter telling me bluntly:

> Mr Packer does not look upon your project favourably and I am instructed to inform you that, should it be completed, your book will be reviewed by our attornies [sic] and, while we reserve all our

rights, any false statement, untrue statement, misquotation, innuendo or any other material contained in the book which is misleading, whether deliberately so or not, and which may or is calculated to produce in the mind of the reader, an unfair or biased view or otherwise derogate in any manner from the good reputation which Mr Packer and the members of his family and the group of companies which he controls enjoy will be prosecuted with the utmost vigour . . .

. . . Any action we may take could comprehend not only yourself and Transworld Publishers but any other person who has any involvement whatsoever in the production of the book and the provision of information to you. You should place such persons on notice of the contents of this letter.

My publishers and I did not go belly up in the face of this bullying, but we did take the warning seriously. We were extremely careful to ensure that everything in the book was meticulously documented, factually correct and defensible in court. We also took a decision to leave some stories out.

This new version of the book is called *The Rise and Rise of Kerry Packer—Uncut* because it is just that. Some of the material that had to be left out for legal reasons in 1993 is now in. In particular, there is a whole new chapter that tells the story of one of Kerry's mistresses, Carol Lopes, who committed suicide in 1991. I have dealt with her story at length—while glossing over most of his extramarital affairs—because Ms Lopes performed services for Mr Packer that went far beyond the boudoir. Essentially, she acted as his madam, procuring women for him and his mates. She also ran a private bordello for him in Palm Beach during the Christmas holidays to which some of Packer's political, sporting and business acquaintances were invited.

I do not know what favours were repaid to or expected by Packer from the powerful people who took advantage of his 'hospitality'. But I am sure he received something in return, even if it was only a hearing. Politicians and businesspeople, of course, had the power to make Packer money by getting decisions to run his way.

Consequently, I make no apology for publishing this story after his death. Carol Lopes's relationship with Kerry was clearly not just a private and personal matter between the two of them. It was, and remains, a matter of legitimate public interest.

I also make no apology for not publishing the story back in 1993. Given the threats of legal action we had received from Packer, and given his record of suing journalists at the ABC and *The Sydney Morning Herald*, it would have been reckless to do so. It would have undoubtedly put the entire book in jeopardy, so that the Kerry Packer story might not have been told at all.

Now at last it can be, complete and uncut.

Paul Barry, May 2007

DEAD LUCKY

*I've been to the other side, and let me tell you, son, there's
fucking nothing there.*

Kerry Packer, October 1990

It is semi-finals day of the Australian Open Polo Championships
at Warwick Farm on the outskirts of Sydney. The date is
7 October 1990, and it is one of those mild spring days when it
feels good to be alive. About 1000 people have gathered to see
Kerry Packer's elite Ellerston White team make off with the title.
The players have come on to the field, warmed up and cantered
around, knocking the ball about with their sticks to get their eye
in. The match has been going for barely two minutes and Kerry
Packer has not yet touched the ball.

Now he canters behind his own goal line, wheels round,
knocks the ball upfield and chases after it to get play restarted. As
he lollops up the pitch to take a second swing, he slumps forward
on his horse. His polo pony, immaculately trained, does just what
it should now that its rider is giving it no signals: it pulls up and
stands stock still in the middle of the pitch. Kerry is lying forward
over the pony's neck, his arms hanging down either side, like a
cavalryman who has been shot by the Indians.

Kerry's son Jamie is the first to reach him, running to his
father's motionless horse from his station as goal umpire only
metres away. A handful of men from the Ellerston contingent are
not far behind. From the end of the ground an ambulance
appears, bumping gently across the grass. As Jamie and the others

arrive and various officials amble across to see what is going on, Packer is pulled off his horse and laid out flat on the ground, a huge man. He does not appear to be breathing, but he may just be winded.

The crowd has no reason to believe that there is anything to worry about. If there's a hush around the ground, it is because people are puzzled. An off-duty ambulanceman with a liking for polo is also in no hurry to get to the small knot of people near the far goal. He is walking across out of curiosity to see if he can help. When he gets close enough for a proper view he knows immediately that Packer has had a heart attack. His presence on the scene is Kerry's first vital stroke of luck. The two junior officers who make up the ambulance team have not diagnosed his condition. They do not realise he is dead.

Within moments it becomes clear to everyone what is at stake. The ambulancemen work desperately to get the heart beating again. One pounds Packer's chest, giving him cardiac massage to make the heart pump. The other holds a mask over his face, with an attachment like a football bladder, to get oxygen into his lungs for the heart to push round the body. But it all appears to be in vain. The heart is quivering but not beating properly. The only thing that will shock it back into rhythm is a defibrillator, or heart-starter, but only one in twenty ambulances in New South Wales carries them, and this ambulance is in the wrong nineteen.

Already the minutes are ticking away and Packer is lying there lifeless. He's not breathing. His heart has stopped. One of the ambos appears to have written him off. In cases of cardiac arrest you have six minutes maximum to get the heart beating again before permanent brain damage becomes almost inevitable. That means the defibrillator needs to arrive in four. They have put out a call for an intensive-care ambulance, but it looks as if the richest man in Australia has just passed the crown to his son.

Onlookers are struck by the fact that Jamie is wearing the mantle well. He has taken control, is giving the orders, and appears calm and collected, whatever he is thinking. The Ellerston contingent is waiting for him to tell them what to do. The young man wants mobile phones; he's yelling for the chopper pilot. Where is the pilot for Kerry's personal helicopter? They put a call out over the PA, as if he could have missed the commotion. They get a mobile phone from one of the cars, then find another when that doesn't work. Jamie is talking to St Vincent's hospital, trying to raise Victor Chang, Australia's top heart surgeon, or Bob Wright, Kerry's personal doctor. It's as if the emergency has been planned for, as if they had expected it to happen. But then this is not the Big Fella's first brush with death.

The ambulance team is still trying hard to revive him. They have put out another call for reinforcements, this time with greater urgency. They are still blowing oxygen into his lungs, then pounding his chest to get the heart pumping blood round his body. They desperately need to get oxygen to his brain. The crowd is keeping its distance; people don't rush forward. It is too ghoulish to push and shove to watch the Big Fella die.

Suddenly there's the sound of a siren. Moments later an ambulance drives through the gates. It is an incredible stroke of fortune, a genuine one-thousand-to-one chance that it should be so close, for this is an intensive-care ambulance, complete with heart-starter and highly trained paramedics. On Sundays there are just twelve on duty for the whole of Sydney and surrounding areas—one-third of New South Wales—yet this one was passing by, on its way back to base after answering a call. It could have easily been busy or half an hour away. Kerry Packer, who loses millions at the races, has had his second life-giving piece of luck.

The first emergency call has not even mentioned cardiac arrest: the message from central control is that someone is unconscious on a horse at Warwick Farm. The second call has sounded more urgent. This time the radio operator has got the details right and asked how fast the paramedics can be there. The driver tells him the ambulance is just passing through the gates. It has taken just three minutes to arrive.

Now the race is on to save Packer, who is lying there with his shirt off. Like a beached whale is the cliché that bystanders recall.

Swiftly, expertly, one paramedic feeds a tube into his lungs to pump in pure oxygen. Then he searches for a vein to give a shot of adrenalin that will stimulate the heart. He can't find one in the arm because it is too flabby so he settles for the jugular instead. By this time the Life Pak 15 is lined up alongside. It takes only seconds to charge up the paddles, smear them with gel, and place them briefly on his chest. The crowd is told to stand back and the button is pressed, delivering an electric shock that jolts the whale into the air and back onto the ground.

Packer looks horrible. He looks like he has gone. He has turned a pale bluey-grey and he's still not breathing. But the defibrillator has shocked his heart out of its reverie. Barely a minute later, the paramedic calls out that he has a heartbeat. Two minutes after that, he announces that Packer has a pulse. It has been six or seven minutes since the ambulance was called, perhaps eight or nine since Kerry collapsed. Eight or nine minutes in which he has, to all intents and purposes, been dead.

In the panic of the moment, Jamie wants his father taken in the helicopter straight to St Vincent's. The senior paramedic, Stan James overrules him: 'If he goes to St Vincent's in that helicopter he'll be dead before he gets there. He's coming with us to Liverpool.'

'By the way,' he now inquires, so that they know where to send the bill, 'have we got a name for this one?' An embarrassed silence falls on the crowd. It seems ridiculous that they don't know who they're dealing with. 'Mr Packer,' someone calls out helpfully, but still it doesn't strike home. 'Packer who?' the paramedic asks. This time there is a ripple of laughter and several people chorus that it's Kerry Packer, you know, the richest man in Australia. 'Oh, yes,' says Stan. 'I've seen him on television.'

As the ambulances depart, sirens blaring, the choppers arrive, pulsing out of the sky. It is like *Apocalypse Now*, only they're shooting film, not bullets. Like crows to carrion, the TV crews have come to pick up the news. Soon afterwards comes Packer's personal doctor, also delivered by helicopter.

Meanwhile the ambulance is on its way to nearby Liverpool Hospital. As it weaves through the traffic, red lights flashing, one of the paramedics leans over the stretcher and tries a standard test for assessing consciousness. 'Open eyes,' he says, 'open eyes.' He gets more than he bargains for. Packer's eyes go wide in response, then he tries to tear the tube out of his lungs and has to be physically restrained.

At Liverpool, Packer is stabilised and sedated. Now unconscious again, he is rushed across the city. By six o'clock he is in intensive care at St Vincent's Hospital in central Sydney. In a facility that normally takes six, he is the only patient. His medical minder Bob Wright, the head of intensive care, already has a team of cardiologists on the case: Packer is a huge donor to the hospital and there are several hundred thousand extra reasons for keeping him alive. Victor Chang, Australia's leading heart surgeon, is also on his way to Packer's bedside, recalled from a business trip to Japan. The word to the outside world is that Packer is in a coma; it seems to be touch and go whether he will live, and the odds are against him making a full recovery. Another top tycoon, Robert Holmes à Court, has dropped dead from a heart attack only five weeks earlier, and Packer is bigger, fatter, seemingly less healthy.

If Packer doesn't recover, it will not just be his relatives who mourn. The institutions who have just pumped millions of dollars into Packer's Channel Nine on the promise that the Big Fella will stay at the helm for the next two years will be sorry, too.

But there is a legend in the making. It takes more than death to stop this man. By next morning, Packer is off the life-support machine and shaking hands with his doctors; soon after, he's sitting up in bed taking phone calls; the next day, he's up and about. Trevor Kennedy, his managing director, goes in to visit him and says he will be back in the office the following week. And this is not just bravado. By Tuesday, Packer is out of intensive care and installed on the tenth floor of St Vincent's private wing. By Friday he has discharged himself, telling people he's not going to lie there and get weaker. The next day, Saturday, he's back at Warwick Farm again, where it all happened the previous weekend, watching the polo.

The TV crews naturally want to get pictures of the man. So do photographers from the daily papers. Not only is he the richest man in Australia and one of the most powerful, he's risen from the grave. He doesn't need to do this much to be news. The cameramen approach him as he sits in his white BMW to ask him how he's feeling. Packer's minders keep the press at bay and the car drives off. But Packer's anger is roused, and before it has gone twenty metres he orders the car to stop. The passenger door opens and Kerry comes almost running out. He looms up to one cameraman with all the subtlety of a nightclub bouncer moving in for the action. 'I'll tell you how I'm feeling. Leave me alone, get out of my way.' A huge face and hand fill the lens and the picture goes spinning.

The television footage is unforgettable. Last time the world saw Kerry Packer he was on a stretcher, huge, pale, unconscious, and apparently dead or a vegetable, with a forest of tubes protruding out of him: now he's charging out of the television screen like a mad wounded animal. He seems vast, superhuman, angry and unstoppable.

Another cameraman has filmed it all. Packer grabs his camera and rips out the film. One of Packer's minders punches the cameraman twice, knocking him to the ground. He gets up dizzily and threatens to call the police. Go ahead, they say. Packer has made his money from newspapers, television and magazines. His editors pay thousands of dollars for paparazzi pictures of the rich and famous or kiss-and-tell stories of sexual dalliance, but his own privacy is jealously guarded. He sees no inconsistency in this.

The next day Packer pledges $3 million to the New South Wales ambulance service to help put defibrillators, now known as 'Packer Whackers', in every ambulance in the state. It is a sad comment on the state of the health service that they don't have them already if this is all it costs, but it shows another side of this enigmatic man. Packer phoned New South Wales Premier Nick

Greiner three days earlier and made the offer. 'Is it generosity or self-interest?' some cynically inquire.

For most, being close to death can be a mystical, life-changing experience. Will Packer now be different after shaking hands with the Almighty? It seems not. 'I've been to the other side,' he informs people, 'and let me tell you, son, there's fucking nothing there.'

Packer has had plenty of time to get used to the idea of dying. He has had such scares before. In 1983 he was rushed to hospital with a suspected heart attack; three years after that he had a cancerous kidney and diseased gall bladder removed in a London clinic. That scare was what made him take up polo in the first place—that and selling Channel Nine to Alan Bond for a billion dollars. Now that the heart attack has given him a good long look at death, he will disengage even further from his businesses. He has never expected to live beyond fifty so he's in the fifth year of borrowed time. All the male Packers, apart from his father, died in their prime. All had heart trouble. So did his mother, who also died young. Kerry has long been overweight, has smoked heavily almost all his life, and has high blood pressure and a chronic heart problem. The heart attack is his third curtain call. And possibly his last.

The brush with death, however, does not seem to have mellowed him. If anything, it has made him angry that he has so little time. As he begins to pull back from his business, preparing to hand it over to James, he begins to fall out with almost everyone who has been close to him. He begins to talk of treachery, of betrayal. He entrusts the running of the empire to a man whose nickname is Chainsaw. A Packer executive, cut down after years of loyal service, blames Kerry's heart attack for the new corporate butchery: 'It made him even more irascible. When it came to the end, anyone who disagreed with him was just swept aside.'

But of course it is not the end. For Chainsaw goes. And the Big Fella comes back, tilting at banks, casinos, Fairfax newspapers, preparing for pay TV, looking for more businesses to conquer. In the next fifteen years he will more than double his fortune to $7 billion and do everything he can to keep death—and his son—at bay.

Back in 1974, when he inherited the empire, they called Kerry Packer the idiot son. More than three decades later, in 2005, when he finally shuffles off this mortal coil, he will be lauded by all and sundry as a great Australian, a philanthropist, a business genius. Politicians will queue up to outdo each other with their plaudits. Only then will the rise and rise of Kerry Packer be complete.

But in the meantime, let us go back to the beginning.

CHAPTER ONE

FORTUNE

*My grandfather went to the races and somebody dropped
ten bob . . . he put it on a horse and it won at twelve to
one. He bought a ticket for Sydney and went into the
newspaper industry and did quite well. That was where
my family started from, ten bob on a racecourse.*

Kerry Packer, 1979

Years before he even dreamed of death, Kerry Packer used to say
that he had had a lot of luck, that it was the most important thing
in life. It was always part of the family credo that the Packers
might all have been broke if things had turned out differently,
and could still end up that way if they didn't hold on hard to
what they had.

In Packer family legend, it was only luck that got them
started. Kerry's grandfather was the son of a Tasmanian customs
official, born in Hobart in 1879, who came to Sydney and made
his fortune in newspapers. But it was only a happy accident that
he got there. At the races one day, as the story goes, he picked up
ten shillings, put it on a horse and won enough to pay the fare
to the mainland. When he arrived in Sydney in 1900 he was
twenty-one, a would-be journalist with barely two bob to rub
together. By the time he died in 1934, he had made and all but
lost a couple of hundred thousand pounds.

At first young Robert Clyde Packer had great trouble finding
a job as a newspaperman in Melbourne or Sydney, because no
one was too impressed with his Hobart qualifications. So after

tramping round all the newspaper offices, he ended up labouring instead, for nine shillings a week, as a powder monkey in a Sydney quarry, even though he had no experience with explosives. When that job ended he got another, wheeling sacks of flour in a warehouse in Sydney's Sussex Street. Then, bored with the mindlessness of manual work, he trekked off northwards to find a provincial newspaper that would have him. Over the next half-dozen years he learned his trade as a journalist on a string of country papers from Townsville to Tamworth.

In 1903 the young man came back from the bush to Sydney for long enough to marry Ethel Maude Hewson and set up house with her at Craigend Street, Kings Cross, where three years later Kerry's father Frank was born. Several years after that, a daughter Kate completed the family.

Kerry Packer's grandmother Ethel was a small, tough, determined woman, an inch over five foot tall, who came from very different stock to her husband Robert Clyde. It was not that he was huge, like his son and grandsons, for he was by no means a big man, but the Packer family boasted that its lineage could be traced back to the aristocracy of seventeenth-century England, to John Packer of Donnington Castle near Newbury, while Ethel's father was a lowly archdeacon from southern Ireland and a political radical to boot.

The first years of Ethel's marriage to Robert Clyde were not easy, for they had little money and were constantly separated, with him scribbling for the country press while she minded the house and child back home. But after five years of living apart, Kerry's grandmother clearly decided that she had had enough of being left on her own. Robert Clyde was by now having a great time editing a newspaper called the *Dubbo Liberal*, which was owned by a young widow. Ethel clearly had her suspicions about what her absent husband was up to, as Frank Packer cheerfully recounted years later: 'My father seemed to thoroughly enjoy that job at Dubbo. My mother thought he enjoyed it a little too much and, on hearing that the widowed owner was quite young and attractive, made a special visit to Dubbo to see for herself.

I was too young to know what my mother saw, but I do know that father immediately left Dubbo and returned to Sydney.'[1]

In 1908, at the age of twenty-nine, Robert Clyde therefore came back to the city for good to a job on Sydney's struggling *Sunday Times*, where he soon built a reputation for himself as a man with a flair for the newspaper business. Within five years he had risen to editor and circulation was climbing impressively, but a violent disagreement with the new proprietor then forced him out. From there he moved to the larger and more prosperous *Sunday Sun*, where by 1914 he was chief sub-editor, and by 1918 editor. He was still at the *Sun* when a fellow journalist asked him to help start a new newspaper and, as it turned out, to make his fortune.

Very few people still remember R. C. Packer, as he was universally known, but those who do say he was a man of great vigour, who made few concessions to convention and cared little or nothing about what others thought of him. He was clearly also an exceptional sub-editor and newspaper manager. One rather extravagant admirer, the journalist and broadcaster Eric Baume, said he possessed 'the greatest newspaper mind of his generation', and compared him to Northcliffe, Molyneux and Schiaparelli all rolled into one. Since the last two were famous dress designers, this was an odd compliment, but R. C.'s special talent was for laying out the news in an attractive and readable way—he was a demon with the scissors and paste.

Others, however, were less impressed. After his death in 1934, a short obituary in the *Bulletin* summed him up rather scathingly as someone with 'great journalistic gifts of a sort—organising ability, energy, and a keen sense of what readers of the mental age of fifteen, or less, want in the way of news and stunts'. A later verdict, untainted by newspaper rivalries, saw him as 'the pattern of the modern newspaper boss ... innovative, cynical, thriving on hard work, inspiring loyalty as well as enmity, politically influential, but chiefly concerned with commercial advantage'.[2]

Sixty years later, one could apply almost identical descriptions to the two more famous Packers who have followed him. And the resemblance by no means stops there. Like his son and grandson after him, R. C. was famous for yelling at people, for firing them and for being obsessively secretive.

Like Frank and Kerry, Robert Clyde had more than his fair share of enemies, but given the way he behaved it was hardly surprising. Even devoted admirers such as Eric Baume conceded that he was an extraordinarily suspicious man, whose habits made him difficult to work with. Like grandfather, like father, like son, he had a temper that could shake the walls, and was given to 'furnace blasts of invective' or fits of rage during which subordinates would run for cover. On one occasion he almost killed a photographer who mixed up his picture captions by hurling a marble clock at him. A notorious bully in his dealings with employees, he was also, as time would show, a buccaneer when it came to business. In the words of one former newspaper colleague, R. C. Packer made Ned Kelly look like the amateur he was.

The Sydney in which young Packer made his fortune was no longer bushranger territory or even frontier country, but it was very different from the place one knows today. In the early 1900s the city had a population of less than 200 000 and was divided by a broad expanse of water that rendered the northern suburbs almost another town. With the harbour bridge not yet built, the horse trams still queued nose-to-tail on the Blues Point Road, McMahons Point, on weekday mornings to catch the ferry to the city. But the railways had arrived many years before, and the town was booming. And if Sydney was still just a distant outpost of the British Empire for the many who looked back to the Mother Country, if it was still thousands of miles from 'Home' and cut off from the rest of the world, it was also an exciting, thriving place in which money was to be made.

Over the first twenty years of the century, one can chart Robert Clyde's steady progress to prosperity, from the seedy inner city round Darlinghurst Gaol to the beachside suburb of Bondi and thence to the rural expanses of Wahroonga on the upper North Shore. But life as a journalist or managing editor never threatened to make him rich. And in the latter years of World War I, the family still seems to have been pressed to make ends meet or keen to have more, for Kerry's grandmother tried endless schemes to bring in money. She kept chickens and sold eggs, then bought bees and sold honey, and finally grew flowers to send to market. None of these projects ever turned a profit, but in the end it hardly mattered. For R. C. Packer eventually made enough for them all, thanks to a flamboyant financier called Sir Joynton Smith.

A man of great wealth, huge nerve and much power, Sir Joynton Smith owned the magnificent Carrington Hotel in the Blue Mountains outside Sydney and several other pubs in the city. He owned a racecourse too, having drained a swamp near Botany Bay to build the track at Victoria Park, which brought him a huge and steady income. Smith's enemies said he was 'a one-eyed cockney crook' but they envied his incorrigible knack of making money. Born plain James Smith in the East End of London, Sir Joynton was the son of a gasfitter who had gone to sea as a galley boy at fourteen and had made his fortune in Australia in the liquor trade. Now he was rich, he affected the habits of an eccentric English Empire lover. He sported a white moustache and a monocle, could not pwonounce his *r*s pwoperly, and smoked large cigars through a gold-mounted lobster-claw holder. In one of his many impulsive moments, he had once offered to buy Runnymede, where *Magna Carta* was signed, in order to present the meadow to the British nation, but the owner had declined to sell.

Smith was an adventurer who loved the *grand geste*, and his decision to start *Smith's Weekly* was just such a stroke. Sydney's newspapers, he complained, published his views only when they agreed with him, so he resolved to launch a paper of his own that would print them regardless.

Packer's introduction to Smith came in 1918 through a fellow newspaperman, Claude McKay, who was drumming up financial support for the last days of the war against Germany. Smith, who had either muscled or charmed his way into being Lord Mayor of Sydney, had been roped in as spruiker to sell the Anzac spirit to patriotic investors and persuade them to put their savings into war loans. McKay, meanwhile, had been dreaming up publicity stunts to get coverage in the press.

With the fund-raising over, Smith asked McKay whether he would like to edit a new newspaper. McKay at once agreed, persuading Smith that they should recruit R. C. Packer, whom he knew as a talented head-kicker and shaper of newspapers, to complete the team.

Packer and McKay gave up their jobs in journalism, hired two attic rooms high above Sydney's Martin Place and engaged a seventy-year-old ex-editor of the *Bulletin* to help them put the new paper together. They then invited contributors to send in articles, pictures, cartoons and gags to fill its pages. It was a modest beginning, but the first issue of *Smith's Weekly* in March 1919 sold 35 000 copies, which was enough to persuade them that a second was worth printing. Meanwhile, they had abandoned good jobs, taken a pay cut from 30 pounds to 10 pounds a week and been given nothing in exchange except Smith's promise of a share in the business if it ever made money.

Claude McKay had assured Sir Joynton that 20 000 pounds would be enough to get the paper on its feet, but by the time *Smith's Weekly* finally broke into profit three years later, the good knight had sunk almost 100 000 pounds of his own money into the venture. He had remained cheerfully unmoved by the risks he was taking; when sales were flagging early on, he told them it was because they were not spending enough. 'Buy the best,' he admonished them, 'or you won't succeed,' so they had taken his cheque-book and spent some more. The day *Smith's Weekly* finally nosed into the black, Sir Joynton summoned McKay and Packer to a board meeting, at which point they dashed off to the pub to speculate on what they might be given.

Packer and I adjourned together to the long bar at the Australia to celebrate . . . On the prospect that we might each get five per cent of the profits, we had a drink. That made things look more rosy, and we had another on the strength of the percentage being more likely to be ten. But even a third whisky didn't lift our optimism beyond that.[3]

When contracts were eventually thrust into their hands several days later, they could hardly believe their eyes. Smith had cut the company into three, giving himself and his partners equal shares. Their backer had no obligation to reward them so generously, since neither Packer nor McKay had risked a penny of his own. But both had played a key part in the paper's success, for McKay was a brilliant editor and Packer an exceptional manager. Before long, R. C. was rewarding himself with a series of big American cars, Mercers and Packards, and moving to one of the best water-front homes in town, at Point Piper in Sydney's eastern suburbs, where Ethel was almost certainly forced to give up keeping chickens.

Under the direction of Packer and McKay, *Smith's Weekly* soon became an important and colourful part of Sydney life. In a city of sober, grey-suited newspapers that used pictures sparingly and cartoons not at all, it was a lively, cheerful rag, full of caricatures, sketches and jokes that earned it admirers around the world. Even on Fleet Street, 19 000 kilometres away, it was said that the *Smith's Weekly* team of black-and-white artists was the best that money could buy. But closer to home, things apart from its brilliant artwork made it sell. It was the spokesman for the common man, as radical as the *Bulletin* had ever been and infinitely more scurrilous. But while the *Bulletin* had been the 'bushman's Bible', *Smith's Weekly* was far more the city man's friend. Proclaiming itself the people's guardian, it exposed slum landlords, profiteers and other public enemies, and cried for justice for their victims. Appointing itself the 'Diggers' Paper', it championed the cause of those who had fought for Empire and come home to less than a hero's welcome, campaigning for better pensions and repatriation benefits. But what marked it out most clearly from its Sydney rivals was its unashamed populism. Where its competitors had long columns of close, grey type, *Smith's Weekly* had pages with pictures and a layout that enticed the reader. Where others served up the stodgy fare of politics, issues and world events, *Smith's Weekly* concentrated on the real-life struggles of ordinary Australians, on the trials of the common man. And the public responded by giving it their custom, taking sales Australia-wide to more than 150 000 copies a week by late 1921.

No sooner had *Smith's Weekly* started to make money than the trio launched a daily paper on similar lines. Once again, it was Sir Joynton Smith who broached the idea, with a proposal to spend 300 000 pounds on a half-share in the old and fading *Daily Telegraph*. But Packer and McKay persuaded him that it would be cheaper to start their own title instead.

Thus in July 1923 the *Daily Guardian* was born. Its first three years were difficult, its first three months disastrous but, once again, Sir Joynton's nerve and money pulled it through as he gaily sank another 100 000 pounds into the new paper during its first year of operation.

Though like *Smith's Weekly* aimed at Sydney's growing urban masses, the *Daily Guardian* was even more tabloid and down-market than its weekly stable-mate, with a mixture of sensational crime coverage and shameless foot-in-the-door journalism combined with the now-traditional trivia of the popular press. A typical early front page featured an eyewitness account of a hanging, reporting in lurid detail the death struggles of a violin-playing murderer who had killed his two young daughters. Later lead stories featured bodies in trunks, cocaine-dealing scandals and exposés of the white slave trade. Murders were always guaranteed a good run if there were some titillating feature in the style of the death.

To give circulation an early boost, Packer and McKay copied the British practice of giving free accident insurance to regular readers, then expanded the offer to include any reader injured on public transport. With the *Guardian*, people were told, they could rest assured: provided they were carrying a copy of the relevant paper when the injury occurred, they would be handsomely compensated. But publicising the scheme proved difficult, because months went by without any accidents. Finally, word came through that a bus had crashed in Mosman. A photographer was rushed to the scene with a copy of Packer's paper to press into the hands of the lone injured man, and a picture was then taken of him holding it. 'The *Guardian* Pays' was the triumphant headline next day above a story of the lucky chap's 250-pound windfall.[4]

While Packer and McKay were shaping the *Daily Guardian* in Sydney, Keith Murdoch was doing much the same to the *Herald* in Melbourne, also keeping more than an eye on Lord Northcliffe's hugely successful *Daily Mail* in London for new ideas to copy. Competitions were Northcliffe's specialty, and they became Packer's, too, first of all with a shopping competition for housewives and then with the 1920s equivalent of the Page Three girl. Pictures of pretty girls had been an essential element in the *Daily Mail*'s success, but Packer's genius was to find a format that married glamour to the competitive urge. This was already an old idea in the United States, where newspapers sponsored the annual Miss America competition so they could splash photos of the pretty contestants across their pages. But it was new to Australia, and that was what mattered to *Daily Guardian* readers. Declaring nobly that Australian womanhood was a match for any in the world, Packer launched the first Miss Australia competition in 1926 to ensure that the nation's young women were given the recognition and attention they deserved. A series of contests in each state soon produced 80 000 pictures of girls in tight-fitting swimsuits, the best of which were printed over the next few months in *Smith's Weekly* and the *Daily Guardian* for readers to study the form. The winners of the state contests were then brought to Sydney for the finals, where in June nineteen-year-old Beryl Mills was crowned the first Miss Australia. Packer's *Daily Guardian*, in its exclusive coverage, compared Beryl's measurements with those of the Venus de Milo and reported that they tallied exactly.

As reward, the delightful Beryl, whose 'cheeks were as rosy as the red velvet coat with which she covered her ivory-beaded romaine frock' was then despatched to America with 100 gold sovereigns in her pocket and a promise to uphold the reputation of Australia abroad. But first, to speed her on her way, she was brought to Sydney's Palais Royal for a glorious send-off. Four thousand people, who had each paid seven shillings and sixpence to get a glimpse of her, were unable to contain their excitement. Before she could complete a circuit of the dance floor, the mob broke through the ring of special constables and 'dangerously pressed around her'. According to the *Daily Guardian*, only the timely playing of a foxtrot prevented Miss Mills and her six attendants from being crushed.

The contest was an incredible circulation success, taking sales of the *Daily Guardian* past those of the *Sydney Morning Herald* for the first time, and marking the end of hard times for the paper, which now began to make healthy profits. But predictably, perhaps, as the business improved and adversity no longer held them together, strains now began to show in the relationship between Packer and McKay, both of whom were powerful, opinionated men, and in 1927 McKay sold out to the other two partners. The row was ostensibly over an article exposing rigged wrestling contests, the promoters of which appeared to be connected to Sir Joynton Smith. But there had been tensions between Packer and McKay, to say the least. And after the breakup, the two became bitter enemies.

The departure of McKay did not prevent the newspapers from continuing to prosper. Later that year Packer and Smith started the successful *Sunday Guardian* as a weekend companion for the daily paper. Then in 1929 they let it be known that they were planning an evening version to take on the *Sun*, owned by their rivals at Associated Newspapers, the mere threat of which was enough to persuade Associated to buy them off. For 575 000 pounds—more than $10 million today—Packer and Smith sold the *Daily Guardian* and *Sunday Guardian* to their biggest competitor and agreed not to go ahead with the evening paper they had planned. A hugely satisfied R. C. Packer pocketed a personal profit of some 200 000 pounds on the deal—

$3.5 million in today's currency—and tucked away an idea of how he might make more money in the future.

As the Packer family began to enjoy its new-found wealth, the Australian economy was already sliding into the pit of gathering world depression. Early in 1929, Australian commodity prices started falling, and wage cuts came hard behind, followed by strikes and lockouts in the New South Wales coalfields and violent confrontations between police and miners when the coal owners brought in scab labour. As the strikes dragged on, there was widespread hunger, poverty and bitterness. In October, the growing economic crisis throughout Australia brought down the federal coalition government, and fresh elections saw Labor returned with the biggest swing ever recorded. The new government was welcomed to office by the sudden and dramatic collapse of the world's stock markets, on the heels of which the Australian economy also went into free fall.

The following year, 1930, Australian export prices dropped by 45 per cent. More wage and spending cuts followed. Sydney became a city of soup queues and beggars, as the ranks of the unemployed swelled to 85 000 people, or more than one-quarter of the working population. Those who could get it lined up for relief work or the dole whenever it was on offer. Paradoxically, the shops and warehouses were full of goods, yet no one had any money to buy them. Evictions became commonplace, with the newspapers full of pictures of families standing forlornly on the pavement, their worldly goods piled up beside them. In the dunes at Brighton-le-Sands and on the foreshore at La Perouse and Clontarf, sprawling shanty towns with one hundred or more makeshift dwellings began to spring up to house the homeless. Meanwhile, the homes from which they had been ousted sat vandalised and empty because no one could be found with enough money to pay the rent.

By late 1930 the fall in export earnings was so great that Australia was unable to meet the interest on its debts without exporting gold reserves. The country had borrowed heavily from abroad in the 1920s to finance expansion, and was now paying the price. A senior British banker, Sir Otto Niemeyer, was sent out by the Bank of England to demand that 10 million pounds in interest from New South Wales be paid on the dot, and to tell all Australians 'with a brutal frankness that shocked his hosts' that welfare programs, wages and public works programs must be drastically reduced because Australia was living beyond its means.

Australia's politicians, bankers and newspaper kings accepted the British demands as the necessary medicine for a spendthrift patient, and called for yet more cuts in wages and public spending. R. C. Packer's papers joined the chorus, even as he laid out several thousand pounds to buy a new racing yacht.

Only in Packer's home state of New South Wales did the British bondholders meet determined resistance. And there State Premier Jack Lang incurred the wrath of the powerful by daring to voice his defiance. Lang promised that while he was Premier there would be no cuts in wages, no cuts in public services and, more to the point, no payments of interest or principal to Britain's bankers unless Australia's workers had been provided for. He promised, too, an immediate moratorium on unpaid rents to stop evictions and an attack on Sydney's slums. Meanwhile, for Australia as a whole, he proposed that interest rates be lowered, the gold standard abandoned, and a program of government-funded public works begun.

The Lang Plan attracted huge public support, with one open-air meeting in Sydney in July 1931 drawing a crowd of more than 100 000 people. But it provoked the passionate opposition of the establishment and the majority of Australia's politicians, who longed to see him toppled. On the fringes of the extreme Right, the militaristic New Guard movement even plotted to remove him by force. Packer's papers, meanwhile, branded him a Communist revolutionary, even though Lang himself was fiercely anti-Communist.

Both the *Daily Guardian* and *Smith's Weekly* had been savagely anti-Lang since the mid 1920s, but they now rose to new heights of abuse. When he proposed in March 1931 to set up a con-ciliation commission to settle industrial disputes, *Smith's Weekly* accused him hysterically of turning New South Wales over to the secret police. Labelling him a 'dictator' and 'mad-dog Premier', the newspaper compared him to Stalin, Mussolini and other great tyrants of history. Between headlines proclaiming a 'REIGN OF SPYING AND PIMPING' and 'BOLSHEVIK METHODS ALREADY HERE', a neatly ruled box summed up the *Weekly*'s considered view of the Premier and his plan.

> Dictator Lang is on top . . . groups of minor Commissars, with full powers of tyranny, espionage and blackmail are about to be created.
> Debts are to be dishonoured and all producers ruined and starved to pay wage-bribes to Government voters. The Soviet Model is complete.

Further down the page, the article invoked the Cheka and the Anti-Christ, and accused Lang of desiring the ruin of the productive farmer, before winding up to a frenzied finale.

> The free spirit of Australians will not long tolerate a Soviet with its bullies and parasites.
> Week by week, the Communist misrule of New South Wales flings more men into unemployment and piles fresh burdens on the productive power of the people.
> The manhood of the nation is in revolt against these evils. They cannot be tolerated . . . Liberty-loving Australians will kick to perdition the attempted tyranny of Lang.[5]

Even allowing for the fact that these were desperate times and that Lang was deeply unpopular with many people, the rabid tone of the piece was quite astonishing, as was the fact that the Premier didn't sue for defamation. But Packer was already famous for such attacks and his son Frank would become even more celebrated for his assaults in later years. There was little doubt that Robert Clyde was personally responsible, for as soon as he left *Smith's Weekly* in 1931 the bombardment stopped. Whereupon, the *Sun* and the *Daily Telegraph*, of which he had become managing editor, took up the offensive, attacking Lang in their columns and refusing to carry advertisements for his political campaigns.

Nine months later, in the run-up to the federal election of December 1931 and three months after Packer took control of the paper, the *Daily Telegraph* splashed a large photograph on its front page showing 'Lenin's Communists machine-gunning the citizens of St Petersburg at the outbreak of the Russian revolution' (fourteen years earlier). A memorable caption informed readers that '20 000 men, women and childen were shot down in two days by Lenin's Communists. There are just 18 746 people in Mr Lang's electorate.'[6]

With this lurid and ominous warning came headlines:

BRUTAL MURDERS IN RED REVOLUTION

IN RED RUSSIA, LENIN SPELT IT PLAIN 'DEATH'

WHAT COMMUNISM REALLY MEANS

AND STILL LANG CALLS THIS BUNK

The following morning's paper had pictures of starving Russian children, the alleged consequence of Bolshevism. And five days later came the explicit allegation, for those who had missed the point, that Lang's Labor Party and the Communists had made a secret alliance. This was both hard to believe and based on the flimsiest of evidence.[7] Six months later, in the final days of the state election campaign, the *Telegraph* claimed it had unearthed an incredible document detailing Lang's plans to depose the governor of New South Wales, close state borders, censor the press, confiscate private property, and suppress political opponents.[8] To say the least, the authenticity of this 'find' was extremely doubtful, but the smear tactics might well have worked, for in both the state and federal elections, Labor was defeated at the polls.

Packer's *Telegraph*, meanwhile, was far more favourable to the potentially fascist New Guard when they broke up two Communist meetings in Sydney in late 1931. Leader Colonel Campbell's speeches were also given huge and uncritical prominence. When New Guard members gathered at Sydney Town Hall in September to hear Campbell speak, the *Telegraph* described it as a 'WILDLY ENTHUSIASTIC MEETING' and reported the New Guard's claim that half-a-million men would rally to its cause: 'Thunderous cheers from 3000 throats shook the Town Hall last night when Colonel Eric Campbell declared: "I openly defy the Socialistic Government of this state to interfere in any way with the New Guard" . . . the only interruptions to Colonel Campbell were salvoes of cheers.'[9]

Four weeks later, the *Telegraph* was endorsing the movement, despite acknowledging its Fascist leanings, on the basis that it was 'made up of loyal Australians who believed that Australia was in danger' and who were 'at least determined to do something for themselves'.[10]

The New Guard was by this stage already attracting the attention of army intelligence who had decided that its militarism was a menace. A secret report dated 26 October 1931 noted that 'Packer, who holds an important post in Associated Newspapers' was a New Guard member.[11] The New Guard appeared to have targeted people with telephones and cars—people with influence in the community. Packer obviously had both and, more usefully, had his newspapers.

Packer's brazen use of the *Telegraph* and his previous papers for political purposes almost proved his undoing. Not surprisingly, Premier Jack Lang was keen to get his revenge for the relentless campaign waged against him and was prepared to hit back just as ferociously as Packer had done. In March 1932 a bill was rushed through the lower house of the New South Wales Parliament that was quite clearly intended to make Packer bankrupt. Against all normal principles of lawmaking, it was designed to render Packer's most lucrative business deal illegal, but retrospectively, three years after the event. Packer was such a scoundrel, Lang told his parliamentary colleagues, that this drastic remedy was more than justified.

> There sometimes arises in a community a scandal so grave that nothing but retrospective legislation can correct it and restore justice to those who have been despoiled ...
>
> The man has committed the most glaring act of robbery and theft that could possibly be discovered in the commercial life of this city, and Parliament must be invoked to make him do justice where justice is due.'[12]

According to Lang, the people whom Packer had robbed were the preference shareholders in Smith's Newspapers Ltd who had put up 300 000 pounds to start the highly successful *Daily Guardian* in 1923, but had received no share in the profits when the paper and its Sunday sister were sold to Associated Newspapers six years later. Meantime, Packer and Sir Joynton Smith had collected 200 000 pounds apiece from the deal. Even worse, said Lang, the sale had deprived the preference shareholders of the very asset that was supposed to earn them dividends, and dividends had now dried up. Only 175 000 pounds out of the total 575 000 pounds sale price had been retained in Smith's Newspapers for the preference shareholders, and most of that money was still owing, with little chance it would ever be paid, since Associated Newspapers was now in deep trouble.

The day after the bill was hurried through the house, R. C. Packer and his son Frank presented a petition to the New South Wales Parliament to argue that they had acted entirely within the law, which indeed they had. Soon after that, the offending legislation was shelved. Two months later, Lang himself was removed from office by the governor of New South Wales and subsequently defeated at the polls, so the danger to Packer disappeared altogether. Packer's *Daily Telegraph* did its level best in the campaign to ensure that Lang was not re-elected.

But while the threat from the bill faded away, the battle between Packer and his erstwhile business partners raged on. Not only had McKay and Smith supported what Lang was trying to do to their old friend, but they were widely thought to have put him up to it. The week after the bill passed through Parliament, McKay commandeered the front page of *Smith's Weekly* to launch a biting attack on his former colleague, proclaiming that Packer had not thrown in a cent of his own money to build *Smith's Weekly*, had not been responsible for its huge success and had been extraordinarily lucky to be given one-third of the shares, which he had received only because Sir Joynton Smith was such a generous man. Packer, he said, had been made 'rich beyond his wildest dreams' but had shown no gratitude for it. He had treated the preference shareholders unfairly, extracted more than the company could bear and then refused to consider giving any of the money back. According to McKay, the auditor of Smith's Newspapers had 'practically demanded' that Packer and Smith each return 75 000 pounds to the company, which Packer had steadfastly refused to do.[13]

The bitter attack on Packer by his two former partners indicated how much they had come to dislike him, but it was also a measure of the trouble that Smith's Newspapers was in. As a letter to R. C. from his son Frank had already made clear, Smith's Newspapers was in financial difficulty from which it might not recover. And without Packer's money, it never did. Between 1932 and 1936 the preference shareholders received no dividends at all, then their capital was halved in an unsuccessful attempt to salvage the company, so that by 1939 their investment had been almost entirely wiped out.

The fortunes of the Packer family, meanwhile, were going from strength to strength, but only after the Great Depression had nearly done what Lang could not. The 200 000-pound profit that they had taken from the 1929 sale had been paid in the form of one-pound preference shares in Associated Newspapers, and by 1931 these had fallen to less than half their face value. Associated itself was in considerable difficulties and there was a real chance that the shares would become completely worthless if the slide were not halted. So in September 1931, R. C. had joined the company, previously his biggest rival, as managing editor, in an effort to save the family fortune. Although he was already seriously ill and in semi-retirement, he felt there was no alternative if he were to safeguard his wealth. Associated had been poorly managed, shirking the tough decisions necessary for survival.

Packer's first act was to close one of the company's unprofitable titles by merging the *Sunday Guardian* and the *Sunday Sun*. His next was to fire off a fourteen-point memo to the board, proposing savage economies and cutbacks. Pulling no punches, he berated the directors for incompetence and blamed the chairman, Sir Hugh Denison, for his appalling management of the company. Three months later, he fired another broadside in which he accused the advertising director, Albert Fordyce Wheeler, of robbing the shareholders of 15 000 pounds a year by overcharging for his services, and suggested that Associated could save a further 7000 pounds by getting rid of Denison's son, who was employed in the newspapers' business department. From there, the confrontations came thick and fast as Packer waged open war with the people who had steered the company into trouble.

Not surprisingly, his attacks gave rise to fierce fights with the people who had hired him, particularly with Wheeler. By mid 1932, according to Eric Baume, Packer's personal assistant at the time, both he and Packer were carrying revolvers around town and taking bodyguards with them wherever they went, although other, common threats might well have prompted such precautions. Finally, in mid 1933, with three years of his contract still to run, Packer attempted to have Denison's son sacked and was effectively turfed out of the company with a less-than-handsome settlement.

R. C. Packer claimed he had suffered constant humiliation and interference, but in the short time he was there he had done what he had set out to do—he had put Associated Newspapers back into profit and restored his family fortune. By late 1933, the ordinary shares had regained most of their value and the preference shares were paying healthy dividends again. Meanwhile, he had all but killed himself through overwork, stress and argument. A sick and disillusioned man, he had fallen out with almost everyone who had ever been his friend.

But despite his worsening health, R. C. still refused to relax. To take his mind off the battles at Associated, he set sail for Hobart in his racing yacht *Morna* with a couple of friends. A strenuous trip at the best of times, it soon turned out to be far worse. Not far south of Sydney, a heavy storm forced them into Jervis Bay to shelter, where the winds were still so strong that the *Morna* dragged her anchor and was thrown against the breakwater. Typically, it was Packer who jumped onto the rocks and struggled to keep the yacht from smashing up. Even then, he tried to continue the voyage, until a second storm off Eden forced them to turn back.

Shortly afterwards, with his health considerably worse, Robert Clyde went to England in search of treatment, but there was nothing the doctors could do. On his way back home by sea in April 1934, three months short of his fifty-fifth birthday, he died of heart failure. High blood pressure was perhaps one reason for this family affliction; a predilection to anger was quite possibly another. But he was neither the first nor the last of the Packers to be struck down in this fashion.

CHAPTER TWO

WILD MEN OF SYDNEY

Q: Can I ask you if you can name anyone you most admire?
A: I really hold no one in higher regard than my father.

Kerry Packer, 1979

Kerry's father, Frank Packer, was a rich man when his father died. There were properties, shares, a yacht and money in the bank to give him a far easier start in life than R. C. had had. And if he had spent some of his youth labouring, driving trucks and working on cattle stations, it was only because the old man believed in typical Packer style that Frank needed toughening up. Already it was clear that he was no intellectual, but it was also quite obvious that he was good at one thing—making money—for, aged twenty-seven, he was well on the way to building a newspaper empire of his own.

While the Packers were a wealthy family, they had lived without display, and young Frank had been anything but spoiled. Indeed, the boy had been given a strict upbringing in which the rod had not been spared, for R. C. was a tough, uncompromising man who stood no nonsense. But the relationship between father and son had been close, if stormy and difficult at times. Robert Clyde Packer was a great bushman and sailor, and would take the boy out on the harbour, roped to the centreboard of his yacht in the early days, or on trips to the bush to shoot kangaroos. He also had an inventor friend who was constantly tinkering with new machines, and when he went to see him he would take his son along. When Packer senior mowed the grass in their orchard at Wahroonga, Frank would be roped in, harnessed to the front of the mower, and pulling, while his father pushed on the back.

Young Frank was a tearaway in spite of his strict upbringing. At the tender age of nine he was expelled from Turramurra College on Sydney's North Shore for taking one of his father's revolvers to school and playing with it in the school playground. Fortunately for him, and for his schoolmates, the bullets he was trying to load into it were the wrong calibre. Thereafter he went to a couple of schools, where he was not greatly successful, before ending up at one of Sydney's poshest establishments, the Sydney Church of England Grammar School, widely known as Shore. There his main achievements were in sport, where he rowed and boxed for the school, but he was never much good at ball games, for he lost ninety per cent of the sight in one eye in an accident chopping firewood when he was eleven years old. Like his son Kerry, he was academically hopeless, failed the equivalent of the New South Wales School Certificate—the most elementary public exam—and claimed to have spent most of his time in class reading detective novels.

At the age of sixteen, Frank and school parted company and he joined his father's new paper the *Daily Guardian* as a cadet reporter, saying later that he had never considered doing anything else. Even at this stage it was readily apparent that he was a chip off the old block. Rough, cheerful and full of energy, he cared as little as his father for the feelings of others. In the words of someone who knew both of them well, 'the Packers did what they chose to do when they wished to do it. They were never hampered by what other people thought of them or by what were in those days pretty considerable restraints.'

Frank had not been a reporter long before his father packed him off to the bush to work as a jackeroo on a friend's property near Cootamundra, in southern New South Wales, where he stayed for eighteen months. Then he came back to Sydney as assistant business manager of Smith's Newspapers where, despite the grand new title, he was made to wrap newspapers and learn his trade. By 1927, still not twenty-one years old, he was promoted to selling advertising, and when his father took closer control of the business soon after, he was promoted again to advertising director.

Already he appears to have had an eye for the deal, for one of his money-making exploits around this time became something of a legend with the *Daily Guardian* staff. As the story was told, young Frank had taken advantage of a bad potato shortage in Sydney to make himself a killing, having been tipped off by the harbourmaster's son, whom he knew from his schooldays, that a big shipment was due to arrive from Tasmania. With great difficulty he had persuaded his father to lend him enough money to secure an option on them and had then onsold them to the merchants of Sussex Street, pocketing a profit of 280 pounds, or roughly twice the annual average wage.

There were other business ventures, more reliably recorded, that did less well, such as Frank's short-lived foray into the roofing-nail business, through a company called Seal-Tite Pty Ltd, and an even quicker dash to the Northern Territory to look for gold. Then, in late 1932, came a remarkable deal in which he really did strike paydirt.

The official version of how Frank Packer got rich, as told by Kerry, is that he decided to start an afternoon newspaper, only to be told by his father that he was crazy because he didn't have enough money. Frank then found himself a partner, 'a great man', according to Kerry, whose only problem was that he was broke too:

> To cut a long story short, they went into partnership and they went and hired a building and they hired some presses and they got the staff together and they were obviously going to go broke, they were going to last two or three weeks because they didn't have the money to do it, and just a week before they're going to produce their first paper and probably their last there was an afternoon newspaper war going on in Sydney and the people who produced the other papers decided they didn't want the interruption, they

didn't realise how broke they were, and they came down and said, 'Well, there's 80 000 quid in it if you don't start the paper.' So by this stage they had got a little bit older, a little bit smarter, they said: 'Done.'[1]

The truth is a little more complicated. And a great deal more interesting.

In late 1932, Frank Packer joined the headlong rush to dig for gold in the Granites, in the arid lands west of Tennant Creek, where many fossickers later tragically died. He had been there a week when he was summoned back to Sydney by his father, who cabled him with the news that a new newspaper, the *World*, was doing so badly that the directors wanted to close it down.

The *World* was a Labor Party daily paper that had been launched less than a year earlier by the Australian Workers' Union and had been a disaster from the very beginning. Within six months of starting up, its directors were steeling themselves to close it because it was losing so much money. Six months later it had run up an overdraft of 60 000 pounds and the AWU's bankers were telling him they could have no more. With only days before the newspaper ran out of funds, the union leaders asked one of their trustees, Ted Theodore, to search for a buyer. As a recently retired Federal Treasurer and co-founder of the AWU, he was someone whose judgment and loyalty they felt they could rely on.[2]

Nicknamed 'Red Ted' for his radical politics as a union organiser in Queensland's mines and shearing sheds in the early 1900s, Theodore was a character whom history has found hard to judge. To some he was a brilliant economist who might have saved Australia from the ravages of the 1930s depression; to others, he was a sharpster or a crook. The truth, perhaps, is that he was both. The son of a Romanian tugboat owner who had come up the hard way, he was Premier of Queensland by the age of thirty-four and Treasurer of Australia ten years later. It was said by his enemies that he had entered Queensland Parliament with nothing and emerged with 100 000 pounds.

Red Ted Thurgood in Frank Hardy's classic Australian novel *Power Without Glory* is unmistakably his fictional double: winning a seat in parliament on the toss of a coin, bribing his way to mining leases and riches and then pushing government money towards companies he secretly owns. Finally, this fictional Red Ted graduates to Federal politics when an associate bribes a sitting MP to relinquish his seat. The associate is John West, a corrupt bookmaker, racetrack owner, violent gangland figure and political boss in the Labor Party machine, based on the infamous Melbourne power-broker John Wren. The real-life version of Red Ted Theodore is pretty much the same, at least to the extent that almost identical charges were raised against him.

In 1928 a royal commission investigated allegations that three federal MPs had been offered money to step down from safe Labor seats in New South Wales so that Ted Theodore could get into Parliament. Theodore said this was 'an absurd statement . . . without a tittle of foundation', but the stories were already common knowledge in Labor ranks. And the royal commission conclude they were substantially true, finding not only that bribes had been offered on Theodore's behalf but also that one MP, Mr W. G. Mahony, had actually accepted 5000 pounds to give up his seat. The other two, who had been asked first, had refused.[3]

Two years later, another royal commission investigated the Queensland Government's calamitous purchase of the Mungana mining leases, which had take place while Theodore was state Treasurer. It was alleged that Theodore had caused the Queensland Government to pay far more than the mines were worth and had profited from the 40 000-pound sale by means of a hidden shareholding in Mungana Mines Ltd. Although nothing on the share register of Mungana Mines linked Theodore to the company, investigation of his income tax records and bank accounts suggested that he had received a share of the proceeds and was a full partner in a scheme to defraud. In any case, the royal commission had no hesitation in finding Theodore 'guilty of fraud and dishonesty' on this charge, and guilty of 'gross impropriety' on another involving government contracts, concluding that Theodore and others in 'high and responsible positions in the state . . . betrayed for personal gain the trust reposed in them'.[4]

Theodore weathered the various scandals surrounding his name with some difficulty, being forced at first to resign as federal treasurer before resuming his position some months later. But the voters were less kind to him than his Labor Party colleagues, and booted him out of his seat in the general election of December 1931, whereupon he quit politics, vowing to make money instead. It was this Ted Theodore, the 'urbane figure of finance', as the papers described him, who became Frank Packer's partner in 1932.

How the two came to join forces remains a mystery but, since Theodore was charged with selling the *World* and Frank Packer was keen to buy it, it is scarcely surprising that they began talking to each other, and it seems the idea of a partnership developed soon after. The negotiations with the AWU were then conducted entirely by Theodore.

According to one version of events, these seem to have been extremely casual, taking place in the bar of Melbourne's King's Hotel, where two of the AWU's most senior officials, Ted Grayndler and Jack Barnes, were downing a few whiskies. According to Grayndler,[5] Theodore suggested that in Frank Packer he had just the person who would take the *World* off their hands, an experienced newspaperman who could make the paper a success. Theodore proposed that he and Packer should lease the *World* for three years, along with the presses that produced the paper and two floors of AWU headquarters, for 4000 pounds a year. In return, they would keep publishing the newspaper, and would 'so far as possible take over and re-employ' existing staff. To the slightly inebriated union officials this must have seemed like an offer they couldn't refuse, for they had already approached other potential buyers without success. They almost fell over each other in the rush to accept. A pound note was plucked from Theodore's pocket to be put down as a deposit on the deal, and another produced on which the bare details of the agreement were recorded and witnessed by the various parties.

Rather more soberly, *Newspaper News* reported some days later that a new syndicate of businessmen headed by Frank Packer had been formed to take over the *World*, announcing that he planned radically to change the character of the paper and to cut its price.[6]

There is considerable doubt about whether Packer and Theodore ever intended to continue publication. But after a formal agreement had been signed in Sydney on 31 October and a 100-pound option fee paid, they gave every appearance of going ahead, forming a new company, Sydney Newspapers Ltd, with an apparently impressive capital of 30 000 pounds.[7] Soon after, George Warnecke, the editor of the *Sunday Sun*, was signed to run the new paper, and several other journalists were persuaded to come aboard. Dummies were drawn up, stories run in the old paper about how the new one would look, and the lease of the *World* taken over with everything apparently on target. Packer and Theodore promised readers of the new daily, to be renamed the *Star*, that it would be 'a brilliant afternoon newspaper ... improved, bright, newsy ... dedicated to the public service'. Far from preaching to Labor supporters and union members, it would be a mass-market daily that would go up against Associated's sole surviving afternoon paper, the *Sun*, in a straight fight for the lucrative Sydney market. What's more, to give it a chance of beating its established rival, it would sell for two-thirds of the price. The *Star* was apparently set for a glorious future. But, as Frank Packer and Ted Theodore knew, its death warrant had already been signed.

Reading one week earlier of a cheaper rival to the *Sun*, Sir Hugh Denison at Associated Newspapers had done what the Packers clearly expected of him. Calculating that it would cost 130 000 pounds a year to the *Sun*'s price to match the competition, he had promptly summoned Ted Theodore to offer the syndicate money to go away. His first suggestion was that they should agree not to undercut the price of the *Sun*, his second was to offer more money if Packer and Theodore would agree not to publish the new paper at all. Then, when this too was rejected, Denison detailed his managing editor, Robert Clyde Packer, to nut out a deal.[8]

How father and son managed not to fall about laughing one can only guess, for R. C. Packer must have known what a weak position the two 'owners' of the *World* were in. As they sat down to talk business, Ted Theodore and Frank Packer had laid out a mere 100 pounds and had not even committed themselves to taking up the lease on the newspaper. R. C. himself could have told them that their 30 000 pounds was roughly one-sixth of what Sir Joynton Smith had spent a decade earlier to launch the *Daily Guardian* in much easier economic times. He could have warned them that, with their limited funds, going ahead would be commercial suicide. He could have pointed out that at the rate the *World* had been losing money, they had just enough cash to last for three months before they went broke. Instead, he now handed over 86 500 pounds of Associated Newspapers' money—more than $3 million in today's currency—to buy them off.[9] With no more than an option on the *World* and its premises, and precious little chance of avoiding ruin, Frank Packer and Ted Theodore were being paid a fortune to be the paper's executioners.

R. C. Packer and the directors of Associated Newspapers were hardly on the best of terms before this incident, but the sight of him distributing large amounts of the company's money to his son must surely have incensed them, and they now consulted their lawyers in the hope of getting out of the agreement, only to be advised that they could not. Meanwhile, Sir Hugh Denison was clearly most unhappy about the size of the payment Robert Clyde had negotiated, and five years later, giving his version of events on oath before the High Court in an income tax case, he said as much:

> Sir Hugh said he was informed by Mr R. C. Packer that his son Frank and Theodore were about to launch an evening newspaper. He had also heard it from other sources and realised the effect it

would have on the Sun. He authorised R. C. Packer to negotiate with Theodore and Frank Packer with a view to preventing the new paper being launched.

When on the golf links one day, said Sir Hugh, he received a telephone communication from R. C. Packer to say that he had signed an agreement with the promoters of the proposed news-paper which provided, among other things, that for the payment of 86 500 pounds, the paper would not be launched.

Sir Hugh said he was very annoyed after receiving this message. He had expected to be consulted before any agreement had been signed.[10]

R. C. Packer's final offer to Theodore and his son Frank was accepted on 9 November 1931, the very day that their company Sydney Newspapers Ltd took up the lease. The first instalment of the 86 500-pound settlement was to be paid the next day. Just four days after that, with plans for the new paper still being trum-peted in the columns of the *World* and rescue apparently certain, the employees were shattered to be told that their paper was closing. The following morning 280 journalists, printers and staff were informed that they had lost their jobs. The newspaper had told its readers on the day that the secret agreement was signed that large additions to the workforce would be made. Now one of the dismissed editorial staff pinned up a notice that summed up their anger.

What a splendid Christmas Box for all . . . Shortly, you will hear honeyed words regarding the damnably rotten deal you have had. Demand the facts of one of the most dastardly deals in high finance, in which you were the meat in the pound-note sandwiches to serve as lunch for the directors.[11]

The editor-to-be, George Warnecke, told journalists he had no idea what was going on or whether the *Star* would be published. Frank Packer meanwhile talked to the printers and delivered a similar message. When asked whether the *Star* would come out, he is reported to have said: 'I don't know. I know no more than you do.' It was hardly the truth, for five days earlier he had agreed to close the newspaper within seventy-two hours of receiving the first instalment of the 86 500-pound pay-off, and it had now been paid. Even as he protested his ignorance, the managers at the *Sun* were telling their printers that the paper's first edition would in future be published one hour later.'[12] They of course knew, as did Frank Packer, that the *Sun* now had the field to itself.

At the time the deals between Associated and Frank Packer could only be guessed at, but *Truth* came closest with the suggestion that Theodore might have pulled off the most gigantic bluff. It would be a typical Theodore *coup de théâtre*, said the paper, to threaten publication of a new afternoon daily so that Associated Newspapers would be panicked into buying them off. But *Truth's* guess was only half right, for the paper assumed that the money had gone to the coffers of the AWU, whereas it had actually disappeared into the pockets of Packer and Theodore. The AWU had been tied into the agreement not to produce a paper for three years but had ended up with nothing, while the paper's printers and journalists had been forced to join the long dole queues of the depression.

One of the key arguments for keeping the *World* going in the first place had been that the AWU could avoid giving out huge amounts in severance pay. The directors of Labor Newspapers Ltd had been told that the deal with Sydney Newspapers would save them a fortune. But now that Packer and Theodore were shutting down the paper and sacking the staff, it became once again the AWU's responsibility to meet most, if not all, of the 10 000-pound bill for redundancies.

At the AWU's national convention two months later, the union officers who negotiated the sale to Theodore found themselves under attack. Accusations of bribery were raised, as were suggestions that it had been a conspiracy from the start. There was more than a little truth in the latter charge. In his unpublished manuscript *Miracle Magazine*,[13] George Warnecke, the man who would have edited the new paper, claims that he and R. C. Packer hatched the plan to take over the *World* with the explicit intention of attracting a handsome takeover offer from Associated. Young Frank, he says, was brought in on the scheme because it was obviously improper for Robert Clyde at Associated to be launching a predatory rival to his own afternoon paper. If this confession is true, it is easy to see where R. C. Packer got the idea, for Associated had bought off several rivals in the past, only to close them down soon after. Indeed, it had done almost exactly that with the purchase of the *Sunday Guardian* and *Daily Guardian* from Robert Clyde Packer and Sir Joynton Smith in 1929. This rather more sophisticated version of the sting had merely eliminated the troublesome step of setting up the newspaper in the first place.

It was predictable that the Packers' arch enemy Jack Lang would not let such dealings pass without comment. When details of the agreement between Denison, Packer and Theodore were leaked to him eight months later in June 1933, he launched a blistering attack on his old enemies, the Packers and Associated Newspapers, in the New South Wales Parliament:

> The city has long since realised that when the Packers and the Denisons get their heads together somebody's money or reputation is in danger. I doubt if anybody realises how infamous was the conduct of these men in the recent transaction which resulted in the closing down of the evening newspaper, the World . . .
>
> In this final act of crookedness, this gang of respectable thieves have excelled themselves. The whole deal was nothing but a swindle, yet these men, because they control newspapers, can go merrily on their way, blackening the reputation and destroying the career of honourable men.

'Honourable men', of course, was a reference to Jack Lang himself, whom Robert Clyde Packer's papers had helped to remove from office exactly one year earlier. But there was more.

> When the scurrilous rags which emanate from this cesspit demand a royal commission to inquire into a statement that somebody told

them that somebody paid two pounds to a public officer, the Government rushes headlong to comply and wastes thousands of pounds on fruitless inquiries . . .

Let it probe and inquire to see how these people, the Packers and their kind, line their own pockets at the expense of their share-holders and the public; to see how they use the tremendous power of the newspapers they control not only to deceive the public, but also to sway the Stock Exchange and the Government's actions for their own personal advantage.

If the Government wants to clean up commercial immorality, I have indicated a wonderful field for its operation.[14]

Although the agreement with Associated Newspapers prohibited Packer, Theodore and Sydney Newspapers Ltd from publishing a morning, evening or Sunday newspaper within 480 kilometres of Sydney for the next three years, it also required them to take up the lease of the *World* so that no one else could produce a news-paper from its presses. As 1933 began, Frank Packer and his partner were therefore left with two empty floors of the AWU headquarters in central Sydney, some idle printing capacity and a talented but disgruntled editor kicking his heels. They also, of course, had a large bag of money to spend.

For a time, Frank and his father pushed round ideas for a publication that would not be banned by the agreement with Associated, while Frank himself toyed with the idea of starting a free shopping magazine to catch the retail ads on a Thursday. But nothing really fired their enthusiasm, and Frank's business partner Ted Theodore certainly had no passion to produce newspapers. He had seen how much money the *World* swallowed up in its one year of operation and had no great desire to repeat the expe-rience. Theodore saw more obvious potential in his three gold mines in Fiji, owned in partnership with the notorious John Wren, and he needed most of his share of the cash from Associ-ated to finance further development. Frank was also excited by the gold mines' prospects and decided to commit some of his own money to the project. So the months ticked by, with Frank increasingly resigned to waiting three years until he was free to produce a daily paper. But then, in early 1933, George Warnecke came up with a better idea.

For several months after the *Star*'s sad miscarriage, Warnecke had worked on concepts for a new women's magazine, looking at overseas titles and playing with different formats and layouts. A great admirer of R. C. Packer, whom he had often heard muse about the possibilities of such a publication, Warnecke had finally put together a mock-up with the help of an illustrator and a photographer friend. And he now took it along to Frank, telling him, perhaps to forestall opposition, that it wasn't so much a magazine as a women's newspaper. Clearly, the stratagem worked.

Frank straightened himself bolt upright in his chair, half-turned to the window and gazed unblinkingly at infinity . . . After minutes of dead silence, he asked: 'What exactly do you mean by women's news?'[15]

Warnecke outlined his vision of a publication that would not only make news out of personalities, fashion, cookery and child care, but would also analyse the headline stories of the week from a woman's point of view. Frank listened sceptically: a women's magazine wasn't quite what he had in mind to launch himself upon the publishing world. But his father was enthusiastic, and so was the advertising agency J. Walter Thompson, to whom Frank showed dummies of the proposed magazine. And the publication had the definite advantage that it would not be proscribed by Associated's ban. So, trusting everyone else's judgment and his own growing enthusiasm, he persuaded Theodore they should risk 25 000 pounds of Sydney Newspapers' money and give it a chance, in the hope that it would at least keep the presses rolling and help pay the rent.

Once again, journalists and printers were hired, dummies drawn up, and the two empty floors of AWU headquarters, MacDonnell House, filled with activity. And this time, seven months after they had strangled the *Star* at birth, Associated did not intervene to kill their new baby. In the second week of June 1933, amid huge fanfares on radio, billboards and in the press, the *Australian Women's Weekly* was launched. Thanks to Frank in particular, who had the brainwave of getting the new magazine to sponsor a popular mystery serial called *The Bamboo Bangle*, broadcast on six Sydney commercial radio stations every day, the publicity campaign was inspired. But it appeared that the product itself was also exactly what Sydney's women had been waiting for, because the first edition of 90 000 was a sell-out within hours. In the *Weekly*'s office, the switchboard almost melted down as newsagents rang in to complain that stocks had run out and they needed more copies for their customers. In response, the presses were started up again and run till the end of the week to crank out another 35 000 magazines, which Packer went down to the basement to help put into bundles. The next week, production was increased further to 160 000 copies, which also sold out with ease.

The first edition of the *Women's Weekly*, as Warnecke had promised, did indeed look more like a newspaper than a magazine, being printed cheaply in black-and-white on forty-four pages of ordinary newsprint. But it was more daring in the use of photographs and illustrations than its newspaper competitors, and bolder and brasher than its staid magazine rivals. Larger than the three other women's publications on the market, the now defunct *Woman's Budget* and *Woman's Mirror*, and the still-surviving *New Idea*, Packer's newcomer was also a penny cheaper, promising the 'Biggest Value In The World' for its two-penny cover price. There was, as Warnecke had envisaged, real news in its pages, presented with flair and a sense of fun, which made its more conservative, old-fashioned competitors look dowdy by comparison. And if it did dish up a familiar diet of fashion, fiction, recipes and tips on baby care, it also threw in more than a sprinkling of women's politics and matters of social interest to give it spice.

The *Weekly*'s first issue even showed a surprisingly modern approach to women's role in society, carrying on its front page a prominent plea for equal pay and equal rights. But it was an indication of the magazine's early schizophrenia that the other two-thirds of the cover was devoted to 'What Smart Sydney Women are Wearing' and to a trailer for knitting patterns, headed 'Unique New Jumpers'.

The *Weekly*'s uncertainties in direction would be quickly dispelled by moving the magazine away from its feminist approach. By April 1934 its columns were already reporting, with no apparent evidence to support the proposition, that 'modern women are earnestly striving to become good housewives again. The back-to-the-home movement has started and is gathering force the world over.'

This article, entitled 'The Swing of the Pendulum', was followed in December 1934 by a more lasting change, in which Warnecke went overseas to investigate new printing technology and take a long rest and Alice Jackson was installed in his place. A pocket galleon of a woman with a proud, substantial bust, she was of far more traditional outlook than Warnecke and almost certainly far more in tune with the majority of the *Weekly*'s readers. Alice had made her name on the *Daily Guardian*'s Shopping Bureau, telling readers where to get the best bargains, but she turned out to be an excellent editor. A stout defender of the family, her views on how women should behave were firmly in line with Frank Packer's own conservative opinions. From then on there was far less stuff about careers and equal rights. There was also no smut, no mention of abortion and, for a time, no advertisements for either alcohol or sanitary towels. After the initial, mainly male launch of the magazine, women were quickly taken onto the staff but, in line with the custom of the day, Alice always insisted that her 'gels' wear hats, gloves and, of course, stockings when they were out on assignment.

With Mrs Jackson at the helm, the *Weekly* steered into safe and familiar waters. Royalty became a regular feature of its columns, with visits even from minor members of the Royal family being anticipated and reported with breathless excitement. Cooking also became a more staple part of the magazine's diet, with occasionally, a triumphant marriage between the two. 'Cooking that charmed a king' was the memorable headline over the *Weekly*'s interview with American divorcee Mrs Wallis Simpson, after her marriage to Edward and his abdication as king of England.

But that was all to come. For the first birthday issue in June 1934, the magazine was still sufficiently broad in its appeal to attract strong messages of support from both the Country Women's Association and the Feminist Club. The public, meanwhile, were flocking to buy it. Its illustrations, in particular, were superb and its articles lively and up to the minute. After its initial launch in Sydney, it was floated in Melbourne three months later, and in Brisbane a month after that, with each a huge success. By mid 1935 the magazine was selling 260 000 copies a week; by 1940 it had almost doubled again to 450 000. From that time to the mid 1950s its climb was relentless, topping 650 000 a week by the end of World War II and almost nudging a million during the Queen's visit in 1954.

The early surge in circulation, paradoxically, was almost a financial disaster for Packer and Theodore, because they had so little capital behind them. And it was touch-and-go whether the magazine would survive. Those who know a little about business will know that rapid growth demands huge amounts of cash to finance it, even when the business is technically turning a profit. And the *Weekly* was not only growing like crazy, it was also making a thumping loss, earning far less per copy than it cost to produce. To attract advertisers at the start, Packer had locked the magazine into two-year rate deals that were absurdly generous, and while some could, with a little rancour, be renegotiated, others could not. Six months after the launch, Ted Theodore was called back from his gold mines in Fiji to look after the magazine while Frank Packer rushed off to England to see his sick father. Theodore had already been asked to stump up more money to keep the magazine growing, but was now horrified to find that the *Weekly* had swallowed 50 000 pounds and was losing more money every day. Since the gold mines in Fiji were also eating up cash, this was courting catastrophe.

Theodore's initial reaction as an essentially conservative financier was that they would have to close the magazine down, or at the very least cut wages and staff, and he at once proposed to cable Frank in London to give him the news. George Warnecke argued vehemently that they should do no such thing, and pledged 1000 pounds of his own to the magazine to help pay its bills. The problem, he said, would not in any case be solved by slashing the wage bill. Frank Packer was equally adamant when he got wind of the argument that they shouldn't pull out just when they were winning, and cheerfully told Theodore that with newspapers 'you just have to keep on spending' if you want to succeed. Theodore, it seems, asked for a firm date when the magazine would start paying its way, then agreed to keep funding the deficit, with a warning that disaster would follow if they exceeded their budgets again. It was probably as well that he then returned to Fiji, for on several occasions thereafter there wasn't enough money to pay the wages. Yet the magazine was selling so well that it was bound to pull through if they could survive long enough to increase advertising rates. And sure enough it did.

By early 1935, the *Women's Weekly* was making money at last and well on its way to becoming the publishing phenomenon that it is today. For the next forty years or more it would be the rock that supported the whole of the Consolidated Press empire, turning out huge profits that financed expansion into newspapers, television and other magazine ventures. It would also become the biggest-selling magazine in Australia, with a market share that no other magazine in the world could touch.

Asked many years after its launch what made the *Weekly* so successful, Frank Packer was wonderfully straightforward about it.[16] To him it was perfectly simple:

Q: Did you at the time you started it in 1933—think it would ever be such an outstanding success?

A: No. I didn't.

Q: Why has it been so successful?

A: Because it's a good paper.

Q: Why do you say that?

A: Because it is.

Having elicited this gem, a somewhat nervous interviewer proceeded to probe Sir Frank about the magazine's cultural impact over four decades, with similar lack of progress:

Q: How great an influence do you think the *Women's Weekly* has in Australia on what women will wear or cook or be interested in?

A: Well I don't know, I'm not a woman.

Q: It seems to me that the *Women's Weekly* does convey the impression that a woman's place is in the home. Do you believe that yourself? What do you think of women?

A: No, I don't think it conveys that impression at all.

Q: You don't?

A: No . . . Personally, I think a woman's place is in the home.

Q: What do you think of things like the women's liberation movement and that kind of thing?

A: Well, I don't know what you mean by women's liberation.

Q: Oh, a kind of aggressive appeal for women's rights. That women should be doing much the same thing as men do, that the woman's place certainly isn't in the home, that they're being kept down by men and by magazines like the *Women's Weekly*.

A: Well, I think predominantly women are going to be concerned with the home because a) they have the kids, b) they've got to rear the kids, they've got to look after them, change their nappies, feed them and do everything else, so I think they're a bit uphill to try to avoid their obligation. After all, I suppose every housewife is a stripteaser, and . . .

Q: . . . You mean inside, at heart?

A: Well, I think, actually.

At which point the interviewer moved on to other matters.

Two years after the *Weekly*'s launch, with profits flowing steadily, Frank began to think seriously again about starting a newspaper. The agreement with Associated was due to expire at the end of 1935 and he was determined to be geared up and ready to go when the starting gun was fired. And suddenly, money had ceased to be a problem.

Even more than the *Women's Weekly*, the gold mines in Fiji had become hugely successful. In the early 1930s, small finds on Theodore's properties had started a gold rush to the hills, with a huge number of squatters fossicking and panning for gold. Most had drawn a blank, but by early 1935 Theodore had clearly struck the jackpot, and later that year he and his partner decided to cash in their chips. In August that year, to realise their profits and to raise new capital for development, the syndicate floated their now-famous Emperor Mine to the Australian and British public. In the prospectus accompanying the share issue, the consulting engineer estimated that there was at least 55 000 tonnes of gold-bearing ore and declared, in most immoderate language for an engineer, that he was amazed at the mine's potential. Frank Packer must surely have been amazed too, for the syndicate of which he was a member now took out 300 000 pounds in cash and allotted itself 600 000 shares in the new company, which were soon trading at twice their ten-shilling issue price. Quite how much he made from it all is less clear, for his shareholding was never on the public record, but he was one of four partners, with Theodore, John Wren and a Melbourne liquor dealer called Cody.[17] It seems probable that Theodore and Packer at least were dividing their profits fifty-fifty, as with the *Weekly*. But however the cake was cut, it was baked to a fine recipe, for Theodore was an excellent miner and Packer a wizard at publishing.

As the deadline for starting a real newspaper drew close, Packer first asked his rival Ezra Norton whether he wanted to sell the weekly *Truth*, but after a few brief discussions about price, that proved fruitless. He then approached Associated Newspapers to make an offer for the *Evening News* building in Sydney's Castlereagh Street, which had been empty since 1932 when Frank's father had closed the paper. Associated replied that they would be willing to sell, but only if Packer and Theodore agreed not to repeat their trick with the *Star* and threaten a paper that would undercut the price of the afternoon *Sun*. Frank refused to agree to such conditions and sat back to await developments, having made it quite clear that he was likely to do exactly what Associated most feared.

It did not take long for the directors of Associated to take fright and make Frank a rather better offer than he had proposed, inviting him to take control of the ailing *Telegraph*, which was losing money and readers at a rate of knots. Given that Joynton Smith had been contemplating paying 300 000 pounds for a half-share in the same paper thirteen years earlier, it was potentially a valuable prize, and when details of the agreement were published in January 1936 after months of negotiations, it was immediately obvious that Packer and Theodore had landed a colossal bargain. The deal would merge the *Telegraph* and the *Women's Weekly* into a new publishing combine, Consolidated Press Limited, under Packer and Theodore's control. And although it required the two men to put 100 000 pounds cash into the new company while Associated contributed nothing, it also gave them two-thirds of the shares and two-thirds of the seats on the board. It provided them, too, with the almost-new *Evening News* building so that they could move out of their rented space at AWU headquarters.[18]

Not everyone was impressed with Packer's judgment in the deal. Referring to it, somewhat perversely, as the new 'Theodore daily', *Smith's Weekly* expressed doubt about whether it could be made to pay, given that its previous proprietors had failed so comprehensively to make a profit. But Frank Packer had no such doubts. The only competition in the Sydney market was the dull old *Sydney Morning Herald*, since all other rivals had perished in the slump, and there was clearly a readership waiting to be served. To his eye, the *Telegraph* was also ripe for improvement. It had struggled along, starved of funds, deteriorating in quality as the months went by, with Associated apparently incapable of action. But there was nothing wrong with it that a good bit of money and a few well-placed skills wouldn't fix. Packer immediately let it be known that he was prepared to pay top salaries for the best journalists in town. He then bought, at great cost, exclusive access to the Hearst International News Service in the USA, to give the revamped paper an edge in foreign news. Meanwhile, Warnecke's world tour had already identified suitable printing machinery, and this was now ordered from Britain to replace the ancient letter-presses that had clanked out the *Evening News* and *Women's Weekly*. Warnecke and Packer themselves set to work remodelling the paper, changing it from a tabloid to a broadsheet, along the lines of Beaverbrook's hugely successful *Daily Express* in London.

The first edition of the new paper was published on 23 March 1936, claiming to be as modern as television, wireless and airmail. There was a page devoted to pictures, stronger headlines, and a far bolder layout than the old-style *Telegraph* it had replaced. There was a full page of cartoons, and a turf section that soon expanded into a twelve-page form guide. But while it was true that the *Telegraph* set the style for today's popular tabloids, in many respects it merely took up where Frank's father's *Daily Guardian* had left off. Free insurance for readers and competitions with large prizes were once again staple features: in later years, they even repeated the quest for surf girls. One of its livelier attractions was its 'Fifty-Word Letterettes' where a provocative letter kicked off debate on subjects of popular concern, such as beach undress, caning at school or the merits of corporal punishment at home. But a more lurid example of what readers could expect was served up on the front page of the first issue, with the dateline Cala, Florida, in the United States (where such stories have always come from). Headlined 'NAILED TO CROSS', it was a model for the popular press for years to come, a veritable classic of its kind.

> Nailed in crucifix fashion to a makeshift wooden cross, J. K. Tiller-man, forty-five, a canal worker, was found on the outskirts of town today.
>
> Thirty penny nails were driven through his feet into the cross.
> His mouth was tightly sewn up.

He had passed through such excruciating agony that he was unconscious when found.

On regaining consciousness in hospital he steadfastly refused to make any statement.

He will not betray his attackers, and offers no explanation of the crime.

Not surprisingly, in view of its racy stories, the *Telegraph* found its readers mainly among the younger working classes. Surveys in 1939 showed that two-thirds of those who bought it were under thirty-five. There was a high proportion, too, of women readers, allowing Packer to entice advertisers to take out space with the cute claim that they could reach the young 'Mrs Spending' rather than the old 'Mrs Spent'.

Like Frank himself, the paper was forthright in its opinions, with its first issue under Packer's banner laying it on the line for readers:

> We make no apologies for being free and frank. We shall apologise
> if we ever become dull, pompously or consciously inaccurate . . .
> No law compels you to read the Daily Telegraph if its views
> conflict with your own.

The *Telegraph* was intolerant of officialdom and inclined to see even the most complex issues in black and white. Its villains were the bunglers, the bureaucrats, the users of red tape. Its gods were quick action, the facts and getting at the truth. There was little room for shades of grey or for right on both sides, for neither fitted well with the expression of strong opinions. Strangely enough, given Packer's own views, which were robustly to the Right, and its rabid anti-Labor stance of later years, it was at first liberal if not Leftish in its approach. In the 1930s it was in favour of disarmament, the League of Nations, modern art and the forty-hour week, to name but a few of its causes. It was against hanging, mistreatment of Aborigines, censorship and prudery on the beaches. Thanks, without doubt, to Warnecke, its early editor-in-chief, it stood for almost everything that the paper and its proprietor would later abhor. But just as Warnecke's views had not been allowed to shape the *Weekly*'s politics for long, so his influence on the *Telegraph* also faded, and he soon departed the scene. Before long, the *Telegraph* was banging the drum rowdily for conservatism, imperialism and the king, in tune no doubt with the approach of war, but also with the prejudices of its proprietor and the majority of its readers.

With Warnecke gone, the *Telegraph* became unquestionably Packer's paper, in that it faithfully reflected his views and nobody else's. Editors either did what they were told or, like the celebrated Brian Penton who took over in the early 1940s, anticipated the boss's wishes. With his black beret and sandals, Penton had cut a glamorous bohemian figure around Sydney in the early 1930s and been a passionate supporter of the socialist cause. But as a Packer editor he soon turned into a virulent union basher and Right-winger, ruling the *Telegraph* with a rod of iron. Whether he had sold out to save his job or had genuinely changed his mind was not clear, but since Frank was known to hate planners, unionists, the Labor Party and Communism, Penton soon ensured that his journalists also attacked these targets.

Penton was academically outstanding and a fine writer, but he was also a cruel and sometimes sadistic disciplinarian whose ill-humour made Frank Packer's outbursts seem almost vaudevillean by comparison. Although fearful to work for, he was a tremendous influence on Australian journalism who made the paper technically the best of its time. With its short, sharp, staccato rhythms, the early *Telegraph* was like the parent of a modern tabloid paper. With Penton as editor:

> You didn't write paragraphs. You wrote sentences. You didn't argue. You made confident and preferably arrogant assertions. Words were used not to persuade but to bludgeon. Governments were not advised to mend their ways, they were told to do this or get out.[19]

In the clear belief that the paper's readers were almost illiterate, Penton's unbreakable law was that no sentence should have more than twenty-five words, no leader more than eighteen.[20] It should always contain the active, not the passive, voice. It should always be pared to the bone. It should state the facts clearly and concisely. It should quote people verbatim wherever possible. There was a fanaticism about these rules and a fanaticism about getting facts right, but they were a vital ingredient in the *Telegraph*'s success. The paper in these years broke a lot of stories. It broke a lot of journalists, too. 'Many a man would break down and cry, trying to get a word out of a sentence,' according to Tom Farrell, the *Telegraph*'s crack investigative reporter in the 1950s and later chief of staff at the *Herald*. Those who disobeyed the rules found their copy sent back. They would be roundly abused for their failures, and before long sacked.

With Penton as editor and Packer above him, the *Telegraph* was almost Victorian in its customs. Journalists were certainly never on first-name terms with the editor or proprietor. Nor was there any discussion about what stories should be covered: staff would sit in a row at the back of Penton's office and be asked in turn for their ideas. Penton would take them down without comment and then after some silent scribbling, allocate stories for each to cover. For many who worked on the paper at the time, though, this was the Golden Age of Australian journalism. The *Telegraph* had good editors, good journalists and high standards. The tyranny produced results, provided you could tolerate the paper's political bias, which became more outrageous as the years went on.

The revamped *Telegraph* was certainly an immediate sales success. At the end of 1935, before Packer took over, it had been selling 96 000 copies a day against the *Sydney Morning Herald*'s 223 000, and losing readers steadily. Within eighteen months of the change of ownership, it had all but closed the gap. So dramatic was its renaissance and so impressive the continuing advance of the *Women's Weekly*, that rival newspaper magnate Sir Keith Murdoch soon expressed interest in adding Packer's publications to his *Herald & Weekly Times* stable in Melbourne. In July 1938, two years after the *Telegraph*'s relaunch, he made an exploratory bid for Consolidated Press, offering 550 000 pounds for a half-interest in the group. Then, when that was turned down, he raised his offer to 800 000 pounds for the whole company. Theodore and Packer discussed it briefly with their lawyers before turning Murdoch away. Although the *Telegraph* was still losing money, the gold mines and the *Women's Weekly* were doing so well that they hardly needed the cash, and there was no other reason for selling.

But Packer was never one to miss a business opportunity. Making use of Murdoch's offer to put the wind up Fairfax, publishers of the *Herald*, he persuaded them to allow the *Telegraph* to raise its cover price so that the Melburnian invaders could be kept at bay.[21] Then, with a spring in his step, he set about polishing his plans for a new paper to attack the Sunday market.

As part of the 1936 deal with Associated, Frank had agreed not to start a Sunday version of the *Telegraph* for three years, in exchange for which Associated had given the *Women's Weekly* a free run of the magazine market, by promising to restrict sales of its most powerful rival, *Woman*. This had allowed the *Weekly* to make even more money just when Packer needed it, yet had not tied his hands at all, since he could not possibly have afforded to launch a Sunday and a daily paper simultaneously, however much he had wanted to. Once again, poor Associated had been taken to the cleaners and Packer had scored a triumph. For now that the *Telegraph* was on its feet and he did have enough cash to start a Sunday version, the agreement had almost expired.[22]

The new *Sunday Telegraph* was launched on 19 November 1939 with a unique sixteen-page colour comic, and it broke through the 200 000 sales barrier after just seven months. By August 1940, Packer was already boasting about its success, with a full-page cartoon in *Newspaper News* depicting his new champion as the heavyweight boxer that knocks its rivals senseless.

A newcomer—young *Sunday Telegraph*—only been in this game eight months but what a wallop he packs in either hand. Came from nowhere to second place in less than a year! They say that he trains on large lumps of reader interest and workouts with brilliant editorial technique, but in the fight just concluded scored a knockout with his new secret punch—four colour Rotagravure. Three outstanding assets are causing the 'fancy' to put their advertising bets on young *Sunday Telegraph*.

The *Sunday Telegraph*'s three assets were its circulation, its high-quality colour printing and its extremely low rates per page for advertisements. But the last of these was really its weakness. Despite its rapid sales success, the *Sunday Telegraph* and its daily brother were both having real trouble attracting advertisers. The paper's top-selling Sunday rival, the *Sunday Sun*, had a firm grip on the big retail outlets such as David Jones, while its strongest daily competitor, the *Sydney Morning Herald*, had an iron hold over the classifieds. This was a situation that fundamentally did not change in all the years that Packer owned the papers. And as a consequence, the *Telegraph*s would never make money, or never make much, and never for long. Frank Packer could outsell or out-shout the Fairfax papers as much as he liked, but he could never match them for financial strength and security.

By the end of the 1930s, however, the *Telegraph*'s proprietor was already a major figure on the Sydney scene, and the Packers as a family had arrived. A year after the launch of the *Women's Weekly*, Frank had married, having caught up with the much-pursued Gretel Bullmore after five years of courting her. It was not clear why she had spent so long saying 'no', or why she had suddenly changed her mind, but she was perhaps reluctant because Frank wasn't quite what the Bullmores were looking for in the way of a son-in-law. The Packers' reputation was that they got what they wanted without worrying too much about the obstacles in their way; as a result, they were on the fringes of polite society. But whatever doubts the bride's family might have had, the engagement was announced on 6 July 1934 and the marriage took place with some despatch, less than three weeks later. It was understandable that the Bullmores regarded young Gretel as something of a catch, since she was tall, beautiful, and a regular visitor to Sydney's social pages, but Frank was also hardly without his attractions, being young, fit and exceedingly success- ful. In some ways, indeed, it was the perfect match, for the Bull- mores had lots of breeding but little money, while the Packers were extremely rich but a little short on class, despite their supposed links to the British aristocracy. Frank's parents had tried to polish the children by sending them to elocution lessons with a famous actress, but in snobbish Sydney circles they were still sniffed at as being distinctly *nouveau*, while Frank's mother Ethel was regarded as plain ordinary. Some of the staff on R. C.'s *Daily Guardian*, who had nicknamed her 'Mrs Fish Shop', to reflect their view that she was a fishwife, believed young Frank to be ashamed of her; it was agreed that the Bullmore family had grace and poise while Ethel, sadly, did not.

Frank and his bride were married on 24 July on a rainy winter's afternoon at All Saints' Church, Woollahra, with Gretel resplendent in a white double-chiffon dress with a long double train.[23] It was a quiet ceremony, yet exciting enough for the social pages to send their spies along and for a small crowd of spectators to brave the wet so that they might see the wedding of 'this well-known girl'. The mothers of the bride and groom, the *Sydney Morning Herald* reported, both wore black, in defer- ence to Frank's father, who had died just three months earlier.

A year after the wedding, the Packers' first child was born and christened Robert Clyde, after his departed grandfather. Kerry followed just over two years later, on 17 December 1937. By this time the couple had moved into a huge house on fashionable Bellevue Hill, which is still the Packers' family home today. Now much expanded, and surrounded by several other properties owned by the Packers, it must be worth $40 million or even more, yet in 1935 it cost Frank just 7500 pounds, paid in cash. It was not the only property he now had around town—there were others in Camden, Narrabeen and Double Bay. Nor was it by any means the full measure of his riches. As always with the Packers, that was kept well hidden.

Frank was already showing a talent that his younger son would inherit for keeping the taxman and other snoopers at bay. There were trusts for the Sydney properties, straw shareholders for Sydney Newspapers and a mysterious Singapore company, TSP Investments, that had collected the profits from the syndicate's initial investment in the Fiji gold mines. Meanwhile, from Emperor Mines itself, there would soon be redistributions of capital instead of dividends so that shareholders could minimise their tax bill.

As for Sydney Newspapers Pty Ltd, the company that had launched Packer and Theodore to success, there was not even a clue to who actually owned it. The seven founding shareholders included a student, a typist, an electrician, a stenographer and assorted employees of the intended newspaper, but not Packer and Theodore. Nowhere in public company records were their names recorded as shareholders, nor was it possible to divine the extent of their investment. There was little hope, either, of getting such information from employees. Sydney Newspapers' articles of association bound directors, officers and auditors of the company to secrecy and required each to sign a declaration that nothing would be disclosed to outsiders.

Frank, no doubt, would have stoutly defended his right to such privacy. In typical Packer fashion he reckoned it was nobody's business but his own.

CHAPTER THREE

THE PACKER PRESS

Dear old Frank . . . a remarkable fellow . . . a wonderful
chap . . . he has been more than fair to me and left me
deeply in his debt.

Sir Robert Menzies[1]

If it was the *Women's Weekly* that made Frank Packer his money, it was the *Telegraph* that gave him his fun. For nigh on four decades he used the newspaper as his own personal soapbox from which to harangue politicians, attack his rivals or declaim on whatever subject had lately caught his eye. He had strong views about socialism, militant unions, the need for stable government, the goodness of America and the divine right of royalty, and was ever keen to voice them. An old-fashioned newspaper baron in the best Hollywood tradition, his view of the world was entirely black and white. There was right and there was wrong: there were friends and there were enemies; there was nothing in between. Neither he nor his papers left anybody in doubt about where they stood in relation to this great divide.

Packer's personal control of the two *Telegraph* newspapers, the *Bulletin* magazine from 1960, and the Sydney and Melbourne Channel Nine television stations from 1956 and 1960 respectively, gave him enormous political power, which he was never afraid to use. And the rules of fair play rarely restrained him. For almost forty years he fought a shameless campaign to keep the Labor Party out of office, denigrating and ridiculing its policies and politicians, while financing and encouraging its opponents. Packer and the politicians in Canberra believed it was within his capacity to make and break prime ministers and to bring down governments, and there was evidence to suggest that they were right. Thanks in part to his newspapers, the Liberal-Country Party coalition remained in government in Australia for a record twenty-three years on the trot, from 1949 to 1972, and on more than one occasion its leaders thanked Packer for their election victory.

The very least one could say about his influence was that he was not someone to cross if one could avoid it—he was a bad man to have as an enemy and a good man to have as a friend. In federal politics, he was on first-name terms with everyone who mattered. He could pick up the phone to Cabinet ministers at any time and expect them to take his call. He would entertain them at his Castlereagh Street offices, his Bellevue Hill home or in Canberra. And he knew them all personally, at least on the Liberal side of politics, which for more than two decades was the only side that mattered.

As befitted a man of his status, he was closest of all to the politicians who dominated Australia in the years after World War II. Packer admired Sir Robert Menzies enormously, counted him as 'a tremendous personal friend' and gave him unstinting support whenever it mattered. Between elections, the *Telegraph* might take one of his ministers to task, particularly if the government was trying to raise taxes. But during Sir Robert's seventeen years as Prime Minister, Packer's paper was unfailingly at his right hand on polling day. And on the vital issues of Communism, socialism, unionism and associated evils, the two men saw absolutely eye to eye. For example, when Menzies proposed in 1950 that the Communist Party be banned, the *Telegraph* enthusiastically concurred. Australia was not the only place in the world where such measures were being contemplated in the early 1950s, for this was the height of the Cold War between Russia and the West. Nor was the *Telegraph* the only paper that supported the ban. But there was an uncomfortable resemblance to McCarthy's witch-hunt in the United States both in the measures that Menzies proposed and in the *Telegraph*'s

49

tub-thumping campaign for Communism to be stamped out.

The Communist Dissolution Bill not only outlawed the party, it also gave the government power to root out Communists from the public service and trade unions. All the authorities needed to do to deprive a person of office was to 'declare' him a Communist. The ban could then be successfully challenged in court only if the accused could prove his innocence. Thus a fundamental tenet of British common law—that someone is innocent until proved guilty—was to be overturned. The law passed through Parliament without problems but was thrown out by Australia's High Court as unconstitutional. Menzies then proposed changes to the constitution so the law could go ahead, and in September 1951 called a referendum to get the necessary approval. The *Telegraph* had given Menzies its raucous support at all stages of the process, as the other papers had done in more measured tones, but as the referendum approached, it pulled out all the stops for a 'Yes' vote, with two memorable headlines:

VOTE YES AND HELP PM SMASH THE REDS

RED HOOLIGANS STRENGTHEN MR MENZIES' CASE[2]

Accompanying them were cartoons showing Joseph Stalin on the phone from Moscow to his Australian fifth column to ask how the campaign for a 'No' vote was going. There were reminders, too, that in Russia you didn't have the chance to vote—you did what you were told or you disappeared. But even in its more sober moments, the *Telegraph*'s summing up of the issues facing the Australian people was just as one-sided. In an editorial three days before the vote, it said that the real issue shone 'bright and clear for rational judgment':

The question is this: Do you approve of Communist sabotage and espionage or not?

If you don't approve, vote 'Yes' and give Mr Menzies the power to put a legal brake on underhand Communist activities.

Remember that Communism was the big issue at two general elections which put and confirmed Mr Menzies in power.

All he now asks is constitutional power to keep his election promises by fighting against Communism without one arm tied behind his back.

Any suggestion that this might have been a threat to civil liberties was peremptorily dismissed. According to the *Telegraph* it was a 'crazy argument ... an attempt to make cheap political capital ... a song and dance ... hot air'. Freedom of speech, freedom of association and freedom of belief were clearly being curtailed, and a pillar of British justice was being toppled. But in the *Telegraph's* view none of this mattered, for only Communists were affected. Far greater threats, it argued, were posed by letting them have free rein.

> If you vote 'No' you will aid totalitarian saboteurs who have no allegiance to this country and whose clearly-stated aim is to overthrow your democratic Governments and democratic ways ...
>
> Should they ever gain power, they would abolish democratic referendums, destroy all organised opposition, and establish an execution squad dictatorship.
>
> That's why Mr Menzies wants to put his heel hard on them from the beginning.

The *Sydney Morning Herald* and other papers also supported a 'Yes' vote, which the Australian public, to its great credit, refused to supply. But Packer's apparent obsession with Communism throughout the 1940s, 1950s and 1960s easily outscored any of his rivals. In the *Telegraph's* columns the Red Menace was never far away, just as it had never been with R. C. Packer's newspapers in the 1920s and 1930s.

Although there was little evidence to suggest that the Communist threat was ever very serious, Frank Packer might well have believed it to be genuine, but both he and Menzies would have been aware of the electoral advantages of regular

Red scares to Labor's opponents. Menzies won the first three postwar elections by 'kicking the Communist can', and Packer's papers continued to put their boot in long after Menzies was gone. According to Fred Daly, a well-respected Labor politician who served in Parliament from 1943 to 1975, the *Telegraph* was consistently 'biased, unfair, and viciously anti-Labor' in its reporting and its editorials. Its tactics were frequently to imply that Labor politicians either sympathised with the Communists or were run by them. Even in the mid 1960s, the leader of the Opposition, Arthur Calwell, was said by the *Telegraph* to decide nothing for himself but to have decisions taken for him by 'thirty-six faceless men' who met behind closed doors and gave him his orders—a reference (which had some substance) to the party's federal conference. Other Labor politicians such as Tom Uren and Les Haylen were more directly accused of being traitors and Soviet stooges. 'I was a former Woolworths' manager, a Mr Average, and in many ways conformed to the system,' says Uren today, 'but you didn't have to be very different in those days to be marked down as dangerous.'[3]

By the 1950s, Packer's malignant hatred of the Labor movement was certainly dominating the *Telegraph*'s political columns, but even in the 1940s, with a war on, the paper was getting stuck into the politicians on Labor's side of Federal Parliament. In October 1944 one of Packer's most famous cartoonists, Will Mahony, was sacked when he refused to keep on drawing anti-Labor cartoons. George Finey, another great cartoonist, then took over from him, only to be shown the door as well when he objected. The *Telegraph*'s attacks clearly hurt Prime Minister John Curtin, for on Curtin's death in 1945 Frank Packer called on Ben Chifley in Canberra, along with Sir Keith Murdoch and Rupert Henderson, general manager of the *Sydney Morning Herald*, to express his sympathy. 'So you bloody should,' Chifley told the trio, 'after all, *you* helped kill him.' It was the *Telegraph*'s cartoons in particular that had so distressed the poor man.[4]

Packer's own politics, one need hardly say, were deeply

conservative. A true-blue Liberal, he was at the small Melbourne dinner in April 1944 that heralded the party's formation, discussing with Bob Menzies and others how anti-Labor forces might be regrouped.[5] A great supporter of Menzies from these early days, and probably closer to the Prime Minister than any other newspaper proprietor, Packer certainly had access to Menzies whenever he wanted it, and saw him socially as well. Menzies was an occasional dinner guest at Packer's home in Bellevue Hill, while Frank was himself a frequent visitor to The Lodge in Canberra. Menzies would at times also stay in one of Packer's Sydney apartments or in his suite at the Australia Hotel. Packer's *Telegraph* would even attack other newspapers for attacking the Prime Minister or the Liberal Party, especially after Menzies knighted him for services to journalism in 1959. Menzies in turn referred to Packer as 'Dear old Frank' and 'a remarkable chap', and described himself as 'deeply in debt' to the man, whose friendship had been 'a great comfort and encouragement to him in many critical periods of his political life'.[6]

Even in the 1961 election when the conservative Fairfax papers deserted Menzies, Packer's *Telegraph* stayed rock-solid behind him. And the newspaper's support was the decisive factor in the Liberal–Country Party coalition scraping back into power with a majority of just one seat, according to Billy McMahon, later Australia's Prime Minister. McMahon was quite convinced that Packer's paper had kept the Labor Party out of government:

> Most of the press were against us in 1961, especially in the very sensitive state of New South Wales. But the Daily Telegraph was our constant supporter and its influence at the grass roots level was substantial. The political popularity of the Liberal–Country Party Government, towards election time, was consistently falling. Had the election been held two weeks later we may have been beaten.
>
> One of the means by which the strong trend against us was slowed was the sustained support of the Daily Telegraph. I believe this to have been the decisive influence.[7]

Certainly the *Telegraph* in this 1961 campaign was scathing in its dismissal of the Menzies coalition's Labor opponents. One of its editorials, written by Packer's editor-in-chief David McNicoll, branded the Labor Party 'a divided, warring, rag-tag outfit, which would have difficulty running a raffle for a duck in a hotel on Saturday afternoon, let alone a country'.[8]

When Menzies retired in the mid 1960s, Packer's support for the Liberals continued as strongly as ever. Indeed, William McMahon, who was Prime Minister from 1971 to late 1972, was an even older and closer friend of the Packer family than Menzies had been, and the *Telegraph*'s support at election time cemented that friendship. When Sir Frank sold the paper in 1972, poor McMahon was quite devastated. The new owner Rupert Murdoch telephoned from Packer's office to reassure him: 'I can promise, Prime Minister, that we will be as fair to you as you deserve.' 'If you do that, you'll murder him,' muttered Frank Packer in the background, though whether this was a comment on the character of Murdoch or the qualities of McMahon was not clear.[9] Without Packer's support, the Liberals in late 1972 suffered their first election defeat in twenty-three years—which is not to say, of course, that Packer could necessarily have kept Labor out if he had still been in control.

In his home state of New South Wales, Frank Packer was naturally an even bigger figure. The state's long-serving Liberal Premier, Sir Robert Askin, who was elected in 1965, was 'one of his courtiers', according to one former *Telegraph* journalist and a regular visitor to Packer's Sydney offices. And Askin had every reason to feel indebted, because Packer helped put him into power. In the 1965 state elections, when Askin was still in Opposition, Sir Frank, as he had become by then, put together some money for the Liberal leader to boost his election chances. As the New South Wales Premier told John Singleton nine years later:

> Sir Frank Packer rang me and said, 'Look you need a supplementary campaign to get yourself into office. You need a couple of guys who can move quick, think, and get their hands on some money quick.'[10]

Packer asked one of his former editors, Donald Horne, then creative director of the Sydney agency Jackson Wain, to run the campaign promoting the would-be premier. The *Women's Weekly* featured full-page photos of Mr and Mrs Askin at home, and presented shopping, housing and education as the election issues. The *Bulletin* targeted a different audience, focussing on law reform and crime. Precisely how much the campaign cost is not clear, but it appears to have been an expensive exercise if you count the free advertising space given to Askin in Packer's papers and the free air time made available on Packer's Channel Nine. Donald Horne's private papers suggest that the total cost was probably around 75 000 pounds or, in today's devalued currency, just over $1 million.[11]

Robert Askin was already well known around town as a ferocious punter and associate of Sydney's 'colourful' gambling bosses. He was later branded as corrupt. According to David Hickie's book *The Prince and the Premier*:

> He was an underestimated man. The real mark he left on this country was considerable—and was never publicly discussed. While Sir Robert Askin was in power, organised crime became institutionalised on a large scale in New South Wales for the first time. Sydney became, and has remained, the crime capital of Australia.
>
> Askin was central to this. His links with the major gambling figures Perce Galea and Joe Taylor and their cohorts allowed the transformation of Sydney's baccarat clubs into fully-fledged casinos. Askin's links with corrupt police allowed these casinos and SP betting to flourish.[12]

Frank Packer used to play poker with Askin at Cairnton, his house in Bellevue Hill, and was also an acquaintance of Joe 'The Boss' Taylor, who ran one of Sydney's biggest illegal casinos. He would almost certainly have shared Askin's view that SP betting and casino gambling were harmless pursuits. But, whether he did or not, he was keen to see Askin elected and the grateful new Premier of New South Wales believed that Packer's support had been vital. After the 1965 victory, Askin wrote to Donald Horne to tell him, 'We could not possibly have won the election without the tremendous contribution made by your organisation . . . You have played a very important part in helping to change the course of events in this state and I will always be grateful.'

Packer's support for Askin was by no means confined to this campaign. One of Frank's close associates says that Packer gave money to Askin every time an election came round. Nor was this limited to paying for pro-Askin advertisements. As the would-be Premier himself made clear, it was far more important to get favourable editorial coverage, and Packer's *Telegraph* faithfully supplied it each polling day. In the 1965 campaign, three editorials in quick succession proclaimed 'RENTS WON'T RISE WITH THE LIBERALS', 'LIBERALS CAN PAY FOR THEIR POLICY', and 'MR ASKIN OFFERS A NEW DEAL'. A fourth accused the Labor leader, Jack Renshaw, of wanting huge increases in taxes that would 'soak' the people of New South Wales and provide a 'bottomless well' for the State Government to dip into. According to the *Telegraph*, Askin was 'on sure ground, wise, constructive, efficient, just, imaginative, practical'. Labor, on the other hand, was 'niggling, negative, bungling, scandalous, wasteful, reckless, intolerable'.[13]

The news columns also gave great prominence to Askin's policy statements, with a similarly favourable slant. A profile of Askin by the *Telegraph*'s political roundsman was headed 'QUIET MAN WHO LIKES TO FIGHT ON HIS PRINCIPLES' and once again all the adjectives were positive: Askin was 'confident, gallant, moderate, principled, prescient, fond of a joke, a reformer'. The Labor leaders weren't profiled at all.[14]

Yet despite his steadfast support of the Liberals, Packer was quite capable of bringing down those within the party he did not approve of. When Prime Minister Harold Holt drowned in December 1967, the *Telegraph*'s influence was thrown behind the successful campaign to install John Gorton as leader. Four years later, in 1971, Packer's senior political writers played an even greater role in removing him. The downfall of Gorton was a messy affair in which his colleagues became so unhappy about his style of government and their standing in the polls that they forced him to step down as prime minister in favour of McMahon, but Gorton was never in doubt that it was Sir Frank who forced his departure. 'Packer decided to get rid of me and set his papers onto me,' Gorton later said bluntly.[15] The editor-in-chief of the *Telegraph*, David McNicoll, even boasted of this fact at the time, telling ABC TV's *This Day Tonight* that he and Sir Frank were indisputably responsible for getting Gorton out and their friend McMahon in.[16]

In the event, Gorton was gone within four days of the Packer press turning its guns upon him—with the most telling blow being dealt by Channel Nine's *Face the Press*. But the dramatic frontal assault merely followed a barrage of whispers laid across Canberra in the previous six months, which had helped persuade rank-and-file Liberals that Gorton couldn't win them the next election. Gorton blames Packer's senior journalists Alan Reid and Ken Schaepel for doing his dirty work, 'lobbying and spreading stories about me'. But the diaries of a prominent anti-Gorton Liberal suggest that Reid at least did even more, actually orchestrating the revolt and galvanising the conspirators into action. This would have been quite in keeping with Sir Frank's view of the proprieties of the matter, for his friend McMahon had always been his first choice to lead the Liberals, and he had only agreed to back Gorton in 1967 if he were prepared to make McMahon Treasurer.[17]

Labor's new leader, Gough Whitlam, also pointed the finger in Parliament at Packer and his men, saying they had become uncomfortable with Gorton and had decided to get rid of him, using the newspapers and *Face the Press* to do it.

Once this decision had been made his doom was fixed. The operation was mounted. As he himself said, there was a command performance. The Packer Press—the *Sunday Telegraph*, the *Bulletin*, the *Daily Telegraph*, and Channel Nine—came into operation. In fact Claudia Cardinale was ousted—an extraordinary metamorphosis—in favour of Mr Reid, Mr Samuel and Mr Baudino. To quote the fallen leader: 'The Packer Press had started a couple of days before: they put on a command performance—a television show—with Alan Reid as the hatchet man and Bob Baudino and Peter Samuel putting the boots in.'

The *Daily Telegraph*, the paper you can trust! Perhaps it's timely to ponder how much the public or Liberal leaders can trust that paper.[18]

Trustworthy or not, Packer's paper was rarely objective on such matters. The hard truth for *Telegraph* journalists was that it was difficult to report on politics, the unions or Labor without one's copy ending up biased or twisted. If mildly pro-Labor sentiments were expressed in stories or the unions insufficiently condemned, they rarely, if ever, ended up in the paper. According to David McNicoll, Packer's editor-in-chief for many years, 'there was always control and supervision of content'. The conservative line was enforced and few reporters tried to breach it. 'They knew the score; they knew the party line existing at 168 Castlereagh Street and they knew they had a watchdog casting an eye over the galley proofs each night.'[19] Not only Packer did the policing. Former *Telegraph* printers who worked 'on the stone' where the final pages were made up say that McNicoll and King Watson, the longtime *Telegraph* editor, were quite capable of rewriting news stories even after they had been set if the political slant failed to match what the boss would have wanted. Labor leaders of the 1950s and 1960s, Dr Herbert Evatt and Arthur Calwell, could therefore do nothing right in the *Telegraph*'s columns. 'Whatever they did, they got slammed,' says one senior compositor. Not surprisingly, the Labor Party loathed the paper, and their NSW State Conference invariably began with a motion (which never succeeded) to expel the *Telegraph*'s reporter. Although it was the working man's paper, the faithful were constantly being exhorted not to read it.

In his own way, Frank Packer was a great advocate of freedom of the press. When Australia's wartime censors used their powers to shield the government from legitimate criticism, it was he who led the press barons into battle.[20] But his version of what this freedom entailed was typically somewhat narrow. It was that nobody should interfere with *him* and tell *him* what to do; it was that his *Daily Telegraph* should be allowed to say exactly what *he* wanted it to, without any threat of interference. Frank loved the sound of his own voice, and was thrilled by the thought that he could have an idea and see it blazoned across the pages of his newspaper the next morning. But his defence of press freedom certainly did not extend to letting journalists express opinions that disagreed with his own. To him, it was the proprietor's privilege to have newspapers that trumpeted his views.

In 1970, in the extremely gentle manner of those days, Sir Frank was tackled by an ABC TV interviewer about how it all worked.

Q: How much does the *Telegraph* express your own political views? I mean do you ever write editorials yourself?

A: Occasionally.

Q: Only occasionally?

A: Well when I say occasionally, I dictate quite a few to McNicoll . . . or I tell them I'd like an editorial along these lines, but I don't have to do that very often. After all, the policies are pretty well ironed out.[21]

Such policies extended to the news columns as well. When a transport strike paralysed Sydney in the late 1950s, stopping the city's trams and buses, Frank decreed that coverage should be kept off the front page to avoid giving publicity to strikers.

It was not often that rogue editorials or news reports slipped through the system but when they did Sir Frank was prepared to take direct action to pull them back. In 1967 he did precisely this with Channel Nine and the *Bulletin*, whose reports on the hanging of Ronald Ryan—the last person in Australia to face the rope—were not to his taste.

Ryan was convicted of shooting a prison warder while escaping from Melbourne's Pentridge jail and, like countless

59

others before him, was sentenced to death for his crime. But, unlike more than fifty Victorians condemned to hang since the last execution had taken place in 1951, Ryan was not reprieved. The Victorian Liberal Premier, Sir Henry Bolte, who had commuted the sentences of others to life imprisonment, was determined that Ryan should swing. The fact that he had killed a prison warder was said to justify this, although the law disagreed. But political considerations also marked him for the gallows. An election was only two months away, rank-and-file Liberal voters would welcome the death penalty for such a crime, and low morale in the prison service might well be improved if Ryan were hanged. Bolte himself had no qualms about it, for like Frank Packer, he believed in the Old Testament code of an eye for an eye and a tooth for a tooth. But he could hardly have anticipated the uproar the decision would provoke.

Melbourne's newspapers, led by the *Age* and the *Herald*, all thundered for the hanging to be halted and were joined by a public campaign orchestrated by the unions. But, more surprisingly, the *Sydney Morning Herald* and Murdoch's *Australian*, in those days almost a radical paper, also joined the throng, arguing day after day that capital punishment was barbaric and a throwback to a bygone era. Only Packer's *Telegraph* stood out against the crowd, making it clear that it believed the decision to be right and congratulating Sir Henry Bolte for protecting those whose job was to safeguard ordinary citizens. To demonstrate that such ordinary citizens wanted Ryan to hang, the *Telegraph* conducted a poll of thirty people to show that two-thirds were in favour of the rope. When campaigners for Ryan's reprieve sent a telegram to the Queen, the *Telegraph* scolded them for their impudence. They must have known, it said disgustedly, that they would 'seriously embarrass' the monach. But contrary to what most proprietors would have done, Packer did not confine his actions to arguing the case in the *Telegraph*'s editorial columns.

On 30 January, the day that Ryan was due to die, 3000 people marched on Pentridge with anti-hanging banners, chanting 'Hang Bolte, not Ryan'. That evening, Ryan's mother Cecilia gave an interview to the newspapers and television stations about what she had been told was her last farewell to her son. In was an emotional, tear-jerking piece that the other channels ran at four minutes but that Packer's Channel Nine cut back to a mere forty seconds. Yet even this was too much for Sir Frank. At around ten to eleven, some fifteen minutes before the late news was due to go to air, the general manager of Packer's Melbourne station, Nigel Dick, was hauled from his bed by a phone call. 'Have you got that interview with Mrs Ryan in the second edition?' Packer asked. Dick replied that he had. 'Well, take it out,' said Sir Frank and slammed the phone down.

Dick telephoned the studio and told them to kill the piece. Fifteen minutes later, Packer rang back in more affable mood. The marchers, he told Dick, didn't care a damn about Ryan being hanged—their mates in Soviet Russia were shot for stealing loaves of bread—they merely wanted to make life difficult for the Liberal Premier. Sir Frank went on to explain that he had rung his friend Sir Henry Bolte to commiserate and to say that he hoped his own 'bloke down there' was 'doing the right thing'. Bolte had told Sir Frank that in fact Channel Nine was running an interview with Mrs Ryan, whereupon Packer had agreed to fix the problem.

Four days later, Ryan was duly hanged. Assuming that the execution would go ahead, Packer's weekly *Bulletin* magazine,[22] which was going to press before the execution but being published afterwards, produced an editorial, 'The Day of the Quicklime', criticising the decision to carry out the sentence. It argued that capital punishment was not a deterrent to murder and that elements of Ryan's conviction were unsatisfactory. And while it was at times a pungent piece, it was hardly unfair.

> So the white hood and rope are lowered over the head of a small-time forger and thief convicted of a fatal act of violence, the hangman pulls a lever, the trap falls, and in a few moments death is seen and certified. The burial in quicklime is apparently intended as a further deterrent . . .

Mr Opas, QC, defended Ryan at his trial and claims that he is not sure beyond reasonable doubt that Ryan did kill Warder Hodson. What is certain is that many witnesses heard only one shot, that a warder fired a shot in the direction of Hodson, that the bullet entered Hodson at an odd angle if Ryan fired it, that the bullet Ryan has been found guilty of firing has never been recovered.

The probability is still strong that Ryan killed Hodson, but there is some doubt, and there is some chance of further evidence being found which will change the balance of probabilities. If that ever happens the Ryan case will become notorious for more murders than one.[23]

On the following page was something that fired Packer's rage even more—a cartoon of his friend Sir Henry Bolte, dressed as an executioner and trailing a noose, with the caption: 'I DO NOT BOW TO MOB PROTESTS—ONLY MOB SUPPORT'. Packer had approved neither the cartoon nor the editorial, but was quick to act when he saw them, ordering all 40 000 copies of the magazine to be pulped. A new editorial was then written and a new cartoon drawn—on other subjects. Sir Frank's own views had been summed up by the *Telegraph* some days earlier—it was right to hang Ryan, hysterical to protest, and admirable of Bolte to have resisted the clamour for reprieve:

Sir Henry had been subjected to pressures which would easily daunt a weaker man. Victorians, no matter how they feel about the Ryan hanging, at least know they have a strong man running their state.[24]

With Packer as its proprietor, the *Telegraph* was often outrageous and always noisy. But at times it also had humour and panache. In many ways the paper reflected the man. Frank himself was outspoken to the point of rudeness and frequently impossible to deal with, but he was also a character, a larger-than-life figure to whom the normal rules of behaviour did not apply. So, on occasions, his newspapers did things that none of his more sober rivals would ever dare try.

The *Daily Telegraph*'s reporting of the death of Stalin in March 1953 is a classic example of vintage Packer style. Headed 'HIS OLD COMRADES ARE PREPARING A WARM WELCOME' and written by 'Our special correspondent', the front page on the morning after the dictator's death began thus:

> HEAVEN Fri.—All hell broke out here today when the news was flashed by electric telegraph that Joseph Stalin, 73, the Kremlin, Moscow, was on his way. Earlier, a stop press report, which was denied by the Grand Schnozzle, had claimed that he had been refused a landing permit and switched to a certain other place . . . There were generals and peasants, clerks and lawyers, workers and scientists, housewives and politicians, secret police and collective farmers. They carried placards which read: 'He liquidated us but we still love him.'[25]

At the top of the page, with an ode to 'POOR OLD JOE' was a large cartoon of a crocodile crying. Inside, in case anyone had failed to spot the irony, the *Telegraph*'s real views were left in no doubt.

> Let's have no sickly sentimentalism over the death of an evil, brutal, corrupt and vicious man . . . Let's face the facts, he's better dead than alive. He enslaved millions, mass-murdered tens of thousands and turned vast areas of Europe into forced labour camps . . . Stalin has so debased every hope of mankind by his ruthless use of power . . . and by his cynical disregard of human values that he has even . . . turned peace into a dirty word. Any sentiment of sorrow that death may bring would be rank hypocrisy.

Few copies of the day's *Telegraph* ever reached the streets because production was halted by a row over the wording of a poster that Packer wanted to accompany the issue. Having helped write the lead story, Frank went off to Prince's restaurant to have dinner and wait for the first copies of the *Telegraph* to come off the presses. Around 10 p.m., proofs of the front page and a poster advertising the next day's paper were brought to his table. 'STALIN DEAD—OFFICIAL' was the banner on the poster. Packer took a pen from the proprietor, crossed out 'OFFICIAL' and substituted 'HOORAY'. Shortly after, as he tucked into pudding, word was conveyed to him that the compositors back at the *Telegraph* had refused to set it. Frank Packer went back to the office, marched down to the print room and ordered them back to work, telling them that he was the one who decided what his paper did and did not do. The approved version of what happened next is that the poster and story were set exactly as Packer demanded they should be, 'such was the force of Packer's presence'.[26] But the editor of the *Sydney Morning Herald* recorded a less glorious account in his diary the next day:

> Today the Telegraph did not come out because Packer had drafted a bill poster saying 'Stalin Dead—Hurrah!'. The men refused to print this vulgar and provocative poster. Packer told them they must and that if Queen Mary dies . . . and he told them to print 'The Old Harlot's Dead,' they must do that too. Finally, he lost his temper and sent them all home.[27]

Nor did Frank's enthusiasm for stirring the possum abate in his old age. The *Telegraph*'s editorial at the height of the 1967 race riots in the United States created far more trouble than the lampooning of Russia's great dictator, and rightly so. Packer didn't write it but admitted he was responsible for it, implying that he had either dictated or substantially amended it over the telephone. Under the headline 'WHY KID GLOVES?' on Frank's favourite front page, the *Telegraph* advised the US authorities to take a harder line with the black rioters. They had caused damage to the tune of hundreds of millions of dollars, and wrecked businesses by the score and thrown America into turmoil. In the *Telegraph*'s view the answer was simple: the rioters needed to be taught a lesson they would not forget.

> If sharks took 14 or 15 people every summer weekend on each of
> Sydney's beaches there would soon be no one surfing.
>
> If every time Negro revolutionaries decided to burn and kill,
> those maintaining the law killed 500 Negroes, the Negroes might
> decide to stop burning and killing.
>
> Surely the time has come for the American nation to take the
> kid gloves off and deal drastically with this lawless minority.[28]

The following day, Packer's paper issued a clarification to say that
it hadn't really meant it. But it was hard to see where misinter-
pretation had occurred. The great strength of the *Telegraph* had
always been its clarity, and in this, as in all things, Frank had made
his views abundantly clear.

Packer used his papers for all sorts of crusades and vendettas
and to ride his own personal hobby horses. At the light-hearted
end of the scale, he maintained a blacklist or hate list of names
that were banned from the paper. He would also use the *Telegraph*
to thunder about things he had heard at dinner. A *Telegraph*
photographer in the 1950s, the late Ted Hood, recalled with a
chuckle in 1993: 'He'd often go to these parties at night, come
back to the office at about 12.30 and look at the front page. He'd
had a few drinks, and he'd been talking to someone who had a
bitch about something, so he'd write a front page story about it.
The next thing you know he'd cop a libel out of it, because he
wasn't in his full faculties, and he wasn't much of a journalist
anyway—he could write well, but he wasn't a journalist. And he
always said the same thing, "Every time I write a story I cop a
libel. I don't think I'll do it any more!"'

On a more mundane level, there were many articles in the
Telegraph about council tips and the nuisance they caused. Journalists believed this was connected with the fact that Packer
owned a company making waste compactors. Similarly there
were surprisingly frequent articles about tenpin bowling, which
Packer's staff reckoned had something to do with his interest in
some Sydney bowling alleys. More seriously, Packer told the
Telegraph's television critic Denis O'Brien that he didn't mind

what he wrote in his column as long as he said nice things about Channel Nine. Nor was Frank teasing, for when O'Brien complained that the commercial stations showed only repeats at Christmas, he was sacked. The gossip columnist on the *Daily Mirror* rang O'Brien to give him the news and to pass on Frank's message that the *Telegraph* didn't need TV columnists like that.

Sometimes, Packer's efforts to use his papers for financial advantage were disguised by an apparently high-minded stance on public affairs. This was certainly true of the *Telegraph*'s vitriolic attacks on Treasurer Arthur Fadden in 1952 over proposed changes to the income tax laws. Though framed in terms of defending the public interest, there was little doubt that Frank's private wealth was the issue, which explains, perhaps, why the assault was so fierce, even by Packer's standards.

The first shots were fired on 28 September 1952 by the *Sunday Telegraph*, which accused Treasurer Fadden in a front page 'opinion' piece of grossly misleading the public, and of 'downright dishonesty'. The column contained the words: 'disastrous . . . contortions . . . highway robbery . . . stubborn refusal . . . indulged . . . confusion . . . error . . . wrong . . . wrong'. The headline at the top was similarly forthright: 'WE CAN NOT AFFORD FADDEN'. Two days later, the *Daily Telegraph came in* on the act, again using the front page. Under the headline 'SIR ARTHUR, CONMAN' it advised its readers that 'the Federal Treasurer Sir Arthur Fadden stands unchallenged as Australia's greatest confidence man'. Once again, a scan of the words would have shown 'iniquitous . . . shady . . . doubly dishonest . . . dupes . . . outcry . . . confidence trick'. The substance of the attack was that retrospective legislation could never be justified and that Fadden was promising concessions while actually increasing tax.

The change that had provoked the *Telegraph*'s fury was both extremely obscure and of no obvious importance to the average reader, who was typically a city-dwelling blue-collar worker. It dealt with the taxation of partnership assets and, in particular, whether a transfer of livestock in grazing partnerships should be taxable—hardly the stuff of which headlines were made. And while it was true that the new law was to be retrospective, which was an important point of principle, there were also to be retrospective concessions to compensate, and almost no genuine transactions appeared likely to be caught by the change. What's more, the new law was merely re-establishing what had been the Australian Tax Office's practice for the previous sixteen years: a practice supported by several public pronouncements of the Board of Review before being overturned in the High Court. The *Telegraph*'s onslaught was therefore bewildering, particularly because its attack on Australia's second most powerful politician, and one of Menzies's ministers to boot, was so vicious.

Later that day, however, some light was thrown on the matter when Fadden was provoked into a response to Federal Parliament. First of all, he dealt with the *Telegraph*'s criticisms by giving an hour-long recital of the tax laws as they related to partnerships that would have had members snoozing in their seats. But then he woke them up with what was, for him, a major outburst:

> I deeply resent the scurrilous attack that has been made upon my integrity ... I tell the House without hesitation that I believe them to have their origin in spleen engendered in the writers because of their failures in the past to divert me and the Government ... from policies which they believe to be inimical to their private interests, and to intimidate both the Government and myself in relation to future reforms.[29]

It was itself a comment on Packer's power that Fadden felt so deeply wounded. The Treasurer had asked his Cabinet colleagues earlier that day to help clear his name and had even offered to resign if that was what they wished. He had then told his fellow government ministers that he believed the *Telegraph*'s motive in attacking him was not to champion the public interest but to preserve the reputation of Frank Packer and his tax adviser, who had run into trouble with the Australian Taxation Office. Cabinet minutes record it thus:

The Treasurer outlined to Cabinet the events which led up to the severe attacks which the Sydney *Sunday Telegraph* and its subsequent daily issues have launched against him in the past few days.

Cabinet had previously been acquainted with tax evasions, and it was the Government's intention to close these loopholes. He had now discovered the 'master brain' behind the largest evasion scheme—Ratcliffe, who was a Sydney taxation consultant and had netted about 250 000 pounds from this to the present. He was associated with Packer of Sydney . . .

The Treasurer was not clear as to whether the *Daily Telegraph* had benefited financially but Ratcliffe was apparently their taxation adviser and Packer was certainly backing him to the hilt.

The Treasurer was prepared to hit back as hard as possible because their scurrilous attack came not so much because of the present amendments which they publicly describe as unjust but because of their fear that they were likely to be exposed for the scandalous scheme mentioned above.[30]

Fadden also told Cabinet that Packer had already used his influence with Menzies to get Ratcliffe a hearing with both the Treasurer and the Prime Minister about the tax scheme in question. But he did not explain exactly what Packer's tax adviser had been up to. However ten days later, after another battering from Packer's papers, he spilled the beans to Parliament. Starting his speech with a promise to say no more about the *Telegraph*'s 'offensive' accusations, he then launched into what was transparently an attempt to discredit the two newspapers and their owner. His aim, he said, was to inform the House about 'certain transactions that have taken place in recent years . . . which are still the subject of legal investigation'.

By an extremely ingenious device, the legality of which is still under question, a very substantial avoidance of income tax has occurred. The object of the various schemes adopted has been to enable certain private companies to succeed in placing current profits in the hands of their shareholders without incurring income

tax at the individual shareholder's rates . . . the essence of each
scheme is an attempt to ensure that the character of trading profits,
when received by the shareholders, shall be changed from income
to capital . . .

The schemes date back to 1949. The Commissioner of Taxation
has reported that one scheme, operated by three associated private
companies in collaboration with two other private companies will,
if successful, deprive the revenue at the expense of other taxpayers,
of tax amounting to 1 200 000 pounds . . . [31]

The names of Packer and Ratcliffe were of course not
mentioned. But it was obvious to all honourable members that
the Treasurer's statement was another salvo in the battle between
the government and 'certain of its critics'. And the battle did not
let up, for the Packer press redoubled its attacks. On 23 October,
the *Daily Telegraph* topped a special front page editorial on the
subject with the headline 'JUDAS GOVERNMENT BETRAYS ITS
OWN SUPPORTERS' and declared that Fadden's bill contained
'some of the most vicious tax proposals ever to come before an
Australian Parliament'. Two days later, the *Sunday Telegraph* led
with the headline 'TREASURER FADDEN IS EITHER A STUPID
MAN OR A LIAR' and devoted most of the front page to a
renewed assault.

By this time, the *Telegraph*'s aim had been broadened to
include changes to the taxation of private companies. Incredibly,
Packer's editorials had declared at the start of the affair that 'none
of the amendments criticised' affected Consolidated Press or any
of its directors. But if that had ever been true, it certainly wasn't
now, for Packer's shares in Consolidated Press were held by
Sydney Newspapers Pty Ltd, a private company of precisely the
sort that Fadden's wider tax changes were targeting. Yet the *Telegraph* now failed to update its original assurance that Packer's
concerns were motivated exclusively by concern for the public
interest.[32]

Packer's month-long campaign against the tax changes was
ultimately fruitless, but it did succeed in upsetting Prime

Minister Menzies, who told his friend to lay off the Treasurer because the pressure 'was killing poor Artie'. Twenty years later, Robert Menzies still referred to Packer's attacks on Fadden as having been hurtful and unjustified.

In 1957, Ratcliffe's tax scheme that had so outraged Fadden was the subject of a famous action in the High Court known as Newton's case. It has gone down in tax history as a celebrated victory for the Australian Tax Office, which used the general anti-avoidance provision, Section 260, to strike down the arrangements made by the taxpayer. The case was appealed all the way to the Privy Council, with the future Australian Chief Justice, Sir Garfield Barwick, appearing for the taxpayer, but the Privy Council, and Lord Denning in particular, backed the Tax Office in no uncertain terms. Once again, neither Ratcliffe nor Packer was mentioned in proceedings, but the company running the million-dollar tax-avoidance scheme in Newton's case was Pactolus Pty Ltd, which Ratcliffe controlled. A separate Pactolus company at around this time was a major shareholder in Consolidated Press. And while Frank Packer was not one of the taxpayers hauled before the courts, it seems likely that he would have wanted to take advantage of the scheme that Newton's case struck down. In this case, he might also have been hit with severe penalties by the Australian Tax Office, who fined the taxpayers in Newton's case a total of 600 000 pounds.[33]

Ever since Frank had started making money, he had certainly spent considerable energy paying as little tax as possible. And while it was hard to work out precisely what he was doing, since he surrounded his affairs with a high wall of secrecy, it was nevertheless pretty clear that he was doing it.

By the 1950s the private companies that owned Packer's shares in Consolidated Press were arranged in what was known among accountants as a 'chain' to avoid paying tax on undistributed profits. Then, shortly after the Fadden tax changes of 1952–3, a major restructure took place in which a series of trusts and cross-shareholdings was created. Earnings from the newspapers were for a few years channelled into a newly formed

Sydney Newspaper Trust, which appeared to take ownership out of Frank Packer's hands. But before the end of the 1950s the cards were being shuffled again.

The precise aims of Packer's advisers would have been a mystery to outsiders, even had they bothered to unearth the documents. But the broader purpose of these extraordinarily complex arrangements was abundantly clear. The Packers thought it mad to pay tax if one could find ways to avoid it. Thanks to their advisers, they usually could.

CHAPTER FOUR

PENNY PINCHING

In our opinion Sir Frank Packer . . . is an odd character
when it comes to dealing with unions. It would be an
understatement to say that he does not like them.

Australian Journalists' Association Secretary, H. G. Coleman[1]

Whatever Frank Packer spent his money on, it was not the comforts of the people he employed. Those who worked at the *Telegraph* in the 1950s and 1960s remember it as a grubby, old-fashioned place, with long wood-panelled corridors and a huge newsroom for the reporters, filled with bare wooden tables and almost nothing else. For the fortunate there were battered chairs to sit on, and maybe even a typewriter. The rest had old butter boxes or the option of standing. On each square table there was one phone and, with luck, a phone book for the use of three or four journalists. The specialist reporters, the roundsmen, did slightly better, getting a tiny office to share among three or four people, but the poverty of the facilities was inescapable. Little, if anything, had changed since the 1930s. Certainly most of the furniture was of that vintage.

If there was one small compensation for those who worked there, it was that the general reporters' room was the perfect venue for Christmas parties because there was no clutter and nothing to get broken. The journalists, photographers and copy boys would simply lay sheets of newsprint on the tables, bring in the booze and get down to some serious drinking. It was Packer's habit on these occasions to appear at around 2 a.m. when the party was in full swing and stand on a table to address the troops. On one famous occasion, shortly after one of his periodic bouts of sacking, Frank told the assembled revellers that it had been a good year: 'If we have another good one, and I don't sack the lot of you, I'll see you again next year.' Amid a hail of paper clips and glue pots, and to a chorus of boos, he then climbed off his perch and disappeared back into his office.

The struggle for better working conditions at the *Telegraph* produced a war of attrition between Packer and the unions that lasted more than thirty years. The archives of the Australian Journalists' Association (AJA) have a heap of correspondence between the union and the company that dates back to the 1950s, with the same basic requests for chairs, lockers, adequate furniture and decent ventilation being repeated time and time again. In the picture they paint, tables are propped up on piles of books because the legs are broken, journalists have nowhere to sit to write their stories and there are never enough typewriters to go round. When reporters bring their own typewriters into work, they are stolen because the company won't provide lockers to keep them in. The letters go back and forth, but the union gets nowhere.[2]

Finally, in 1967, the AJA took Consolidated Press to the Arbitration Court, where its secretary, H. G. Coleman, recited the long saga of struggle.

> The history of the accommodation in the office goes back into the 1940s. There have always been promises of a new building, new facilities, and new furniture . . .
>
> In 1953 the matter was taken up with the company by myself personally, and in 1954 it was an issue before Mr Commissioner Blackburn. We were then told that new building projects were in mind . . .
>
> By 1957 nothing had been done and on 31st October that year I again interviewed the company and received the same assurances—that things were moving right away.
>
> On March 19th 1958 I went back to the company . . . Nothing happened.

73

The members stirred very violently and on April 30th, a little more than a month later, I was back again and was once more given the same assurances. In May 1958 I was back again and still nothing had happened, but we were given assurances that the building was about to start.

On 6th April 1959 I interviewed the company again and was told the same story. On 12th February 1960 I again interviewed the company . . .

By 1962, nothing had developed . . . Sir Frank Packer promised to look into the subject of furniture and the difficulties of reporters but again nothing happened and there was no improvement whatever . . .

In 1965 we reached a stage where a petition came to the office, and I have it here. I have cut the signatures off for obvious reasons . . . Nothing developed . . .

In 1966 I had several interviews with Mr McNicoll on the matter of accommodation. The members were protesting to the district committee, and during this period I had quite a number of telephone calls to my home late at night, such as, 'There is not a chair in the reporters' room and there are three members wanting to do their work. What will we do?' I said, 'Have you spoken to the chief of staff?' The answer was, 'Yes.' I asked, 'What was his reply?' and they said, 'He said to ******* go and find one somewhere, I haven't got one.'

When the union finally managed to gain an audience it fared no better, for Sir Frank opened the batting by saying that he didn't like unions, and he especially didn't like unions interfering. As for his journalists suffering a bit of discomfort, that was positively to be encouraged: 'My experience of journalists has been that the more they whinge, the better they work.'

Frank's attitude was that it was his business how he treated his employees and nobody else's. If they didn't want to work for him, then they knew what they could do. Finally, in December 1966, he even wrote to the union to tell them so:

It is our affair if we choose to continue to use tables that are old tables or chairs that are old chairs. That is our affair. As for type-writers . . . surely it is the employer's privilege to decide what typewriters he provides for reporters?

His verdict on lockers was similar: he didn't like them cluttering up the place, and he couldn't possibly provide them for everyone.

It is not clear from the AJA files how the dispute ended, but it appears to have been a triumph for Packer. After the Arbitra-tion Court hearing in February 1967, he agreed to a date on which a deputation would come and inspect the premises. The day before its arrival, to everyone's amazement, new chairs suddenly appeared in the newsroom. The journalists had appar-ently won a famous victory. The union inspection team duly turned up and was taken to Sir Frank's office, where the AJA's Jim North outlined their complaint. 'Not enough chairs, what bloody nonsense,' said Frank. 'McNicoll, go out there and count the chairs.' Sure enough there were plenty and the union team beat a retreat. The new chairs were then taken upstairs again to the clerks' office whence they had all been borrowed. After that, the journalists gave up hoping for improvements.

As the AJA's secretary said rather plaintively to the Arbitration Commissioner, Packer was a difficult man. He absolutely refused to give in, was impossible to argue with and placed the unions high on his hate list.

We feel that we can be pardoned for saying that in our opinion Sir Frank Packer—and not in our opinion alone, but also in that of other unions—is an odd character when it comes to dealing with unions. It would be an understatement to say that he does not like them.

It was not just unions that Packer detested, it was anyone who forced him to do anything. Whether it was the taxman, the censor, the government or the unions, he resented anyone who interfered with his affairs. He wanted to run his life and his business entirely as he saw fit. He insisted that he was in control, that handouts and pay rises were given on his terms, at his discretion, with his largesse.

Ron Saw, who worked for the Packers for thirty-three years, had a more trivial but equally revealing example of this philosophy in action. There was a big party at the *Telegraph* offices for the young cadets on the paper, where vast amounts of alcohol were consumed, a lot of noise was made and things got out of hand. The night watchman kept coming in to quieten things down but no one took any notice, so he called the police. The next day he reported it to one of Packer's executives, whose first question was: 'Who called the cops?' When told it was the night watchman, the executive's response was to tell him: 'Right, you're fired. Get out of here and don't come back.' Says Ron Saw: 'That was how they were. It was their newspaper, their business. They didn't want anyone interfering.'

Among the *Telegraph* staff, Frank Packer was jokingly referred to as 'God'. And in his own limited universe it was perhaps only a mild exaggeration; not much went on that he didn't know about, nothing went on of which he disapproved. Thanks in part to his temper and in part to his physical appearance, he was viewed with a mixture of fear and awe. He was a huge man, in good condition, built like the heavyweight boxer that he had been in his youth, when he had briefly been amateur heavyweight champion of New South Wales. 'Tall and thickset, with a fist that could fell an ox and a boot that could kick a mule,' he was a man with great presence and, if he cared to bestow it, great charm.[3] When he was in a good mood, according to Alice Jackson, editor of the *Women's Weekly*, he could charm a monkey out of a tree. But he could just as often be quite terrifying.

Frank Packer and the much younger Rupert Murdoch were, in their own ways, both enormously successful newspaper men by the 1960s. But their styles could hardly have differed more. Murdoch would come into an editorial conference and apologise; Packer would come in and expect everyone to salute, which is almost what they did. Even the *Telegraph's* editor King Watson

A lonely boy. Sent to Cranbrook at the age of five, Kerry Packer was 'a bit of a laughing stock' with schoolmates because he was 'academically stupid'. Struck down by polio, he spent six months in an iron lung. His upbringing was exceptionally strict.

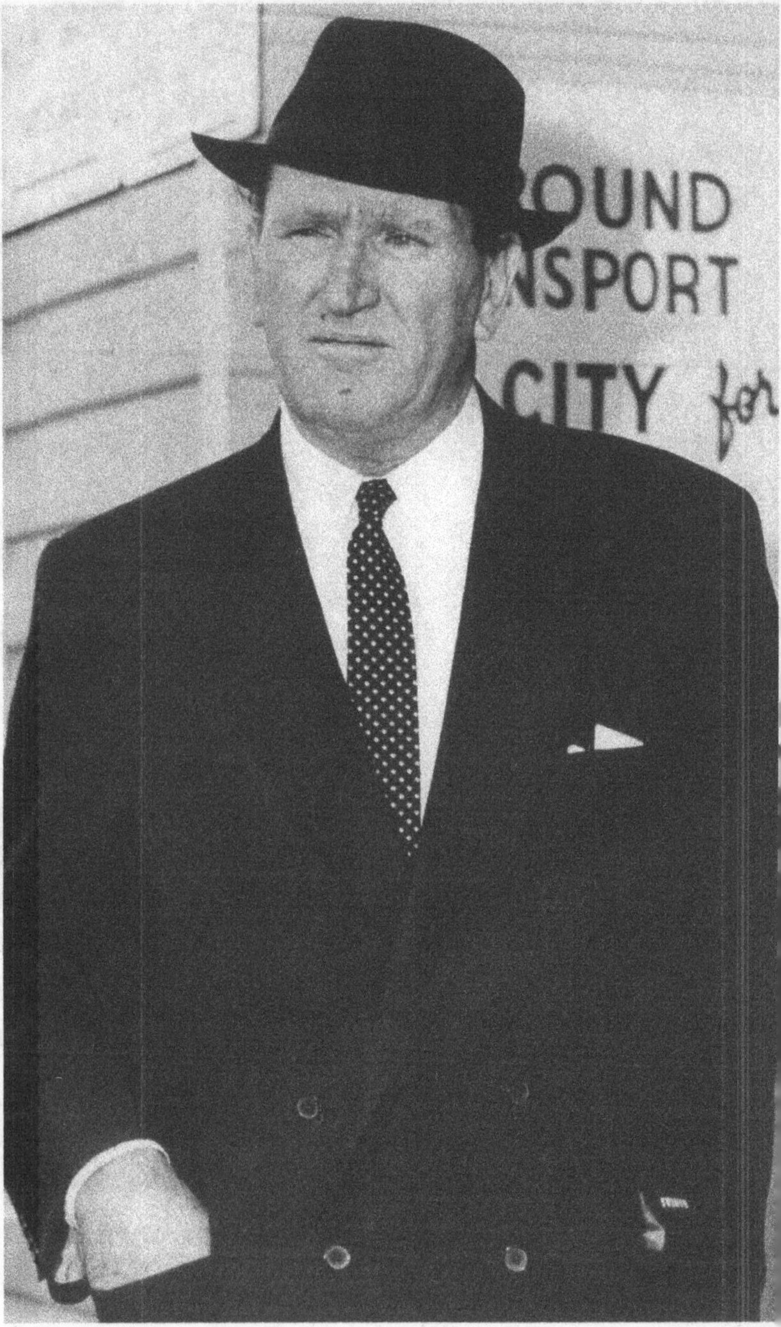
OUND
NSPORT
CITY for

Frank Packer was a big man, in more ways than one. Gambler, boxer, America's Cup challenger, and scourge of politicians, the newspaperman was a bully and a bastard to some, a fine man and great employer to others. All agreed he was a remarkable, larger-than-life character.

A failure at school, young Kerry lived his life for sport. He was a low handicap golfer and had a good eye for most ball games. *Above:* With older brother Clyde and father Frank at Gleneagles in 1959. *Below:* In the 1955 First XI at Geelong Grammar, where he played cricket and football for the school. *Right:* At twenty-five years of age Kerry married Ros Weedon, a doctor's daughter from Wagga Wagga, in 1963.

CITY FORECAST: Fine
and mild, with light
winds

DAILY
MIRROR

Special Lottery
6B4: P.34
TV, Radio Guide P. 34
Crossword .... P. 34

P'MATTA
WEST
COMFORT
NEWS TIPS!
2-0924

Saxon
SHIRTS
LATEST FASHION
For
BUSINESS & LEISURE
with
PERMANENT STAY COLLAR

PHONES: Editorial, Business, Advertising 2-0924 (97 lines); Circulation BX4101, 14 lines.

No. 5906.   SYDNEY, WEDNESDAY, JUNE 8, 1960.   PRICE 5d. Registered at the General Post Office, Sydney, for transmission by post as a newspaper.

Mr. Clyde Packer, son of Sir Frank Packer, forcibly ejecting the general manager of Anglican Press Ltd. (Mr. J. Willis) from the premises. Other pictures, Page 3.

KNIGHT'S SONS
IN CITY
BRAWL

Mr. Clyde Packer and Mr. Kerry Packer, directors of Consolidated Press and sons of Sir Frank Packer, managing director of Consolidated Press, attempted to take over a church printery last night.

The printery is Anglican Press Ltd., Queen St., Chippendale, printers of The Anglican and other publications, including the independent magazine Nation

assumed the proportions of a brawl.

In a series of sensational happenings the Packer brothers and several other men entered the premises when a door was momentarily left unguarded.

Soon after they forc-

one stage he was on his back in the middle of the street.

Later, his eyes were almost closed and his shirt was torn.

Mr. Clyde Packer

No executives of John Fairfax and Sons were at the scene, but it is understood they were kept informed of the proceedings.

Left and above: Newspaper wars, Sydney style. In 1960 the Packer boys seized the Anglican Press printery and were caught in the act by Murdoch's *Daily Mirror*. The premises were retaken by force – with help from heavies hired by Murdoch – and the Packers ejected.

Right: Older brother Clyde *(above)* should have taken over the Packer empire, but in 1972 he argued with his father and was disinherited. On Sir Frank Packer's death in May 1974, it was the 'idiot son' Kerry *(below)* who took charge.

An early success. In October 1975 Kerry Packer's Channel Nine bought television rights to the Australian Golf Open for $1 million. Packer, seen here with Jerry Pate, spent a further $1 million having Sydney's Australian golf course redesigned to put the competition in the top rank.

and editor-in-chief David McNicoll stood to attention when Packer came into the room, and those who refused to follow risked verbal or physical abuse. When the writer and adventurer Francis James failed to stand for Frank's entry, the old man went bright red with rage and kicked him hard in the backside.[4]

Like Packers before and after him, Frank's temper could erupt at a moment's notice. It was wise not to be around when something went wrong. The less you saw of him the better, says one photographer who worked for him for many years. 'If you didn't run into him you didn't cop an earful.'

His saving grace was that he could be extremely funny. When he wasn't sounding off against politicians, bullying his staff or charging around on the polo field, as Kerry later did, he treated life as a constant jest. Cross-examined by Dr Herbert Evatt (former Deputy Prime Minister of Australia) in a 1956 court case, he was asked:

> You went into the newspaper industry as a very young man and have been a newspaper executive almost from the beginning—trained for the position—and you are essentially a person with special experience and skill in the conduct of newspapers? Is that correct?

Packer replied drily: 'Well, I am on oath. I cannot deny it.'

There was no question that Frank Packer had a sense of humour, although its style was not to everyone's taste. He was a great practical joker and a great teaser, who delighted in provoking people to see how they would react. On one occasion he persuaded a policeman to handcuff him and lead him up to his office on the third floor at Park Street, causing great alarm to his staff who naturally thought he had been arrested. On another, he seized his secretary by the hand and led her upstairs to the sauna room in the *Telegraph* building. Ordering her to stand outside the door and watch, he flung it open to reveal the naked figure of one of his senior executives, who was sitting inside. Frank thought this sort of thing hugely funny.

In yet another episode, Packer was watching the opening ceremony of the 1956 Melbourne Olympics with a number of photographers from the *Women's Weekly*. The magazine had sent a team of four and planned to make a great splash in the next week's issue. As the parade marched past Frank Packer picked up the phone in the press box and rang through to his Sydney office to tell the *Weekly*'s editor Esmée Fenston that it was raining hard in Melbourne and the light was so bad they wouldn't get any photographs. He then put the phone down abruptly, rang through to Sydney again and got his personal secretary, Fairy Faircloth, on the phone. 'Take a double brandy up to Mrs Fenston,' said Packer. 'I believe she's just fainted.' Meanwhile in Melbourne, the sun was shining brightly.

Packer's jokes tended to be cruel, at other people's expense, variations on the banana-skin trick. But he behaved with similar disregard for people's feelings when he wasn't joking, and was famous for not caring what people thought of him. He was, as McNicoll put it, 'seemingly impervious to any resentment about his personal behaviour'. Thus, he might lay into the British High Commissioner at lunch if he had complained about something in Frank's papers, or march out of a dinner when they refused to toast the Queen. 'No Queen, no Packer,' was one of his more famous remarks. But he didn't only pick on people his own size. When dealing with his own employees, for example, who had precious little chance to answer back, he could be quite sadistic.

On one visit to Packer's office Francis James was asked whether he wanted to meet Packer's leader writer. Sure, said James. A timid man was then marched into his office. 'Stop,' said Packer. The man stopped. 'Turn around,' said Packer. The man turned round. 'Stand in the corner,' said Packer. The man stood in the corner. 'There,' said Frank, turning to James, 'that's my leader writer.'[5]

Packer's old friends such as David McNicoll liked him in spite of such things, and endeavoured to understand and explain him to others, but even they accepted that he behaved quite dread-fully at times. According to McNicoll, Frank could be heartless, cruel, harsh and unbending, yet was also capable of great kindness. 'He longed to be popular,' said McNicoll, 'but could never understand that his behaviour frequently made him the reverse.'[6]

Another friend, jeweller Barton Fairfax, told Frank's official biographer rather more one-sidedly, 'He was the finest man I have ever known,' adding that 'he has his faults of course. Who hasn't? But they're the kind of faults real men, manly men, are proud to have.'[7] Quite what these faults were one hesitated to ask, but Frank was rough, tough and stood no nonsense. And being a manly man, he farted in male company and swore like a trooper.

A dictator and a tyrant at the best of times, Frank Packer was quite impossible when he had had a few drinks. He was fond of martinis at lunchtime and scotch in the evenings, and became fonder of both as he got older. His office was on the editorial floor, and after a few whiskies he would wander round the reporters' room looking for people to argue with. At nine o'clock he might discover a journalist working on a story. 'What time did you start?' he would ask. 'Twelve o'clock, this morning,' the journalist would say. 'You're fired,' Packer would reply, 'if it takes you nine hours to write a story and you still haven't finished, then you're no good as a journalist.' And then he would lurch off to pick on someone else. David McNicoll would go round after him, patching things up, telling Frank's victims to disappear for a couple of days and wait for the storm to blow over. But on occasions there were purges, as in 1961–2 when, as a result of a severe credit squeeze, six or seven cadets got the boot, along with a dozen photographers. And then no one could save them. The AJA was too weak to fight and didn't generally even raise its voice.

Almost everyone who worked for Packer has his story of being sacked by him. Ron Saw, a famous columnist on the *Telegraph* and *Bulletin*, and Denis O'Brien, for many years the *Telegraph*'s television critic, were each sacked five times. Packer seemed convinced that O'Brien was a Communist. But few stories are better than Donald Horne's account of his first dismissal. Summoned to Packer's office after organising a successful promotion, the *Sunday Telegraph* Beach Girl Quest of 1947, he was expecting congratulation for a job well done.

I went along the forbidden corridor and through an empty anteroom into what, with the books lining its walls, seemed to be a gentleman's study. There Packer sat, behind a desk the size of a dictator's in a movie . . .

He began shouting as soon as I reached the door. As I stood in front of his desk the room seemed to shake as if it were a hurricane and I was in the ship's cabin with a mad Admiral. Why had I taken a car to Cessnock? . . . The car was authorised and I . . . Where's the authority?

. . . Well, I had spoken to . . . I'm telling you there wasn't an authority . . . What I was trying to say . . . I don't care what you were trying to say! Why would you want a car? What's wrong with the bus? . . . There wasn't a spare seat on the bus . . . You didn't need a seat! You could have stood up . . . Well, I thought there were laws against that . . . Don't try to be smart with me, Mr Horne! You're sacked![8]

Horne spent the weekend trying to engineer his re-engagement, which his fellow journalists believed to be a foregone conclusion, and on Monday morning turned up for work in an optimistic frame of mind, his only concern being to help his awkward boss out of his embarrassment. His hopes were soon dashed. He could have his job back, he was told, only if he stumped up fourteen pounds to cover the cost of taking the car to Cessnock. Angrily he refused, collected his back pay and was ushered from the building. The next day a telegram arrived from the *Telegraph* chief of staff, summoning him to Packer's presence. And thus followed encounter number two:

Packer stands up when I come into the office, face all smiles. He motions to a chair. We sit down together, two men talking together reasonably. He had the wrong picture in his mind the other night but he's banged a few heads together and he's found out the truth. (Smile.) He wants me to come back. (Smile.) A great future awaits me at the *Daily Telegraph*. (Stand up.)

Most of those who worked for the *Telegraph* have similar stories to tell, for this was the way in which Frank behaved. Anyone who mattered in the organisation was sacked regularly and, in legend, Packer was said even to sack people who worked for others. There are any number of versions of the story, perhaps because Frank himself used to tell it with great glee and couldn't remember or didn't know whom he had actually fired. But it may be that more than one is true, for it involved a young man misusing the lift, on which subject Packer's sensitivity reached unusual heights. He would push people out of the lift on the Elizabeth Street side of the *Telegraph* building because he regarded it as his own. And while the lifts on the Castlereagh Street side were for public use, Frank was convinced that people kept their fingers on the button, forcing him to wait for far too long. One evening, perhaps after a whisky or two, he worked himself up into such a state watching the lift go up and down that he was quite beside himself when a young man eventually stopped it at his floor. 'What's your job?' thundered Packer to the startled occupant. 'Post boy, sir,' came the reply. 'How much do you earn?' retorted Packer. 'Thirty bob,' came the answer. 'Right, here's two pounds, now get out, you're sacked.' Whereupon the young man, who was not a Packer employee at all but worked for the Postmaster-General's department, fled the building, never to be seen again.

David McNicoll's version, which claims to be firsthand, has Packer sacking one of his own employees but picking on the wrong man.[9] The lift confrontation, however, is much the same. Once again, the lift went up and down past Packer's floor, causing him finally to chase it downstairs where he intercepted the fellow he believed to be the culprit:

By this time Frank was shaking with rage. He grabbed the young man by the shoulders and said, 'What is your name?' The man told

him and Frank said, 'What do you do?' The chap said, 'I'm a reader.'
'You were a reader, you mean. Collect your money tomorrow,
you're finished.'

A little later, Packer and McNicoll came back to the office after
a spot of bacon and eggs to find the presses stopped and a posse
of union men demanding the innocent man's reinstatement.
Frank naturally refused to back down and the next day's paper
was lost. Thereafter notices appeared by the lifts to the effect that
it was safer to take the stairs.

Another classic showdown between Packer and his staff came
in 1957, when several gangs of Sydney waterside workers
unloading a cargo of rusty pig iron were dismissed for laziness.
Keen to prove that his journalists could do a better job than the
wharfies, or as the *Telegraph* put it, wishing as part of its public
duty to find out who was right, he persuaded the Macquarie
Stevedoring Company to let a party on to the Glebe Island
wharves to try their hand. But getting the journalists to play the
game proved more difficult. Six of the *Telegraph*'s brightest and
best, including Ron Saw, Peter Bowers and Frank's son Clyde,
were detailed to report for duty to the *Telegraph*'s garage at 9.45
a.m. and briefed by David McNicoll on the nature of the job.
Packer wanted them to demonstrate how slow the wharfies were,
he said, and they shouldn't have much trouble. In Packer's view,
a bunch of Girl Guides could do it quicker.

But the journalists did anticipate a great deal of trouble from
their fellow workers in the Communist-led waterside unions. It
was already an inflammatory dispute and Packer's intervention
would be as good as throwing petrol on the flames. So, not
surprisingly, all six journalists, with the exception of young
Clyde, complained to the AJA and were instructed not to go. The
following morning, all were dismissed, whereupon Frank, Clyde,
David McNicoll and two senior executives set off by themselves,
only to be turned away by a group of irate wharfies who had
been tipped off to expect visitors.

The formal disputes procedure then swung into action, with

the New South Wales Labor Council instructing all members at Consolidated Press to strike if no settlement were reached within forty-eight hours. Things were not looking good for Packer; it was a crazy argument and the unions were unlikely to back down. But he was a man who hated to lose, and he was determined to negotiate a victory if he could. His first ploy was to offer to reinstate the sacked journalists if they would agree to 'unload' the pig iron at the *Women's Weekly* printing plant. His next stratagem was to goad each one into resigning, telling them that if they didn't like working for him, they should leave. And one of them, Peter Bowers, later a senior writer on the *Sydney Morning Herald*, was unwise enough to accept.

> I said, 'Reinstate me on my former status and I'll resign.'
>
> Mr Packer said, 'Sold.'
>
> I then left the conference.
>
> Later I handed Mr Packer my written resignation which said: 'Following my reinstatement on my former status I now tender my resignation. The resignation will apply immediately.'
>
> After reading the resignation Mr Packer said, 'That's all right. See me at two o'clock and I'll re-engage you.'[10]

Twelve hours later the dispute was settled, with Frank backing down. But Bowers was not re-engaged. The young reporter then decided on a personal appeal to Packer to ask for his job back, choosing a Saturday morning before the races, when Frank was always in a good mood. 'Just admit you were wrong,' said Frank, 'and I'll take you back.' Bowers, however, would not. 'It's not done you any good, you know,' said Frank, taking another tack. 'I've already had other proprietors on the phone, asking for your names, and I could easily tell them you were one.' Bowers still stood firm. And with the first race drawing closer, Packer relented. 'All right, have your job back,' he barked as he went out the door. 'But . . .' He stopped and turned round for an exasperated last word: '. . . but I don't like it.'

Why Frank Packer behaved like this was a mystery, but it seemed that he couldn't help it. Even to those who knew him well, he appeared to have difficulty in making relationships on anything but a master–servant basis. Perhaps because of this he got on much better with the printers, where he and they both knew their place. Frank would greet the older printers by their first names, but rather as a feudal lord might address his peasants, or an aristocrat bid 'g'day' to his gardener. He was arrogant, aloof, patrician, and they were working-class and proud of it. Yet for the most part they rubbed along fine, with a degree of mutual respect. And in many ways, theirs was a much more equal relationship. Not only did the printers have much stronger union backing than the journalists, but they were essential to producing the paper which, in Frank's view, the scribblers were not. In any case, Frank knew better than to try to sack them. And for all his little ways, the printers loved him, at least in hindsight. 'A beautiful man ... a great employer ... nothing but praise ... the most remarkable man I've ever met' are some of the phrases they use. Frank was a straight and honest man, all of them agree, 'as hard as nails, but absolutely fair'.

Packer could be unusually generous both to his partners and his journalists, as scores of those who worked for him will testify. This was, if you like, the benevolent side of feudalism. He would meet legal fees for employees if they got into trouble and pay for medical treatment when they or their families got ill. He would lend money at nominal rates of interest, to finance houses, cars or school fees for those who asked. If his employees died in the Packers' service, he would offer a job for life to their closest relatives. In Frank's great book of obligations, debts to his father's staff were also honoured without question. When one of the *Daily Guardian*'s photographers was killed on assignment in the 1920s, Robert Clyde Packer had promised there would always be a job for his son on the paper. Some years later, it was Frank who honoured the commitment, decreeing that the young Ron Berg was to be taken onto the payroll and kept there. Berg became a top photographer for the *Women's Weekly* and stayed with the

Packers for forty-nine years. But that was a bonus: the fact that people had once been good to him or his family was enough for Frank. It was his duty to repay the debt.

Joyce Bowden, a senior journalist on the *Women's Weekly* for many years, spent three decades working for the Packers and loved it. Early in her career, she was rushed into hospital for a serious operation on the eve of her vacation. When she woke up, she found a huge bouquet of flowers next to her bed, with a 'get well' message from Frank saying: 'Sorry to hear you're ill but delighted you decided to arrange it in your holidays.' It was, of course, a Packer tease, for he paid her full salary all the time that she was away, even though there was no statutory sick leave. According to Joyce, two other staff members on the *Women's Weekly* later contracted multiple sclerosis and were paid a pension until the day they died. Again, there was no legal requirement for Packer to do so.

Before agreeing to such things—paying pensions, meeting medical bills or putting people on the payroll—Frank would ask only one question: 'Is this person a loyal employee?' If the answer was, 'Yes,' he would say to his managers: 'Well, you fix it. You do the necessary.'

But there was another, darker side to Packer's ledger. Those who left his service often found their benefits summarily withdrawn, and few were ever forgiven for going. When the famous foreign correspondent Richard Hughes parted company with Frank Packer in 1960 to join his young rival Rupert Murdoch, he left with the words 'On your way, Judas' ringing in his ears. To join the enemy, as Hughes was doing, was to Frank the most grievous of crimes.

To most of those who observed him, Packer was a puzzle. Although he was capable of extreme generosity, he was extraordinarily suspicious and a great hater. In his eyes, people were generally regarded as guilty until they had proven themselves to be innocent. Though hugely rich in his later years, he was also tight-fisted to the most absurd degree, and had an obsession with waste that was nothing short of paranoid. He would wander round the *Telegraph* offices turning off lights, raging at anyone he suspected of leaving them on. Though the business was worth millions, he still scrutinised all reporters' expenses and delighted in striking out the things they had claimed. He demanded that his reporters catch trams or buses to assignments, and insisted that they attach tickets to their expense claims to prove that they hadn't cadged a lift with someone else. When tram fares went up, he even sent his staff a memo telling them to walk to the next stop to absorb the increase. Another memo suggested that photographers and models going on a fashion shoot should also take trams: there was no need to take the office car unless they had a lot of clothes and gear, and there was never a need for a taxi. Nor was any of this in jest. When one manager allowed excess tram fares in a reporter's expenses, Packer fined him two and sixpence.

Even his wife Gretel did not escape. In the late 1950s, Verne Toose, the manager at the printing works where the *Women's Weekly* was produced, got a call from Gretel asking whether he had a container she could use for mixing garden manures. Toose said he could find one, then had his engineers drill a hole in the side of an old forty-four-gallon drum and fix a top onto it. This was delivered to Bellevue Hill, with strict instructions to the driver that Lady Packer was to be asked for one pound as payment. The next day an angry Frank Packer was on the phone demanding an explanation. 'What the hell do you mean by getting men to do things for my wife for nothing?' Toose was expecting the call and had guessed how Frank would react. 'I charged her a pound for it,' he told his irascible boss. 'Oh, did you?' said Frank, taken aback. 'Oh well, that's all right, then. But I won't have anyone doing anything for nothing. Is that understood?'

In the early 1960s Bruce Gallard, the shipping roundsman, had his claim for a three-and-sixpenny taxi fare struck out by Frank and was so livid that he resigned. He had hauled himself out of bed before 5 a.m. to catch a train and a pilot boat to meet a steamer arriving in Sydney harbour at the crack of dawn, and had taken a cab to the station because it was too early for the buses to be running. Before leaving the building he typed out a blistering farewell letter to Sir Frank, telling him what a sour old bastard he was and where he could put his job. He then delivered it to Sir Frank's secretary Fairy Faircloth and departed for the pub. An hour or so later, the good Fairy came out to the reporters' room with the message that Sir Frank wanted to see him. A friend duly descended to the pub to give Gallard the news, to be told that Bruce would be happy to see his ex-boss when he had sunk another four or five schooners. An hour later, Gallard rolled into Frank's office for a showdown. His colleagues by this time were fearing the worst, but when the door opened some ten minutes later it was a beaming Bruce Gallard who emerged. Sir Frank's opening gambit had been that his star reporter was clearly the victim of an injustice; his next had been to return the cab fare; finally, he had granted him six months' leave of absence to go round the world on a P&O liner.

It was characteristic of Frank that his bark was often worse than his bite. He seemed to like playing the role of the old bastard, only to give in when he had had his fun. Tom Farrell, the *Telegraph*'s top investigative reporter in the 1950s, tells a story of how he persuaded Frank to put money into a car for the Redex motor trials. Ford provided the vehicle, Farrell drove it across Australia and Packer footed the bills. The exercise was a success, bringing a small amount of prize money, a creditable finish and valuable publicity for Ford. At the end of it, Ford offered as a reward to sell Farrell the car for a knock-down price that would give him a handsome profit. Having no money himself, he took the idea to Packer and proposed they split the profits fifty-fifty if Frank would fund the deal. Packer agreed, took a wad of cash from the safe, and Farrell bought the car. Sometime later he came back with Packer's share of the profit.

'Now just remind me,' said Packer. 'What did we agree to?' Farrell recalled the fifty-fifty arrangement.

'Yes, yes. Well, how much have we made?' Farrell explained it was some five hundred pounds, after all necessary repairs to the car had been carried out.

'Well, come on, then, let's see the bills,' demanded Packer. They then solemnly went through the receipts, with Packer adding it all up to check that the figures were correct.

'Okay,' he said. 'You keep all that. Don't bother about my share. I just wanted to make sure you weren't rooking me.'

A well-known photographer, Johnny Smith, who also used to work for Packer, tells a similar story from 1972 when the *Telegraph* was sold to Murdoch's News Limited. Smith asked whether he might hang on to his company car. Packer asked him how much he thought it was worth, to be told by Smith that $1200 would be a fair figure. 'My, you're a good poker player, aren't you,' said Packer. Smith explained that the car had travelled a few miles and wasn't in the best of condition. 'Well,' said Packer grumpily, 'I'll have to think about it.' A short time later, Smith found out the title to the car had been transferred to his name for just one dollar.

There was both an element of teasing and an element of paranoia about Frank's behaviour, but he was genuinely concerned that people were trying to do him down. For someone who was worth several million dollars, it was an extraordinary obsession, but it was obviously pathological. 'The more people I employ, the more people rob me,' he told veteran photographer Ted Hood on one occasion, after they had downed a couple of whiskies in Frank's office. 'That's all my employees do. They take my pens and pencils, pinch my copy paper. They all rob me.' Nor was it said light-heartedly. Frank really worried about it. There was even a rule at the *Telegraph* that reporters had to hand in their old notebook or pencil before they could get a new one, so that Frank could be sure they really were finished.

In later years, the obsession with avoiding waste and saving money was bad for the paper. On the grand scale Frank might still authorise a million dollars for new presses, but in smaller things he was increasingly reluctant to give staff the tools for the job. The contrast with such rivals as Murdoch could hardly have been greater. In the 1960s, when Ted Hood was running the photo-graphic department at News Ltd. Murdoch was happily spending hundreds of thousands of dollars to re-equip the *Daily Mirror* with 35 millimetre cameras and automated processing equipment, to keep pace with the revolution in techniques at the time. Only months before, Packer still needed to be bullied to buy the basics. 'If we could convince him to buy a seventeen-inch telephoto lens for football or something,' says Hood, 'he'd buy just the one. We had to pass the damn thing around, and the pictorial editor would have to make a decision about which job we should take it on.' Ron Berg remembers running into Frank on occasions at Prince's or Romano's, fashionable Sydney restaurants where he would be sent to take photographs of the society ladies. Frank would often be dining there and would beckon him over: 'How much do those flash globes you're using cost?' he would inquire. On hearing they were two bob each, he would tell Berg he had taken enough pictures and send him back to the office.

Among Frank's other eccentricities was that he was a stickler for rules about appearance. He insisted that all members of his staff, journalists and copy boys included, wear a suit and tie to the office every day. When one reporter turned up sporting a loud check sports coat instead, he called him off the editorial floor and led him away to his office. Sitting him down, he told him, 'That's a fine coat, Jim, a particularly fine coat . . . don't wear it in the bloody office.' He stipulated that everyone wear a hat when out on company business, and would haul in offenders to upbraid them if he spotted people hatless. Even his more senior executives were sent stiff memos to warn that their pay would be docked if they didn't comply with the rules. There was only one exception to the hat decree—one could go bareheaded to social functions in the evening. Evening, as Frank's memo to his staff made clear, was defined as one hour after sunset.

Frank also got worked up about the length of his male employees' hair, and would tell reporters and executives alike to get their hair cut if he considered it too long. Once again, he would fire off memos to this effect, warning the younger members of staff to cut their hair to a reasonable length—reasonable, that is, to Frank's one eye—or face dismissal. On receipt of this instruction, some of Frank's young journalists decided they preferred their locks to their labour and opted to leave, where-upon McNicoll and Watson had to convince Packer that the best of them should be persuaded to return.[11]

There were other ways in which working for Frank's papers was an experience few have ever forgotten. There was, for example, a special reason why the night shift on the *Telegraph* was referred to as the 'dog watch'. Frank had been passionate about dogs since his childhood and had a habit of adopting strays, which he then brought to his office, where they terrified staff and snapped and growled at visitors. One of his favourites was a big black Alsatian cross, which he had rather pointedly named Henry after his chauffeur. Henry was prone to go walkabout, particularly during the night when the dustbins were out, as the police roundsmen on the *Telegraph* knew to their cost.

Ced Culbert, the *Telegraph*'s police roundsman from the mid 1950s, remembers one famous chase which started with a late-night call from the boss, who had obviously been drinking. 'I want you to go to Paddington Street, Oxford,' slurred Sir Frank, getting street and suburb mixed up. 'Henry's being fed by a woman there, and he keeps running over to see her. Go and pick him up and bring him back to the Taj.' Ced and his photographer dutifully hopped in the police rounds car with a driver and started cruising the streets. Before long they found the hound in one of the side roads off Oxford Street, persuaded him to jump in the back seat, and ferried him back to Bellevue Hill, where they got Sir Frank out of bed to open up. No sooner did they open the door to let Henry out of the car than he shot off down the drive and disappeared. 'Don't just stand there, get after him,' bellowed Sir Frank, and the chase was on once again. It was well past midnight and Bellevue Hill was trying to sleep, but before long half the neighbourhood had been woken up by Ced and his companions clambering over fences, beating the bushes and calling for Henry to come home. The dog, however, gave them the slip, the hunt was called off, and Ced took the rounds car back to the office. Later that night, as he went home to Bondi at around 3 a.m., he ran into Henry again, nosing round the bins of Oxford Street. This time he delivered him safely back to Bellevue Hill and took him up to Frank's bedroom on the first floor. Frank had left the door open just in case.

It was clear to all that Frank adored his dogs. He showered them with love and spoiled them dreadfully. Some of his senior staff observed unkindly that he got on better with them than he did with humans, and perhaps it was true. He seemed to be a man who was at odds with the rest of the world, unsure how to make his peace. The same could be said of relations with his family. It was quite possible that he loved them all deeply. But if he did, he certainly found difficulty in showing it.

CHAPTER FIVE

YOUNG KERRY

*So what was my father? What were my feelings towards
him? I was a bit scared of him. He was a strong man.
He was a just man.*

Kerry Packer, 1979[1]

Frank Packer devoted up to twenty hours a day to his business,
and his two young sons paid the price. Kerry and his elder
brother Clyde had an unhappy childhood. Not only was Frank
an absent father, he was also a harsh one. When he and his
children did cross paths, he was hard and unrelenting and the two
boys bore the brunt of it. But it seemed to be a hallmark of
Australian newspaper dynasties that the children should suffer in
this way, for both Rupert Murdoch and the young James Fairfax
had remote, over-powering fathers who made their sons' lives a
misery in one way or another. Frank Packer was possibly the
hardest father of the lot—even his approved biographer noted
that he gave his boys an 'exceptionally strict' upbringing.[2]

Years later, Clyde confessed that his was a childhood he would
not wish on his own son. In private, Kerry would express similar
feelings, which in public he would qualify by saying that his
parents were not to blame.

> I had a disrupted childhood, which was nobody's fault. It wasn't a
> matter of neglect, it was a matter of circumstances. My father
> worked bloody hard to survive, and I didn't see him because he
> paid a price for success . . .

My mother was one of four daughters in her family and a woman of beauty and intellect. She was devoted to her husband. He came first, as is right. I don't mean by that she neglected us—she didn't. She believed that her function in life was to look after my father and I don't disagree with that. I think you do what you can for your children but you don't devote your life to them. When they grow up, as they must, and move away, as they should, an enormous vacuum appears. So I didn't really see much of my mother or father until I left school.[3]

Kerry's mother Gretel, according to the adults who knew her, was a good, gentle woman of charm and beauty. But Clyde's and Kerry's schoolmates found her cold and distant. And as her son observed, she was not an obviously doting mother for, like many other women of her class and wealth, she had better things to devote her energies to. She believed her first role in life was to look after her husband, and her next, or so one might surmise, to enjoy the things that her position and wealth had brought her. As a girl she had enjoyed Sydney's social whirl, going to charity balls and having fun. Once married, she became a great hostess and passionate gardener, and spent her time entertaining, gardening, doing good works and living the life of a society lady.

The social pages of the *Sydney Morning Herald* and Frank's own *Telegraph* in the 1930s and 1940s tactfully omitted to mention the activities either of their rivals or their owners, but one can plot Frank and Gretel's progress round Sydney's high spots in the pages of the *Bulletin* and the *Mirror*, or in the pictures snapped by their fellow partygoers. There were fancy balls at the Fairfax mansion and great parties at the Packer household, with evening dress and formal gowns the uniform for all. Gretel, who had been one of the darlings of the social set before her marriage, took such occasions seriously enough to buy all her party dresses in Paris and to send them back there for dry cleaning. She and Frank were also regulars at the polo and the races, Sydney's great daytime social pastimes for the well-to-do, at which Dior outfits were also *de rigueur* for women whose husbands had the money to buy them.

With their parents so busy at work and play, the two Packer boys were naturally brought up by nannies instead, as were the children of most of their rich neighbours:

> There was a whole team of nannies in our suburb, only we didn't call them Nanny, we called them Nurse. Our Nurse, Inez, was known as Nurse Packer. Then there was Nurse Fairfax who brought up the Fairfax kids, Nurse Watt who brought up Suzie Watt who's now the wife of Chief Justice Street, Nurse Lloyd Jones. They ruled the eastern suburbs and were almost more important than the families. They decided who was in and out, which parties to go to.[4]

When Nurse Packer was called up to go to war in 1942, the young boys were sent to boarding school, to Cranbrook, just down the road in Bellevue Hill. Clyde would say later that it was the saddest day of his life, and Kerry can hardly have liked it more, for he was just five years old. For the next four years he and his parents were almost constantly separated. Between the ages of five and nine, he saw his mother perhaps half a dozen times, and his father, it seems, not at all.[5]

Cranbrook was only a stone's throw away from the Packer family home, so it would not have been difficult for Kerry and Clyde to be ferried to the school gates every day. But Frank was by this time helping with the war effort and Gretel was working full-time for the Red Cross, and it would perhaps have occurred to neither of them that they might look after the children themselves. Barbaric as it may seem nowadays to treat such young children in this way, there are plenty of others who have experienced it. Indeed, the British Empire was built by men who were educated that way. It was said to toughen children up: after a couple of months of tears and cold showers, one could cope with anything and feel for nothing.

After only a year at Cranbrook, Kerry was packed off to live with his aunt in the southern highlands of New South Wales. The fear of Japanese invasion was growing and it was thought prudent to get him out of harm's way. Many of the rich families in Sydney's eastern suburbs had already sent their women and children down to the country properties. Cranbrook itself had even talked of closure, and had opened an annex in the Blue Mountains after Japanese midget submarines had shelled their Rose Bay playing fields in 1942. Aged six, Kerry joined the exodus.

> I was sent to live with my mother's sister and two kids in Bowral and I went to school there. It was wartime of course and hard to get into a school, so I went to a girls' school with my aunty's daughters.[6]

Not surprisingly, Kerry disliked this school even more than Cranbrook, but the country had its compensations. In the absence of Gretel, his aunt Mary Hordern, her sister, was an excellent substitute. He remembers her as 'a wonderful woman' and the biggest adult influence on his early life. But he had not been in Bowral long before his life was disrupted yet again, this time by severe illness.

> I lived there for two years until one morning I got out of bed and just fell flat on my face. I had polio and rheumatic fever, and I was sent straight down to Sydney. They put me in hospital there for about nine months in an iron lung. I don't remember much about it except having lumbar punctures—that's the most vivid recollection . . . I was lucky that my problem was diagnosed quickly and that I didn't try to strain myself, because I understand that's where the damage is done. But I couldn't walk, and they thought I was trying to get out of school, because I loathed school.[7]

The early symptoms of infantile paralysis, as it was more commonly known in those days, were headache, fever, and weakness in the limbs, so it was quite easy to mistake it for malingering, but the doctors' diagnosis would have been made easier by the fact that there was a polio epidemic in 1945, the year when Kerry was struck down, and Sydney's hospitals were full to overflowing with small children suffering from the virus. There were outbreaks every year in those days, since vaccines were still a decade away, but that autumn's crop of cases was the worst in New South Wales history, with more than two hundred sufferers in the Royal Prince Alfred and Royal Children's hospitals by mid May and a total of five hundred cases recorded across the state. Young Kerry was obviously one of the more severely ill, for iron lungs, or respirators, were used only in cases where the patient's life was threatened by inability to breathe.

'No other disease strikes with more terror than infantile paralysis,' an American expert on polio observed in 1946. 'Nearly every father or mother whose child succumbs has no doubt that the child will be left a cripple.' Polio did not in fact leave all its victims crippled for life, but it was a disease for which there was no cure, and it was undeniably both frightening and dangerous. It killed between one in thirty and one in ten of those who contracted it, and left roughly half its victims with permanent muscle damage. And there was nothing one could do except let the illness run its course, although proper treatment of the patient was essential to minimise eventual damage.

The prognosis for children like Kerry, whose breathing was affected, was considerably worse than average, in that they were more likely to be crippled and less likely to survive. The newfangled iron lungs, first used in America less than twenty years earlier, were still primitive and rather dangerous machines whose prototypes had killed more patients than they had saved. They were also in short supply in New South Wales and needed experts to work them, so not all children got them when they needed them. But Kerry was either rich enough or sick enough to get the best treatment, and had the luck of which the Packers often speak, for he emerged from the illness physically unscathed, apart from a palsied cheek and a damaged eye. It would have been a horrific experience for a small boy, nevertheless. The orthodox treatment of the time required children to be kept immobile for months, and often demanded that legs and arms be splinted and that the child walk with a frame.

Perhaps even harder to bear would have been the emotional trauma of what happened next, for no sooner was he out of hospital in Sydney than he was packed off again, this time to Canberra, where he spent the next two years being looked after by a private nurse. The altitude was supposed to be the right thing for his recovery, but it must have been bewildering for such a small child, aged only seven or eight, to be exiled from his mother and father yet again. And with his aunt Mary no longer there to take their place, there was a vacuum in his life where a parent should have been. As Kerry would afterwards confess, it was 'a lonely, difficult period'.

By the time he came back to Cranbrook almost two years later, at the age of nine, he had already been to four different schools and, not surprisingly, was hopelessly behind everybody else. He had terrible problems reading and was awful at both writing and spelling. He became a loner with few friends—the class dunce. Although no one realised it, he suffered from the reading disability dyslexia, which can make perfectly intelligent kids look utterly brainless, but that didn't protect him from the ridicule of his schoolmates or the indignity of being the class idiot.[8] Even according to his own description, he was 'academically stupid, a dolt'. In his last year of junior school at Cranbrook, he was required to repeat a year, and in third form of senior school, it happened again. He became, as he put it, 'a bit of a laughing stock', frequently left behind as his classmates moved on. It was, as he later admitted in a strange, somewhat detached way, 'a very tough period for a kid. It was probably the hardening of the shell because kids are very unkind to kids.'

His defence was to display an ostentatious lack of interest in learning, and this at least brought him some admirers. He would sit at the back in lessons, making occasional sarcastic comments that disrupted the class. Sometimes he would cause hilarity with his apparent inability to do what was asked of him, and come in for a spot of target practice with the blackboard rubber because of it. But his real means of survival was to lose himself in sport. He was big and athletic with a good eye for a ball, and talented at almost everything he tried. Aged five, he had run away with Cranbrook's under-seven sports cup; aged six he had won the under-eights' freestyle at the Combined Prep Schools' swimming competition. And now, on his second spell at Cranbrook, he played in the junior school's first football team and won the boxing championship. His struggle with polio had not destroyed his athletic prowess.

Not all his boxing was confined to the ring. He was big for his age and seemed huge and intimidating to most of his classmates. Like most boys, he got into a fair number of fights and, because of his size, he almost always ended up the winner. Some thought him a bully because of it, but there was no malice in him, no joy in hurting others. He was just a big boy who used his size to get what he wanted, who was keen to be king pin, in much the same way as did the man he later became. Kerry, according to one boy who knew him well, wanted to be at the centre of things: 'he tried to imitate his father, he wanted to be the leader . . . to run the pack'. The trouble was he was always something of an outsider. He couldn't run the pack because he wasn't in it.

He had some close friends in Cranbrook, all the same, who would go back to the Packer home in Bellevue Hill and muck around in the huge garden, which would have been a small boys' paradise. They remember birthday parties there, quite formal affairs, with fifteen to twenty kids running round screaming at the tops of their voices and a butler hovering on the fringes. In their memory, Kerry's parents were never much in evidence; the housekeeper looked after the Packer boys and their visitors and made sure they had something to eat. Gretel was often there but always seemed pretty distant. Sir Frank was rarely around, and when he was he seemed strict, a disciplinarian, a frightening figure who was tough on his sons.

Frank was a great believer in the benefits of corporal punishment, and his two boys came in for a fair few beatings, as Kerry has told a number of interviewers.

Q: Was he a strict man with you?

A: Yes, he was very strict. But he was very fair. He used to sentence me to going upstairs and waiting for him where he used to come and er . . . he used to use a polo whip very well. I got a lot of beltings, because I wasn't a very good child, but in all the times I can remember that I got a belting from him I never got one I didn't deserve, and there were quite a few I didn't get that I should have got.[9]

Frank's fairness, according to Kerry, manifested itself in allowing the boy his very own appeals procedure, though some might argue that this made the whole process even more premeditated.

I remember in my early life he took me aside and said: 'Sometimes I have a bad day at the office and I'm angry. I'm going to come home and if you believe that what you've done isn't worthy of the punishment I think you should have, you can have a stay of execution. All you've got to say is, "Look, I think you're in a bad mood and I'd like to discuss it with you tomorrow," and that'll stop it.' He said that it may not alter the punishment—that he may decide on the next day that I was wrong and he was right—but I had that option.[10]

Kerry never put his father's promise to the test, but says he never needed to. In the words of the classic saying, Frank was a hard man, but fair. And despite his strict regime, the boys either loved or feared him enough to show him affection in public. When he came back from overseas trips they would go to the airport to meet him, and kiss him. Kerry would say years later, in a Pollyanna sort of way, that he had been a lucky child—lucky to be born with all the advantages, lucky to survive his illness, lucky to have so many good things happen to him, lucky to have such fantastic parents. Defiantly, almost, as if saying it would make it so, he said that he had a stack of happy memories, marred only by one thing, the loneliness of his childhood. He was shunted around from school to school and place to place so much that he had no opportunity to make friends. The holidays at home in Sydney with his fantastic parents could be especially lonely, but that, he said bravely, was just the luck of the draw.

After five years at Cranbrook, Kerry was packed off to another boarding school, more than a thousand kilometres away down south, to Geelong Church of England Grammar School, where Australia's rich and famous often sent their sons. His brother Clyde had been sent there two years earlier on the advice of Cranbrook's principal, Sir Brian Hone. Both children had been living at home, and Hone was worried about Frank's treatment of Clyde in particular. Bullied by his father, the elder boy had started to take it out on his fellows at school. At the age of fourteen, he was already more than six feet tall (1.82 metres), 95 kilograms in weight and hard to handle. He appeared to have little respect for prefects or teachers, was widely disliked and constantly in trouble. Kerry, meanwhile, was learning nothing, was also huge and also seen as a bit of a thug. One older boy who knew both Packers well says they were big, obnoxious, dirty-minded boys who thought they could get away with anything. But Clyde, in particular, stood out.

Away from his father, however, Clyde soon flourished, and before long was enjoying a brilliant career. At Geelong, he played the double bass, starred in the school's production of *Macbeth*, turned out twice for the First XV Rugby team and eventually became a house prefect. His academic record also improved: shortly after arrival in 1951 he did so badly in his exams that the school wouldn't let him proceed to matriculation. Not much later, he was winning house colours for work, matriculating, and even landing a Commonwealth scholarship to stay on an extra year, although the Packers can hardly have needed the money.

Sadly, the move to Geelong worked no wonders for Kerry. As at Cranbrook, he was academically hopeless and suffered the same gibes from teachers and pupils about his lack of ability. Once again, he took little or no interest in his studies, trailing a radio out of the window at the back of the class to listen to the Melbourne Cup or some other sporting event, but rarely working. One classmate, Chris Forsyth, who later worked for Kerry's World Series Cricket, remembers him sitting in economics lessons, openly reading pulp novels by Carter Brown. Forsyth took the precaution of also reading the economics textbook, but Packer never bothered, not even considering it necessary to own one.

> I recall once he actually picked up my copy, hefted it and remarked: 'How can you be bothered reading this boring shit?'[11]

Packer, who was doing economics for the second time around, failed it again. But this was the pattern across all the subjects. It took him six years to complete four years of senior high school and, like his father, he seems to have failed to pass the Leaving Certificate at the end. Yet, like his father and several others who come to mind, his academic incompetence was no barrier to eventual success. Nor did it necessarily indicate that he was slow-witted, for as those who met him in later life realised, he was not. Once again, no one understood enough to realise that Kerry's fundamental problem was dyslexia, so he was assumed to be unco-operative, uninterested in scholastic pursuits and, to put it bluntly, simply thick.

As at Cranbrook, he took refuge in being tough, which was not difficult for someone his size, and in being good at games. In his own words, he lived his life for sport. He played football, cricket, rugby, and golf well; he boxed and swam. But although he was good at most sports, he was brilliant at none, and he had to work hard for his success. He played for the First XV in football and the First XI in cricket, but only after working his way up from B grade and serving time in the third and second teams. At cricket, he is remembered for crashing a quick twenty or thirty before getting himself out, but looking through the scores it is hard to find matches in which Kerry scored runs. He approached batting as he did most other things, with an athletic swagger and an apparent arrogance. Only at boxing did he really excel, as his father had done before him; helped by the fact that he was larger than almost anyone else, he punched his way to be the school's heavyweight champion in 1956 at the age of eighteen.

Whether this was adequate compensation for being an academic failure is doubtful. Geelong's famous headmaster of the 1950s, Sir James Darling, was convinced that Kerry continued to regard himself as a reject, and that several of his classmates reached the same conclusion. 'I think he felt the failure of not being up to standard at school work,' said Darling. 'Of course, he put a lot of effort into games and got satisfaction from that, but I don't think that made up for being no good academically.' Accomplished though he was on the games field, Kerry was certainly not feted as the school's sporting hero. Nor did his all-round sporting prowess make his masters or peers noticeably better disposed towards him.

Fortunately, Kerry's housemaster at Geelong, Vic Tunbridge, did like him and wasn't afraid to show it. Like Frank Packer, he was a forthright man, who believed in discipline and plain speaking, and did not suffer fools, but he was kinder and more sympathetic to the Packer boys than Frank ever was. According to James Darling, Tunbridge and his wife were devoted to Kerry, who looked on them as surrogate parents. Jane Stoddart, the matron in Kerry's house, was another who liked him and got close to him in a way that most of his fellow pupils did not, finding him polite, gentle and considerate.

Sir James Darling confessed that he didn't particularly *like* either of the Packers, and in any case preferred Clyde to Kerry, because he was more sensitive and self-aware. Yet he still had some kind words for Kerry, saying that he was without malice, even if he was one of the school tough guys: 'He was a simple chap and a good chap.'

According to Chris Forsyth, his classmates and those who had to teach him liked him far less.

Packer was not popular. Despite his size, or perhaps because of it, Packer was considered fair game for spiteful shafts about his father's money. Teachers baked him, possibly getting even for what they saw as lack of respect—and Packer did not bother to hide it . . . 'Just because your father's got money you think you can get away with it' was the favourite phrase they tried to belittle him with. In a school where everyone's father had money, this was a curious attack. Yet they singled him out.[12]

It might have been the way that Kerry's father made money or the vulgar power of Frank Packer that upset his schoolmates. Or it might simply have been the fact that his family's money was new rather than old—Kerry certainly reckoned the people at Geelong were a bunch of snobs—but it was particularly unfair to attack Kerry for being rich, for his father hardly spoiled the child or gave him reason to think that the Packer wealth entitled him to privileged treatment. Far from it, in fact.

One famous summer holiday, the young Kerry returned home from school in Geelong without his tennis racquet. According to Kerry's telling of the story, he had only been back in Sydney for a couple of hours when his crime was discovered. He was downstairs in the billiard room, playing a game with his father, while upstairs his mother unpacked his bag. It was a close game, the two men were trying to concentrate and, in Kerry's version, Gretel wouldn't give them any peace.

> Every time Dad was about to take a shot, Mum would yell out from upstairs, 'Where's your so-and-sos?' And as I say, the match was pretty tight. Eventually the old man's done his lolly at this; he said, 'For Christ's sake Gretel, do you want me to send him back to pick it up?' And she's not going to be outdone at this stage. She says: 'Yes.' And the next thing I know I'm on my way back to Melbourne.[13]

The train fare no doubt cost a great deal more than the tennis racquet, yet Frank Packer obviously believed that the lesson he was teaching his son was cheap at the price. Many would doubtless admire him for not spoiling the boy, or would merely find the episode amusing, but only a determined man could have put such an impulse into effect. One can imagine how the timetable would have had to be consulted, the car and driver ordered, the journey to the station made, the ticket bought, the train boarded, the farewells said. One can imagine how there would have been numerous opportunities to forgive and forget, yet none was taken. Once the decision had been made, in Kerry's romanticised version, in a moment of understandable annoyance, Frank either would not or could not accept his chance to back down. And Gretel, if she wanted to, was unable to make him. Twenty-four hours later Kerry cabled to his father from Victoria: 'Arrived Melbourne safely. No love, Kerry.' One imagines that he found his racquet and remembered to take it home.

Years later this whole incident could be treated as a joke, as Kerry did when recounting the story on television, but it would surely have been less funny at the time. Frank Packer, according to Kerry, was a just man, a fair man, and an honest man. And no doubt he meted out this and other punishments in the name of honesty, fair play and just deserts. But he would have been a hard man to have as a father, nevertheless.

As a boarder at a school more than a thousand kilometres from Sydney, Kerry once again saw his parents only in the holidays or on the rare occasions when Frank made the trek down to Geelong. Even then, his father seems to have been visiting James Darling, the headmaster, as often as his sons, for the two men had official business to discuss. When the Australian Broadcasting Control Board was set up in 1954 to advise the government on who should get the first commercial television licences in Sydney and Melbourne, Darling was made chairman. Packer, predictably, headed one of the consortia bidding for the Sydney licence. There was therefore plenty for the two men to talk about, apart from Frank's younger son's lack of progress.

They would have been interesting meetings, for the contrast between the two men could hardly have been greater. Darling was English, courteous, loved learning for its own sake and believed that the privileged had a duty to do good. Frank could be outrageously rude, held intellectuals in contempt and was firmly convinced that making money was the highest moral pursuit. But on top of these differences in style and creed, there was also a clash of egos. Headmasters are accustomed to commanding considerable respect, and Sir James Darling as head of Geelong would have been used to receiving more than most, but Frank bowed to no one. Darling later could not remember the subject of the blazing row they had, but the memory of losing it has not faded. 'He's the only person ever to have rolled me out flat in my own study,' he said. There's no doubt that Frank Packer was an honest man, said Darling, 'but he was a thug'. The venerable headmaster admitted that even he was somewhat afraid of Packer senior. One needs little imagination to divine how fearsome a figure Frank must have seemed to his sons.

CHAPTER SIX

THE IDIOT SON

What are you like at fixing blueys?

Kerry Packer to the *Daily Telegraph* police roundsman, 1956[1]

Even before he left school in 1956 at the age of nineteen, Kerry was being made to work at the *Telegraph* in his holidays to get a taste of the family business. And as soon as he finished at Geelong, he was required to resume that education. It had never occurred to him to do anything else, but it would probably have made little difference even if he had, for he would never have dared defy his father.

Just like Frank thirty years earlier, he was forced to start at the bottom on the most menial jobs, unloading newsprint, cleaning the machines, filling the ink drums and stacking newspapers as they came off the line. Doing such menial work was an important lesson for someone who had had lots of privileges, but Kerry certainly didn't think so at the time. He loathed what he was doing. It was mindless and boring, the hours passed slowly, and he felt aggrieved that he should be asked to suffer it. To Kerry, the fact that he was undergoing this pointless indignity must have seemed doubly unfair, because his elder brother had escaped scot free. The brighter, more successful Clyde, who everybody said was being groomed for the succession, had spent a short time at university in Canberra before being taken on as a reporter and was now working upstairs while Kerry laboured in the basement.

Nevertheless, the printers who worked with Kerry found him good-natured enough, if somewhat lazy, and got on with him well. Typically, Frank had given strict instructions that he was to be shown no favouritism and spared no hardship, that he wasn't to have an easy life just because he was the boss's son, and at first this caused some trouble. When young Kerry was told to help one of his new workmates wash down the cylinders on the printing presses—a filthy job that involved sliding under the machines to clean off all the ink—Kerry refused to have anything to do with it, and was promptly told by the foreman, Jack Rodney, that he would do as he was told or go home. According to the story that went round the subsequent night shift, Kerry fired back that he would do better than that, he would go and see his Dad. And off he marched in his ink-stained overalls and dirty boots. One can only guess at the reception he got, but ten minutes later he was downstairs again, 'like a mongrel dog with his tail between his legs'. After that, it seems, Kerry did as he was asked and the printers had little trouble with him.

In Kerry's four months in the machine room, and subsequent periods learning the trade elsewhere in the bowels of the *Telegraph* building, his father certainly showed him no favours. Indeed, he seems to have subjected the boy to some petty humiliations. When the other printers lined up on Friday for their wages, for example, young Kerry had to go knocking on his father's door to collect his money. Nor was this arranged so that Frank could give his son a bonus, for he paid him no more than a printer's wage and almost certainly paid him less. Indeed, when Kerry moved over to the *Women's Weekly* printing plant a little later, Frank demanded that he hand five pounds of the nine pounds eighteen shillings in his pay packet straight back to him. Presumably this was to cover his accommodation at Bellevue Hill but, according to the *Weekly*'s production manager Verne Toose, it was just typical Frank, a perfect example of how tough the old man was.

Kerry's first contact out at the *Weekly* was Bill Hudson, who was standing by his machine one morning, watching the big paper reel feeding onto the presses when Kerry came up to him.

'Is your name Bill?' Kerry asked.

'Yes,' Bill replied, aware that he was talking to the boss's son.

'The old bastard has sent me out here and says I've got to spend two weeks on every job in the place. It's going to take me a year, and I'm starting with you. You're my boss.'

Kerry gave his new master no trouble, and the two of them got on well together. But he turned out to be none too keen to learn, was apt to be late, and in Bill's opinion 'didn't have too much brains'. He had apparently decided that he already knew quite enough about the business and could therefore take it easy. One morning he came in complaining of feeling crook because he hadn't been to bed. 'Isn't there a place you can have a siesta around here?' Kerry asked. No, there wasn't, Bill told him. If you had siestas, you got the sack.

Whether Kerry had already found a place to kip down, or whether this was the start of his quest for one is not clear, but others were obviously more lenient than Bill, for before long Kerry had found a way of passing the time and catching up on his beauty sleep. As Kerry later explained, he needed to save his strength for the more important things in life.

I was having a very torrid love affair with a very beautiful lady from overseas. I was working from seven o'clock in the morning till three in the afternoon, and she was working till eight o'clock, she was a mannequin. And by the time I was getting home which was about four o'clock in the morning the hours of sleep had been contracted to a point where they were almost non-existent . . . and of course I was going to sleep every time I sat down. Eventually, they took compassion on me, the fellas, and they said, 'We'll cover up for you', and they took me down where all the big bales of paper were, and they got opened up and inside there was a very comfortable bed, and they used to let me have an hour's kip and someone would keep watch for me in case anyone was after me.[2]

When he wasn't chasing young women or sleeping off the evening's exertions, Kerry seems to have spent a fair proportion of his time driving round in powerful sports cars, often with three or four young friends in the back. One old printer remembers him roaring into the loading dock in a red two-seater, and Frank, either watching or hearing the noise, declaiming to anyone who would listen: 'Here comes that silly maniac son of mine. He'll kill himself in that thing before long.' One of Frank's executives remembers being driven down Sydney's Captain Cook Drive by Kerry at 160 kilometres per hour and being booked for speeding. Others who were passengers with him at the wheel record that he had only two speeds: flat out and stop. Clearly, he often drove his cars fast enough to attract the attention of Sydney's traffic cops, for when he met the *Telegraph*'s young police roundsman Ced Culbert in the pub in the mid 1950s, the first thing he asked was: 'What are you like at fixing blueys?' (slang for speeding tickets). A few years later, he boasted to one of his passengers that he had found someone who could deal with them. Whether that was just bravado, of course, was another matter.

The teenage Kerry was regarded by journalists at Consolidated Press, and perhaps by Frank himself, as the black sheep of the Packer family. It was common knowledge, so everyone said, that he was a mad punter who had run up large gambling debts that he couldn't pay off. And some of the rumours were obviously true, for he was certainly in debt to an SP bookie named Lou Samuels, or Louis the Letterbox. In the late 1950s, before any sort of off-course betting was legal, Lou Samuels was the *Telegraph*'s bookie, the one whom everyone in the building used, from the editor-in-chief, David McNicoll, another avid and unsuccessful punter, down to the lowliest copy boys. People would ring through their bets to Lou and then settle up or collect their money on Tuesdays when he came into the *Telegraph* offices, and young Kerry was a regular customer. According to Bill Whittaker, one of Sydney's most respected racing journalists, Lou claimed that Kerry ran up a large debt with him while still in his teens. His father was paying him ten pounds a week or less, yet Kerry's habit was to punt in hundreds, so naturally when the luck ran against him, there was no way he could pay his debts. Lou let the matter ride till the tab reached 1000 pounds, which in today's currency might be ten times that, and then arranged to see Frank Packer in the hope he could get his money back. When he explained to the big man that his son owed the book 1000 pounds, Lou was told by Frank Packer to 'piss off' and was thrown out of the office, with the declaration that he wouldn't get a penny and how dare he take bets from a boy. But by the time Lou got home, Frank's anger had obviously cooled, for Lou found a message to ring him at the *Telegraph*. Frank told Lou that he had made inquiries, was satisfied the money was owed, and would honour his son's commitments. But with the promise of payment came a warning: 'If I ever find you taking bets from my son again,' said Frank, 'I'll have you run out of the SP business and run out of town. And don't you ever set foot in my building again.'

Verne Toose, who knew Frank well, remembers how on this or another occasion Kerry ran up 600 pounds in gambling debts, and sought Frank's help to pay them off. Frank, who was himself a demon punter, was furious and refused to bail him out. 'You've got a car, you can sell that,' he supposedly told Kerry. The car in question was a prized Ford Falcon, 'the greatest souped-up motor you ever saw' according to Toose, which only Kerry and his driver were capable of handling. This was duly disposed of to keep the bookies at bay.

In these young days, like most young men, Kerry also drank and by all accounts drank heavily. Ted Hood, who died in 2000 at the age of eighty-nine, was in charge of the darkroom at the *Telegraph* until late 1955. He remembers having to chase Kerry round the local pubs while he was supposed to be learning about photography. His first memory of the boy was of a huge, quiet, poker-faced figure, dressed in a big blue boiler suit, who stood sheepishly by his father as Frank made the introductions and gave Ted his marching orders.

'Here you are, Hood, this is my son, Kerry. He's yours for a month,' said Frank. 'I want you to teach him all you know about photography.'

'Thank you, Mr Packer,'Ted Hood replied.'We'll get along fine.'

'I'll tell you something, it's not as easy as you think,' Frank went on. 'You've got to look after him, too. If I find him in a pub, never mind whether he's with you or not, you can snatch it.'

'But Mr Packer, that's not very fair, he's a big bloke. How am I going to stop him?'

'Never mind how,' Frank replied, 'you look after him,' and with that he walked off.

Ted liked Kerry and thought him a nice young man: 'You couldn't find a nicer bloke,' he told me. But he could never take his eyes off him, for the moment he did, the boy was out the door and off to the pub. He was barely eighteen at the time, but Ted couldn't keep him off the booze. 'I wouldn't wait for the lift. I'd run down the stairs and duck into the three pubs that were out the back. And when I found him, I'd say he had to come out or he'd get me sacked. He'd just thrust a beer into my hand and say "Ah, bugger it, relax and get this down you."'Ted Hood only looked after Kerry for a month, but he chased him often enough to be almost a nervous wreck by the end.

Later in life, Kerry never touched alcohol, but few people know why. He told one interviewer in 1977 that drinking knocked him about more than it did other people and that he was not capable of doing it in moderation so he had ceased altogether.[3] A case of flat out or stop once again. But there has always been a rumour that he became an abstainer after a bad car accident in which three people were killed, and that is the explanation that Kerry himself gave to Phillip Adams, to whom he was close in the late 1970s. The New South Wales state coroner's files confirm that the accident took place, that three people were killed, and that Kerry Packer was at the wheel.

The accident happened in September 1956 on the Hume Highway just south of Goulburn. Kerry was eighteen at the time, still a schoolboy at Geelong, and had been on a skiing holiday in the Snowy Mountains. He was driving back to Sydney a Mrs Ash, the wife of a wealthy Newcastle timber merchant, and her two children, all of whom were asleep. It was just after one o'clock in the morning and had been raining. Kerry had been driving for some forty minutes. As he drove north, another car approached, travelling south. Shortly after the accident, Kerry told police what he believed had happened next:

> I remember coming along a stretch of practically straight road where I saw some headlights. I think they were about 200 yards away when I first saw them. I was driving well over to the left . . . As they got nearer I noticed that they were drifting towards me. Then I thought that they were coming right at me. I still thought that they would go back to their correct side. I had dimmed my lights previously. When we got very close and I saw there was no possibility of them returning to their own side of the road, I attempted to swerve out and around them. That was just before the impact . . . I think that the approaching vehicle was travelling fast. The impact was a very serious one.[4]

Despite the severity of the crash, Kerry never completely lost consciousness; it was the passenger's side of the car that took the biggest battering. But as he came to his senses he realised the car was filling with smoke. Mrs Ash was trapped in the front passenger seat, there were two children in the back and their door was jammed. Flinging open his own door, he leaned back into the car to try to get them free before the lot went up in flames. Then, realising that the smoke was clearing, he sat down on the car's running board with his head in his hands until a passing motorist discovered the scene. The three young boys in the other car were already dead.

The garage man who towed the cars away said it was the worst accident he had ever seen. The car in which the three boys had been killed was a write-off, the whole of its engine and bonnet pushed back into the passenger compartment. Mrs Ash's Rover 90 had taken more of a glancing blow, but was badly smashed on the passenger's side, its heavy construction almost certainly saving her life, and perhaps Kerry's as well. She would be too badly injured, according to her lawyers, to appear at the inquest in Goulburn four months later. Kerry would spend eight weeks in hospital and several months more on crutches, while a dislocated hip and broken femur mended. The two young Ash boys, fortunately, were shocked but not badly hurt.

Frank Packer was at the races when he got the news. Bill Whittaker, then a cadet on the *Telegraph*, remembers being thrown bodily out of the phone cubicle by the big man so that he could use the phone. He immediately flew up to Goulburn in a chartered plane to see his son, take charge of the situation and, perhaps, to smooth things over. He would have been anxious for the accident to get as little press coverage as possible, and in that he certainly succeeded. Neither his own papers nor his rivals gave it more than a mention. And none was so tasteless as to highlight the involvement of Frank Packer's son, even though a triple fatality in which he was involved would have been a big story.

Strangely enough, there is no evidence that anyone at the eventual inquest asked whether Kerry had consumed any alcohol on the evening of the crash. A blood test had not been taken at the scene of the accident, since Kerry was too ill and the breathalyser had not yet been invented. Nor had the police made any enquiries. Yet Kerry told the inquest that he and Mrs Ash had stopped twice on the way home—first at the Kosciusko Hotel, which in those days was only a bar, at around 5 p.m., and later for dinner in Cooma. It would have been a natural line of investigation to follow, but it was clearly deemed to be irrelevant. The police were obviously in no doubt that the driver of the other car, and not Kerry, was to blame. And in this, the coroner unhesitatingly agreed.

> It appears that the car in which the deceased were driving was definitely on the wrong side of the roadway and this was the real cause of the accident. The extensive damage to the two vehicles indicates that one or the other was travelling at a fast speed and this may be a contributing factor. I cannot attach any blame to Mr Packer.[5]

While Kerry was in hospital, the Packer empire was pushing back its frontiers. Perhaps Kerry even watched as he lay in bed with his leg in traction, but on 16 September 1956, a week after his accident, the first television broadcast in Australia was made from Frank Packer's Channel Nine studios. It came from a makeshift set-up in a church hall in the inner Sydney suburb of Surry Hills, whence a visibly nervous Bruce Gyngell, 'a well-spoken man with a raw deal from the make-up department', welcomed viewers with the magic words, 'This is Television'. Packer's TCN 9 had beaten its three rivals in Sydney and Melbourne to the punch by almost two months.

Television's first night was an amazing occasion. A visit from the Martians could hardly have attracted more interest. Although there were only 3000 TV sets to tune in to the inaugural broadcast, more than 100 000 people crowded round them to watch. Crowds of up to 1000 people jammed the showrooms of metropolitan and suburban radio dealers or pressed their noses against the glass to catch a glimpse of this new phenomenon. Families made special trips to the city to watch through the windows of department stores. Others, who had the money and foresight to have bought a set already, held parties to impress their neighbours and friends. In streets that were normally deserted on a Sunday night, queues of cars and throngs of viewers held up traffic. As the *Telegraph* reported it, there was chaos everywhere:

The TCN Channel Nine opening caused a traffic jam on the Pacific Highway seven miles south of Newcastle. More than 400 people crowded round a set in the window of a store owned by Mr A. S. Pickering. The crowd jammed the highway and held up cars each side of the shop for several hundred yards. Mr Pickering said afterwards: 'The picture was perfect and the sound just like that from a local radio station.'

Another traffic jam occurred in King Street, Newtown, where 400 people tried to see the programme.

About 1000 people packed Goodwin's Showrooms, Railway

Square, and hundreds were turned away. Mr Goodwin said: 'We have twenty-five sets going and it's still not enough.'

The Lord Mayor of Sydney (Alderman Hills), his wife and their five children, watched at a radio store. Asked if he would buy a TV set, Ald Hills pointed to his five children, sitting fascinated before the set and said: 'Just look at them. What can I do about that?'[6]

Clearly, the forecasters of demand for TV sets had not spoken to parents or to their square-eyed offspring, for television mania soon gripped Australia. Although there had been little interest before the first broadcast, dealers were saying within days that they had run out of stock. The cheapest sets on offer were two hundred guineas, the price of a fortnight's holiday for four on Hayman Island, for which one bought a black-and-white set with a tiny screen. But already architects were designing lounges with TV viewing in mind. Within four years, roughly three-quarters of the homes in Melbourne and Sydney had television. Frank Packer by this time had added a Melbourne television station, GTV 9, to his Sydney property, TCN 9, and was sitting on a cash machine that rivalled the *Women's Weekly*.

Frank had invested in television reluctantly, having no idea what a money spinner it would become, and had done so more for the sake of insurance than anything else. He was worried that it could take revenue away from his newspapers and he wanted to ensure that any gains still flowed to the coffers of the Packer empire.

Like all the other applicants, Consolidated Press had been allowed to pitch for only one of the four television licences on offer but had picked up one of the two Sydney licences with ease. Packer's political influence would have made it hard for the Menzies Government to refuse him the prize in any case, but he had won fair and square, getting the nod from a selection committee that included Kerry's Geelong headmaster James Darling. In copybook Packer fashion, Frank had ensured that his bid had the right technical expertise, financial backing and political support. Among the shareholders of his new Television Corporation Ltd were the British newspaper group Associated Newspapers, the Dutch electrical giant Philips, the Church of England Property Trust and the Sydney radio station 2KY. The church gave Packer's bid gravitas and moral rectitude, while 2KY gave his consortium pretensions to represent the people, since it was owned by the New South Wales Labor Council, the supreme body for the state's trade unions. Packer's dislike of trade unions was well known, but in this case his love of money was more powerful.

Before long, television was bringing huge profits to the Packer empire. But even though it coined him money, Frank never became a convert. Unlike his young son Kerry, he always preferred the printed page. As with the *Telegraph*, however, he realised he could have fun with it and treat it like a toy. In the early days when it was still a novelty, he rang the Channel Nine control room twice in one evening to stop a movie that was being shown. Frank had guests for dinner and wanted to show them his horse winning that afternoon at Randwick, so the movie was twice interrupted to have the race re-run.[7]

Apart from these unscheduled repeats, the initial program diet in these early years was extremely wholesome by comparison with today's fare—a mixture of American sitcoms like *I Love Lucy*, quiz shows like *What's My Line*, variety in the shape of *The Johnny O'Connor Show*, and a modest ration of solid British drama. But the day after the first night's broadcast, the *Telegraph*'s reviewer was already hinting at what the public wanted more of. Having noted one 'alluring chanteuse', he went on to praise the charms of 'that singing rage' Miss Patti Page, an American who had also graced the opening night. Whether she had sung the hit that made her famous, 'How Much is that Doggie, in the Window', the reviewer did not relate, but that was perhaps because he was more interested in watching her perform.

Miss Page, a young and extremely come-hither young lady, presented an attractive quarter-hour in which she not only sang but wobbled her bust (on my set anyway) in quite a fascinating manner.[8]

There wouldn't be too much more of that sort of thing if the Australian Broadcasting Control Board had its way. Anything blasphemous, indecent, obscene, vulgar or suggestive was ruled out by strict program guidelines, which also contained an instruction that appeared to have direct relevance to Miss Page and her wobbly bits.

> To preserve decency and decorum in production, and so avoid embarrassment or offence to viewers at home, the presentation of all performers must be within the bounds of propriety. Special care must be taken as regards costuming, movements of dancers and others, and selection of camera angles.[9]

Certainly Packer's *Telegraph* assured its readers that at least two of Channel Nine's directors would be taking such matters seriously. The Reverend Father Martin Prendergast and Major-General the Reverend C.A. Osborne promised that they would 'pay strict attention to the moral and cultural standards of telecasting', and ensure that programs neither offended Christian teaching nor offered harm to the developing characters of children. Meanwhile, in these early years, each night's viewing was preceded by a live religious talk. How, oh how, such times would change.

Three years later, the pattern was already much more recognisable. Packer's TCN 9 was increasing the amount of American programming and going down-market in the search for popularity. Like the rest of his businesses, it was run on a shoestring, but run well. It was said to be the most profitable station in Australia.

While Kerry idled his way through life, with few expectations that he would ever be called on to do more, his elder brother was fast climbing the journalistic ladder. This, though few people realised it, was obviously ruled out for Kerry because of his dyslexia. The two brothers had never been close, but the difference in their treatment might well have pushed them further apart, for Clyde was seen by Kerry and others to be the more favoured son. As the elder, of course, he was also heir to the Packer fortune.

In 1955, at the age of twenty, Clyde started his career with the company as a sub-editor on the *Telegraph*. By twenty-two he was Donald Horne's second-in-command at *Weekend* magazine. A year later, in 1958, he was promoted to be managing editor of all the group's magazines, except the *Women's Weekly*. Then, after a spell of six months in England working for the *Daily Mail*, he was made news editor at the *Telegraph*. Those who worked for him found him capable, intelligent, a good sub of other people's copy, and a nice bloke. Most journalists and printers liked him: he never pulled rank and was ready to discuss things, being far less didactic than either his father or his brother. He was also, union men would later report, compassionate. When it came to closing a magazine he ran in the 1960s, Clyde made a real effort to find work outside the organisation for the people who were being put off.

But young Clyde was not without his trials, either. When he sounded off about Kerry in front of his father, he was suspended from the payroll for ten days. And the fact that he was the favourite son, at least in terms of privileges, did not protect him from Frank's angry outbursts. Even when he and Kerry were in their twenties, their father treated them both very hard on the job. If he felt they hadn't produced he would blast the daylights out of them in front of everyone. And Clyde in his role as make-up sub on the *Telegraph* seems to have come in for the worst of it, although Kerry was by no means spared. Poor Clyde would be bawled out and bullied despite the fact that he was good at his job, a good newspaperman. The printers who had to witness it found it uncomfortable to watch, for Clyde in particular seemed really scared of his father. Usually Frank's rages concerned the newspaper, but sometimes they were about leaving the lights on at home or trivia like that, which made Frank almost more annoyed. 'You blokes think I'm made of money,' he would thunder at his sons.

On one occasion in the mid 1950s, Ted Hood went out to the Packer home at Bellevue Hill to take some pictures of Gretel for a *Telegraph* gardening feature. After the session was over, she invited him in for a cup of tea, and before long the conversation turned to Frank and Clyde. Above the back door was a single light that illuminated the area around Cairnton's five garages. Clyde, it transpired, had come home late the previous night, parked his car in one of the garages, and gone up to bed without turning it off. 'That got under Frank's skin,' says Ted Hood, recounting what Gretel told him. 'He got up in the morning, saw that bloody light on and he went for Clyde. He took his licence away, and the keys of his car, and he grounded him for a month, all because of that one 75-watt globe being left on.'

So what did Gretel think of all this, one might ask? Ted didn't have to wait long to find out. 'He's a mad dog when he gets anything between his teeth, isn't he?' she said. 'I've been trying to talk him out and quieten him down. I might be able to get Clyde his keys back. I just don't know.'

There is little doubt that there were difficulties in Frank and Gretel's marriage, for which no one believed Gretel was to blame. The editor of Packer's *Sunday Telegraph*, the late Cyril Pearl, claimed he had witnessed Frank strike Gretel in public. Plenty more had seen him abuse her verbally. And almost everything about Frank suggested he would be nigh on impossible to live with. In a celebrated argument early on in their marriage he had demolished a door at Sydney's sumptuous Australia Hotel.[10] But if Gretel was a tolerant and good-natured woman, which she doubtless needed to be to live with Frank, she was also capable of giving as good as she got, especially when she had had a drink or two, which she often had. In one fit of temper, she particularly impressed an observer by stubbing out a half-finished cigarette in a jar of cold cream. On another occasion, during an argument in the car, she wound down the window and flung into the street an expensive ring that Frank had just given her. In yet another famous confrontation, when Frank refused to give her the money to redecorate the upstairs part of the house, she was said to have confiscated all Frank's trousers in retaliation and forced him to give in. So, despite the rows, they were in some ways not unfairly matched. In any case, they stayed together, regarding marriage as a partnership and a binding contractual commitment. The fact that one of the partners did not observe all the terms of the engagement, however, was noticed. 'Had he been the gentleman that she was the lady,' as one of her friends put it, 'they would have made a lovely couple.'

If anything did threaten the Packers' marriage, apart from the general difficulty of living with such a man, it was Frank's affairs. While he was both a puritan and a prude in his public life, especially in his rules about what the *Women's Weekly* might write, he had always been fond of pretty women, and as a young man had got himself into a scrape or two. Years later, when introducing himself to the British newspaper magnate Cecil King, who owned London's *Daily Mirror*, he shook him warmly by the hand and announced: 'I'm interested in girls and horses, what are you interested in?' Cecil King, who was by no means a stuffy person, confessed that he was slightly taken aback by this directness, for this happened in the 1940s or 1950s when Frank was still married to Gretel.[11]

Certainly, a man with Frank's riches and working patterns had no shortage of opportunities to pursue the first of his expressed interests. He kept a permanent suite at the Australia Hotel on the corner of Sydney's Castlereagh Street, just down the road from the *Telegraph* offices, and there were also various apartments around Sydney that could be useful for dalliances. London, of course, gave him additional scope. Frank went there regularly, spending three or four weeks in England most years as part of his annual routine. He had tried Acapulco once and found it not to his liking, because nobody recognised him or knew who he was. In London, on the other hand, he was someone. He kept a suite at the Savoy where he was treated like one of the family and could hold court in the lobby in his shirtsleeves, to the amazement of his more formal English visitors. He would go to Ireland to buy racehorses, to Scotland to play golf, and anywhere he fancied to have fun.

One of his affairs, with an overseas fashion designer, appears to have become rather more than a diversion, starting when she brought a collection out to Australia for the *Women's Weekly* and continuing for some years thereafter. According to the late Francis James, who was a close friend of Clyde Packer in the late 1950s, Gretel was sufficiently angered by it to leave the family home and take off to England herself for six months, accompanied by young Clyde, who went with her despite his father's threats that he would be disinherited. Another long-running affair was with a journalist at the *Women's Weekly*, Maisie McMahon, who was fiercely jealous of her foreign rival. Maisie was reported to be so upset that she made an effigy of her, stuck pins in it and put it in her bottom drawer. Shortly after, the fashion designer was said to have fallen down the stairs.

It was around this time, in the late 1950s, when the difficulties over the fashion designer arose, that Frank's state of mind began to preoccupy his executives. He had become even more irascible and dissatisfied than usual, and all remedies, from golf to chess lessons, had failed to improve him. Donald Horne, sitting next to him at a dinner party one night at the Packer family home, found him in a particularly black mood. As the conversation flowed around him, Frank was heard to ask his plate: 'What does a man do when he can't get on with his family?'[12] Presumably, he found the answer, for he and Gretel were eventually reconciled.

Not long after, in August 1960, Gretel died. She had been ill for some time, and extremely ill for a year or more. Frank had done everything he could to find her a cure and to make her last months comfortable. Finally, he had agreed she should be flown to the Mayo clinic in Minnesota in the mid-west of the USA. Surgeons there attempted to replace her main cardiac artery in a major operation, but it was not a success. She died ten days after admission, with her husband and two sons by her bedside. She was only fifty-three. Heart disease ran in her family too, as it did in the male Packer line.

When Sir Frank launched a campaign shortly after her death to tilt at the great prize of yachting, the America's Cup, it was only natural that he should name his challenger yacht after her, as he did once again when he took a second run at the cup in 1970. But he also paid her his respects in a more remarkable way. When the challenge was announced, his station managers at Channel Nine in Sydney and Melbourne were sent a memo to tell them that their businesses would each be required to contribute a quarter of a million dollars to the cost. The Melbourne manager, Nigel Dick, who was co-ordinating the television coverage, promptly set about raising some of the money by selling advertising to Ampol and W. D. & H. O. Wills, who were sponsoring the Australian challenge. Ads were duly signed up and prepared for inclusion in the first hour-long documentary showing preparations for the race. A day or two before this film was to go to air, Sir Frank telephoned to check on progress. It was fine, he was told, it was looking good.

'We're not going to have any ads in it, are we?' Frank inquired.

'Well, yes, Sir Frank, we are,' Dick replied.

'Get them out, I don't want any,' Packer ordered.

Dick then said that if Packer wanted to cancel the advertisements he had better ring the sponsors to tell them, whereupon Sir Frank, calling his manager a 'gutless swine', rang off. Ten minutes later, he rang back to say he had fixed it and to explain.

'This boat is named after my dear departed wife,' he told his manager. 'I don't want any advertisements sullying her name.'

It was typical of Packer that he was prepared to sacrifice hundreds of thousands of dollars for a principle in this way. Typical, too, that he hated such sentimentality to be exposed to public view. In characterising him, it was difficult to say much more than that he was impossible to characterise.

Four years after Gretel's death, Sir Frank announced that he was remarrying; his driver, George Young, believes he could no longer bear to be alone. A month before the wedding, which took place in London in July 1964, he was at the Commonwealth Press Union's annual dinner in one of the city guildhalls. After the Royal toast was proposed, Lord Astor, the owner of London's *Observer*, got to his feet. He was not going to make a speech, he explained, but he wanted to congratulate his

Australian colleague, Sir Frank Packer, who had recently announced his engagement to the delightful Florence Vincent. There was applause, a chorus of 'Hear, hear,' and Sir Frank stood up to reply.

It was very kind of them, said Packer, to offer their good wishes, and they were right to say that Florence was a good sort, but he wondered whether he might have been a bit premature. He had not realised, he said, when he proposed to Florence, that Lady Beaverbrook would be coming onto the market. It was a joke, of course, since Lady Beaverbrook was an old woman, well beyond marriageable age but it was received with an appalled and awful silence. The celebrated press baron, Lord Beaverbrook, had died that morning at the age of eighty-five and was not yet in his grave.

Even in his sixties, Sir Frank Packer still had an eye for a pretty girl. Sandy Symons, who started on the *Telegraph* in the 1960s and later edited *Mode* for Consolidated Press, remembers meeting him in the lift when she was a copy girl. As the lift doors closed he turned his rather shortsighted gaze upon her and stared. She was wearing a red double-breasted suit, with buttons that began at her breasts and went down to her waist. 'You look nice today, girlie,' said Sir Frank, and pressed her buttons with a stiff finger, one by one, as the lift descended.

Most women at the *Telegraph* found Frank gallant and charming despite his roving eye. To the more senior ladies, he was always a gentleman. He would send them flowers if they were taken ill, arrange cars or cabs for them to be driven home if they were working late at the office, and look after them in a considerate and old-fashioned way. Frank, they said, knew how to behave. It seemed that on occasions he simply forgot.

CHAPTER SEVEN

PACKER BUSINESS

*There is only one bloody Packer and that's me, and don't
you forget it.*

Sir Frank to senior executives responsible to
Clyde and Kerry

Few people at Consolidated Press took the young Kerry Packer
terribly seriously. The printers rubbed along with him okay, but
the photographers and reporters thought him a galoot and
regarded him as a bit of a joke. Several of them remember him
in unflattering terms, as 'a gangling dill', as one senior journalist
put it, 'He was bombastic, not too bright, and not what you
would call lovable. He was well cast as the boss's son.'

Now in his twenties, Kerry seemed to have great difficulty
keeping boredom at bay, and even more difficulty applying
himself to work. At lunchtimes he would be seen playing three-
penny poker in the canteen. In the office, he was often found
with his feet up on the desk, keen for a chat. Meanwhile, it was
stories of his cars and conquests that filtered up to the girls on
the *Weekly* or the women's section of the *Telegraph*, rather than
tales of his executive skills or addiction to effort. Like all his
father's male staff, he had to wear a hat when going out to meet
clients—he would take tea with the people from Grace Brothers
and Farmers to drum up business or maintain good relations—
but he carried his in protest because he hated it so much. At one
point, like everyone else in the building, he was sacked by his
father. As the legend goes, he then walked into a Sydney adver-

tising agency and got himself a job, where his tenure lasted as long as the agency's ignorance of his disagreement with Frank. Thereafter, he found all doors in town closed to him.

Among the staff at Consolidated Press it was sometimes said that Frank had been unlucky with his sons. Others added unkindly that the old man was such a bastard he deserved it. He seemed disappointed with the way Clyde and Kerry had turned out, and occasionally remarked that he wished that they would show more drive. No one was prepared to tell him that his sons were unlikely to display much initiative while he bullied them so much, or to excel when he gave them no opportunity to do so.

Young Rupert Murdoch was far closer to Frank's idea of what his sons should be like.[1] Brash, confident and aggressive, just as Frank had been at his age, he was also a creator and a gambler, who cared little about the rules or the obstacles in his way. Only six years older than Kerry and four years older than Clyde, he had by the age of twenty-nine already quadrupled profits on the Adelaide *News*, taken over Perth's *Sunday Times* and the magazine *New Idea* and opened Adelaide's first television station. Now, in 1960, he was ready to muscle in on the rich Sydney market, the biggest in Australia, where the Packers would be forced to defend their territory against his invasion.

There was a long history in Sydney of brawls between rival newspaper owners, with a highlight being the notorious Derby day punch-up at Randwick in 1939 between Frank Packer and Ezra Norton, who owned *Truth* and the *Daily Mirror*.[2] But the scraps with Murdoch were at least about something more substantial than ego. There were rich prizes to be won—in television, the dailies, and suburban newspapers—and much to lose as well. And from the start, in February 1960, when Murdoch declared war on the Packers, both sides played rough. Murdoch's initial act of aggression was to buy a company called Cumberland Newspapers Pty Ltd, which published a number of free sheets in the western suburbs of Sydney. Four months later, the famous battle at the Anglican Press was the result.

Sydney's suburbs in the early 1960s were growing fast, new regional shopping centres were opening up and there was the promise of a vast new advertising market to tap into. The Packers and Fairfaxes naturally wanted a share of it but, just as importantly, they wanted to protect their existing domination of the city, in which the *Sydney Morning Herald* and *Daily Telegraph* carved up the classified advertising between them. Murdoch's newly acquired giveaway papers, operating on the fringe of their territory, obviously had the capacity to steal their customers. So the Packers and Fairfaxes formed a joint venture to fight him off by publishing their own suburban papers. Their initial plan was to use the *Daily Mirror*'s presses to print them during the idle day shift, but Fairfax soon upset this by selling the *Daily Mirror* to Murdoch, in the vain hope that they might sink him with the huge debts he would take on to buy it.

This ill-advised move left the Packers without a printing plant, only weeks before the launch of their first paper, and forced them to find an alternative. It was immediately clear that the Anglican Press, of which Clyde was a director, was the best on offer. It was close to the centre of town and had a huge composing room that could be used to put the papers together. Even better, it was in receivership and up for sale. The Packers made a bid of 50 000 pounds, were told that it would be accepted, and assumed they had the matter sewn up. But they had reckoned without the company's managing director, Francis James, whom Clyde Packer was unwise enough to tell about the deal the night before it was due to be signed.[3]

Francis James was one of Australia's great eccentrics. A flying ace in World War II, he had been shot down over Germany, and escaped twice from prisoner-of-war camp before succeeding at the third attempt. After that, he had been sent down from Oxford University, made his fortune in fishing trawlers on the west coast of Australia and written leaders for the *Sydney Morning Herald* from his 1928 Phantom II Rolls-Royce, which had a fold-down writing desk in the back. Subsequently he became editor and owner of the *Anglican*, which he turned into a controversial and successful Left-leaning newspaper. The Anglican Press, which printed the paper, was a separate company, but James carried enough influence with the bishops who controlled it to persuade them that they shouldn't sell to the Packers. Within twelve hours of Clyde telling him that the deal was on, James had successfully ensured it was off by persuading the bishops to sack the receiver of the Anglican Press who was about to sell the company to Sir Frank.

Not surprisingly, the Packers were livid when they heard the news. But on the principle that possession is nine points of the law, they resolved to seize the premises. At quarter past nine in the evening of 7 June 1960, a *Telegraph* staff car rolled up outside the Anglican Press building in the grimy inner suburb of Chippendale and disgorged Kerry and Clyde Packer onto the street, together with their lawyer Fred Millar and a couple of *Telegraph* employees. Waiting to meet them was the new receiver of the Anglican Press, Harry Reid. As Millar brandished a document that purported to show that the Packers had bought the printery, Clyde demanded to be allowed into the building. By way of reply, Reid handed them his letter of appointment, telling them that *he* had done no deal to sell the assets, and informing them that they most certainly could not go in.

Clyde and Kerry and the rest of the Packer party then sauntered round to the back entrance on the pretext of inspecting the premises. Reid went through the front door, locked it, and made his way back to his office. There he was surprised to find Clyde Packer already installed in his chair, telling him that he could not make a phone call because the lines had been disconnected. Reid summoned the police, who soon came and went after receiving assurances from the Packers' lawyer that their presence was unnecessary, and then nipped out of the building to make a phone call. When he came back, he found that he had been locked out. Clyde and Kerry had clearly planned the invasion, for they had brought a locksmith with them to change the locks, and also barricaded the windows to make the building apparently impregnable. Reid stood there on the pavement, wondering what to do. As he pondered, the front door was flung open by the huge figure of Clyde Packer and the Anglican Press's one-legged general manager, John Willis, was lobbed unceremoniously onto the street.

While all this was happening, Francis James was having a quiet dinner on Sydney's North Shore, half an hour away, but a call from Reid soon put a stop to that. James first phoned a group of his old RAF mates and arranged to meet at a church near the besieged building. Next he got on to Murdoch to tell him what had happened. Murdoch insisted that this was a job for Frank Browne, an ex-boxer, notorious Sydney character and sworn enemy of the Packers. Shortly after midnight, they met on the steps of Sydney's Town Hall where, in James's version of the story, Browne was accompanied by four of the biggest bruisers he had ever seen. Rupert Murdoch was also there, pressing several hundred pounds in ten-pound notes into Francis James's hands to pay the pugs before he departed.

Reaching the Anglican Press at around 1 a.m., James and his commandos were confronted by a huge factory-like building, with barred windows three metres off the ground, and doors that had been locked and barricaded. But round the back was a smaller toilet window that offered a far better chance of entry. Though only thirty centimetres square, it was large enough for a slim man to wriggle through, and its fearsome iron bars had been adapted by James, in a bout of prison paranoia, to swing back on a hinge. Thus, the plan was hatched: while one team made a noisy attack on the front door, the other, led by James, would go in through the window. In the confusion that followed, all hell broke loose, but the Packers were outnumbered and soon ejected. As James burst into the print room he was greeted by the sight of Clyde Packer in his shirtsleeves being chased round the layout tables by Browne and his boys, who had battered through the front door. From one of Clyde's shoulders, according to James, a huge heavy red-feathered dart was hanging, while two others were stuck in his ample posterior. The battle then spilled into the street, where Browne turned his attentions to Kerry. It was an unfair match, even though the boy was big and a good boxer, for Browne had been a soldier and professional fighter. Kerry was knocked to the ground. Eyes half-closed, shirt torn, he was then picked up by his seconds, bundled into one of the *Telegraph* cars and driven off. Two other cars, their tyres let down by the attackers, were left behind.

Accounts differ as to whether Kerry was badly hurt, but since both sides were armed with monkey wrenches and similar implements, there is every chance that he was. One journalist at the *Telegraph* saw him a couple of days afterwards wearing large black sunglasses, with his face a mass of bruises, and looking as if he had taken a terrific beating. Various photographers were on the scene, yet no pictures of the assault ever saw the light of day. One *Daily Mirror* photographer, who was unquestionably there as Browne laid into Kerry, is reliably reported to have caught three good shots, but the negatives and prints were handed over to Murdoch early the next morning and subsequently disappeared.

The morning after the fight, Murdoch's *Mirror* gave the story the full treatment, though naturally with the proprietor's particular bias upon it: 'KNIGHT'S SONS IN CITY BRAWL' was the headline across the front page, taking advantage of Frank's new honour, bestowed six months earlier for services to journalism. Alongside was a large photograph of Clyde Packer about to launch the Anglican Press's general manager into the street. There was no mention of Browne and his bovver boys or of Rupert's role in the night's activities, though he and Frank Packer had both kept in touch with the battle over their respective cars' two-way radios.

Sir Frank, in fact, had risen from his hospital bed to take command of operations—he was frequently laid up in later years as he battled different illnesses—and had gathered his senior executives in the boardroom at the *Telegraph*. Donald Horne was one of them, suitably armed in case they were called on to join the fight. But neither they nor Frank had been able to avert defeat. Nor could they now avoid further damage in the courts.

The owners of the Anglican Press won orders banning the Packers from the premises and requiring the return of any documents they had removed. An affidavit from the company's general manager alleged that the steel safe had been forced open and the cash book, ledgers and various documents taken. Three employees subsequently brought actions for assault and battery against the Packers, which were settled out of court. They had received quite enough bad publicity already without having the full embarrassing story come out.

Despite the surrender of their bridgehead at the *Anglican*, the Packers and Fairfaxes still managed to get a new suburban paper afloat only two weeks later. The first edition of the *St George & Sutherland Shire Leader* appeared on schedule at the end of June 1960. Its 75 000 copies had been printed at Consolidated Press, transported to a triple garage hired for the occasion and bundled up by Clyde and his team. Sir Frank and Henry the chauffeur helped load up the trucks that shipped the papers out to the newsagents. Watching over them were six large Italian gentlemen, hired by Clyde from a nightclub in Double Bay, to ensure that there was no repeat of the trouble.

A year after the engagement, the Packers and Murdoch sat down to talk peace and agreed to carve up the Sydney suburban market between them. By this time the Packers had opened another three newspapers in Sydney's western suburbs: the *Northern Star* at Ryde, *Inner Western Times* at Burwood, and the *Parramatta Mail*, which were handed over to Murdoch in exchange for his papers in Rockdale, Kingsgrove, Hurstville and Campsie. With the swap came a twelve-year agreement not to encroach on each other's territory. It was blatantly anti-competitive, though not illegal, but for the Packers in particular, it was an excellent deal. By the mid 1970s, they had fifteen suburban newspapers in Sydney, cranking out pre-tax profits of around half a million dollars a year between them. Had Murdoch not challenged them, they might have devoted far less energy to succeeding in the market.

But of far greater strategic importance than this tussle over suburban newspapers was the battle for supremacy in television. Given that Channel Nine would eventually make Kerry a billionaire, the significance of the campaign to the Packer empire can hardly be overstated. When they launched Australia's first television service in 1956, the Packers had a 30 per cent share in just one television station, Sydney's TCN 9. Eleven years later, Channel Nine was not only the dominant force in Australian television, with the Melbourne station GTV 9 also in its fiefdom, but the Packers had increased their share of it all to 80 per cent. That they had done so was thanks entirely to Sir Frank, who had both outfought and outfoxed his opponents.

The first vital victory was scored in July 1960, with bruises from the *Anglican* punch-up still fresh, when Sir Frank snatched Melbourne's GTV 9 from under the noses of his rivals. The station's existing owner, Sir Arthur Warner, had just sold his Electronic Industries business to the UK electrical group Pye, but needed a separate buyer for GTV 9 because new rules had been passed to prohibit any foreign company owning more than 15 per cent of an Australian television station. Packer, Murdoch, the Fairfaxes and the Melbourne *Herald* all leaped into the bidding as soon as they discovered that the station was on the market, but it was the wily Sir Frank who emerged victorious, even though his rivals were prepared to pay as much.

When he heard that Sir Arthur Warner was thinking of selling GTV, Packer was about to depart for the USA and Warner was on his way back to Australia from England. They agreed to meet in Hawaii, where Packer offered Warner six pounds a share, or six times what the station had cost him three years earlier. This was an excellent price, working out at 3.76 million pounds for Warner's 62 per cent holding, but there was one big snag. Sir Arthur had already twice given assurances to Rupert Henderson, the managing director of Fairfax, that he would sell to him if ever he put GTV on the market, and they had even discussed a price of four pounds a share. Given that Fairfax's Sydney station ATN 7 was also GTV's network partner, Henderson had every reason to expect Warner not to sell to his rival.

Inevitably, Henderson soon heard of Packer's bid and rang Sir Arthur Warner to remind him of their agreement, offering both to match what Packer had offered and to stump up cash in payment. Warner presumably agreed for the third time to deal with Fairfax, for Henderson then had the ANZ Bank reopen its safe after hours and write out a bank cheque for the 10 per cent deposit, which was then sent express mail to Sir Arthur. But by the time it arrived Warner had changed his mind again, and had disappeared. One version says that Packer had whisked him away to his house on Bellevue Hill to get him out of Henderson's reach. Another, which does not necessarily conflict, says Sir Frank was in the room while Warner and Henderson were apparently reading their new agreement. But whichever way it was Sir Frank Packer came out ahead.[4]

Having secured the Melbourne station for the Packer empire, it was then a simple matter to smoke out GTV's other main shareholder, David Syme & Co., owners of the Melbourne *Age*. Packer paid them such meagre dividends over the next six years that they decided to quit the company because it was giving them such a poor return on their investment. In 1966, in some frustration, they agreed to sell their shares to Consolidated Press, leaving Packer in sole control.[5]

Rupert Murdoch had been as keen as anyone to get his hands on Melbourne's GTV 9 and, having failed, was now desperate to succeed in Sydney instead. His small station in Adelaide, which was making a 40 per cent return on capital every year, had already taught him how profitable the television business could be. So, when a third Sydney TV licence came up for tender in 1963, he was quick to apply, putting maximum effort into getting the judges' nod. Failure to win that third licence caused him to look for another way into the market, and before long he was repeating the trick he had tried with the suburban newspapers and attacking the Packers from the flank. In 1963 a new television station had been set up in the steel town of Wollongong, 100 kilometres south of Sydney. The population there was too small to attract a man with Murdoch's ambitions, but WIN 4 had a powerful transmitter on top of a large hill, whose signal was strong enough to reach Sydney.

A year after its launch, this same station was in need of rescue from a spot of bullying by the big boys. Sir Frank Packer's Channel Nine had teamed up with Channel Seven, the other Sydney station, owned by Fairfax, to deny WIN 4 access to decent overseas programs. The big two in Sydney had told the American program suppliers that they could sell either to Sydney or to Wollongong, but not to both. The little guys in Wollongong had then complained to the government and started action in the courts, but were getting nowhere fast and going broke in the process. Murdoch's solution to the problem was to buy a strategic stake in the Wollongong station and fly to New York with chequebook in hand. There he splashed out one million pounds on 2500 hours of programs produced by the American Broadcasting Corporation, including the high-rating *Phil Silvers Show* and *Ben Casey*. Next, he flew back to Australia to announce that he would be aiming these marvellous programs at Sydney's southern suburbs, to give the big two stations a bit of competition. 'There are two million Sydney viewers within WIN's range, and we intend to go after them.'[6]

Whether this was a serious threat or not, and it is doubtful whether Sydney's viewers would have chosen to turn their aerials southerly to pick up the signal, Sir Frank's antennae certainly did get the message. He decided to buy Murdoch off, offering him two seats on the board of Television Corporation and 25 per cent of the shares. It was not exactly surrender, in that Murdoch handed over the American programs, shares in the Wollongong and Adelaide stations and enough cash to bring the consideration up to $4.5 million, but neither was it what Packer would have chosen to do had he been in a position of strength. Those who let Murdoch in the front door, as Packer would surely have known, can soon discover they are being whooshed out the back. And the Packers, with only 35 per cent of the shares in Television Corporation, were certainly not secure against hostile takeover.

Three years later, however, Sir Frank found a way to throw the gatecrasher out, with an ingenious offer that had both Murdoch and Henderson completely fooled. The bait he dangled before them was the chance to buy the two *Telegraph* newspapers and all Australian Consolidated Press's magazines. To the two gentlemen concerned, the deal must have appeared as safe as it was alluring, and a perfectly genuine proposal. After all, Sir Frank had turned sixty, was in extremely poor health, and was known to have doubts about the mettle of his sons; it was natural that he should want to pass on his publishing empire to someone who would run it as well as he had done. In any case, Murdoch and Henderson both jumped at the chance, offering $22 million and $24 million respectively. They then flew independently to London, where they began to discuss the possibility of splitting the empire between them, with Murdoch taking the newspapers and Fairfax the magazines. As the two neared some sort of agreement, Murdoch was surprised to learn from Sydney that Television Corporation had called a board meeting without inviting him. He must have been even more surprised when he heard soon after that the directors had agreed in his absence that Television Corporation should itself buy the same Packer newspapers and magazines that he had been offered. The board had been forced to admit that they were getting a bargain, for $21 million was less than the Packers had already been offered by the two mugs in London. The auction had been nothing but a charade from the start, designed simply to satisfy the Australian Stock Exchange that Packer was shuffling his assets at a proper price.

When he dined with his journalists that night, Murdoch seemed quite amused that he had been shafted, but he had every reason to be upset. Not only had he missed out on owning the two *Telegraph* newspapers, which must have annoyed him but, more significantly, he had lost any influence in Packer's Television Corporation. The company had taken over the newspapers and magazines by issuing new shares to Consolidated Press Holdings, which had tightened Sir Frank's grip on the television empire, exactly as he intended. Consolidated Press now owned 62 per cent of the shares in Television Corporation and Murdoch only 25 per cent. He could either stay locked in to the company and be denied a decent dividend, as David Syme & Co. had been, or he could ask Sir Frank to let him out. Wasting no time, he made for the exit, selling his shares to Packer for $1 million less than he had paid four years earlier. Sir Frank, no doubt, chuckled all the way to the bank. Getting Murdoch out had left him in total control of the Sydney and Melbourne stations, with all but a handful of Television Corporation's shares.[7]

Although he had been taken for a patsy, Murdoch appeared to harbour no grudge. He still saw Sir Frank and the boys socially and continued to do business with them. And five years later, he came back for a second bite at the newspapers, this time with more success.

As the 1970s began, both *Telegraph* newspapers were losing money, but they now needed vast amounts spent on new presses. There had also been a string of damaging and energy-sapping strikes by the printing unions. Kerry in particular was keen to get rid of the papers, though beginning to suspect that Sir Frank would rather die than see them go. Even as a youngster he had told the printers that his father was sitting on a gold mine with the *Telegraph* building but that the old man couldn't see it. He would tell senior production staff at their regular meetings that they ought to get shot of the paper: 'It's not worth a cracker, this place,' he would say, 'it loses money all the time, we'd do better to sell the thing and rent out the building.'

Whether he dared talk to his father in such terms is extremely unlikely, for Sir Frank was still indisputably the boss, and Kerry unquestionably the junior. Even though he was thirty-five or more, Kerry was still not seen to challenge him. Someone setting up a deal with Frank in the early 1970s remembers a number of meetings at which father and son were present: 'When we discussed business, Kerry didn't speak. If Sir Frank left the room, Kerry would have an opinion. If Sir Frank came back, he would shut up completely.'

Frank would often take a breather during negotiations by this time, because he was a sick man. In his absence, his executives could often be persuaded to support a point of view. But if Frank expressed the opposite opinion when he returned, neither Kerry nor anyone else would raise a voice against it. And the son would always stand with the rest of them when his father came into the room.

Ian Kennon, who later worked for Kerry, would occasionally see Sir Frank and his two sons in the early 1970s having lunch at the Garden Court restaurant in Sydney's Sheraton Wentworth, one of the old man's regular haunts. Oblivious to the fact that it was a public place, Frank would treat them in appalling fashion. 'They were huge grown-up men and Frank would yell at them like they were naughty little boys.'

But a mountain of money eventually did what Packer's sons could not and persuaded the old man to let the *Telegraph* be sold. It was May 1972 and Kerry was coming back from a boxing match with Murdoch, who was already well on his way to being top dog in Australian newspapers. As they sat in the big Packer Mercedes outside Sydney's Town House hotel, the deal was done.

> My father was sick and said, 'Take Rupert to the fight for me.' So we sat in the car together and talked of many things. The conversation started on the basis of why don't you buy 49 per cent of the Telegraph and we'll buy 49 per cent of the Mirror and we'll put them out of one office because there's no way we can compete coming out of two offices against the Sydney Morning Herald and the Sun coming out of one.
>
> And then it progressed until eventually Rupert said, 'What will you take for the goodwill, just the mastheads?' We came to the figure of $15 million and he said, 'Are you setting me up?' And I said, 'No, I'm not.'
>
> Because remember, he had been set up once before. And I said, 'I'll use my best endeavours to see it's accepted.'[8]

Frank did accept, but reluctantly. The price was twice what the *Telegraph* would have fetched if the Packers had made the first move, and such a good one that he couldn't possibly refuse. He was being invited to unload an unprofitable paper for almost ten times what Rupert had paid for the *Mirror a* dozen years earlier, and he was old, sick, and tired of the continual fights with the printers. But even if he had been perfectly fit he might well have made the same decision, for it would have been a matter of principle that he could not turn such a good offer down. There were fifteen million reasons why he couldn't say no. As one observer put it, he didn't need the money, and it 'couldn't console him for the loss of the unique pleasures the *Telegraph* had given him' but it was too much 'to be refused by someone who saw profit as the prime mover of human affairs'.[9]

The deal was done in a matter of days. The various parties flew down to Canberra to sign the documents, to avoid paying stamp duty, then flew back for a celebration in Sir Frank's Park Street office, where Kerry suggested that a call to Billy McMahon, Australia's Prime Minister, might be a good idea. In view of Packer's unshakable support for the Liberals over the years and his help in getting McMahon into the Lodge, it was a dreadful shock for the Prime Minister that the *Telegraph* was falling into other hands. Understandably shaken, he said that he would like to see Sir Frank that evening, and suggested the newspaperman come round later to the McMahons' Bellevue Hill home. Packer pleaded that he was too ill to make the journey, and suggested that the Prime Minister come round to him instead. It is perhaps an indication of Sir Frank's power that the Prime Minister was persuaded to go up the hill later that night to the Taj, as Packer's mansion was known.[10]

The sale of the *Telegraph* put some 300 printers out of work. The fortunate few received an envelope signalling their transfer to Murdoch's headquarters at Kippax Street, but the rest were paid off. Later, memories differed as to the manner in which it was done, but for some the bitterness remained. They recalled being locked out of the *Telegraph* building in the pouring rain and being made to file in from Castlereagh Street one by one to get their pay. Others remembered a more civilised sendoff, and said that

Kerry came down to say goodbye, wish them good luck, and offer an apology for the ill fortune he had brought them. But with or without bitterness, all regretted the era's passing.

The printers liked Sir Frank and were sad that the game was up. Even though they had sparred with him and thought him a tyrant, they had always felt part of the business. It was like a family to which they all belonged. They had their rows and behaved unreasonably quite a lot of the time, just like families do. But they fought about simple things like money and conditions, and they respected each other as worthy opponents. Frank was a character, who could make life fun, unless you happened to be related to him. He would amble around the machine room, chatting to the old hands, would allow people to stay with the company into their seventies, rather than make them leave, and would always look after those who had helped him build the business. And if he was a bastard, as almost everyone agreed he was, he wasn't a bad old bastard.

Twenty years later, the printers who were lucky enough to get jobs with Murdoch still looked back on their years at the *Telegraph* with nostalgia. But their longing for the good old days was perhaps as much for a bygone Australia as it was for Frank Packer himself. People helped each other in those days, they said, talked to the bosses, did what the foreman told them, worked as a team. It had become impersonal, remote, more automated. There were too many different nationalities working on the floor. The good old days had gone.

The sale of the *Telegraph* was no less painful for Sir Frank himself, for all the money it made him and for all that it was sound business sense. For two weeks afterwards he wandered round the building a 'shambling drunk' in the words of one of his old friends. As Kerry said later:

> Emotionally it tore him to shreds. But he stood back from it as a businessman and said, 'It's a good deal. If I want this company which I have built to continue to prosper and grow, it's a deal I should make.'[11]

Even more graphic was the description given by Donald Horne, by this time editor of the *Bulletin*:

> His reaction to this sacrifice was so great that people wondered if it might kill him. Several times he cried when he spoke of it; his face was pinched and his gaze distracted; he walked slowly like a wounded man, his hand on a helpful shoulder; his words wandered; he spoke of the dead as if they were still alive, and gave orders to men and machinery that it was no longer in his power to give.[12]

For years it had been Frank's habit to come into the office on Saturdays to get the *Sunday Telegraph* out. Even after he had sold the papers, he found it almost impossible to stay away. There was nothing for him to do there, no journalists to bully, no editorials to write, nor even lights to switch off. Yet he still came in, a sad and lonely figure in the old empty offices, with no one's company but his own.

> He loved the *Daily Telegraph*. It lost money all the time; perhaps no one apart from Packer himself and a few of his court esteemed it; many derided it; by the kindest standards it was humdrum; but Packer loved it. It seemed like power to him; he would think of something and the next morning there it was in the paper. It appeared to give him political influence. It gave him interesting guests to invite to dinner, esteem when he was in London and New York, his knighthood. But I think he also loved it for itself—its racing news, the printing presses in the basement, the ledgers upstairs recording its failures, the comic strips, the newsagents' accounts, the sub-editors at their semi-circular desk, the attacks on the Labor Party, the teleprinters, the scruffy typography, the stereo department, the stock exchange reports, the letters to the editor, the lift-drivers (until he sacked them).[13]

With his beloved *Telegraph* gone, it was inevitable that Frank would turn his attention to the television stations in Sydney and Melbourne and begin to interfere more with their running.

Inevitable too perhaps that his meddling would eventually lead to a confrontation between him and his elder son, Clyde, because the pressure had been building up for some time. Earlier in 1972, in a row between Clyde and his deputy at Channel Nine, Nigel Dick, Frank had ruled in favour of his son, telling Dick that he had to understand that blood was thicker than water. Now, when faced by a similar argument with Clyde, those same family ties meant nothing. What was at issue as far as Frank was concerned was obedience: Clyde had to do what he was told. As he had often warned his executives when they had acted on instructions from one of his sons which he had not vetted: 'There's only one bloody Packer, and that's me. And don't you forget it.'

There was in fact plenty of the Packer in young Clyde, in that he had the capacity to bully and belittle with the best of them. And there were some, like Ron Saw, who thought him a clone of his father. But he was also the softest of the family and certainly the most intellectual. Those who knew all three Packers said that he had a sensitivity and a capacity for objectivity that his father and brother lacked. He was capable of discussing ideas, of arguing about philosophy, and of keeping an open mind. Although politically well to the Right, he was also a committed defender of civil liberties, which made him not exactly a chip off the old block.[14] Certainly he had little in common with his younger brother Kerry, apart from a grab bag of shared experiences and the common trauma of having Frank as a father. And by the 1970s, the two young men rarely talked to each other; they were definitely not friends.

As a child, Clyde had suffered even more than Kerry in fights with the old man. He was more sensitive, more vulnerable, less thick-skinned. He was also a fat boy who became an even fatter man, and his father made no secret of the fact that he hated obesity. If, as some suggested, he had become the more favoured son, it was largely because he had worked at it. He was ambitious to do well in the business and always keen to please. For twenty years Clyde had been uneasy about his role as a Packer. He would tell colleagues wistfully that he wished he had secured a university degree and settled down as an ordinary suburban lawyer. But his father had made that impossible. And Clyde had allowed him to.

> My father thought universities were a waste of time. He said: 'You go to work for me. You'll learn far more in the school of hard knocks' . . . I tried to go to Sydney University but the old man made it too difficult. I felt very awkward being the boss's son. I never really knew what to do. There was a big strike but I could hardly join the picket line.
>
> The period of disillusionment hit me when I was about thirty-five . . . I'd had to suppress a large part of my personality. I'd always been interested in human relationships but working for a father-tycoon this part of me was denied.[15]

The change in Clyde's life and the split with his father had begun after the break-up of his first marriage in 1969. Frank thought the idea of divorce a disgrace and refused for some time to stump up any money for the settlement, provoking a huge confrontation with his son. Frank's suggested recipe for dealing with such problems was for Clyde to set up his mistress on the other side of town. But this marital breakdown also had a dramatic effect on Clyde. His circle of friends narrowed, as did his interests, and he began to wonder what he was doing with his life. He began to reassess. He had been seeking power and suddenly began to wonder why he needed it. He began wondering, too, whether it was worth paying the price that the business and his father demanded. As he grew older, working for Frank was becoming increasingly difficult. Even in his late thirties Clyde was still treated like a boy, and a stupid, disobedient one at that. In public, as well as in private, he would be treated to the most embarrassing dressings-down from the old man. 'Is he a saint or an imbecile?' asked one of Sir Frank's barons, having watched Clyde's smile persist like an Etruscan deity's through calumny that had put everyone else off lunch.[16]

The showdown finally came in August 1972 with a row over the running of Channel Nine, where Clyde was managing director. Fortunately for Clyde, there arose a clear-cut principle on which he was able to stage his exit. With an election drawing close, an eight-week strike by oil refinery workers had brought most of Australia to a standstill. Petrol supplies were practically exhausted, and businesses were laying off thousands of workers. McMahon's Liberal Government had, not surprisingly, backed the oil companies against the unions. Given Frank's views about publicity for strikers, it was predictable that he would object to Bob Hawke, then President of the Australian Council of Trade Unions (ACTU), being given time on his station to present supposedly sensational evidence about the behaviour of the oil companies. It was also predictable that he would stop it going ahead, which is precisely what he did. Having watched Australia's future Prime Minister on the nightly news, he rang through to Clyde to tell him that Hawke was a Communist, and was on no account to appear on the Packer channel.

Soon after, Nine's top gun interviewer Mike Willesee was called in to Clyde's office to be told that the segment featuring Hawke on *A Current Affair* had been vetoed by Sir Frank and would not go to air. There was a fierce but brief argument, at the end of which Willesee resigned, saying that he was not prepared to accept the diktat. Clyde thereupon walked across the room and shook him by the hand. 'Congratulations on your integrity,' he said to the bemused journalist. 'I've just completed my last official act as managing director. I resign, too.'

Clyde was no fan of Bob Hawke, but he liked censorship a great deal less. And after eighteen years of working for his father, he was fed up with being pushed around, fed up with the bullying and the interference. Aged thirty-seven, he resigned not only from Channel Nine but from the Packer family. It was not a problem for him that Willesee later made it up with Sir Frank, at least for a time, because this was just the opportunity he had been looking for.

That wasn't the cause, it was only the trigger. I don't want to go into it. Basically my father and I didn't handle our relationship very well. The main thing I objected to was that he couldn't draw a distinction between work and family. You were always on deck, night and day. Probably I should never have gone to work for the business.[17]

Sir Frank said publicly that they parted with regret, but his actions suggested otherwise, and Clyde was in no doubt that he left with good riddance, telling one interviewer, 'He was as glad to be rid of me as I was to be rid of him.'[18] Never one to forgive those who crossed him or who left the tribe, Frank immediately amended his will to cut Clyde out of the succession. The split was complete, and clearly bitter.

Clyde, for his part, now set out on a path that was calculated to push Frank's blood pressure off the dial. At the age of thirty-seven, he took to wearing caftans to parties and living the life of an overgrown flower child. The late Ron Saw, who used to live almost next door to Clyde in Sydney's Woollahra, would come across him often after the fall. He would look from his window and 'see him walking across Queen Street, this great ambulant tent, with vast striped muu-muus, puffing clouds of smoke from a huge joint'. This did not endear him to his more conservative brother.

Clyde, as his friends now saw it, set out on a personal quest to discover life and to enjoy himself. After almost forty years of his father's disapproval and restrictive rules, the release must have been extraordinary. As he himself later described it, he wanted to have all the sweets in the shop at once, and by all accounts did his best to cram them in. He gathered around him a salon of young people from the arts world in which ideas were freely discussed, and experimented with sex: 'Hair-raising tales are told about his quest for sexual novelty and the scope of his conquests,' one magazine reported in its preface to an interview with him, even though (it continued) 'commonsense suggests that an 18-stone frame that gets little exercise and is regularly dosed with blood-pressure depressants isn't suited to the exacting program of a playboy stud'.[19]

He also teamed up with his friends Mike Willesee and John Cornell[20] to set up the sex magazine, *Forum*, in Australia. The magazine lost money heavily for two years, and Clyde was eventually left to carry it alone. But despite dire predictions that it would fail, it eventually turned a reasonable profit and, perhaps more importantly for Clyde, proved that he could carve out success in the face of family opposition. The style of the magazine, which aired people's sexual problems in lurid detail, certainly did not find favour with Kerry, or with Sir Frank, who must have been near to apoplexy.

Forum's outrageous tone even played a small part in Willesee eventually being pushed out of Channel Nine in late 1973, although he and Sir Frank might have had enough differences without it. Ostensibly their parting came over a row about money, but in reality the argument between them had been bubbling away for a long time. Frank hadn't even wanted Willesee to come to Nine in the first place. 'He's a Communist,' he had told Clyde in 1972, and he had clearly felt, since then, that his fears had been confirmed. Willesee had survived the row over Hawke, when Clyde had departed, because the old man had backed down.[21] He had then won a second battle to interview former Prime Minister John Gorton, which Frank had also tried to veto. But he wasn't going to be allowed to win a third.

In April 1973, a memo winged its way from Frank's Park Street office across to Channel Nine's general manager, George Chapman, on the subject of politics and sex.

MEMO: MR CHAPMAN

I am receiving a lot of complaints about the Willesee program on two scores.

1. That it is politically biased and slanted towards the Labor Party, and from my own observation I believe that there is a certain amount of truth in this . . .

2. More disturbing than that is the type of material that is going over which is quite unsuitable for 7 o'clock telecasting. This particularly applies to the segment on Forum . . .

If it becomes necessary, we will have to tape the Willesee program so we can see it before it goes to air, unless Willesee is prepared to become more cooperative.

Willesee was clearly not prepared to fit in with Packer's definition of becoming more co-operative, for in late 1973 came a third confrontation between the two. This time, Willesee wanted to broadcast an interview with two Sydney jockeys involved in an industrial dispute, and Packer was adamant that it would not run. Not only was Sir Frank an avid punter and racehorse owner with little sympathy for the jockeys' cause, he was also a member of the Australian Jockey Club committee, which was the other party to the jockeys' dispute. There was no way that he would give air time to these strikers. Willesee bowed to the inevitable and dropped the segment, but protested vigorously and subsequently refused to sign his contract. The dispute then descended into farce, with Packer getting his newsreader to read derogatory comments about Willesee on air and Willesee replying with an ad-libbed attack on Sir Frank. Finally, with a week to go before *A Current Affair* finished for the year, Kerry was sent over to Channel Nine with a letter cancelling Willesee's contract and demanding that the show finish that night. As this last program went out, Kerry stood in the control room ready to pull the plug if Willesee said anything about Frank's actions. Willesee did not, apart from making a snide remark to Kerry off air about him being an expensive messenger. But he was soon plying his lucrative trade for Channel Seven instead.

Frank, meanwhile, saw to it that the *Bulletin* published his version of the story, including *Forum* memo and details of Willesee's contract demands which, he maintained, were for an annual fee of almost $500 000.[22] Now it was Clyde's turn to be angry. When a journalist from the *Australian* rang for a comment on the article, Clyde for once agreed to talk. 'The thirty-eight-year-old millionaire was clearly disturbed, a very angry young man, ready to break his long years of tight-lipped loyalty to his father,' the newspaper reported dramatically the next day. But that was all a bit of an overstatement, for by comparison with what Clyde could have said it was pretty tame stuff. He called his father's action 'unethical' and 'gutless', but phrased his criticisms largely in terms of the public duty of proprietors. Paraphrased, it might have said that Sir Frank can't use Channel Nine in the way he used the *Telegraph*.

> Television is a completely different ball game from newspapers. It has a responsibility to present programs the public wants and not to ram its own viewpoint down their throat . . . If Channel Nine continues to take politically provocative actions there might be a public investigation into it. What Nine is now trying to do to Willesee, what they tried to do to Hawke, and what they did to the New South Wales Labor Party builds up to a pattern.[23]

Sir Frank had indeed tried to use his television stations like his newspapers, but Clyde had missed out the most blatant example. In the election of November 1972, which saw Gough Whitlam and Labor voted into power after twenty-three years of Liberal government, Channel Nine in Sydney had given a large amount of free advertising to the conservative and confusingly named Democratic Labor Party in the hope that it would split the Labor vote and let the Liberals in. The actual amount, some $19 000, sounds insignificant by today's standards, but it was enough to buy eighty-nine sixty-second slots on Australia's highest-rating TV station. Nor was that all. In a much more direct effort to get McMahon re-elected, Packer's Channel Nine stations in Melbourne and Sydney had also run two unprecedented election editorials attacking the Labor Party. Written by David McNicoll, they came at 7 p.m. at the beginning of *A Current Affair*, one of Channel Nine's highest-rating programs, and poured scorn on the country's prime minister-to-be in an updated version of the vintage Packer style:

> It will not take the solid middle-of-the-road voter long to work out which policy—Mr Whitlam's or Mr McMahon's—is the best

146

for Australia and for him ... Mr Whitlam's speech sounded like the marijuana dreams of a Utopian Disneyland.[24]

In Gough's Disneyland world, the editorial went on to say, there would be no strikes, no wars, and no need to work. Everything would be paid for by squeezing the taxpayer. In contrast, under McMahon's realistic government, which had cut taxes, law and order would be upheld and 'Australia's onward march to greatness' continued.

There was a predictable outcry from Labor politicians and the Australian Broadcasting Control Board, who decreed that Nine would have to give the other political parties a chance to reply. Whitlam's staff then spent the next week preparing their own three-and-a-half-minute editorial and sent it to Channel Nine for broadcast. Sir Frank, however, took not the slightest notice. Ignoring what the regulators had instructed him to do, he simply refused to give it air time, on the grounds that it did not answer the specific points raised. Then, to add insult to injury, Nine broadcast a second editorial, giving Labor another blast. If Labor did get elected, said Packer's penman this time:

> Mr Whitlam would be Prime Minister in name only ... the real course would be set by people now trying to hide in the wings ... Mr Bob Hawke and the other union bosses.[25]

It was a cry that Packer's *Telegraph* had made familiar over the years with the references to the 'thirty-six faceless men' of Labor's federal executive committee, but it was a new departure to say it so bluntly on television, and to do so in the face of stern official disapproval. There was dark talk among Labor politicians of taking Packer's television licences away if Whitlam were elected, but it remained just talk, even though Labor did get in. When the next election came round in mid 1974, Packer's Channel Nine did not attempt a repeat performance, but perhaps only because by then Sir Frank was dead.

The old man had been unwell for ten years or more, suffering his many and various ailments with great stoicism, despite the fact that he was often in pain. Heart problems had caused him to have a pacemaker fitted; continual throat infections brought chronic lung congestion and made him wheeze, gasp and gurgle as he talked. His doctors had at one stage 'tubed' him like a race-horse, inserting a silver pipe into his windpipe in a rather ghastly attempt to alleviate his breathing, but it had not been a huge help. In the last few years, coughing fits became frequent, as did the need for oxygen, which he kept constantly at hand in his office and his car. For a man who had been so strong and fit in his youth, it was a sad and cruel decline. Already almost blind in one eye, he gradually lost the sight of the other as he got older, and peered out on the world through thick pebble glasses. He became a more regular visitor to St Vincent's hospital, where his arrival was generally preceded by a refrigerator and followed by cases of beer and whisky. On one occasion, he collapsed at the office late at night and was carried downstairs by Kerry, to be rushed by car to St Vincent's. Whatever had caused the crisis, it was thought to be serious enough to see him off. That weekend, one of Randwick's leading bookies, Les Tidmarsh, offered 2/1 on 'No Packer by Monday'. Frank got wind of it and rang him up to say he'd like to have a bet.

Try as he did to maintain his particular brand of humour, Sir Frank cut himself off in these later years from most of his friends, spurned invitations to cocktails and stopped going out to parties. He tried to console himself with his own morose company, but with no great success.

His last years were sad ones for a man who had been a sought-after social figure as well as a newspaper tycoon. He spent the days seated at his desk in his office. He spent the nights seated at his desk at the Taj, phoning people, watching TV, often dropping to sleep for hours until his faithful butler, Alfred, would insist he went to bed.[26]

Even his wife couldn't keep loneliness and disappointment at bay. His driver George Young remembers celebrating Lady

Florence Packer's sixtieth birthday in a Chinese restaurant with just the three of them to keep each other company. And a maudlin occasion it was too, with Frank wheezing and Florence complaining repeatedly that she was getting old. Frank's father, Robert Clyde, had died a bitter and disillusioned man some forty years earlier. Frank departed in much the same frame of mind.

Sir Frank Packer eventually died from heart failure on 1 May 1974 at the age of sixty-seven. On his death, his Consolidated Press empire comprised two television stations, five radio stations, nine provincial newspapers and the biggest magazine publishing company in the country. There were also extensive property interests, shares in the Fiji gold mines, three hotels in the snowfields, a stud, some racehorses and a ragbag of other businesses and investments. Taken together, they were probably worth around $100 million. But Sir Frank's estate was valued for probate purposes at only $1.3 million; in death, as in life, he escaped the taxman. Even half the garden at Cairnton was outside the taxman's grasp, because it was owned by Australian Consolidated Press. One Labor Senator, Arthur Gietzelt, was sufficiently angry to draw attention to the matter in Parliament and to ask how Packer had done it.

> Will the Government indicate the ways by which Sir Frank Packer was able to divest himself of most of his fortune during his lifetime for the purposes of the Estate Duty Act, while retaining absolute control of his vast empire?
>
> Will the Minister assure the House that the Government will take steps to stop such wholesale manipulation of assets by the rich to avoid taxation?[27]

The hapless minister, Senator Wriedt, answered that he knew nothing about Sir Frank's tax affairs and that his government had endeavoured to close the legal loopholes. He would, he said, forward any more information to the senator, if he could obtain it, but he never did.

Sir Frank, of course, had organised it cleverly and with the best legal advice. Neither the shares in Consolidated Press nor the television stations were part of his estate because they were held by a company called Sydney Newspapers (Canberra) Pty Ltd. The shares in that company weren't part of the estate either, because it was owned by Sydney Newspapers Pty Ltd. Similarly, Frank owned no shares in that one, because they were held by the Packers' master company Cairnton. Sir Frank certainly controlled this entity, but the millions of dollars profit that the Packer empire earned every year was not paid to him. It went through Cairnton to the holders of the company's B preference shares, who in 1974 alone netted some $400 000 in dividends. The recipients were half a dozen trusts set up in 1954 to get the Packer family fortune out of the taxman's reach. Not for the first or the last time, the Packers had craftily given the taxman the slip.[28]

Three days after his death, more than a thousand people turned out to St Andrew's Cathedral in Sydney to wish the old man goodbye, packing all the available pews, standing in the space at the back, and overflowing into the street outside. He had been married in the rain, now he was buried in it. Tributes poured in from politicians across Australia: his friend Bob Menzies promised to remember him with affection, his mate Bob Askin, the Premier of New South Wales, said with feeling that Sir Frank would be sorely missed. But it was one of Sir Frank's old rivals, Sir Vincent Fairfax, who gave his funeral oration, describing the old man as one of the most colourful characters of the time—a great and strong Australian possessing deep understanding, loyalty and great compassion, a buccaneer businessman, who had played the game to win as well as for fun.

The funeral cortege, accompanied by police motorcycle outriders, drove at speed out of Sydney, with Frank's two black Mercedes 600s following the hearse. At every intersection there was a policeman to hold up traffic and give the motorcade a clear run. Whether out of respect or because of a power cut, all the lights were out of action.

To those who had witnessed the occasion, with its celebrities from the Age of Menzies, it seemed like the end of an era both in journalism and in the tooth-and-claw capitalism that Frank had represented. Packer himself had felt the same. Four years earlier he had given a rare interview to ABC TV for its series of *Profiles of Power*, in which he had been asked about the future. Would Packer and Co. prosper when he had gone, or would the business he had nurtured be broken up? In line with his low opinion of the worth of his sons, he had seemed fatalistic, almost pessimistic about its prospects.

Q: Do you feel that the day of the family newspaper empire is over?
A: I think ultimately the day of the family business is over alto-gether, whether it be newspapers or anything else. It's getting so big.
Q: Well if we look back at your family, your father was a pioneer, and you have become a legend. What is left for your sons to do?
A: Oh well, they'll own quite a sizable stock holding in the Tele-graph, in Consolidated Press and TV and everything else, and I suppose it will be up to them what they do, whether they go on or whether they sell out, or what they do. I suppose they'll wait till I peg out before they decide to dispose of it or they may decide to keep going. I think they will.
Q: Would you like to see them keep the family business together?
A: Of course I would.[29]

The day after his death, the obituary notices said nothing of Clyde's role, past, present or future. He had been reconciled with his father on the old man's deathbed but not reinstated as heir to the empire. A one-line announcement stated that Frank's younger son Kerry would be taking over as chairman of Consolidated Press.

CHAPTER EIGHT

KERRY TAKES CHARGE

Shirtsleeves to shirtsleeves in three generations.

Proverb

The old adage about dynasties is that it takes three generations to go from nothing to nothing. The first makes the fortune, the second builds it up and the third fritters it away; thus, the cycle from shirtsleeves to shirtsleeves is complete. By birth, Kerry was cast in the role of loser, and his upbringing would surely have helped convince him that he was made for the part. At school, he had been taunted by teachers and classmates for being an idiot and made to believe that he was a failure. At home, his father had criticised him, pushed him, punished him, and referred to him quite openly as 'Boofhead'. And in his eighteen years in the family business he had rarely, if ever, been encouraged. Frank had continued to dress him down in public, rebuke him in front of others, and deny him the responsibility that would have given him confidence in his own abilities.

Given the way in which the old man had brutalised him and humiliated him, even as an adult, it was not surprising that Kerry told his closest friends he wasn't sad to see him go. In fact, he confessed, the day his father died was the happiest of his entire life. He was sick of being bullied, sick of being bossed about, sick of being paid a measly wage, and sick of waiting to become a man.

By the time he got his first taste of real power, his first real freedom from his father, Kerry was already middle-aged. Thirty-seven years old, he had married Rosalind Weedon, a doctor's daughter from Wagga, eleven years earlier and had two young children of his own. Yet within Channel Nine and Consolidated Press he was still widely regarded as Frank Packer's idiot younger son. Given the way in which his father had dominated every aspect of the business, it was natural that people could not envisage life without the old man, that people would worry about whether the empire could survive his death. But it was not just Sir Frank's departure that caused concern, for looking at Kerry, few people considered that he was up to the job. There was a common view that he was not only stupid, but lazy and good-for-nothing as well.

It was true, of course, that Kerry had always found fast cars, women and gambling more interesting than playing second fiddle to his father in business. But there was, in spite of that, a hard core inside Kerry not normally to be found in the third generation of a wealthy dynasty. He was no dilettante, no lover of the arts, no slave to fashion or ideas, and most important of all, no believer in the idea that making money was unimportant. If his father had passed on one quality to his son, it was the belief that it was a man's duty to multiply his wealth.

There were other ways in which Sir Frank's harsh tutelage had equipped him well. He had toughened him up to believe that life isn't easy, and had taught him three basic rules for success: be loyal to your friends, tough on your rivals, and care not what others think of you. Kerry had spent years at his father's knee watching him work and had been through every part of the business to learn his trade. He had inherited, too, Frank's strength of character and lack of fear. He had needed it to survive.

He was convinced, all the same, that he was no match for the old tycoon, and never would be, as this 1979 exchange with TV interviewer Michael Parkinson makes clear:

Q: You live very much in his shadow, don't you?
A: I hope so.
Q: Why?

A: I think he was a very great man. There are people who create things . . . perhaps fifty or a hundred in every generation. I'm not one of those. He was. I'm very proud of him.[1]

Kerry liked to say that while his father could build jumbo jets, all he could do was fly them. And it was very much as the pilot of his father's enterprise that he saw himself. Unlike Rupert Murdoch, who was forever expanding his business empire, creating, acquiring and pushing back the frontiers, Kerry's aim was to keep the inheritance intact. He was conservative, lacking in confidence, ever worried that he might lose it all and let his father down. The thought that he could ever surpass his father's achievements would never have occurred to him.

Given his upbringing, it was natural that he should feel this way, but there were already signs that he underestimated himself. One or two of those who had observed him at the *Bulletin* with his feet on the desk had noticed that the circulation graph had started to rise soon after his arrival. Others who had seen him sell advertising knew that he was a terrific salesman. And those who had been involved with the launch of Consolidated Press's new magazine *Cleo* in 1972 would have gleaned something else: he had nerve. The significance of *Cleo* was quite simple. It was the first significant project in the history of the company that had proceeded without Frank's active support. He had for once allowed Kerry to back his judgment, and the new magazine had proved to be a stunning success.

The original impetus had indeed come from Sir Frank, who had organised for Consolidated Press to bid for the Australian rights to publish the Hearst-controlled American magazine *Cosmopolitan*. But negotiations had collapsed at the last minute, with Hearst opting to deal instead with the Packers' arch-rivals at Fairfax magazines. It was then Kerry who had decided that they should publish a home-grown rival instead. Ita Buttrose, who had already been lined up to edit *Cosmopolitan* on the assumption that the project would go ahead, was called downstairs to be told that the deal had fallen through. There she was confronted with the large and irate figure of the boss's son.

> Kerry was very angry, and Kerry Packer angry is not a pleasant sight. He puffed angrily on several cigarettes ... Having broken the news of the disaster to me he sat silent, glaring into space and smoking away like an incinerator. I waited, dismayed and disappointed. Kerry broke the silence: 'Have you got a magazine upstairs that we can do?' 'Well, yes, we have,' I said. I got the *Cleopatra* dummy and showed it to him. He liked it. Smiling for the first time that day he said, 'Right. We'll publish this one. I want it on the streets six months before the Australian edition of *Cosmopolitan* comes out.'[2]

Ita Buttrose had started with ACP as a secretary on the *Women's Weekly* at the age of fifteen, tagged along with journalists on her day off to see how stories were put together and made it to the rank of cadet within a year. Never backward in coming forward, she had written to David McNicoll to recommend herself as editor of the *Telegraph* women's page and been given the job at the age of twenty-three, after promising Sir Frank that she wouldn't start having babies, a prospect that apparently horrified him. An ambitious, talented, self-promoting woman, she was regarded as insufferable by some of her colleagues. But she had done well with the women's page and scored again in 1971 with the launch of a new magazine for the *Sunday Telegraph*, which was also a success, despite arguments with people at Consolidated Press.

Ita and Kerry's new magazine, *Cleo*, also met with concerted opposition, both from inside and outside the company. The Packers' advertising agency J. Walter Thompson thought little of it. The 'progressive women' on whom the advertisers tested it thought even less. It was going to bomb, they said; the project should be canned, and the name *Cleopatra* was a disaster. Kerry's most important contribution to the success of the project was to take no notice of all these jeremiahs. His gut feeling was that the magazine would sell, just as *Cosmopolitan* was selling in the

United States, so he heeded the warnings only to the extent of shortening the name to *Cleo* and ignored the rest of their advice. Wisely, he also decided to keep the market research and the advertisers' misgivings from his father, instructing Ita to take the panning from J. Walter Thompson and stuff it in a drawer, well out of sight.

Sir Frank was not only sure that the magazine would fail, he was also deeply perturbed by its contents, which explored new territories of sexual excitement and titillation that he believed women should not be allowed to read about. In his view, a woman's magazine should contain knitting patterns, recipes, stories on the Royal family and romantic fiction, and this had none of them. What's more, he liked the new name of *Cleo* little more than the old one, favouring a more traditional title like *Women's Monthly*. It was left to Ita Buttrose to point out that it was perhaps unwise to call a periodical by a name that applied to periods, and after this Sir Frank's opposition grew quieter. As the first issue of the new magazine went to press, he even sent Ita a telegram, wishing her luck, adding somewhat tartly that the magazine would need it. He apparently hoped the project would fail.

At the heart of *Cleo's* first issue was a male centrefold of actor Jack Thompson, posed in the style of Titian's famous painting 'Venus of Urbino', and sporting nothing more than a hand to preserve his modesty. Soon after came articles about female masturbation as an aid to conquering frigidity, and practical guides to such matters as 'What turns a man on?' Ten years later, such subjects would be commonplace, with articles telling women how to brush up on their technique in oral sex, but for its time, the new magazine was both daring and revolutionary. It was the first time that Australian women could read a magazine that wrote about their bodies, about sex, about careers, about some of the things that really concerned them, in a grown-up way. And as a result its success was dramatic.

The advertisers had been promised that the first issue would sell 80 000 copies. In the event, it did better than that, selling out the print run of 105 000 within two days. Three issues later, the presses caught up with demand, at 150 000 copies. It was better than anyone had dared hope, but it was only the beginning. Within five years it would be the fifth largest-selling magazine in Australia, with more than 250 000 sales per week, well ahead of *Cosmopolitan*, the magazine the Packers had intended to buy.

Sir Frank was generous in accepting defeat, if that's how he saw it, cabling Ita afresh to tell her that she was talented as well as good-looking. But whether he passed on the same sort of praise to Kerry is another matter. And his concerns about the magazine's content certainly didn't abate. In his time he had cancelled advertising contracts for the *Women's Weekly* because the pictures revealed too much, and had instructed his *Telegraph* columnist Ron Saw that he wasn't to write about public lavatories. 'We don't want any of that bullshit and filthy stuff,' he had told him. With *Cleo*, he insisted on being given a rundown of the magazine's contents prior to publication, and would call for the full text of articles that he didn't like the sound of. Whatever the public's taste, he was not going to abandon his duty to keep smut at bay.

When Sir Frank died two years later *Cleo* was going from strength to strength, yet Kerry still lacked confidence. Fortunately, he was not left entirely on his own to run the empire. In 1969, the Packers had taken on a new finance man whom everybody regarded as brilliant. Harry Chester had been lured across from Fairfax on a much-increased salary to add strength to the management at Consolidated Press, and was now charged, after Sir Frank's death, with keeping an eye on Kerry and the business. A tough, clever man, he had rapidly become a key figure in the company, such that Sir Frank had rarely acted in his last years without consulting Harry first. There had been talk that he would even take over as chief on the death of the old man, but Sir Frank had not gone quite that far. His will had been amended in late 1972, after the split with Clyde, to make Chester a joint governing director, with Kerry and Lady Florence, of the Packers' master company Cairnton Pty Ltd, through which the whole empire was controlled.[3]

Chester had already brought a far more professional approach to the running of the business. Before his arrival, financial control had been primitive at best. Vast amounts of cash had sat around in bank accounts without earning interest and investments had gathered dust for years without being reviewed. Sir Frank, meanwhile, had been busy fretting about increases in tram fares and the rising cost of rulers, or doing battle with his enemies and rivals on the national stage. Chester quietly began to change all this, focussing management attention on the things that mattered in the business, and the company began to prosper and expand as a result. Kerry, according to Ita, 'adored Harry' and regarded him like a father. He was said to be the only man who could make Kerry change his mind, the only one he would ever defer to.

But Chester's nicknames of Hatchet Harry and Harry the Axe were also well earned, and he was by no means universally liked. He had a reputation for ruthlessness and strong views about homosexuals in particular. 'Is that bloke a poofter?' he asked one of his accountants one day, indicating a broker with a powerful whiff of aftershave, who had been brought in to monitor the price of Packer's share portfolio. The opinion was proffered that he probably was. 'Then get rid of him,' came Chester's response. 'I don't want him back here.' Another of his fierce dislikes was Kerry's elder brother Clyde, who returned his antipathy in good measure. Clyde's split with Sir Frank in 1972 had been preceded only three weeks earlier by an attempt to get rid of Chester, who now played an important role in cleaving the two brothers apart.

The first signs of the split came in December 1974, seven months after Sir Frank's death, when Clyde resigned or was removed from the board of Sydney Newspapers Pty Ltd, an important private company in the Packer domain. Eighteen months later, in April 1976, the rift opened wider as Clyde was kicked off the board of Consolidated Press Holdings Limited. Shortly after, he upped sticks and went off to Los Angeles, leaving Harry and Kerry in control. It seemed that he had wanted to get back into the family business, but had been rebuffed by both of them. He left with relief, all the same, and when he was later asked why, he replied he could no longer hack being a Packer. In Sydney, he could approach no one and do nothing without everyone knowing who he was and reacting accordingly, usually with antagonism.

> The Packer name . . . followed you around wherever you went. You couldn't even go into a pub for a drink without copping it, so I left Australia.[4]
>
> I was sick of lugging this Packer persona around with me. It was like going away for the weekend with three steamer trunks . . . I suppose it was privacy I was looking for.[5]

Later that year, 1976, a settlement was negotiated to buy Clyde out of the company, and the elder brother went off to his new world. The separation was complete.

> When I came to America, Kerry said, 'I'd better buy your shares.' I resigned as a director of Consolidated Press Holdings and there was a very amicable separation of interests. The details have never been disclosed, and they are quite complex. But I left Kerry totally in charge and I now have no shares in the company.[6]

Clyde sold out for some $4 million and handed over his roughly one-eighth share of the Consolidated Press empire to Kerry's control.[7] The deal would cut Clyde out of his brother's eventual billions, yet he never seemed to mind. There's only a certain amount of wealth that makes a difference, he would tell friends—after that, it's all about ego and power. He had seen enough of both to know that he didn't want the Packer life for himself or his son, and that he was prepared to pay for his freedom. Having seen it close up, he was quite happy to let Kerry take over from his father as the tycoon.

> The thing about tycoonery—and I'm not attacking Kerry because his family life is most important to him—but the more a person

159

gets involved in being a tycoon, it chews up so much of him there is less of the real person left. Being a tycoon is not a real thing. We're all expendable, all fallible, but tycoons believe they're not— or maybe they worry that they are.[8]

The drivers at Consolidated Press were happy that Clyde hadn't stayed on to run the empire, for they had never much liked him. In their opinion he was reserved and arrogant. Unlike Kerry, who would always sit in the front of the car and chat with his chauffeurs, Clyde would invariably get into the back. Those who travelled overseas with him and liked him better also found that his treatment of underlings could be an embarrassment. If anything went wrong he would shout at waiters or airline ticket clerks. He could be quite brutal.

Clyde spent the next 25 years of his life in California with his second wife, Kate, a former Sydney model, dabbling in film production and running a small magazine business, Western Empire Publications, that published volleyball, bodyboarding and surfing magazines. He continued to play host to a stream of visiting Australians, and claimed to be happy to have walked away from it all. But those who knew him well suggested he found the going tough in one respect. Clyde was an intellectual who liked to talk about books. People in Santa Barbara, where he lived, did not talk about books, said one close friend; they did not even have them in their houses. Asked once to write his own book about the Packer family, Clyde replied that he wasn't ready to write fiction. Pressed to give a more serious answer 'the smile faded and he looked uncomfortable again. "I'll never write the real Packer story. It would hurt too many people."'[9]

With Kerry in charge at Consolidated Press, things soon began to change. The shabby old Park Street office received a smart new fit-out, Jaguars replaced Frank's two huge Mercedes and in the directors' dining room chops and sausages ceased to be the only dishes on the menu. For a time, the tomato sauce bottle even disappeared. The style of the company changed too. Kerry was far less patrician and far less distant than his father had been. He mixed much more. Whether it was a difference in character from his father or just a difference in generation, he would talk to people and tell them what was going on. One year he even ventured onto the Big Dipper at Luna Park with his staff when they held the Christmas party there. In much the same fashion, he and Chester set about sharing financial information with their executives and editors, at least to the extent of letting people know what their budgets were, whether they were losing or making money, and what they might do to improve matters. Under Sir Frank, all this had been kept in a black book which the accountants had brought to him every day, but whose contents had remained a secret. Now managers were allowed to discuss strategy, marketing and money with an openness that Sir Frank would have found quite alarming.

One such matter that had already been talked about quietly before Frank's death was the old gold mine the *Women's Weekly*, where the seams that had financed the empire for so long were nearing exhaustion. Sales were down because the magazine had lost touch with its readers and the competition, and because the world had changed while the *Weekly* had not. Magazines that last forty years, like gold mines that bear ore that long, are a rarity, so the trusty old *Weekly* had done well to stay in production, but its days as a cash provider were numbered unless new shafts were sunk.

The *Weekly*'s main problem was that it looked old-fashioned alongside its more modern rivals. It needed a facelift and an update of its contents. *Cleo*, which had been launched in a smaller 'standard' size on new glossy paper, had taught Consolidated Press a lesson about what magazines should look like, and its thundering success suggested that the *Weekly* could only benefit from its own new set of clothes. But it wasn't just that sales were falling, for the *Weekly*'s dwindling revenues were being rapidly engulfed by rising costs of production. Its larger 'tabloid' size made it expensive to produce because it did not fit neatly into the dimensions of the newsprint roll. There was waste, too, on the page itself, since the designers left large margins with nothing to fill them. Even more to the point, there were huge gains to be had by going smaller: if one halved the size of the pages, increased their number, yet still persuaded advertisers to pay almost the old page rate, profits could be increased dramatically.

Kerry calculated that the various changes, taken together, would yield the company an extra $2 million a year, some of which could then be used to print the magazine on glossy paper. This left only one worry—whether its loyal readers would stay with them. Ita Buttrose remembers Kerry, even before Frank's death, cutting down copies of the *Weekly* to see what it looked like in different sizes. 'What do you think of that?' he would ask her. He hadn't bothered to ask his father, since the response to such a radical change would have been 'over my dead body'.

It is a tenet of magazine publishing that you normally make changes subtly, bit by bit, so that your old readers don't desert *en masse* before you attract new ones. But the mess that the *Weekly* was in demanded a braver approach. While there was a danger that the magazine would die on the operating table if the surgery was radical, there was a certainty that its life would drip slowly away if drastic action were not taken. Not surprisingly, Kerry was nervous at the prospect of what had to be done, for he was refashioning his father's most successful creation, the magazine that had launched the Packer publishing empire forty-two years before. The nerves showed in his somewhat erratic behaviour. In the very last weeks before the launch, he sacked J. Walter Thompson, the advertising agency which had been with the Packers for twenty years, and gave the job to his friend John Singleton at Doyle Dane Bernbach. Then, almost immediately, he changed his mind again and gave Thompsons the job back. His worries showed, too, in the way he treated his employees, at whom he would rage and shout if things were not entirely to his satisfaction. On one occasion he reduced Ita to tears over a photograph she had chosen for the cover, screaming at her and abusing her, and stopping only when she asked for the tissues; on another she remembers going downstairs to his secretary's office to find one of the doors kicked off. She can't remember now what had annoyed him.

The changes they were making did not come cheap. The new printing press clocked in at $2 million, the binding and wrapping machines at another $1 million and the promotion campaign at a further $1 million on top of that. But it ensured the product was good and the public would know about it. As D-day approached, the new *Weekly* was everywhere—on billboards, in newspapers, on radio and television, and on trains and buses in all the major cities. Because of her success with *Cleo*, Ita had been given a free hand to bring the magazine's editorial content up to date. More controversially, she was also given the job of presenting the television ads for the new magazine. She would soon be promoting its stories regularly on television, with the trademark lisp that the advertisers thought quaintly marketable.

Outwardly, Kerry was certain that the new-look *Weekly* would succeed. When Barry Porter of the Australian Journalists' Association said that he hoped the changes would work, Kerry told him brashly: 'They'll work. No one knows more about advertising than I do, and I'm telling you, they'll work.' But inwardly, according to Ita, he was extremely nervous, and talking of pulling out even in the last weeks before the launch. By this time, though, the money had been spent. It was too late.

True to Kerry's public pronouncements, the relaunch was a triumph. The first edition of the new-look magazine topped the million mark for the first time, outselling even the record Coronation issue of 1953. Just before it went on sale, Kerry had sent Ita a very personal note of thanks to tell her how important she had been in the project and how close she had become to him:

Ita,

Forty-two years ago we launched the *Women's Weekly*. Forty-two years later we relaunched it. I know it is going to be a great success and you are the person who is going to make it that. If anybody has asked me what your nickname should be I would have told them 'A Jewel Beyond Price'. From the bottom of my heart, thank you.

Kerry[10]

The success of *Cleo* had already made Ita powerful within Consolidated Press, but the even greater success of the *Weekly* made her star rise still further. By 1976 she was editor-in-chief of both publications, and by 1978 publisher of all the group's women's magazines, putting her second only to Harry Chester in importance in the company and in her ability to command Kerry's ear. The following year she was given the OBE for services to journalism and voted the most admired woman in Australia, having become a celebrity in her own right. By this time she was even employing a speech writer for her frequent public appearances. But if the women of Australia approved of her, many fellow journalists did not, arguing that her changes had modernised the *Weekly* but trivialised it, too. Even those that merely poked fun, such as aesthete Phillip Adams, in Melbourne's *Age* newspaper, did so rather cruelly, mimicking her ubiquitous television ads and the *Weekly*'s new modern approach with a wicked sense of satire.

Hello. Thith ith Ita Buttrothe, editor of the Authralian Women'th Weekly, thitting here in the thtudio, thmiling at you from the thcreen. I'd like to tell you about thith weekth thuper ithue. It'th full of wonderful thurpritheth and thintillating featureth . . . We show you how to teach your cat to thing opera; how to propagate garden gnometh; how to turn your Great Dane into a chihuahua by employing anthient Japanethe bonthai techniqueth; how to glue lawn-clippinth to your lino as a low-cotht thubthitute for carpet; how to develop an attractive lithp; how to uthe a thimple pieth of thtring to thave your huthband from the embarrathment of premature ejaculation, while adding lotth of fun to your marriage; how John Thingleton found God; what Kamal wearth under hith caftan; how Raquel Welch prayth for motherhood.[11]

Those who interviewed her were often even less kind in their treatment. They called her hard, ruthless and demanding, and mocked her dress, her attitude and her ambition. Male colleagues, unused to such a powerful woman, claimed to find her cold, selfish and insufferable. Others, however, found her wonderful to work for. Ita put criticism down to envy and continued on her way, but this was not a happy time for her. When the executives of Consolidated Press gathered in the taproom next to Kerry's office for drinks in the evening, she was not spared the male banter in which they almost all engaged. Nor did many go out of their way to make her welcome. Ita felt she was being ostracised, and complained to friends. What perhaps increased male jealousy was that she was perceived as being extremely close to the boss. On occasions, as at a big party in 1976 at London's Savoy Hotel, she even acted as hostess at Consolidated Press's public functions, with Kerry as host.

Kerry's wife Ros appeared to have no interest in playing such a role in the business. But by all accounts she was charming and delightful. A strong-minded, down-to-earth country girl with no pretences, Ros Packer spent her time padding round barefoot, dressed in jeans, doing the gardening. She reminded many of Kerry's mother Gretel, but was less involved in her husband's public life than her mother-in-law had been. She was no society lady and no dazzling political hostess. She stayed at home, lived a normal life insofar as she could, and concentrated on her dogs, her homes and her children—Gretel, named after Kerry's mother, born in 1966, and James, born two years later.

The Packers had enough money to dine on champagne and caviar every night, yet Kerry preferred junk food to anything else. He liked hamburgers, milkshakes, hot dogs and Fanta, with Chinese meals for treats. When they went out for office celebrations he would order sweet and sour pork with double pineapple sauce and would complain loudly if others took too much. He had a great sweet tooth, with a weakness for ice cream, puddings and fizzy drinks. He also smoked sixty to eighty cigarettes a day and was rarely seen without three packs on the table in front of him. Often he had two or three cigarettes burning at once.

Not surprisingly, since he took little exercise, he battled constantly with his weight, and struggled with diets. Ron Saw recalls writing an article for the *Bulletin* about a weight-loss merchant who had a magic formula for injecting drugs into fat people to make them thin. Kerry saw it and decided to give it a try. With Saw beside him in the office he had his secretary ring the Sydney Hilton arcade where the quack was to be found. 'Packer here,' he said when the call was switched through, 'get round here and show me how this business works.' According to Saw, there was then some explanation from the other end that clients normally came to them, not the other way round. 'Look,' Packer growled, 'do you want this job or don't you? Right, well get round here in half an hour.' Packer then put the phone down with an evil look in his eye, and explained to Saw: 'When you've got a lot of money, you can behave like that.'

The tales of Kerry's temper were legendary, but that didn't make them any less true. He had trouble sleeping, took Mogadon regularly, and was at his worst when the tablets didn't work. On these 'Mogadon days' there was only one safe answer for staff, and that was to stay out of his way. 'He had a foul temper, such a foul temper,' according to Ita, and seemed to enjoy grinding people into the dust, to see them squirm. He was also on a hair trigger, needing the lightest of touches to set him off. His driver, George Young, found him the easiest bloke to work for as long as one was on time and didn't make mistakes, but if something went wrong, Packer would explode. When he did erupt there was nothing to do but wait for the storm to pass, for if you argued back he would just swear more loudly. Asked once why he shouted at people, he thought for a long time and then said that he supposed it was because he didn't know what to say to them.

Given his childhood, it was hardly surprising that he had difficulty in making relationships and that he was shy and isolated. Being rich and powerful made it no easier, for he could never be sure who his real friends were. But as he explained drily to

Michael Parkinson in a television interview on the ABC in 1979, the Packers both expected hostility and planned for it.

> My father always said, 'Son, by the time you get to thirty-five, thirty-six years of age they won't let you into any bloody clubs, so join early. You're going to be treading on too many corns and there'll be too many people who don't like you at that stage. You'll never get elected.' So he put us down for a whole series of clubs when we were eighteen or twenty years of age, so we got in before anyone didn't like us too much.[12]

So far so funny, Kerry had great timing and a sharp wit; the television studio audience laughed loud. But Parkinson then asked him a question that stopped him in his tracks. Thus far there had been a sunny gloss on everything, but this cracked it to reveal glimpses of a deep gloom inside.

> Parkinson: Do you make friends easily? I mean, what's your first move towards somebody when you first meet them?
>
> Packer: Er . . . No. I don't make friends easily, Michael. Er . . . I'm . . . I'm . . . I've had my share of being attacked, nobody likes being attacked, and of course you get very defensive, and then I saw my father being attacked by a lot of people. I'm not trying to get sympathy, we're quite capable of doing a bit of attacking ourselves, but there is a stand-off thing. Basically, when I meet people, I don't expect to like them . . .

It was almost painful to listen to Kerry's sad siege mentality being laid bare. Even then, he believed the outside world was out to get him, to rip him off, to take him for a sucker. He saw himself as an object of hatred. He had to be on his guard.

At Consolidated Press, every night after work, there would be drinks in the taproom next door to Kerry's office. All the senior executives were expected to attend, or let Kerry's secretary Pat Wheatley know that they weren't going to be there. Kerry would preside perhaps three nights out of five and was frequently the last to leave. At eight o'clock, when everyone else had gone, he would still be going strong. Ian Kennon, who was in Kerry's inner circle for a brief time in the mid 1970s, would sometimes go to dinner with him afterwards, where he would order the best food and the best wine and just talk. They would still be there at 2 a.m., with Kerry wanting to chat about politics, television programs, television schedules, the world or anything else that came to mind, and one night even working out how to grab the takings from the ski resort of Perisher Smiggins by hijacking the armoured truck that took the money down the mountain. He seemed, for all his wealth and power, to be a desperately lonely and unhappy man. He liked people around him all the time, and was always ready to sit up and talk till the small hours if he could find someone prepared to listen. In one such late-night conversation with Phillip Adams, they got round to the subject of astronomy and black holes. Adams explained what they were and Packer said, 'That's what I have: a black hole inside me.'

To keep boredom and loneliness at bay, he needed constant excitement. Sometimes, as with the relaunch of the *Weekly*, he got his kicks from business, but he also gambled more than ever, leaving himself constantly short of cash, for all the huge Packer family wealth. Though nearing forty, he was also as passionate about cars as he had ever been in his youth. Needled, it was said, by being overtaken by Porsche 911s on the Newcastle expressway, he had bought a Jaguar XJS and spent $50 000 to have it modified, fitting the car's V12 engine with twin turbos that boosted its output to 1000 horsepower or forty per cent more than the Le Mans-winning Jaguars of the late 1980s. Those who went in it were scared witless: one moment the car was going along quietly, then the turbos kicked in and the telegraph poles flashed by like a picket fence. Sadly, it was not much fun to drive, and it spent almost as much time off the road as on it, because the gearbox couldn't cope with the power of the motor.

When Kerry relaxed, he could be both charming and fun to be with. He had an obvious grasp of the media business and business in general. He was funny, a good raconteur, and undeniably sharp. He was straightforward, one of the boys. Most of his staff liked him. Most of his staff were also scared of him.

There were echoes of his father in the way he behaved. When he had nothing better to do, which seemed to be quite often, he would prowl round the *Women's Weekly* offices asking why people weren't there. One morning when a sudden downpour had snarled up Sydney's traffic, he cruised into the advertising sales area barely a minute after 9 a.m. to find several empty desks. Having asked where the hell everybody was, he ordered all late arrivals to be sent down to see him as soon as they came in. Thus, before long, senior managers and junior sales staff trickled down to his office in twos and threes to be shouted at. According to one of them who suffered the dressing-down, it was just like facing the headmaster—fine if you didn't try to make an excuse, but terrible if you tried to talk your way out of it.

His dealings with staff had never been subtle. As far back as 1972, when the *Telegraph* had been sold to Murdoch, it had been his job to persuade the journalists to transfer to News Ltd. Most hadn't been keen to go: 'We liked working for Frank Packer, mad though he was,' says Ron Saw, 'so a lot of us said no, you can go to buggery.' Kerry had summoned the objectors one-by-one to his third floor office to give them their marching orders, where his talk with Ron Saw, who was ten years his senior, had gone something like this:

> Kerry: Right son, I want you to go to Rupert.
> Saw: No, Kerry, I don't want to go.
> Kerry: Well, if that's the thing, son, you can go on writing your column every day, we'll take it and throw it in the garbage can. And you'll never get another job in Australia.

He would employ similar tactics in negotiations over business. In the mid 1970s, when chat show host Mike Walsh was getting itchy feet at Channel Ten, Kerry summoned Walsh's lawyer up from Melbourne to talk about the star coming over to Nine. His opening gambit was to lay down the rules of engagement, which went: 'At the end of the day you'll either sign a contract or you won't sign. And then you'll walk out of here. If you don't sign, I'll tell Channel Ten that we've had discussions and they've got nowhere.' Walsh's lawyer was taken aback—the normal rule of such talks is that one treats them in the strictest confidence, for obvious reasons—so he ventured the opinion that Packer was not being fair. Kerry had to this point been waving a golf club as he watched his own Australian Open on his own Channel Nine. Now he banged the golf club down on the table and shouted at the poor lawyer, 'Don't you fucking tell me what's fair and what's not fair. I should be down at the Open now, and instead I'm here talking about making money for your fucking client. Now do you want to talk or don't you?' By eight o'clock that evening contracts had been signed, and Channel Nine had a valuable new property. The verdict of those who saw it was that it was brilliant negotiation. It was also typical of Packer's style.

When Sir Frank died in May 1974, no one at Channel Nine had been too keen that Kerry was taking over. Even those at the television station knew his reputation of being the dumber son, and for the first few months there was little to calm their fears. Some felt he was playing the role of TV proprietor, throwing his weight around, yet knowing little about the business. They could hardly have been more wrong, for Kerry would eventually leave Channel Nine unchallenged at the top of the ratings, yet some of his first acts suggested that he would ape the worst aspects of his father's behaviour. It was not just the little things, like keeping his driver sitting outside the whole night while he talked about his ideas for television. It was that while other stations were increasing staff, Kerry set about cutting numbers with some vigour. It was also that he appeared to show no concern for what the outside world thought of him. Just like his father, he seemed to believe that this was nobody's business but his own.

One such example came in August 1974 when a parliamentary committee published a damning report on the practices of the soap powder industry. The report recommended a cut in prices and an examination of the 'ambiguous and misleading' advertising claims made, largely on television, by Colgate-Palmolive and Unilever. As the report pointed out, the two companies controlled 80 per cent of the Australian soap powder market, earned profits three times the Australian average for manufacturing, and used advertising to create artificial differences between similar products. Channels Nine and Ten both sent a crew to film the Minister for Science, Bill Morrison, who spent the whole interview attacking the deceptive advertisements. Somehow, neither story made it to air. Channel Ten's film was 'spoiled in processing', while Channel Nine's story in Sydney was pulled on the instructions of Sam Chisholm, the network's sales director, who said words to the effect that there was no way they were going to show it. The reporter who prepared the Channel Nine story, Derek Maitland, bravely allowed himself to be interviewed on ABC TV that night, whereupon Packer ordered him to be sacked.

Gerald Stone, who was about to become Channel Nine's news director, then attempted to persuade Kerry to change his mind, arguing that Channel Nine should be seen to defend the independence of journalists from commercial pressure. Packer's answer was a blunt 'Fuck it, he's going.' The fact that the journalist had been disloyal overrode all other considerations.

There was another episode that made the people at Nine wonder what sort of proprietor they had been landed with. In late August 1975, the former Portuguese colony of East Timor erupted into civil war. With refugees bringing tales of massacres and beheadings, all the television networks were keen to get in to cover the fighting, but the Portuguese were denying visas to journalists, and the Australian Government was doing its best to ensure that nobody broke the ban. Nine beat the blockade by joining a medical mission run by a freelance Right-wing entrepreneur, Michael Darby, and the Australian Society for Inter Country Aid to Timor (ASIAT), his hastily-formed charity. ASIAT was confident they could get in, but they needed money to charter a ship. For $1000 a day, with $6000 cash down, they offered Nine a great story—an Australian humanitarian mission to Timor—and a way into Timor that would otherwise be denied. They offered, too, the hope of some protection, since ASIAT's doctors had made friends with the people from Fretilin and the UDT, the two warring sides, on a previous trip. Gerald Stone, by this time Nine's news director, asked Kerry whether he was prepared to put up the money and was told that he would be happy to, but only on one condition: that he came along, too. Stone was none too thrilled about having the boss along on the trip, but there was not much he could do about it, and so the deal was sealed, Kerry included.

Since a similar offer had already been made to Channel Seven, the journalists at Nine reckoned they had to act fast to avoid being scooped on the story, so everything now became a mad scramble. ASIAT's doctor, John Whitehall, who was waiting in Sydney for word that the trip was on, was told to get on the next plane to Darwin. The following day he was in a motel room in the Territory's capital, being introduced to Packer and being sworn to secrecy. Kerry was stretched out on a bed, with very little on, 'like a great beached whale' as Whitehall recalls it. Whitehall mentioned that Channel Seven was still keen to get in on the act and might be able to match what Channel Nine had offered. Kerry's reply, still lying flat out, was to kick an aluminium box full of banknotes across the floor and say: 'Let's see if they can fucking get above that.'

The ship they had chartered, the *Konpira Maru*, was hardly an ideal choice for the trip, since she was at the centre of a row with the Australian Customs Service, but there was no other boat in harbour big enough to make the journey. A twenty-four metre ex-Japanese fishing vessel that had been washed onto Bathurst Island during Cyclone Tracey in December 1974 and salvaged by a couple of Darwin seafarers, she was technically an illegal import, but had been given Panamanian papers in an attempt to stave off a demand for $468 000 in unpaid import duty. Now registered as a foreign ship, she had been banned from working in Australian waters, but that hadn't deterred her owners from accepting the offer of an illicit trip, for they needed the money badly.

Fortunately, the ASIAT party had only a few teachests of medical supplies to smuggle aboard, but there were several boxes of Channel Nine's camera gear and a spanking new Zodiac rubber dinghy that Kerry had bought for the occasion, so it must have been difficult to depart without attracting attention. But the authorities were probably glad to see the back of them. Giving customs the cover story that they were going crayfishing in Indonesian waters, since they had been refused a visa, they left Darwin under cover of darkness at 7 p.m. on 26 August 1975. The next morning they sent a radio message to say that they had changed course and were bound for the East Timorese capital of Dili.

Kerry did not get on well with his fellow passengers or the ship's crew on the two-day voyage. He had pitched up at the dock with six cases of Fanta and a Portuguese bodyguard named Manuel, who everyone was informed had been a mercenary in Angola and Mozambique, and he soon made no bones about the fact that he thought everything on the ship was shit. He refused to eat the food and installed himself in his rubber dinghy up on the deck, where he both slept and had all his meals, which consisted of big hunks of salami that he cut off with a Bowie knife. He argued constantly with the crew, telling them what to do and how to do it, and complaining that they weren't going fast enough.

He and Manuel had brought an armoury of guns between them, enough to start their own war, as one fellow passenger put it, and Kerry was keen to try them out. As they cruised through the Timor Sea, John Whitehall and another man were deputed to throw cans off the stern while Packer attempted to blast them with his hi-tech buffalo rifle. Whitehall remembers that he wasn't much of a shot, and kept missing but, even worse, the gun kept jamming so that Kerry was soon in a rage. The final straw was when the ship's mate, John Chatterton, produced an old .303 with a back-sight fashioned out of a piece of tin and had a can thrown for him, which he hit first time. The game was then terminated as Kerry packed up his gun and stumped off. In all the time that they had been throwing targets off the back, he had never invited anyone else to have a go.

They reached Dili at dawn two days after they set off to find it fairly peaceful, with only a few desultory fires burning at one end of the town. They had taken the precaution of flying a makeshift Red Cross flag, but they scarcely needed it. As they hove to outside the reef, a couple of Australians in an aluminium dinghy came roaring out to meet them and guide them into the dock. One was the local hotel owner, a man of some influence, who had told the Fretilin soldiers not to shoot.

The worst of the fighting was already over, but there was still the odd sniper to contend with and scores of casualties in the town's hospital, where there were people lying in the corridors and almost 100 cases awaiting surgery. The place was filthy, the staff had run away and the one remaining doctor was drunk. There was plenty for Dr Whitehall to do, and more than enough for the television crew to shoot. For the next three days they went their separate ways, each racing the clock to get the job done.

Stone and Packer then arranged to fly back to Darwin to get the story to air as quickly as possible. Since the RAAF was unwilling to fly into Dili this involved going to the nearby island of Atauro, which was still under Portuguese control, so the *Konpira Maru* was once again pressed into service. This time four Australians who had been stranded by the fighting came with them. One of them, geologist Alex Grady, had shot some super 8 footage of the fighting, with pictures of casualties, refugees and the like, which Packer understandably wanted Channel Nine to have, to retain its 'exclusive'. Grady sat next to him on the flight back to Darwin and was bullied for three hours to give up his film. Money was never mentioned as an inducement; Grady was simply told by Packer that he owed a debt of gratitude and that he had a moral obligation to hand over the footage. 'You wouldn't even be here if I hadn't taken you on my boat,' Grady remembers him saying. Grady resented being hectored in this manner and hung on to his footage, eventually giving it to the ABC instead.

As Packer flew back to Darwin, the *Konpira Maru* returned to Dili, where several hundred Chinese refugees were desperately waiting to leave. Most had lost their businesses in the fighting, then seen friends and relations killed in the crossfire when the dock area had come under Fretilin bombardment. Now they jostled and fought and offered their worldly wealth to get on board, under the watchful and unsympathetic eye of the Fretilin soldiers. Almost 200 women and children managed to clamber onto the decks whereupon the *Konpira Maru* filled to bursting, made its way back to Darwin with its precious human cargo.

Kerry's role in this mercy lift, such as it was, received little attention at the time. But twelve years after the event, under a headline worthy of Sir Frank's old *Telegraph*, 'GRATEFUL REFUGEES BLESS THE DAY PACKER SAILED INTO WAR', the story was told in Brisbane's *Sunday Mail*. It was a fascinating example of how myths can be made when you are rich and newsworthy, for it portrayed Kerry as a bashful saint, a big man with a bigger heart, too shy to tell people of the good deed he had done.

> Only a few people knew Packer sailed into Dili harbour in former Portuguese Timor only days after a coup d'etat had plunged the island colony north of Darwin into civil war. The day Packer went to war he didn't wear a uniform, didn't carry a gun, and he didn't stay long.
>
> But he stayed long enough to ensure that 187 frightened Timorese had a safe passage to Australia.
>
> The 187 included five pregnant women and 60 children. They may well owe their lives to Packer who, known to bet millions on racecourses, that day bet his life.
>
> Characteristically, he never boasted of that fact.[13]

There were elements of truth in this account. But Packer the bashful saviour is not the man the *Konpira Maru*'s master remembered. At the age of 85, Syd Hawkes was still complaining that Packer owed him $3000 for the trip. What is more, he maintained that the money was never paid because the *Konpira Maru* carried the refugees without Packer's authorisation. Whether that is accurate or not, it is clear that the Timor trip ended with recriminations and accusations on both sides, for Kerry's prize rubber dinghy and powerful outboard were never returned. Kerry naturally wanted his property back; he might also have felt that he had paid in full, even though the *Konpira Maru* had been away from Darwin for nine days and he had paid only for six. In any case, his office sent Hawkes a reply-paid telegram soon after, demanding: 'Return dinghy and outboard by air Kingsford Smith.' Hawkes' young partner John Chatterton opened it and cabled back two words: 'Get stuffed'.

Tales of Kerry's exploits in Timor soon got back to journalists and executives at Channel Nine and doubtless added to his reputation. The rubber dinghy and Packer's pot shots off the ship before long passed into legend. But it is unlikely that they would have persuaded the people in his newly inherited television empire to take him more seriously. They would soon realise, however, that behind the bluster and the bullying there was a sharp brain and an instinct that few of the professionals could match. As they soon discovered, Kerry was much more interested in television than his recently-departed father had ever been. He had ambitions for it, and was prepared to spend money to make things happen.

CHAPTER NINE

HOWZAT?

Q: Is it right that you went into the Supertest business to
make money?
A: Of course, I have never said anything else.

Kerry Packer, cross-examined by Michael Kempster QC,
September 1977

Nowadays the TV networks will tell you that international
cricket is ideal for commercial television. It has bright colours,
gladiatorial action, Australian nationalism, thumping the Poms
and sixty seconds of advertisements at the end of every four-
minute over. But best of all it is extremely profitable, because it
is tremendously cheap to broadcast and rates better than almost
anything on the dial.

Yet in the mid 1970s none of the commercial television
moguls except Kerry Packer had the faintest idea of the game's
potential as a TV sport. Had you asked them in 1976 whether
they were interested in televising Australian cricket, they would
have barely stifled a yawn. Why, they would have inquired, would
we want to cover a Test match grinding out over five days to a
draw while nobody watches? No thanks, they would have said,
we'll leave that stuff to the ABC. Which was precisely what they
had done.

Packer, however, had other ideas. He had lived his life for sport
at school and followed Rugby League, cricket, tennis and golf
passionately as an adult. As an avid sports fan and confirmed television addict, it was only natural that he would want to get these

games onto Channel Nine and jazz them up a bit to make them less boring. But as a sports fan who also owned a network, he appreciated better than most television executives how sports coverage would be transformed by having colour pictures, which were spreading across Australia in the mid 1970s at tremendous speed. It would take just three years, from 1975 to 1978, for two-thirds of Australian viewers to buy themselves colour television sets. And games that had once seemed dull and lacklustre would suddenly come alive on the screen. It wasn't just the cricket that Packer coveted—he tilted first at tennis, Rugby League and golf, with varying degrees of success. But it was only in the stuffy cricketing world, with its vestiges of British Empire rule, that his approach caused such turmoil and uproar.

Ever since 1956, when television was first introduced into Australia, cricket had always been the preserve of the ABC, who had covered it in a hushed and gentlemanly fashion that struck a chord with the traditions of the game. The commercial stations had been invited to bid for the television rights in the early days but had shown little enthusiasm, and in 1961 the Australian Cricket Board had given up talking to them, so the ABC had always got the coverage cheap. The board offered the commercial stations the opportunity every year to televise the same matches, once a deal with the ABC had been struck, yet the offer was hardly ever accepted. According to Ray Steele, manager of Australia's touring teams in the 1960s, and one of the Cricket Board's negotiators:

> The commercials were a bloody nuisance because they didn't want to televise cricket, except when England came out or the West Indies came out and there was an exciting test, or something like that . . . the ABC, on the other hand, they always televised cricket right throughout the country, and they not only televised Test cricket, they televised Sheffield Shield cricket, which was great for the game.[1]

With this twenty-year history in mind, the Australian Cricket Board didn't take too much notice when it received a phone call from an executive at Channel Nine in March 1976 to say that Packer's station was interested in bidding for the cricket rights. According to Ray Steele and Bob Parish, the Australian Cricket Board's two key negotiators, there was absolutely no mention of the ABC being excluded, nor was there a formal approach by letter to spell out Channel Nine's intentions. Steele and Parish therefore filed the approach in their bottom drawer and did the usual deal with the ABC, selling them rights to televise Australian cricket for the three years until May 1979 for $207 000. In June 1976 they notified the commercial stations that they were prepared to deal with them on the same terms. Soon after, they received their second phone call from Channel Nine, this time to say that Kerry Packer wanted to see them.

The offices of the Victorian Cricket Association, where the meeting took place, were housed in an elegant Edwardian building in the shadow of the Melbourne Cricket Ground. The walls were covered with trophies and pictures of winning teams down the years. As you would expect from such an organisation, there was a quiet air of tradition and history about the place, and Packer was about to shatter it. As Ray Steele tells the story:

> Kerry walked into the room and said, 'I want totally exclusive television rights.'
>
> And he was told. 'Sorry, Mr Packer, but you can't have that.' I'm sure he knew, because we'd written to him and told him that we had done a deal with the ABC.
>
> And he said, 'Come off it, you haven't signed that agreement with the ABC.'
>
> And he was told, whilst we hadn't signed the agreement, we had virtually shaken hands on the deal and there was no way we would go back on it.
>
> Well, he was bloody irate. His reply to that, I'll never forget it, was, 'We're all harlots, how much do you want?'

Packer's version was that he said, 'There's a little bit of the whore in all of us. Gentlemen, name your price.' But whatever the precise words, the Australian Cricket Board officials were taken aback. No one had asked for exclusive rights in twenty years, nor had anyone spoken to them like that. Packer told them he was prepared to offer $500 000 a year, more than seven times what the ABC was paying, but the officials were powerless to negotiate. There was no point, said Parish, in even taking the proposal to the Board, because they were morally bound by their agreement to sell the rights to the ABC. They promised Packer to consider granting him exclusive rights in three years' time, but he was not to be mollified and left in high dudgeon.

It was typical of Packer that he would have no truck with non-exclusive rights, for he always wanted monopoly or market dominance, but it was a wise decision to demand them, because the ABC had built up a loyal audience over the years and viewers were unlikely to watch cricket on a commercial station if they could watch it uninterrupted on another channel. Channel Seven discovered this the following year when it bought rights to the Centenary Test in Melbourne and was beaten hands down by the ABC, which picked up two-thirds of the audience. Packer was therefore determined to get exclusive rights or nothing, and he was not used to settling for nothing.

Several months later he was offered a chance to get even. John Cornell, a former Channel Nine producer who had launched Paul Hogan's career in showbiz, suggested that they should stage their own one-day matches for television. Since he was already marketing Australia's firebrand fast bowler Dennis Lillee, wicket-keeper Rodney Marsh and a swashbuckling young batsman called David Hookes, he knew that cricketers would be eager for the money. Packer was immediately taken with the idea. 'Why not do the thing properly?' he asked. 'Why not get the world's best cricketers to play the best Australians?'[2] So World Series Cricket was born and the signings began.

Kerry Packer's idea of doing things properly had already been made clear during Nine's coverage of the Australian Open Golf championship, which in 1975 had been in need of a sponsor and looking as if it might go under. Packer had agreed to put in

$1 million in prize money, and had picked up three years' television rights in exchange. Most sponsors would have stopped there, but Packer wanted to make the tournament one of the top five in the world, along with the British and US Opens, the US Masters and the US PGA, and decided to spend a further million dollars to make it the best. He insisted that the Open should have a new permanent home, at Sydney's Australian Golf Club, and hired Jack Nicklaus to redesign the course. Artificial hills were added as vantage points for spectators and a vast network of underground cables laid to improve communications. When Packer's Open first hit the screens in October 1975, the television coverage was as good as, or better than, anywhere else in the world. For the first time in any tournament anywhere, there was a camera on each of the eighteen holes. Naturally the viewers approved, so ratings were good. But the innovation made sound business sense, too, for it attracted eighteen separate sponsors who wanted their name in lights. Since W. D. & H. O. Wills had already coughed up $150 000 as a secondary tournament sponsor, this put Packer well on his way to getting his money back.

The changes to the course made the Australian among the best in the country but also, by common consent, one of the hardest. A welcome by-product of this, as Kerry told Ita Buttrose and Harry Chester over lunch one day, was that the course would now be too difficult for women to play on. According to Ita, Kerry and Harry both loathed women on the golf course and laughed as this observation was made. They laughed even louder as Ita predictably objected. Some of the professionals also found the revamped Australian nigh-on impossible, but Nicklaus did not, and won the tournament. Kerry could hardly have wished for a better result, for Nicklaus was then the dominant figure in world golf. And his involvement had already guaranteed a record turnout from the top American professionals, who could not fail to be impressed by what they saw.[3]

By comparison with what Jack Nicklaus picked up for his Open victory, the great stars of Australian cricket were appallingly badly paid. While golf and tennis stars were making a fortune out of their skills, only a handful of cricketers in the mid 1970s were making more than a living. Australian Test players on the tour of New Zealand in 1977 would receive just over $2400 for 35 days work; if they were picked for the ensuing tour of England they would get another $11 000 for a further 134 days. And that was far better than previous years, thanks to a lucrative new sponsorship deal struck with Benson & Hedges in January 1977. England's Test players at the time were earning even less, receiving only the equivalent of $5000 for a four-month tour of Pakistan and Australia, or $350 per match in England. The typical county crick-eter in England pulled in less than the national average wage and worked in the winter to make ends meet, coaching in South Africa if he was lucky or bricklaying if he wasn't.

It was hardly surprising, then, that cricketers fell over each other to sign for Packer. Although they were hardly being offered a fortune, $25 000 for twelve weeks' work must have seemed like one, particularly for those who believed they would be able to play regular cricket as well. Packer told the High Court in London later that year that the players had accepted with fright-ening alacrity. But it was hardly surprising, as Gary Sobers pointed out: 'If somebody comes along and offers you five or six times the money to play against the best players in the world, I believe you're mad not to think about it.' The players would make in twelve weeks what he had made in his first ten years. As it turned out, only one of those approached said 'no', and that was the English Test star Geoffrey Boycott. Even he said 'possibly'.[4]

The signings took place amid the utmost secrecy, which was needed if the plan was to have any chance of success. Those who were invited to join were asked beforehand to take a vow of silence. As Kerry later recounted, he would say to those he was trying to recruit, 'I have a business proposition I want to put to you. You must give me your solemn oath not to discuss it with anybody, win, lose or draw.' This, he maintained, was essential if the project was to get to first base.

Obviously, if you're going to start something which is going to be controversial, and all the cards are held by the other party . . . you would be some form of mental deficient if you went along to the other party and said, 'Look, this is what I think I'm going to do.' Of course I was secretive about it, but I have been secretive about every business deal I've ever been in to start with, as has everybody else who has ever done something successful.[5]

To Kerry, of course, it was second nature to keep his lips sealed, but the players also managed to keep their mouths shut, and not a word leaked out. When Richie Benaud was approached in April 1977, six weeks after the mass signings of Australian players had begun, he had not even heard a whisper. Yet the mustering had taken place under the nose of the cricket authorities. On the last day of the Centenary Test in Melbourne, in March 1977, even as Australia and England were celebrating 100 years of white-flannelled struggle, World Series Cricket's Austin Robertson was handing out money to people for agreeing to play Packer's pyjama game.

The game was over. Australia won by 45 runs and they were all in the dressing room—Parish, Steele, players, officials, the lot—and so was I, with $75 000 in cheques in my briefcase.

The cheques were all in individually addressed envelopes—to Walters, Davis, Walker and so on. And right there, under all their noses, I was moving round handing out the cheques, saying things like, 'Hey Doug, there's your theatre tickets,' and passing over his envelope and then moving on. That's how we did it, and though it seems unbelievable, no one suspected a thing.[6]

It was not till May 1977 that the story of the signings broke, by which time the Australian cricket team was in England, about to play four Jubilee Tests, and Packer had secured the services of thirty-five players. There was an immediate outcry, especially when it was discovered that thirteen of the seventeen-strong Australian touring party, including team captain Greg Chappell, had already joined the enemy.

Three members of the English team, including captain Tony Greig and two key players, Alan Knott and Derek Underwood, had also signed up. Greig had not only taken the Packer shilling but had also acted as a recruiting sergeant for the other English players, for which he was immediately condemned. Here was a man who had earned his living and fame from the official game conspiring in secret to take its best players hostage. Greig was respected by most of his fellow cricketers but he could be brash, outspoken and occasionally stupid, and his past excesses were now recalled to show that he had always been unsuitable—he had threatened to make the West Indians 'grovel' when they played England in 1976, had run out Alvin Kallicharan in a Test match the previous year as the batsman walked to the pavilion after the last ball of the day and, worst of all, had been a South African all along. Now he was branded a traitor and a mercenary, and summarily sacked as England's captain. 'No one is likely to be convinced that he has acted less than miserably,' commented *The Times*. It had taken just three days for the authorities to dump him.

Secrecy and treachery were predictably the issues that the cricket faithful chose to emphasise. But their real sense of outrage was about far deeper concerns. It was about 100 years of tradition, about an invader on cricket's hallowed turf, and in England, where the opposition to Packer was at its most choleric, it was also about an Australian trying to take over the sport that England had given to the rest of the world. To the diehards at Lord's, the home of the Marylebone Cricket Club, where one still needs permission to take one's jacket off on a hot day if watching from the pavilion terrace, there was far more than just a game at stake. Cricket, played in the proper way by proper people, was a way of life, a religion. To talk about setting up a rival church, run by an Australian of all things, was quite simply heresy.

No doubt some of the members at Lord's would have been happy to see Kerry burned at the stake, in the way that heretics of old were dealt with, but in the meantime they opted for ridicule to drive him away, with the full support of the Fleet

Street press corps. From day one, Packer's plans were dismissed as 'just not cricket', and as a common entertainment. 'TESTS HAVE NOTHING TO FEAR FROM THE CIRCUS' was the headline in London's *Times* the day that Packer's plans were leaked, followed by a scathing dismissal by the paper's distinguished cricket correspondent John Woodcock.

> To say that the creation of a circus of international cricketers, expected to be announced from Australia tomorrow, will wreck the future of Test cricket is a wild exaggeration. The Royal Variety Performance at the London Palladium is all very well, but it is not the real thing . . .
>
> . . . The modern cricketer will do a lot for money. He will hawk autographed miniature bats in Calcutta, one of the world's most impoverished cities, at 15 pounds a time. When they are scarce, he will flog his complimentary tickets at more than the going rate. He will charge for having his picture taken by a professional photographer, even if the only trouble he has to go to is to leave the swimming pool . . .
>
> I can see no long-term future for a side of touring cricketers.[7]

In England, it was hard to find any sympathy in the sports columns for Packer or his players, and when he came to London almost two weeks later the reception was almost uniformly hostile. He had offered almost daily to talk to the cricket authorities to settle the storm, but they had ignored him. Installing himself in a suite at the lavish Dorchester Hotel, he now waited to be summoned. For several days, the cricket authorities did their best to pretend he wasn't there. Finally, they acknowledged his existence and agreed to talk, just as he was catching a plane to leave.

Three weeks later he flew back to London again to a meeting at Lord's on 23 June with cricket's governing body, the International Cricket Conference or ICC. As the distant sounds of leather on willow floated in the window of the committee room, five points were read out to Packer, reasserting the authorities' right to run cricket on their terms, with their rules and by their consent. The key to these conditions for peace was his World Series Cricket matches that southern summer should run for six weeks only and not be represented as Australia versus England or as a genuine clash between any national teams. Packer replied that he was prepared to compromise: he would consider letting them have his players for their matches, he would consider limiting the series to six weeks if they would give him what he wanted. On only two issues was he immovable. He wanted a pledge that there would be no victimisation of those who had signed for him, and a guarantee of exclusive television rights in Australia from 1979.

Packer and his party went off to inspect the Lord's pitch while the ICC debated his offer. Before long, he was summoned back to be told that it was 'totally wrong in principle' that exclusive television rights should be made a condition of negotiations, and that if he insisted it be so there was nothing more to discuss. Packer's response was to utter a curt 'Well, that's it, gentlemen,' and walk out the door. If there had been any confusion before about what was at issue, neither the cricketing authorities nor the press was now in any doubt. As Packer left the meeting, he told waiting journalists that Australian television rights were the sole reason for the fight. Had the ICC promised him a monopoly, he said, he would not only have played the game their way, he would have been prepared to withdraw from cricket altogether: Now he would most definitely not. As far as he was concerned, it was 'Every man for himself, and the devil take the hindmost. I will not take steps to help anyone.'[8]

Even as Packer had been talking peace, he had been planning for war. Back in Australia his management team had been looking for umpires, trying to secure Brisbane's Gabba ground for the fifth Supertest, working on budgets and designing clothing. Now, with hostilities declared, the preparations became far more urgent. It was almost July and the campaign was due to start in November, only four months away. And they hadn't yet sorted out anywhere to play.

Within a month of the meeting at Lord's, all the official grounds in Australia had barred their gates to the Packer 'circus' after pressure from the cricket authorities. Various football grounds had agreed to let them in at a price, but none was ideal for spectators and, more to the point, none even had a cricket pitch. In Sydney, the best they could come up with was the Showground, which was rutted, bumpy and possibly dangerous because of the horses and wagons driven over it each Easter at the annual show. But at least, with Sydney's climate, it should be possible to produce a serviceable wicket in the four months available. Growing pitches at VFL Park in Melbourne or the AFL ground in Adelaide, however, was an altogether different proposition. Winters down south are wet, cold, and can seem to go on for ever. What's more, they bring only a couple of hours of weak sunshine a day. Even in July, the growing season for the fine grasses of which cricket wickets are made was five months away. And Melbourne had had its wettest June for years. It seemed that nothing short of a horticultural miracle would save the Packer Supertests.

While they pondered what to do, an army of groundsmen went to work in Sydney, laying heating cables under the soil at the Showground to speed the growth of the grass that they now planted out in the middle. With luck and a mild Sydney spring, it might just be ready in time. But for Melbourne and Adelaide more drastic measures would be necessary. The only hope was to try to grow the grass indoors, under glass, just like early season vegetables. So two big greenhouses were hurriedly erected and huge 56 000-watt sodium lamps wheeled in. They would have to put electric underblankets into the soil to keep it at 30 degrees Celsius, then flood the scene with artificial light to fool the grass into thinking that summer had arrived. Then all they could do was to hope like hell it would work. They would need five wickets in all like this—two for Adelaide, three for Melbourne.

But getting the grass to grow would be only the start of their worries. They would then have to get the turf out of the greenhouse and into the middle of the football grounds. They could hardly roll it up in strips and re-lay it in the square, because it would be like playing cricket on a patchwork quilt. But neither could they shift a complete wicket, all twenty-five metres of it, in one piece. The best they could think of was perhaps being able to move it in two sections if they were lucky. So, gambling that they would find a way, they planted thousands of tiny sprigs of couch grass in huge concrete trays, roughly twelve metres long and four metres wide. Filled with layers of gravel, sand, loam and black river soil, they weighed 52 tonnes each. No one had yet figured out how to get the trays from the greenhouses to the pitch, but they would have four months to come up with an answer. And, to look on the bright side, if the grass didn't grow, they wouldn't have to worry about it.

Till now, they had intended that World Series Cricket's games should dovetail with Australia's official Test matches against India, but since compromise now seemed impossible, Packer decided to put the contests head-to-head. Details of the new schedules were sent to the owners of VFL Park and Adelaide's AFL ground and soon fell into the hands of the press. On 24 July 1977, only two days before a new meeting at Lord's was set to decide whether the Packer players should be banned from official cricket, Melbourne's *Sunday Press* led its front page with 'CRICKET CIRCUS WAR', breaking the news that the matches would clash, and drawing the obvious conclusion.

> This can only mean the disqualification of every Packer cricketer in this country. They cannot possibly play for the cricket circus and Australia too. This settles the whole question of country versus money. And it means total confrontation between TV magnate Kerry Packer and the Australian Cricket Board.[9]

Two days later, with the London papers echoing these sentiments, the ICC did what was predicted and declared that it would ban all Packer players from official Test cricket. In formal terms, anyone playing in a Packer match after 1 October 1977 would be considered a 'disapproved person' and would therefore be excluded. It was akin to a racecourse 'warning off' a crooked punter, jockey or trainer. And to Richie Benaud in particular, who was named along with Packer as being one of the first to be 'disapproved', it was a blow that hurt. A widely respected man who had done as much as anyone for the good of the game, he was being branded an outcast. It was true that there were provisions to lift the ban, but an ICC spokesman made it clear that it was 'going to be tough to get back'. For those who were to be cast out, it looked like a ban for life.

The English Test and County Cricket Board immediately followed up by banning the Packer players from all domestic competitions under their control. This was a real threat to Packer's plans because nineteen of his West Indian, Pakistani, South African and English players made their basic living from county cricket. Forced to choose between their steady jobs and twelve weeks with Packer, some would be tempted to break their contracts. The Australian fast bowler Jeff Thomson, who didn't play county cricket but was worried about an end to his international career, immediately announced he would do exactly that. In September England's county cricketers, most of whom had not been invited to join the party, backed the ban on the Packer players, whereupon World Series Cricket took the Test and County Cricket Board and the International Cricket Conference to court to have their ban declared illegal as a restraint of trade.

In the month-long legal battle that northern autumn in London's High Court, a wonderful Gothic pile at the top of the Strand, cricketer after cricketer spoke eloquently of the rotten life of a professional sportsman, poorly paid, separated from the family, with little to fall back on in retirement. Packer's legal team helped paint a compelling picture of the near-workhouse conditions that cricketers toiled under. Packer meanwhile presented himself as a businessman doing the best for his shareholders, and keen to do a good turn for cricket and cricketers in the process. Asked by Michael Kempster QC whether he had gone into the Supertest business to make money, he replied disarmingly, 'Of course, I have never said anything else.' He was an impressive witness, even if he did tell the court, somewhat puzzlingly, that television rights had almost nothing to do with his fight.

By contrast, the British cricket establishment was dull, less than eloquent, and repetitive in defence of its actions, even on the evidence of its supporters. Years of unchallenged authority had never caused its members to question their right to rule, nor had they ever seen the need to practise persuading people who did not already agree with them.

But in any event the authorities had a poor case to defend. The first issue was whether the International Cricket Conference had induced the Packer players to break their contracts. Shorthand notes of the crucial meeting suggested that they had sought to do precisely that. The Test and County Cricket Board's Doug Insole, in particular, had said quite brutally to the ICC committee that it should vote on whether 'the players contracted should be banned from first-class cricket unless they rescind their contracts with Packer'. On that evidence, the ban was quite clearly intended to induce the Packer players to desert, whether or not it had had that effect.

The second key issue was whether banning county cricketers from playing for Packer in the winter months, when the counties did not wish to employ them, interfered with the players' freedom to make money from their skills. And there was no question that it did. The authorities sought to justify the ban by arguing that it was vital for the game of cricket that it be maintained. But it was hard to show that both public and players would suffer if the ban were lifted—indeed, the opposite seemed true. Stripped of the emotion and rhetoric about the future of the game, it seemed a fairly simple case. What was puzzling was why the establishment had thought it had any chance of winning in the first place, but that was the arrogance of power. The hearings took a month; the deliberations would take longer. Meanwhile, the show had to be put on the road.

By now the Packer camp was presenting a confident face to the world and Kerry himself was optimistic. He had signed fifty of the world's best players and was sure the public would flock to see them play. His television chiefs, led by Sam Chisholm, assured him that viewers would also switch on *en masse*. But the organisation itself was in chaos. With only a month to go, the groundsmen were convinced that the pitches would not be ready on time, while details of who was playing whom, ticket prices and itineraries had still not been finalised. To cap it all, World Series Cricket's general manager Verne Stone was on the point of resignation because he was under so much strain. They were facing other legal challenges, too, from the New South Wales Cricket Association over whether they might still use the Sydney Cricket Ground, and from the Australian Cricket Board about whether they were entitled to call their contests Test matches. And while neither was a matter of life and death, they both added to the feeling that the team was under siege. Meanwhile, Kerry himself was as much a hindrance as a help. His public threats to the authorities had won unerring bad press, while his dictatorial management style had paralysed his subordinates.

Richie Benaud and John Cornell were the only ones who seemed prepared to stand up to him, but each had commitments that prevented him taking command. Elsewhere, it was the familiar tale of management by bullying—Packer bullied his executives, who in turn bullied those beneath them. According to Chris Forsyth, Kerry's old classmate turned PR chief for World Series Cricket, Packer in his worst moods was 'a ferocious, cruel, shouting tyrant', unable to distinguish between what was important and what was not, while 'his quick savage temper, puckish humour, sudden whims, free-handed generosity and brutal rages' made dealing with him 'like handling the ends of a broken power cable with the current turned on'. Yet without his approval, nothing could be done. All was dependent upon his whim, when he was around to have one.

> Packer was personally in command. Where Packer went, so went the centre of power. In other words, everything—all effort, all advice, all support—was concentrated around Packer.[10]

But for long periods Kerry was absent. He was in London fighting the court case or in Sydney worrying about the result, while most of his management team were either in Melbourne or Perth. In one compartment, the television plans might be proceeding well under David Hill (not the David Hill who was managing director of the ABC), in another, the promos going great guns with John Cornell. But overall, no one was managing, solving the day-to-day problems. There was no one around to knock heads together if the television people clashed with the few who knew about cricket.

But with little more than three weeks to D-day, by far the biggest worry was the state of the pitches. Sydney's was thriving in the middle of the Showground, but the Melbourne and Adelaide wickets were still sweating under glass. It was true that they were only a few hundred metres from their ultimate destination but that was little comfort, for a Supertest could hardly be held in a greenhouse. They had pinned their faith on turning the trays into hovercraft for the short journey, but the attempt was a fiasco. They had invited the sporting press to watch but had then thought better of it. Fortunately, only Kerry Packer, Harry Chester and Verne Stone were there to witness the disaster.

Having already rejected conventional methods because of the damage they might do to the outfield, the Packer team now called in Brambles, the heavy haulage experts, to see whether they had any ideas on how to move them. Before long, a steel runway was being constructed from the greenhouse outside VFL Park to the cricket square. A week after that the two sections of the would-be pitch were being trundled towards the middle of the ground, aided by a gaggle of cranes, low-loaders and heavy trucks. And this time there was no disaster. With just fifteen days to go to the much-publicised first match, they jiggled the Melbourne wicket into place. They wouldn't have time to roll it properly to get the moisture out, so it would be a bit puddingy, but they could tolerate that. They could also ignore the join in the middle and the fact that the newly turfed surrounds were higher than the pitch, for they now had a wicket they could play cricket on. The show might yet be a disaster, but at least it would go on.

Two weeks later, on 24 November 1977, World Series Cricket lifted its skirts to the press for what was supposed to be the inaugural match. Packer had bet that 15 000 people would be there to watch, but in the event there were almost as many journalists and officials as paying spectators. From the top of the huge stands at VFL Park, some 30 kilometres from the centre of Melbourne, as the South African Mike Procter loped in to bowl the first ball, one could see acres of empty seats. In a stadium that held 90 000 people, just 200 had turned up to watch the toss, and by the end of the day, still fewer than 2500 had filed through the turnstiles. On the boundary fence the advertisement hoardings had to be shrouded in plastic because no one had bought the space. Outside, the vast car parks were deserted. The local press, knowing how hard it would be to entice people to watch cricket at a football ground miles from the middle of town, were remarkably restrained in their reviews. But the English papers had a field day. This was supposed to be D-day for Packer, and it had been D for Disappointing, if not D for Disaster. They were told, however, that they had got it all wrong: this had been only a practice match.

If Packer and his team were downcast by the small number of spectators and the gloating of the scribes, there was one bit of good news to cheer them up. Two days later, in the small hours of the Australian morning, the judgment in the London High Court case was handed down, giving Packer total victory. Not only did it declare the ban on his players illegal and award World Series Cricket 250 000 pounds in costs, but it also provided Packer with a public relations coup. Neither he nor the players, it said, could be criticised for the secrecy in which they had signed contracts, because the authorities had made it quite clear they would have done all in their power to kill it. Nor was his action without benefit, it added, for World Series Cricket had already increased earnings during the winter for fifty cricketers, attracted new sponsors to the traditional game, increased public interest in cricket and brought back to the game some stars who had left. The authorities could hardly have been given a sounder or more public thrashing.[11]

But important though this was, the war would be won only by getting people to watch, and that looked like being a far tougher fight. Nine days after the initial debacle, the players trooped back to VFL Park for the First Supertest between an Australian XI and a West Indian XI. Two years earlier, almost exactly the same teams had attracted 85 000 people to the first day of the Test match at the Melbourne Cricket Ground. At VFL Park that day only 3000 turned up to watch the Supertest equivalent, and as the first ball was bowled only 400 were in their seats. It was, in the memorable words of John Thicknesse, cricket writer for the London *Evening Standard*, 'like confetti in a graveyard'. The cricket, not surprisingly, lacked tension, atmosphere and almost everything else. In London that afternoon, the *Evening Standard*'s banner headline told cricket fans 'IT'S A SUPER FLOP', and continued, 'Even the most loyal Kerry Packer yes-man had to stop pretending World Series Cricket was a certain winner today.' More soberly but no less emphatically, *The Times*'s John Woodcock wrote, 'He would never admit it, of course, but Kerry Packer must be a worried man tonight.'

The establishment-minded Woodcock could not resist telling *Times* readers how symbolic it was that the sight screen had come crashing down in the middle of the game. So confident was he that World Series Cricket was doomed, he even offered to eat his hat if a fight to the death left Packer the winner.

But as he read the papers back in Australia, Kerry Packer had other worries to contend with. Dawn had broken with news of the resignation of John Curtain, one of World Series Cricket's middle managers, who had used his departure to say that the outfit he was leaving was disorganised and incompetent. The previous day Ian Redpath, one of the older-guard Australian recruits to Packer's army, had damaged his leg so badly that he seemed unlikely ever to play again. Meanwhile, the official Australian Test team, or the third team as Packer liked to call them, was doing far too well, fighting its way to a stirring victory against India in Brisbane and attracting crowds of 10 000 a day.

The Test matches were winning the television battle, too. Channel Nine had picked up a measly 5.3 per cent of the audience for the opening day of the 'Superflop' and had been beaten into third place. The ABC's coverage of official cricket had outscored it comfortably and Channel Seven's tennis had hooked almost four times as many viewers. Nor would matters improve for Packer as the season progressed, for by the time the third Supertest came round World Series Cricket was stuck on 5 per cent, while the Test matches on the ABC were attracting three times as many viewers and the Australian Tennis Open on Channel Seven four times as many.

Meanwhile, despite the declaration that a ban was illegal, the Australian Cricket Board had discovered a perfectly legitimate way to banish the Packer players. It had simply asked them to sign an exclusive deal with the new sponsor of official cricket, Benson & Hedges. Since the Packer players were unable to do this because of their existing commitments to World Series Cricket, they had automatically excluded themselves. Many now found they were also shunned. Some were sent to Coventry by their former state teammates, who were instructed not to talk to them. Others were barred from their local clubs and couldn't even play grade cricket or use the practice nets. Ian Redpath, who was an honorary life member of South Melbourne, was told he could never again play for the club.

For the rest of that first summer of 1977–78, almost nothing went right for Packer. Australia's official Test players, captained by a born-again Bobby Simpson, beat India 3–2 and produced some of the most exciting cricket since the classic Tests of 1960–61 against the West Indies. They attracted good crowds, too, with the deciding match in Adelaide, where India nearly snatched a stunning victory, pulling in more spectators in one day than Packer's Supertest in Perth could manage in five.

By the end of the first season, the whole future of Packer's brave venture seemed in doubt, especially from the point of view of those working for it. Because World Series Cricket had failed to attract decent gates and television audiences, it had sold hardly any time to advertisers. It was therefore losing a vast amount of money. From inside Consolidated Press there were warnings that the haemorrhage of cash was risking the future of the whole Packer empire; there were also reports that Hatchet Harry Chester wanted the whole thing wound up. Expenses were huge, revenues almost non-existent. Not only had two teams been flown around Australia all summer to play to a couple of hundred spectators in the country towns, but the Supertests in the cities had also played to almost empty houses. John Cornell had forecast they would top 100 000 spectators in World Series Cricket's first five days, but five complete Supertests had been necessary to do it. The television experts had insisted that viewers would switch on in droves and that advertising would bring a bonanza. But it had proven almost impossible to get sponsors for the telecasts. The original plan had been to find nine sponsors at $400 000 each, for a package of advertisements worth three times as much. But despite the big discounts on offer, they had found no takers. They had then cut the price again and still found only six willing to buy. Packer had blamed the sales force at Channel Nine for this failure and gone out on the road himself. But super salesman though he was, even he had done no better. In mid 1977 Harry Chester had forecast that World Series Cricket would make a profit of $1.5 million in the first year. By mid 1978, they were staring down the barrel of a $6 million loss.

Packer's bullish public statements gave his opponents no clue that the year had been such a disaster. Nor did his demeanour within the company suggest that he had any intention of giving up the fight. According to Andrew Caro, who took over as managing director of World Series Cricket in March 1978, Packer was determined not to be beaten. His attitude appeared to be that money was no object and that they must win, whatever the cost, and this was the face he presented to the world. He had told the press that he had more money than his opponents so he was bound to win. And it was important that they continue to believe it.

Fortunately for him, there were signs even now that some of his opponents were beginning to crack. Pakistan, for example, wanted to select its three Packer players for the Test matches against England starting in June 1978. The West Indies, meanwhile, had actually played its five Packer players against Australia in the Caribbean Tests that began in March.

Both cases would end with a hardening of attitudes against the Packer players, but they signified growing disquiet about not being able to select first-choice teams. The Pakistanis were told they had to play in England without their Packer players and were thrashed as a result. The West Indians, with their Packer stars shining, won the first two Tests in magnificent style, but were then beaten in the third when the Packer players and three others were left out. The West Indian authorities had tried in the interim to secure commitments for the tour of India in November on dates that clashed with Packer's Supertests. This hard line had prompted three more of their players to defect.

The West Indies second team had managed to recover to win the match, but had only been saved from humiliating defeat in the fifth Test by the crowd invading the pitch and bringing the game to a halt. After the massacre, Packer was asked by a local journalist whether he intended to destroy Test cricket. His reply was to throw the ball back at the authorities: they themselves would kill Test cricket if they maintained the ban on his players.

Packer: The image of Test cricket will be destroyed in the minds of spectators once the Boards continue to play boy scouts in test matches . . . The very meaning of the word Test, which is the highest standards between nations, will be destroyed by those who have built it up over the last hundred years or so.

Q: Are you really as confident of the future as you come over as being?

Packer: When the people who run traditional cricket see that we are a fact of life and that we are going to succeed in providing the

most exciting cricket, they will want to become involved, and at
that time I am sure that compromise will come about.[12]

Even as Packer made the prediction, World Series Cricket was
coming closer to being a fact of life. After a season in which his
players had been forced to play on the back blocks, two of the
traditional grounds in Australia had decided to throw open their
gates to his so-called 'circus'. One was the Gabba in Brisbane
and the other, far more significantly, the SCG in Sydney. Their
blessing would bestow on Packer's Supertests the legitimacy and
prestige that cricket's authorities had fought so hard to deny
them.

Kerry Packer knew that he had one man in particular to
thank for this breakthrough, the Labor Premier of New South
Wales, Neville Wran, whose government had done its utmost to
help.

At the launch of World Series Cricket in May 1977, Packer
had been asked what would happen if he was denied access to
traditional cricket grounds such as the Melbourne Cricket
Ground and the SCG, to which he had replied prophetically,
'They were built by governments for the use of the people, and
if the people are angry enough and want the grounds enough
I'm sure the governments will come to some arrangements.'[13]

It was debatable whether the public had expressed its anger
vigorously enough for the New South Wales Government to
notice or whether, as seemed more likely, Neville Wran had seen
political advantage in giving one of the state's biggest media
proprietors a hand. But when the SCG Trust barred its doors to
World Series Cricket, Wran's Government had lost no time in
coming to Packer's rescue.

The Sydney Cricket Ground Trust had written to Packer on
25 July 1977, the day before Lord's banned his players, to say that
it could not entertain World Series Cricket at the SCG because
it had 'long-term contractual commitments' to the New South
Wales Cricket Association, to whom the law required it give
preference. The very next day, Wran's Sports Minister Ken Booth

had announced that the law would be changed and the thirteen members of the SCG Trust compulsorily retired; or, in words of one syllable, sacked. Packer naturally welcomed this move and congratulated the Premier for making it, saying: 'I give Mr Wran full marks for this, he is a very shrewd politician and I would have thought he would have seen the public groundswell against the existing situation.'[14]

Whether such a groundswell had really built up in twenty-four hours was a moot point, but perhaps the Premier, with his sensitive antennae, had anticipated one. In any case the SCG Trust, whose chairman Pat Hills was also a senior minister in Neville Wran's Government, soon had a change of heart and decided that World Series Cricket should be allowed to have the Sydney Cricket Ground after all. Since Packer was offering $260 000 for thirteen days' use compared to the few hundred dollars they earned from the New South Wales Cricket Association, it made sound financial sense for them to do so. And since Packer's dates did not clash with any regular cricket fixtures, there seemed no logical reason why they should not. In the event, the NSW Cricket Association succeeded in keeping Packer out for the 1977–78 season by mounting a successful court challenge. Wran's Government then changed the law, as it had promised it would, and by April 1978 World Series Cricket had been given permission to play at the SCG.[15]

But helping Packer gain access to the Sydney Cricket Ground by changing the law and replacing almost all the members of the SCG Trust was not the full extent of Neville Wran's contribution to Packer's ultimate success. The one bright spot in a dismal first season for World Series Cricket had been the day–night games played under lights. The first match at Melbourne's VFL Park in December 1977 had attracted 7000 people and later ones had done even better, with one scoring a crowd of 24 000. They were more popular because people didn't have to leave work early to see them, but also because the lights created a sense of theatre that the Supertests so manifestly lacked. There was also, of course, the excitement of a guaranteed result. In sum, they offered the one glimmer of hope for Packer and his cricketers, but it would be impossible to hold day–night matches at the Sydney Cricket Ground unless someone put up lights for the 1978–79 season.'[16] And here, once again, the Wran Government was able to help.

Packer's people were already planning in early 1978 to erect lights at the Showground next door, and had even signed a $1 million contract with the German electrical giant Siemens to provide them. Now that the SCG was available, they naturally wanted the lights to be put up there instead. Sure enough in May, Pat Hills announced that six massive light towers would be built at the Sydney Cricket Ground as part of a deal for Packer to use the ground. It soon emerged that two-thirds of the bill, which eventually came to $1.3 million, would be picked up by members of the SCG, many of whom were bitterly opposed to Packer, while the other third would be borne by New South Wales taxpayers. World Series Cricket had been asked to contribute nothing. Quite extraordinarily, after weeks of negotiations in which the subject of money had not been mentioned, WSC's managing director, Andrew Caro, was told by Pat Hills, 'Of course, you realise these are our lights.' Caro was happy to agree that he did. He had assumed all along that World Series Cricket was paying for them. It had, after all, been their idea to have them.

Whether the Wran Government believed it to be sound public policy to subsidise World Series Cricket fans, or merely a good idea to have Mr Packer the powerful media man on side, was again not clear. But the very fact that the lights attracted a grant suggested that the SCG was not convinced they were a commercial proposition. In the long run, they proved of great benefit to cricket fans. In the short term, however, they helped Packer immeasurably in winning his fight with the world's cricket authorities.

The first game of the 1978–79 season was an unqualified success. A day–night game at the Sydney Cricket Ground with the new lights blazing, it attracted an incredible 50 000 people, more than double the previous season's best. There had been a

barrage of publicity and promotion beforehand, for, after the first
season's huge losses and dreary crowds, all Kerry Packer had
gambled was at stake. But the match was everything that its pre-
decessors had not been. The atmosphere was fantastic, the razzamatazz and excitement quite unlike anything cricket had ever
seen before. Packer and his party of celebrities surveyed it all
from the executive room, once the opposition's citadel, high up
in the Members' Pavilion above the brightly lit ground. Gazing
down on the invaders was a picture of Australia's greatest
cricketer, Don Bradman, snapped for posterity as he scored his
hundredth century. Outside, to complete the sense of conquest,
the 10 000 seats of the Members' Pavilion were almost deserted.
In the early evening, it was decided that the mob should be
allowed to occupy them. Even if the members didn't want to
watch the game, there were hordes still coming to the ground
who did. After it was over, according to an unusually flowery
Adrian McGregor in the *National Times*:

> The slimmed Kerry Packer stood arms akimbo, presiding fondly
> over the sea of humanity seeping from that enthralling scene . . .
> The popularity he desired was now his. The incongruity of it all.
> That Packer at that moment, so absolutely removed from hoi
> polloi, should have tapped the Australian egalitarian myth and
> achieved the proletarianisation of cricket. He had enticed sports
> fans out of the pubs, away from drive-in cinemas into the sports
> arena, transforming the subtleties of traditional cricket into the
> spectacular that is night cricket.
>
> At that moment . . . it seemed World Series Cricket had struck
> a stunning blow against its rival.[17]

The traditionalists would have been horrified, had they been
there to watch. A golf buggy darted out occasionally to bring
drinks to the players. Big pictures of the three World Series
Cricket captains, Ian Chappell, Clive Lloyd and Tony Greig,
loomed large on the boundary fence. And loud music hailed the
teams—a calypso for the West Indians, and the new anthem,

'C'mon, Aussie, c'mon' for the Australians. The ball was white with green stitching, and the players' caps brightly coloured. But what would have horrified the purists more than anything was that the occasion was so obviously a triumph. The stands were full of young people, old people, people who had never seen a cricket match before, and most had obviously adored it.

That night, as the crowds drifted away, Andrew Caro gathered his team of workers to congratulate them and to break open the champagne. To his chagrin, Packer had already left without thanking them. Now, to his annoyance, the steward informed him that the drinks were under Mr Packer's control. It seemed a good time to celebrate and to relax, for they had been working eighteen-hour days for the last six months, and could sense victory for the first time since the whole venture had begun, so the steward was overruled and the champagne flowed. The next day, Caro breezed into Packer's office, expecting to be told how well he had done. Instead, he was reprimanded for holding the party. It was the sort of reception that would have done Sir Frank Packer proud. Even now, in the midst of success his son found it hard to celebrate, congratulate or give credit, but easy to find fault and blame.

Yet this had been the turning point for World Series Cricket. As the crowds continued to roll in, it soon became clear to everyone that Packer was not going to go bust or throw in the towel. It also became obvious that his opponents were keen to settle. They had suffered financially by having to share cricket's revenues with a rival, and were mostly tired of selecting their second teams and being beaten. Australia's reserves had acquitted themselves reasonably well, but the Ashes tour of Australia that summer now brought defeat after defeat and dwindling crowds.[18] The Australian Cricket Board had expected the series to be a triumph, creating so much interest that Packer's games would remain unwatched. Instead, with gate receipts sharply down, the state cricket associations realised they were facing financial troubles for the first time in years. Meanwhile, as World Series Cricket played its matches at the recognised grounds and

Channel Nine's audience increased, the Packer players looked more and more like Australia's first team.

By March 1979 there were signs that a deal was in the wind as the Australian Cricket Board's negotiators began to soften their public line. Bob Parish made it clear to one journalist that he wanted an end to the war, and suggested that everyone in cricket wanted a solution. Ray Steele made it even plainer, going so far as to heap praise upon Packer:

> He has helped build up the tremendous interest in cricket that exists today . . . He has taught us a lot in promotion . . . I would love to see Packer's skills and money used in . . . official cricket.[19]

As he was uttering these emollient words, the Australian Cricket Board had already received a conciliatory call from one of Packer's lieutenants and was sitting down to talk peace. It was obvious what the price would be, for television rights were due for renegotiation again. But the traditionalists were now prepared to pay it. Obtaining permission to deal from the International Cricket Conference, Steele and Parish reluctantly agreed to give Packer what he had wanted from the beginning.

The armistice was eventually signed on 30 May 1979. Packer agreed to pull stumps on World Series Cricket and give his players back to the authorities. In exchange, the Australian Cricket Board agreed to give Packer's company PBL Marketing Ltd exclusive rights to organise all televising, merchandising, marketing and sponsorship of cricket in Australia for the next *ten* years. It also gave Packer's company a virtual guarantee of exclusive television rights for any Tests played overseas by the Australian team. Never had a more complete victory been won. Two years previously, the Australian Cricket Board and the ICC had said that they would not negotiate with a gun to their heads, yet they had now done just that, giving away far more in terms of promotion rights and control of the cricket timetable than they would ever have contemplated at the beginning. It was possible, as some did, to regard the settlement as a monumental capitulation. Indeed, it was difficult to see it as anything else.

Having signed the treaty, the Australians now had to sell the peace to their allies. A hostile reception greeted Steele and Parish at Lord's a few days later; the English in particular were unhappy about the conditions that Packer wanted them all to accept. The Australian Cricket Board had agreed to arrange a program of twenty one-day internationals in Australia every year, to run from November to February, starting that summer, and had vowed to do its best to persuade the other countries to play ball. It had also agreed to accept one-day cricket in the Packer style and to sell these changes to the other participants. As a result, the future would be one of day–night matches with white balls, coloured clothing and black sightscreens, and a seemingly endless stream of one-day contests to feed the appetite of Packer's Channel Nine. The English baulked at some of these changes, but eventually gave in.

Exactly how much Channel Nine had paid for the television rights remained a mystery, because Packer's lawyers succeeded in keeping the agreement confidential, despite court challenges. But since the authorities were anxious to settle, it was unlikely to have been much more than the $500 000 a year that had been offered in 1976. And according to Steele, it was 'no bonanza'. Packer's PBL Marketing, however, did famously out of the deal, for they also gained the right to merchandise all goods and services concerned with Australian cricket and won a share in gate receipts, said by some to be 20 per cent and by others to be nearer 50 per cent. These two sources of income brought PBL $600 000 in 1980 alone. In later years it was much more.

PBL, meanwhile, appeared to recoup all the money it paid to the Australian Cricket Board for the television rights, and perhaps more, by selling them on to others.[20] The BBC in England chipped in for the UK rights, while the ABC in Australia paid heavily to relay Channel Nine's coverage to the country audience that Packer's network couldn't reach. The ABC's management was extremely reluctant to do so, taking the view that it should not have to pick up Packer's butt ends and certainly should not have to pay for them. But the men who held the ABC's purse strings thought otherwise. The ABC's chairman, John Norgard, was called to see Tony Staley, Fraser's Minister for Posts and Telecommunications, and told in no uncertain terms that the ABC should buy Nine's signal. The ABC then paid a ridiculous sum of money for the privilege of delivering Packer's cricket to the bush and solving *his* political problem, which was that his own network couldn't reach there. Remarkably, the previous minister had intervened in a similar manner two years earlier.[21]

In years to come, cricket became a gold mine for Packer. By the 1990s, Tests and one-day internationals on Channel Nine were winning their slot 99 per cent of the time and pulling in, typically, between half and three-quarters of the available audience. Cricket was also achieving its ratings at minimal expense for, compared with almost every other sort of television, it was fantastically cheap. A mini-series with similar ratings cost eighty times as much to make, while even soaps cost some sixteen times as much.[22] Cricket therefore became a major factor in Nine's high profitability. And in the 1990s, Nine still got it for a song, paying probably $1 million or $2 million a year. By comparison, Seven's coverage of the Olympics in 1992, which established new ratings records, cost the channel an almost incredible $60 million for two weeks' coverage.

But aside from making him money, Packer's wider achievement was that he had brought cricket to the masses. A survey of one-day matches at VFL Park in late 1978 showed that 40 per cent were attending a cricket match for the first time and 90 per cent would come again. Fourteen years later, the Melbourne Cricket Ground chalked up a crowd of 87 000 for the World Series Final between Pakistan and England, and a gate receipt of $1.5 million in one day—a testimony to the excitement of the one-day contests and the power of marketing. Only a few months after that, a superb Test match between Australia and the West Indies played to an almost empty house over five days at the Gabba in Brisbane, even in the final nail-biting sessions.

In 1993, some blamed the supposed decline of traditional cricket on the rise of Packer's fast-food alternative. But away from the Members' Pavilion or the saloon-bars of Home Counties England, there were few complaints. Perhaps surprisingly, Bob Parish and Ray Steele, the men who initially denied him the television rights in 1976, had no regrets. Parish, who had hardly started out as an enthusiast, said that Packer's brand of one-day cricket had saved the traditional game by picking up the ever-mounting bills. And all but the stoutest member of the establishment agreed that he had greatly improved television coverage of the game—excepting the commentary.

As for the man himself, he will be remembered for defeating cricket's colonialists. But whether he got what he really wanted was another matter. His old schoolmate Chris Forsyth believed he was after adulation and approval, and that he had risked his $15 million 'to buy a place for himself in Australian public esteem. Not the forelock-tugging kind that goes with being a millionaire, or the cringing kind that accompanies a television mogul, but the fullblown respect and admiration that Australians are reluctant to bestow even on the genuine originators and creators.'

The press certainly hadn't given it to him—he hated their criticisms and their failure to give him whole-hearted approval. Nor, it appeared, had the public, for the surveys suggested he was not greatly loved. During the exercise, Consolidated Press had considered launching a magazine called 'Packer's' but market researchers had said it would meet serious consumer resistance.

In almost every other respect, though, Packer's assault on the cricketing world had been a resounding success. He had seen off the establishment, altered the face of the game and built a lucrative property for his television stations. He had also, in Tony Greig and some of the other cricketers, made lasting friends. What was more, in his constant battle to live up to his father's expectations, he had shown that he could create something from scratch. Yet he apparently found it hard to rejoice in victory. After the settlement, he threw a lavish party for his players and the staff at World Series Cricket to celebrate. He took a lot of trouble to see that everything was right, even getting limbo music for the West Indians. But as everyone else danced and drank into the night, Kerry Packer sat quietly in his office, away from the throng.

CHAPTER TEN

BACKING WINNERS

His old man was a one-party man, a Liberal Party man.
One can't say that of Kerry. He prefers winners to losers.

Bob Hawke[1]

The Wran Government's vital support for World Series Cricket was the first time that Packer's cosy relationship with the New South Wales Labor Government had been laid bare. But ever since his father had died, all politicians had been keen for his support. Given the way in which Sir Frank Packer had used his *Telegraph* and Channel Nine to make or break governments, it was inevitable that this should be so. If state or federal politicians of either party could do favours for Kerry Packer without compromising their principles, or without compromising them too much, they would invariably be eager to do so.

Consider this parable of politics.

Once upon a time in New South Wales, there lived a fishmonger who leased his shop from the State Government, which the Labor Party controlled. Then one day a public servant decided to increase the fishmonger's rent. The next morning he got a phone call. The secretary of the Labor Party wanted to know why the fishmonger's rent was going up. 'This man is a good friend of the Party,' said the secretary, 'we don't want to offend him.' The public servant explained that it wasn't just the fishmonger whose rent was being increased, but all the tenants that this government body had. The Party secretary was satisfied and went away.

The next day, the phone rang again. The minister was on the line. 'What's going on with this man's rent?' the minister asked. 'He's a good friend of the Party, we don't want to offend him.' Once again the public servant explained that all rents were going up, and the minister went away satisfied.

But the next day, the phone rang once more. 'Hello,' said the caller, 'it's the Premier here. Now, what is going on with this man's rent? He's a good friend of the Party.'

Now it was the public servant's turn to ask what was going on. What exactly had this fish-shop owner *done* for everybody? The disturbing answer would have been that he had bribed all these politicians and was calling in his favours. But the more disturbing answer was that he had done no such thing. The extent of the Labor Party's debt to him was that he dumped a free box of prawns outside their door every week. That alone had been enough for him to mobilise this extraordinary political support—although not, in this case, to prevent the rent being raised.

The parable is a true story and, like all parables, it has a message. For if this was how high the politicians of New South Wales would jump for the fish-shop owner, how much higher might they be willing to go to please a powerful press proprietor like Kerry Packer?

Neville Wran's success at the polls in New South Wales in May 1976 put Labor back in power in the state after eleven years in the wilderness. Coming only five months after Gough Whitlam's crushing federal election defeat, which had left the faithful anticipating twenty years on the Opposition benches, it was a victory that testified to Wran's great personal charisma. Unusually talented for a state politician and exceptionally marketable, with a rare blend of earthiness and charm that gave him wide appeal, Wran's working-class pedigree from inner-city Balmain was impeccable, while his self-made riches and dark lawyer's suits testified to his undoubted abilities. In 1986 when he stepped down from the premiership after ten years, some would remember him as a great Premier, others for the allegation of interference in a court case that had at one stage threatened to topple him. (Wran was cleared by a royal commission.)[2] But none would deny that Nifty Neville, as his friend the disgraced solicitor Morgan Ryan had nicknamed him, was an astute and effective political leader. And nowhere was this astuteness better demonstrated than in his management of the press and proprietors such as Packer.

Neville Wran was convinced that hostile press coverage had brought down the Whitlam Government and was determined that the same fate would not befall him. Even before he came to power, he therefore made it a central part of his political strategy to get the press on his side. And Packer's ownership of Channel Nine made it particularly important to secure his support. Wran's advisers had read the research showing that people relied increasingly on television for their news, and this had convinced them that television was where the battle for votes would be decided. Packer also had around a dozen suburban and country newspapers covering roughly one-third of the seats in the state, and owned the country's biggest magazine empire to boot. His support, Labor strategists believed, could make the difference between the party staying in power and being expelled at the first electoral challenge.

Packer, as it turned out, was happy to back Wran. Unlike his father he had no political loyalties; he liked winners, governments, people who could give him what he wanted. In polite terms, one would have called him a pragmatist. More bluntly, he saw it as the job of governments to help people like him get things done. Since parties in Opposition had no such power to assist, it was natural that he should become friendly with governments.

For the first two years of the new Labor Government in New South Wales, from 1976 to 1978, Wran clung to office with a majority of just one vote in Parliament, and then thanks only to the support of the Independent MP John Hatton. It was therefore hardly surprising that the new Premier was preoccupied with staying in power. But it was an early sign of what he was prepared to do to secure his position that he offered Hatton a ministerial post, an unusually large expense allowance and an official car and driver in an attempt to buy his support.[3]

Similar pragmatism, if that's what one wants to call it, was displayed in his dealings with the press. From the beginning, Wran's Government managed the news in a more professional, more concerted and more manipulative fashion than anything Australia had seen before. Immediately after the election, most of the Liberal Government's press officers were replaced by Labor sympathisers but, more significantly, a new supremo, Peter Barron, was appointed to oversee them. Barron later became chief political minder to Prime Minister Bob Hawke in 1983 before joining Packer's Consolidated Press as a lobbyist in 1986. It was Barron's job to ensure that the government's good news came out in a steady stream, rather than in an occasional unnecessary flood, so that journalists always had something positive to report.

Wran's big press-feeding machine concentrated more on television than on newspapers. Invitations to the Premier to attend public functions were typically accepted if cameras were going to be present and turned down if they were not, while announcements were always planned with television firmly in mind. There were cameras in the Premier's wing of the State Office Block almost every night, with interviews timed to coincide with the news bulletins so that the Premier would have to broadcast live. Wran was the master of the thirty-second grab in which he could push the government line and say whatever he wanted, irrespective of the question that had been asked, and live crosses ensured that he would not be edited. As for formal press conferences or speeches on the hustings, Wran's staff minimised the risks of reporters picking the wrong parts by distributing his speech in advance with the key thirty-second bites highlighted so that television reporters would know when to turn on the cameras.

But there was another more cynical way in which Wran's press minders sought to secure friendly coverage. According to

Wran's chief press secretary Brian Dale, they were always happy to help out journalists they liked.

> 'It's contract time' was all that was necessary for a television reporter to say in order to get two or three weeks of nice and exclusive stories from the government. A run of good stories usually resulted in the reporter in question receiving a more lucrative contract than a reporter without such a run of good luck and good contacts.[4]

This presumably also resulted in good press for the government, for journalists would not be stupid enough to bite the hand that fed them such tasty morsels.

The same theories of mutual benefit could be applied equally to the press proprietors, whose support Wran also desired. Three in New South Wales were to be cultivated—Packer with Channel Nine, the *Bulletin* and a dozen suburban and country papers; Murdoch with the *Mirror*, the *Telegraph*, the *Australian* and Channel Ten (after May 1979); and the Fairfaxes with Channel Seven, the influential *Sydney Morning Herald*, and a half-share in the Packer local papers.

Of these three organisations, only one appeared to be a lost cause. In all its 146-year history, the *Herald* had never advised its readers to vote Labor in a New South Wales state election, and had only once advised them to vote Labor in a federal election (in 1961). Nor did its behaviour in the 1976 campaign encourage Neville Wran to believe that it could be induced to change its ways. Long before polling day arrived, he was angered by the *Herald*'s suggestion that Labor might have to raise taxes to pay for its election promises. Foreshadowing later outbursts against the ABC, Wran buttonholed the *Herald*'s state political correspondent, John O'Hara, at a pre-poll party and told him, 'As for you O'Hara, you can get fucked.'[5]

The would-be premier's fury was doubled on polling day when he read the *Herald*'s front-page editorial, advising readers that it would be an act of madness to vote Labor. The Whitlam

Government, it opined, had already proved that socialism, that reliable old bogy, didn't work:

> In a very real sense the voters of New South Wales who go to the polls today have already given their verdict. They gave it when they turned thumbs down on Mr Whitlam, socialism and government by crisis last December. Mr Wran is simply Mr Whitlam writ small; the party he leads is Mr Whitlam's party committed to the same objectives of socialism, class war and strangulation of the states, of expansion of the public sector and squeezing of private enterprise. It would be remarkably unrealistic if NSW, having kicked socialism out the front door four months ago, were now to admit it by the back. It would be remarkably foolish to ignore the recent object lesson of how the Labor Party behaves when it gets to power . . .
>
> There is the same spate of expensive promises, the same dribble of ideas about footing the bill for them . . . There are the same crowds of squabbling place-seekers, ready to tug at the leader's coat tails and demand their cut of the cake, the same factions ready to jostle for pre-eminence. And in the shadows behind the reassuring front man, with his lawyer's plausible tongue and his Darling Point address, loom the same realities of Labor politics and power, the inescapable 'platform', the contentious Caucus, the party machine, the Trades Hall manipulators, the militant unions.
>
> New South Wales cannot afford Labor policies and attitudes any more than Australia found it could.

It was almost worthy of Sir Frank Packer's *Telegraph* in its heyday. Understandably furious, Wran phoned the *Herald*'s editor, Guy Harriott, at home, eventually hanging up in a rage.[6] And so ended any faint possibility that Labor would try to get the *Herald* on side. From this point on, Wran would have to look to Packer and Murdoch, the state's two other media proprietors, for press support.

So close was the 1976 vote that it took ten days before Wran knew whether he would be able to form a government. In the nail-biting hours, as he waited to hear, he discussed with his press secretary Brian Dale the *Herald*'s hostility and how to counteract it, eventually telling him. 'The others weren't for us but they were never totally against us. If we win we should try and defuse their hatred for us. It may be a vain attempt, but we'll try it.'[7]

'The others', of course, were Packer and Murdoch. Wran had known the Packers since 1973 when Sir Frank had invited him in to lunch at Park Street, but he now set about wooing Sir Frank's son, Kerry, making it obvious that he wanted the Packer organisation's support. Exactly how the approach was made is not clear, but Trevor Kennedy, the *Bulletin*'s editor, had excellent contacts in the Labor movement and may well have helped to smooth the path.

The Labor Party's connections with Channel Nine in Sydney would also have been useful.

It was a happy coincidence for both sides that Sir Frank Packer, that great hater of socialism, had been canny enough to include Labor's Sydney radio station 2KY in the consortium to form TCN 9 back in 1956. Under this arrangement, the secretary of the powerful NSW Labor Council, the supreme trade union body in the state, had always occupied a seat on Channel Nine's board. Now, three months after Wran's election, this seat passed to John Ducker, state president of the ALP, secretary of the NSW Labor Council and *eminence grise* of Labor politics in New South Wales. If there was anyone more powerful in state Labor politics, it was Premier Wran himself. And Ducker had played a vital role in installing him as leader.

According to Ducker, there was no point in the Labor Party seeking support from the *Herald* because the paper and its managers were 'steeped in class-war hostility'. But Packer was 'more pragmatic' and 'prepared to do business'. Exactly what 'doing business' meant in practice, Ducker did not make clear, but on the principles of relationships between governments and powerful media proprietors, he told me in 1992 that 'if you spit in someone's eye, they'll spit back. If you give them a fair go, they'll give you one, too. I can see nothing wrong with that.'

Like many of the powerful on both sides of politics, Ducker regarded it as a fact of life that governments around the world trade favours with press proprietors. In his view it was naive to expect otherwise. As long as the public didn't suffer, he argued, there could be nothing to complain about. It was simply a transaction between politicians and businessmen in which both sides benefited, just as nations might gain from trade. The Wran Government wanted to stay in power and needed media support. And if Packer and Murdoch, as powerful media proprietors, gained valuable contracts from the Wran Government, what was the problem? Nobody was bribed, nobody was killed, nobody suffered. Packer and Murdoch were probably the best candidates anyway. So what could there possibly be a fuss about?

When the Sydney Cricket Ground Trust barred Packer's World Series Cricket from the SCG in July 1977, it took less than twenty-four hours for Wran's Sports Minister, Ken Booth, to announce that the law would be changed and the trust reconstituted. For the rest of that year Wran's Government did its utmost to push the new legislation through State Parliament in time to give Packer access to the ground for the crucial first season. Only the opposition of the state Liberal Party in the NSW Upper House prevented that from happening. Several months later, in May 1978, when the SCG had been secured and day–night cricket beckoned as a possible saviour of World Series Cricket, the Wran Government stepped in again with money to help erect the SCG's lights. The pay-off for Wran, in terms of favourable coverage from the Packer press, followed almost immediately.

In July 1978 the resignation of Sir Eric Willis from Parliament brought the first electoral test for the Wran Government in the two years since its election. Willis's seat of Earlwood in southwest Sydney was already in Liberal hands, so there was no danger of the government falling if Labor lost, but victory was naturally to be preferred and Wran told his supporters to go all out for a win. By a lucky coincidence, the key newspaper in the constituency was Packer's *St George & Sutherland Shire Leader*, which weighed in enthusiastically in support of the Premier. Its final election editorial, published three days before polling day, contrived to make no mention of the Liberal Party at all. Instead, the Packer paper praised the Labor candidate, local solicitor Ken Gabb, and extolled the virtues of Neville Wran's Government. It was certainly a far cry from what it would have said in Sir Frank's day. It was also hardly what one might have expected from John Fairfax & Sons, the paper's part-owners, whose managers were extremely angry when they saw what had been published:

> All the signs point to a victory for the Wran Government in Saturday's Earlwood by-election.
>
> A round-up of views within the Earlwood electorate shows that the people have a high regard for Premier Neville Wran and are prepared on Saturday to give him a vote of confidence.
>
> Many have commented on the Premier's 'stable and moderate' style of government and are satisfied with it at this stage.[8]

After opening with this endorsement, the editorial listed some of the achievements of the Wran Government: lower fares, no increase in taxes and greater spending on transport, particularly in the Earlwood area where half-a-million dollars had been spent on rail-track upgrading and forty-nine new Mercedes buses. Next it repeated the ALP's promises to abolish death duties and not raise taxes, and pledged they would be fulfilled. Finally, it came to the subject of Neville Wran himself, noting his fine personal qualities and particular concern for the *Leader*'s readers:

> Mr Wran has thrown himself into the local campaign and has been available to consult with local groups whenever requested. He has had discussions with local P&Cs, the Earlwood Caring Association, the Cooks River Valley Association, the Canterbury Community Aid Bureau, education authorities, senior citizens and others.
>
> Many of those who have spoken of their problems with Mr Wran have been surprised that he has not made the usual political promises because there is an election on, but has instead taken the problems away for some proper constructive study.

All in all it was an amazing eulogy, made more remarkable by the fact that Labor politicians assumed it had been written by the paper's editorial director, Tom Mead, a staunch Liberal supporter, and old friend of Sir Frank's and former state Liberal MP. So remarkable were Wran's achievements, it was said, that even Tom had become a convert.

But the truth was both grubbier and more interesting. The editorial looked as if it had been written by the Labor Party because it had been. The man who had penned it was Peter Barron, the operator of the Wran Government's press machine, who had produced it at the Premier's request. It had found its way into Kerry Packer's newspaper through the hands of the proprietor himself. Packer had handed the sheet of paper on which the editorial was written to the managing director of his suburban papers, David Halliday, telling him that it was to run in the *Leader*.[9]

The seat of Earlwood fell to Labor with a huge 9 per cent swing, far more than anyone had expected or hoped for. A jubilant Neville Wran, interviewed in the tally room as the result came through, declared it 'bloody marvellous'.

Two months later, Wran called a press conference to announce a general election for 7 October. By this time, the ALP already had its campaign commercials made and ready to run, along with a special thirty-minute television package put together by Labor's press people. It was normal practice for the networks to shunt such things off into late-night viewing so as not to interfere with their top-rating programs, and this is what Channels Seven and Ten did. Channel Nine, however, asked for permission to break the 8 p.m. embargo and show it in prime time. Thus the top-rating six o'clock news and *The Sullivans* were respectively shortened and postponed so that Wran's election speech could go to air. The effect of this, of course, was that the maximum number of Nine's viewers was captured for the Labor message.

The Liberals, however, did not get thirty minutes on Packer's channel to reply. Nor did they get the same invaluable opportunity that Wran had been given of broadcasting in prime time.

But in the hurly-burly of the four-week election campaign, they didn't feel there was much point in complaining. And, amazingly, Nine had no legal obligation to give them equal treatment. It was merely required by the Broadcasting and Television Act to 'afford reasonable opportunities for the broadcasting or televising of election matter to all political parties'. In this New South Wales election of October 1978, Packer's *St George & Sutherland Shire Leader* once again banged the drum for Labor, as did the other key suburban paper in his stable, the *Manly Daily*. Between them, the two could reach voters in almost one-sixth of the state's seats, including some of the key marginals. Both carried identical editorials just before the poll, which were remarkably similar in context and style to the previous leader written by Barron. Again, they read like a Labor press release:

> It is traditional in Australia that governments are given at least two terms to put their programs into action.
>
> The Wran Government in New South Wales seems certain to continue the tradition by winning its second term at Saturday's general election.
>
> The electorate has been obviously impressed with the Government's stable and moderate approach, and the Premier has already made his mark as the most popular leader in the country.

As before, there was a recital of the Wran Government's achievements in transport, praise for its refusal to make dramatic promises and congratulation for its 'outstanding success' in economic management. Finally, there was a prediction.

> On Saturday, it seems that the Wran team will be rewarded for two and a half years of steady consistent government with a healthy majority in the new Parliament.
>
> There is every reason why it should be.

None of Packer's other local papers carried election editorials that year, so there were none to blow the trumpet for the

Liberals. It was hardly surprising, therefore, that Wran was happy with Packer. 'There was no doubt,' says Wran's speech writer Graham Freudenberg, 'that Kerry was our favourite proprietor.'

Packer's *Bulletin* magazine was also a constant supporter of Wran's Labor Government, if only because journalists on the magazine got the message that the Premier and their boss were the best of mates. Packer did not interfere directly in what they wrote, but did not need to do so, because his views were obvious. The subeditors, however, were always careful to refer copy concerning the Premier to the *Bulletin*'s editor Trevor Kennedy, believing, as one puts it, that they would get kicked to kingdom come if they allowed anything negative to get through. The *Bulletin*'s opinion polls were also supplied to Wran's office on a regular basis. There was nothing remarkable in this, perhaps, except that Wran's people saw them before publication while the Liberals had to buy the magazine.

One *Bulletin* story concerning Wran does appear to have been ordered by Packer. In 1980, Wran's Ministerial Advisory Unit briefed Bob Carr (then a journalist, but later Premier of New South Wales) on Wran's improvements to the state transport system. Carr was already a Labor stalwart and would have been disposed to view Wran's record favourably in any case, but he left the Premier's staff in no doubt that he was only writing the piece because Kerry Packer wanted him to.

By the late 1970s, if not well before, Wran had become a regular feature at Channel Nine functions, and Packer was clearly impressed with the Premier's approach. 'Kerry had a lot of respect for Neville,' says Ita Buttrose, 'we talked about him very favourably.' Inside the Packer organisation, which had opposed Labor unrelentingly for fifty years, Sir Frank's old retainers were alarmed at the support that Kerry's papers and Channel Nine provided to the New South Wales Labor Government and at the close relationship the two men appeared to enjoy. They also believed it was founded on mutual self-interest, although one or two of them described it less politely than that.

There were few things Packer and Wran had in common apart from 'doing business' together, but they were both anti-establishment, even though they belonged to it by virtue of their standing. They were also essentially pragmatists. And as anyone who dealt with them knew well, they talked the same direct language. Or to put it more bluntly, they were both foul-mouthed to an extraordinary degree. Labor's other great New South Wales power-broker Graham Richardson, who donned John Ducker's mantle in the late 1970s, once gave a memorable description of a row in Neville Wran's office in 1980. He had come to introduce a new back-bencher, Jim Curran, to the Labor Premier, only to be greeted by a torrent of abuse. Wran's reported language was quite extraordinary. But so was Richardson's apparent pride in telling the story.

> No one can say 'fuck' more in sixty seconds than Neville, no one. I'm good at it, so's Keating and so's Hawke actually, but no one could say 'fuck' as often as Neville.
>
> So I sit down with Jim Curran and Neville, and Neville's saying: 'Listen you fucking cunt, I won't fucking wear what you're fucking trying to do,' and so it went on.[10]

Those who knew both men said that Packer was at least the equal of Wran in the profanity stakes. Nor did he let the presence of secretaries or female executives cramp his style. In any case, he got on well with Wran and had a real affection for him, even if the friendship between the two men did not really blossom till late in Wran's term as Premier.

In the ten years that Wran ruled New South Wales, Packer had frequent dealings with his government, mostly over development projects in Sydney or at the snowfields. Several of the Sydney decisions where Packer was in partnership with Malcolm Edwards's and Neil Ohlsson's Essington group were the subject of critical parliamentary comment at the time.[11]

There were also rumblings about the deals Packer was able to negotiate for his ski resort at Perisher in the Kosciusko National

In 1977, amid great secrecy, Kerry Packer signed up fifty of the world's best players and declared war on the cricket establishment by staging his own rival matches. Two years and $7 million later, he emerged the victor, securing Australian television rights for all first-class cricket for the next ten years.

The first Supertest in December 1977 was a disaster. The pitch at Melbourne's VFL Park had to be grown under glass, then wheeled into place. And on the first day only 400 people were at Melbourne's VFL Park to watch the first ball being bowled. It was like 'confetti in a graveyard', said London's *Evening Standard*. Twelve months later, the first day–night match at the Sydney Cricket Ground was a sell-out. Lights and access to official grounds worked wonders.

Above: Kerry Packer runs the gauntlet after giving evidence to the Costigan Royal Commission in February 1984.
Right: Costigan wanted Packer investigated in connection with alleged corporate fraud, tax evasion, drugs, pornography and even murder. Packer said the allegations were ludicrous and his innocence was easily established. In 1987 he was officially cleared of all 'allegations and insinuations made against him'.

Prime Minister Bob Hawke shares a joke with Kerry Packer at the Australian Business Top 500 Awards in June 1987. Hawke told the gathering that he counted Packer as 'a close personal friend' and 'a very great Australian'. Packer confided to a friend that he wished Hawke wouldn't be so deferential in public.

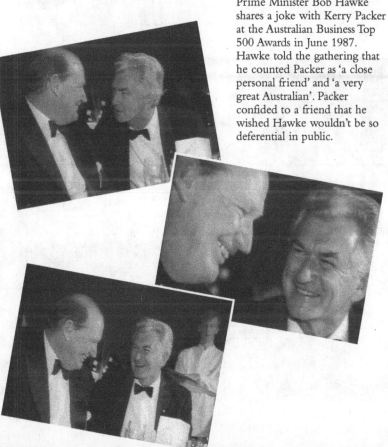

'You only get one Alan Bond in a lifetime' said Kerry Packer after selling Channel Nine for $1 billion in January 1987. Shortly afterwards, Packer lost $19 million in a night's blackjack at London's Ritz casino and threw $60 million at the bookies during Sydney's autumn racing carnival – but to him it was just small change.

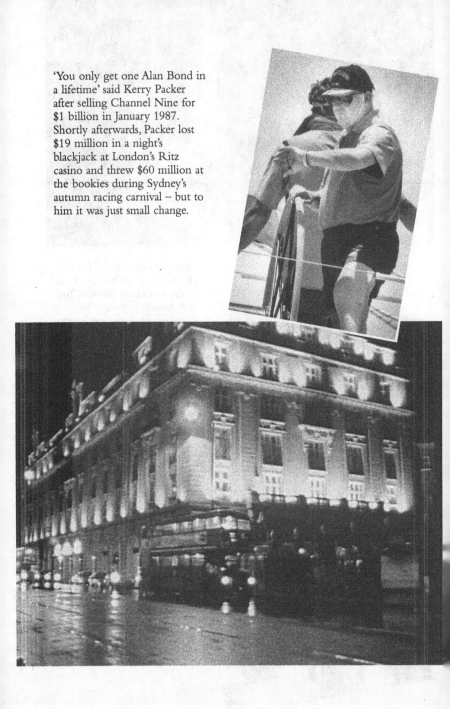

Kerry Packer and ocker adman John Singleton at a Warwick Farm polo match in 1990. The two men had been good mates since the 1970s.

Park, in southern New South Wales. Shortly before the 1978 election, Packer's Murray Publishers group was granted a twenty-five year extension of its lease there on what seemed to be favourable terms. Five years later, after concerted lobbying from Packer and other interested parties, Wran's Planning Minister Eric Bedford attempted to overrule a proposed ban on further development within the Kosciusko National Park. He was persuaded to change his mind after senior officials argued that it would be electorally inadvisable for him to intervene.

But by popular consent, the biggest thing that Packer got from the Wran Government was the contract to run the new Lotto gambling game in New South Wales in July 1979. For the company that got the job, running Lotto looked like being a bonanza. Given that it was expected to gross $100 million in the first year and $250 million a year by the fifth, of which the operator would take around 7 per cent, it appeared to be a licence to print money. Unless the operator was extraordinarily incompetent, it seemed guaranteed to turn a handsome profit for whoever won the prize. The contract went to a consortium that comprised the pools operator Robert Sangster and Wran's two favourite media proprietors, Rupert Murdoch and Kerry Packer.

The saga of Lotto has produced one of the more outlandish urban myths that plague Packer, for there is a lawyer in Sydney who claims to know for a fact that Packer gave Wran a million dollars to swing the decision in his favour. He claims that a policeman watched Packer take the money out of a Sydney bank and drive across town to the Premier's office to deliver the money. This is an obvious fantasy on the lawyer's part, yet, like all good urban myths, it has a basis of truth on which the fantastic superstructure is built. Five years after the Lotto contract was awarded, Packer appeared before the Costigan Royal Commission in secret session and was asked about his withdrawal of $1 million in cash from the CBC Bank in Sydney's Pitt Street in October 1979. Packer then raised the subject of Lotto himself, telling Frank Costigan QC:

I want you to know so far that money has been reported in rumour as being used to bribe Neville Wran for Lotto. It has been reported to the Prime Minister of Australia, Malcolm Fraser . . . as me taking the money out for me to bribe Wran.

Costigan replied soothingly, in an attempt to reassure him, 'Mr Packer, let me say this, a public figure like you is always subject to all kinds of rumours . . . I will act only on evidence, not on rumour.'[12]

Strangely enough, Packer's withdrawal of this $1 million in October 1979 had only come to light because the bank manager asked the police armed robbery squad to stand guard in case there was a heist. So the urban myth was true to the extent that the police had watched it all take place. But the money had been withdrawn three months after the Lotto contract was awarded, and the cash, in $50 notes, had neither been picked up by Kerry Packer nor taken across town to the Premier's office. It had been bundled into an airline bag by Packer's secretary Pat Wheatley and Portuguese bodyguard Manuel Petasi (who had accompanied him to Timor in 1975), and then thrown into the boot of his white Mercedes. There was not the slightest evidence or suggestion that it had been delivered to Wran. But almost as bizarrely, as far as the rumour mongers were concerned, Packer said that he had put it in his office safe so that he could use it for gambling.

The fact that gossip should knit together the rumours of this cash transaction with the awarding of the Lotto contract said something about the awe in which rich men like Kerry Packer were held, and something about his extraordinary lifestyle in which such huge sums of money were toted round in bags, but it also said something about the process by which Lotto was handed out to the consortium of which Packer was a member. Put bluntly, that consortium, Lotto Management Services, might well have been the best candidate for the job, but the result still sparked huge public controversy, thanks to the way the selection process began.

The proposal to introduce Lotto came in 1977 from the New South Wales Treasury, who saw how much the game was raising in Victoria, where it was bringing in more than $1 million a week for the State Government. Wran's advisers and then Wran himself soon recognised that it would be a sure-fire winner in New South Wales. Wran's 'Mau Mau' (Ministerial Advisory Unit) did some homework on it and told the Premier that only two organisations were capable of running it, both of whom were in the private sector. One was Tattslotto from Victoria and the other Australian Soccer Pools, then owned jointly by Robert Sangster and Rupert Murdoch.

The Murdoch–Sangster consortium was probably quite capable of winning the contract in open contest, but invitations to tender were framed in such a way that the two leading public sector candidates, the New South Wales Lotteries Office and TAB, were denied any chance of even competing. All applicants were required to have a 'proven record in operating successful Lotto or pools-type competitions', which the TAB and Lotteries Office did not. The field was thus narrowed down to private sector organisations that had already run Lotto-type games, which virtually guaranteed that the Murdoch–Sangster consortium would win, since Tattslotto was almost certain to be ruled out by the fact that it ran a rival Lotto game in Victoria.

The announcement that Lotto would go to a private company was made on 28 February 1979 by Wran's Treasurer Jack Renshaw. His prediction that the winner would be announced within four weeks suggested strongly that the result had already been decided. This, however, took no account of the reaction from the Labor Party, who greeted with outrage the exclusion of the NSW Lotteries Office from the race. There were immediate protests from the unions and strikes at the NSW Lotteries Office, followed by angry scenes at the ALP State Council meeting two weeks later. And as anger within the party bubbled over, Wran was forced to back down to avoid revolt.

The deadline for tenders was extended by three weeks and the terms changed to allow applications from the TAB, the NSW

Lotteries Office, and anyone else who felt they were competent to run the game. Belatedly, an independent committee was set up under the chairmanship of businessman Sir Norman Rydge to assess the applications.

When the Rydge Committee reported to Wran in July, three months later, it made no recommendations about who should win the contract, but praised the quality of the TAB's application and highlighted Lotto Management Services' proposal as outstanding. Wran duly awarded the Murdoch–Sangster company the prize, calming the political row by giving the NSW Lotteries Office a role in the distribution of coupons.

What caused almost universal surprise, however, was the presence of a third shareholder, Kerry Packer's PBL Ltd, in the winning consortium. It was not clear at what stage Packer had been admitted or at whose behest, since the documents recording shareholdings in Lotto Management Services, the winning tenderer, were not lodged until the day after the contract had been awarded. But there had been no hint of Packer's involvement in the preliminary discussions with the Mau Mau six months earlier, and Wran's advisers had certainly not suggested that the Murdoch–Sangster bid was defective without him. Nor did it seem likely that Murdoch and Sangster had come to the sudden conclusion that they needed him, for they had already applied in 1978, without his assistance, for the Queensland Lotto licence.[13]

Strangely enough, Packer's involvement as one of the tenderers had been a secret even to John Ducker, despite the Labor man's seat on the board of Packer's PBL Ltd, the company that ended up with a one-third share in Lotto's operation, and despite his role as a mediator between the party and the Premier over the issue. In half-a-dozen meetings of the PBL board during the first half of 1979, Ducker says the subject of Lotto never once came up. He only heard of Packer's involvement on 24 July 1979, as the public did, when the official winner was announced.

Those who were close to the decision have no doubt that Neville Wran was happy with the eventual result. As one insider put it: 'The group that Neville wanted to get it got it.' Packer was also happy. On the day the Lotto decision was made, Phillip Adams happened to visit his office in Park Street. As he arrived, he bumped into Premier Wran, who was leaving. Kerry was pleased with himself, according to Adams, who warned him, 'You shouldn't do this, Kerry. You don't need the money and people won't like it.'

'It's not the money,' Packer replied.

'What is it then?' Adams inquired.

'I just wanted to see if Neville could deliver,' said Kerry.

It all fitted nicely with Packer's idea of what governments were for. 'They're there to do things for you, not to you,' he told Adams.

Given Packer's pragmatic approach to governments, it was not surprising that he supported the Liberal Prime Minister, Malcolm Fraser, at the federal level, rather than any of Wran's Labor running mates, because Fraser was a winner and Labor quite clearly was not—especially after its thumping defeat in 1975. But Packer also believed that Fraser was the best man for the job, and his natural sympathies (as distinct from loyalties, which he lacked) lay with the more conservative Liberal Party in any case.

When Kerry first took over from his father in May 1974 there had even been signs that he would follow the same political course that Sir Frank Packer had set and use his newspapers in an anti-socialist crusade. Two weeks after the old man's death at the beginning of May, there had been a federal election in which the Packer newspapers in suburban Sydney and country New South Wales had run blistering editorials telling people not to vote Labor. The text of the leaders in all the ten-or-so papers was identical, and utterly familiar to those who had followed Sir Frank's career.

Australian people will go to the polls tomorrow in what is probably the most important election to face the nation since Federation . . .

In reality what this election is all about is simply whether we want to exchange the freedom of democracy under which Australia has become great for the totalitarianism and tyranny of socialism.

225

Make no mistake, Australia has moved so far to the left that its traditional friends now regard it with a very suspicious eye. We are virtually one step removed from socialism, and those who reject that theory do so with their heads in the clouds.

We have seen the greatest run of socialist ideas in 17 years than ever before in history . . .

If the Whitlam Government is returned tomorrow, Australia will rush headlong into socialism. The states as we have known them, with their safeguards, will cease to exist, and everyone will have to pay homage to the all-powerful Canberra dictatorship. The first thing to be done will be to muzzle the freedom of newspapers to criticise freely.

It will be the Big Brother of George Orwell's *1984*, ten years early, if the Liberal–Country coalition is not given the Government benches by the electors on Saturday.

The choice is yours—Freedom or Tyranny.

The editorial had been written by one of Packer's local newspaper editors and then toughened up by the Liberal Premier of New South Wales, Bob Askin, who had been invited to run the pencil over it, whereupon all the papers had been instructed to run it in their leader columns. But much as it may disappoint the conspiracy theorists, Kerry was not responsible for this particular Packer assault. In the absence of Sir Frank, it was his old yachting pal, David Halliday, who had ensured that Labor was given its usual blast. Halliday shared Frank's views on the evils of socialism and the need to speak up, and as managing director of Packer's suburban and country papers, he had commissioned the editorial without consulting Kerry. Yet in view of some of Packer's later political activities, it is unlikely that the leaders upset him, and he did not complain to Halliday. He was certainly no fan of Whitlam, whose Labor Government he regarded as dangerously socialist and an economic disaster. And before long he had become close to Malcolm Fraser.

According to Ita Buttrose, when the Governor-General Sir John Kerr dismissed Whitlam's Government in November 1975,

Fraser rang Kerry Packer to tell him that he feared there would be 'blood on the streets', whereupon Packer went down to Canberra at once to talk to him. At the long meeting they held that evening, or shortly after, Packer made it clear to Fraser that he was keen to see a Liberal Government in power. During the subsequent campaign, Packer saw Fraser a number of times and gave him 'a great deal of moral support', according to one senior Liberal adviser. His papers, meanwhile, gave Fraser a great deal more than good wishes.

With Kerry at the helm, the Packer press was nothing like as stridently anti-Labor as it had been when Frank was in charge, but it was still abundantly clear who they wanted to win. In the regional papers in particular, the Packer organisation's opposition to Whitlam was uncompromising, with even the news columns running headlines like 'GOUGH'S GOTTA GO', 'LABOUR CAUGHT ON THE HOP' and 'DID GOUGH ENGINEER HIS OWN DISMISSAL?'. Some of the papers carried editorials developing the theme, like this one from the *Maitland Mercury*.

> Let's cut out the hysterics.
>
> The Governor-General, Sir John Kerr, has done what he believes is right.
>
> He doesn't make the rules, he just applies them. And in with-drawing Mr Whitlam's commission and dissolving both houses of parliament he has shown great personal courage . . .
>
> He's in the firing line today, shamefully ridiculed by the Prime Minister, without hope of defending himself, for doing nothing more than his job as he saw it. What's happened to our principles? Fair Go Australia.

Packer's *Bulletin* also made it quite clear that it didn't favour Whitlam, although it was more subtle in its barracking than Sir Frank's *Telegraph* had ever been. Its pre-polling day cover featured rapturous crowds with a huge Cecil B. de Mille banner proclaiming 'LANDSLIDE TO LIBERALS', which was re-run as an advertisement for the magazine in the Packer regional papers. The four other campaign issues splashed Fraser on the cover twice, with one bearing the headline 'FRASER HITS THE FRONT' to report his improvement in the opinion polls. Its only cover picture of Whitlam was a satirical cartoon.

The paper's contents were dismissive of Whitlam—the *Bulletin's* chief political correspondent Alan Reid made damaging new allegations about the Khemlani loans affair, an episode in which the Labor government had made itself look ridiculous; meanwhile, a profile of Whitlam by David McNicoll concluded, 'It is not hard to despair of Gough. He sounds so sincerely insincere.' The Liberals were dealt with by profiling Malcolm Fraser at the depths of his popularity in mid-November, with a mildly critical article that described him as 'the man in a muddle' but did not question Fraser's role in the dismissal of the Whitlam Government. Interestingly, its author (and now novelist) Robert Drewe raised one matter relevant to Packer himself:

> Subtly I ask whether he regularly discusses his tactical moves with the Press proprietors, as has been suggested, 'I discuss things with a great many people, not only newspaper proprietors . . . Obviously, you're pleased if you get their support. Whitlam takes the view that if the editorials support me I have spoken to the proprietors. That's not necessarily so.'[14]

It might not necessarily have been so, but Fraser had in fact spoken to Packer several times before and during the campaign. Yet, as one of Fraser's Cabinet ministers, Peter Nixon, later pointed out, there was a long tradition of such things:

> Media owners always had good relationships or kept up relationships with the Prime Ministers . . . all the Prime Ministers I served under. And they had influence, there's no doubt about that . . . they always had the ready ear of the Prime Minister of the day. I mean, that goes back to the Menzies day and it occurred right through every Prime Minister I've ever known. They are powerful figures in the community and the Prime Minister is a

powerful figure in the community. They had a lot in common, so they used to meet often.

Q: Were you ever aware of occasions on which those sorts of bi-lateral contacts between media bosses and Prime Ministers might have had a bearing on policy in those areas?

Nixon: Well, if I did, I'm not about to repeat it.

Q: Well, as a general observation, do you believe . . .

Nixon: There's no doubt at all, for example, that Rupert Murdoch and Kerry Packer impacted on Prime Ministers, both Liberal and Labor, no doubt about that.[15]

Unusually, in this 1975 campaign the *Women's Weekly* was also wheeled in to have its say. Packer's chief political correspondent, Alan Reid, wrote a sixteen-page supplement to explain the loans crisis and blocking of supply in the Senate by the Liberals, which he believed sealed Whitlam's fate. Like the rest of Packer's papers, it was certainly pro-Fraser. There was no suggestion that the Opposition leader was wrong to have brought the government down. Nor was there any hint that the Governor-General could be criticised for sacking an elected Prime Minister. But the pictures also told a powerful, if subtle, story. There were big photographs of the Labor ministers Rex Connor and Jim Cairns with a caption 'MISLED THE PARLIAMENT' for each. Further on, a half-page picture of Fraser had him addressing an enthusiastic crowd holding huge placards such as 'GOUGH'S GOTTA GO', while the corresponding photograph of Whitlam showed him apparently pacifying an audience that looked bored, even hostile. Significantly, none in the Whitlam crowd carried banners or placards, so one didn't get the favourite Whitlam slogan, 'SHAME, FRASER, SHAME'.

Whether Kerry Packer himself was responsible for any of his magazines' pro-Fraser bias was another matter. But it was well known to *Bulletin* journalists that their proprietor was not a Whitlam supporter. Ita Buttrose at the *Women's Weekly* was even more aware that Kerry was backing Fraser and had visited him during the campaign. As for the *Bulletin*'s editor Trevor Kennedy, he could hardly have been ignorant of Packer's chinwags with, and support for, the Liberal leader.

In television, Kerry did intervene directly on Fraser's behalf, or so insiders at Channel Nine believe. On 10 December 1975, three days before polling day, the Whitlam forces staged a huge carols-by-candlelight service on the steps of Parliament House in Canberra as a climax to their campaign. Advertised as a 'Vigil for Democracy' it was guaranteed to attract big crowds and good television coverage, and was clearly calculated to win votes for Labor. Even though it was in the middle of a non-ratings period, when TV stations typically serve up second-rate fare or repeats, Packer's Channel Nine ran an extremely expensive first-run movie, *Young Winston*, to blow it out of the water. The normal soapies were shunted aside so the film could go to air at 7.30 p.m. as the carol service got under way. Insiders at Nine are sure that it was Kerry's decision to alter the schedules in this way. In Packer's television empire, it was inconceivable that something like that would be done without his consent.

Whether Packer got anything from Fraser in return for his support is debatable. But his power as a media proprietor and backing for the Liberals at election time gave him a sympathetic hearing from Fraser's Government whenever he wanted it. And with a personality as forceful as Packer's, that guarantee of access was a pretty good start. He played a heavy hand in argument, even though he was capable of great charm. One Fraser minister who dealt with him was left with the impression that he would do anything, including using his magazines and television stations, to get his way.

In the late 1970s and early 1980s some political decisions certainly fell Kerry's way. In December 1976, for example, the Packers' old friend Bruce Gyngell was appointed chairman of the Australian Broadcasting Tribunal (ABT), the new regulatory body for the television industry, after Fraser intervened to veto the candidate put forward by his own Minister for Posts and Telecommunications, Eric Robinson. Gyngell was a consultant to Channel Nine at the time and had been a close friend of the Packers for more than twenty years. He had visited Kerry in hospital in 1956 after his terrible car accident, had been Sir Frank's protégé at Channel Nine shortly after, and had then run TCN 9 in Sydney for most of the 1960s. His wife Anne was godmother to Kerry's son James, and her interior decorating business had Consolidated Press as a major client. Gyngell himself drove a Jaguar provided by Packer in his early days at the Tribunal and moved into a Packer-owned house in 1980, six weeks before he quit as Chairman.

One of those pressing Fraser to put Gyngell in charge of the new ABT was Ian Sinclair, who later became leader of the National Party. He had been friendly with Gyngell and Packer for many years. Also batting for Bruce was Packer himself, as one prominent commentator reported.

> The most widely accepted version of Gyngell's appointment is that Kerry Packer, who enjoyed ready access to Fraser, pushed Gyngell's claims, and that Fraser, running out of time to produce an alternative to the nominee he had vetoed, accepted this suggestion.[16]

The potential conflict of interest that Gyngell's appointment created was highlighted in 1977 when the ABT was asked to decide which of four applicants would get the lucrative radio licence for the western region of Sydney. Gyngell permitted sharp criticism of Fraser's favoured candidate, Metro-West Broadcasters, and was congratulated for his political independence. But his tribunal then awarded the licence to the Liverpool Broadcasting and Transmitting Company Ltd, controlled by Consolidated Press. No one suggested that the victor was unworthy of the prize, for if it were Packer-run it was likely to be good, but as one respected critic remarked, the government should never have allowed a position where Gyngell's previous employer could be a beneficiary of his decisions.[17]

Nine's commercial rivals had been appalled by Gyngell's appointment because of his links to Channel Nine. But they would end up happy with his chairmanship. For as Packer surely knew, he favoured keeping regulation of the commercial stations to a minimum and did not interfere in the same way as some of his more troublesome successors. Gyngell made no secret of the fact that this would be his approach, telling Packer's *Bulletin* magazine shortly after his appointment that he believed in a *laissez-faire* approach, self-regulation and persuasion, and was 'entirely sympathetic' to the commercial stations' viewpoint, adding that he thought nothing of quotas, bureaucrats and well-meaning intellectuals.[18]

But the most important thing Packer got from the Fraser Government was a commitment to a national communications satellite that would carry Nine's television signal across Australia and tip the balance of power dramatically in favour of the big-city stations.[19] Although Packer did not realise it at the time, the Fraser Government paved the way for him to become a billionaire. Packer, however, was unhappy that Fraser's Cabinet did not give him more and would not provide the sort of satellite service he was after. He was also deeply unhappy with the Liberals in New South Wales for opposing World Series Cricket's access to the Sydney Cricket Ground in late 1977 and one of Fraser's advisers says Packer was disappointed that Fraser refused to kick them into line. Most date his disillusion with the Liberal Party from this point. Even though Packer was still talking of Fraser as Australia's best-ever prime minister in 1982, his links with federal Labor politicians were growing.

Packer's real political views were deeply conservative. Like most rich businessmen he complained regularly about government waste, official stupidity and the excessive power of the unions, and his immediate circle of friends and colleagues clearly held similar views. Indeed, his mate John Singleton and brother Clyde felt so strongly about such things that they had run their own campaign in the mid 1970s to keep Whitlam out of office— even spending money to do so, as Sir Frank had so happily done most of his life.

Singleton first came into the Packer orbit in the early 1970s, by which time he was the *enfant terrible* of Australian advertising, a role that he hasn't relinquished. With his shock of blond hair, toothy grin and boyish charm, he was in some ways an attractive and likeable man. But his public persona was quite the opposite. He came over as the king of ockerdom, a professional lout, the antithesis of restraint and good taste. Crocodile Dundee without the parody, and the self-appointed champion of all Australian nationalism, he was a man's man and proud of it: drinker, womaniser and loudmouth.

In the mid 1970s Singo, as he has been typically called, wrote a column for the *Nation Review* which delighted in its lack of literary pretension. In an average week he would manage to include three 'wanks', two 'fucks', two 'ratshits' and one 'bullshit'. His brief flirtation with a wine column was even more bizarre. When asked to write about sherry, he crossed swiftly to the subject of the winos who drink it, in a style that Barry Humphries' hero Barry McKenzie could not have bettered.

> And as I said the other day, as I passed the sherry to the lady sitting in the middle of the seat in the park, it just doesn't seem fair. But unfortunately she couldn't reply, as she was chundering down the pie and the sherry and simultaneously pissing down through the slats in the seat.[20]

By the end of 1974, if not before, Singleton had become a close mate of Kerry Packer's and had lined up a campaign to increase sales of the *Bulletin* magazine, which he succeeded in doing.[21] In mid 1975 he was hired to help relaunch the *Women's Weekly* and considered for the job of handling all the Packer group's advertising. By this time he had already teamed up with Kerry's brother Clyde to run an unofficial campaign for the Liberals in the 1974 federal election.

As Singleton tells the story, the saga began just before Easter in 1974 at a dinner with Clyde and several others, when he complained about the Labor Party, socialism and how awful Whitlam's re-election would be. Clyde had asked him why the hell he didn't do something about it, and then phoned the next morning to say he had arranged an appointment with New South Wales Premier Robert Askin. Packer had told the Premier that Singleton would be able to raise at least $250 000 for an advertising campaign to help the Liberals. The following day, Singleton walked into Askin's office, where Askin told him of the previous help he had received from the Packer clan.

You know John, it reminds me of when I first got elected in 1965. Sir Frank Packer rang me then and said, 'Look, you need a supplementary campaign to get yourself into office. You need a couple of guys who can move quick, think, and get their hands on some money quick.'

You know, John, it's a funny thing that Clyde should now ring and say the same thing.[22]

Within days, Singleton had made seven TV commercials. Their aim was simple: to show a series of people who had voted Labor in the previous election but now wanted to change. But in practice most were Singleton's friends and employees or friends thereof, giving vent to their anti-Labor views. One featured Peter Sawyer, the English owner of a company called the Sales Machine, which later handled the public relations for Packer's Australian Golf Open and World Series Cricket—he subsequently married Ita Buttrose and handled PR for Christopher Skase and the Queensland property developer Mike Gore. His contribution went like this:

I am one of the great majority of Pommies who came to Australia and love it without reservation. But unfortunately too many of my countrymen seem to be here with the apparent intention of turning Australia into the very sort of socialist society that we had hoped to leave behind in Great Britain. I firmly believe in the union movement as a principle, but most of the union leaders I have met here or read about or heard on TV aren't Australians at all. They seem to be mainly embittered and vicious British immigrants, the second-rate ones. I have heard them: 'Those in favour on the left, scabs on the right.' Australia is the last of the great free countries in the world. We shouldn't even consider letting social-ism take that freedom away from us.

But the testimonial that caused the most trouble was from the 'Estonian Lady':

> I came originally from Estonia, the Baltic state. I escaped about thirty years ago when the Russians took over my country for the second time. I have lived enough under communist regime so I left and came to Australia.
>
> My husband and I we worked very hard and we did well. We brought our children up so that they are well educated and they have a good living standard. Then about 16 months ago the Labor Party came to power. And I thought: 'So it is still a free country.' But now I can see how wrong I was.
>
> Today I can see Labor is disguised socialist, but for me it is disguised communist. Many Australians can't understand. They haven't seen it happen. I've seen it in my country, Latvia, Lithuania, East Germany and Poland, and now I can see the same thing happening here.

Despite the advertisements, or possibly because of them, the Liberal Party lost the election.[23] Singleton, meanwhile, survived death threats and the burning of his Rolls-Royce (the latter of which apparently had nothing to do with the campaign) and went on to greater things.

This involved, in the November 1975 election, starting the oddly named Workers' Party. It was odd in the sense that a millionaire like Singleton with his fiercely anti-union views should identify himself with the working class. As Fraser and Whitlam battled for the main prize, Singleton and his fellow workers campaigned on such issues as getting rid of bludgers, no-hopers and parasites, cutting taxes, chopping off branches of government, scrapping regulations and attacking union power. Singleton accepted that many people thought he was on the lunatic fringe, but said it was all common sense. In his world view, as in Kerry's, governments were generally incompetent and unnecessary. They stifled initiative, reduced people's freedom and got in the way of business. His Workers' Party promised to cut back free education and government handouts, force criminals to repay society, and allow free enterprise to reign supreme. Interviewed by the *Australian*, he summed up his political views:

> The Workers' Party stands for less government, less tax, less inflation and more freedom ...
>
> Australia is being ruined by socialists, who are bums. We would abolish government welfare and get back to the friendly ways of old country towns, where neighbours cared about each other ... If someone was sick, Aunty Flo made soup for them and did their washing.

Aside from Singleton, the Workers' Party included another of Kerry's friends, Sinclair Hill, who stood as one of the candidates. Eleven years later, he would teach Packer to play polo. And while there was no evidence that Kerry himself took any part in the campaign, he would certainly have agreed with its view that taxes were too high, the unions too powerful and governments generally a nuisance. Like Singleton and a mutual friend Brian Ray (who organised and helped fund the 'Joh for Canberra' push in 1987), Packer was also a fervent admirer of the ultra-conservative Queensland Premier Joh Bjelke-Petersen, who really knew how to take care of business and get things done. Joh was anti-socialist, anti-union and anti-handouts, a champion of the old values. And to judge by Kerry's regard for Joh, and his own support for an anti-strike campaign in the late 1970s, his views would not have been violently different from Singleton's or those of others on the far Right.

In July 1979 a series of strikes in the public sector over wage claims and cuts to the public service led to confrontation between the Fraser Government and the unions. When work bans in Telecom and the postal service disrupted telecommunications and delivery of mail, Fraser threatened to invoke new emergency powers that would enable Telecom to stand people down—which in due course he did. The day after his threat was made, the high-profile radio talkback show host John Laws, a friend of both Singleton and Packer, leaped into the fray, calling for the public to petition the Prime Minister to do something. Packer heard Laws on the car radio as he was being driven in to work and decided to help by throwing the full resources of Consolidated Press behind him. With extraordinary speed that led some to wonder whether the operation had been planned in advance, Packer's presses printed 120 000 copies of the petition and distributed them to newsagents across the state, all for free. Simultaneously a senior producer at Channel Nine, Peter Meakin, was detailed to write a commercial that Laws would deliver on Channel Nine, again without charge. Broadcast that weekend, it went like this:

> Strikes, strikes and more strikes. It's easy for us to treat strikes like the weather, something to grumble about but totally out of our control. Well, not any more. This petition is your opportunity to do something to tell the politicians and the unions that you've had enough, that Australia deserves better. You sign it and I'll take it to the Prime Minister personally.

A week later, after union complaints to the New South Wales Labor Council and an approach to Packer from John Ducker, the unions were allowed the right of reply. Ducker's Labor followers had instructed him to get equal air time or resign from the board of PBL Ltd, through which Channel Nine was controlled. Packer wanted to avoid such a split, for Ducker was a powerful man, and he rarely allowed his political sympathies to override his loyalties. Those, of course, were to his shareholders, number one of whom was himself.

Despite his public support for the Laws petition and his continued backing of Fraser at the federal level, by the early 1980s Packer was getting acquainted with the new generation of federal Labor politicians, the most powerful of whom had their roots in the New South Wales Right. There were several points at which their paths were bound to cross. Paul Keating and Graham Richardson were both protégés of John Ducker and powerful in the New South Wales Labor Party. Bob Hawke, for his part, was close to Sir Peter Abeles, with whom Kerry had often played poker in the 1970s. And both Hawke and Keating were mates with Trevor Kennedy, the editor of Packer's *Bulletin* magazine, who was one of Kerry's few close personal friends.

At Kennedy's fortieth birthday in 1982 at the Imperial Peking Harbourside restaurant in Sydney, the special brochure to celebrate the occasion carried a picture of Bob Hawke and Trevor Kennedy on a fishing trip together back in the 1960s when they had been starting their respective careers as union leader and journalist in Western Australia. Packer was naturally at the party too, and made one of the speeches. Indicating Bob Hawke and Paul Keating, both future Labor prime ministers, who were among the select band of guests, he said that his father would be turning in his grave if he knew that his son was mixing with the enemy.

Although Packer was naturally a conservative he liked the raffishness of these Labor mates, who were hardly socialists in any case. He had never been comfortable mixing with the establishment and he shared the Labor working-class dislike of snobbery and pretence. With Hawke in particular, a punter, sports fan, womaniser and drinker, he had several things in common. Unlike the Liberals with their rules and their private school educations, the Labor mates were larrikins like him, outsiders, united against the rest, on the make, his sort of people. More to the point, they would soon be in power, winners like him. They would then be the people who could give or deny him the help he wanted from government.

Like Fraser and Wran before, and other politicians before that, Hawke and his Labor colleagues would always be ready to listen to what a powerful media proprietor like Packer had to say and would be keen to give him what he wanted if they could. As far as Kerry Packer was concerned, that was what governments were for: to help businessmen like him create wealth, and of course to make him rich in the process.

As Bob Hawke, Prime Minister from 1983 to December 1991, put it, Kerry was never a one-party man like his father. He was always more interested in who was going to win.

Only winners could do him a good turn.

CHAPTER ELEVEN

MAKING MILLIONS

*A very wise old man who taught me about TV once told
me if you can be right 60 per cent of the time, you'll own
the world.*

Kerry Packer, BBC TV, 1987

From the beginning, to the delight of his executives, Kerry took
television more seriously than his father and the other old-style
newspaper proprietors had ever done. When asked by a journalist in 1977 whether he regretted no longer having interests in
print, he replied scathingly that newspapers were now 'the
second-class media, whether you like it or not. Your influence is
nowhere near as great as that of the broadcast media. So, having
a reasonable voice in the broadcast media I believe I am much
better off than having a voice in the newspaper business.'[1]

Kerry believed in the value of television as against newspapers
because he watched it all the time. More importantly, he knew
what the masses wanted because he shared their tastes. His
greatest asset as a proprietor was that he disdained all things
artistic and intellectual. He liked movies and sport, and hated
culture and the arts: 'The ultimate purgatory would be to go to
the Opera House and hear Joan Sutherland sing,' he told one
interviewer.[2] At the end of a hard day's work, he liked nothing
better than to come back home, slump in a chair and watch
Charlie's Angels or *Starsky & Hutch* on television; by this time he
had done all the talking and all the mixing he wanted to do, and
by implication was too tired to talk to his family. He never read

because he was dyslexic, rarely went out because he didn't drink, and had time on his hands because he was a lonely man with few friends. Instead of books, his library at home had videotapes. So each evening he would sit on his sofa and watch television. At the office, there would always be a screen playing in the background. He would boast of his viewing habits to rival executives, claiming that he always watched at least four hours of television a day.

Kerry's other strength as a proprietor was that he was not prepared to put up with Channel Nine being second best, which it was threatening to become in the mid 1970s after almost two decades of being number one. Not long after his father's death, he called in his Sydney general manager Sam Chisholm to tell him, 'I want a station to be proud of, a station that is top of the ratings.' After six months working twelve-hour days, seven days a week, without even a blip on the ratings chart, Chisholm came back to suggest that the station could make plenty of money without actually taking the top spot. 'Listen, son,' said Packer, 'you get to the top of the ratings or else you don't have a job.' By 1977, this had been achieved, thanks as much to Packer as to his TV deputy.

The Packer recipe for increasing ratings and profits was to give the public a diet of sport, news and game shows, which rated extremely well, yet were relatively cheap to produce. As time went on, Channel Nine concentrated more and more in these areas. In 1979, for example, sport and news on Nine took up little more than 10 per cent of program time; by 1986, more than 30 per cent of its output was devoted to these two items, with the cheapest shows like *Midday* and *Today* running a total of three-and-a-half hours every weekday, dominating in terms of time. Channel Nine spent a lot of money on news by comparison with its commercial competitors and did everything well, but it was able to recycle its material from show to show at low cost and fill the rest with chat. Most of its international coverage came from American or British news services rather than from its own correspondents. And news, like sport, cost far less than home-produced drama or documentary, which all but disappeared from Nine's schedules.[3]

Another key to Nine's success was Packer's willingness to import American programs and ideas. Never afraid to copy what others were doing, *Channel Nine News* was a keen imitator of the American style, and *60 Minutes* went even further, taking an American program and cloning it for the Australian market. *Sunday*, borrowed from CBS, was another successful American program that was copied by Nine. In all these copycat operations, Packer was said to be the initiator and driving force. 'I want one of those,' he would tell his television producers, pointing to a successful American product. He would then get it, right down to the titles, content, and even the set.

60 Minutes, launched in early 1979, was perhaps the best example of his talent for picking winners and a timeslot in which they would succeed. The program was a proven success in prime time in the United States, but there was no guarantee it would repeat the trick in Australia, especially since Packer wanted it to go out at 7.30 on a Sunday evening to compete against the popular family entertainment shows *This is Your Life* and *This Fabulous Century*. The critics predicted it would fail and tut-tutted knowingly as the first two programs pulled in less than 10 per cent of the audience. But within six weeks it was Packer who was smiling as the show pulled up into the twenties, making it already a commercial proposition. It is one of those hoary old myths that Packer poured money into the program and that only his strong nerve allowed it to pull through. In fact, it was rating above 30 per cent within a year, by which time it had knocked its more frivolous rivals into second and third place.

By comparison with most current affairs programs, *60 Minutes* was, and still is, extremely expensive to produce. In an era when the other commercial stations in Australia hardly ever sent crews overseas, *60 Minutes* did so every week. And if stories didn't come up to scratch, the program canned them, whatever the cost. By definition, it was Packer's decision to give it the money it needed. But credit for the program's success should also go to its

American-born executive producer Gerald Stone, who was responsible for getting the formula right and, it seems, for taking it further down-market than Packer had intended.

Stone was one of the few people prepared to stand up to Packer, which was made easier by the fact that he had a clear idea of what he wanted to achieve. But there were naturally some heated disagreements. A few weeks before the launch, the boss summoned Stone to ask why they weren't covering the British elections, making it clear that he believed they should. Stone argued that it wasn't what *60 Minutes* should be doing, but when that cut no ice he told Packer that they had only three crews, none of which was in London. 'What do you mean, you've only got three crews?' asked Packer. 'I told you to get four.' Stone explained that he had decided to spend the money on an extra producer instead. 'Well, if you're not going to listen to me,' Packer exploded, 'then you can forget the fucking program altogether.'

'Are you serious?' inquired a bemused Gerald Stone. 'You've spent one and a half million dollars on it.'

'You're dead right I'm serious,' Packer replied, indicating that the conversation had ended. A somewhat dazed Gerald Stone then removed himself from Packer's office. Some time later, he was persuaded by colleagues to go back to Packer and apologise. A fourth crew was then added, the British elections covered and *60 Minutes* survived, as did Stone. But even then, the style of the program's election coverage did not impress the proprietor or his old friend Bruce Gyngell.

The British election of May 1979 was the one that brought Margaret Thatcher to power after the country's famous 'winter of discontent'. Prolonged strikes by the public sector unions had cast the country into darkness for several weeks, left the streets filled with garbage, and brought the transport system to a standstill, as workers demanded higher wages. Stone and his producer Peter Meakin decided that *60 Minutes* should profile an individual British shop steward to illustrate the 'I'm all right Jack' attitude of Britain's unions and demonstrate what the election was about. But Packer and Gyngell thought the program light-weight and said so.

Stone believes that his boss wanted *60 Minutes* to be more like the long-running ABC program *Four Corners*, but that sort of approach would never have delivered the huge audiences that *60 Minutes* has been able to command. More than 30 years after its launch, it still ranks in the top ten most-watched programs in Australia and is often Channel Nine's best performer. Certainly, the show had, and still has, its critics—it has always been tabloid, often trivial and occasionally trite; increasingly it concentrates on celebrity and human interest stories, and the personalisation of the most complex issues—but at its best it can still be compulsive viewing and its pulling power remains unbeatable in terms of Australian TV current affairs.

After the fracas over the British elections, Packer issued only one direct instruction to Stone in the ten or so years that he ran the program and this came some four weeks after the launch. The first four shows had for some reason carried three stories on prisoners. Packer thought that was enough and told a staff meeting that he didn't want to see 'any more fucking prisoner stories'. But the fact that he issued no direct instructions did not mean that he left Stone and the other journalists at Channel Nine alone. There are numerous stories of producers being rung up during or after their program by an irate proprietor, telling them that an item was 'shit' or asking them 'why the fuck' they had shown a particular interview. On one such occasion, Kerry caught Stone off guard just after *60 Minutes* had gone to air. 'What did *you* think of that Negus interview?' Kerry inquired, in a tone that suggested he didn't like it at all. Stone replied angrily that he thought it was good, which was why he had run it, and then told Kerry none too politely what he could do with himself. 'I've got four million viewers out there, and you're just one of them,' he said. There was a silence on the other end of the line. 'Oh,' said Packer, 'I thought at least I might count for two.'

Packer was a hard taskmaster, who could be rude, opinionated and a bully. But he was prepared to let his executives take risks and would spend whatever was necessary to get things done. His only proviso was that they had to be done well. Mistakes or failure, it was understood, could mean instant dismissal. Success, on the other hand, brought great financial rewards, admission to an inner sanctum and the satisfaction of a challenge survived. It was management by fear but it clearly worked, for Nine was a tight, professional, profitable outfit, the best in town. Some certainly found the Packer style abhorrent and left, others simply copied the boss and passed the bullying down the line. There were plenty who refused to contemplate working for Nine because of its aggressive macho atmosphere, but others enjoyed the tension and ended up regarding Packer with respect, admiration and even affection. In some ways he was easy to work for— he never left you in any doubt about what he thought and he didn't dither around. Nor did you need to go to five different committees to get a decision. You just went to Kerry.

Because of his dyslexia, in all business dealings he did everything face-to-face or on the phone. There were no board papers or minutes, no lengthy memoranda. If you tried to give him more than one page to read he would shout and throw it back in your face. He demanded that all legal documents be read to him, and had a remarkable ability to focus on the spoken word. He had been amused when the High Court of London had asked for all the documents involving the setting up of World Series Cricket; while the other side had wheeled its papers into court on a trolley, he had ambled in with one slim file tucked under his arm. Despite his difficulties with reading, or perhaps because of them, he had a ferocious memory and grasp of detail. He was also, for all his reputation as Frank's idiot son, sharp, articulate and good at numbers.

According to one banker who dealt with him, he was opinionated, decisive, a hands-on manager, a proprietor in the old style. The good thing about him was that his word was his bond, the bad thing that if he said black was white, that was the way it was going to be. Even his more senior executives lived in fear of his temper and would leap into action as soon as the Packerphone rang on their desk. Few liked to be bearers of bad news because he tended to shoot the messenger. One or two stood up to him, and prospered in spite of it. But for the most part, he was surrounded by yes-men, eager to jump at his command. Few of his executives had the courage to find out that he respected those who were prepared to fight him. But that was not surprising, for once he spotted fear in an opponent he would take great pleasure in crushing him. It was an easier option for executives never to take him on.

Yet his management formula appeared to work. In the year that Kerry took over from his father, the Packer empire had made a profit of $2.7 million after tax. Eight years later, in 1982, it was making almost exactly ten times as much. It was true that inflation had made the increase in earnings look twice as good as it really was, but fivefold growth in less than a decade was still pretty remarkable.

Kerry was incredibly proud that he had done better than his father, and he liked to draw attention to the fact. Interviewed by the *Financial Review* in December 1982 he pointed out that the company had grown at 30 per cent a year since his father had died in 1974.[4] And talking late at night with Phillip Adams he repeated the exercise, showing Adams the company's profit figures and indicating the year of his father's death as the time when the graph had started rising fastest. Yet in spite of this undeniable evidence of his skills, he still seemed to doubt his abilities, inquiring earnestly whether Adams thought he could have succeeded without the start his father had given him.

A more relevant question, perhaps, was whether he could continue so successfully without the help of Harry Chester, the financial wizard whom Frank had hired at the end of the 1960s. Rightly or wrongly, there were still plenty of people at Consolidated Press who thought that Chester's brilliance was the cause of the company's success. But they would soon be given the chance to test their theories, for in October 1979 Chester died of a heart attack by the side of his swimming pool. His death at the age of fifty-eight was both unexpected and a great loss to the Packer organisation.

Immediately before the heart attack, he had been preparing annual reports for the four companies in the Consolidated Press group. Ten days later, the directors of each company met to approve them. The reports had been completed by one of Chester's staff, who had worked through the night and weekends to do so. 'Why haven't I seen these?' asked Packer angrily as the reports were laid before him just as the first meeting was about to start. 'How do I know what the bloody company's done if I haven't read the report?' The accountant apologised, explaining that he didn't know they had to be shown to Packer first and that Harry Chester usually did the job. 'Harry's not around any more,' snapped Packer.

There were four meetings in quick succession that morning, with different directors for each company. Before every meeting, Packer repeated the performance, rendering the poor accountant a nervous wreck by the end.

But Packer missed his mentor terribly, whatever impression he might have given to the contrary. On the day of Chester's death, the flag at the group's Park Street headquarters was flown at half-mast, and for a month afterwards Kerry sported a black armband and kept the blinds of his office drawn. At the funeral, John Ducker found him in a driveway, crying. And he was not the only one who witnessed tears in the weeks that followed. Others couldn't help noticing that he looked really upset. In fact, Kerry was shattered by Chester's death. According to Ita Buttrose, he had loved Harry like a father. Harry had encouraged him, nurtured him and built him up, which his real father had never done.

With Chester gone, his brother Clyde abroad and Sir Frank long dead, Kerry was now on his own at the helm of the empire. He was quite capable of steering the television and publishing businesses by himself, as time would show, and the ship was undoubtedly sound. But the old streak of Packer pessimism was never far below the surface. Perhaps it stemmed from the family's troubles in the 1930s depression or from Frank Packer's perennial fear of losing everything, but Kerry seemed always to believe that there were rocks ahead or storms beyond the horizon. In late 1982, with the recession deepening in Australia, he was asked by the *Financial Review*'s Kieran Kelly why Consolidated Press had increased its borrowings by $90 million. He explained that he wanted to be safe—his companies didn't need the cash, and were investing it at a loss, but Ol' Man Trouble was never far away:

> Packer: I have thought we are heading into a depression for the past eighteen months to two years. But we have all the money we need to ensure that if others go broke, we won't. That is what the increase in borrowings is all about.
> Kelly: Have you borrowed more than you need?
> Packer: Absolutely. If the international banks do go broke and there's a depression, not a recession, those merchant banks out there might not have the money. They are in a far weaker situation than I am. So I intend to have my money locked up, and can afford to pay the extra half-a-per-cent interest.[5]

In fact, by 1982, the group did have problems, which might perhaps have been avoided if Chester had still been alive. Television and publishing were doing fine, although profits were down, but several of Packer's investment ventures were in a mess. In 1980, four months after Chester's death, Consolidated Press had made an expensive foray into coal mining, spending some $30 million to $40 million to buy two-thirds of the Forestwood Group, which had mines at Muswellbrook in New South Wales's Hunter Valley. The decision had been made at the height of the resources boom and coal prices had crashed soon after. In two years the mines had lost more than $9 million, while a further $9 million had been written off to close the company's salt and tin mines.[6]

Property had also proven a costly mistake. Packer had tried to ride the real estate boom on Queensland's Gold Coast, but again had jumped on too late. With more than $50 million invested in high-rise apartments with the Raptis Group and two subdivisions with Alan Bond, he had made some early profits and hoped for more, apparently convinced, for all his professed gloom, that prices would hold up. In early 1982, six months before the slump, he had still been confident there would be no crash, but it had come all the same, and the Packer empire was facing losses of almost $10 million.[7] To his credit, he moved quickly and decisively to get his money out, sacking his investment chief, Russell Knowles, as he did so. It was the style of the Packer organisation that someone had to pay for the mistakes. Success was rewarded, failure punished. It was how the world worked, or so Kerry's father had always taught him. Yet some of the blame was also his, for he was the boss and had approved the decisions.

In business as in life, Kerry's views were simple, etched in black and white. Like his father before him, he had a tribal vision of the world that divided people into friends and enemies, members of the tribe and outsiders. If you were within the tribe he could be fantastic to work for because loyalty was rewarded generously and benefits showered upon you. If your health became bad or your children got into trouble, Kerry was always prepared to help. Bills would be paid, doctors found, money provided, all quietly and without fuss. But if you left the tribe, the life support would be cut off and the friendship severed.

Like father, like son, he was fiercely loyal to anyone (except politicians) who had done the Packers a good turn in the past. In the mid 1970s, the group's biggest advertiser, Reckitt & Colman, suggested to Kerry that they were his most important client because they spent far more than any other company to advertise in his magazines. Packer put them straight in no uncertain terms. His most important client, he said, was not the largest. Years ago, the biscuit manufacturer Arnotts had taken the back page of the *Women's Weekly* every week, supporting his father when he needed help. Now they were the son's most important and valued customer.

In one way, Kerry was more generous to his employees than Frank Packer had ever been. In the forty years that his father ran the business, senior executives had received cash bonuses at Christmas time, and sometimes even a car. But the largesse had never penetrated to the lower levels of the company. The journalists had made do with a party and a speech from the boss, while the printers had each got a bottle of warm beer. Kerry's more democratic approach was to give everyone a Christmas hamper.[8] These were good enough to make people come in on their days off and queue to pick them up. There were cold ones and hot ones, and the cold ones were better, but you had to get in early to be sure of landing one.

But there was a price to be paid for this beneficence, as there had been in his father's day. For one thing, Kerry insisted on knowing where his executives were at all times, in case he needed to reach them. The switchboard at Park Street was open twenty-four hours a day and, according to Ian Kennon, even if you were going out for a drink, you would have to tell the operator where you were: 'It might be ten o'clock at night, but you'd have to phone in that you were just leaving Darcy's and were on your way to the Sebel Town House. He demanded to know where you were, so that he could always get hold of you.'

Kennon recalls a somewhat chilling first day at Consolidated Press when Packer came into his office to give him the official welcome.

> He sat down, put his feet on the desk and summoned in the woman who was going to be my secretary, Mrs Robinson. Then he asked her how long she'd been with the company and she said twenty years. So he said: 'That's pretty good, isn't it? Mrs Robinson has been with the company twenty years, and do you know, son? If I ring her up any time and she doesn't know where you are, I'd have to fire her.'

Luckily, Mrs Robinson never lost track of Kennon's movements, so the seriousness of the threat was never tested. But Kerry appeared to believe that he owned his employees, just as his father had done. In the words of one editor who was with Consolidated Press for many years: 'When you worked for the Packers, you were their property. Their attitude was that they made you what you were, so that if you left you were stealing from them. Even when you were there, your spare time was not your own; it was regarded as time in which you could recover so that you might return refreshed to their service.'

Ita Buttrose's twenty-three years at Consolidated Press led her to similar conclusions.

> The Packer organisation behaved as though it possessed you, and intruded into every aspect of your life. If I went on holiday, Kerry had to know where I was going. If I went out at night I had to leave a phone number where Kerry could call me in a crisis. If I went out to lunch I had to leave the name of the restaurant and its phone number. This reflected the style in which Sir Frank had run the company, and Kerry followed in the old man's feudal footsteps.[9]

When Kerry went overseas, as he often did, he would demand that his senior executives have lunch with him the day he returned. This could be difficult because neither his executives nor his personal staff knew exactly when to expect him. He would frequently appear with the minimum of notice, perhaps because he liked to keep people on the hop, and would be outraged if people were absent. According to Ita, he was also outrageous when they were not: 'He always returned with jet lag, tired and bad tempered, and was rude and angry all through lunch.' On one occasion he came back to Sydney to find five senior executives out of town, and promptly fired off a memo to tell all his top people that it wouldn't happen again. Ita kept her copy, which read:

> On the day I return from overseas, I expect all my executives to be here so that they can inform me immediately of what has been happening during my absence. If not, I expect to know why they will not be available before I go away. World tours and other trips will be cancelled.[10]

If a member of the Packer tribe decided to leave, retribution could be swift, savage and enduring. On the death in 1974 of

Alice Jackson, the former editor of the *Women's Weekly*, it would have been natural for Consolidated Press to send flowers to her funeral and for the Packers to attend. Sir Frank decreed that there should be no flowers and that no one should go. Alice Jackson's crime had been to leave him in 1948 to work for his arch-rival, Sir Keith Murdoch, taking some of her best staff with her. It meant nothing to him that she had spent fifteen years with the *Weekly* and contributed enormously to its success, nothing that the circulation had trebled to more than 750 000 in her time as editor. Frank had been variously reported as 'bitterly angry' and 'beside himself with rage' at her departure, and twenty-six years later he could still not forgive her.

Similarly, in 1981, when Ita signed up with Sir Keith's son Rupert to edit the *Daily Telegraph*, Kerry seemed determined to punish her. Like Alice Jackson, Ita had helped make the Packers a fair chunk of their fortune through her part in the launch of *Cleo* and the relaunch of the flagship *Women's Weekly*. She had also been personally close to Kerry and a member of the inner circle. But after twenty-three years with the company she was not even allowed back into the building to say goodbye to staff, and had to return on Christmas Eve to collect her belongings. She was given a week to return her company Mercedes, then told two days later that she must surrender it immediately. The same day she was asked whether she and her children would get out of their company-owned house in Woollahra 'right away'. Even then, the battle did not let up: when she tried to rent another house, she found that a Packer employee was also after it, offering to top the advertised rent by $100. It was hardly surprising that there was a saying in the Packer organisation: 'They can sack you as many times as they like. But you only resign once.'

Tribalism apart, Kerry was old-fashioned, straitlaced and somewhat Victorian in his ideas. He believed in sobriety, honesty, hard work, and being thankful for what life had given him. He talked of fair play, obeying the umpire, and offering a straight bat, yet when it came to a fight, he behaved as if the rules meant nothing. According to Chris Forsyth, who watched him wage war with the establishment over World Series Cricket, he was 'indifferent to most civilised forms of conduct' when it made the difference between winning and losing. He told journalists in the course of these battles that he was deliberately tough and hard. And he justified his business philosophy to Michael Parkinson in similar terms.

> I don't believe you're employed to be popular, you're employed to get a job done . . . I think you have to be diligent about the firm's money. I think you have to take hard decisions and unpopular decisions even with people you like within a business.
>
> In your own private life you have the right to choose your friends and ignore their weaknesses . . . In your own private life I believe you have a completely different set of standards.[11]

What was fascinating about Kerry's credo was not just that he believed there were two different sets of rules for different spheres of life. It was also that he felt that money carried a moral imperative of its own: if you had money as he did, you had a duty to be brutal in the fight for more.

If this was what Kerry thought, it was hardly surprising that he professed not to care whether people liked him and that he behaved in business as he did. Even in the presence of outsiders, he treated his executives without mercy. One relatively junior manager remembers being called down to Packer's office in the late 1970s to be confronted by an array of Packer's senior executives, including Trevor Kennedy, Ita Buttrose, Graham Lawrence, Rob Henty and others. Packer beckoned him in, lined him up before the assembled company and said, 'These cunts are trying to get at me. Will you find out what they're trying to do?' And with that, everyone was dismissed.

A government minister who dealt with Packer on several occasions recalls a similar performance during a meeting with him and his senior advisers. 'Tell the minister where we stand on this,' said Packer. The three advisers duly laid out their view of what their boss was after. When they had finished, or perhaps before, Packer exploded, 'Jesus Christ, why I employ fucking cunts like this I wouldn't fucking know. Let me tell you what the true position is.' To the minister's amazement, the three men simply sat there and took it. He could only explain it by assuming that Packer must pay them spectacularly well.

On occasions, Packer showed a similar impatience with politicians or government officials, and he sometimes lost business because of it. In 1979, the Queensland Government decided it would boost revenue and attract tourists by licensing two casinos in the state, with one above and one below the 23rd parallel which runs through Rockhampton. The Gold Coast licence in particular was likely to be a prize worth winning.[12] Packer teamed up with his friends at Essington, with whom he was also doing property deals, to form the Majura syndicate and make an unsuccessful bid for the licence. According to the Queensland Treasurer, Sir Llew Edwards, who scrutinised the tenders, Packer's high-handed attitude was a major reason why his syndicate lost.

According to Edwards, there were a number of problems with the Majura proposal. The reviewing committee felt that its plan for a 300-bed hotel and casino complex on the old Surfers Paradise racecourse was vague on detail and a second-rate construction proposal. But what killed the syndicate's chances as much as anything, says Edwards, was Packer's arrogant, uncooperative approach: 'We were concerned by his born-to-rule attitude.'

Edwards and his public servants wanted a proposal with everything settled so that arguments about detail could not lead to political pressure to bend the rules. But when pressed by the committee, Packer was aggressive and overbearing, and answered questions by asking his own. He seemed to Edwards to think it beneath him to be questioned by officials of the public service when he could talk to their political leaders instead.

There were echoes of his father in this, as in so many other things. But if the two were alike in numerous ways, there was also one key difference. Despite his undoubted respect for money and belief in the goodness of profit, Frank Packer had always been a newspaperman first and an accumulator second. But with Kerry there was no hesitation in putting money above all other gods, perhaps because he saw it as a way of measuring his achievements against the Packers who had gone before him.

This third-generation Packer was extremely generous in negotiating employment contracts and was never obsessed, in the style of Sir Frank, with paper clips or expenses claims. But when the sums of money became larger he was as tight and as tough as his father had ever been. Those who dealt with Kerry said that he not only hated to lose, but hated even to risk losing. Hence he often appeared greedy, for he was so determined to win that he rarely left anything in the deal for anybody else. Perhaps it was what made him so successful, but his idea of cheap, as one banker put it, was to buy something for $100 million less than it was worth. And this, in 1983, was precisely what he managed to do with his own company, Consolidated Press, when he took it back into family ownership.

Extraordinarily enough, no one had even realised during the 1970s that the Packers owned only one-quarter of Consolidated Press's shares. It was abundantly clear that they had always controlled the empire, for Kerry and his father ran it like a corner store, but the secrecy surrounding the group had concealed the true ownership position. Only the Packers and their advisers knew for sure what had taken place and why, but Sir Frank and the Packer family had owned almost half the business until 1972. Then, apparently to raise cash, they had sold half their shares, or roughly one-quarter of the Consolidated Press empire, for just over $3 million.

They had maintained their iron grip on the group, in spite of this divestment, by selling their shares to Consolidated Press itself, which had rather bizarrely left the company owning 23 per cent of its own share capital.[13] This 1972 transaction and incestuous cross-shareholding had remained hidden until October 1980, when Kerry had attempted to buy back the shares. Discovery had then provoked some anger among institutional shareholders, who were unhappy that it had happened in the first place, doubly unhappy that they hadn't known about it and unhappiest of all that they were now being offered what they considered a miserable amount of money to untangle it.

This first 1980 effort to buy back part of the empire therefore failed. Kerry offered $4 million less for the shares than they would have fetched on the stock market and the institutions made it clear they wouldn't sell, so the deal was scrapped. Almost three years later Packer came back for a second more ambitious attempt, this time to buy all the shares in Consolidated Press held by the public or, in other words, to take the company right back to being a family business. 'The days of the family business are over,' Sir Frank had lamented in 1970, but oh, how wrong he had been.

There were a number of reasons why Kerry was so keen to put the empire back in private hands,[14] but fundamentally he hated busybodies, regulators and all those who told him what to do. Undoubtedly, he also wanted the business for himself, and this was the perfect time to make the move. The share market was down, the company's profits had taken a hammering, Australia was in the throes of a deep recession. It would never again be as cheap as this to buy the public out.

In city legend, Packer's second and successful attempt at privatisation began with him leaning over his back fence one weekend late in 1982 to ask the merchant banker who lived next door whether he wanted to handle the campaign. Mark Johnson of the now-extinct Australian Bank agreed to give it a try, even though he didn't believe the deal could be done. The problem quite simply was that Packer was determined to get it on the cheap. He had told Johnson that he was prepared to pay $5 per share and not a cent more, and Johnson did not believe this would be enough. Although on the face of it the offer looked generous, since the shares were trading on the stock market at less than $3, the market price was only depressed because the company had always been mean with its dividends.

Packer's advisers' calculations on the back of an evelope suggested that the shares would normally fetch $9 or $10 in such a takeover, or almost twice what Packer had offered. So it would not only be hard to get institutional shareholders to sell, it might also be impossible to find an independent expert who would say that the deal was kosher.[15] In valuing the shares the experts were required to use guidelines laid down by the National Companies and Securities Commission, and these would unquestionably yield the conclusion that $5 was not enough.

Packer's advisers, however, came up with two cute answers to the problem. The first was to reduce the proportion of shareholders they needed to win over; the second was to structure the deal so that the $5 became worth considerably more in the hands of the only shareholders with power to kill the deal—the institutions.

David Saunders, head of corporate finance at the Australian Bank, came up with a scheme that solved the first part of the puzzle. 'I've got it, I've got it!' he remembers shouting as he ran into Johnson's office, 'I know how it can be done!' The National Companies and Securities Commission's rules required a takeover to be approved by 90 per cent of a company's voting shares. Saunders' idea was to convert the shares beforehand into preference shares, which would need only 75 per cent of the votes cast at an extraordinary general meeting. The beauty of this ingenious scheme was that Packer would be allowed to vote his shareholding in favour of the conversion, virtually guaranteeing that it would go ahead.[16] Buying the preference shares at $5 apiece would then be a formality and the takeover a *fait accompli* because the preference shares did not have a vote.

The second part of the puzzle was much easier. The institutions could be persuaded to support the deal by being offered a stream of tax-free dividends instead of a lump sum. This would pump up the value of the $5 cash offer to around $8 or $9, which was almost what the institutions were looking for.[17] If the big shareholders were still not thrilled by this offer, they could be told quite bluntly that they had no choice. The alternative to acceptance, it could be emphasised, was being locked into the company for evermore, with its low dividends, poor share price and tight Packer control.

A more serious problem was that the deal had to be scrutinised by independent experts, who were required to say whether or not the offer was a fair and reasonable one. This task was given to the accounting firm Coopers & Lybrand, whose conclusion quite simply was that it was not. The experts' report valued Consolidated Press shares at $6.89, admittedly less than Packer's advisers had feared, but still way above Packer's offer of $5. On this reckoning, the experts could only conclude that Packer's bid was both unfair and unreasonable, which they did.

Amazingly, however, it was still possible for the deal to go ahead, for the experts were also required to tell the independent directors of Consolidated Press whether they would be justified in recommending the offer. And the brutal truth was that the shareholders would not do better elsewhere. The offer was 28 per cent higher than the share price had been before the bid, and there was no prospect of any other bidders appearing. Nor was there any chance of the company being liquidated and the shareholders getting their money that way. Unfair as it was, this was the best offer that shareholders were likely to get. Coopers & Lybrand duly gave Packer's $5 offer the green light, telling the independent directors that they could recommend shareholders to accept. Translated into the vernacular, the message to the shareholders was simple: Kerry had them by the short and curlies.[18]

As so often before, there were two sides of Packer to be seen in the course of the transaction. When it came to handling the people who were bolting the deal together he could be dreadful, 'the biggest bastard you've ever seen'. According to one who was closely involved, he would bully, scream blue murder, accuse people of not knowing what they were talking about and generally throw his considerable weight around. But when it came to persuading Westpac, Citibank and a syndicate of bankers that they should put up the money to fund the takeover, he was magnificent. Called in by the advisers to give the bankers a pep talk, Kerry was the perfect salesman, saying all the right things, massaging the egos that needed to be massaged and charming the pants off the rest of them.

But with his advisers he was never so deferential. On one occasion, needing to see him on a Friday afternoon, they finally tracked down Kerry's secretary Pat Wheatley, who told them that he was having a golf lesson and was expecting them out at the course. Saunders and Johnson duly drove out to the Australian Golf Club to see him. As they parked the car they were greeted by the sight of the club secretary running towards them. 'You must be for Mr Packer, he's waiting for you out on the course.' The two pin-striped bankers with their polka-dot ties were bundled into a golf buggy, armed with an umbrella as it was starting to rain, and given directions to where they would find their man. Sure enough, Packer and the professional were discovered working on the big man's iron play. Packer barely looked up as they approached, and certainly made no move to stop what he was doing. As they huddled together in their city suits under their umbrella, Packer continued to hit shots, firing questions about the deal as he did so. Finally, when he had heard enough, or decided that his golf was up to scratch, he suggested that he had better buy them a drink. They piled back into their golf buggies, with Packer leading them behind a copse to where the Channel Nine helicopter was parked. There, they were subjected to the same barrage of questions all over again until Packer looked at his watch and announced that it was time to go. 'Sorry about the drink, boys, I've got to be in Palm Beach by five o'clock.' And with a clatter of rotor blades he was off, leaving them standing in the downdraught. It was the sort of power play be loved. On another occasion, when Kerry was recovering from a heart scare, they were summoned to his home in Bellevue Hill and ushered into his bedroom, to be quizzed on the deal's progress. Kerry was lying, apparently naked, under a thin sheet as they paraded before him, once again in full city dress. It was most embarrassing.

Characteristically, Packer had last-minute nerves about the deal, just as he had had with the launch of *Cleo* in 1972 and the relaunch of the *Women's Weekly* three years later. A week before the button was to be pressed, Packer asked his advisers to fly to the USA to explain the deal to Jim Wolfensohn, the man who had guided him and his father since the early 1960s; he had never made a major move without consulting this financial wizard and this was no exception, so Saunders and a colleague duly caught the plane to New York. It seems unlikely that Wolfensohn understood the nuances of it all, given that its design owed much to a desire to skirt Australian regulations, but he was obviously satisfied that it was a good move for Packer to be making, and gave the deal his blessing.

Although the design was ingenious, it still needed only two major institutions to vote against for the whole scheme to fail, and the biggest and most influential of them all, the Australian Mutual Provident Society (AMP) seemed set to oppose it. As the deadline drew near, Kerry himself went in to do a bit of persuasion, telling the AMP that the future prospects for television were terrible. This clearly did the trick. When D-day dawned at the extraordinary general meeting, the AMP voted in favour and the scheme was approved by more than the requisite 75 per cent of votes cast. Even so, it had looked in doubt to the last minute. And Packer was sufficiently nervous about the outcome to vote his own shares in favour of the proposal, which his advisers had counselled him not to do.

For Packer the deal and the timing were brilliant, for he picked up assets worth more than $220 million at less than half-price. More to the point, he laid out none of his own money to do so. In the words of one of the bankers who designed the scheme, Packer went from owning less than 25 per cent of the company to owning the whole lot without even putting his hand in his pocket. The $110 million it cost to buy out the public shareholders was put up not by him but by Consolidated Press Holdings and its subsidiary companies. These in turn were financed by the banks, who were happy to lend money on the security of the group's extremely valuable assets.[19]

The assets acquired in the deal soon rose in value dramatically. Within three-and-a-half years, Packer was selling the two Channel Nine television stations to Alan Bond for $1050 million and pocketing all the proceeds himself. Within a further five-and-a-half years, he was selling half the company's Australian magazines in a deal that valued the full magazine business at another $1175 million. Thus, in just two deals over the next nine years, the privatisation paid out more than $2 billion on a punt that Kerry had essentially had for free. Only seven years earlier in the mid 1970s, he had moved from an eighth share to a quarter share of the empire for just $4 million when he bought out his brother Clyde.

Ironically, such was his hatred of debt and fear of losing it all, according to Malcolm Turnbull, then company secretary at Consolidated Press Holdings, that he worried about how much the group was borrowing to enable the privatisation to go ahead.[20] He even told his wife Ros, in a style reminiscent of his departed father, that she would have to be careful not to leave the lights on at Bellevue Hill. It did not appear to Turnbull that this was meant as a joke.

But even if Packer had no inkling of how rich the deal would make him, even if he lacked the true entrepreneur's boundless optimism that things would always turn out fine, he must have known one thing: that even by his own exacting standards, he had repossessed the Packer empire at a bargain basement price. He had not done a better deal before and, Alan Bond aside, he would not do a better one again.

CHAPTER TWELVE

COSTIGAN INVESTIGATES

Each and every one of the allegations made against me in the
National Times *article are false and demonstrably so. It is*
extraordinary that this disgusting publication should place me
in a position where I effectively have to prove my innocence.

Kerry Packer, 28 September 1984

One of Packer's reasons for taking his companies private in 1983 was to put his affairs out of the reach of busybodies and prying eyes. But in this respect he was spectacularly unsuccessful. For in September 1984, leaked documents from the Costigan Royal Commission exploded into the public arena through an article in the *National Times*. The newspaper had not intended to identify Packer but many of Australia's lawyers, journalists and politicians knew instantly to whom the Royal Commission's sensational 'confidential case summaries' referred, and the rest were told soon afterwards.

The central character in Costigan's rogues galley was identified in the *National Times* by the codename 'Goanna' and portrayed as being involved in pornography, tax evasion, drug importation, corporate fraud, money laundering and even murder. Despite the wildness of these alleged crimes and the fact that the royal commission's original codename of 'Squirrel' had been changed, it was obvious to those who had followed its investigations over the previous year that the caricature referred to Packer.[1] In case there was any doubt, however, he made a public statement two weeks after the article appeared, admitting that he and the 'Goanna' were one and the same, before proceeding to tackle each of the allegations head-on in devastating style.

The article dropped like a bomb onto Packer's life—it is not every day that one is branded a drug baron and gangster. But the shock waves were felt as far away as England, where his cricketing escapades had made him famous. And to the end, almost twenty years after Packer's official exoneration, the battle damage remained. As with the famous Chamberlain case, most Australians probably now accept that Packer was an innocent victim, unjustly and wrongly accused of crimes he never committed. But a sizable minority doubtless still believe that there can be no smoke without fire, that some of the allegations must have been true and that Packer was in some ill-defined way a sinister and evil man.

One of the ironies of the whole Goanna episode is that the royal commission on the activities of the Federated Ship Painters' and Dockers' Union, to give the Costigan inquiry its full name, was set up on 1 October 1980, in the wake of revelations made in Packer's own *Bulletin* magazine. A series of articles on the Melbourne waterfront had cracked the dockers' code of silence and revealed evidence of corruption, violence and murder. These had raised the circulation of the magazine, delighted its proprietor and embarrassed the Fraser Government into establishing a royal commission to recommend what might be done. Francis Xavier Costigan QC, a tenacious, Jesuit-educated Melbourne lawyer, had been chosen to run it and asked to investigate whether the union or its members were engaged in illegal activities relating to shipping. His inquiries soon took him much further than that.

Knowing that his investigators wouldn't get anywhere by putting painters and dockers in the witness box, Costigan followed the document and money trail through a maze of $2 companies and bank accounts, and uncovered evidence of drug trafficking, pornography, SP bookmaking, massive tax fraud and murder. The money trails went in several directions, but one in particular in early 1983 led from the wharves of Melbourne to a branch of the Bank of NSW (now Westpac), at Comalco House in the centre of Brisbane. Further investigation led Costigan to a huge network of companies and a massive bottom-of-the-harbour tax fraud.

The term 'bottom-of-the-harbour' was coined to describe the tax scams that became extremely popular in the late 1970s that are thought to have cost the government between $500 million and $1000 million in lost tax.[2] But although almost everybody has heard the phrase, few people realise how the scams worked or why they got their name. Quite crudely, the schemes involved ripping the cash out of companies with large tax liabilities and then deep-sixing the companies to the metaphorical bottom of the harbour where the taxman couldn't find them. The clients of these remarkably simple schemes (which the promoters claimed were entirely legal) included some of the nation's wealthiest families. They might well have thought the promoters had discovered some sophisticated way of losing their tax liability—though most preferred not to inquire—but in fact there was nothing so clever. The tax was simply not paid, while the company was made to disappear so that the taxman could never come knocking for the money. The promoters, meanwhile, became extremely rich.

To take an example of how it worked, a company with profits of $1 million in cash could be sold to a tax 'promoter' for around $900 000. He would then strip the cash out of the company, keep the balance of $100 000 for himself and dump the empty shell out of the taxman's reach. The original owner, of course, would escape paying tax because the company now belonged to others. Deep-sixing the company was a relatively simple matter, although it involved laying a complicated and confusing trail. Normally, the name of the company and the address of its registered office would be changed several times, while it would be shunted simultaneously through a bewildering array of new directors and shareholders. Finally, it would be dumped on people who had no assets and no idea that the company still owed huge amounts of tax. This was where the painters and dockers came in, for they were prepared to sign thousands of company documents for a small fee yet ask no questions about what they were doing. Many used false names anyway, and most were so tough that the taxman thought twice about getting heavy with them.

The particular bottom-of-the-harbour scheme uncovered by Costigan was run by an accountant named Donald Lockyer who, as time soon revealed, was a remarkable character. (He was jailed for bankruptcy offences in 1983 and 1984 and jailed again for tax fraud in 1986.) Three times a bankrupt, yet also a multimillion-aire, he owned vast amounts of property around the world, while his wife Suzi wore jewellery worth millions of dollars, ran three Rolls-Royces and a yellow Maserati. Lockyer himself had paid no tax for twenty years, yet the Australian Taxation Office had never caught up with him. But more to the point he had, during the 1970s, controlled a network of 1000 companies that had assisted other people in evading at least $100 million in tax. Lockyer, in short, was one of Australia's leading bottom-of-the-harbour tax practitioners.

His partner was Ian Beames, an accountant well known in Brisbane as a designer of dodgy tax schemes and as a business-man of doubtful repute. A millionaire by the age of thirty, he had in the mid 1970s been the whizz-kid responsible for a company called Comfin Australia, one of the shooting stars of the stock market. Comfin had made fortunes out of land speculation, share trading and asset stripping until the property collapse had sent it crashing in 1977 with a deficit of more than $2 million. This was shortly after Beames had told everyone how well the company was doing. A lengthy investigation by police had followed and Beames had been charged with three counts of fraud, on which he was jailed in March 1980. No sooner had he got out than he was jailed again on separate fraud charges, and he was still in prison in 1983 when Costigan caught up with him. Though less flamboyant than Lockyer, he too had a remarkable pedigree, for before going to jail he had worked with the king of Australia's bottom-of-the-harbour schemes, Brian Maher (jailed for five years for fraud and tax fraud in 1985). And investigators believed he had taught Maher his trade.[3]

Beames's involvement in tax schemes in the late 1970s had encompassed a Queensland property developer named Brian Ray, with whom he had been friends since 1975. And it was not long before this man also came to Costigan's attention. There are several ways in which this might have happened, for Beames was giving secret evidence to Costigan as early as April 1983, but the official story is that Costigan's investigators decided to tear the Brisbane bank branch apart to look for drug money and in doing so discovered large movements of cash involving the two men. Three cheques totaling $225 000, signed by Brian Ray, had been drawn on the account of a Beames company called P&S Meats and then picked up in cash. But what had happened to the money thereafter was a mystery. Costigan believed Beames to have connections with drug dealers and suspected (incorrectly) that the cash was financing drug shipments. He therefore commanded Beames's friend Brian Ray to appear before his royal commission and give evidence, which on 4 October 1983 he did. And it was here that the trail to Kerry Packer began.

The Costigan inquiry had by this time been performing in public for three years, and Brisbane was only a sideshow to Melbourne's main attractions, so there was no great interest in the day's proceedings. The weather was also unseasonably hot, and the morning had seen a succession of minor witnesses so, by the time the afternoon session arrived, the sole journalist was almost asleep in the front row of the press box. Then an exchange between Ray and Doug Meagher QC, the counsel assisting Costigan, snapped him out of his reverie.

Ray had already been questioned about a man called Richards who had picked up $120 000 in cash from another Brisbane bank branch and couriered it down to Sydney. Ray had signed the cheque and the money had been drawn from the bank account of a company belonging to him. Yet he had claimed to have no idea who the man was and where he had taken his money. Ray had then been asked whether others had ever picked up money for him, and had replied that Ian Beames had once collected $50 000 from the Comalco House branch and delivered it 'to a friend'. At this point Ray's lawyer had leapt to his feet and begged that the answers be given in secret session. This application had been refused. And the story of what Beames had done with the money had then been allowed to emerge:

> Meagher: Where did he take it after he collected it?
> Ray: He delivered it to a friend of mine.
> Meagher: Was it ultimately delivered to you?
> Ray: No, it was not. It did not ever go through me.
> Costigan: Where was that friend? Sydney?
> Ray: Yes . . .
> Meagher: Did you give Mr Beames instructions as to who he was to deliver the money in Sydney?
> Ray: Yes.
> Meagher: Who did you tell him to deliver it to?
> Ray: Mr Kerry Packer.[4]

Costigan claimed in his report that he was surprised to hear Packer's name dropped, bombshell-like, into the proceedings, but he could hardly have been as shocked as the journalist, who realised immediately that he had a scoop on his hands. This was sensational evidence that would run in every paper in Australia the next day and send reporters hotfoot to Brisbane for the revelations. And sure enough, they were not disappointed, for the next day Ian Beames came to the stand to confirm that he had couriered the money to Packer. He remembered the amount as being $100 000 but agreed that he had definitely picked up the cash from the bank manager's office in Brisbane and taken it down to Sydney on the plane:

> Meagher: And when was that?
> Beames: It was in February 1980. It was on a Friday afternoon.
> Meagher: And why did you collect it?
> Beames: I was asked to collect it and deliver it in Sydney.

Meagher: Who asked you to collect it?

Beames: Brian Ray.

Meagher: What did he say when he asked you to collect it?

Beames: To cash the cheque, collect the money, and I would be met at Sydney airport.

Meagher: By whom?

Beames: By Mr Kerry Packer's chauffeur . . .

Meagher: How did you carry it down to Sydney?

Beames: In a brief case, I presume.

Meagher: And you took it out of your brief case and gave it to him?

Beames: Yes.[5]

Between them, Beames and Ray agreed, they had filled their cases with a total of $225 000 in cash which had been delivered on three separate occasions to Packer or his driver. Costigan quite naturally wanted to find out what the money was for and why it had been done in such a clandestine manner.

Brian Ray told the commission that the money was a loan from him to Packer. He said he had not been given a receipt for the $225 000 because he didn't feel he needed one. Nor had he documented the loan in any way. What's more, he agreed, it was entirely unsecured and there was no set repayment date.[6] This was an odd explanation, since Ray had been essentially bankrupt at the time, and either was or should have been penniless. In more precise terms, he had been in a scheme of arrangement with his creditors, paying off debts of $3 million at the rate of one cent in the dollar. Yet, he had not only had a spare $225 000 to help his mate but, generously, had been able to provide the cash to Packer interest-free. Three-and-a-half years later, by which time some $90 000 interest would normally have been coming his way, the loan had still not been repaid.

According to Ray, it had been Packer's idea to have the money in cash so that no one would find out about it. But he claimed to have no idea why:

Meagher: Did Mr Packer explain to you why he wanted this kept quiet?

Ray: No, he did not.

Meagher: Was it his idea to be kept quiet?

Ray: It was something we agreed upon ... certainly I wouldn't have minded it being ...

Meagher: Right, so Mr Packer wanted it kept quiet?

Ray: Yes.

Commissioner: Why, did he tell you?

Ray: No.[7]

When Packer finally gave evidence four months later, after doing his utmost to avoid appearing before the commission, he echoed Ray's story. According to Packer's public evidence, he had suffered a bad run on the horses, been short of funds, and mentioned the matter to his friend in the course of a casual conversation:

My recollection of it is that we were talking on the telephone ...
and he made the remark, 'How are things going?' I think I said,
'Well, it has not been a good week.' 'What is wrong?' I said, 'I lost
too much at the races' or whatever it was. He said, 'Do you want
some money?' I said, 'Yes, have you got any?' He said, 'Yes, I have
got a bit.' I said, 'Have you got any to spare?' He said, 'I certainly
have.'[8]

The counsel assisting Costigan, Doug Meagher QC, then inquired, as he had earlier of Ray, why Packer had asked for the money in cash, only to be answered in the inimitable Packer style:

Packer: I did not realise it was illegal to do so.

Meagher: Yes, but why did you ask for it to be done in cash rather than just by way of a cheque?

Packer: Well, are you seeking an explanation from me, or do you just want a yes and no answer?

Meagher: I will go back a step. Did you ask for it in cash?

Packer: Yes.

269

Meagher: Why did you ask for it to be in cash?

Packer: Because I wanted it in cash.

Meagher: Why did you want it in cash?

Packer: Because I like cash. I have a squirrel mentality. I like to keep money in cash. It is by no means the most cash I have ever had in my life.

Meagher: What did you do with it?

Packer: I put it in a safe place.

Meagher: What does that mean?

Packer: Well, I do not know.[9]

On this version, offered by Ray and Packer, the money couriered down to Sydney in cash had been a loan made by a bankrupt to a millionaire. Beames, however, told a very different story. There was no dispute that the $225 000 delivered to Packer had come from the bank account of his company P&S Meats. Beames's understanding was that the money was *repaying* a loan that Packer had made to the company to fund an unsuccesful tax-avoidance scheme. Packer, Beames believed, had provided almost $1 million for this purpose).[10]

The two differing accounts were never reconciled, but some things were beyond dispute. As all three men would eventually testify, Beames and Ray had visited Packer in his Sydney office in August 1979 to ask him for a million dollars to fund a scheme that involved minimising income tax by 'investing' in film copyrights.

The fact that the property developer and his bottom-of-theharbour friend had even got through Packer's front door suggested that he already knew one of them well, and this was so, for Kerry and Brian Ray had been good mates since the late 1960s or early 1970s when they had been introduced by a mutual friend, John Singleton, who had known Ray since they were at school together. The two had since done business on several occasions and Ray was now one of a string of people who brought Packer deals. It was one of Packer's characteristics that he often seemed most comfortable with people from the wrong end of town. It was to do, perhaps, with his dislike of the establishment as much as his love of money, but his close business associates included a gaggle of property developers, tax promoters and fast-money merchants whose activities he was often happy to finance. Brian Ray, for example, had already introduced him to Malcolm Edwards of Essington, whose record in the 1970s included a couple of business failures and some withering official criticism.[11] Within eighteen months he would introduce him to Phillip Carver, then facing fraud and arson charges, to whom Packer would provide funds to market a miracle 'youth drug'. And now he brought him Ian Beames, failed businessman, soon-to-be-convicted fraudster and bottom-of-the-harbour tax promoter. Packer had never met the man but apparently trusted Ray's judgment enough to be incurious about his background, for he would tell Costigan that he did not know in 1979 that Ray's friend was facing imminent trial on fraud charges.[12]

The film scheme that Beames and Ray wanted Packer to finance was not so outrageous as any of the bottom-of-the-harbour scams around at the time. Indeed, two tax barristers had sprinkled holy water over it by declaring it quite legal. But it was not exactly as clean as a whistle either, for it was a blatantly artificial arrangement that exploited a loophole in the law for the sole purpose of avoiding tax. As a guide to its artificiality, 'investors' were told they could claim a tax deduction of six to forty times their actual investment. For just $15 000 of real money, they would receive a tax deduction (if all went well) of $100 000, with the gap being filled by funny-money loans that did not have to be repaid.[13]

The films that they would be funding with their inflatable dollars were low-budget twenty-minute shorts planned by companies on the Gold Coast, with titles such as *Hidden India*, *The Australian Success Story—In Space*, and *Anatomy of an Island Resort*. There is some doubt about whether all of them were ever shot, and considerably more about whether they were ever shown. But the salient point was that the copyrights had been acquired by Beames's and Ray's companies for $100 000, yet would be parcelled out to investors for a total of $19 million. This remarkable inflation of their value would be achieved by sending them through a couple of $2 companies that would buy and sell the films with fictitious 'round-robin' loans. Packer was undoubtedly aware of this aspect of the scheme, and would have needed to be blind not to see that it was close to the line.

When Packer eventually gave evidence to Costigan in February 1984, he said that he had refused to finance the scheme. And he said this again in a public statement soon after the *National Times* published its sensational 'confidential Costigan case summaries' in September 1984:

> Evidence has been given at the Royal Commission by me that I was approached by Mr Brian Ray and Mr Ian Beames to provide finance for a tax minimisation scheme centred upon the acquisition of copyright in Australian films. I was advised at the time that this scheme had been approved by experienced tax lawyers, but nonetheless I did not provide the funds they sought.
>
> Two companies of mine did however invest in the scheme by purchasing film copyrights and claiming tax deductions accordingly. Each of these deductions were rejected by the Taxation Department. An objection was lodged by each of the companies and subsequently withdrawn. The tax was then paid in full and the net result of each of those two companies was that they were worse off than they would have been had they not entered the scheme.
>
> The decision to withdraw the objections was made in 1982, long before I was ever mentioned before the Costigan Commission in October 1983. Each and every one of the allegations contained with respect to that film scheme are false, at least so far as they refer to me.[14]

Packer was always on the lookout for ways to minimise his tax, in the belief that anyone who did not was a fool, and he was easily the largest investor in the scheme as well as one of the most favourably treated by the promoters. Two of his private companies, Cairnton and Dealer Holdings, attempted between them to claim a total of $1.8 million in tax deductions for an investment that had cost just $68 000 in real money. This, one imagines, would have brought Packer savings of around $1 million in tax if the scheme had been accepted, but the most these two companies could scrape up in income for their supposed $1.8 million 'investment' was a ridiculous $37.32. And not surprisingly the taxman rejected the claim, as he did with the 170 other investors, who had hoped for almost $19 million worth of tax deductions. Packer therefore ended up out of pocket to the tune of $68 000,[15] while the other investors waved goodbye to the $2 million they had contributed. Roughly half of their money or around $1 million ended up as profit in the hands of the promoters.

The scheme was quite obviously a dreadful rort, but that did not mean it was criminal. Packer's accountant, Bill Harrington, who had invested in the scheme himself, told the Australian Broadcasting Tribunal in 1985 that the deductions had only been rejected by the taxman because they hadn't produced assessable income, and that the scheme itself was perfectly legitimate. This, he claimed, was demonstrated by the lack of official reaction:

> No penalties were charged by the Taxation Department and at no time has it been suggested to the companies that the scheme was fraudulent or unlawful in any way.[16]

Costigan, however, had no doubts that the scheme was illegal and said so quite bluntly. In the confidential Volume 9 of his report he concluded that 'the scheme was a fraud on the Revenue' and 'deserving of prosecution as a conspiracy to defraud the Commonwealth'.[17] In a public exchange with one of the men who marketed it, the Sydney solicitor Henry Kelly, he had already said much the same:

> Costigan: It was an absolute fraud, was it not?
> Kelly: No, sir, I do not accept that.
> Costigan: A man paying $15 000 out of his pocket and then claiming $100 000 by use of legal documents which appear on

paper to represent substance but were just hollow. You know that as well as I do. It was a fraud.

Kelly: Your worship, I simply cannot accept that, it is a very technical piece of legislation.[18]

Costigan's view that it was fraudulent made it particularly relevant to know whether Packer had financed the scheme, for if he had the royal commission might wish to recommend he be prosecuted. By October 1983, four years after the meeting in his office, Australia's bottom-of-the-harbour practitioners were being very publicly pursued. Beames's partner Donald Lockyer had already had his assets frozen by the NSW Supreme Court, while his former employer, Australia's biggest tax promoter Brian Maher, had been arrested and charged with a total of twenty-four counts of fraud and tax fraud. Retrospective legislation had also been passed to knock out several types of tax-avoidance scheme. So there was a climate of prosecution and persecution of tax cheats. And even though the film scheme had been blessed by tax lawyers, there was still a risk that its promoters might be pursued.

Costigan clearly believed that Packer had financed the tax scheme. The Queensland fraud squad would come to a similar conclusion in February 1985 when they reviewed all the documents held by the National Crime Authority. And Robert Redlich QC, the Special Prosecutor charged with pursuing various tax matters arising out of Costigan, would agree with them both in August 1985 when prosecuting Ray for conspiracy to defraud the Commonwealth.[19] Costigan made it clear in Volume 9 of his final report that he personally had no doubts about the evidence, saying: 'I am satisfied that Mr Packer was involved both as a participating client and as a financier.' As to Packer's public denial that this was so, Costigan's report said he was satisfied that the denial was 'false'.

As designer, operator and promoter of the scheme, Beames told Costigan he believed that Packer had financed it. It was no secret that Packer had funded other projects that Ray had taken to him and had picked up half the profits. In fact, when Beames and Ray walked into his office in August 1979, the fifty–fifty partnership arrangement with Packer applied to all the projects that Ray was involved with.[20]

Beames's clear understanding, as the accountant who drew up the books of P&S Meats, was that the fifty–fifty arrangement had been applied to the film scheme too. The profits of the scheme had ultimately been divided into three, with Beames getting a third and Ray getting two-thirds. Beames believed that $223 000 (one-third of the total profits), which had been paid to one of Ray's companies, had ended up with Packer.

> Meagher: . . . you prepared on your list Mr Packer getting $223 000?
> Beames: Yes.
> Meagher: Have you got Mr Packer's name on that document?
> Beames: Yes.
> Meagher: What is the word to the left of his name?
> Beames: D-i-s-t.
> Meagher: What is that?
> Beames: Distribution.
> Meagher: Distribution of profit?
> Beames: Yes.
> Meagher: What is the amount on the other side?
> Beames: $223 000.
> Meagher: Does that not mean $223 000 distribution of profit to Packer?
> Beames: It appears that way . . .
> Meagher: That is what you thought was its ultimate destination?
> Beames: It went through one company not controlled by me. What happened when it got to this company I have no control over.
> Meagher: That is where you expected it to finish up?
> Beames: Certainly.[21]

Whoever had lent Beames's company the money to operate this tax-avoidance scheme was also in line for interest and fees totalling $293 000, according to Beames's evidence, putting the annual cost of the money at an extraordinary 100 per cent. Beames said he believed this also went to Packer:

Meagher: Who did the interest get paid to?
Beames: As far as I know it was paid at Brian Ray's direction to Mr Packer.
Meagher: All of it?
Beames: Yes.
Meagher: So in addition to that $223 000 you have $293 000 of interest?
Beames: Yes . . .
Meagher: The total amount is paid?
Beames: To Packer.[22]

Packer and Ray denied this, with Packer adding that he had told Ray three minutes *after* their August 1979 meeting that he could not, as director of a public company, get involved in anything so sensitive. Beames was not privy to this conversation, but one year after giving sworn evidence to Costigan and a week after publication of the royal commission's final report, he made a statutory declaration denying his original testimony. This said that he had learned 'subsequently' that Packer had 'declined to provide any financing for the transactions'.[23]

But whoever had put up the money, there was no dispute that it had come through tortuous channels. Packer had directed Brian Ray to talk to his Sydney solicitors, Allen Allen & Hemsley, who had directed Ray to a trust company in Hong Kong called Universal Corporate Services that had acted in the past as an offshore trustee for Packer. They in turn had arranged for the funds to be provided from Singapore through a shelf company activated on Aliens' instructions, Progress Credits Pte. In mid November 1979 Progress Credits had sent $922 000 to Australia which had been paid into Brian Ray's account.

One of the strange features of this story was that only a small part of the loan had ever been secured and then in somewhat lackadaisical fashion. Since Ray was in a scheme of arrangement with his creditors to whom he owed $3 million, and had no assets, he was not obviously a good credit risk, so it was odd that he could get the money at all, and odder still that he could get such a large amount without security. Indeed, it was an extraordinary story, and Costigan suspected that the whole arrangement with the Singapore company was a sham. His suspicions, however, were considerably heightened by what happened next.

Having given evidence for three days in a row, Brian Ray had signed an authority on 6 October 1983 permitting Costigan to take possession of any documents relating to the four-year-old Progress Credits loan. These were likely to tell Costigan beyond doubt who had channelled the money into the film scheme. On Ray's authority the solicitors Allen Allen & Hemsley in Sydney, accountants Touche Ross in Singapore and law firm Johnson Stokes and Masters in Hong Kong were all requested to forward their files to the Royal Commission.

On the day the authority was signed, the crucial loan file was still in Allens' Sydney office. By the time it was actually delivered twelve days later, far from being surrendered to Costigan, the file had been sent out of the country, to Singapore. A week after that, in late October, Costigan set off after it, along with two lawyers assisting the Royal Commission, Lex Lasry and Rick McDonnell, and a member of the Victorian police, Chief Inspector Frank Green.

Their first port of call in Singapore was the offices of the accountants Touche Ross.[24] When they arrived there unannounced on 27 October 1983, there was pandemonium. They were soon told that the man they needed to talk to was in a meeting. A little later, they saw him hurrying out of the building. After an hour of negotiation they persuaded a helpful clerk to produce a file marked Progress Credits Pte and let them have access. While he would not let them see the documents he was for some strange reason prepared to read them out. As he did so, instructions were being sought from Hong Kong by his superiors about whether the file should be turned over. As the contents of the documents were revealed, the investigators listened with mounting frustration, for the file contained exactly what they wanted—some two centimetres of letters and telexes relating to the Progress Credits loan.

Outside the office afterwards, by which time the file had been locked away again, Lasry and McDonnell started to curse their bad luck. But they were soon calmed down. 'Don't worry,' said Chief Inspector Green, 'I've taped everything he said.' The policeman had brought with him a special briefcase fitted with tape recorder and external microphone and had a record of the file's contents. According to Costigan's confidential Volume 9, these made it clear that 'Progress Credits was to be used for only one purpose, being the transmission and disguise of the funds'.[25]

The following day, Costigan's investigators were told officially by Allens' man in Singapore that none of the documents in the Progress Credits file concerned Brian Ray, so they had no authority to examine them. But by now the file had in any case been spirited away again, to Hong Kong. So, once again, the investigators got on a plane and went after it.

At the Hong Kong law firm of Johnson Stokes and Masters they were again denied access, on the basis that the file was no longer Brian Ray's property. Although this contradicted what he had told the commission in early October, he had changed his mind on 'legal advice'. They were then shown a telex suggesting that someone had beaten them to the documents, for Johnson Stokes and Masters had been informed by Allens in Sydney that:

Mr Bruce McWilliam of this office will be in Hong Kong today and we would be grateful if you would give him access to all documents and correspondence in relation to Progress Credits, etc. Also, he will have instructions for you concerning the files held by Universal Corporate Services on behalf of the trust set up by you. (Mr Ray, we understand, relinquished any interest he may have had some time ago.)[26]

Green, Lasry and McDonnell decided to confront McWilliam about their failure to see the Progress Credits file and to ask him why he was shadowing their moves. Before long, they had traced him to a hotel and discovered that he was booked on a flight back to Australia at 9.30 that evening. They decided to tackle him at the airport. But this was easier said than done, for although they knew they would find him in the Qantas departure lounge, they had no idea what he looked like except that he was said to be slim, of medium height and curly-haired. The only solution they could think of was to call out 'Hi, Bruce' to any Anglo-Saxons who looked suitably legal and answered to this rough description. They tried it with several people who failed to respond. Then, eventually, one did. They surrounded the man, with Green brandishing his Victorian Police badge, and introduced themselves as being from the Costigan Royal Commission. 'Shit,' said the poor man, 'what have I done?' Sadly, it was not Bruce McWilliam at all. Profuse apologies were offered, and they tried again.

Subsequently their cries of 'Hi, Bruce' did locate McWilliam just as he was about to board the flight. They accused him, without ceremony, of removing the documents they had come to Hong Kong to see. He denied that he had and invited them twice to search his luggage, which they declined to do. When they asked him why he was in Hong Kong looking at the documents, he refused to tell them, knowing as a lawyer that he didn't have to.

Back in Sydney five days later, McWilliam admitted in court proceedings that he had gone to Singapore and Hong Kong on Kerry Packer's instructions. He again denied having concealed or removed any documents or instructing others to do so.[27] Costigan, meanwhile, had already accused him in a public statement of preventing the investigators from getting at the truth:

> In Brisbane sittings I sought from Brian Ray his consent for me to obtain files from him in Singapore and Hong Kong ... and in due course he signed an authority which confirmed that consent ...

Pursuant to that, I went to Singapore last week for a few days . . . Both in Singapore and Hong Kong the commission was met with a blank wall . . . orchestrated from Sydney and quite deliberately intended to keep from the commission's eyes the documents which it had previously been indicated and authorised that I could have.

In addition to that, Mr McWilliam was flown from Sydney to Singapore last Sunday and then to Hong Kong on Monday, clearly playing a part in the instructions issuing from Sydney to hide from the commission's eyes the documents which had previously been authorised.[28]

Costigan later repeated this allegation in terms that related specifically to Packer, and which referred back to the original removal of the file from Sydney, saying in his final published report:

I conducted private examination of his [Packer's] lawyers concerning the removal of a file from their offices to Singapore and Hong Kong . . . I conclude that the removal of the file was deliberate, and was for the purpose of frustrating my inquiries and was at the specific instructions of Mr Packer.[29]

His confidential Volume 9 went even further, saying that:

The file contains documents which are material not only to my Commission, but are relevant to the criminal investigation that I recommend should be undertaken in respect of the film scheme.[30]

Packer denied he had had anything to do with it. He and his emissary McWilliam maintained that the documents were neither Packer's nor under his control. Brian Ray, meanwhile, had already said that he had been mistaken in thinking the file belonged to him. The question of who was behind Progress Credits remained a mystery.[31]

Further light was shed on it, however, almost two years later in mid 1985, when Brian Ray, Ian Beames and Donald Lockyer appeared in court in Melbourne on charges of conspiracy to defraud the Commonwealth. After fifty-four days of evidence, Packer's friend Brian Ray was committed for trial on the 'exceedingly strong probability' that he was involved in a 'dishonest and unscrupulous scheme . . . to deprive the Commonwealth of income tax'.[32] Beames and Lockyer had already entered pleas of guilty and were sentenced to two years and two years eight months respectively.

The fraud charges related to Lockyer's bottom-of-the-harbour scheme to strip companies of their profits and then dump them, rather than to the film scheme that Costigan was targeting. But the prosecution made it clear that it believed the two schemes to be interwoven. Lockyer and his wife Suzi had pocketed most of the proceeds from the bottom-of-the-harbour scheme, garnering at least $12 million between them. But according to the prosecution case as summed up by the magistrate, Beames and Ray had also benefited, and so had another 'silent partner':

> It is said to be clear from the evidence that . . . Ray and another person (not a party to these proceedings) acted in silent partnership with Beames as financiers of the scheme.[33]

The prosecution strongly suggested that the silent partner was Kerry Packer. A key part of the prosecution case was that the illegal bottom-of-the-harbour scheme was financed by the very same money that had funded the film scheme (which Packer denied having provided). The prosecution's evidence showed that some $922 000 had been sent in from Singapore on 21 November 1979 for Brian Ray after he had approached the Sydney lawyers Allen Allen & Hemsley for help in arranging a loan. This marked it unmistakably as the money from Progress Credits. The prosecution then commented on why they believed such a roundabout route had been chosen:

> The money that Ray and his partner put up came, as the evidence discloses, from Singapore. One might well ask . . . why it was

necessary to bring in money from Singapore for this purpose and for the purpose of the film scheme. The answer we say is obvious, because it thereby achieved to hide the identity of the third party involved.[34]

But there was more direct evidence than this. It was not disputed by the defence that Beames had collected one-third of the profits of the partnership, while Ray had collected the other two-thirds. The prosecution maintained that one half of Ray's share had gone to his silent partner. And the magistrate had agreed that it seemed likely, saying that there was 'credible evidence' that

> Ray and another person (or perhaps persons) associated with Molland Pty Ltd took a charge securing the assets and income of Halboham Pty Ltd, a company used by Beames to market a film scheme and to acquire current-year-profit companies which for the most part were subsequently disposed of in a way dishonestly designed to defraud the Commonwealth.[35]

Halboham Pty Ltd, according to the magistrate, was a Beames company that had been central to the bottom-of-the-harbour and film schemes, and had derived its assets and income from precisely these tax-dodging activities. Its ill-gotten gains had been mortgaged jointly to a Ray company called Savannah Investments Pty Ltd and a Packer company called Molland Pty Ltd, which was the trustee of several Packer family trusts. Molland's two shareholders were Kerry and Clyde Packer, while Kerry Packer was also a director. The clear implication was that this Packer company was entitled to a share in the profits of the film scheme or the bottom-of-the-harbour scheme, or both.

But again there was more, for there was also 'credible evidence', according to the magistrate, that a key Lockyer company in the bottom-of-the-harbour scam owed money to the same two Ray and Packer companies:

Famiti Pty Ltd, which Lockyer used as a vehicle for the purposes of his nefarious current-year-profit scheme, jointly owed Savannah and Molland $175 000 for 'services rendered'. The irresistible inference of this piece of evidence is that Savannah and Molland were assisting Lockyer to implement his scheme, and receiving fees for that assistance.[36]

Or, to put it more bluntly, the magistrate believed there was 'credible evidence' that a company owned by Kerry Packer and his brother was profiting from an illegal bottom-of-the-harbour scheme that had defrauded the Australian taxman.

None of this, of course, demonstrated that he was guilty of fraud or that he even knew the money was being used in this way. And it is essential to point out that no charges were brought against him. But if the magistrate's findings were accepted, there was support for Costigan's belief that Packer had lied to the royal commission.

CHAPTER THIRTEEN

THE GOANNA

*Every statement in the 'Goanna' case summary is
fallacious . . . It is extraordinary that these grotesque
allegations could ever emanate from a royal commission.*

Kerry Packer, 28 September 1984

Costigan's belief in 1983 that inquiries into Kerry Packer were
worth pursuing was heightened by the big businessman's obvious determination to avoid being questioned. By the time he
did eventually take the stand it was mid February 1984, three
months after he had first been subpoenaed to appear, and
Costigan was running short of time to complete his inquiries.
Packer had turned up in November, accompanied by Australia's
highest-paid QC, Tom Hughes, but had refused to answer questions that weren't specifically related to the painters and dockers.
He had then waged war on Costigan in the courts in an unsuccessful attempt to have the original subpoenas set aside. His
lawyers and alleged partners, Ray and Beames, had joined him
in this action.

By the time Kerry Packer did finally walk up the steps of
Melbourne's Hawthorn Magistrates Court to answer Costigan's
questions, there was nationwide interest in what the showdown
might bring. But those who had been expecting a public spec-
tacle were soon disappointed, for most of his evidence was taken
in closed session. The public examination dealt only with the
$225 000 cash payments from Beames and Ray, Progress Credits
and the film scheme, and produced answers that covered little

fresh ground, while the confidential examination remained, for the moment, just that.

By this stage, Costigan had only four months left to wind up the commission, but new investigations into Packer's affairs now spread so rapidly that they soon occupied the bulk of his work. By April 1984, his interest had expanded to cover all of Packer's ventures with Ray. To these had been added a hashish importation inquiry from 1978 that had been dug up and resuscitated, and the reported suicide of one of Ray's former employees. There was also the withdrawal of a million dollars in cash from a Sydney bank by Packer's chauffeur and secretary that Packer said he had used for gambling, so that there were five or six different matters on Costigan's books involving Packer. In Costigan's view each of these merited a major investigation by his commission, yet there was time to complete none of them. In fact, three or four of Costigan's more serious allegations that were eventually made public were subjected only to the most cursory examination.

Costigan would later complain that Packer's reluctance to give evidence had delayed him so much that his investigations could not be completed. And certainly the pressures of time became intolerable when the Royal Commissioner was put out of action for several weeks by illness, after being rushed into hospital over Easter. But while this may have explained the thinness of some of Costigan's allegations against Packer, it only made it more important that they should not be made public. Yet that was precisely what happened next.

Shortly after the royal commission was wound up at the end of June 1984, forty confidential 'case summaries' were handed over to the National Crime Authority, amid grumblings by Costigan's staff that they needed more time and complaints that the NCA wasn't competent to complete the investigations. Some two months later there was still no news about which ones the NCA would accept, and rumours were spreading that some of the cases would be buried.[1] Then, in early September, correspondence was tabled in Federal Parliament revealing that Costigan had warned Prime Minister Bob Hawke on several occasions that the NCA would be unable to pursue his inquiries properly because he had never had enough time to brief its investigators.

In this climate of rumour and excitement, Costigan's sensational and highly confidential 'case summaries' were leaked to the *National Times*, whose editor Brian Toohey had no hesitation in publishing them. Amazingly, both Costigan and his leading counsel Doug Meagher QC say that they were given advance warning that this was going to happen, yet decided that it was unnecessary to take action. A week before the case summaries were published, Brian Toohey flew down from Sydney to have lunch with Meagher at Melbourne's Jade Lotus restaurant. According to Meagher, Toohey not only revealed to him that he had copies of the royal commission's confidential case summaries, he also disclosed the name of the person who had leaked them. Meagher says he then reported this conversation to Costigan. Costigan confirms this.

The events are somewhat bizarre, for there is no question that the lunch took place or that Toohey and Meagher were there, but it seems odd that an experienced journalist should give a senior officer of a royal commission the chance to stop publication of such highly sensitive documents and even odder that he would put his source in danger. Toohey today denies absolutely that he told Meagher the name of the person who leaked him the documents or that he revealed the fact that he had them. He says they merely discussed the work of the royal commission.[2]

Meagher's account of what happened next is also remarkable. Here was the editor of a newspaper that had been fearless in publishing such leaks allegedly warning that he possessed highly secret and highly damaging royal commission documents that he quite clearly intended to publish. Meagher says his response to this was to report back to Frank Costigan QC that he did not believe that Toohey was telling the truth. According to Meagher (and again Costigan confirms this), he and Costigan discussed the matter at length and concluded that Toohey could not in fact have the documents because security had been so tight. Therefore no action was taken to prevent publication.

Meagher believes that it would have been a simple matter to stop the article had they chosen to do so—the Attorney-General could have sought (and would surely have gained) an injunction from the courts to prevent publication. But the Attorney-General was not asked to go in to bat, and publication went ahead.[3]

Even if you didn't know who they referred to, the Costigan case summaries made for pretty stirring stuff. But if you did (as everyone soon would), they were quite incredible. Reprinted verbatim by the *National Times*, with almost no editing, they focussed on a character called the 'Goanna' and dealt in crudely-simplistic terms with the allegations that had been made against him. History does not relate Packer's reaction on reading them (or having them read to him) but he would have been entitled to feel suicidal or homicidal or both, for some of the allegations were quite outrageous. The 'Goanna' summary opened with allegations about drugs and pornography and movements of large amounts of cash, and went on from there. The following extract gives some idea of its flavour:

There are circumstances giving rise to suspicion that a group of people including the Goanna and three partners may be involved in the importation and distribution of drugs. Similar suspicions arise as to their involvement in the importation and distribution of pornographic video . . .

There are large movements of cash. There is an instance of the Goanna cashing a cheque for a substantial sum. His explanation defies logic or understanding. Indeed, he asserted he applied the money to paying gambling debts, not wishing to reveal his gambling habit to the bank. Examination of his bank accounts reveals no such reluctance.

The Goanna's lifestyle is flamboyant and very expensive. While he has considerable assets, it may be doubted whether they are sufficient to provide the cash resources to support his gambling habit and lavish living. The style of living suggests resources beyond those which are overt and legitimate. They may be met by provision of money from schemes adumbrated in other relevant criminal activities noted with this, but even those would seem unlikely to generate the returns necessary . . .

The importation of drugs reveals substantial planning. It was in commercial quantities. It was cleverly concealed . . .

There were several other allegations involving the Goanna that were listed under different case-names, most of which made the case against the Goanna appear strong, if not cut and dried. In a section headed *Code: Playhouse*, which dealt with the film scheme, he was accused of involvement in 'fraudulent tax evasion and currency violation'. In another section headed *Code: Monarch*, which dealt with some of Packer's ventures with Brian Ray, there were allegations of involvement in real estate fraud and further tax evasion. Finally, in *Code: Parricidium* there were allegations that 'the Goanna's partner' was one of the main suspects in a murder.

Aside from the 'murder', the most serious charge against the Goanna was that he was engaged in drug trafficking on a grand scale. And it is worth setting this out in more detail for it was probably the most damaging of Costigan's 'allegations' or 'suspicions' yet also one of the most absurd. In April 1978, a large quantity of cannabis oil had been discovered in more than a hundred condoms hidden in the walls of two packing cases at Sydney's Maynair bond store. The cases had been consigned from Katmandu to Kerry Packer, Chairman of World Series Cricket, and opened by the customs agents working for Australian Consolidated Press. Inside was a collection of brass figures and a smattering of cricket books, including several copies of Alan Knott's book on wicket-keeping. One of the customs agents had thought that the walls of the boxes looked thicker than usual and had poked a spike through the side of one, whereupon a thick brown liquid had started oozing through the hole. The Narcotics Bureau had immediately been called in and had interviewed a number of people, including Kerry Packer himself, but had closed down the investigation soon after for lack of leads. At no stage had Packer been a suspect—and even Costigan had made this clear when questioning him in confidential session—yet the allegation had achieved great prominence in the case summaries handed over to the NCA. Apart from anything else, the charge appeared to be a gross insult to Packer's intelligence, for he would have needed to be breathtakingly stupid to have had the package addressed to him if he really had been a drug importer.

The only other 'evidence' to suggest that Packer was involved in drugs appeared to be even more tenuous. His name had been discovered in the teledex of the well-known Sydney crime boss George Freeman when it was confiscated by police, and his so-called 'partners' at Essington had paid money into the notorious Nugan Hand bank during 1978 at supposedly significant times to supposedly significant people, at around the time when the cannabis shipment had arrived. (Nugan Hand was later the subject of inquiry by another royal commission that investigated its involvement in drug financing and money laundering.) But even if this 'evidence' were to be taken seriously, none of it would have been enough to get Packer within a hundred miles of a court of law on drug charges. And yet, with no other apparent basis, drug importation had become the central (and ultimately very public) allegation against Packer and the one that supposedly explained his lavish lifestyle and frequent large dealings in cash.[4]

Shortly after the *National Times* article was published, graffiti began to appear around Sydney identifying the Goanna as Kerry Packer. But it was already an open secret among journalists, lawyers and politicians that this was so. Before long, the possibility was aired that his name might be revealed under the cover of parliamentary privilege, and at this point Packer sensibly decided to go on the attack, issuing an 8000-word public statement on 28 September 1984 that denied all the material allegations and addressed the injustices in the way in which he had been treated. The following deals with the drug charges, together with Packer's reasons for breaking silence.[5]

My identity as the Goanna has become well-known by word of mouth and veiled hint through the media. Initially, I did not believe one should dignify these sort of gutter allegations with any response, but sadly, I feel I owe it to my employees, my business associates and my friends to make an answer.

More importantly, perhaps, I owe it to my family to respond to these disgraceful allegations. These innuendos and allegations emanating from the inquiries of the royal commission have caused immense suffering on the part of my wife and children for nearly a year. They have been fuelled by what I believe has been malicious rumour and innuendo in newspapers controlled by commercial rivals of mine, John Fairfax & Sons Ltd. My children, who are still at school, have had to endure cruel taunts and insults. I do not believe that I should permit that to continue.

Each and every one of the allegations made against me in the National Times article are false and demonstrably so. It is extraordinary that this disgusting publication should place me in a position where I effectively have to prove my innocence. However, so ludicrous and misconceived are the allegations that my innocence is easily established.

The first allegation made against me is that I have been involved in the financing of drug importation. The bulk of the allegations made against me are of a completely general kind. This makes them virtually impossible to refute. If I am accused of 'financing drug trafficking' without being given any particulars of the particular drug importations that I am alleged to have financed, how am I to refute that other than in equally general terms? The only particular reference made about me in the National Times material concerns a drug importation in 1978. It is suggested that I was involved in that drug importation, that it was not properly investigated and that I had tried to explain it on the basis of it being common practice for drug importers to address their deliveries to persons other than themselves. The facts of that importation are as follows:

In 1978, the customs department at Australian Consolidated Press Ltd was notified that there was a large box at the airport addressed to me as chairman of World Series Cricket. The box had been consigned by someone in Katmandu, Nepal.

The ACP customs department contacted my office and were advised that I did not know anybody in that country. The normal practice of the ACP customs department is that when parcels arrive at the airport addressed to a Consolidated Press Group company that the customs officers are advised of the contents of the parcel and duty is then paid on the basis of that advice. It is rare that boxes are opened to be inspected, given the good working relationship that exists between the ACP customs department and the customs officers at the airport. The ACP customs department advised Customs at the airport that they did not know what was in the box and that it should be opened and inspected. Therefore it was in fact as a result of a request by the ACP customs department that the box was opened.

The box was opened at the airport and was found to contain some bronze statuary and, as I recall, some books on cricket. The walls of the box were also found to contain hashish oil.

I was interviewed by officers of the Narcotics Bureau as indeed were members of my staff. The universal conclusion was that someone was either trying to embarrass me (and it must be recalled that at this stage the World Series Cricket controversy was at its height and in certain quarters I was a most unpopular person) or that somebody with access to the Consolidated Press building was importing drugs and hoped after the box had been emptied to take it away and remove the hashish from the walls of the box. At no time did anyone suggest that I may have been involved in this importation. I imagine it would be a quite unusual thing for a drug importer to address his importations to himself.

In February of this year I was questioned in confidential session at the Costigan Royal Commission about this importation. The royal commission showed me a film of the box which had apparently been taken by the Narcotics Bureau at the time it was discovered. In the course of that confidential session Mr Costigan made it quite plain to me that there was no suggestion that I was involved in the import- ation of these drugs. He said to me: 'I just hope you understand that so far as the commission is concerned it is not making allegations against you of that kind at all.' Indeed Mr Costigan explained his interest in the importation by telling me that the company which at the time had the contract for cleaning the Consolidated Press building employed certain persons who were associated with the painters and dockers. I took it from that that Mr Costigan suspected that one of the painters and dockers in the cleaning company had arranged for the importation in the expectation that once the box was unpacked it would be disposed of with the rest of the rubbish and therefore could be recovered by one of the cleaners . . .

The 'Goanna' case summary goes on to say 'at the time of the [1978 drug] delivery, two of the partners paid substantial sums of money to Nugan Hand as a deposit'. I understand that the two 'partners' referred to are two Sydney businessmen with whom I have recently been associated in some major commercial activities. It is true that they had placed money on deposit earning high rates of interest with the Nugan Hand bank in 1978. It must be recalled that Nugan Hand was regarded as a high-flying merchant bank in the days before it crashed. They had \$100 000 on deposit with that bank at the time it crashed, and they are, unfortunately for them, amongst the long list of unpaid creditors.

Both these men have been interviewed by the Royal Commission and at no time did the Royal Commissioner put to them any suggestion that their dealings with Nugan Hand had anything to do with drugs.

But there is another defect in the case summary. Whilst it may be true to describe those gentlemen as partners of mine as of today, I believe that in 1978 I had not met either of them. Certainly, I did not become involved with them in any commercial activities until early 1980. Accordingly, it is quite false to say that these people were 'partners' of mine in 1978.

The 'Goanna' material goes on to suggest that I have a lavish and expensive lifestyle and that my considerable assets are insufficient to provide the cash resources necessary to support both my lavish living and my gambling. As anyone who knows me would attest, both my lifestyle and my gambling are well within my means . . .

Having covered drugs, Packer's statement went on to deal in detail with the allegation that he had been involved in the importation and distribution of pornography. Costigan's investigators had received a tip-off about this just before the commission was wound up, and had not been able to establish whether there was any evidence to support it. It then dealt briefly with tax and alleged fraud in real estate, before making a scathing rebuttal of alleged strong-arm tactics by a solicitor said to be close to the Goanna. Finally, it rounded off with a general condemnation of Costigan's work.

> It will be seen from the foregoing that every statement in the 'Goanna' case summary is fallacious. They are based on either a deliberate misinterpretation of the facts as known to the commission or careless conclusions reached with reckless indifference to the facts.
>
> It is extraordinary that these grotesque allegations could ever emanate from a royal commission . . .

A month after Packer's statement, at the end of October 1984, Costigan's final report was published. There was no repetition in the public volumes of the allegations about drugs, and little about tax schemes or real estate frauds, but the public was told that three confidential volumes were devoted to Packer and his associates, and Costigan made it clear that he anticipated 'proceedings in the courts' once investigations were complete. These three volumes, 9, 10 and 11, were said to be 'substantial'.[6]

Surprisingly, the public report did deal with the death of a former Queensland bank manager who had shot himself, or been shot, while working for Brian Ray. This was the 'murder' that the *National Times* 'case summary' *Code: Parricidium* had referred to, in which the Goanna's partner was alleged to be one of the main suspects. Costigan recommended that the death be investigated by a special task force that would gather evidence for an inquest. This inquest would be held in Brisbane in early December 1984.

But it would not turn out to be the trial of Kerry Packer, as some expected, so much as the trial of Francis Costigan, for it would provide a crucial test of the royal commission's findings.

CHAPTER FOURTEEN

MURDER OR SUICIDE?

*However Mr Coote died, I had no involvement in his
death in any way. Mr Costigan has never explicitly
alleged that I did have such involvement. However, he has
by wicked inference suggested that I had some unspecified
connection with the death of this man.*

Kerry Packer, 2 November 1984

Ian Coote had been shot dead on 16 December 1982, the day
before he was to be charged with nineteen counts of fraud by the
Queensland fraud squad. After a brief investigation, the police
had decided that his death was quite obviously suicide. Costigan
was equally sure that it was murder, and devoted confidential
Volume 10 of his final report to the shooting.

Until two years before he died, Coote had been manager of
the Capalaba branch of the Bank of NSW in suburban Brisbane,
where Brian Ray kept his accounts, and in this capacity had
played an important role in facilitating the notorious film tax-
avoidance scheme. He had also arranged large amounts of cash
for delivery to Brian Ray, and had later become a director of
several of Ray's companies.

While most of the details of Coote's death were kept confidential by Costigan, the royal commission's public report referred
to it in the context of investigations into Ray and Packer, and
Costigan stated quite baldly that he was 'satisfied' that Coote had
been murdered.[1] Coote's wife June immediately fanned the
flames by telling a Brisbane newspaper that she had never

believed that her husband had committed suicide, saying: 'I know he did not kill himself. I did not believe it when the police said he had shot himself and I said so at the time. It's time there was an inquiry into the whole filthy business.'[2]

Packer, for his part, had already dealt with the suggestion that it was murder in his long September statement answering the allegations in the *National Times* case summaries, saying:

> I was informed that the facts relating to this death which pointed to suicide were as follows:
>
> 1. The deceased had been accused of defrauding the Bank of NSW whilst he was a manager of a Queensland branch. The alleged defalcations did not relate to me, nor, I am informed, to any of my 'partners'.
>
> 2. He was due to be questioned by the Queensland Fraud Squad in relation to these allegations the following day.
>
> 3. He had been extremely depressed and anxious about these allegations, and those people working with him had noticed the effect these allegations had had upon his demeanour.
>
> 4. He had deliberately placed all his affairs in order prior to his death.
>
> 5. He was killed with a blast from his own shotgun . . .
>
> It is . . . a monstrous injustice for this sort of allegation to be published without any evidentiary basis. As I understand the facts concerning this man's death, every piece of evidence points to suicide.

Coote's body had been discovered nine days before Christmas on a piece of waste ground just off the Pacific Highway in the Brisbane suburb of Loganholme, some two hours after dark. Police had received complaints that a car had been abandoned with its headlights on, and had arrived to find Coote's Holden Commodore with the driver's door open and the former bank manager lying beside it. He had died from a single gunshot wound near the top of the ribcage which had severed a major artery. Next to the body and partially covered by it was a .410

small-calibre shotgun, whose barrel was pointing towards Coote's chest. On the ground was a mark in the dirt that could have been caused by the gun's recoil. It appeared to police that he had pressed the barrel against his chest, leaned over and pulled the trigger. The gun was his, and the open boot of the car contained an almost-full pack of cartridges. The investigating policeman wrote in his notebook that there were no suspicious circumstances. Eight days later, his report recommended that no inquest be held since it was a clear-cut case of suicide.

To those who knew him, Coote had been a kind, considerate and helpful man with a happy outlook on life but a tendency to fuss. Married with three children, he had appeared to be a typical suburban bank manager, treading his unremarkable path through life. But there had been warning signs that not all was well. He had been overweight and drank too much, and had seemed insecure. Mild-mannered and retiring, he had also had few friends to share his troubles with and had never discussed business with his wife. Yet he had been a worried man, who would have been an important witness in Costigan's investigations if he had lived long enough to testify. It was this that was supposed to have provided a motive for murder.

As manager of the Capalaba branch, Coote had been at the centre of one of the more bizarre transactions that Costigan had investigated, in which $120 000 had been picked up by a mysterious 'Mr Richards', who had stuffed the money into a suitcase in the bank manager's office while a taxi waited outside.[3] But, just as importantly, Coote had arranged the funny-money financing that had made the Beames–Ray–Packer film scheme possible, sometimes leaving the bank exposed to the tune of several million dollars. In addition he had granted unorthodox loans to buyers of houses on the Victoria Point estate in Brisbane, which Ray and Packer had developed together, and in which Costigan believed (incorrectly) that fraud was involved. Then, after leaving the bank in late 1980, he had worked for Ray as financial controller, allegedly acting as his bagman and twice delivering suitcases full of cash.[4]

In addition to the dodgy things Coote had done for Brian Ray, he had cost the Bank of NSW a lot of money by giving loans to several of his customers without proper security. And this had got him into trouble with the police. His prime motive had not been gain, for he had received no kickbacks, but the bank had lost some $350 000 through his actions and the rules had been broken. He had also betrayed his employer's trust by lending himself money for a bit of property speculation on the side. Worst of all, he had forged documents and altered entries in an attempt to cover his tracks. The bank had first raised the matter in May 1980 when an internal report had questioned his lending practices, and only six months later Coote had left, perhaps because he feared that the game was up. The bank had then conducted a special audit and called in the fraud squad, news of whose investigation had been broadcast on the radio in August 1981 and brought to Coote's attention.

After leaving the bank, Coote had gone to work for Brian Ray, and both men had tried hard to find out what the police were after. Coote was quite naturally worried that they were on to him, but Ray also had good reason to be concerned. Coote had rung his colleagues at the bank; Ray had phoned a detective inspector in the fraud squad; everything had then gone quiet for fifteen months. Finally, on 6 December 1982, ten days before Coote's death, Sergeant Hilary Huey of the Brisbane Fraud Squad had rung to ask him to come in for an interview. They had already drawn up charges which they intended to lay regardless of anything he might say in his defence. On the morning the interview was due to take place his solicitor, Jeremy Charlston, phoned the police to say that Coote had shot himself.

In the minds of the investigating police, Coote's death was unquestionable suicide. It was his gun, they were his cartridges, there was no sign of anyone else being involved, and he had been found lying across the gun barrel. But, apart from that, he appeared to have had good reason to take his life, insofar as anyone could have. It was clear for a start that he had known for fifteen months about the fraud squad investigation and had been anxious about it. It was clear, too, that he had forged documents and knew he could go to jail. He also had cause to worry about what the bank might do to recover its $350 000 loss, for there was every chance that it would seek compensation. Two weeks before his death he had read in the local paper that another bank manager on the Gold Coast had lost his house when the bank took court action against him to recover monies. Only days after that, when the police had told him they wanted to interview him, he had become worried and depressed, according to Ray's secretary Gayle Coward, and had said that he could lose everything if he were charged.

Before he died, Coote had taken steps to tidy up his affairs. Two days before his death he had paid off a bridging loan on the house. The next day he had closed his joint bank account and paid all the money into his wife's personal account. Finally, only hours before the shooting, he had obtained a bank cheque payable to the Australian Taxation Office to meet an outstanding tax bill. As a bank manager, he would have known that a cheque signed by a dead man was likely to be dishonoured. Back at the office, according to Ray and Coward, he had brought the cash books and files up to date, entered the account balances on the company cheque stubs and cleared all the rubbish out of his drawers. He had left his desk clear of everything except a calendar and accessories. He had then placed a Christmas card for Brian Ray and presents for the Rays' two children on the desk and left a card for Coward on top of the filing cabinet.

Taken at face value, this evidence suggested that Coote was indeed planning to take his own life. But there were other reasons to believe it to be so. He was a man who had cared about appearances and security, yet had been facing shame, financial ruin, and possibly jail. Even if he had defeated the fraud charges that were to be laid against him, legal costs of $50 000 could have forced him to sell his house, while conviction could have brought prison, bankruptcy, and eviction for his wife and family. Conviction would also have lost him the proceeds of a valuable life insurance policy, which had been taken out by the trust company that employed him and was valid only while his employment continued. Suicide, on the other hand, ensured that his wife would be able to collect the full $181 000, as she later did.

Although Costigan's investigators were aware of most of this evidence, they had dismissed the notion of suicide almost out of hand. Before they had even challenged the police or pathologist on the forensic and ballistics evidence, they had reached the firm conclusion that:

> The suicide theory may be rejected. The evidence not only fails to support it, but shows it is a most improbable explanation for his death . . . Murder is the only alternative.[5]

Looking at the *Squirrel Analysis*, which was the commission's working document on Packer-related matters, it is hard to understand how Costigan's investigators had come to this conclusion. But they seem to have reached it in spite of the evidence rather than because of it. And they appear to have been determined to believe that a murder had occurred, taking an extremely sceptical approach to the police version of events.[6] It is hard to summarise all their reasoning convincingly, since some of it is extremely tendentious, but they pointed to several things that threw doubt on the suicide theory. In the first place, Coote had left no note to explain his action, which seemed odd for a man who loved his family; he had also promised on the morning of the day he died to take his son Christmas shopping after work. Even stranger, only hours before supposedly killing himself, he had changed the time of an appointment for the next day, and had telephoned his accountant, promising to have a Christmas drink with him. The accountant and several others, including his wife, had found him cheerful before he died, had not noticed that he was depressed and had not thought of him as someone who might kill himself. So on these accounts, it was argued, Coote had not appeared to be a man who planned to take his own life.

But it is hard to believe that these circumstances would have been taken so seriously if Costigan's investigators had not already been convinced that there were powerful people who wanted Coote killed. If they hadn't, in other words, already made up their minds.

The *Squirrel Analysis* identified two people as the 'murder' suspects: one was Packer's friend and partner Brian Ray and 'those he represents'. The other was Ray's brother-in-law Phillip Carver. Costigan's confidential case summaries, printed in the *National Times*, did a similar job, noting that 'two avenues' were being pursued 'to determine responsibility for the murder', and adding that the second led directly to 'the Goanna's partner'. It needed no great skill to work out, as many did, that this description also referred to Brian Ray, and Costigan's public report soon made this abundantly clear.[7]

Phillip Carver's alleged motive for murder, according to Costigan's analysts, was to prevent the former bank manager giving evidence against him on fraud charges. Carver was alleged to have defrauded Packer and Ray during one of their more bizarre business ventures involving a 'youth drug' called Provital, to which Carver had introduced them. Packer and Ray had poured hundreds of thousands of dollars into this project of Carver's in the belief that this supposed wonder drug would earn them a fortune, and had backed a huge television advertising campaign featuring Cary Grant that would sell it to Australia. But their dreams had been dashed by the New South Wales Health Department, which had soon revealed that it had banned all advertising of the drug three years earlier until the claims that it made people 'younger' could be verified. The whole Provital episode hardly spoke volumes for Packer and Ray's business acumen or, indeed, for their choice of business partners, since Carver was already facing fraud charges when they began the project together in January 1980, to which arson charges had been added a few weeks later.

But more to the point, as far as the death of Coote was concerned, this Provital venture was supposed to have given

Carver a motive for murder, for soon after the setback, Ray and Coote had discovered that Carver was embezzling the company's funds, and had called in the fraud squad. Coote had then given important evidence against Carver at the committal proceedings and had told police that he feared for his safety as a result. Brian Ray, meanwhile, had also expressed fear of what Carver might do and had accepted police protection for his family for two days while he was away from home. The New South Wales police already suspected Carver of planning to kill the key prosecution witness in the arson case, and had a note from him allegedly demanding the return of $10 000 from a hit-man who had accepted the contract but not carried it out.[8]

Costigan's alternative, and apparently preferred, theory was that Coote had been killed on the orders of Brian Ray to prevent him telling the police about the supposedly fraudulent tax-avoidance scheme and an alleged fraud to do with Ray and Packer's real estate development at Victoria Point. Or as the *National Times*'s 'confidential case summaries' put it:

> One explanation for his death is that some people were anxious to prevent him talking. There were a large number of matters which the Goanna's partner would have strongly wished the dead man would not speak about.[9]

The evidence for Ray wanting Coote silenced was largely supposition, and supposition of the flimsiest kind. But insofar as there was any, it came from Carver, who had told Costigan's counsel, Doug Meagher, about a phone call he had made to Coote two days before the shooting, in which the former bank manager had supposedly said his life was in danger:

> Carver: He said he had been threatened; people had been to his home. He talked about a person with a gun.
> Meagher: Did he name the person?
> Carver: No.

Meagher: So a man had come to his home with a gun?

Carver: He did not say singular. He had been threatened many times. He said I do not want you to become involved.

Meagher: Did you understand that he was conveying to you that he had been threatened as to his life.

Carver: Yes, yes, definitely . . .

Meagher: He put it to you to stop having anything to do with it. If you talk you are going to suffer what I am suffering?

Carver: That is right. He said that, you know, it is a dangerous world. You do not know what you are playing with. It is too big or too dangerous for you to understand. He said think about it before you do anything. He was worried. He said, it is all happening. He started crying then. He just said he had been a good man.[10]

The thrust of Carver's evidence, which Costigan appeared to take seriously and even accept, was that Brian Ray and Packer had powerful friends and would stop at nothing. To put it as Packer would have done, Costigan and his investigators had begun to believe their own conspiracy theories.

When the inquest into the death of Coote was finally held in December 1984, the policeman who had investigated the shooting, Detective Senior Constable Gary Wilkinson, was asked by Packer's counsel Malcolm Turnbull to recall a conversation he had had with Doug Meagher QC, counsel assisting Costigan. According to this evidence, Meagher had told the policeman during a break in the commission's proceedings that they were determined to nail Packer.

Wilkinson: He said he was involved in organised crime in Australia. He said that they were going to get him or words to that effect.

Turnbull: Can you remember the exact words he used? Just think for a moment.

Wilkinson: I can't remember the entire context of the conversation but one part I do remember. He said: 'He's a prominent criminal and myself and the Commissioner intend to destroy him.'[11]

Ray's specific motive for wanting Coote silenced was alleged to be a major fraud involving Victoria Point, Packer and Ray's housing development in Brisbane, which had been one of the matters referred to in the *Code: Monarch* case summary reported in the notorious *National Times* article. Ray had learned from Coote that the fraud squad intended to take action over loans the bank had made there, and Ray told Costigan he thought he had mentioned this to Packer.[12] Costigan had also 'received information' that the police had been ordered from on high to terminate their inquiry into Victoria Point after intervention by Ray.

Even if this were true, however, it was still a big leap to suggest that Ray would be so concerned about it that he would want Coote killed. And the members of the fraud squad conducting the inquiry said that it was in fact quite false to suggest that they had been called off. Furthermore, neither the police nor the Bank of NSW internal auditors shared Costigan's belief that there *had* been a major fraud. The bank's auditors had looked at Victoria Point during their investigation of Coote, but had not bothered to complain to the police. And the fraud squad had never pursued the matter in any depth. Neither believed that the trail led to Packer or Ray in any case. According to Ian Scotney, the man in charge of the audit, no evidence had been discovered at any time of a 'fraudulent connection between Ian Coote and Kerry Packer'. Nor did he believe that Ray was implicated.[13]

Such avenues aside, the only suggestion that Coote's life *might* have been threatened by Ray came from Carver himself, and he had not even identified the source of the threats. What was more, a less reliable witness could not have been imagined. He had been convicted on fraud charges in late 1982, charged with setting fire to his business to destroy the records (though acquitted), and was now facing further charges of defrauding Ray and Packer. The detective responsible for both fraud investigations, who had known him for four years, had talked to his friends, acquaintances and colleagues, and had interviewed him at length, was quite damning about his lack of credibility, and told the inquest:

I am of the firm opinion that Carver has little, if any, respect for telling the truth either privately or in public. I believe that he would not hesitate to say anything that he believed would be to his own personal advantage, either financially or otherwise, whether or not it was the truth . . . A significant number of former employees and business associates have expressed the opinion, in one form or another, that Phillip Carver is a person of low integrity and one whom, having encountered once, one would not trust again.[14]

In view of Carver's subsequent record, this was perceptive. Jailed in 1987 on forty-one counts of fraud relating to the Provital venture, he was to face charges in 1993 of obtaining property by deception in relation to $65 million of policyholders' funds that were lost in the aborted sale of the Occidental and Regal Life insurance companies in 1990. Given that he was already facing fraud charges in 1980, it seemed odd that Packer and Ray had ever done business with him.[15]

It seemed just as odd that Costigan's investigators had relied on Carver to such an extent. Given that Costigan believed Packer and Ray were involved in fraudulent tax schemes or worse, it was perhaps understandable that his sleuths thought that Coote might have been murdered. It is, after all, the job of investigators to have such nasty thoughts. But it was extraordinary that they had reached a firm conclusion on the basis of Carver's testimony and a few circumstantial titbits. It was also extraordinary that they had then gathered support for the murder theory in either the most unlucky or the most incompetent fashion.

In June 1984, as the commission was winding down, Costigan's investigators conducted their own ballistics tests to see whether they supported their conclusion, already reached in the *Squirrel Analysis*, that Coote had been murdered. The results of these tests gave Costigan his most potent argument for rejecting suicide as the cause of Coote's death, yet, incredibly, they were based on information that was completely wrong. Costigan's ballistics expert was told that the shotgun had blasted a hole in Coote's chest measuring 8 centimetres by 7 centimetres, which was almost the size of a tennis ball. In fact, the wound was not much bigger than a shirt button. This, as one might imagine, was a mistake of the utmost importance, for if the hole in Coote's chest was no bigger than the barrel (and it was not) then it was obvious that the gun had been fired at point-blank range or in contact with the skin. If it was the size of a tennis ball, as Costigan's investigators believed, it was clear that it must have been fired from some distance away.

How this mistake came about is difficult to understand, but it had been a comedy, or perhaps a tragedy, of errors. The pathologist who conducted the postmortem examination of Coote's body had recorded 'a large defect in the chest wall, measuring 8 centimetres x 7 centimetres', and this had been backed up by the police report prepared eight days after Coote's death, recording an '8 centimetres x 6 centimetres hole in the rib cage directly behind where the pellets entered'. Neither, however, had actually noted the size of the entry wound. And there was some doubt about whether the policeman who investigated Coote's death had attended the post-mortem at all.[16]

Reading back over the evidence and looking at the police photographs of Coote's body, it is almost impossible to comprehend how the mistake was allowed to endure. The pathologist, the policeman and a ballistics expert were all summoned to the stand in June 1984, yet none took the opportunity to set Costigan straight. The pathologist had left his notes in Brisbane because he had not been able to find them in time, the policeman had left his report in Brisbane because he hadn't been asked to bring it, and had not measured the wound himself anyway, while the ballistics expert assumed that the others must have got the measurements right, even though the police photographs suggested that they had got them wrong. Crucially, the pathologist failed to produce photographs of the wound taken in the mortuary that showed beyond any doubt that the hole in Coote's chest was tiny.

Thus, the real size of the wound was never discovered and, on the basis that it was the size of a tennis ball, Costigan was able to conclude with absolute certainty that Coote could not possibly have killed himself. Costigan's confidential Volume 10, Chapter 10, entitled *Cause of Death*, summed it up thus:

> From the ballistics evidence, I conclude that the muzzle of the weapon was between 500mm and a metre from Coote's chest at the time of discharge.
>
> This renders impossible the conclusion that he committed suicide and leaves as the only other rational conclusion that he was murdered.[17]

Fiction writers would not dare to dream up such a ridiculous scenario, but fact, as they say, is stranger than fiction. The enormous irony of it all was that the Institute of Forensic Pathology in Brisbane had actually taken close-up pictures of the wound in Coote's chest for teaching purposes, because the puncture represented such an excellent example of an entry wound from a .410 shotgun fired at very close range or in contact with the body. The photographer had no trouble recalling that the size of the wound was around twelve millimetres (or half an inch) in diameter. But he was never asked to supply his photographs to the Costigan inquiry or give evidence. He did, however, give evidence to the inquest into Coote's death in December 1984.

When produced to the inquest, the pathology photographs were impossible to argue with, showing beyond doubt that the hole in Coote's chest was no larger in diameter than the barrel of a .410 shotgun. The coroner therefore had a simple job, as Costigan would have done had the mistake not been made, in finding that:

> The wound in question was made when the shotgun barrel was in contact with the deceased's body. Upon the evidence before me there can be no doubt whatever on the issue. I am satisfied that it would be impossible for this particular wound to have been inflicted by the particular shotgun from a range of 500 millimetres to one metre.[18]

Having demolished Costigan's assertion that it would have been *impossible* for Coote to have committed suicide, the coroner found that there was nothing of substance to suggest that he had been murdered.

> There is a complete lack of evidence to support murder . . . the evidence clearly supports the view that the deceased did deliberately take his own life . . . I am satisfied that the deceased's death was self inflicted and that no other person was directly or indirectly responsible for his death.[19]

But in case there was any lingering doubt about Packer's innocence, the coroner now quelled it.

> I am aware that suggestions have been made that Mr Brian Ray or Mr Kerry Packer may have been in some way associated with the deceased's death. However, upon the evidence before me, there is no basis whatever for that suggestion. In my view it is not reasonable to entertain any suspicion in relation to such persons in relation to the deceased's death.[20]

But the damage to Costigan's theories did not end there, for the coroner had a further message about the credibility of Carver. As well as suggesting that Coote might have been murdered, Phillip Carver had been a key source for several of the fraud allegations against Packer and Ray and had given evidence to Costigan of large amounts of cash being moved offshore. But his evidence, according to the coroner, was simply not to be believed. Carver had told the inquest about notes that had now disappeared, conversations that his solicitors could not remember, and telephone calls to Coote's office that no one had witnessed or could recall. It even seemed likely that he had lied about his sensational call to Coote two days before the shooting. He had originally claimed to have phoned at 3 p.m. or 4 p.m., yet Coote had not returned from Sydney till much later. He had claimed that Coote had been deeply upset, yet his wife remembered no call. The coroner was not persuaded by any of it:

> Mr Carver was questioned at length before me and I found him an evasive and unimpressive witness upon whose evidence I could not rely. There are a number of sections of Mr Carver's evidence that I find quite unreasonable and improbable . . . Bearing in mind the lack of credibility of Mr Carver and the improbability of some of the facts outlined by Mr Carver, I am not prepared to find that such a phone call was in fact made.[21]

The coroner emphasised that he was not criticising Costigan's work and did not intend that his remarks should be so construed. Yet his findings carried the clear message that Costigan had got one of his most serious allegations totally wrong. Packer's counsel Malcolm Turnbull couldn't resist the opportunity to press home the attack:

> The decision here today and its evidence constitute a savage indictment of the disgraceful way in which Mr Costigan conducted his inquiry. Every aspect of his reasoning has been demolished and disowned, even by his own experts. Even the most basic inquiries were not made.
>
> He is not just unjust, he is incompetent, as has been revealed today. He and Meagher have set themselves up as amateur sleuths, but the way they have done their job would be a disgrace to any policeman in any jurisdiction.
>
> Mr Costigan's work is worthless because he has not done it in a competent manner, and that incompetence has been demonstrated today.[22]

It was not true that all the rest of Costigan's allegations were based on such flimsy stuff, but there was one sense in which Turnbull was entirely right, for after this defeat the royal commission's credibility was shattered. From December 1984 it was much more difficult for anyone to take Costigan's

allegations about Packer seriously. It was also much more difficult to argue for extensive investigation or prosecution. Few
public servants or politicians would want to risk being on the
end of another rout like that. The political battle for Packer was
therefore already half won.

Packer's reaction to the news, however, was neither cheerful
nor charming. In Adelaide the next day to watch Australia play
the West Indies at cricket, he was approached by a photographer
and a reporter who wanted a picture for the Sunday papers. The
big man, whose $350 million empire was built on his media
businesses, told them to leave him alone. The photographer, Paul
Lakatos, then tried to get some pictures through a telephoto lens
as Packer walked along the towpath by the side of the River
Torrens. Packer soon spotted him and gave chase, apparently
spitting with rage. When he caught up, he grabbed Lakatos by
the throat and ripped the camera from around his neck,
knocking him to the ground in the process.

Minutes later, when Packer's fury had subsided and he had
thought better of throwing the camera in the river, Lakatos
complained that he had been assaulted and his tooth broken.
Packer replied that he had only been after the camera and hadn't
hit the photographer, adding that if he had, the young man
would 'certainly have known about it'.

The historical parallel almost certainly escaped Packer's
notice, but forty years earlier one of Ezra Norton's bodyguards
had dished out the same sort of treatment to a photographer
whom Frank Packer had sent to snatch a picture of the *Truth*
proprietor at Darlinghurst courthouse. The bodyguard had been
unlucky enough to be sentenced to three months in jail for
assault. The difference was, perhaps, that Norton's minder had
never apologised. Kerry Packer, however, rang the Adelaide
Advertiser later that day to say sorry and to offer to meet the
dental bill.

CHAPTER FIFTEEN

ENTIRELY INNOCENT

An incalculable and unwarranted damage has
been done to Mr Packer . ... he is entitled to be
regarded by his fellow citizens as unsullied by
the allegations and insinuations which have
been made against him.

Attorney-General Lionel Bowen,
26 March 1987

Seven months after the publication of Costigan's final report, and almost a year after the handing over of his confidential case summaries, there was still no formal response from the government or the extremely secretive National Crime Authority, and it was anybody's guess what had happened to the recommendations about Packer and his partners. An election had intervened to slow things down, and the NCA had also not given these particular investigations top priority. Then, when the response did finally come, it was hardly illuminating. On 21 May 1985 the Attorney-General, Gareth Evans, told Parliament in a marvellously empty phrase that matters requiring further investigation had been referred to the appropriate authorities.

One of those 'appropriate' authorities was the Queensland fraud squad, which had been asked in October 1984 to look at Costigan's allegations against Ray and Packer and was still going backwards and forwards with the NCA seven months later about what should be done. During this time, it had made no investigations at all of its own, and had merely analysed the material

Costigan had collected. Its investigators had reported first in December, after reading confidential Volumes 9 and 10, that it looked as though there were grounds for suspecting fraud, tax and currency offences, but had emphasised that they hadn't seen enough to make a proper assessment.[1]

Two months later, in February 1985, they had become more confident, after spending a week with the NCA in Melbourne examining around 150 files and 2000 documents, and had reported that they endorsed Costigan's view that investigations would be likely to lead to prosecutions. They could now confidently state, they said, that 'numerous offences, both Queensland and Commonwealth, have been committed by various people either individually or in concert with each other', adding that the 'possible offenders' included:

PACKER, Kerry Francis Bullmore
RAY, Brian
BEAMES, Ian Robert ... [2]

This second report made it quite clear that there was still insufficient evidence for charges to be laid against anyone, but recommended an 'extensive and thorough investigation' by the NCA and Queensland fraud squad to collect the necessary material. The committee overseeing their efforts then asked a number of pertinent questions which appear to have made the policemen think harder. And by the time they wrote their final report in July 1985, they were a great deal less sure, saying cautiously that they were now unable to comment on the culpability of any particular person because there wasn't enough evidence.

This final report still exuded confidence that offences had been committed, but also rejected some of the 'frauds' that Costigan had alleged. In their judgment it did not appear that there had been a fraud with the real estate development at Victoria Point, or at the development involving Ray and Packer at Mt Crosby near Brisbane, or in the liquidation of Ray's company Donlan Developments (which had been alleged by

Phillip Carver). In fact, as they now made clear, the film scheme was the *only* matter that they felt justified further investigation. The major offence here, if there was one, was likely to involve tax, which would have been a Commonwealth matter, and outside their jurisdiction. But the fraud squad believed that a Queensland charge of conspiracy to defraud investors should also be pursued, on the basis that the people who had put their money in the film tax scheme had thought they were investing in epics worth $19 million, when they were actually buying low-budget movies that had cost $100 000.[3]

The recommended investigation was never carried out, or not by the Queensland fraud squad, and seems to have sunk without trace, even though the fraud squad argued strongly that it should be pursued. But conspiracy to defraud investors was arguably a bizarre offence to allege anyway, at least as far as Packer was concerned, for he had invested in the film scheme himself and would therefore have been a victim as well as a co-conspirator. What was more, investors had been after the huge tax deductions that the films had promised rather than a share in the profits, so they wouldn't have cared what the films had cost, provided the 'investment' had reduced their tax bill. And it was far-fetched to suggest that the promoters had known that deductions would be disallowed.

While the fraud squad and NCA deliberated about what to do, a less appropriate authority was also being asked to investigate Packer. When Channel Nine's television licence came up for renewal in autumn 1985, it was suggested to the unfortunate Australian Broadcasting Tribunal (ABT) that they should consider whether Packer's behaviour might render him not a fit and proper person to hold a television licence. This suggestion, from the Public Interest Advocacy Centre, eventually elicited some fascinating information from Channel Nine's lawyers about how the film tax-avoidance scheme worked and how much tax Packer had hoped to save, but did not get the station's boss onto the stand, for the ABT understandably took the view that the National Crime Authority had been set up to pursue precisely this sort of investigation and should be allowed to get on with it.[4] Interestingly enough, though, it appeared that the tribunal was persuaded by the argument that Packer had acted at all times on professional advice, had no understanding of tax schemes and, as a consequence, couldn't possibly be blamed for anything.

All investigations of Packer and Ray by the NCA, however, continued to take place behind closed doors, so that there was little action in the public arena after the middle of 1985. What there was came in titbits, released in the committal proceedings against Ray, Beames and Lockyer on the tax fraud charges relating to the bottom-of-the-harbour scheme. In fact, it would have been impossible even to be sure that investigations were taking place if Channel Nine's lawyers had not confirmed to the ABT that the Australian Federal Police and NCA were carrying out various inquiries, in which Packer was providing the 'utmost assistance'.[5]

For two-and-a-half years the silence continued, by which time most people who remembered the row over Costigan had assumed that the matters were dead. Then, in March 1987, Attorney-General Lionel Bowen made a statement to Parliament to the effect that Packer had been cleared of any suspicion arising out of Costigan's inquiries. Bowen told several people that he had been under strong pressure from Prime Minister Bob Hawke to issue the statement. And it was certainly extraordinary for such public declarations of innocence to be made. But the allegations made against Packer since the start of the Goanna affair had been extraordinary, too, and many felt that the balance had needed to be redressed.[6] Bowen's statement certainly did its best to achieve that:

First, an incalculable and unwarranted damage has been done to Mr Packer.

Second, there is no basis to justify any charges being brought against him.

Third, he is entitled to be regarded by his fellow citizens as unsullied by the allegations and insinuations which have been made against him.[7]

313

In fact, the NCA had investigated Packer for twelve months and had then passed the papers to the Commonwealth Director of Public Prosecutions Ian Temby in early 1986 for a decision on whether Packer should be prosecuted. It had taken almost a year for the DPP to reach a final decision not to charge him. Temby had sought an outside opinion from Ken Handley and Margaret Beazley, both of whom are now judges, who had advised that charges would be unlikely to succeed. Packer's lawyer, Malcolm Turnbull, had also sought opinions from three QCs on whether the film scheme was fraudulent, and all had concluded that it was not, at least as far as Packer's conduct was concerned.[8]

The NCA, however, was unhappy that the decision whether or not to prosecute Packer had been taken out of its hands. In mid 1987, the parliamentary committee overseeing its operations asked the NCA to comment on a draft version of a report entitled *The National Crime Authority—An Initial Evaluation*, in which it was proposed to say among other things:

> Of its completed investigations, no charges resulted from one. The subject of the investigation—Mr Kerry Packer—was cleared of any wrongdoing and a statement made to that effect by the Attorney General on 26 March 1987. The Commonwealth Director of Public Prosecutions decided not to lay charges against two other principals, and a third principal died.[9]

The NCA responded tartly in a letter that:

> The reference to Mr Packer, and by inference, the Authority's role is inaccurately put. The Authority would much prefer that no specific reference be made to him.

And as a result, the offending passage was amended, so that the report merely stated: 'Of its completed investigations, no charges resulted from one.'[10]

Packer responded to Bowen's statement with a brief one of his own, saying that he had made his position clear 'on these trumped-up charges' a long time before, but was happy that the charges had been officially dismissed, adding: 'A very unhappy chapter in my life and my family's life is now closed.' He also declared himself delighted that the government had sought to prevent it happening again—which was presumably a reference to Bowen's condemnation of the *National Times* (and any other paper that emulated it in the future) for publishing allegations from a royal commission for which it had no independent evidence.

Packer had been under huge strain while the hue and cry was at its height and had been depressed and almost suicidal, according to friends. He had never courted publicity, to put it mildly, and had hated being caught in the spotlight over World Series Cricket, but the terrible experience over Costigan would leave an indelible mark on his life. Whatever view one took of his reluctance to pay tax, his strange dealings in cash and his involvement (or not) in dodgy tax schemes, it was impossible to deny that he had been appallingly served. But there were one or two observations worth making in Costigan's defence. He had not intended the Goanna allegations to be published, and the substance of his confidential reports was considerably more impressive than the crass 'case summaries' that had been leaked to the *National Times*. Costigan had been reluctant to produce these summaries in the first place, and argued in his final report that it was the fault of the legislation that his 'suspicions and allegations' had to be committed to paper in this brief form for the NCA's consideration.[11]

Another argument of Costigan's was also worth considering. In his public volumes he made it clear that he believed Packer had deliberately attempted to frustrate his inquiries. In the confidential Volume 9 he went one step further. Talking about how he had first investigated the $225 000 delivered to Packer by Ray and Beames, he wrote:

Packer was anxious to deny that moneys were used for drugs, as were the others. Their problem was their reluctance to disclose the

315

real purpose of the cash payments, for fear that on exposure they would be prosecuted: thus the half-truth, not the whole. For the investigator, a half-truth is worse than a complete lie. It is easy enough if he knows which half is untrue. If he does not, he must explore it all to make this distinction. This was my onerous task. Those who purvey half-truths have only themselves to blame for the consequences.[12]

Setting aside the lasting damage to his reputation, if it was possible to do that, Packer had in fact won every single public battle over the Goanna allegations. Shortly after the original article was published by the *National Times*, he had sued the Fairfax organisation for defamation, and this had eventually produced a five-star apology. It would not have made up for the story being printed in the first place, as far as Packer was concerned, but it must have warmed his heart a little all the same, for it could hardly have been more complete. Published in April 1985, six months after the initial article, it acknowledged that Packer had always strenuously denied the allegations, emphasised that the newspaper had never endorsed them, and concluded:

> John Fairfax & Sons Limited accepts and recognises that it has no evidence, nor is it aware of any evidence, to support the allegations in the Costigan case summaries.
>
> John Fairfax & Sons Limited sincerely regrets and apologises for the embarrassment and hurt caused to Mr Kerry Packer and his family by the article.[13]

If there were room for irony in the whole experience, it was that Packer had suffered at the hands of the same weapon that his father had used to attack such people as Artie Fadden, Les Haylen and Tom Uren. For it was the stories in the press that had bruised him. And the newspapers had reported the allegations so prominently because he was rich, powerful and a public figure.

Packer certainly believed that some of his mates had accepted the allegations as true and was sure that many of his staff had too. When Christmas came round in 1984, three months after the Goanna allegations were published, the traditional Packer hampers at Australian Consolidated Press had turned up with a message from the company instead of from Kerry himself. When asked why this was so he had supposedly remarked that staff would not want anything from him because he was a 'bad man'. In fact, a number of his employees gave him their support by signing a letter to say that they couldn't believe the accusations about drugs and murder to be true.

His feelings of paranoia had already been fanned by his own *Sunday* program which had produced a *Hypothetical* on the media in April 1984, some months before the whole Goanna affair had burst into the public consciousness. The program's moderator, Geoffrey Robertson QC, had been asking various journalists on the panel whether they would run stories on people whom they discovered to be using cocaine, and had taken a High Court judge and a cricketer as his first two examples. The journalists had agreed that they would print the allegations and name the people because both were public figures. Robertson had then turned to Packer's lieutenant Trevor Kennedy and suggested that he had been given a secret tape-recording by the cocaine dealer, and that it contained a surprise:

Robertson: You listen to the tape, you recognise the voice: 'I want fourteen ounces and I want it quickly.' Trevor Kennedy, it's your proprietor, Kerry Murfax. Is he a public figure?

Kennedy: Yes.

Robertson: You're going to expose him?

Kennedy: Well, we've certainly got a problem. [Laughter] That's obviously a decision which, in the final analysis is going to be made by the proprietor.

Robertson: So you're going to ask the proprietor, 'Do I expose you, sir?'

Kennedy: Well, it begs the question, certainly.[14]

317

The hypothetical proprietor had been christened Kerry Murfax to make him an amalgam of Australia's three big press barons, but the first name made it easy to assume that it was Packer, since he was in fact Kennedy's proprietor and Costigan had made it clear in November 1983 that he wanted to question Packer about big cash payments in the context of his drug investigations.[15] There was a sharp intake of breath from a number of the panel members at the audacity of Robertson's question, but this was nothing compared to the horrified reaction of Channel Nine executives when they heard about it.

When the program's executive producer, Peter Luck, came into the studios the next day to edit the footage, he was surprised to find that the camera tapes had all been confiscated. Discussions had then followed with Nine's boss, Sam Chisholm, in an effort to get a compromise program to air, but the episode had been canned on Packer's express orders. The next *Hypotheticals* program had only got to air by virtue of being edited in twenty-four hours while Chisholm was away in London watching Wimbledon, and the series had been dumped soon after. The item's executive producer Peter Luck had left the network soon afterwards when his contracts expired.

With Packer's clearance in March 1987 there also came good news for his friend Brian Ray, who was acquitted on charges of conspiracy to defraud the Commonwealth after one of the longest and most expensive trials in Australian legal history. The magistrate at his committal in August 1985 had been persuaded that the case against Ray was strong, and had been severely critical of Ray's truthfulness, noting that he was 'compromised by his demonstrably false denials concerning his relationship with Lockyer' and pointing out 'myriad inconsistencies and demonstrable falsehoods' in his affidavit and interviews. He had then listed half-a-dozen examples to support his conclusion, in which he characterised Ray's assertions variously as 'totally false', 'demonstrably false', 'extremely prejudicial' and contradicted by 'a wealth of evidence to the contrary'.[16]

The jury had clearly taken a different view and found Ray's defence to be credible. This was that he had only taken an active part in the bottom-of-the-harbour scheme to help his friend Ian Beames while the latter was in jail, and had never realised that the scheme was fraudulent.

Ray's release was celebrated with a party at his home on the Gold Coast attended by his old and good friend Sir Joh Bjelke-Petersen, as well as Kerry Packer and John Singleton, who reportedly ran for cover when a press photographer happened upon the gathering.[17] Sir Joh had already indicated that he had never doubted Ray's innocence. 'I have always been proud to have Brian as a friend and to know he is on my team. Early on in the piece, I questioned him on his involvement in the various different matters and I was completely reassured.' Ray himself had something to say of the strain he had been under:

> All these matters have taken a toll. I would not be human if that were not so ... My wife has sat through five years of court proceedings praying it would come out right. Only a fortnight ago, I took a walk along the beach with the older children to explain that I might go to jail ... I still believe in our system of justice because it worked for me.[18]

His acquittal was not celebrated by Labor's maverick Finance Minister, Peter Walsh, who made a number of uncomplimentary remarks about Sir Joh and his financial backers, of which Ray was one, under the cover of parliamentary privilege. Referring to Ray as a 'scumbag', he opined that Ray's acquittal 'says a great deal more about the difficulty of getting a conviction on conspiracy than it does about Mr Ray's guilt or innocence'.[19] He declined to repeat the comments outside Parliament where he would be required to prove them to be true.

Packer's public statement of 3 November 1984, in reply to Costigan's final report, had accused the Royal Commission of adopting a forensic version of the old music hall song, 'I danced with a man who danced with a girl who danced with the Prince of Wales' to justify investigations of his affairs. The same statement had accused Costigan of using the technique of guilt by association to smear him. Whether this was fair comment or not, it was hard to deny that Packer kept strange company.

In the late 1980s, he would sit next to the Queen in the Royal Box at Windsor as they watched polo together, while the boards of his international companies would bristle with the great and the good, including such people as Vernon Jordan, later a senior adviser to American President Bill Clinton. But in the early years of the 1980s he was still doing rather more than dance with a number of people whose pedigree was far less impeccable.

Brian Ray, for example, had caused him to do business with Phillip Carver, con-man and fraudster, with whom he had gone into partnership, and had introduced him to Ian Beames, bottom-of-the-harbour promoter and tax scheme designer, who also ended up in jail for fraud. Beames in turn had been close to Lockyer and Maher, Australia's two leading bottom-of-the-harbour tax promoters.

Two more of Ray's friends, who also had dealings with Packer were Malcolm Edwards and Neil Ohlsson of the Essington group. Ray introduced them to Packer some time around 1978, and Packer became a partner in many of their business ventures soon after. Their partnership lasted till the end of 1986, when Ohlsson left Essington. Packer then took a share in the group and continued his partnership with Edwards until 1990.[20]

One of their joint ventures came under the spotlight in February 1985, only three months after the publication of Costigan's final report, when the Victorian Government announced that a company called EKG Developments had won the $400 million contract for its huge Victoria Project to re-develop Melbourne's Museum railway station. This was to be the most expensive and glamorous construction project in the history of the state, featuring an 84-storey office tower and the world's biggest glass dome. One of the major shareholders in EKG was the Japanese construction giant Kumagai Gumi, but the other four were all Australian, comprising Essington Securities, a company called Toaz Pty Ltd (owned fifty–fifty by Essington and Kerry Packer), and the two respective family companies of Malcolm Edwards and Neil Ohlsson. Less than a week after the contract had been announced, amid great fanfare, Melbourne's *Age* newspaper led its front page with a story that two business-men dealing with a large government project had been savagely criticised by Costigan's confidential Volume 9.[21] The *Age* did not name the businessmen, but opposition politicians and other journalists soon worked out that it was referring to Edwards and Ohlsson of Essington. Extraordinarily enough, the Victorian Government, which had established the Costigan Royal Commission in the first place, had been entirely unaware that Costigan had recommended the two men be the subject of a thorough investigation.

As the inevitable row intensified over the Victorian contract, a New South Wales politician also turned the fire hose on Packer's partners, making a string of allegations in the New South Wales Parliament in which he suggested that Australian police forces were conducting four separate investigations into Essington companies or personnel, in addition to any inquiries being handled by the NCA. The member for Pittwater, Max Smith, also gave Parliament a hint of what the confidential Volume 9 contained on the subject. Costigan had been told by the notorious Phillip Carver that he and Ian Coote had twice collected suitcases containing large amounts of money and ferried them to Essington's offices. In relation to this evidence, Smith asked Parliament:

> Has any effort yet been made to seek an explanation for the mys-
> terious movement of large bags of money in 1981 between a Surry
> Hills address and the Essington offices in Crows Nest, referred to
> by a witness before the Costigan Royal Commission?[22]

Two months later, in April 1985, the leader of the Victorian Liberal Party (later State Premier), Jeff Kennett, provided a fuller version of Costigan's views on the company to the Victorian

Parliament, telling them that Costigan had reported Essington was 'expert in the movement of money and has sufficient overseas connections to provide an international money laundering service'. He then went on to read a passage from Volume 9 that referred to Costigan's findings on Essington and the alleged cash deliveries, in which Costigan had said:

> I conclude that all these movements of cash were for illegal purposes. In my view the Essington group justifies an inquiry in which it is the centre of investigation. That group has been operating since the demise of Nugan Hand and is still operating today. By the manner in which it carries on its business it warrants close and intensive investigations. It may be expected that a central feature of such an investigation will be taxation fraud.[23]

Whether Costigan's suspicions were well founded was another matter, for no prosecutions ever resulted and no subsequent inquiry made adverse findings, but even if none of them was true there was enough in the careers of Essington's two principals to unsettle the Victorian Government, which decided later in 1985 to deny EKG any management role in the Victoria Project and to limit the company's share of the action to 10 per cent.

One of Essington's two key men, Malcolm Edwards, was the son of a scrap metal merchant who had trained as an accountant and gone into business in the early 1970s. His first venture had come in May 1971 with a company called Roward Pty Ltd, a finance broker which had operated from offices in Sydney's swanky Gold Fields House in a smart part of town near Circular Quay. Edwards was one of the two founding directors and shareholders of the company. Within two years of being established the company was in trouble, and within another year it was on its knees. Finally, in 1975, it was put into liquidation. In three years of finance brokering, in which it was supposed to be finding large amounts of money for people to borrow, it had racked up expenses of $415 000, yet earned income of only $900. According to the man in charge of clearing up its mess, liquidator John Walker:

If I may be pardoned for an indulgence of levity, the company's performance presents the elements of 'A Fairy Tale' rather than the normal management of a limited-liability company.[24]

In its short and inglorious life, Roward's performance, according to the liquidator, had been 'a repetitive history of unproductive loan negotiations from various overseas sources'. Malcolm Edwards had led people to believe that Roward had access to huge sums of money. A large number of people or companies had lined up to apply for a total of $1 billion in loan funds, and all, without exception, had been disappointed. The liquidator searched for evidence of any money being lent to the company's hapless clients but could find none:

> I wish to report, having collected a large volume of files and papers relating to this company, and in support of my statement as to the unproductive nature of loan-seeking, that the 174 files examined contained not a single advice from the dozens of supposed lenders that the desired loans will be provided. Such applications totalled about 125, and the correspondence between the applicants and Roward Pty Ltd would average about twenty letters on each matter.[25]

Describing how Edwards would lead people on, he cited a couple of cases where people had been taken on a wild goose chase in the promise of being supplied with funds:

> The time wasted by applicants was of considerable dimensions. For example, Mr Ingall was required to meet Mr Edwards in London for the purpose of collecting the 'loan' of $5 million, and after eight days he concluded he was the victim of a misleading 'approval' . . .
>
> Having been advised to collect an approved loan of $14 million, Mr Smedley spent seventeen days in London on behalf of his company, Doujema Pastures Pty Ltd. I understand that Mr Smedley, in consequence of the said loss, suffered severe financial embarrassment.

In all his career, the liquidator said, he had never seen such exploitation of would-be borrowers. Not only had they wasted their time and never got their money but they had also been fleeced on the way, being required to put down a non-returnable deposit, or commitment fee, as a condition of applying for the loan. They had never seen this money again. While they had waited patiently for the loans that they had been led to believe would come, Malcolm Edwards's Roward Pty Ltd had paid some $90 000 to other companies with which he was associated.

When Roward had got into difficulties in 1974, Malcolm Edwards had left the country. Over the next few years he had written several letters to the liquidator from the Empress Hotel in Hong Kong, suggesting that a deal or a solution was only weeks away, but none of these deals had ever materialised and creditors never got their money. They were still owed some $250 000 in 1980 when Edwards and Packer started doing business together. One of Roward's would-be clients in the early 1970s had been the Republic of Togo, which had thought it was borrowing $50 million and had allowed Edwards to set up an International Bank of Togo in Sydney in consequence. An internal Australian Treasury report in 1975 highlighted the fact that Edwards and Roward had also had 'loan dealings with Bolivia and Ghana'. Indeed, Edwards had even tried to arrange a loan through Roward for the Australian Government, offering to lend $2 billion for a period of thirty years. Fortunately, the Australian Government had not paid a commitment fee and he had not got past first base.

Strangely enough, Edwards's eventual partner in Essington, Neil Ohlsson, had also tried unsuccessfully on several occasions in the early 1970s to arrange big loans for the Australian Government, offering in June 1975 to provide $1 billion over twenty years, interest-free until 1995 when a sum of almost $5 billion would have to be repaid. Ohlsson's share of this deal which, like Edwards's effort, had never borne fruit, would have been a commission of $2.5 million. According to Max Smith in the New South Wales Parliament, an internal memo to the Treasurer on 3 July 1975 had been scathing in its comments, describing the offer as 'a classical funny-money proposal'. The Treasury memo also pointed out that Ohlsson had 'a reputation as a fringe operator in loan markets'.

At the time the loan offer was made, Ohlsson had been a director of the ill-starred Dollar Fund of Australia, a mutual fund-cum-tax minimisation scheme that had been set up in 1970. Ohlsson had been on the board since the beginning, but would leave in mid-1976, some 18 months before the fund was put into liquidation.

Two months after Ohlsson ceased to be a director of Dollar Fund, he was photographed in San Francisco by an FBI surveillance team, meeting a US mafia figure called Rudy Tham. He had met Tham on several occasions, along with a California mafia hitman, called Jimmy 'the Weasel' Fratianno,[26] having been introduced to them by Dollar Fund's principal Bela Csidei. Csidei, who was suspected by the FBI of drug smuggling, was facing charges under the NSW Companies Act at the time of the trip with Ohlsson. Two years afterwards, in 1978, he was jailed for cultivating marijuana in the Northern Territory. Ohlsson's connection with this group of people was to advise them on business deals. He said he was unaware of their mafia connections.

The relationship between Ohlsson and Edwards dated back to 1975 when they had come together in Hong Kong as partners in Essington. Some three years later, they had been introduced to Packer by Brian Ray. Deals had followed soon after, giving Essington a tremendous boost to its business career. On their own, Ohlsson and Edwards might have found it hard to get significant finance, but Packer's presence made that easy. One of their first joint ventures was the redevelopment of Sydney's Sebel Town House in 1980, but other property projects came thick and fast after that, with the bulk coming in New South Wales, where many of the developments were on government-controlled sites. This attracted comment from Max Smith, the MLA for Pittwater, who in addressing the New

South Wales Parliament in February 1985 about Essington's mention by Costigan also said:

> What worries me is the remarkable success which Essington has had in obtaining government contracts, in spite of the controversial background of one of its principals.[27]

Smith's particular criticism was directed at two Sydney sites in which Packer was a co-venturer. One was a proposal to build a 700-space car park near the Regent Hotel in the Rocks area of Sydney. The other involved a site off Pitt Street in Sydney's central business district, owned by the Joint Coal Board. Shortly after expressions of interest in this second site had been invited from developers in late 1983, New South Wales Premier Neville Wran had announced (during a trip to Japan) that it had been sold to Essington. This had amazed the company's competitors, many of whom who were still preparing their tenders. Smith commented:

> The outstanding aspect of this contract is the haste with which the tendering was opened and closed. Indeed, I am aware of developers who were told by the Joint Coal Board or its agents not to bother. Without proper tendering, how are honourable members to know that taxpayers received full market value for the property? The people of New South Wales are entitled to a full and open inquiry into the awarding of the Joint Coal Board contract.
>
> The Regent Carpark site was awarded to Essington under equally mysterious circumstances.
>
> I am advised that the Valuer-General supplied the Sydney Cove Redevelopment Authority with a valuation of the three proposals on 8 June 1982, and that Essington's bid was worth about $15 million less to the government than the highest tender, put in by Mirvac. I am informed that the Chairman of the Authority communicated to the Minister that Essington's offer was a guaranteed minimum, while Mirvac's offer was only illustrative. That is a highly debatable distinction, but in any case, the former Minister

needs to explain why, if the Government received market value, Essington was, within days, trying to resell the site for substantially more than it would pay.[28]

Malcolm Edwards told the *National Times* six months later that he had discussed the Joint Coal Board proposal with Wran and the JCB chairman shortly before the Premier's trip to Japan, at which time the Premier had told them he thought it a very good project. Journalist Wendy Bacon tried to confirm this with Mr Wran's office, but to no avail:

> Some weeks ago, this newspaper asked Wran whether this meeting had occurred, whether any other discussions took place, and when the agreement with Essington had been reached.
>
> We received no reply. Finally, Wran's press secretary David Hurley said he had consigned the questions to the waste-paper bin without reading them. He told this writer not to waste further breath asking more questions as they would be consigned to the same place.[29]

Before their joint venture in the Victoria Project, Packer and Essington had formed a syndicate to bid for the Gold Coast casino licence, in which they had been unsuccessful. Packer had also put up money for an Essington venture into the fast-food and baking businesses. Here, Ohlsson and Edwards had suffered a rapid corporate collapse, with their Heraton Food Group being forced into liquidation after only two years of trading, in which time it had managed to lose $8 million. Packer had backed the company with more than $1 million, secured by a personal guarantee over Edwards's assets, which he perhaps hoped to recover in future deals. Some 230 trade creditors were told in May 1983 that they could expect nothing from the wreckage. Despite optimistic noises from Edwards, many received only part of what they were owed or nothing at all. Australian Guarantee Corporation, which had lent Heraton $3.2 million, was not paid out. Nor was Ferrier Hodgson, the accounting firm which acted as liquidator for the company. After the liquidation of Heraton, some of its businesses continued to trade through a new company called Culinaire Pastries which, to the anger of creditors, was part-owned by companies in the Essington Group.

Despite criticism from Costigan, adverse press comment and Essington's appalling corporate record, Packer continued to do business with Edwards throughout the 1980s before selling his shares in the group in 1990. Almost all the Essington companies eventually went into liquidation.[30]

The largest of them, Essington Ltd, which was also the group's holding company, had an estimated shortfall of $153 million. Not surprisingly, Packer and Edwards ceased to be bosom buddies after that. Kerry also fell out with Brian Ray, and did not speak to him again until they were reconciled shortly before Ray's death in a plane crash in 2005.

CHAPTER SIXTEEN

MEDIA MATES

*Loyalty is a two-way thing, Kerry. You've
certainly given it to your people. I hope you
feel that all of them and all of your friends
have stuck by you. You deserve it.*

Prime Minister Bob Hawke, April 1987

In June 1987, three months after Packer's clearance by Costigan, Prime Minister Bob Hawke was guest of honour at the Australian Businessman of the Year Awards, sponsored by Packer's *Australian Business* magazine. The two men sat next to each other throughout the evening, laughing and joking together, with Hawke leaning over on occasions to whisper a quiet word into Kerry's ear. Then came Hawke's turn to sing for his supper, bringing from the nation's most powerful politician a testimonial of fulsome praise:

> It is, ladies and gentlemen, a real pleasure for me as Prime Minister
> to be here and sit next to a person whom I'm pleased as Prime
> Minister of this country to count as a close personal friend and to
> measure as a very great Australian, Kerry Packer.[1]

Packer had already told ABC Radio in a snatched interview as he came through the door that he believed Hawke's Labor Government had done great things for business and would be returned at the forthcoming election, adding that he would certainly be giving them his vote. Hawke would pick up on this support the next day with great enthusiasm, especially since Packer had branded the Liberals' promised tax cuts as a 'sham', but in the meantime he was full of back-slapping bonhomie. One veteran Channel Nine journalist was left in no doubt as to who was the senior partner in the relationship. Packer, however, did not appear entirely comfortable with Hawke's admiring attention, muttering to a friend as he left the room that he wished the Prime Minister would not be so deferential in public.

One of the stars of the night's festivities was another of Hawke's favourite entrepreneurs, whose public profile was a great deal higher than Packer's. For the journalists and their advisers at *Australian Business* had selected the bouncing figure of Alan Bond to receive one of the evening's minor awards—for 'Best Merger' of the year. This modest bauble was in recognition of his intrepid takeover of the brewing group, Castlemaine Tooheys, almost two years earlier. But most people at the dinner were keener to talk about his more recent and more glamorous dive into the media business. On the very day that *Australia IV* had been bumped out of the America's Cup challenge off Fremantle in January 1987, the still-brilliant Bond had scored a publicity coup by announcing that he had bought Channel Nine from Kerry Packer for more than a billion dollars. Ironically, in view of what followed for the two men, almost all Australia's financial commentators had greeted this as a splendid victory for the man from Western Australia.[2] In fact, the deal helped make Packer the richest man in Australia while it propelled the insatiable Bond ever closer to his inevitable bankruptcy.

Packer and Bond had first had secret talks about the future of Channel Nine in London in mid 1986, and had followed up with a second round of meetings at Sydney's Intercontinental Hotel in January 1987, in which they had settled the sale in just two hours. At the outset, Packer had been considering retiring from business altogether, but as the year wore on he had become more attracted by the idea of grabbing Bond's two Channel Nine stations in Perth and Brisbane. In the end, any doubts he had about which way to jump had been rapidly settled by Alan

Bond's claim that his two provincial properties were worth $400 million. Packer's response had been to tell the eager entrepreneur that at those prices his own big-city stations in Sydney and Melbourne must be worth at least a billion dollars. And Bond, amazingly, had taken the figure seriously, topping the asking-price with an extra $55 million. 'You only get one Alan Bond in your lifetime,' Packer said later, 'and you certainly didn't turn him away. A billion dollars was around twice what the stations were worth. In fact, Packer's own executives at Nine had told him that he could expect the pair to fetch no more than $400 million.

Since he had valued them himself at around half that figure in 1983, and had effectively picked them up for nothing in the privatisation deal that year, even $400 million might have been an attractive proposition. But a billion dollars was an offer Packer could not possibly refuse. Indeed, it was one of the most spectacular deals of the decade. Yet such was the climate of the times, or such the gullibility of journalists and bankers, that many believed Bond had won. The rewards of owning a television network were seen to be limitless, the 1980s boom was at its height, everyone was borrowing big and buying bigger. And nowhere was there a crazier scramble taking place for assets than in television and the media. Here, new laws introduced by Hawke's Labor Government had sent the prices of newspapers and television stations sky high by permitting the creation of true television networks in Australia for the first time. There would be only three such networks to cover the country, and there might be only one chance to buy in. So the mad rush to stake a claim had begun.

For twenty years the size of the Packer, Murdoch or Fairfax television empires had been limited by a law that stopped anyone owning more than two television stations. With this old rule now scrapped, there was going to be almost open slather. According to the professional media analysts, the changes had added $600 million to the value of Packer's two Channel Nine stations alone. And Bond was clearly of the same opinion, as were Christopher Skase and Frank Lowy, who soon offered similarly ridiculous amounts for Channels Seven and Ten respectively.

The changes to the media laws, which had been tossed around in Hawke's Cabinet for the best part of a year, had caused a very public and very damaging split in the Labor Government, in which a couple of ministers had accused the Prime Minister of wanting to tailor the new rules to suit Packer and Murdoch. But there was also no question that the previous Liberal Government had played an important role in bringing Kerry and Rupert their bonanza, for the pressure to introduce nationwide television networks to Australia had started with a decision of Malcolm Fraser's Government nine years earlier. Changes that Fraser had set in motion, under strong pressure from Kerry Packer, had been the vital first move in the enrichment of these two media proprietors.

In October 1979, the Fraser Government had committed Australia to launching a multi-million-dollar communications satellite, whose chief purpose was to carry television signals across the nation. The satellite had given Packer and Murdoch the capacity to beam their television programs to several million new customers but, more to the point, had made it almost inevitable that they would eventually be allowed to do so. Once a decision had been taken to put the satellite in the sky, the logic led inexorably to nationwide television networks, for without them the satellite would have virtually no customers and no hope at all of earning enough to wash its antennae.

The story of how Kerry persuaded the politicians to invest hundreds of millions of taxpayers' money in a satellite to deliver TV pictures is a sad tale of Australian policy-making gone wrong, for while it made Packer rich, the project rapidly became a financial disaster for the taxpayers who were funding it. When Aussat, the company that owned and operated the satellite, was sold to the new private carrier Optus in 1992, it had racked up losses and debts of $800 million and had needed continual injections of public funds to save it from bankruptcy. Although there had been warnings of such an outcome from the very beginning, the politicians had ignored them.

The saga of the Packer-inspired satellite began in 1976, when Kerry was setting up World Series Cricket and looking for a reliable way to send live television pictures around the country. In Australia, there was nothing that could do the job properly, but in Canada and the United States there was just the thing—a satellite system set up for the television networks to carry their signals across the continent. Packer was quick to realise that a similar gadget in Australia's skies would allow him to transmit not only his cricket pictures but all his television programs round the country, enabling his Sydney and Melbourne stations to tap into an audience of millions that they hadn't already reached.

There was one small obstacle in the way of this idea. An official inquiry, set up by Telecom Australia, had just spent five years looking at whether Australia needed a satellite and was about to publish its conclusion that it did not. Packer decided that it would be a good move to talk to Prime Minister Malcolm Fraser, who had actively sought his support in the 1975 election campaign, and convince him of the project's merits. Unlike Alan Bond, then a struggling property developer, who always got shuffled off to public servants or junior ministers, the powerful media boss had no trouble getting Fraser's ear. And neither did he have any difficulty persuading the Prime Minister that the satellite was a must for Australia. For, as Packer later explained, Fraser thought it was a marvellous idea:

> To his undying credit he grasped on to it immediately and said, 'Of course it's what we want. It's exactly the sort of thing we need to stop the drift of people into the urban areas . . . Can you do more for me on this?'[3]

There were political advantages for Fraser which may have struck him as even more obvious than the satellite's dubious capacity for stopping urban drift, for the project would deliver a choice of high-quality television pictures to voters outside the capital cities who had to put up with an inferior service. As Packer doubtless pointed out in their chat, four million Australians were forced to make do with only one commercial channel and to wait months for episodes of their favourite soaps,

333

while many were denied the right to watch live sport on commercial television at all. Yet another half-million people in remote areas were still more disadvantaged, in that they had no access to television of any sort. A communications satellite, Packer told the Prime Minister, would enable the networks to break this terrible drought, to bring much-needed pictures to those who had none. And some of those four-and-a-half million people, Fraser may well have surmised, would surely vote Liberal out of gratitude.

Having received an enthusiastic response from Fraser, Packer hired an American called Donald S. Bond to explain in greater detail why Australia needed such a system. His expert report of August 1977 waxed lyrical about harnessing the Space Age to bring 'immediate and tangible benefits for the peaceful needs of mankind'. But the more sober paragraphs made clear that the primary purpose of a satellite next to the Southern Cross was rather more mundane. It was simply to bring 'diverse colour television programs of excellent quality to all the citizens of Australia'.[4] In a foreword to the report Kerry Packer spelt it out even more explicitly, arguing that Australians had a right to equality of television service (which one might have paraphrased as saying that they should all be allowed to watch Channel Nine) and adding:

> In particular, I believe that television services should be provided to areas not at present served and that all four networks should reach all the nation's citizens.

Packer then handed the report to Malcolm Fraser and his Minister for Telecommunications and waited for action.

He did not have to wait long. Within five weeks an official task force had been asked to examine the feasibility of Packer's proposals. Soon after, it came up with a recommendation to go full steam ahead. Packer's American expert had argued that the satellite should be built as soon as possible 'to fulfil urgent public needs'. And even though it was not in the least clear what these urgent needs were, the majority of the task force readily agreed that a satellite should be despatched into orbit without delay. They also accepted that new commercial television stations should be created in the country areas to transmit the big-city stations' programs—which was the crucial first step towards national networks.[5] The task force took an extraordinarily short time to reach these conclusions, barely eight months from start to finish, but that was because it was not allowed any longer. Amazingly enough, it did not even consider the essential question of whether a satellite could be justified, because it was not specifically asked to do so. Nor did it apparently inquire why the five-year Telecom study had rejected one. Finally, it ignored the warnings of the Department of Finance, whose dissenting report had argued that the satellite 'would be very difficult to justify' and should not proceed. The Department of Finance had counselled that the improvement in communications would be marginal and the cost enormous, and had pointed out that satellite systems in the United States, where the market was far bigger, had failed to make a profit. Yet the enthusiasm of the other members of the task force and the positive nature of its terms of reference had allowed any doubts to be buried.

Despite the warnings and an estimated cost of up to $400 million, Fraser and his communications minister, Tony Staley, were also extremely positive about the project. And it was soon being taken as a *fait accompli* that it would go ahead. But the Labor Party did at least raise public doubts about whether the satellite was a good idea, arguing that it could not be justified on economic grounds. Labor's spokesperson, Senator Susan Ryan, was also unhappy that the scheme gave so much to Packer:

> Put simply, everything that Mr Packer asked for in his submissions, the task force provided . . .
>
> It is he who emerges as most favoured by the task force recommendation that the Broadcasting Act be radically changed to permit a national commercial television network.[6]

By the time the formal go-ahead for the satellite was given in October 1979, after a second positive report from the task force, the Prime Minister's own department had joined the ranks of its detractors, and the Department of Finance had warned even more sternly that it would not pay its way. In a climate of cutbacks, in which the government was still slashing at public spending, Fraser and his ministers were now committed to splashing out hundreds of millions of dollars on a piece of hi-tech space junk. Yet even at this stage it was not clear who really wanted it. Telecom was saying it would have little use for it, the international carrier OTC indicating it would have rather less and the Department of Defence suggesting that it might not use it at all. The satellite and its TV pictures would please people in the bush and the politicians who coveted their votes; it would also please Kerry Packer who was determined it should happen; but there was little else to explain why the enormous expense was being contemplated. Looking back, one can only imagine that the politicians were dazzled by the sheer whizz-bangery of it all, by the talk of communications revolution, interactive data transmission and the like. To them, perhaps, it was the 1970s equivalent of turning the rivers westward, a marvel that a grown-up country like Australia could not be without.

But not only was Fraser's Government backing the satellite, it was supporting the establishment of television networks as well, which, after all, was the satellite's *raison d'être*. Tony Staley, the minister responsible, had instructed his department to find a way to give country television viewers more choice of programs, and in early 1980 the bureaucrats came up with an acceptable scheme. This provided for the creation of two supplementary licences in each local television area, or in simpler terms, sixty-eight new television stations across Australia. These would be sixty-eight new buyers for the networks' programs. Kerry Packer was reported to be 'heavily behind' this concept, which was not surprising, since it had been his idea in the first place. The only difference was that he had wanted at least one hundred and twenty.

The regional television operators had already made it clear what they believed would happen to them if Packer had his way and these new stations were introduced. Nigel Dick, managing director of the Victorian Broadcasting Network and a former manager of Sir Frank Packer's GTV 9 in Melbourne, had told an industry conference in Canberra in early 1979 that 'the Packer Plan would send my television complex bankrupt, just as it would bankrupt every other television station outside the capital cities'. It would bankrupt them, Dick argued, because the same amount of advertising revenue would have to be shared with a vast number of new television stations, who would be likely to grab the biggest slice of the cake.[7] This would starve the existing stations of money, so that they would either go out of business or cut back their local programs. Either way, the principle on which Australia's broadcasting laws had been built would be betrayed. Since the introduction of television to Australia in 1956 it had been a cardinal aim of the legislators to encourage and protect local programming, to allow each television station its role as a latter-day parish pump. The Packer plan would put an end to this.

The huge row and fierce lobbying that followed the government's plan for sixty-eight new regional stations caused several agonised reappraisals and endless delays. As a result, Fraser's Cabinet had still not got round to implementing the policy by the time of the 1983 election. The Liberals were then voted out of office and were able to wash their hands of the problem, no doubt with a sigh of relief. Fraser had come under 'severe and significant pressure' from Packer to shape television policy and the satellite in a way that would favour Channel Nine, but claimed to have resisted it.[8] But while Packer had certainly become very angry by early 1983 that he had not been given what he wanted, it had been Fraser who had said 'yes' to the Packer-inspired satellite in the first place, and Fraser who had rushed the taxpayers into building it. And by March 1983, when the Hawke Labor Government came to power, it was too late for the charabanc to be halted. Even though the expected cost had now risen to $650 million and the expected loss over its seven-year life to more than $460 million, the Department of Finance advised that too much money had been spent to make it worth pulling out.[9]

If the new Labor government wanted to avoid complete financial disaster for Aussat, which had been set up with the aim of making a profit, it was also too late to avoid the creation of new regional stations and television networks. The satellite needed revenue so it had to have customers, and the Melbourne–Sydney television combines were the only ones in sight.[10] They in turn needed someone in the country areas to send their signals to, and that meant new stations who could buy their programs. The only issues for the policymakers to settle were what form networking should take, how many new stations there should be and how fast the changes should be introduced.

In practical terms, Hawke's Government had to judge whether Packer-style networking really would bankrupt the regional stations. In political terms, its task was much easier. It was being asked to choose between two rival commercial groups, the regional operators and the big-city combines. Since the latter group included two of the most powerful media proprietors in the country, Kerry Packer and Rupert Murdoch, it was pretty obvious which one was going to win. Murdoch had savaged Labor in the past but was still dangerous enough to be worth keeping on side, as was Packer. And Kerry's helping hand for Neville Wran in New South Wales almost certainly qualified him as a mate who deserved good treatment. Politically, therefore, the choice was clear.

Hawke's natural sympathies seemed to lie with Packer in any case. From the early days of the debate, his opinion quite clearly coincided with the one Kerry had expressed since the mid 1970s, that there should be national networks supplied by satellite. Hawke would complain that when he went home to The Lodge in Canberra he could get only one-and-a-half channels on his set, one being the local commercial station, which picked from the various networks as it wished, and the half being the

ABC, for which Hawke had scant regard. An avid sports watcher and punter, the Prime Minister was an unashamed fan of Channel Nine. He was an unashamed fan, too, of Kerry Packer.

Hawke's chief political adviser, Peter Barron, was possibly even more pro-Packer than his boss. It was he who had written the strongly pro-Labor editorial in Packer's *St George & Sutherland Shire Leader* during the 1978 Earlwood by-election campaign, when he was running Neville Wran's press machine. A key member of the NSW Right and a close friend of the Labor party's kingmaker Graham Richardson, himself a Packer friend and strong supporter, Barron would often tell Hawke and his ministers what a good man Packer was, how he was a philanthropist and much misunderstood. Barron held a powerful position at the heart of the Hawke administration and was particularly important in the politicking over television policy. It was no surprise to colleagues when he left Hawke's office in the middle of 1986 to join Kerry Packer as his chief political lobbyist, and perhaps not even to Hawke.[11]

Barron's role as Hawke's political minder, put bluntly, was to persuade him to follow policies that would get the government re-elected. And a big part of such a strategy was to have powerful media barons such as Packer and Murdoch on Labor's side. In Barron's time with Neville Wran, the contract for Lotto in New South Wales had helped tie them into supporting the State Labor Government. It would make sound political sense now, for the same reasons, to deliver a television policy that the same two media proprietors would like.

The main obstacle to achieving this goal was a former suburban solicitor named Michael Duffy, who was nominally in charge of television and media policy. A tough, independent-minded fellow, Duffy remained the only minister in Hawke's Cabinet who had never aligned himself with any of the organised factions of the Right, Left or Centre. One colleague said jokingly when he took the Communications portfolio that all he knew about it was how to turn on the television set. But he soon formed strong views about what the policy should and should not allow. Duffy favoured greater diversity in the media and did not want to see the big boys get bigger. Nor did he want the regional operators to be forced out of business or turned into slave stations for new national networks. And he had a stubborn streak that made him prepared to fight for his policies.

The first strategic battle, however, ended in a major victory for Hawke and the big-city television stations, for in 1985, after a heated face-to-face argument late one night, Duffy was forced by his Prime Minister to make a public promise that all Australians would be able to receive all three commercial television channels within three to five years. There was nothing wrong in principle with this, and a lot to gain politically—Hawke's calculations obviously matched Fraser's in reckoning that there were votes to be had for any party that brought television to the bush. But the promise appeared to preempt the argument about national networks and the risk of bankrupting the regional stations in favour of Packer. From here on, networking of some sort was guaranteed, provided Labor stayed in power. Packer had already got most of what he wanted.

The intellectual challenge for Duffy's bureaucrats was to find a way of fulfilling the promise without impoverishing the regional stations. And after much head-scratching, they found one. Since the overriding problem was that most of the local television areas were too small to support more than one station, Duffy's department suggested that the answer was a policy of 'aggregation'. Instead of creating a host of new stations, they would merge the local areas into bigger markets for which the existing operators could compete in a three-cornered fight. The regional stations would still have a good chance of making money, but country viewers would get a choice of three different signals. The regionals, no doubt, would have preferred the status quo, but could live with this aggregation if they had to, while the Sydney-Melbourne combines thought it a marvellous idea. As long as there were three stations in each area, they would be blissfully happy, for each of them—Nine, Ten and Seven— would have a captive customer who would be forced to buy their product. Packer's people therefore lobbied hard for aggregation to be rushed in. But Duffy still had some doubts.

While aggregation was a better answer for the regional operators than Packer's original 1977 plan of creating new television stations, it would still cause them heartache, for they would have to buy more powerful transmitters to reach their new customers. These could cost them around $600 million and throw up interest charges that would wipe out all their existing profits. Meanwhile, they would also come under pressure from the big-city program suppliers who would be able to put up their prices now that the regionals were forced to buy from them.[12] Duffy therefore decided, as minister, that the move to aggregation should be phased in over ten years, much to the network's displeasure.

But almost out of the blue, he now set his heart on something else that posed a far greater threat to Packer and Murdoch. The shake-up in television policy had caused his department to look at a complete overhaul of Australia's ageing legislation governing ownership of television stations, and the beacon of greater diversity and competition in the media had beckoned bright. A group of television proprietors from the smaller capital cities, including Alan Bond, Kerry Stokes, Christopher Skase and Robert Holmes à Court, had been lobbying for the chance to compete on more equal terms with the big-city stations so that they could become program makers too. And Duffy and his department were sympathetic to the idea. The new boys on the block argued they should be allowed to have the same financial muscle and audience reach as the existing Sydney–Melbourne combines, which they were prevented from doing by a twenty-year-old rule that prohibited anyone from owning more than two television stations. This two-station rule had the perverse effect of allowing Packer and Murdoch (who each owned a Sydney and a Melbourne station) to broadcast to 43 per cent of the Australian viewing audience, while limiting the smaller capital-city operators to a maximum of 16 per cent of the audience (which was all one could get with the two biggest cities, Adelaide and Brisbane, combined). Duffy and his department were excited by the idea of greater competition, and thought it fair to replace the old two-station rule with a limit on audience reach alone. Crucially, they suggested that this should be set at 43 per cent, which would prevent Murdoch and Packer, with their Sydney and Melbourne stations, getting any bigger, but would allow the newcomers to catch up if they could.

Labor's backbench Caucus was so enthusiastic about Duffy's proposal and the increased competition that it promised that its members immediately voted for an even more drastic change, recommending that the limit on audience reach should be set even lower, at 35 per cent. This, if accepted by Cabinet, would make it impossible for anyone to own both a Sydney and a Melbourne station and would ultimately bring the break-up of the Packer and Murdoch television empires. Reluctantly the backbenchers agreed that it would be necessary to have a grandfather clause allowing the two gentlemen to keep what they already had so that neither would be forced to divest. But they made it clear that they would not countenance the two proprietors selling their stations as a pair. Once again, if this were accepted by Cabinet, it would have the effect of seriously reducing the stations' value.

Far from having their position enhanced, as Hawke's and Duffy's promise of three-channels-for-all had earlier suggested, Packer and Murdoch suddenly found their privileges under attack from both the minister responsible for media policy and the ALP's backbenchers. It was no longer just a question of whether the two men would get what they wanted; it was a question of whether they could hang on to what they already had. The stage was now set for a huge confrontation in Cabinet. It was inconceivable that Hawke would allow his government to get the two powerful media barons off-side.

The battle was due to be fought in Cabinet on 9 December 1985. But the first skirmish came in committee the week before, with victory to Hawke. Riding the issue uncharacteristically hard, he not only argued for aggregation to be brought in immediately but also pushed for Packer and Murdoch to be treated as a special case under any new ownership rules, making it clear that he would accept the Caucus proposal of a 35 per cent limit on audience reach, but only if Packer and Murdoch were exempted. Hawke proposed that they, and they alone, should be allowed to own both a Sydney and a Melbourne station, but that they should also be allowed to sell them as a pair. Finally, he suggested a move that would entrench their advantage still further, arguing for a rule that would prevent anyone owning more than two capital-city stations. This would make it impossible to build a rival network from the smaller capital cities, as Bond, Stokes, Skase and Holmes à Court were all hoping to do. Indeed, it would make it virtually impossible for them to build a rival network at all. If Hawke were to get his way, it would effectively be one rule for Packer and Murdoch and one rule for everyone else. And after a four-hour struggle in Cabinet committee, this was how the policy stood.

Hawke, Richardson and Barron now set about lobbying for the more important fight to come, emphasising to Labor ministers the political advantages of their approach—which was that they could expect support from the two powerful media barons in return. But it soon became clear that it would be a far harder task than it had been in committee for the Prime Minister to get his way. Having ruled by consensus since he came to power, Hawke was now asking Cabinet to push through a policy that the minister responsible bitterly opposed. Not surprisingly, in view of this fact and in view of the nature of the proposals, the battle produced one of the roughest encounters that the Hawke Government had seen. For three hours the discussion went back and forth like a marathon tennis rally, with Duffy and Hawke giving few others a chance to speak. As other ministers watched and listened, one or two got the feeling that the real issue was not even in play. Senator John Button, Duffy's ally at the time, was direct enough to serve it up. Turning to his prime minister in frustration, he asked: 'Why don't you just tell us what your mates want?'

'It's nothing to do with *my* fucking mates,' an angry Hawke is said to have replied, 'they're the only ones we've got.' After that, the debate did not get much further. With the match still to be decided, it was resolved to try again at a special session of Cabinet the following Sunday.

It didn't take long for news of the battle to reach Canberra's press gallery. The next day saw the first of a stream of articles outlining the history of the fight and accusing Bob Hawke of doing Packer and Murdoch's bidding. Before long, details of Button's clash with Hawke were public, and a dozen political commentators were reporting as one that Hawke faced the most severe test of his authority since he came to office. Almost all agreed that victory for Duffy's forces was likely. When Cabinet reconvened on the Sunday, Bob Hawke laid the offending newspaper articles on the table one by one, holding them up first for all to see. He made it clear that there would be no witch-hunt and no search for the leakers. But he also ruled that there be no further discussion of the issue that day. It would be handed over to a Cabinet committee of four, comprising Hawke, Paul Keating, John Button and Michael Duffy, to look for a solution.

There then followed a year of stalemate, with Duffy on the brink of resignation and Hawke immovable in defence of the Packer and Murdoch television empires. In early 1986, however, it became possible to reach a compromise on the question of a timetable for aggregation, because Duffy was essentially forced to back down—the regional operators refused to make any concessions or accept that aggregation was going to happen, and Duffy could no longer defend them.[13] But the problem of ownership limits proved a much tougher one to solve. It seemed to be a stark choice between entrenching Packer's and Murdoch's privileges and opening the market up in competition. The rift in the government therefore remained. Caucus became increasingly hostile to Hawke's position, while Hawke refused to budge, even though it appeared he would never be able to muster the numbers to win.

As the months of 1986 drew on it became more urgent to reach a resolution, since the satellite was now in the sky, yet the four-man Cabinet committee either did not meet or did not invite Duffy to attend if it did. Towards the end of the year, a date was finally set for the policy to be presented to Cabinet a second time, and with no movement taking place, the experts were again certain that Duffy would win through. The Left wing of the party and the ALP Caucus were both supporting him, while only the New South Wales Right was solidly behind Hawke. Then, almost as D-day dawned, a new idea emerged to break the deadlock. As a back-bencher, Paul Keating had argued for a law that would prevent media proprietors wielding power in television and print at the same time; as Treasurer years later, he had presided over deregulation of the financial system. Now he threw the two ideas together to offer a way out of the impasse. Keating suggested that ownership limits on television should be scrapped altogether in exchange for a simple rule that prevented anyone from owning a television station and a major newspaper in the same city.

The attraction of this compromise was that it would give something to everyone. Bond, Skase and Holmes à Court would have the chance to build their networks, which was what Duffy had been pushing for. Packer and Murdoch would be denied any special treatment, so Caucus could no longer complain. The economic rationalists in the party would get the deregulated market that they had always cherished. And even the Left, who hated the idea of greater concentration, would get the cross-media rule they had wanted for so long. But best of all, without doubt, there would be an end to the internal strife and bitterness of a year-long fight.

Sold on those terms it was unquestionably a winner, and Keating pushed it energetically, lobbying harder than he had for anything else in his ministerial career except the consumption tax he had once so much wanted. But it soon became clear that he and Hawke also had their sights set on the political advantages of the move. Keating had dined with Murdoch in New York to put him in the picture and had also told Packer of the proposed new rule. And, perhaps as a result of these conversations, when the scheme finally came to Cabinet on 24 November 1986, he was able to tell fellow ministers enthusiastically that the scheme would be welcomed by both men. Hawke had lobbied his fellow ministers in similar terms before the decisive vote, telling them that if Keating's proposal got up, the ALP would be guaranteed to win the next election because it would have the media barons' support.[14]

Duffy was left with only a handful of ministers in Cabinet still backing him. He tried hard to persuade them that they should accept the cross-media rule while maintaining an audience limit of 43 per cent to encourage new players in the industry. But his fellow ministers had heard enough. Eventually Cabinet settled for a limit of 75 per cent, to split the difference between the figures that Duffy and Keating were putting forward. In practice, one could easily control the market without growing that big.[15]

Whatever the politicians thought, it was immediately clear to most commentators that the new rule would bring unprecedented domination of the television industry by three all-powerful networks, one of which was certain to be Packer's Channel Nine, for it had essentially removed all significant limits on their expansion. It soon became just as obvious, as Murdoch launched a $2 billion bid for the *Herald & Weekly Times* empire in early December, that it would do exactly the same for Australia's newspaper business. But by this time the die was cast. Labor's back-benchers vented their unhappiness about the huge increase in market dominance that it had unleashed, but to no avail.

It was clear that there were winners and losers in all of this which seemed to correspond to the political allegiances of the various proprietors. Those who had done bad turns in the past, such as the Herald & Weekly Times Ltd and John Fairfax & Sons Ltd, had been punished, while those who might do good turns in the future, such as Murdoch, had been rewarded. The Herald & Weekly Times Ltd would be forced to sell either its Melbourne newspapers or its television station HSV 7 to comply with the new cross-media rule, while Fairfax would have to sell either the *Herald* and the *Sun* or its Sydney television station ATN 7.[16] But the main winner was unquestionably Kerry Packer. The cross-media rule did not affect his magazines, while his Channel Nine now had carte blanche to gobble up the rest of the stations on the network. In the press the next day it was dubbed the Packer package. Instantly, the stock market analysts were on hand to say that it would boost the value of metropolitan television stations by more than 100 per cent. Whether this was true was extremely doubtful, but since buyers like Alan Bond believed that it was, that hardly mattered.

It took Bond just five weeks to make up his mind that he wanted Channel Nine rather than any of the cheaper stations on offer and to clinch a deal that would pay Packer $1055 million, of which some $800 million was in cash. To this point, Packer had been just an ordinary rich man with only a couple of hundred million to his name, but now he was rich beyond comprehension.

Such was the excitement of the 1980s buying binge that few realised it at the time, but this deal summed up perfectly the difference between the two businessmen. It was no coincidence that they were on opposite sides or that Packer was the one who prospered, for Kerry Packer knew when to sell and when to buy and Alan Bond clearly did not. Packer had no dreams, no illusions, no ego to blind him, no attachments to businesses that money couldn't loosen. It did not matter that he had built up Channel Nine himself, because anything was for sale if the price was right. And a billion dollars most certainly was.

But the whole episode revealed another way in which the two rich businessmen were poles apart, for Bond had regularly sought the ear of governments but had never really possessed it, while Packer, as a big media proprietor, only needed to whisper to get what he wanted. In fact, of course, he had argued tirelessly since the mid 1970s for the changes that had made his stations worth so much. But by the mid 1980s it was getting to the point that politicians almost anticipated his demands. They thought about his reaction when they framed the policy.

Michael Duffy says there is no doubt that the politicians gave Packer what he wanted because they felt it was good politics to do so. Asked whether Packer had power, he told me:

> Of course he has power. Anyone who denies that is having himself on. Packer has power because politicians think it's a good idea to give him what he wants, because it's a good idea to have him on side.[17]

Almost throughout the debate, Packer had a strong supporter for his case in the prime minister's office. Peter Barron had constantly argued to public servants, Duffy's advisers, Duffy and other ministers that Packer's arguments should be accepted. Barron's version in 1985–86 of what television policy should be was the same as the version being advanced by Channel Nine, sometimes absurdly so. Tom Burton, later a journalist with the *Australian Financial Review*, was on Duffy's staff throughout the debate and remembers Peter Barron coming into Duffy's office one day clutching a piece of paper and saying, 'This is what the boss wants,' or words to that effect, as he thrust the paper towards him. Burton couldn't help noticing that it was a fax from Channel Nine. It seemed odd to him that Hawke's supposed 'recommendations' had not even been transferred to the Prime Minister's notepaper.

Barron argued to a number of ministers that giving Channel Nine what it wanted would keep Packer friendly and help the ALP retain office. According to Duffy, he was Packer's ally at the centre of power,

> 'putting Packer's point of view all the time. If a proposition came forward that wasn't acceptable to Kerry, then it wouldn't get up.'

Duffy was no less straightforward about Bob Hawke. In the course of the debate, Hawke and Duffy travelled up to Sydney together from Canberra to an appointment at Kirribilli House. Duffy had been told not to bring advisers. On arrival, Duffy found himself ranged against the top men from the three capital-city networks, Sam Chisholm for Channel Nine, Ken Cowley for Murdoch's two Channel Ten stations and Gerald Carrington from Channel Seven. Also present was Bob Hawke's adviser Peter Barron. Hawke apparently took little part in the discussion as the men from the networks once again put their case for the imme-diate introduction of networking to the industry. Duffy had listened to their arguments ad nauseam; he had seen them so often that his eyes were falling out, yet here he was being asked to go through it all again in the presence of his boss. Duffy could see only one purpose in this meeting, for him to be brought into line. In his view, it was 'unbelievable' that a prime minister he in fact respected should have put him in this position. As for Hawke's role in the whole debate, Duffy said:

> The truth is that no government has stood up to these people. Not one since the advent of television. The economics of the satellite were always questionable but Fraser swallowed it. And Bob Hawke was no different.

The lesson of the whole satellite and television networking saga is perhaps that one should never underestimate the insecurity of Australia's politicians. They are convinced that the media has the power to make or break them, and convinced that the crucial decisions to do so are made by the proprietors themselves. It hardly matters that in Packer's case this has only occasionally been true, for the politicians treated both him and Murdoch as if it were. And nothing that has happened since suggests that it will change. Packer and Murdoch both lobbied politicians in Canberra to get what they wanted and were rarely denied. But Packer was both more persistent than Murdoch and had greater pulling power. He kept a house in Canberra's embassy district of Red Hill for entertaining, to which he invited small groups of the most powerful Cabinet ministers a couple of times a year for dinner. And once politicians were face to face with him, his ability to get his way was remarkable. It was harder to say no to Packer than it was to Murdoch, because he was so much more frightening to deal with.

On several accounts, Packer treated politicians much as he treated everybody else, which is to say that he abused them whenever he felt it appropriate. In the early 1980s, Senator John Button, Labor's Shadow Minister for Communications, turned up for lunch at Consolidated Press in Sydney to be met by Packer and his executives. 'G'day Kerry, how are you?' the diminutive Senator Button genially inquired. 'I was a fucking sight better till I read that bullshit you've been writing about media policy,' replied his host, towering almost 45 centimetres over his head. Later, according to someone at the lunch, Button was brave enough to venture a joke at Packer's expense. The media boss had just been to the Soviet Union and was regaling the assembled company about how he had been trailed by a KGB agent posing as a cultural attache. Button remarked that the Russians were a subtle lot, attaching a cultural guide to Kerry—who was not known for his love of such things. There was a clatter of cutlery as knives and forks were put down, then a terrible silence. Around the table, people had gone white, waiting for the big man's response. Fixing his eye on Button, Packer said: 'You'll keep.'

This small tale of bluster and bullying was not an isolated example. As his friend Graham Richardson admitted, Packer was wont to go 'off his brain' if he didn't like the way a policy was shaping up. He did so with Richardson on pay TV in 1992 and on changes to tariff policy in 1991. On this latter occasion, Richardson told colleagues that Packer had vowed never to invest in Australian manufacturing industry again. But there are others who have been on the wrong end of a Packer tirade. John Dawkins, for instance, came in for a huge blast from Packer while dining at the Prime Minister's official residence, The Lodge. Memories of the cause of the attack have faded from those who witnessed it, but the style of it has not.

While the Hawke Government was in power, Packer undoubtedly had the capacity to summon ministers to his presence and expect them to obey. 'If Packer rang Hawke and said he wanted to see me,' says one minister, 'then I'd be on the next plane to meet him.' And that was the way that it usually happened. He rarely, if ever, went to see anybody, whether it was politicians, bankers, or even the Pope. They came to see him, and did so at a time of his choosing. He was available when he wanted to be, rather than when others wanted to see him.

Despite a perception to the contrary, however, he was not a close personal friend of Hawke in the way that Sir Peter Abeles, the head of TNT, undoubtedly was. Unlike Sir Peter, he neither called at the Prime Minister's office nor phoned up most days to have a yarn about policy. 'He was not mates with Hawke and didn't want to be. He just used him' is the rather bleak verdict of one of Packer's senior journalists. Yet the Prime Minister seemed keen to be in his good books, ringing him in hospital in 1983 to wish him a speedy recovery from illness, and portraying him in public on occasions as his bosom buddy. Hawke says that he deliberately emphasised his friendship with Packer at public functions because he felt that his treatment at the hands of Costigan had been so outrageous.[18]

In April 1987, three months after the billion-dollar sale of Channel Nine to Alan Bond, the network's stars threw a party at the Sydney studios to wish their old boss farewell. To mark Packer's passing, a special video was shot for the occasion. Even allowing for the fact that he had treated them well, paid them a fortune and made them famous, the big names at Nine seemed genuinely to regret that he was going. In some of the goodbyes there was real affection, and in almost all there was respect. Sam Chisholm, Nine's managing director, set the tone, perhaps more effusively than most, by telling Packer:

> The great thing about Channel Nine is the enormous sense of family feeling that we have. That is quite unique. And the reason that it exists is because of you . . . Nobody has ever got near what

you've built and put together and been responsible for. You should be enormously proud of it, as we all are.

Next came Gerald Stone to talk of Packer's flair for backing programs and seeing ideas to fruition. Filmed on the set of *60 Minutes*, Nine's top-rating current affairs show, he said Kerry had been the driving force behind this program and several other successes. Kerry had decreed 'Let there be *Sunday*, and out popped *Sunday*,' while the *Today* show had been his kind of *Today* show, and it was he who had made Nine's news competitive with the best in the world.

After that came a cavalcade of stars, Mike Willesee, Ray Martin, Brian Henderson, George Negus, Mike Gibson, Ian Chappell, Richie Benaud and more, sporting shades as they parodied the World Series Cricket anthem, with a performance of 'Come on Kerry, come on'.

But one man eclipsed them all. Introducing the testimonial video from his garden at Kirribilli House, where he had been filmed specially for the occasion, was Prime Minister Bob Hawke himself. Straight to camera, one powerful man to another, it was a personal, almost embarrassing endorsement. 'G'day, Kerry,' said Hawke for openers, 'I don't think anyone has made a greater contribution to television news and current affairs than you.' After an interlude with the stars, the Prime Minister was back again for an emotional and clearly heartfelt homily on the subject of Packer's treatment by the Costigan Royal Commission. Packer had been cleared by the statement in Parliament less than a month earlier. Hawke summed it up thus:

> OK, that's the fun side. When we're talking about Kerry don't let us ever forget the sad side. I don't think any figure in Australia has had to bear such a burden as Kerry Packer, with the unjustified innuendos, slanders, the malicious gossip. And it was all untrue. Loyalty is a two-way thing, Kerry. You've certainly given it to your people. I hope you feel that all of them and all of your friends have stuck by you. You deserve it.

Australia's prime minister was allowed the last word for a sign-off to his mate. 'Good on yer, Kerry,' said a smiling Bob Hawke, 'you've been true blue.'

CHAPTER SEVENTEEN

BONDY'S BILLION

You only get one Alan Bond in your lifetime,
and I've had mine.

Kerry Packer, 1987

Soon after the sale of Channel Nine to Alan Bond for a billion dollars, John D'Arcy, the managing director of Melbourne's *Herald & Weekly Times,* rang Packer to congratulate him on the deal he had done with the bubbling entrepreneur, and to ask him what he was going to do next. Packer gave him this reply: 'Sport, first I'm going to take three years off and get fit. Then I'm going to come back and buy television stations for half the price their new owners just paid for them. Then, son, I'm going to have some fun.'

The sale of Channel Nine had not only delivered Packer a huge sum of money, it had also given him the opportunity for a much-needed break. He had been going to the office every day for thirty years and was fat, out-of-condition and very bored. What's more, he had just suffered a major health scare. In May 1986 he had been rushed to Princess Grace private hospital in London complaining of severe stomach pains, having collapsed on the golf course at Gleneagles, just north of Edinburgh. The doctors had opened him up to find a diseased gall bladder and a cancerous kidney, both of which they had then removed. According to his brother Clyde, who dined out on the story, Kerry had been angry enough to send the offending organs to his doctors in Sydney with a note demanding to know why they had not detected the problem. The brush with death had clearly given him a shock, for he later told Ian Wooldridge from the London *Daily Mail*: 'It brought me up with a jolt. I'm not a great ponderer, but the operation made me realise that life isn't a dress rehearsal.'

Having realised that he might not have long to live, Packer had decided to enjoy himself and had discovered a passion for polo. One of the advantages of this, as he told anyone who would listen, was that he would be able to keep away from the stock market for a time and prevent himself from buying anything. In early 1987, some six months before the October crash, his friend Jimmy Goldsmith, a long-standing member of the billionaire businessmen's club that Kerry had just joined, was selling his investments and cashing up. Packer shared his apocalyptic view that trouble was on the way, and wanted to be out of the office so that he couldn't spend his billion-dollar windfall—not on business, at least. And polo provided the perfect answer.

Few men can ever have pushed themselves so hard in the pursuit of fun, for Packer took to the game with a savage determination to get good at it, fearing that he would be laughed at if he did not. But he had good reason to be worried, for polo is a game that is normally played by lithe, snake-hipped young men who can swivel and swerve at will, while Kerry, after thirty years sitting in a chair, smoking eighty cigarettes a day and feasting on milkshakes, ice cream and hamburgers, was a lumbering 130 kilograms and easily puffed. He had a couple of advantages, however, that gave him a start: he was good at ball games and had been a decent rider as a boy, almost forty years before, when his father had made him ride in jumping competitions at Sydney's Royal Easter Show every year and abused him roundly for not living up to expectations.

All the same, turning a bloated billionaire businessman with high blood pressure, heart problems and recent major surgery into a born-again sportsman was still going to take some doing, no matter how determined Kerry was.

First of all, Packer set about losing some weight and learning to ride again. Then he persuaded his old friend Sinclair Hill, who

355

had once been a brilliant polo player, to teach him the rudiments of the game. And after that, it was just practice, practice, practice. He spent countless hours on a wooden polo horse in his driveway at Palm Beach, sitting in the saddle and swinging the mallet, and countless more hours riding around on the real thing to get his eye in with the little white ball. In Sydney he would take off to Centennial Park each morning at the crack of dawn with his son Jamie for sessions with Sinclair Hill, and the rest of the time he was out in the paddocks at Ellerston, his huge property in the Hunter Valley. At the end of the day he would come in sore and chapped, with no skin left on the more tender parts of his body, yet next morning he would still go out for more. Eventually, his driver George Young passed on the old jockey's trick of wearing pantyhose under his jodhpurs. A dozen extra-large pairs were purchased and training resumed, with Kerry more suitably protected.

His father had been mad keen on the game all his life, and had played for more than twenty years, but he had never taken it that seriously. Like his son, he had always been too big to be much more than a trier. At 115 kilograms when fit, Frank had been a heavy load for his ponies to carry and, according to his polo groom, would cause their backs to bend as he settled into the saddle. Once mounted, he was said by an unkind friend to look 'more like an elephant than a man' and to be 'just as dangerous'.[1] A 1935 match report in the now defunct *Sydney Mail* suggested that it would have been unwise to get in his way when in full flight, for Packer Senior had spent the game charging around, 'hitting the ball with fearful force and bumping his attackers out of the way like chaff'.

Polo in Frank's day had been far more knockabout than the game Kerry was set to play on the international polo circuit, but it was common to both that there was as much action off the field as on it. The polo set in Sydney in the 1930s and 1940s had given young men and women of the moneyed classes the chance to meet up and have fun, and the chukkas had needed to be squeezed in between frequent rounds of cocktails and parties.

Frank, according to his polo groom, tended to hit the cocktails a bit too hard to be at his best on the field. Coming to mount his horse before a match one day, looking a little the worse for wear, Frank asked jokingly which horse he should mount, to which his groom replied, 'If you reckon there's two of them, I shouldn't get on either.'

Sydney's great polo occasion in the 1940s was the annual Packer Cup at the Royal Easter Show, in which Frank always played, and which was normally reported prominently in his newspapers. One year he took a tumble early on in the game and his *Daily Telegraph* reporter dutifully recorded the fact in his copy, writing 'During the first chukka, Mr Frank Packer fell off his horse.' By the time it appeared in the paper this had been thoughtfully amended to a more acceptable and dignified version, which in view of his size may well have been more accurate: 'During the first chukka, Mr Packer's horse fell from under him.'

One of the *Telegraph* photographers, Johnny Smith, also had a memorable encounter with Sir Frank, as he was by then, at the Packer Cup in the 1960s. Smith had been detailed to cover the event for the paper, as per usual, and had set himself up behind one of the goals in the hope of getting some really good pictures. Sure enough, play soon came his way, with the horses thundering down the field in full cry. Just as the goal was about to be scored, he jumped out to snatch the perfect action picture. The next thing he knew, he was waking up in hospital, with the vivid memory of half-a-tonne of horseflesh bearing down on him. He'd been told that horses always swerve to miss people, but the flash had blinded both horse and rider, and he and his camera gear had been knocked flying.

Seated at a table nearby as this had happened was Sir Frank Packer, who was acting as timekeeper. In an instant he was on his feet and running to Smith's side, greatly agitated, but not out of concern for his unconscious employee. 'For Christ's sake,' yelled Packer, 'clear this photographer off the field, he's holding up the game.'

Smith was well enough the next day, despite an injured shoulder, a hairline fracture and an armful of stitches, to cover the Sydney races for the *Telegraph*, where the man who had run him down sought him out to make his apologies. Sir Frank, however, neither offered his condolences nor mentioned the incident again. The Australian Journalists' Association told Smith he should make a formal report in case it came to an insurance claim, so he duly notified Packer's editor-in-chief, David McNicoll, of what had happened. This produced from McNicoll the immortal response: 'God, John, what do you want us to do, sue the polo pony?'

Although Frank had been crazy about polo, he had always approached it in an entirely amateur fashion, but Kerry immediately set about it as though his life depended on it. Whereas Frank had only ever owned half-a-dozen horses and paid no more than three hundred pounds apiece, Kerry was soon spending a fortune on every aspect of the game, 'doing things properly', as he would have put it. When he first took up polo in late 1986, the going rate in Australia for a decent pony was around $5000. Five years later, after Packer's entry to the market, the same sort of animal cost more like $20 000, with prices propelled upwards by the sheer weight of his money. More shockingly, as far as the purists were concerned, he had introduced his own unconventional ideas about stock breeding. One of the ways in which he had celebrated the sale of Channel Nine to Alan Bond was to spend $2 million on a champion English racehorse called Longboat, which he hoped might win him the 1987 Melbourne Cup.[2] Sadly, the horse was injured soon after arrival in Australia and was forced to end his illustrious racing career, whereupon, to the horror of pony breeders and racing fans, Packer put him to stud with pony mares to see whether the racehorse could produce bigger, faster polo ponies.

But it wasn't only on horseflesh that Packer spent money, for he was soon hiring the cream of Australia's polo players to play for him and run his operations, and pumping close to $150 million into a series of private polo complexes from which to stage his assault on the game. Unlike his earlier attack on the cricket world, there was no ulterior motive in this massive expenditure. He had no plans for televised polo or a world polo circus. He just wanted to have fun. Those who dared ask him how much it was costing and whether it was worth it were told to 'get stuffed', in perhaps more direct language than that.[3]

Packer's huge building program began at Ellerston in the Upper Hunter Valley, where his father had first bought some land in 1973. Over the years, Kerry had vastly expanded the property by buying out his neighbours, to the point where he owned 28 000 hectares of some of the best land in Australia. Set in a magnificent stretch of country on the Hunter River, where the grass grows brilliant green after a winter's rain, Ellerston was slap in the middle of one of the world's biggest horse-breeding areas—outhoofed only by Kentucky for the number of brood mares in residence—which made it perfect for polo. And here in 1987, sparing no expense, Kerry set about building a dream.

The transformation he wrought was breathtaking, for within five years a new model town had been created. Behind several kilometres of 2.5-metre-high fence, with its privacy-protecting security guardhouse, was a network of roads, all kerbed and guttered, and clusters of perfect cottages, guesthouses, five-star stable blocks and other immaculate buildings, all of which were spotlessly clean. At the centre of it all was the Packer homestead, built on a grand scale, with thirteen bedrooms and a 1.2 hectare manmade lake, complete with waterfall.

Nearby, the main polo field sat in a perfect natural amphithe-atre, surrounded by jagged hills, like a giant billiard table, with grass so smooth you could play lawn bowls on it. Further on were four more fields, each close to 300 metres long and 200 metres wide, on which Packer and his teams could practise and Ellerston's annual polo competition could be played. For days when it was pouring with rain, there was a vast indoor arena, the length of five cricket pitches, with a black rubber floor.

Packer's 160 polo ponies were housed in huge cathedral-style stable blocks, air-conditioned for the horses' comfort, and kept free of flies by a computerised insecticide mist-release system in the roof. There was a special horse hospital, complete with surgical unit, X-ray room and laboratory, with heated floors and hot-and-cold showers for its equine patients. There was also a private racetrack, where the 200 quarter horses that Packer bred on the property could be put through their paces.

For commuting to and from Sydney, there was an airstrip that could take light planes, and a pad for helicopters. A huge hangar housed the fleet of cars, bikes and all-terrain vehicles used on the property, and a collection of boys' toys that Packer and his guests could have fun with. Among these were an ultralight aircraft Kerry had learned to fly, without taking lessons, and a gaggle of go-karts in which he and his mates could tear around Ellerston's private track. Naturally, the track had been designed to be as testing as possible, with humps and hollows and adverse camber on the corners, separated by long straights where the 500cc carts could get up to 160 kilometres per hour. Naturally, too, Kerry liked it best when the tarmac was wet.

For him and his polo teams to keep fit, there was a gymnasium complete with parquetry floor and ballet barre, aerobics area, weights room and squash court. For less strenuous recreation there was a private cinema seating one hundred people, which could be used by the Packers for private viewings or by the estate's employees. For visitors, there were two luxurious guest-houses fitted out with seventeenth-century antiques, plus an Olympic-sized swimming pool and a couple of tennis courts. Later on, Ellerston would also have its own championship golf course, designed by Greg Norman and built at vast expense, which was solely for the use of the Packer family and their guests. Those who were lucky enough to play on it reported that it was right up there with the best in Australia.

Conditions for the hundred or so people who were brought in to live and work at Ellerston as grooms, blacksmiths, polo players, groundsmen and staff were almost as remarkable. There was a registered club, or pub, filled with rosewood furniture and leather lounges, where employees and their friends could while away the long winter evenings, drinking, watching videos, or playing billiards. There was also a huge restaurant-cum-cafeteria, in which everyone who worked or stayed at the property could get breakfast—steak, bacon and eggs, whatever they wanted—for free. Lunch and dinner were also provided gratis to anyone who came along, until some of the locals started taking advantage of Packer's generosity and deep pockets.

For shoppers, there was a general store-cum-supermarket with a baker and butcher, while for the children of employees, there was a school right in the middle of the property. Also bene-fiting from Packer's largesse, it was perhaps the only one in Australia that had a swimming pool whose length in metres (25) was greater than the number of pupils on the roll (21).

In spending the $30 million, $50 million or $100 million that it cost to realise his dream, Packer went to great lengths to get the locals on side, and not just by giving them the run of their teeth at breakfast time, for he bought locally and employed local workers whenever possible. Not surprisingly, they were grateful for the prosperity he brought to the district, as were the 200 or so builders who worked on the construction and the bulldozer drivers who scraped away the top of a hill to make room for one of the polo pitches. Even the local taxi driver managed to cash in, making the 140-kilometre and $140 round trip from Scone to Ellerston to deliver Packer's papers whenever the big man was in residence.

Packer proved a good neighbour, too, according to local farmers, helping out with feed in times of drought, and with water and fire-fighting gear when bushfires struck. Conse-quently, none had a bad word to say about him, even if they were shocked by the way he and his polo players would hop into the chopper for a quick dash to Sydney's Palm Beach, 170 kilometres away, for a summer swim.

To ferry the polo teams to matches around New South Wales, Packer bought a huge fifteen-seat Sikorsky helicopter (because his Channel Nine chopper was far too small). The horses were sent by road in a fleet of Mercedes prime movers decked out in

the Ellerston livery of a black 'Z' on a white background, representing Packer's two teams, Ellerston Black and Ellerston White.
There were two teams because he had bought one for his son
Jamie as well. Father and son both played polo during the spring
and autumn in Australia, hosting their own tournament at Ellerston in March that has since become a regular fixture in the
Australian calendar.

For much of the rest of the year, Kerry travelled the international circuit, to England in May, France in July, and Argentina
in October, which kept him out of Australia for five months on
the trot. To play the game properly he established an equestrian
headquarters on a par with Ellerston in each of these countries—
apart from the base in France, which was much more modest.
The last of these polo complexes, in Argentina, was slightly less
of a strain on his pocket than Ellerston, but still set him back
some $20 million for the buildings on top of the $10 million that
he spent on acquiring the land. Packer's English headquarters
probably also cost a good $30 million when all the bills had
been paid.

His base there was the fabulous Fyning Hill estate in the heart
of rural England, perched on top of the South Downs near
Midhurst in Sussex, with superb views to the south coast. In the
usual Packer style, it was aggressively private, surrounded by huge
fences, high walls, tall trees and regular notices advising people to
keep out or instructing visitors to report to security. The estate's
previous owner, a friend of Jordan's King Hussein, may well have
been initially responsible for creating these defences, but Packer
certainly did not throw open the gates when he moved in. The
estate cost Packer some $15 million in May 1989 but he imme-
diately set about spending more money on it, ripping out the
gold taps, building a clay-pigeon shooting tower in the grounds,
extending the seven staff cottages and building a new stable
complex to house more than a hundred horses. He also spent
several million dollars bulldozing land to make way for polo
pitches at Great House Farm, which he also owned, in the
nearby village of Stedham.

Packer bought Great House Farm for a mere $1.5 million, shortly after he purchased the Fyning Hill estate, paying more than the asking price to ensure that he secured it. It was perfect for his needs, since it had some 37 hectares of land, almost all of which was extremely flat and fertile. And just as importantly, it was only a few kilometres down the road from Britain's premier polo ground at Cowdray Park.

The saga surrounding this farm, though utterly trivial at one level, provided a fascinating insight into what a rich man like Packer would do to get what he wanted. Days after he bought the property in 1989, with no word to the locals, he sent a dozen giant earthmovers lumbering in to level the farm's fields. These were beautiful lush water meadows, right on the edge of Stedham village, that had remained untouched for hundreds of years. An ancient footpath ran across them to a neighbouring hamlet, the occasional cow chewed the buttercups, and the odd villager struck out across them with a dog. But apart from that, they had seen nothing much happen since William the Conqueror's men had put the village in the Domesday Book. For the next four months, Packer's bulldozers worked from dawn till dusk, throwing up great clouds of noise and dust as they scalped the ancient greenery, while the villagers became more and more irate.

In England, one needs planning permission for building works or changing the use of land, and it can be hard in historic villages like Stedham to get approval for simple things like erecting a shed or changing a window frame. But Packer did not bother with such niceties, even though he was moving half-a-million tonnes of earth. At a public meeting called by his agent, Pat Tudor, to calm the locals' anger, villagers were told that planning permission had been neither granted nor sought, because none was necessary. This was because the property was still to be used for farming, as an 'experimental turf farm' to be precise. The locals weren't fooled; lasers were being employed to level the land and a tarmac road was being built across it, and they knew full well that Packer loved polo.

For several months, Pat Tudor swore black and blue that there would be nothing played on the 'experimental turf farm's' fields apart from a bit of 'stick and ball with chums' to see whether the turf stood up to wear and tear. But soon an old barn on the site had been converted into a clubhouse for players, and flags were being used to mark out the pitches. Shortly afterwards, the cars, the spectators and competition polo arrived, and thus came an inevitable confrontation between angry English peasants and their arrogant Australian squire. As the first match got under way, a band of villagers set out to walk the footpath that led them right into the thick of the game. They were met halfway by Kerry Packer himself, who came across to ask what they thought of the development. When told they didn't like it one bit, he asked them why. 'You've destroyed the village,' said one of them.

'But it's still there,' replied a puzzled Packer, adding for good measure: 'Only an arrant moron would say that.'

After a two-year battle between Packer and the villagers, permission for the English polo complex was finally sought and received from the planners in 1991, albeit with conditions attached. Competition polo was not to be played on the pitch that straddled the ancient footpath, while helicopters, grand-stands, public-address systems and television cameras were all banned. But in Stedham the bitterness remained. There was no chance of the old meadows being put back, the new road being dug up or the brick-and-wood barn being restored to its original rustic state.

Packer's spending spree certainly brought him success at the game, even though his own handicap never exceeded a modest one goal, out of a maximum possible ten.[4] But this was because he always bought the best. In the early 1990s, for example, there were only eight ten-goal polo players in the game, yet Packer had two in his four-man team. For a fee said to be 300 000 pounds apiece, Kerry secured Argentinian brothers Gonzalo and Alfonso Pieres to ride for Ellerston White during the two-month-long British summer season. Later in the decade, he had the world's best player, Adolfo Cambiaso, on his side.

Polo in Great Britain is run by aristocrats and ex-army officers, and watched by people with cut-glass accents, yet Australia's richest man was welcomed warmly to their club. This was understandable, since Kerry was charming and could behave like the perfect gentleman. And the game had always catered for people like him, with a handicap system that allowed the rich to actually take part, which is more than one can say for ocean racing. Teams in polo are traditionally based around a wealthy *patron* (pronounced in the French manner), who pays mercenaries to fight on his side. And *patrons* have often been foreigners, whether Arab sheikhs, eastern sultans, Indian princes or Australian media moguls. Some have even had more money than Packer. The Sheikh of Abu Dhabi, for example, used to have a Boeing 747 for commuting to Windsor from his emirate, which had been specially fitted out with stables for his polo ponies and a parking space for his favourite Rolls-Royce. So Kerry's massive expenditure was not unprecedented.

In July 1991, ABC TV's *Four Corners* filmed Packer playing in the final of the British Gold Cup at Cowdray Park and found it to be a truly international event. The balls had been flown in from Dallas, Texas; the two teams' *patrons* were Packer and a Greek-born shipping magnate called Embiricos; and four of the remaining six players on the field came from Argentina or Mexico. The mainly British spectators were adamant that Packer had been 'jolly good for polo' because he had put a lot of money into the game, brought jobs to the area, and been prepared to have a go. 'I think he's done awfully well,' was the almost-unanimous verdict of the upper-crust polo fans as they tucked into their strawberries and cream, with one adding that they thought a great deal of another famous Australian, Alan Bond.

Packer's presence at this climax to the British polo season was impressive. As in Australia, huge black-and-white articulated horse floats had ferried some forty ponies to the field, so that Kerry's four-man team could all be offered a change of mount at the end of each chukka. His white V12 BMW 750, which he used when he was in the country, as opposed to the black

Bentley Turbo he normally kept in town, was parked near a brace of Range Rovers that had brought his family and their friends to cheer him on. In their polo gear, blue blazers and flowing summer dresses, with their picnics and easy chairs, they fitted in perfectly with the surrounding scene.

It would be an exaggeration to say that Packer played well in the match, for he was probably the worst of the eight players on the field and was certainly handicapped by his bulk, which made it hard for him to turn as sharply as the best can do. But for such a big man, giving twenty years' start to the others, and with health problems that would have consigned most ordinary people to the sidelines, he was quite astonishingly good. One can't be sure what Genghis Khan would have looked like on horseback but one suspects that Kerry would have cut an equally impressive figure at the head of the Mongol army. He was quite obviously an excellent horseman with a good eye for the ball. In full flight, as he thundered down the field, fiercely aggressive and remarkably fit, he looked much as his father must have done, like a train at full tilt; formidable, unstoppable and a sight to behold.

At the time, Packer was bidding for the Fairfax newspaper group, as part of the Tourang consortium. After the game, I asked him whether he would be prepared to talk to the ABC about it. The conversation went like this:

Barry: Mr Packer, hello, I am Paul Barry from ABC TV, I wondered if you might be prepared to say something about the Fairfax bid.
Packer: I have nothing to say to the ABC . . . ever.
Barry: Not even about the polo?
Packer: And get your bloody cameras out of there. Take them away. Just leave me alone.

Packer then pushed on to where his party was sitting, at which point his polo manager, Jim Gilmore, a Queensland farmer and six-goal polo player, came up to offer some rather less friendly advice, which, shorn of a few expletives, went like this: 'Fuck off.

Just fuck off. Get out of here. Or you'll get my fist in your face. Get right out of here or I'll spread your face.' I pointed out that it was a public place, that we had permission to film and that I had merely asked Mr Packer whether he would mind talking to us. The threats of physical violence were repeated half-a-dozen times, even after I made it clear that we would leave.

Even though he had the estate at Fyning Hill, Packer maintained a tradition of staying at London's Savoy Hotel during the English polo season, taking several suites for the entire summer. Stories varied as to what he had from year to year, but in 1986, when he was recuperating from his stomach operation, visitors described it as half a floor, some of which had been redecorated for him and fitted out with his own furniture. In 1990, he was reported to have eight suites for three months, at a cost of $40 000 a week, while in 1992, he appeared to one visitor to have taken the whole of one wing overlooking the river, or about twenty rooms. His polo team, meanwhile, was being accommodated in lavish style at the Dorchester Hotel in Park Lane, with their every need catered for.

To play polo in Sussex, Packer would be driven across the Thames in his Bentley to Battersea heliport, choppered down to his estate to play a few chukkas, and then choppered back to London, where the Bentley was waiting to pick him up again. You could tell whether he was in residence at the Savoy because his distinctive car with its equally distinctive number plate, 80 AUS, was usually parked right outside the hotel's front door.

While he was in London, the Savoy served as Packer's office, with a string of merchant bankers, media men, Channel Nine executives, television stars, stockbrokers and business rivals trooping along to see him. They were generally received by a man in polo whites or a tracksuit, throwing a football around or practising his putting. Few were greeted with great enthusiasm, to judge by the tales they told or by Packer's own public pronouncements. He told one journalist he no longer 'gave a stuff' about business, spent all his time thinking about polo, and resented having to waste even a minute on managing his business affairs.[5] But as his son James would soon discover, it was impossible to stop Kerry running the empire, wherever he was and whatever he said about being bored by it all.

CHAPTER EIGHTEEN

THE MIDAS TOUCH?

My father was a gambler. Every man who
ever created anything was a gambler. I am
also, but there's a difference . . . I've never
risked the lot. I've never risked anything that's
going to put Consolidated Press at risk.

Kerry Packer, 1979

In mid 1986, as he recovered from his cancer scare, Packer had summoned his friend Trevor Kennedy to his bedside at the Savoy Hotel and anointed him managing director. Kennedy had run Packer's magazine business since 1981 and was now, or so he hoped, being given the chance to run the entire empire. Certainly, if the Big Fella dropped dead in the near future, Kennedy would be left in charge, for Jamie Packer was still only nineteen years old.

Six months later, after selling Channel Nine to Alan Bond, Packer was claiming he would retire. But his resolution to stay away did not last long. Like Frank Sinatra and Dame Nellie Melba, Packer found it hard to leave the stage, and he was soon back again, looking for excitement. As he quickly discovered, even having fun could lose its thrill, and there was nothing like the thrill of the deal to get the adrenalin pumping again.

Physically, Packer was often absent from the office, especially after the sale of Channel Nine, but he was never far away from the action and he was always on the end of the phone. He was rarely out of contact with Kennedy for more than a day or two and was always involved in the major corporate plays that Consolidated Press was making. The company, he said later, was run from wherever he happened to be at any particular time.[1]

What rendered retirement impossible was that Packer could never find enough people to play with, to keep boredom at bay. Polo went some way to keeping him occupied but he really wanted four or five mates in Australia who could match him in money, intellect and desire to have fun, and they simply didn't exist. When he came back home after his overseas trips he would sit up at Ellerston for a few days, firing rifles off his back verandah or at the pop-up buffalo on his private firing range, and racing round in go-karts or playing paintball. Then he would roar down to Sydney to throw some money at the bookmakers, fire a few copyboys or spend a few million dollars on buying something, just to make life interesting again. He craved action and excitement, and business was the place where it could always be created.

The sale of Channel Nine had given him some $800 million in cash to play with, and a simple way to amuse himself was to spend it. For most of 1987 the stock market was rising, and property started booming after that. Then there was the wreckage of the recession in which to search for bargains. And so began a spending spree such as the Packer empire had never seen before. Typically, given his love of bargains, there was little logic to it all. One of Kerry's weaknesses as a businessman was that he was prepared to buy anything, and could be led astray by 'mates' who came to him with deals. In the past he had backed youth wonder drugs, automatic pineapple peelers, piemakers and potato farms, and he now went shopping with one main rule to guide him: if it was cheap, it was fair game, whether it was a Chinese laundry, a merchant bank or a chemical company.

Packer even spent much of 1986 trying to buy newspapers. As he recuperated in his Savoy Hotel suite in June he made a rather half-hearted attempt to get control of London's *Today* newspaper, an ailing tabloid daily owned by Eddie Shah, which had been driven to the brink of bankruptcy by Shah's fight with the printing unions. Packer talked to Shah about the possibility of bailing him out in return for a controlling stake in the business, but the talks eventually came to nothing. In the meantime, between taking his medication and nipping out to the casino, he was making daily phone calls to a far more important newspaper boss in Australia.

Packer had been approached at the start of 1986 by John D'Arcy, chief executive of Melbourne's huge Herald & Weekly Times group, to see whether he would sell his suburban and country newspapers in New South Wales, where the Herald was keen to get a foothold. Characteristically, Packer had said he would be happy to sell if the price was right, for he had never loved newspapers and had no emotional attachment to these ones. So, after the accountants and advisers had given their opinions of the papers' worth, the two had sat down in Packer's office in Sydney to sort out a price. Neither had been keen to name a figure and each had tried to persuade the other to start the bidding.

'You're the vendor,' said D'Arcy, 'you should say what you want for it.'

'Oh no,' said Packer, 'you came knocking on my door. You tell me what you think they're worth.'

Eventually the matter was settled by Packer producing a 20-cent piece from his pocket and saying: 'Tell you what, sport, I'll spin a coin to see who bats first.'

The doubtful privilege of opening fell to D'Arcy, who pushed forward with a bid of $90 million. No, said Packer, that was out of the question; he wanted $125 million or he wouldn't let the papers go. Five minutes later, the deal was done and a price of $100 million agreed.

But these negotiations merely raised the prospect of a much bigger deal that interested Packer far more. Why, he suggested, didn't the Herald & Weekly Times, with its 142 newspapers and commercial radio stations, join forces with Consolidated Press, with its television stations and magazines, to form a media group that would dominate Australia? Between them, they could be number one in newspapers, magazines, television and radio all at once. D'Arcy was keen on the idea because he was fairly sure the Herald & Weekly Times would be ravished by someone else if the merger didn't go ahead and because the company's share price was riding high, which made it an opportune moment to strike a deal.

But D'Arcy's directors at the Herald & Weekly Times were far less keen on joining up with Packer, whom some of them regarded as not their sort of person. Even though his money was sixty years old, it was still Sydney money and its makers had always lacked a certain gentility. Put bluntly, they also knew that Packer would be the largest shareholder in the new group and might ride roughshod over them if he took control. And their fears were probably justified. In one of Packer's many telephone conversations with D'Arcy while the Herald board deliberated, Packer told his new-found friend, 'When this is all tied up, we'll get rid of those fucking dickheads on that board of yours.' D'Arcy, who did not entirely share Kerry's views on the subject, had to tell him to calm down and play it cool.

By mid 1986, despite some directors' reservations, it began to look likely that the merger would go ahead, with Packer taking the chairman's job and receiving 30 per cent of the new company, subject to a prohibition on him increasing his stake by more than 3 per cent a year, to stop him throwing his weight around. Then, just as the deal seemed settled, both Packer and D'Arcy were struck down. Packer was rushed to the London clinic to have his left kidney removed, while D'Arcy went into a Melbourne hospital to have a small melanoma seen to. There doctors found he had a large tumour buried like an iceberg beneath his skin. And suddenly everything ground to a halt.

Having survived the surgeon's knife, Packer rang Australia almost every day for six weeks to urge D'Arcy to get a move on. D'Arcy meanwhile was struggling into his Melbourne office minus most of his hair, thanks to his daily dose of radiation, and trying to get the deal moving again. But by this time momentum had slowed and doubts had begun to creep in on all sides. One section of the Herald board, representing the Adelaide *Advertiser*, had commissioned an expert report that suggested the Herald might have better options to pursue. Packer, in response, soon brought his own expert adviser, Jim Wolfensohn, in on the act and demanded that he should be allowed to move faster to full control.

When the crunch finally came in late 1986, the Herald & Weekly Times board was almost evenly divided as to whether in principle the deal should go ahead. And after a full day of argument a formal vote had to be taken to break the deadlock. In the end, the verdict could quite easily have gone the other way but Packer's merger proposal was defeated by the narrowest of margins. Thus a deal that would have changed the face of the Australian media and allowed Packer to dominate the scene to an extraordinary extent only just failed to proceed. Packer was bitterly disappointed, for he had been sure of success right to the end. D'Arcy was even sadder, not least because his fears of a takeover were proved right a couple of months later when Rupert Murdoch captured the company. Perhaps if Kerry had been prepared to pay top dollar—as Rupert was—the Australian media landscape would now look very different. But with Packer, price was always paramount.

For all his professed desire to be playing polo and his declared boredom with business, Packer wasn't only talking to D'Arcy in late 1986 as the fate of their plan for the Herald & Weekly Times was decided. He was also deep in discussions with the colourful entrepreneur Warren Anderson and touring Papua New Guinea with him in the search for gold.

Warren Anderson was one of those people from the wrong side of the tracks with whom Packer so loved to do business. A rough, aggressive, self-made man who had made money fast, he had the reputation of being one of the smartest property developers in Australia. Before making his fortune in Perth, he had been a wheat grower, kangaroo shooter, shearer and bulldozer driver. Then in the late 1970s, after a prosperous and private decade building shopping centres for Coles New World, he had moved to New South Wales and become famous, though not perhaps in the way he would have wanted.

In his newly adopted state, Anderson had made connections right across the social spectrum, from enforcers and criminals on the one hand, to powerful politicians in the New South Wales Labor Party on the other. At one end of the scale he had become friends with Paul Keating and Graham Richardson and two New South Wales Cabinet ministers, Rex Jackson and Eric Bedford. Towards the other he had employed gentlemen such as Tim Bristow and Tom Domican to visit people opposed to his projects and persuade them to change their minds.[2]

Anderson had received a lot of unwanted publicity over these social and business connections, both in the press and in the New South Wales Parliament, but none of it had stopped him getting richer. All it had done was increase his contempt for parliamentarians and magnify his hatred of journalists so that it matched Kerry Packer's.

Anderson, like Packer, was a determinedly private man who lived the life of a semi-recluse when he wasn't doing business. Such reticence was unusual in a boots-and-all Western Australian entrepreneur, as was the style he displayed in spending his enormous wealth. In the subtropical north of the Northern Territory, Anderson owned a huge cattle station called Tipperary, which was probably the only property in Australia capable of giving Packer's Ellerston a run for its money. The 40-kilometre drive from the main highway to the Anderson homestead was lined with 2000 specially planted palm trees, while the house itself, sited on an artificial lake, had been built with stone carted across the continent from the coast of New South Wales. The property covered around 5000 square kilometres and was almost unbelievably lavish, with its own abattoir, show rings, private zoo and an airstrip that could handle planes as big as a Boeing 707.

Anderson's pied-à-terre in his old home town of Perth promised to be almost as impressive if it were ever completed. In the centre of Peppermint Grove, the fanciest suburb in the city, he had bought up eleven properties surrounding his house and knocked down ten of them to make a garden at a cost of some $10 million, in the middle of which he was building a huge Federation-style stately home. Meanwhile in Sydney, where he was now spending more of his time, he had yet another two places to rest his head. On the harbour front at Elizabeth Bay he owned a pink art deco Spanish villa called Boomerang, said to be worth another $10 million, while out to the west of Sydney towards Penrith he had a magnificent old property called Fern Hill, with its own stables and racetrack and another private zoo, which was reckoned to be worth considerably more.

As well as being a collector of houses, the culture-loving property developer was a connoisseur of antiques, which were cared for by a full-time restorer he had brought over from England. This pastime gave him something in common with Australia's prime minister-to-be Paul Keating, who had shared a Paris shopping trip with Anderson to look for trinkets and had stayed in his Sydney waterfront house for several weeks while the Keating home was being renovated. The future Labor prime minister had also visited Anderson several times at Fern Hill, to which he had been ferried on one occasion in the developer's helicopter.

Anderson's other passions—guns and money—had helped bring him close to Packer. Included in his multi-million-dollar collection of some 600 antique weapons were a pair of pistols that Napoleon had given to Josephine, a selection of rare Colts in mint condition and the sword once used by Colonel Custer. But Anderson liked to use his guns as well as look at them. He was said to have hunted everything in the world that was huntable, shooting polar bears in the Arctic, stalking deer in New Zealand and potting pigs from a helicopter in the Northern Territory with Packer and Keating.

Anderson's style in business was to work ferociously hard and take real risks. In the words of a rival developer, he was 'a real double-or-nothing merchant', someone who was prepared to put his 'balls on the block' to make money. And he had an enviable record of picking winners, which was doubtless what persuaded Packer to join him in November 1986 in an extremely risky new venture, looking for gold on the Pacific rim. Unfortunately for Packer, however, it was not just Anderson's tender bits that ended up being crushed in this case.

Looking back with only a modest degree of hindsight, it is hard to see how Packer could have been so rash as to throw almost $200 million at a bunch of unexplored jungle properties that might or might not produce gold. But he would doubtless have looked brave and brilliant had he struck lucky. And even if the road to Eldorado was jammed with fools, others had hit the jackpot just before him, which was why a new gold rush had started in the mid 1980s to the remote mountainous regions of the western Pacific along what is glamorously known as the Rim of Fire.

On this side of the ocean, the Rim of Fire stretches in an arc from Kamchatka down to New Zealand, through the Philippines, Indonesia and Papua New Guinea, along a ridge of volcanic activity that several geologists thought was a dead cert to contain gold in commercial quantities. Two big finds had already been made in PNG by a geologist called Peter Macnab who had made the discoveries for Kennecott Copper. It was Macnab's judgment that Packer was essentially relying on, for he had selected most of the areas in which Packer's money was to be punted.

But it was Warren Anderson who was responsible for bringing Packer and Macnab together. Anderson had already formed a joint venture to look for gold with a company called Pacific Arc Exploration that had been floated on the stock exchange by Macnab and a Brisbane used-car dealer called Eddie Stoyle. Anderson had apparently agreed to pay the exploration costs and throw in some good prospects in Indonesia, where he had powerful friends, in return for a majority share in the operation. Anderson had a local partner in Indonesia, who had perhaps helped persuade President Soeharto in late 1986 to grant them exploration areas 'under the hand of the President'.

Packer was therefore buying into an existing partnership that owned rights to explore for gold in various parts of the Philippines, Papua New Guinea and Indonesia. All of these were greenfield sites, where it was impossible to be sure there would be any gold at all. In other words, Packer was risking everything he staked on the venture.

On paper, it cost Packer $107 million to take part in this corporate gold rush, but none of his initial contribution appears to have been in cash. Payment was made by surrendering shares in his mining company, Muswellbrook Energy and Minerals (MEM), to Pacific Arc Exploration and a Hong Kong company called Asiamet Resources (apparently owned half by Anderson and half by Consolidated Press). But real money was then pumped in to fund exploration and was soon disappearing down the drain. Not to put too fine a point on it, the whole exercise was a disaster in double-quick time. Eighteen months after Packer joined the treasure hunt, $62 million of the original investment had been wiped out, while all six of the original exploration areas in Indonesia and all but one of the five sites in Papua New Guinea had been abandoned. Nor did things improve. Five further exploration areas in Indonesia, acquired in late 1987, also proved to be duds, so that by 1989 the balance of the $107 million investment had been all but written off. Even worse, by the end of the search another $88 million had been spent to discover that the prospects did not contain enough gold to be worth mining, if indeed they contained any at all.

The main losers in this sad debacle, apart from Packer himself, were 1300 small shareholders in Muswellbrook Energy & Minerals, who lost virtually everything they had invested in the company. Before the deal was announced in April 1987, their shares had been worth $1.40 and the company $100 million. By the time Packer swept up the remains in mid 1991, their shares were down to 5 cents and the company was all but worthless.[3] Several financial institutions also came out severely bruised after putting up $50 million in a private placement of Muswellbrook shares in early 1987 to fund the exploration expenditure.

Before the ink had dried on this Rim of Fire deal (and long before it became clear that it had been such a disaster) Packer was joining Anderson in more conventional property development ventures. The first such project, in March 1987 in Melbourne's Bourke Street, did little better than break even when they sold the site to National Mutual in 1988. Subsequent property ventures in Perth's central business district, however, turned out to be a second huge loser for the Anderson–Packer team, costing Packer some $200 million and wiping out Anderson's fortune completely, of which more in due course.[4]

But it wasn't just newspapers, gold or property that caught Packer's eye as he tried to spend Bond's money. In early 1987, shortly after the Channel Nine sale, Packer called in a team of analysts from Melbourne's IBIS consulting group and sat them down with his executives for a two-day session in Sydney. He told them he wanted to turn his $1 billion into $5 billion within five years, and asked them to figure out what he should invest in. Their advice was that he should consider putting money into chemicals, mining and rural investments. And so, before long, he was busy buying in all these areas.

In late 1987 Packer bought Australia's biggest cotton processor and farmer, Auscott, for $80 million and simultaneously took a stake in the country's second-biggest grower, Colly Farms Cotton, with the intention of marrying the two. The plan was for his Consolidated Press group to become the controlling shareholder in Australia's most powerful and lowest-cost cotton producer, which would also be one of the biggest in the world. But just as the marriage was about to be made, the October stock market crash upset the nuptials. Packer's rules in making money had always been to buy and sell at the right time and to get things cheap, and the dive in share prices meant he was suddenly committed to paying too much. Then in early December 1987 cotton prices dived as well and the deal began to look doubly dangerous. Packer was lucky enough to find a rival bidder for Colly Farms Cotton who needed his shares, and in February 1988 he was able to escape from the deal with the unexpected bonus of a $10 million profit. Two years later he sold out of Auscott as well, taking a further profit of $33 million in the process and ending his short flirtation with the cotton industry.

Packer's foray into chemicals lasted longer and was much more successful. If he had any rules in business apart from picking up bargains, it was to buy companies that had a monopoly in their market or a dominant share. Chemplex fitted this requirement perfectly, being the only major Australian producer of the packaging material styrene monomer, with 75 per cent of the market. Packer paid Chemplex's American owners, Monsanto, $150 million for the company in March 1988 and then watched it produce after-tax profits of $55 million the following year, when styrene prices rose crazily. In later years Chemplex made less money, but it was sold in 1993 for more than it had cost, even though Consolidated Press retained valuable waterfront land in Balmain, Sydney, that had come as part of the parcel.

Throughout 1987 Packer was also extremely active in the share market, despite his habitual pessimism about the world economy. One of the more successful plays was with the British merchant bank Hill Samuel, whose shares he started buying early in the year until he built up a stake of around 12 per cent of the company at a cost of around $100 million. The pundits then predicted a Packer takeover, possibly with help from Larry Adler of Australia's FAI Insurance, who had simultaneously acquired a similar stake. But if this was ever a serious option it was abandoned after a frosty reception from the Bank of England, and once again Packer was extremely lucky to unload the shares when he did. Both he and Trevor Kennedy became bearish about the stock market in the middle of the year, but it was Kennedy who decided the shares had to be sold and who got on a plane to London in late September 1987 to find a buyer, hiring the British merchant bank Robert Fleming to help. Two weeks later, Fleming called Consolidated Press to say that the Trustee Savings Bank, a new British bidder for Hill Samuel, was keen to buy them out. Packer and Kennedy took the money and ran, pocketing a handsome profit of around $80 million. A further two weeks later, in mid October, the world's stock markets crashed and the share price went plummeting.

These share market plays were fun and frequently profitable, but they could not make Consolidated Press worth $5 billion in the time Packer wanted, even if they all came off. And the losses in gold and property with Warren Anderson were big enough to more than cancel them out. But by 1989 Packer was getting involved in far bigger corporate adventures that at least had the capacity to make him as rich as he wanted to be.

In the early 1980s, Packer had teamed up with his friend Jimmy Goldsmith the British financier and the banker Jacob Rothschild to mount raids on a couple of big American multi-nationals, with a view to taking them over and shaking up their management. And the three had generally made money even though they had never quite hit the target. In 1984, for example, they had picked up a quick $70 million profit after grabbing a stake in the big St Regis Paper group and selling it back to the company. Two years later they had repeated the trick and picked up a similar profit from an attempted takeover of the huge American tyre company Goodyear.

These corporate war games had come to a halt at the beginning of 1987 when Goldsmith disappeared into self-imposed exile in Mexico to avoid the global depression he believed was coming. But after two years building a mansion to rival Britain's Blenheim Palace in 25 000 hectares of idyllic forest, he had become bored, as all self-respecting entrepreneurs seem to do, and decided it was time for action again. In January 1989, he summoned Packer and Rothschild to his Mexican hideout to identify new targets for the team, and proposed an attack on the massive food, tobacco and retailing group British American Tobacco. In March 1989 the trio flew into London and loosed off a few warning shots, capturing 29.9 per cent of another British food company, Ranks Hovis McDougall, for $880 million. Then in July, they came back into town to announce the big one.

Kerry Packer in full flight on the polo field.

Polo was Packer's passion. His Ellerston estate in the NSW Hunter Valley has air-conditioned stables for 160 polo ponies, five full-sized pitches and a private racetrack. There are similar complexes in England and Argentina. And the cost of it all? Best guess, around $100 million.

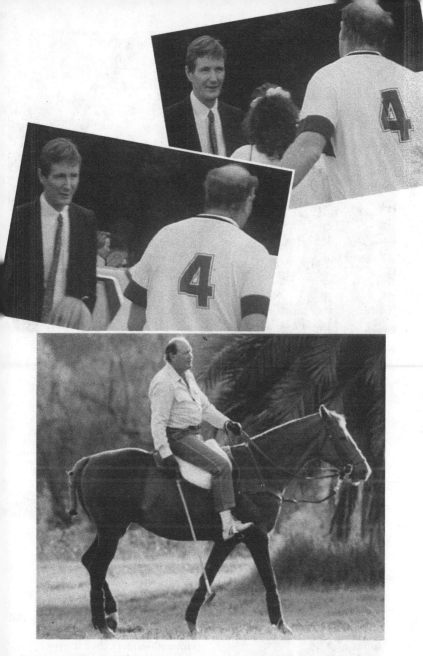

A very private man. 'Get your bloody cameras out of here . . . leave me alone', said Kerry when I approached him at a polo game in England in July 1991. His minder then warned me to 'fuck off' or he would 're-arrange my face'.

Proud father, happy bride. Kerry's daughter Gretel was married in July 1991 in Sussex, near the Packers' magnificent English estate, Fyning Hill *(right below)*. Old friends at the fifteenth-century church service included rival tycoon Rupert Murdoch *(above)* and former NSW Premier, Neville Wran *(left)*.

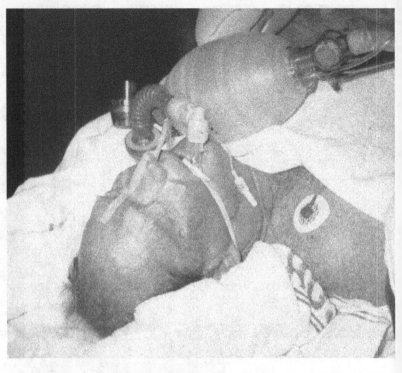

Rising from the dead. Kerry Packer 'died' for eight minutes in October 1990 during a cardiac arrhythmia.

Six days later he was back, mixing it with cameramen at a polo match and telling them, 'Get out of my way. Leave me alone.'

Sharks – Kerry Packer and Greg Norman won the AT&T Pro-Am at Pebble Beach in California in February 1992, breaking the tournament record by six shots. Packer, off 16 handicap, improved on Norman's score 38 times in 72 holes.

Even on the opening shot of $28 billion, the bid for BAT was set to be the second-biggest takeover the world had ever seen, outgunned only by the 1988 move on RJR Nabisco, which it almost matched in size. And the potential profit was extraordinary, too, offering an expected $14 billion or more in gains from the planned sale of BAT's individual businesses.

As Goldsmith outlined the strategy and Rothschild helped with the numbers at the London launch of the bid, Packer sat chain-smoking in the background, demonstrating that tobacco companies did still have a future. Having said nothing throughout the proceedings, he was asked by one journalist about his role. He replied helpfully that he liked doing business with the other two and had always wanted to go to a press conference like this one. He had played little part in the detailed planning but had been happy to lend his financial muscle. As one of his top executives put it, 'Packer thought Goldsmith was the brightest, smartest man on earth' and was happy to back his friend's judgment.

It had not at this stage cost him much money to do so, for the beauty of the deal was that the Goldsmith team was putting little more than promises on the table. They were launching the bid with only a token 1.25 per cent stake in the company, which had cost them a mere $260 million. If the bid succeeded, they would then have to fork out another $500 million each in cash. But this would bring them fabulous rewards that, according to BAT's analysis, would give them $360 million of every $1 billion profit that the BAT break-up produced and deliver them a $5 billion windfall from the anticipated gain of $14 billion.

BAT's shareholders would also reap their share of these profits but in the meantime they would have to accept junk bonds from Drexel Burnham Lambert and shares in a new Goldsmith company called Anglo Group for the bulk of their $28 billion investment. The reaction from BAT's management to this part of the proposal was both scathing and aggressive, and few of London's stock market analysts liked it either. They were suspicious of junk bonds, had concerns about Drexels and thought

Goldsmith and his partners were taking too big a share of the spoils. But in the end, BAT shareholders were never required to make up their minds.

First, the prospect of the bid succeeding was diminished by a decision of the US regulatory authorities to investigate the planned sale of BAT's American insurance company, which was an essential part of the takeover strategy. Then came disaster for the Goldsmith team as Drexel Burnham Lambert went bust in spectacular fashion. For several months the BAT bid remained suspended, despite repeated promises that it would be relaunched. Finally, it fizzled out in April 1990, ten months after the fireworks of the initial launch.

In terms of collateral damage, Packer escaped lightly compared to the others because of the way the consortium was structured, and he emerged from the raid with a loss of only $15 million. But the team's assault on Ranks Hovis McDougall proved a more costly failure. When it was finally abandoned in February 1991 without a formal takeover being attempted, Packer suffered a further hit of around $60 million. There were other losses around this time, however, that hurt even more. A dive into the waste business in the USA, for example, cost Consolidated Press around $100 million, while a similar sortie into the US oil business produced losses almost as large. And, of course, there was the $200 million he had lost with Anderson, which brought the total up near half a billion dollars.

The truth was that Packer was not 'THE MAN WITH THE MIDAS TOUCH', as the headline writers liked to call him. Nor did he have a grand strategic vision of how his empire should grow. He was essentially a conservative and cautious businessman who confined his gambling to the casino and the racetrack. Unlike Murdoch and Goldsmith, who had built empires from scratch, and whose vision he envied, he never took risks in business that could make or break the company. Nor did he like going out of his comfort zone. In the mid 1980s, his American adviser, Jim Wolfensohn, suggested he should buy the ailing CBS TV network in the USA (of which Wolfensohn was a director), but

Packer could not be tempted. He liked being a big fish in a small pool and did not relish the financial gamble he would have to take by getting deep into debt to buy the network.

But Packer did have undoubted strengths: he listened long to his advisers and then acted fast and decisively. He had brilliant timing, great instincts, strong nerves and superb negotiating skills. And his winners usually made up for what he lost on the also-rans.

One of these big winners was the Fairfax magazine empire, which he bought in early 1988 for the bargain price of $212 million. Packer had acquired an irritant stake in the John Fairfax group in late 1987, while young Warwick Fairfax was trying to privatise the company, in the hope that he could pick up the *Financial Review* in exchange for selling his shares without making a fuss. But when that was denied him, he was more than happy to settle for a quiver of magazines that included the top-selling *Woman's Day*, *People*, *Cosmopolitan*, *Dolly* and *Good House-keeping*. These additions made his Australian Consolidated Press unassailable as the leader in magazine publishing, with more than 50 per cent of the Australian market. And Packer's management promptly increased this dominance by improving sales and revenue for almost all the titles they acquired.

A second big winner was Australia's largest engineering company, ANI, bought by Packer for $380 million in April 1989.[5] When companies hit hard times or were buried in a blizzard of bad publicity, Kerry was often a buyer, and this was a classic example. The shares had taken a hammering over the company's investment in the collapsed Spedley merchant banking group, which was set to cost ANI more than $200 million, and Packer had decided they were oversold. Few agreed at the time (though all accepted he was brave) but Packer proved them wrong. In the next fifteen months companies were sold, factories closed and excess management cut away, with the effect that debt was reduced from $570 million to $240 million and profits increased. Eventually ANI's shares responded to the improvement and Packer was able to sell out in 1991 with a profit of $180 million. Sadly, many employees lost their jobs in the process.

The third win was the best of all, paying off handsomely enough to wipe out all Packer's losses in one big hit, and this was the American coupon insert manufacturer Valassis, bought in December 1986 for US$365 million (A$520 million). Valassis made its living by printing and selling space in promotional brochures that were inserted into the middle of Sunday newspapers. Big consumer-goods manufacturers such as Kellogg, Nabisco and Colgate Palmolive used these brochures to launch special offers and issue coupons that gave customers discounts on their products. This was a fast-growing business in the United States and Valassis was the dominant player, with almost 50 per cent of the market.

In the first three years that Packer owned the company things did not go well. Valassis built up losses of US$121.5 million (A$174 million) before tax and must have looked like a turkey. Then, quite suddenly, its fortunes changed. Over the next two years it recouped all its losses and more, by making a pre-tax profit for 1990 and 1991 of US$147.9 million (A$211 million). This transformation turned the company into an immensely valuable commodity.

The difference between profit and loss was simple, and it owed more than a little to a powerful Australian Packer had known for many years. Soon after Packer bought Valassis, its rivals in the market, Quad Marketing and Product Movers, started discounting prices heavily. Then late in 1988 the two companies were taken over, and almost immediately the price war ended. In the following fiscal year, Valassis's revenue increased by a remarkable 40 per cent, 'primarily from substantial price increases', and the company went soaring into profit.[6]

The purchaser of these two rival companies was that well-known Australian businessman and long-time friend of the Packer family, Rupert Murdoch. It was his arrival in the market that helped turn Valassis into a company worth US$1200 million (A$1710 million)—or more than three times what Packer had paid for it—in early 1992, (at which point Packer sold 50 per cent of his shares for a huge tax-free gain).[7] It was an interesting example of what could happen in a market that these two powerful businessmen dominated, and in view of their ambitions in the Australian media industry in the 1990s, whether in newspapers or pay television, it was one worth remembering. It was also enough to help Kerry double his fortune between the late 1980s and early 1990s, so that he was now worth more than $2 billion.

Packer's business secret, apart from cosy deals with his rivals, was that he knew when to buy and when to sell—his timing was generally spot on—so he got in when prices were low and sold when prices were high. He was also prepared to back his judgment. Trevor Kennedy tells a story of how, at the Bing Crosby golf tournament one year, he and Packer met the owner of the Burger King hamburger chain, who offered them the Australian franchise. Driving back to the hotel afterwards, Kerry spotted one of their restaurants at the roadside and pulled in. He and Kennedy then sat themselves down at a table, next to a rubbish bin, while Kerry ordered two of everything on the menu. For the next 40 minutes, the pair munched their way through a couple of dozen burgers, pies and patties—tossing them in the bin after taking a bite—before the Big Fella announced he had had enough. As they got back into the car, he decreed he wouldn't buy Burger King because he didn't like the product. Other businessmen would have called in consultants and spent a fortune on number crunchers to see whether the deal was worth doing. Kerry was just happy to trust his gut.

Another talent of Packer's was that when he bought established businesses he almost always improved them. Jobs might be lost, factories closed, but the cost-cutting process left a better managed, more valuable company at the end of it. Unlike Alan Bond, who loaded new acquisitions with even more debt to fund the next purchase, Packer was always looking to get the borrowings of a business down. He might borrow to acquire a company, but would always be aiming to pay the banks back.

Here his great strength lay in what he didn't do. Bond and the other entrepreneurs who went bust in the crash of the late 1980s perished because they couldn't stop buying. Packer could stop, at least in terms of buying on a grand scale. Bond Corporation, for example, grew twentyfold in the boom between 1983 and 1988, because Alan Bond always piled the winnings of one bet onto the next. It was therefore only a matter of time before he came unstuck. By contrast, Consolidated Press in its peak period of growth expanded only fourfold in size between 1986 and 1991 (at a time when there were far more bargains to be had).

The downside of this was that Packer would never be a Rupert Murdoch. He lacked the vision and the derring-do, and he did not have the confidence to strut the world stage. He was a gambler but he never risked the lot. And he always knew when to cut his losses, unlike on the racetrack or in the casino.

CHAPTER NINETEEN

PRINCE OF WHALES

Like many other Australians, I like to bet.

Kerry Packer, 1984

When Packer was not chasing deals, playing polo or racing around in go-karts, he often dashed off to the races or the casino to gamble. In London, he made regular forays from his Savoy suite to play the tables, winning or losing in one session more than most people earn in a lifetime. As one of his executives put it, he gambled when he was bored, and he gambled often because he was often bored. Kerry had been a big punter in one way or another for as long as anyone could remember, but after the billion-dollar deal with Bond his stakes became quite ridiculously large. In March 1987, two months after selling Nine, he reportedly lost 8 million pounds ($19 million) playing blackjack in one night at the Ritz.[1]

Packer's exploits in casinos in London and Las Vegas in the 1980s and 1990s became the stuff of legend, earning him the nickname the 'Prince of Whales'. And most of the tales were true. From the 1980s until his death he was one of the biggest—if not the biggest—casino gamblers in the world. He bet bigger than arms dealer Adnan Khashoggi, bigger than the Sultan of Brunei, and bigger than any of the oil sheikhs or Asian high rollers. What's more, he remained on the scene for a great deal longer.

In his $19 million tangle with the Ritz in 1987, Packer lost the money playing blackjack in a private room on the casino's ground floor. According to an eyewitness, he played two tables at a time and moved from one to the other to place his bets, playing all seven hands at each table and staking 10 000 pounds per hand. As he lost, he repeatedly signed the casino's house cheques for more chips, at 200 000 pounds a time, but the chips didn't come fast enough. Eventually, he tired of signing his name and handed over a cheque for 1 million pounds instead.

In London there were only three or four casinos that could handle him, such were the amounts that he demanded to bet in.[2] And even for them it could be a terrifying or thrilling experience. If he had a bad night at the tables, he could transform a dull year for the casino into a brilliant one. If he had a good night he could win enough to hijack the year's profit and maybe even to break the bank. When London's most exclusive casino, Aspinall's Club, ran out of money in May 1990 and was forced to shut down there were reports that Packer was responsible. One London gossip column claimed he had gambled there the previous week and won 300 000 pounds, which had forced them to close their doors.[3] This may well have been urban myth, for neither the casino management nor Packer would confirm the story, yet the principle of him being richer than the casino was absolutely accurate. On another occasion, he was barred from the London casino Crockfords for winning too much. According to his right-hand man and partner in fun, Trevor Kennedy, he had won 'about 10 million quid' in the previous few weeks and the casino had tired of it. The manager took Packer aside, offered him a free dinner, and then politely requested he gamble elsewhere. According to Kennedy, Packer came back 'with a big grin from ear to ear', saying it was the thing he had always wanted: to be banned from a casino for winning too much.

Clearly, Packer had the firepower to bankrupt even the richest London casino if he got lucky, so the owners always wanted to know when he was about to visit. If he was planning a foray to the tables they liked to have at least half an hour's notice that he was on his way. Packer's aides would ring in advance to say he was coming and to make sure that he got good service. Once he was through the front door, the key staff would be alerted through personal bleepers and told 'He's in, he's in.' Often he came mob-handed, in a party of seven or eight, but almost always he gambled alone. He was as likely to come in mid afternoon and stay till ten o'clock as he was to come in late in the evening and stay till the small hours. He was rarely ecstatic when he won, but he was always extremely cranky when he lost, because he hated losing. This was a particular problem if he was back in Australia (and had lost, say, a couple of million dollars at the races). According to Kennedy, he would arrive at the office in a foul temper and set about trying to sack people, on the pretext that he had seen too many standing round doing nothing. It was just like Sir Frank had been in days gone by.

Kerry occasionally played roulette and punto banco, but his favourite game was blackjack, which he played well. According to croupiers, he knew the basic strategies of when to split, when to twist and when to stay, which allowed him to reduce the casino's advantage to around 1 per cent (as against a house advantage of 5 per cent when a player plays badly). But he did not count cards and was not good enough to turn the odds in his favour. Nor did he win as much as he lost, despite his occasional huge wins. The fact that the top casinos rolled out the red carpet for him proved they were more than happy to see him. Those who gambled with him said he chased his losses and hated to give in. As in the rest of his life, he did not easily admit defeat.

Packer told people on occasions that gambling was a disease from which he suffered. And it certainly caused him problems over the years. Once during the mid 1980s, he told one of his accountants in Australia to transfer to London what seemed to him a vast amount of money to settle a gambling debt. The accountant made a few inquiries and discovered to his surprise that a couple of other people in Consolidated Press had been asked simultaneously to do the same thing. The accountant was sufficiently concerned about the effect the gambling was having on the company that he told the Reserve Bank what the funds transfer was for. It was his way of trying to get Kerry to kick the habit. A minor row ensued, in which Kerry's response was reportedly: 'How can I help it. You shouldn't have left me in London over the weekend.'

Over in Las Vegas, Packer was as much a figure on the gambling scene as he was in London, and there too he was welcomed by croupier and casino owner alike. When he won, he tipped the croupiers handsomely, which he was not allowed to do in Australia or the UK, and when he lost, the casinos cleaned up. In November 1991 he gave the Las Vegas Hilton a hammering while he and his polo team were on their way to Argentina. Stopping off for a few days of fun at the hotel, he won $7 million one night playing blackjack in the public section of the casino at a table roped off from regular punters. Next year, the Hilton won it all back again, taking US$10 million off Kerry in a two-day session in a special room built for him to gamble in. In May 1995, he was back on the right side again, winning US$20 million at the MGM Grand. On this occasion, he arrived in the early hours of the morning and demanded that the entire floor of the casino be cleared so he could play by himself. Witnesses said he then went from table to table, playing eight hands at once at US$250 000 apiece. Within forty minutes he was US$25 million ahead, having apparently won twenty hands on the trot in one lucky streak.

After this win, he left a US$1 million tip to be split between the dealers. But even when he was losing, he could be remarkably free with his chips. Often he would dish out US$100 000 to his polo players and tell them to enjoy themselves. Sometimes he would pay cocktail waitresses US$50 000 to sit with him while he gambled. Other times, he would pay girls similar amounts of money to dance with him all night. In one of the most frequently told stories, he bought a Mercedes-Benz during a visit to Vegas and gave it to a valet parker. Another time, as legend has it, he paid off the US$150 000 home mortgage of a female croupier who was deeply in debt.

One version of this story, which was told in Packer's own *Bulletin* magazine after his death, had the woman refusing his gift on the grounds that all tips had to be pooled and shared. The Big Fella then called her manager and demanded she be fired, threatening to take his business across the road if his wish was denied. After some hesitation, the croupier was duly dismissed, whereupon Packer pressed the pile of chips into her hands, before turning to the manager and insisting she be rehired.

Whether this was Packer being generous or just showing off, it is hard to be sure. But there's no doubt that Packer loved the power that his huge wealth afforded him. On another famous occasion, he got into an argument with a big Texan gambler at Steve Wynn's Bellagio casino, where both men were playing poker in the high-rollers' room. According to the casino's CEO, the Texan asked to join Packer's table and was told he could not. When he persisted in asking, Packer asked the man how much he was worth, to which the unfortunate gentleman responded, 'One hundred million dollars'.

'Well, son,' Packer replied, 'if you're so keen to play, how about I toss you for it?'

In Australia, Packer rarely gambled seriously, because no casino would let him stake the sort of amount he required. But he did bet on the horses in a major way, from the time he was a teenager. Like polo, backing horses was a habit he had picked up from his father, who had been a mad punter in his day. Sir Frank had been a passionate racing man who bred and kept racehorses with notable success, in particular with his 1947 Caulfield Cup winner, Columnist. Packer Senior liked to back his horses heavily when they ran and would often get one of the *Telegraph*'s turf correspondents to put on his bets for him. Keith Robbins, who was the paper's turf editor for many years, remembers being rung one morning from the USA by Sir Frank, where he was challenging for the America's Cup, and being asked to back one of his runners with what in those days was a large amount of money: 'The bet would change by the hour depending on how much the old boss had had to drink. It'd go from twenty thousand to thirty thousand and back in from forty thousand to thirty thousand if he'd sobered up a bit.'

Sir Frank had loved to gamble and loved the thrill of the chase. And Kerry had undoubtedly inherited his passion. But while Sir Frank seemed to know when to stop, Kerry had always had a bit of a problem. There was a story from family friends that Frank had set up a series of trusts for the two boys that matured at five-year intervals. On at least one occasion, it was said, the proceeds of Kerry's trust had been corralled by the old man to pay off his gambling debts. There were also stories of Kerry visiting his brother Clyde late at night on a couple of occasions in the early 1970s, white faced and apparently desperate for money because he was in debt to bookmakers who were determined to collect.

In the late 1960s and early 1970s, it was certainly accepted by racing journalists and bookies that young Kerry was the biggest gambler at Sydney's Harold Park trotting races. And even in those days he was reckoned to be staking as much as $10 000 on a single race. Almost always he seemed to be doing battle with the famous Waterhouse clan. In those days Big Bill Waterhouse was unquestionably the biggest bookmaker in Australia and thought to be one of the richest in the world, yet Kerry appeared to be determined to take him on and try to beat him. Given his later pronouncements about how much he lost over the years as a gambler, it seems unlikely that Packer gave Big Bill much of a bruising. Some years later, the Costigan Commission received evidence that Packer's bankers had been cautioned in 1974 against granting him an overdraft, on the basis that he owed $360 000 to Sydney bookmakers.[4] This would have been at a time when his duels with the Waterhouses were at their height. But whether this banking 'intelligence report' was correct or not, Packer certainly didn't succeed in driving the Waterhouses from the field of battle.

That defeat was inflicted by the Australian Jockey Club in 1971, which did put Big Bill Waterhouse out of business for a short time. Ironically, it was then Kerry Packer's father Frank, a member of the AJC committee, who came to the colourful bookmaker's rescue, supporting him in his eventually successful bid to get his bookie's licence back. It was a shock to people in the racing game that the two men should be on the same side.

But perhaps Frank Packer considered himself, like Waterhouse, to be an outsider.

The cost of Kerry's gambling certainly mounted over the years. Costigan's confidential Volume 9 revealed that Packer had made payments of $4 million to an SP bookie called John Rogan during an eighteen-month period in 1980–81. In the same period, Rogan had paid Packer only $1.2 million, suggesting that he had gambled away some $3 million in that time. Previously, in October 1979, he had withdrawn $1 million in cash from a CBC branch in Sydney and put it in his office safe. He told Costigan he had used this money to meet his betting losses so that his bank manager didn't think he was 'some form of mental deficient for going to the races'.[5] In a public statement in November 1984, after the publication of Costigan's final report, he explained his need for this million dollars by saying that he had always been a substantial gambler. 'The fact is that I, like many other Australians, like to bet. The fact is that I, like many other Australians, have put a good percentage of my bets on in cash and have settled a proportion of losses and winnings in cash.' The fact was, however, that he was not at all like most Australians, for unlike them, he could afford to gamble and lose a million dollars.[6]

Packer claimed periodically that he had kicked the habit, telling the *National Times*, for example, in 1977 that it was impossible to win as a gambler, and adding ruefully: 'It cost me a lot of money to find out, and it's something that I no longer do. Basically, I don't bet any more.'[7] But his resolve to stay away from the track did not last, for he kept on coming back.

In the late 1970s and early 1980s one could see him often at the track with John Rogan, who was both a friend and his commission agent (who put on bets for him). The two of them would stand in the middle of the ring at Sydney's Randwick races, surrounded by half-a-dozen gofers, while a crowd of onlookers strained to hear what he was going to back. Then the big man would give the word, the gofers would go running in all directions, and the bookies would be hit with an avalanche of money. Whatever horse Packer was backing would instantly become unbackable as the bookies slashed their odds to try to balance their books, so the key to success was for all the gofers to arrive at once. Anyone who tried to have a bet after them would be hard pressed to make money. If Packer was backing a horse for a million dollars, you needed great faith in your own judgment and an extremely strong nerve to back another horse to beat it, since it seemed obvious that anyone staking a million dollars must have some pretty good information. If you decided, on the other hand, that it made sense to follow him, it was impossible to get a decent price, because his money turned anything except rank outsiders into short-priced favourites.

Once the bets were on, Packer would stand back and watch it on the television monitor, often without saying a word, and rarely with any display of emotion. In the late 1980s, he placed most of his bets himself with Dominic Beirne or Bruce McHugh, and one observer remembers him standing watching a race with the latter, possibly with millions of dollars riding on the result. At the end, as the horses flashed by the post, it was quite impossible to know who had won and lost. Neither smiled, neither reacted. Packer gave a quick nod to McHugh, who barely acknowledged it in return.

As Packer got richer, so the stakes naturally became larger, just as they did in the casino. And once again, the sale of Channel Nine to Bond signalled a massive betting spree. In April 1987, three months after the deal, and a month after his $19 million setback at the Ritz, Packer was at Sydney's Rosehill track for one of the biggest two-year-old races of the year, the Golden Slipper. Betting from a private box high up in the new stand, where the biggest Sydney bookies have agents to phone bets down to the ring, he is said to have had $2 million on his horse Christmas Tree in the big race, only to see it come in fourth. Several of his fancies in other races, interstate, trailed in behind the field too, causing him to lose a great deal more money. Two days later, the *Telegraph*'s experienced turf editor, Keith Robbins, the same man who had placed Sir Frank's bets twenty years earlier, reported that the bookies had held a world record $20 million in their satchels, and that Packer had finished $7 million down.[8]

Two weeks after that Packer was at it again at Randwick races, backing the Tancred Stakes winner Myocard to beat his own horse Major Drive in the Sydney Cup. The whisper round the course was that he had staked $3 million on the horse at 3–2 on (to win $2 million), and was sure it couldn't be beaten. But on the well-known principle of Murphy's Law, Myocard came in fourth and Kerry's own horse got up on the line at 7–1 to snatch the race. It was a good five minutes later when an angry Packer finally appeared in the winner's enclosure to greet his horse and jockey. Visibly fuming, he roundly abused Robbins, who had written the story about him losing $7 million at Rosehill two weeks earlier, when he had seen Myocard win so convincingly.

This, however, was just the start of what must be the biggest betting splurge the world has ever seen, for in three days of racing at Randwick's autumn carnival that month, Packer is believed to have staked $55 million, almost all of which was placed with the Sydney bookie Bruce McHugh. Naturally, neither Packer nor McHugh ever confirmed the fact, since the first was passionate about secrecy and the second was sworn to it, but the AJC's official figures for betting turnover make it obvious that Packer's spree took place. In the six years from 1986 to 1991, the typical total for the first four days of Randwick's carnival meeting was around $35 million. In 1987, the year that Packer let rip, it was just over $100 million, or $65 million more than usual. That year stands out like a beacon, and if any doubt remains that the vast bulk of this extra money came from Packer, then there is one other compelling piece of evidence: on the one day out of four in 1987 that Packer wasn't there, the betting turnover was virtually unchanged by comparison with the other five years.

These figures strongly suggest that Packer was losing heavily at some stage, for the turnover could not possibly have climbed so high if the bookies had not already won a stack of his money—Bruce McHugh could not possibly have stood Packer for $60 million because he wouldn't have had it to lose. The figures also suggest that McHugh offered Packer the chance to win most of it back. And this is precisely what the racetrack gossip reported. The buzz round the tracks was that late on the second Saturday, the fourth and last day of the 1987 carnival, Packer was $28 million down to McHugh. He then persuaded the bookie, so the story goes, to take him on for a maximum of $10 million per bet, against the previous limit of $5 million, and pulled three straight winners out of the bag. One of them, New Atlantis at 11–4, in the last race at Randwick, won by a short half-head or, in layman's terms, by a whisker. Whether these details are entirely accurate or not, the experience is said to have shaken McHugh to his boots, and on the Monday morning two days later, he walked into the offices of the Australian Jockey Club at Randwick and handed in his book-maker's licence. He denied that he was retiring because his nerve had gone and denied that he had been cleaned out by Packer. But his fellow bookies would have sympathised if either was true, for betting against Packer was a dangerous business even when you were ahead. He insisted on betting in telephone numbers, which made it impossible to lay the money off with anybody else. And when he lost he was keen to double the stakes and chase his money. If, as his bookie, you allowed him to do that, it was only a matter of time before he would get it back. McHugh wanted to get out before Packer put him back on the milk round.

Once McHugh had packed his stand, there was a brief flurry of excitement in racing circles about who would take his place. Never shy of publicity, the flamboyant bookie-cum-punter Mark Read claimed he was coming out of retirement and selling everything to take Packer on. The colourful Gold Coast bookie Terry Page also offered to stand him, at up to $500 000 a bet. But in the end there was only one whose wallet was fat enough and whose nerve was strong enough, and that was a Parramatta Road car dealer called Harry Barrett. Until then Barrett had been the leading bookie in the interstate ring and excluded by AJC rules from taking bets on the Sydney races. These rules were now waived to accommodate Kerry Packer.

Like McHugh, Barrett was sworn to secrecy about the bets he took from Packer, but he was doing well enough a few months later to pay $6.2 million for a house on Sydney's glorious Point Piper, one of the swankiest pieces of real estate in town, which he was buying as a present for his wife.[9] Not long after that, he was mixing it with Packer at Randwick where, on the second Saturday of the Spring Carnival in April 1990, he was reported to have held stakes of $9 million, most of which had come from Packer, who whispered in his ear at intervals during the afternoon. Barrett's smile at the close of play suggested to racing journalists that Packer was on the losing end again. As before, the AJC's betting turnover figures confirmed the essence of the story, showing a $7 million increase in stakes from a typical year. Put bluntly, Packer's duel with Barrett had doubled the usual amount wagered by the several-thousand-strong crowd. As one fellow bookie put it, looking enviously at Barrett's apparent good fortune, poor Kerry had never been a lucky punter.

Packer's former Channel Nine star Mike Willesee has a story that illustrates the big man's punting style. Standing in the ring at Rosehill one day, Willesee had eight strangers come up and tug his coat tails to tell him that he should get on 'the best bet of the year' that was running in the next race. None of the tipsters was known to him, but he had seen the game played before and knew that it was likely to be a set-up. Moments later, Kerry Packer crashed into him going full tilt towards the bookies. 'Have you backed this?' Packer asked, stabbing his finger at the card. 'This is the best bet this year.'

Without thinking of the consequences of depriving his once and future boss of a big victory, Willesee told him that the horse had no chance: 'Kerry, the horse can't win.'

'How do you fucking know, son?' was Packer's reply.

'Well, Kerry, I've just had eight strangers tell me to back it. That alone is enough: the horse can't win.'

Willesee steered him towards a horse that he was thinking of backing each way, whereupon Kerry discarded his 'best bet of the year' and went off to tickle it with a small each-way wager. The horse duly came second, returning Packer his money, while the paddock's hot tip crawled in last. As Packer pushed off through the crowd, he called out cheerfully to Willesee, 'No fucking harm done there, son.' Perhaps a thankyou would have been more appropriate, but Packer's mind, it seemed, was already planning the next tilt at the windmill.

Packer was never a great mixer or socialiser at the track. And according to his chauffeur of twenty years, George Young, he was bored by horse racing. He kept to himself at race meetings, often left early, and on occasions came off the course in a filthy mood. Given the size of the losses he suffered, that was perhaps not surprising.

CHAPTER TWENTY

KERRY AND THE TAXMAN

We are proud of being Australians, we're prepared to pay
our taxes as Australians and we are prepared to contribute
to the country that has given us everything. Now that is
an old-fashioned stupid idea, if you like. But that is the
way I was brought up, that's the way my father was
brought up and that's what I believe in.

Kerry Packer, May 1977[1]

By 1990 Packer was so rich it was hard for him to do anything but become richer. Provided his main businesses stayed healthy and he didn't punt the whole company on trying to turn his $2 billion into $10 billion, he was likely to have more money at the end of each year than he had at the beginning. There was certainly no way his everyday spending could make a major dent in his fortune, however much he lost at the blackjack tables or squandered on polo and luxury yachts. To Packer, losing $1 million at the races was akin to the average punter losing $100—the sort of thing one might get annoyed about, but of no real importance. And even blowing $100 million was not going to send him to the brink of bankruptcy. As for the little luxuries of life, these scarcely registered as petty cash.

If he wanted new shirts he could have them made to measure in London's Jermyn Street by Harvie and Hudson and sent out by the score. If he wanted the latest Rolls-Royce or Mercedes he would walk into a showroom, write out a cheque and drive out the door. He could have a $200 000 BMW in England and an identical car in Australia. He could have matching Bentley Turbos in each country as well, if that was what he wanted. He could buy two Nissan GTRs after their Bathurst victory and roar round the racetrack at Sydney's Oran Park with his son Jamie. Yet none of it would seriously damage his wealth. In terms of his fortune, purchasing all these things together meant as much to Kerry as a couple of meals at the local Pizza Hut meant to the average Australian family.

Naturally, all the trappings of corporate success were also at his beck and call—the drivers, the servants, the helicopters and the corporate jets. But unlike the high-flying Australian entrepreneurs who had possessed these things until they went down in the crash, the bills were all paid with his money, which was certain to last. And even on their terms Packer could outdo them. While Alan Bond and Laurie Connell had Gulf Stream or Falcon business jets to fly them round the world, he had traded up to a long-range DC8 to nip over to Las Vegas for a night on the tables or to ferry his polo teams around the world. Reputedly leased at a cost of $4 million a year, the Packer jet was fitted out with a huge double bedroom and en-suite bathroom for the boss, a dining room with a table that seated twelve people, a big lounge for relaxing and separate staff quarters and bathroom. So large was the Packer airliner that it had to be kept in the Qantas hangar at Mascot because it was too big to go in the area reserved for executive jets.

Nor was he short of decent digs. The houses at Packer's end of Bellevue Hill were huge, embassy-sized villas in vast English-style gardens that caught the northern sun in winter and cool sea breezes in summertime. Cairnton, as Kerry's house was called, was a huge old Victorian mansion with sweeping tree-covered lawns that in other suburbs would have been split up to accommodate eight apartments or knocked down and replaced by four ordinary dwellings. It had been in the Packer family since Kerry's father acquired it in 1935 for a mere 7500 pounds. Twenty years later, Sir Frank had also snapped up the huge block next door and demolished the two houses that stood on it to make his garden bigger. His wife Gretel had always been keen on gardening.

Only ten minutes from Sydney's central business district, Cairnton was a magnificent property to have so close to the city, yet it was only one of several that made up the Packer compound. Clustered around Cairnton and its ample estate were four other houses that Kerry had purchased in the late 1980s to accommodate his son Jamie, his daughter Gretel and the usual complement of staff and visitors. These four more normal-sized houses were bought from Kerry's erstwhile neighbours for a total of more than $9 million, giving the Packer family more than 1 hectare (more than 2 acres) of land in one of Sydney's most expensive residential areas, worth around $20 million in total. But to put this in perspective, it was less than one-hundredth of the family fortune.

To the passer-by, the Packers' Sydney stronghold had the bearing of a stately home or perhaps even a castle. Its frontage to Victoria Road, where even the most modest houses fetched several million dollars, was almost 100 metres long and fortified by walls and fences that towered in places to around 6 metres high to keep out intruders. Two security gates guarding the openings were watched silently by video cameras perched on top of a long pole, and were floodlit at night.

The high walls at Cairnton also served to protect the Packers' privacy, in which department Kerry and his father had never needed any prompting. To one side of the house, running up the hill, was a public footpath where for some reason the fence was less than 2 metres high. Here, those who tried to get a good view of the Packer property were sadly disappointed. Standing on tiptoe to peer over the palings one was confronted by a wall of dense foliage and trees that blocked out all but the most fleeting glimpse of the house's upper windows.

Cairnton was by no means the only spread the Packers owned in Sydney. Ten minutes away by Packer helicopter there was a magnificent mansion at Sydney's Palm Beach, right on the ocean shore, bought for just over $1 million in 1981 when that sort of money meant something. Built on a large double block, it was a big, sprawling umber-coloured house set back beneath the palm trees, but here there were no high walls and no TV cameras. During the 1980s, when Kerry's helicopter was still allowed to land on nearby Pittwater, you could even see him in the surf at Christmas time, usually swimming with a party of people. Often his dip was preceded by a small tractor dragging the jet skis and other beach toys down to the water.

Another half an hour north of Palm Beach was the Packers' superb Ellerston estate in the Hunter Valley, where Kerry spent more and more of his time. Yet even this was not the last (or the biggest) of their Australian homesteads, for almost as a sideline in his thrust to get richer, Kerry had become one of Australia's largest landowners and cattle barons. Ellerston itself doubled as a working farm, with around 15 000 sheep and 12 000 cattle on its 28 000 hectares. Several hundred kilometres further north, in the south-western corner of Queensland, was another huge holding called Nockatunga, bought for $13.2 million in August 1990. This was a record price for a Queensland rural property, yet Kerry had not even bothered to inspect it before buying. In London for the tail end of the polo season, he had given it the nod on the recommendation of his cattle manager after watching a video sent to his suite at the Savoy.

Further north again, in Queensland's central west, Packer had another prime rural property on the Barcoo River just south of Longreach. Isis Downs had long been famous for its merino sheep and could carry 90 000 head on its 192 000 hectares. It also had an old Queensland homestead with long deep verandahs and a celebrated semicircular woolshed, erected in 1914 by the British company that built the Sydney Harbour Bridge. Kerry had bought the property in September 1987 for $10.3 million at the top of the wool market after prices had doubled. Six years later they had fallen to record lows.

In nearby Winton, also in Queensland, there was yet another Packer property, Mimong, with a further 10 000 head of cattle. And near the coast to the south, just below Rockhampton, there was a Brahmin stud that bred stock for despatch to Kerry's key cattle properties in the Northern Territory. The chief of these was Newcastle Waters, which was one of the most spectacular in Australia.

Newcastle Waters covered 10 350 square kilometres, or more than a million hectares, of prime land on the western edge of the Barkly Tableland, between Tennant Creek and Katherine. In the midst of the red desert of the Northern Territory, it stood out like a vast green oasis. It was harsh country, with mid-summer temperatures above 40 degrees Celsius and 200 days a year rated 'uncomfortable for humans'. But Packer's property had a permanent water supply that ensured around one-fifth of its enormous area was covered year round with lush pasture. Roughly one-third of the property was semi-desert but the rest was fit for grazing cattle, and Kerry had ensured that all this usable land was watered and paddocked. As one local expert pointed out, this was 'a helluva lotta work', given that the property was bigger than Cyprus and more than half the size of Israel.

Kerry had bought Newcastle Waters in 1983 for an undisclosed sum. Within eighteen months he had spent $2 million on fences, stock traps and almost seventy artesian bore holes that he named after famous cricketers such as Benaud and Thomson. Another $7 million was laid out to upgrade the herd, with the purchase of 25 000 Brahmin heifers that Packer's managers could cross with Santa Gertrudis bulls to achieve fast-growing calves.

Expenditure on the house that Packer built was even more amazing. According to Nigel Austin, then the rural writer for the *Australian*, who visited the property in late 1984, it was the most lavish homestead to be built in Australia for half a century, and it looked the part.

Approaching Newcastle Waters in the early morning the shimmering roof of the new station becomes visible in the distance, its breathtaking size a symbol of the enormity of Northern Australia and of Mr Packer's ambitions—and resources.

The luxurious 150 square home will be completed by Christmas. The eight bedroom, air-conditioned mansion is the grandest ever built on a cattle station in the Territory. No expense has been spared.

The architect-designed homestead is crowned by a 20-metre high steel roof, which stands as a monument to the Packer endeavour to harness the vagaries of the North.

Why Kerry needed such a huge house in the Northern Territory was something of a mystery—and in later life he hardly went there—but he presumably used it for entertaining. A favourite Packer pastime was pig shooting, which he liked to do with friends. He and his guests could easily fly direct to the property because Newcastle Waters had a landing strip, built in World War II, that was large enough to take almost anything.

In the 1980s, Kerry had also snapped up cattle stations at Dungowan, Kirkimbie, Powell Creek, Tanyidgee and Humbert River that brought his total landholdings in the Northern Territory to a whisker under 20 000 square kilometres, or 2 million hectares. Special dispensation from the Northern Territory Government had been required for Packer to exceed the limit of 12 950 square kilometres set down in section 38A of the Northern Territory's Crown Lands Act, but the government had been only too happy to give it to him. Packer was committed to the cattle business, was prepared to improve the land and had unlimited funds. He was also, of course, not a man to whom one liked to say 'no'.

Taken together, Packer's Australian properties covered an area bigger than Belgium, yet their total value (even when added to his houses in Sydney, Melbourne, London and elsewhere) still came to far less than a tenth of his enormous and ever expanding fortune, which by 1993 was around $3 billion.

Nor was he stumped for cash, because his private companies typically paid him an annual income of around $50 million in dividends. Yet, in spite of these almost incredible riches, Kerry appeared to have very little trouble with the taxman. Indeed, he almost certainly paid a lower rate of income tax than his gardener, or should one say gardeners. In 1977 he had boasted to an interviewer about his family's tax-paying record, claiming that the Packers were 'proud to be Australian' and happy to pay their fair share. He had even commented:

Now that is an old-fashioned stupid idea, if you like. But that is the way I was brought up, that's the way my father was brought up and that's what I believe in.[2]

But his celebration of old-fashioned Australian values was bullshit. The truth was that Kerry and his father hated paying tax more than almost anything else in life and had always devoted a great deal of their considerable energies to paying the absolute minimum. Sir Frank had used all sorts of artificial devices in the 1950s and 1960s, including (it seems) the scandalous dividend-stripping scheme designed by his tax adviser John Ratcliffe that had so angered Federal Treasurer Arthur Fadden in 1952.[3] And Kerry was even more determined to find ways of giving the taxman the slip. In the late 1970s he engaged in a series of complicated tax avoidance schemes that were so successful (until challenged by the Australian Taxation Office) that he amassed more deductions than he needed to wipe out his tax bill—or so Costigan's analysts believed. But this obsession with making his tax bill disappear also landed him in serious trouble. He was a whisker away from prosecution for tax fraud in the mid 1980s (for financing the notorious film scheme in which he claimed $1.8 million worth of fake tax deductions for his companies), and suspected tax evasion was at the root of almost all his troubles with Costigan. What is more, it caused the ATO's investigators to sit on his tail for much of the 1980s, chasing at least two schemes that they believed to be fraudulent.

It is a regrettable or laudable feature of Australian law (depending on your point of view) that it is almost impossible to publish the details of investigations into people's tax affairs, especially when they are alive and can sue you for defamation.

Section 16 of the Income Tax Assessment Act draws a cloak of secrecy around such matters and prescribes criminal penalties for anyone who dares to leak information. It also makes it illegal for officers of the ATO to give evidence in court in support of a story, even when journalist, taxpayer and investigator all know that it is true. But occasionally the veil lifts a little, when disputes between taxpayer and taxman come into open court. And in the 1980s this happened twice with Kerry Packer and his companies. In April 1984, for example, the ATO beat off a legal challenge from Packer in the Queensland Supreme Court and won access to various ledgers and trust accounts of companies connected to Kerry and his friend Brian Ray, relating to what the ATO described as an 'offshore auctions scheme' to minimise tax.[4]

Three years later, Packer and the taxman were revealed to be at war again, this time in the American courts, over access to bank accounts and documents held in the United States. After a request for help from the ATO in January 1987, the US Internal Revenue Service's Criminal Investigation Division issued summonses against Bank One of Ohio, the Mellon Bank in Philadelphia and another American bank to produce documents relating to 'accounts held or controlled by or on behalf of Kerry Packer for the period 30 June 1980 to 30 June 1985', in connection with an investigation of Kerry Packer's tax affairs in Australia. A letter to the US authorities from Assistant Commissioner Michael D'Ascenzo made it clear that the ATO believed Kerry Packer and Brian Ray were evading (as in illegally avoiding) Australian tax, which was something Packer always denied doing.[5]

The ATO wanted to look at these American banks accounts so that it could get to the heart of a 1983 transaction involving Packer's Australian Consolidated Press, which had claimed a $5 million tax deduction in Australia for purchasing a patent from a company called Grintonland, run from the tiny Turks and Caicos Islands in the British West Indies. According to documents filed in the US courts, the ATO suspected that this $5 million purchase was in fact a sham that had allowed Packer to dump a large tax liability in the Turks and Caicos Islands tax haven, while the money was bouncing round the world and back from Australia.

Whether the taxman had any evidence to support these suspicions was never tested in open court, but the ATO was determined to get its hands on the US bank records, and Packer's lawyers were equally determined that the taxman should not be allowed to. And from that, you may draw your own conclusions about whether Packer had anything to hide.

The first round in this 1987 argument went to Packer, and access to the American bank accounts was denied. The second round was set to be fought in Australia in April 1988, when Assistant Commissioner D'Ascenzo was due to give evidence to the Australian Capital Territory Supreme Court. A few days before his examination was to take place, the two parties came to a settlement that appeared to give the tax office what it wanted. Since the ATO needed only to demonstrate that Packer's tax affairs were being investigated and that the bank records were required as part of its investigation, it seems probable that it succeeded. But history does not relate whether the $5 million deduction was disallowed or whether any penalties were levied. Clearly, there was no prosecution of any sort.

Some years before this investigation came to light, and before Costigan started his inquiries into Packer, Kerry was involved in two another tax-minimisation schemes that were designed to wipe out any tax on profits made by his share-trading company, Dealer Holdings. One of these was the celebrated film scheme, which was investigated by the ATO and disallowed before Costigan got to look at it. The other involved the purchase and leasing of three English stallions for which Kerry and his company claimed tax deductions of around $900 000. Packer told the ATO he had bought the three ex-racehorses, Speedy Dakota, Compte de Loir and Farolo, from a stud in Newmarket, England, for $1.75 million and was using them for breeding. But the tax office suspected it was all just a tax dodge. Neither he nor his company had earned any income from this enterprise, and there was doubt about whether Packer had actually paid the leasing fees. But the biggest problem was that $1.75 million was six or seven times what blood-stock experts believed the horses to be worth. In the words of an internal tax office report on the scheme, written in 1982: 'It seems certain that the cost price of the stallions has been inflated'. And as the ATO commented bluntly, the purpose of this was 'patently obvious'. It was to evade tax.

At this stage, the ATO had no proof that it was a rort: the English invoices supported Packer's claim to have paid $1.75 million for the stallions, they had been insured for that amount and duty had been paid on the full value. But the ATO's investigators had just busted the vendor, a well-known breeder with a stud in Australia, for lying about the cost of another batch of horses he had brought into the country. And the Packer trans-action looked equally suspicious. It was financed by $1.4 million worth of loans from two offshore companies, Swiftsure Credit Facilities in Vancouver, and East Coast Mortgage Indemnity Co in New Jersey that could not be found in any phone book or business directory; the 'loans' had never turned up in the bank account of Dealer Holdings, to whom the money was suppos-edly being lent; and at least one of the companies, Swiftsure, was controlled by John V Allen, who had been Kerry Packer's tax adviser until the early 1980s.

The tax office appears to have spent two or three years investigating Packer over this transaction with the help of tax authorities in the UK and Canada. And US court documents reveal that its inquiries led to another Turks and Caicos Islands company called Tintagel, which was linked to Allen. But only a handful of people could testify what the endgame was. We do know that Packer was not prosecuted, despite the ATO's suspi-cions, but it's a fair bet that the scheme was knocked back. The tax office was planning to disallow the deductions anyway on the grounds that Kerry's supposed horse breeding had not produced any income. Once again, we do not know if he was forced to pay any penalty.

Several years before this tussle with the tax office, Packer had been investigated over yet another tax scheme in which money was shuffled between him and his family trusts in Australia and Hong Kong. Back in the 1960s his father had arranged ownership of the Packer empire so that it rested with a number of Australian-based trusts, of which Kerry and his brother Clyde were the primary beneficiaries. After Clyde sold out, Kerry had remained liable to tax on dividends paid into these trusts from the Packer business empire, and in December 1974 he had adopted a scheme designed by his lawyers Allen Allen & Hemsley to reduce his tax bill. Its aim, as so often in such schemes, was to transform taxable income into a non-taxable capital receipt. The scheme, which was extremely complex, had Packer surrender his rights to income from the trusts in return for a $650 000 capital sum, which was paid to him by a new set of trusts called the Puckeridge Settlements. These new trusts then borrowed an identical sum of money from a newly created offshore trust called the K2HK Trust in Hong Kong (of which Kerry Packer was again the primary beneficiary) and paid interest to Hong Kong, where (crucially) it was not taxable. Back in Australia, these payments counted as a tax deduction for Puckeridge Settlements, wiping out some or all of its Australian tax bill. Packer, meanwhile, had no personal tax liability on the large capital sum he had received. In this way, everyone was a winner. Except the Australian taxpayer.

The feature of the scheme that fascinated the ATO was that the interest due to the Hong Kong trust was actually paid into a bank account in Sydney and re-lent interest-free (without ever leaving Australia) to one of Packer's private companies in Australia, so Kerry continued to have use of the money. Despite the fact that the funds appeared (on paper) to have been sent out of the country, no money was ever remitted to Hong Kong.

Once again, we can't be sure whether Packer was eventually forced to pay up. But in 1990 the Federal Commissioner of Taxation was taken to court by a taxpayer who had engaged in an almost identical pre-paid interest scheme in 1979. In his case, the ATO had disallowed the tax deductions, as it almost certainly did with Packer. But when the ruling was challenged in court, the ATO was defeated and the scheme was ruled successful.[6] Packer, however, did not take his case to court. And on that basis, one can probably assume that the tax office won the day.

There was never any suggestion that this particular Allen Allen & Hemsley scheme used by Packer was illegal—unlike the film and bloodstock schemes. And if any of his tax dodging raised moral questions, Kerry Packer did not seem to be in the least bothered by them. In November 1991, he appeared before a parliamentary inquiry into the Australian print media and was asked whether his tax arrangements were contrary to the spirit of the law. He replied contemptuously (and famously) that what he did was perfectly legal and that one had to be crazy not to be doing it.

> I am not evading tax in any way, shape or form. Of course, I am minimising my tax. Anybody in this country who does not minimise his tax wants his head read. I can tell you as a government that you are not spending it so well that we should be donating extra.[7]

Packer was certainly no fool. Indeed, if efforts to reduce one's tax bill were a measure of wisdom, he was one of the wisest and sanest men in Australia. But I must confess that I am stupid and old-fashioned enough to believe what Kerry said in 1977: that the super rich should pay their share of tax just like anybody else. It's a well-known fact, of course, that the rich have always been able to rort the system, and there will always be an army of highly paid lawyers and tax advisers prepared to push the law to the limit. But it is odd that so many small taxpayers applauded Kerry Packer for his reluctance to pay his dues. Tax, after all, pays for the society we live in—for our roads, our hospitals, our doctors, our pensions, our soldiers, our government and our unemployment benefits. By making such an art of minimising his tax, Packer was also minimising his contribution to the running of Australia: the country that, by his own admission, had given the Packers 'everything'.

Nor was it just personal tax that Kerry managed to avoid. His companies were as keen to minimise tax as he was, and just as successful. In the financial year 1991–92, his privately owned Consolidated Press Holdings group earned a profit of $623 million before tax and had a positive cash flow of almost $2000 million, yet its provision for income tax was a mere $5 million, or less than 1 per cent of profits. Its actual tax payment made during the year was an almost identical $6 million.[8]

Taking the six years from 1987 to 1992, the position was slightly less spectacular but still very similar, in that the Packer empire earned $1445 million in profits and paid $91 million in tax, which worked out at almost exactly 7 per cent of its profits. This compared with a nominal corporate tax rate of 39 per cent and an average tax rate paid by the top 100 Australian industrial companies of around 30 per cent. Few if any of these could match the achievement of Packer's businesses in earning so much and consistently paying so little. Most of the entrepreneurial companies that had paid virtually no tax in the late 1980s went bust in the crash, reflecting the fact that their profits were a fiction in the first place. But Consolidated Press went from strength to strength and there was certainly never any suggestion that its profits were a fantasy.

Interestingly enough, the Packer group's low tax performance dated from 1984, before which it had paid around 40 per cent of its profits to the taxman. In 1983 two things of significance had happened: one was that the Consolidated Press empire had been privatised and taken back into Packer family ownership; the other was that Bob Hawke's new Labor government had come to power with a plan to deregulate Australia's financial markets. Deregulation in 1984 had allowed the free flow of money into and out of Australia and had helped greatly to enrich Kerry Packer.

The opportunity presented by deregulation had been seized upon by Packer and his advisers who had immediately moved some of the financing of Consolidated Press offshore. By 1986 this was producing considerable tax benefits and helping to reduce the group's tax rate from 39 per cent to 14 per cent, but by the late 1980s far bigger dividends were being reaped. In the last three years of the decade, when Consolidated Press's main businesses were in Australia and the USA, Packer's group managed to earn big profits tax-free in the Netherlands Antilles and Hong Kong. Most of these profits were made by UK companies based in London, which on close examination were non-resident companies run from a tax haven.

Just down the road from the British Museum in the heart of London's Bloomsbury district there used to be a small shop with a barometer in the window. Set in an eighteenth-century brick terrace with an olde-worlde feel about it, the shopfront looked like an antiquarian bookseller or a dealer in fine arts. But in the late 1980s the only fine art on sale from these nondescript premises was the art of international tax avoidance, for these were the offices of a firm of solicitors called Bishop & Sewell. Between 1984 and 1990 this small shopfront played home to a number of Consolidated Press's offshore companies, making it in effect Packer's international headquarters. In the last four years of the 1980s these UK companies earned some $370 million in tax-free profits at a time when the Packer empire employed only a handful of people in the United Kingdom doing business. While the various companies were nominally based in the UK, they were in fact run from Hong Kong. As a result, they were not required to pay UK tax. Yet for reasons that the ordinary person might find hard to grasp, they also paid no tax at all in Hong Kong, because they did not actually do business there either.

International tax law is a weird and wonderful thing, and Packer's tax lawyers have been smarter than most in making it work to their client's advantage. In the late 1980s they managed to arrange a number of Packer's international business activities to operate beyond the reach of taxmen anywhere in the world. Exactly what these various companies did to earn their money was something of a mystery, and one that Packer's people were in no hurry to clear up. In mid 1991 ABC TV's *Four Corners* program paid a visit to Hong Kong and approached two of the key directors of Packer's offshore business empire. After several attempts, I succeeded in talking briefly by telephone to Miss Catherine Sham, a director of forty of Packer's international companies, who gave the remarkable answer that she couldn't say what the companies did because she didn't know and wasn't involved—even though she was a director. It was still possible, however, from accounts published in the UK, to build up some picture of how these companies made their money.

In principle, it appeared that these tax-haven operations earned their profits by financing and owning Consolidated Press businesses in the United States and elsewhere. In return for lending money (that was often sourced from Australia), the tax-haven operations collected interest payments or dividends from companies like Valassis in the USA, reducing the empire's taxable profits in America and accumulating the money tax-free in Hong Kong. Over the seven years from 1984 to 1990 three of Packer's UK non-resident companies run from Hong Kong earned tax-free profits of A$210 million from financing Packer's offshore businesses.[9] Meanwhile, his Australian companies attempted to claim tax deductions onshore (for lending money to the tax-haven companies) to reduce the Consolidated Press group's Australian tax bill.

One of the more intriguing and more profitable of these offshore companies was Consolidated Press International Holdings UK, set up in February 1987 after the sale of Channel Nine to Alan Bond. According to its accounts, this company traded through two subsidiaries in the Netherlands Antilles, making money in commodity futures and foreign exchange. It seemed to be speculating on an enormous scale and to have been brilliantly successful, chalking up profits of A$189 million in 1988 and 1989, half the total profit of the Consolidated Press group in those two years. But it may also have benefited from some of Packer's successful share plays.

413

In July 1990 changes were made to the Australian tax system in an effort to stop Australian companies from using international tax havens to dodge Australian tax. As Treasurer Paul Keating told federal parliament in characteristically colourful language when introducing the bill, the government would not tolerate companies ripping off the rest of the community. In theory this new law was quite simple: profits earned in tax havens by Australian-owned companies would be taxed after July 1990 as if they had been earned in Australia. But in practice the new regime was extremely complex and it was by no means certain that it would do the job, at least as far as Packer's companies were concerned.

Four months before the new tax law came into operation (but almost a year after it had been foreshadowed) Kerry Packer moved his international corporate headquarters and all his offshore assets to the Bahamas. The UK non-resident companies were put into liquidation and the Hong Kong operation run down. Once again Packer's advisers were in no hurry to explain the reasons for the change, but the very fact that they had demolished one international structure and replaced it with another suggested that they had found a chink in the tax laws that Packer's companies could squeeze through. The additional fact that the new international structure used old Australian trusts set up by Kerry's father, Sir Frank, tended to confirm that impression.

The new ultimate holding company for the entire Packer group (including the Australian assets) was the Nassau-based Consolidated Press International Holdings Ltd, set up in March 1990. This new master company was in turn owned by half-a-dozen trusts of which Kerry Packer was the primary beneficiary, namely Custodian Settlements No. 6 and No. 8, Genetout Settlement No. 6 and the K2, K3 and K4 Trusts.[10] The first three of these had been set up in the 1950s and 1960s by Sir Frank Packer, who had died in 1974. Now, the significance of this can only be guessed at. But the new tax regime was targeting *Australian*-owned companies in tax havens. And there was some question whether the new law defined this new Bahamas company as Australian-owned, because its owner was a discretionary trust set up by someone now dead (Sir Frank).[11]

Whether the new Bahamas arrangement did squeeze through this tax loophole was a matter of conjecture, but Packer's advisers certainly managed to keep Consolidated Press's tax bills down, even after the new tax laws came into effect. In the two financial years immediately after the new regime was introduced in July 1990, Consolidated Press earned profits of $825 million yet paid just $27 million in tax.[12] In the second of these years, a Dutch-based company called Conpress Investments BV, owned through the Bahamas, recorded a profit of $1272 million from dividends paid on the sale of half of Packer's American coupon business Valassis (and perhaps from the sale of other companies). This profit was evidently tax-free.[13]

Following a question to Packer at the House of Representatives inquiry into the print media in November 1991 about whether Packer's tax arrangements were contrary to the spirit of the law, the ALP's John Langmore tried to press for information on Packer's corporate tax payments. Packer's response was that he and his companies paid whatever tax the law required and he was not going to discuss his tax affairs with anyone. When asked whether it was true to say that the Consolidated Press group had paid tax at 10 cents in the dollar between 1987 and 1990, Packer professed ignorance:

Packer: I do not know—it's your story, you go ahead with it.
Langmore: You do not know?
Packer: No, I do not know. I do not do the tax returns.
Langmore: It seems a surprising thing that, with your company, you do not know how much tax you pay.
Packer: Well, I do not.
Langmore: What do you estimate it to be?
Packer: I do not estimate anything.
Langmore: What do you think then is the . . .?
Packer: I do not think about it either.

Langmore: You mean you're not prepared to answer questions on this subject?

Packer: I have already given you the answer on this subject. I have told you that I pay whatever tax I am required to pay under the law—not a penny more, not a penny less. The suggestion that I am trying to evade tax—which is what you are putting forward—I find highly offensive. I do not intend to co-operate with you in the blackening of my character. You ask whatever questions you like, but my memory's gone.[14]

Australia's fearless political investigators left it at that. If Kerry Packer didn't want to answer questions put to him by Australia's parliamentarians, it seemed there was nothing they could do about it. It was a sad comment on the power of parliament and of Packer that they believed this to be so.

But the ATO was not so easily dismissed. As Kerry smirked at the defeated politicians, the ATO resolved to conduct a wide-ranging audit of his tax affairs. For the next three years, its senior investigators combed through Packer's personal and corporate tax returns and camped out in his Park Street offices. Finally, just before Christmas 1994, the taxman issued a demand for $260 million in back tax, including some $52 million from Kerry in personal income tax for the years 1989 to 1992.

The mother of all legal battles then broke out, raging all the way to Australia's High Court in 2004, at which point, both sides claimed a sort of victory. The ATO was able to highlight the judges' decision that Packer's financing of the attempted BAT takeover in 1989 had breached the anti-avoidance provisions of Part IVa of the Tax Act. Packer, meanwhile, was able to boast that his Bahamas reshuffle had been deemed to be both within the law and not taxable.

But there was no doubt about who really won. The ATO's demand that Packer stump up $52 million in unpaid income tax was settled before the matter even came to court for the princely sum of $32.93, the price of a good bottle of wine. And despite the ATO's claims of success, it appeared that Packer's companies escaped without paying any more tax than they had before the audit took place.

But in some ways all of this was a sideshow, for Packer's personal tax bill would always be remarkably low, thanks to something called 'dividend imputation', which the Hawke government introduced in 1987. This allowed Kerry to receive millions of dollars in dividends every year from his publishing empire, yet pay tax at a maximum rate of only 9 per cent, giving him several million reasons to be thankful to the ALP. The system was eminently sensible in its aim to prevent double taxation of dividends, but it did not look good when applied to cases like Packer's.

Because of the way dividend imputation worked, Packer could claim a credit against his personal tax bill equal to the amount of *all* the Australian tax paid by his companies. This amounted to millions of dollars every year, even though the group's tax rate was only 10 per cent (or less) thanks to its use of tax havens. So Kerry Packer was able to pay himself a dividend of $35 million a year in the late 1980s yet pay only $3 million in income tax, or 9 per cent (which was then the difference between the personal and the corporate tax rates). After 1994, when the Packer empire was re-floated on the Australian Stock Exchange as Publishing & Broadcasting Ltd, Packer's key private companies also derived massive benefit from dividend imputation, so that Consolidated Press Holdings normally paid no tax at all. In 1999, for example, CPH earned $1.25 billion in profit, yet paid not a cent in tax. It had also managed to pay no tax on $600 million earned in 1997 and 1998. This was entirely within the rules. But it appeared to be incredibly unfair. As the head of the National Tax & Accountants' Association remarked to the *Sydney Morning Herald* in an article headed 'Earn $1.2 billion, pay no tax', it was enough to make the ordinary PAYE taxpayer sick.

Packer was so outraged by this criticism he sued the newspaper, claiming it portrayed him and his companies as trying to evade their tax obligations, in a way that was 'nauseating'. Kerry's lawyers realised that if they were to pursue the defamation action, the Big Fella would have to surrender all his tax returns. Not surprisingly, he was extremely reluctant to do so. Seven years later, after Packer's death, the case was still sitting before the Federal Court.

418

CHAPTER TWENTY-ONE

KING KERRY

That's God, but we have to humour him because he's
got a bit of a problem. You see, he thinks he's
Kerry Packer.

Packer joke, 1990

Less than three years after the sale of Channel Nine to Alan Bond, Packer was knocking on the door to get back in again. He had accepted $200 million of the $1 billion sale price in the shape of an IOU from Bond, or more precisely in the form of Bond Media preference shares that fell due for redemption in March 1990. And as this date drew closer it became more and more obvious that Bond would not be able to find the money.

By this stage of his rapid corporate decline, Bond was busy trying to persuade his creditors to settle for a fraction of what they were owed, but it was against Packer's nature to do such things. He wanted his money back.

The idea that Packer might have to force his way back into Channel Nine to collect the cash was first put to him in late 1989 by his former adviser (turned merchant banker) Malcolm Turnbull, and he was less than thrilled at the prospect. He was far more interested in playing polo than in coming back to Australia to run a television network, even if he could get his old stations back for next to nothing. But he was soon persuaded there was no other way to be sure of his money.

The strategy Turnbull outlined was to push the TV network to the brink of bankruptcy and force Bond to negotiate. If that move failed, Bond Media's inability to find the $200 million would compel the banks to step in and take control. Channel Nine would then almost certainly be put up for auction, and Packer was virtually assured of winning. Not only were Australian financial institutions keen to bankroll him back into television because of his undoubted abilities, but he had a huge financial advantage over all other potential bidders. Anyone buying Channel Nine from the receivers would be forced to add Packer's $200 million to their bid, but he could simply wave that money in the air and put it back in his pocket. It was therefore almost inconceivable that anyone would be able to match what he was prepared to pay.

The campaign to regain control of the network took nine months, but by July 1990 Packer was back in the driving seat and happy to be so, having decided in the heat of the battle that he wanted Channel Nine back after all. Having sold out for more than $1 billion in early 1987, he was buying in again for just $200 million. Or to put it even more graphically, having walked away from the original sale with $800 million in cash in his pocket, he was now taking a controlling share in the expanded network for nothing.[1]

No sooner had the deal been signed than Packer began to make himself felt. Eleven days after Bond Media shareholders had given the thumbs up to his return, Kerry's big white BMW 750 pulled into the car park at Nine's Willoughby headquarters with driver George Young at the wheel. In the passenger seat was the network's old proprietor, back to teach the boys a lesson, while behind him in the back was young Jamie Packer, who was soon following his father at a respectful distance towards the foyer. It was precisely 7.30 a.m., the sort of time when most television executives are still struggling to get out of bed.

In case anyone failed to get the message that the boss was back, Packer soon installed himself in the managing director's huge office and waited for the rest of his executives to show up, summoning them to his presence as they did so. The first edict that came down to the program makers, as they drifted in later that day, was that all alcoholic drink was to be thrown out of the building and all fridges cleared. The second was that all staff would in future take only one hour for lunch. The third was that each program must find a 10 per cent cut in its budget. And the fourth, which all had expected, was that there were going to be job losses on a grand scale.

Under Bond's ownership, expenditure at Channel Nine had gone crazy, or so Packer believed. A new third floor had been added to the studio building and fitted out with plush executive suites. There was a new marble foyer, a spectacular glass lift and a vast green marble bar in the chief executive's eyrie. There at the end of each week, Packer's old deputy, the diminutive Sam Chisholm, would hold court to his senior staff, doling out chardonnay and champagne from bottles in a large glass-fronted fridge. These drinks sessions had supposedly kept up morale but they had also helped earn Nine the nickname 'the Bollinger channel'. After the Bond takeover in 1987 the French champagne had flowed freely, for in its vast collection of bank-funded assets the Bond Group was fortunate enough to have had the Australian Bollinger franchise.

But apart from its expenses, which were high, and its debts, which were huge, Channel Nine had actually done well in Packer's absence. And Chisholm was the man responsible, for he had gathered a talented team of people at the station and had kept his stars happy, not least by paying them outrageous salaries. In fact, since Packer's departure the network had improved its earnings before interest each year, consolidated its number-one spot in the ratings and grabbed 40 per cent of national TV advertising revenues. But in Packer's view there was nothing at all to be happy about. The people who worked for the station had had their snouts in the trough, as he elegantly put it, and he was going to take the trough away.

Three weeks after Packer's dramatic comeback, forty-seven people were sacked in the first wave of economies, with most of the cuts coming in news and current affairs, where program makers and front people took most of the casualties. As these new recruits to the dole queue left the Channel Nine studios, time-and-motion men from Coopers & Lybrand were still running their rulers over the rest of the business. Known as the Mormons because they always wore suits and travelled in pairs, they were soon recommending that further cuts be made to staff in administrative areas, and over the next few months at least another hundred employees departed. Channel Nine's super-expensive stars had already been told to contribute to the savings by taking a pay cut. It was said that Jamie had been counting BMWs in the car park and had found too many for his father's liking.

Before long, Sam Chisholm was also saying his farewells. Even though he had been made managing director of the new company, it was almost inevitable that he would depart once Packer was back in charge. He had fought hard to stop Packer coming back, albeit in the interests of saving Bond Media, and was too closely identified with the old free-spending style. But even more to the point, there was no room for a king below Kerry. Chisholm stayed for a month to listen to Packer's contemptuous condemnations of the network's extravagance and then accepted an offer to run Rupert Murdoch's British pay TV service, the newly merged Sky-BSB.

Thereafter, Packer was rarely in occupation at Channel Nine but his family pictures remained on the walls of Chisholm's empty office while he played polo overseas, if only to remind the people at Nine that the business was to be run for its shareholders rather than for its employees. Packer, of course, being the largest shareholder of all.

Despite his King Kong behaviour, or perhaps because of it, there were people at Channel Nine who were happy to have Packer back. He promised to lower debts, cut costs and increase the network's profits, restoring value to the enterprise once more. And that certainly went down well with Channel Nine's bankers and shareholders. At the first general meeting of the new Packer-controlled company at Sydney's Darling Harbour, there was no pomp and circumstance, no razzamatazz and not even a chairman's address. The business of the meeting was all over in fifteen minutes. Packer congratulated his new directors on being in charge of a company with no money and announced a $600 million pre-tax loss for the financial year just ended. As was the habit on such occasions, his accountants had thrown in all the losses and write-downs they could find to ensure that the future would only get better. Bond had been incompetent and profligate, Packer told shareholders, but the new team was not. 'I can assure you that there will be no money wasted and no one will be touching you. You will not have anyone dipping in your pockets here,' said Packer. 'I came out of retirement to make sure these things happen and they will happen.'

No one doubted that they would. But some of the people in the audience who applauded his speech may have believed that the man could walk on water. For the myth of Kerry Packer's invincibility was growing fast by this stage. It was not just because his 1987 prediction of buying back Channel Nine at half-price had come true, although that was impressive enough; it was also that he had suffered a massive heart attack in October 1990 while playing polo and had 'died' for seven minutes, yet was still around to tell the tale. It seemed that nothing and no one could now stand in his way.

Packer's so-called heart attack was more properly described as a cardiac arrhythmia in which his heart had gone haywire: beating too quickly to pump blood round the body. But there was no doubt that he had come back from the dead in double-quick time and with terrific style. One minute the cameras had snapped him flat-out on a stretcher with tubes up his nose, apparently in a coma as he was taken into hospital. The next moment (or so it seemed) he had been storming across a polo field to attack another batch of cameramen who were eager to record his remarkable recovery. The morning news bulletins on 8 October 1990, the day after his collapse, had warned that he might have brain damage or even be rendered a vegetable by the seven minutes in which he had been 'dead'. The evening news bulletins five days later showed unmistakably that he was as angry and as alive as ever.

In fact, Packer had had heart problems before, which had given him cause to believe his days were numbered. In 1983 he had been rushed to Sydney's St Vincent's Hospital complaining of severe chest pains, after collapsing on The Australian golf course. He might easily have felt then that the end was nigh, because he had suffered an attack of angina, which strikes in the centre of the chest and can be so savage that people often think they are dying. At that stage he had not needed surgery, but it was pretty clear he soon would. He was unfit, grossly overweight, loved junk food and had extremely high blood pressure, all of which increased his risk of heart disease. Plus, there was a history of heart problems on both sides of his family. Worst of all, he smoked like a chimney. Indeed, he smoked so much he did not care what brand he used because he couldn't taste the difference, which was convenient, since he regularly ran out of cigarettes and cadged from his employees. Given that he smoked three packets a day, this was hardly surprising.

In an effort to get Packer to kick the habit, which was clearly putting his life at risk, his doctors in 1983 called in Renee Bittoun from St Vincent's Smokers Clinic, who was famous for her ability to get people to quit. But Packer was obviously not one of her conquests, for he struggled to give up over the next seven years without lasting success. Visitors to his Park Street office throughout the 1980s recall him shouting to his secretary Pat Wheatley to get him a 'fucking cigarette', or rougher versions thereof.

According to his long-time driver George Young, Packer tried constantly to stop smoking and was quite unapproachable whenever he did so: 'You couldn't get within twenty feet of him without getting your head ripped off,' George reported. After being lectured at St Vincent's one day on the dangers, Packer reeled out of the hospital vowing he would never touch another cigarette in his life. He then ripped open the glove box, in which his driver had stored six packets of cigarettes in case they ran out, and threw them all out of the window. As they drove off from the hospital, he grabbed George's cigarettes as well and flung them out, too, along with all the lighters and matches he could lay his hands on.

Two days later, George picked him up off the chopper from Ellerston. 'Christ, give me a cigarette,' said Packer, as soon as he got into the car.

'Sorry,' said George, 'you threw them all away.'

'Give me one of yours then,' Packer pleaded.

'Sorry boss,' said George, 'you threw them out, too.'

In his first bid to give up in 1983, Packer took to chewing Nicorettes and bought them by the truckload. There were boxes of them everywhere, so that George Young ended up taking them home to store in his garage. But neither the Nicorettes nor horror films about smoking did the trick and it wasn't till three months before his brief 'death' in October 1990 that Packer supposedly succeeded in giving up. Even then, his abstinence didn't last for long.

Packer's heart scare in 1983 gave the medical staff at St Vincent's their first sight of Packer as a patient and it wasn't always pretty. He could be heroically charming to the nurses, but appalling if he did not get his way. One junior doctor recalls seeing him on a trolley in the Intensive Care Unit, naked to the waist, brandishing a large paper cup of Coke and snarling at the nursing staff, 'I told you I wanted cubes in this, not fucking crushed ice.'

Packer's arrival in intensive care on that first occasion was heralded by all manner of commotion, with frantic phone calls to say he was on his way and a bevy of people fussing around him. Calls from the press came flooding in soon afterwards. The doctor in charge, Bob Wright, who was summoned down to meet him, was baffled by it all because (amazingly) he had no idea who Packer was. Somehow, he had managed to be the only person in Sydney who had never heard of him. But over the next dozen years Wright and Packer became almost bonded at the hip, because he effectively became Kerry's personal physician. Packer, it seems, did not have a regular doctor, so he started using Wright (who was Director of the Intensive Care Unit) as his first port of call. Occasionally, it was serious. More often, it was stuff a GP could have taken care of. If Kerry needed an eye test, his secretary Pat Wheatley would ring up and get Dr Wright to arrange it. If Kerry had a rash, Dr Wright would fix for him to see a dermatologist.

This bizarre arrangement was tolerated, one imagines, because Packer gave large amounts of money to the hospital, starting with his very first visit in 1983, when Dr Wright suggested he could buy St Vincent's some new heart monitoring equipment, on the basis that he would soon be needing it himself. Packer asked him which company made the best product, and was told it was Hewlett Packard. 'Then get me the head of Hewlett Packard on the phone,' he barked. Sure enough, the boss of Hewlett Packard was soon on his way up from Melbourne with a couple of minions, for a private presentation at Packer's bedside.

'I'll tell you right from the fucking start,' Packer began, 'I've never paid the full price for anything in my life. Now, where's the quote?' Packer then took the piece of paper that was handed to him and scribbled on it, before starting again. 'Right. I've written a figure here. If you can get underneath it, you can have the business. If not, you can forget it.'

The guys from Hewlett Packard went in to a huddle for a couple of minutes in a corner of the ward and then bobbed back with an offer. Luckily for St Vincent's, it was low enough for Packer to say yes, and the deal was done. After they had gone, Packer grinned at Wright, telling him, 'There you are, son. That's a lesson in how to do business.'

Packer and Wright got along reasonably well, with Wright matching him for bad language and directness whenever necessary. 'If he swore at me, I swore back at him,' he says. But the doctor found him a handful. 'It was easier to look after twenty intensive care patients than one Kerry Packer,' he says. There was a non-smoking rule in the hospital, for example, but Kerry ignored it, and no one wasted their time trying to enforce it. He was also incredibly demanding—as only a billionaire can be. And, just like in business, he would walk over anybody (particularly men) who did not stand up to him. Often he would have meetings at his bedside and (as one observer put it) 'bash the shit' out of his unfortunate executives.

On the other side of the coin, most of the nurses liked Packer, and the money kept flowing in. Shortly after the Big Fella's heart attack in 1990, Bob Wright organised for a superintendent of the Ambulance Service of New South Wales, Val McMahon, to visit Packer's bedside and show him the defibrillator that had saved his life. 'How would you like to put one of these machines in every ambulance in New South Wales?' Wright asked.

'How much would it cost?' Packer replied.

'$5 million,' came the answer.

'Get me Greiner on the phone,' said Packer. And within minutes he was talking to the premier of New South Wales. 'Look, I'm putting $2.5 million into buying these things,' Packer told the premier. 'How about you go the other half?' And thus the deal was done.

Two weeks after his collapse on the polo field Packer underwent a triple heart bypass operation, which took veins out of his leg to bypass the clogged-up sections of his coronary arteries. He was also prescribed drugs to combat a recurrence of the arrhythmia, adding to the pills he was already taking to keep his blood pressure down. But he did not do the other things the doctors ordered—like quit smoking, get fit, lose weight or change his diet—so it was likely to be a matter of time before his heart gave him trouble again.

Even as a younger man, Packer had often told friends that he did not expect to live beyond fifty, and his latest health problems had hardly given him grounds for great optimism. Indeed, on his own predictions, he was already living on borrowed time, for by December 1990 he was fifty-three years old and would soon have outlasted both his mother and his grandfather. His mother Gretel Packer had died of heart disease at fifty-three, while one of her sisters had also died young from cardiac trouble. His grandfather, Robert Clyde Packer, had died of a heart condition at the age of fifty-four after several years of illness. And few on the male side of the Packer family had lived past sixty. In fact, Kerry's father Sir Frank Packer had been a rare exception to the rule, living to the age of sixty-seven, when he, too, died of a heart attack. But Sir Frank's last ten years had been plagued by constant illness. It was no surprise that Packer's friends reported him to be scared of dying and convinced he would not live long.

There was a joke that now went around Sydney about Packer going to heaven, which went like this: Packer was standing in line at the Pearly Gates waiting to be let in when an old man with a beard jumped the queue. Packer marched up to St Peter who was guarding the gates to ask what the hell was going on. 'Oh,' said St Peter, 'that's God, the bloke who owns the place.'

'Oh, yeah?' asked Packer. 'Well how come he doesn't line up like everybody else?'

'Ah well,' said St Peter, 'we have to humour him because he's got a bit of a problem. You see, he thinks he's Kerry Packer.'

Joking aside, Packer's most recent brush with death did not seem to have softened him. In fact, it appeared to have made his temper worse. It was as if it no longer mattered to him what people thought, since he wasn't going to be around much longer. But is was also that he now knew there was no God. He told his old friend Phillip Adams that his brief journey to the other side had been a revelation: 'There's no one waiting there for you . . . There's no one to judge you, so you can do what you bloody well like.' As if he hadn't done already. So he now went about his business in even tougher fashion than before, if that were possible.

With the Nine Network back under his banner, Kerry set about making it pay, as he had promised the banks and shareholders he would do. Having put the fear of Packer into his executives in Sydney and Melbourne to get costs down, he now sent a message to the people who bought Channel Nine's programs, the regional television stations operating under the Nine Network, that he wanted them to contribute more. On one well-documented occasion, the pitch went something like this: 'You've had it easy in the past and got your programs cheap, but we're the new kids on the block, and we're going to make you pay your fair share.'

The style of the Packer approach to one regional affiliate of Channel Nine was recorded verbatim in documents filed before the Australian Broadcasting Tribunal (ABT), which gave an extraordinary insight into the way that Packer's people did business.[2]

On 1 January 1991, Telecasters North Queensland (TNQ) was all set to become the Nine Network's flag carrier in a newly aggregated area covering the whole of rural Queensland. But one key matter had not been settled—the price that the station would pay for Channel Nine's programs under these new arrangements. Negotiations on this began just a month after Packer's heart attack with a meeting in Townsville on 9 November 1990 between Jack Gleeson and David Astley of TNQ, and Nick Falloon and Lynton Taylor from Channel Nine. After a few preliminaries, Taylor got down to basics, telling the two men from TNQ that Channel Nine intended immediately to raise prices for its programs fourfold compared with what the station had paid under the old arrangements, when it had bought from all three networks. Taylor made it quite clear that TNQ would lose all access to Channel Nine's output if it was not prepared to pay these prices, because there was another operator in the wings ready to fly the flag instead.

But there was even worse to come. While Channel Nine wanted an immediate 25 per cent of TNQ's gross revenue, which would come through raising program prices fourfold, its real target was 40 per cent of TNQ's revenue, to which it intended to move within five or six years. It didn't matter, said Taylor, that TNQ had done a good job in the past or that it was the best station in the area; Channel Nine wanted more money and it meant to get it.[3]

Astley and Gleeson of TNQ were shocked and appalled by this demand. Handing over 25 per cent of TNQ's revenues to Packer would in their opinion drive the company into bankruptcy. They protested strongly that they couldn't afford it. But

Packer's man Lynton Taylor was not impressed. He told them bluntly that their costs were too high and that they made too many local programs. Cut the number of local programs or cut them out altogether, Taylor advised, and pass the savings on to Channel Nine. As for local programs, he said, the government wasn't interested in local programming and nor was he: 'Localism will have to disappear for you to survive.'

According to TNQ's evidence, Astley and Gleeson countered that they were required to provide local programs to satisfy their obligations to the public and to the ABT. Taylor said he might be able to help on this if the ABT started giving TNQ a hard time, because Channel Nine could make 'the right noises in the right places'. But really, said Taylor, he couldn't see any need for concern about the ABT taking TNQ's licence away just because the station ignored the ABT's guidelines—it had certainly never done so to other stations in the past.

The directors of TNQ were given three weeks to respond to Channel Nine's proposed price increase and its accompanying ultimatum, which was to pay or be damned. But they were advised by their lawyers that they could not accept, since they believed it would bankrupt the company. Astley and Gleeson put up a counter offer to give Channel Nine an 80 per cent increase in revenue. This was instantly dismissed, and Packer's people then made good their threat to sell the programs to someone else. The 'new kids on the block' struck a deal with Bruce Gordon, a former director of Channel Nine and protégé of Sir Frank Packer, who was already flying Nine's banner over his WIN 4 station in Wollongong.[4]

It has never been revealed how much Bruce Gordon's company was asked to pay for Channel Nine's programs in Queensland, but his general manager John Rushton rejected suggestions that prices were raised to their WIN 4 station by even 100 per cent. 'Certainly not,' he told the *Sydney Morning Herald* in January 1991. 'I don't think any business can suffer 100 per cent increases in operating costs.' He then added a note of sympathy for TNQ and its shareholders: 'In a small, little corner of my heart I feel sorry for the poor buggers because I know how I'd feel in that position.'[5]

There was nothing that TNQ could do. The massive changes to television introduced by the Labor government in 1986 had put the regional stations at the mercy of the big-city networks, just as people had predicted they would. And if TNQ's experience was any guide, they were particularly at the mercy of Channel Nine, which was the most successful network, the most powerful and the least squeamish about throwing its weight around.

Having lost its affiliation to Channel Nine, TNQ was forced to buy programs instead from the less successful Ten Network. By mid 1992 it had lost audience and advertising revenue, sacked 10 per cent of its staff and cut local programming from seven shows to two shows a week. But according to Gleeson, even this was better than giving in to Packer's demands.

Shortly before the TNQ episode, Packer had played just as tough with the people running the Ten Network, which was in dire financial trouble. As a preliminary to the battle he had phoned Ten's chief executive Steve Cosser in May 1990 to tell him he was unhappy about a plan that Cosser had put forward to merge Channel Ten and Channel Seven to get them both out of trouble. Cosser had suggested forming one super channel that would have the pick of Seven and Ten's best programs and almost certainly knock Packer's Channel Nine into second spot. Cosser was at home in Sydney's Vaucluse one Saturday morning when the phone rang. It was Packer, calling from the Savoy Hotel in London where it was still the middle of the night. He was obviously extremely angry. After the conversation, one statement in particular stuck in Cosser's mind, which was this: 'If you think there's no fucking difference between being number one and number two in a fucking two-station market, then you be fucking number two.'

Two months later, Channel Ten's chairman John Gerahty also received a call from Packer, to request a chat, and duly visited the Big Fella in his office at Park Street. According to Gerahty's account to his fellow directors, it was an extraordinary meeting, in which Packer's manner was threatening and his language coarse and abusive. Packer's message was that Channel Ten ought to 'know its place'; it had to stop trying to be number one and accept that it was the number three station. It should stop bidding against Channel Nine for programs and talent and should come to a sensible arrangement. It should also give up its valuable rights to televise Australian Rugby League. That way, said Packer, it might get its costs down. As it was, he couldn't understand why the Ten Network wasn't already in receivership.

Gerahty had been a merchant banker for twenty years and was used to dealing in a quiet businesslike fashion. A small, calm man, he had never experienced anything in his life like this warning from Packer. Nor had he ever met anyone who used his power so bluntly. When two journalists from the *Sydney Morning Herald* interviewed Gerahty four months later he appeared to be still shaken by the memory and refused to talk about it. Packer had warned him he would be sued if he did.

One month after his chat with Gerahty, Packer's prediction that Channel Ten would be put into receivership came true when Ten's principal banker, Westpac, pulled the plug. Given that the network was losing $2 million a week, it is understandable that they should have done so, and there is no suggestion Packer had any part in their decision. But some people in the industry questioned whether Westpac could take a truly objective view when Packer's Consolidated Press was their biggest customer and Packer's former cohort Malcolm Turnbull was advising the bank on Channel Ten's rescue and restructuring.

Turnbull had proposed a no-frills service for Channel Ten that would allow the network to make money with a much smaller share of the audience, and this plan was essentially adopted by the receivers when they took over in September 1990. One month later, the expansion-minded Steve Cosser was sacked as chief executive and replaced by Gary Rice, another ex-Packer man who had been advising Westpac since leaving Channel Nine in August. Three weeks after that, Channel Ten lost its rights to televise the Rugby League. Kerry Packer had warned John Gerahty in July that this would happen, telling him that Ten had been paying a silly price for the League coverage and would be forced to get rid of it. Channel Nine's connections with the Rugby League, said Packer, were better and he could afford to pay more. Sure enough it ended up with Packer, just as he predicted.

Channel Ten had bought the TV rights in July 1989 on a three-year contract at $16 million a year, which, indeed, was more than it could now afford. But in October 1990 the NSW Rugby League had offered to renegotiate, provided Ten stumped up the latest instalment of $2.6 million. According to Cosser, the money was in the bank to make this payment, which had already been authorised by the receiver James Millar. Millar and Cosser had also met the NSW Rugby League's general manager John Quayle and its chairman Ken Arthurson at half-time in the Grand Final in September and assured both men that Channel Ten intended to keep the contract.

But Ten's new chief Gary Rice clearly had other ideas. On 19 October 1990, three days after Steve Cosser's dismissal, Rice and Millar met Quayle and Arthurson in the League's Sydney offices and told them that Channel Ten was prepared to pay only $4 million for the next year's television rights. They were told bluntly that this was a ridiculous offer and the NSW Rugby League would not even consider it.

Even though the network now faced the certainty that it would lose its most valuable property, Channel Ten's bid was not increased over the next three weeks; nor was the outstanding $2.6 million paid. As a result, the contract lapsed and the rights were sold to Channel Nine in an auction at which Packer's network was the only serious bidder. Packer paid the NSW Rugby League $6.5 million for the rights, offloaded the international matches to Channel Seven for around $1 million and then sold the club matches back to Channel Ten for $7.7 million.[6]

It was both a remarkable deal for Packer and a disaster for Channel Ten. Packer showed a profit of more than $2 million on

433

the $6.5 million he paid the League and yet kept the matches that he really wanted, which were the three State of Origin clashes between New South Wales and Queensland. Channel Ten, meanwhile, bought the club matches for almost twice the $4 million it had been prepared to bid for the entire package of Rugby League games, including the valuable State of Origin clashes. These matches were year in, year out the most popular programs on Australian television, pulling in more than 50 per cent of the audience in Queensland and New South Wales and breaking all ratings records in 1992 when broadcast on Channel Nine.

Negotiations to buy Perth's West Australian Newspaper group in April 1991, in which Packer put his size fourteen boots on the table and told his opposite number how things had to be, provided another example of the man's business style. West Australian Newspapers was at this stage in the hands of the banks, which had been left with the wreckage of Alan Bond's corporate empire. And as usual, Packer was determined to buy for a rock bottom price. Bond had stuffed the business, Packer told the banks' adviser Mike Tilley from Lloyds Corporate Advisory Services, just as he had stuffed up Channel Nine, and they were lucky to have him as a buyer. The newspapers needed a lot of money spent on them and he was prepared to pay no more than $160 million, of which half would be in cash and half would be paid in the future. 'You can take it or leave it,' he told Tilley. Since this would have involved the banks in a loss of almost $100 million, Tilley said that he was sure the banks would leave it.

Up to this point in the negotiations, Packer had been charming, but he now became angry. According to Tilley, Packer told him that his proposal was the best the banks were going to get and they had better wake up. Rupert Murdoch had been in his office the previous day, Packer said, and the two of them had a game plan for the future of the Australian newspaper industry. Murdoch had agreed, said Packer, that he wasn't going to bid for the *West Australian*. What's more, if anyone else except Packer did bid, there was no doubt Murdoch would crush them, destroying the newspaper's earning ability, reducing its value and ending any prospect that the banks would be repaid. Tilley was sufficiently upset by this conversation to commit the details to paper as soon as he left Packer's Sydney office. Not long after, his file note was published in full by the new monthly *Independent* newspaper. One passage in particular summed up the message Tilley had received from the meeting. Tilley had suggested that the *West Australian* had already shown itself to be capable of surviving in the face of competition from Murdoch's *Sunday Times*.

Mr Packer suggested that this was bullshit; that he and Mr Murdoch had developed a plan for the newspaper industry in Australia which he described as 'a game plan' and that under that game plan there was no room for the *West Australian* to be owned by anybody else or operated successfully in the face of the onslaught that would be forthcoming.[7]

Whether or not Packer and Murdoch did have such a game plan for Australia's newspapers, Packer's warning that Murdoch would not bid for West Australian Newspapers was right.[8] But the banks still managed to sell the business for $260 million and the *West Australian* did not get crushed. In fact, the purchasers got themselves a bargain, for by 1993 the newspaper group was worth some $400 million on the stock market.

Packer's golden rule in business was said to be that the one with the gold made the rules. And invariably, it was he who had the gold. But it was possible to stand up to him and survive. Few who dealt with him, however, were brave enough to go on record. 'He's a bully and a bastard and this is a small town,' said one Sydney banker when I interviewed him for this book, 'so it doesn't make sense for me to be as honest as I would like to be. In fact, it doesn't make sense for me to talk to you at all.'

'He's ugly, he's unpleasant, he's every bit of a thug, he has no humility at all,' said another business executive who dealt with him, and who also insisted on anonymity. Foreign television executives, meanwhile, shook their heads and reported that he was the rudest man they had ever met.

Yet virtually everyone who dealt with Packer said he could also be an Olympic charmer. Malcolm Turnbull's verdict in the early 1990s was: 'He has the capacity to be very amusing, very kind and very generous. He is also very clever, and all of that makes him a very interesting person to work for. He has got a pretty rough side to his character, too, but I didn't see very much of that personally. I've heard a lot of horrific stories about Kerry roaring at people and so forth, but I've only ever witnessed him lose his temper two or three times. I know that sounds unlikely but it's true ... and I cannot recall an occasion when he screamed at me. I would have screamed at him.'

Others who knew Packer well said that he used charm and terror in equal measure to secure what he was after, using whichever he thought was appropriate. One former Packer editor said he was never afraid to use the full range of human emotions to get what he wanted. He was his own tough guy, nice guy act. In the middle of perfectly normal negotiations with one merchant banker in the late 1980s Packer suddenly lost his cool: 'What do you fucking know about it? If I never have to fucking deal with you again, it's no skin off my fucking nose.' By the time the meeting was over, he was behaving as if they were best of friends again.

If this was a deliberate negotiating technique of Packer's rather than uncontrollable temper, it was pretty effective. He could be so rude, so overbearing, so aggressive that it was very hard to stand up to him. But it did not win him many friends.

CHAPTER TWENTY-TWO

APPALLING PEOPLE

*Kerry Packer loathes the Australian
media . . . he regards Australian newspapers in
particular as completely irresponsible.*

Packer's *Bulletin* magazine, November 1989

Packer's style was certainly not calculated to put people at their
ease. Visitors to his office in Park Street were confronted by a
huge bull elephant staring at them from a painting on the wall
behind his desk, alongside a portrait of a large rampaging male
lion. Between the two loomed the scarcely less frightening figure
of Kerry Packer himself. But Packer rarely sat at his desk to interview visitors, especially if they were his own employees. While
executives trooped in in their business suits to perch on the edge
of chairs, Packer was frequently to be found lounging on the
sofa, munching a chocolate bar or popping Minties, which he
hardly ever offered to share.

Those who sat in the anteroom outside the Packer den,
waiting their turn for an audience, were able to get in the mood
for their encounter by gazing at another wildlife painting in
which a pack of dogs tore a sheep to pieces. One such visitor
remembers staring in wonder at this picture as the sounds of a
hapless employee being given the Packer treatment came wafting
through the door.

Strangely enough, the safest strategy was to visit Packer alone,
because he was always worse when he had an audience to play
to. On such occasions he would pick out the weakest person in

the room and bully him unmercifully. It was almost as if he could smell fear, according to those who worked with him. And he never liked to pass up an opportunity. One former top executive recalls how a programmer at Channel 9 became a particular target and was turning into a nervous wreck because it was so stressful. The executive told Packer he had to stop tormenting the man, and the Big Fella did then lay off, but only after one last hurrah, in which he paused at the height of his performance to wink at his captive audience. Many people told similar stories. It was clearly one of Kerry's favourite tricks.

Packer also had a habit of keeping his visitors waiting. In the mid 1980s his TV executives came to Park Street once a week for management meetings and commonly found they had to kick their heels for an hour or two before gaining admission. One regular participant remembers a meeting that was due to start at 9.30 a.m. and eventually got under way six hours late. Packer spent the morning in his office chewing the fat with one of Channel Nine's female stars while the cream of his executive talent sat waiting outside. Two of them had come up from Melbourne and had got out of bed at 5.30 a.m. to be there on time. Packer appeared briefly around 12.15 p.m. on his way to lunch with a politician and finally summoned them in at 3.30 p.m. One or two had bragged that they would tell Packer how outrageous it was they had all been kept waiting so long, but when they came face to face with him, not one of them uttered a word.

Few if any of Packer's executives were prepared to confront their boss, and it was not a good move to argue with him. But there were plenty of Packer clones in the television and magazine hierarchy who aped his behaviour and dished out similar treatment to the people below them. David Dale, editor of Packer's *Bulletin* for two years until he was sacked in 1990, says, 'I sometimes thought sitting in group lunches with executives just below the Packer level that the way to success in that organisation must have been your capacity to fit the word "cunt" into the sentence more often than the next person. It was really a boys' club of fellows who liked to show the boss how much they could bully each other. The pecking order is clearly established from the top down. Person A bullies person B who bullies person C.[1] Channel Nine was just the same, although there the magic word was 'fuck'.

At Consolidated Press's head office in Park Street, all Packer's top executives and editors had a yellow hotline or Packerphone on their desk on which the boss could ring through. The executives and editors could also talk to each other on this telephone, but the system was designed so that Packer could override anyone talking on it and butt into their conversation. All lived in fear of the hotline ringing and Packer being on the other end, but there were also great possibilities for practical jokes. The editors in particular used to play tricks on each other, ringing up to shout down the phone at their frightened colleagues. Jim Hall, who became editor of the *Bulletin* in April 1990, had been in the job for several months and had never heard a word from Packer about what he thought of the magazine's progress until one day the yellow phone went off on his desk. It was obviously the great man at last. Hall picked up the phone to hear a voice at the other end yelling, 'What the fuck are you doing to my fucking magazine?' Hall was dumbstruck; this was the fearsome Packer of legend. 'What the fuck are you doing to my fucking magazine?' the voice roared again, whereupon Jim Hall realised that perhaps he was being had. Sure enough, it was not Packer at all but one of his television executives, Ian Frykberg, on the line.

David Dale got a similar fright one day when the yellow phone rang and, once again without preliminaries, the voice on the other end said, 'I want you down in my office immediately.'

Dale said, 'Well, yes, I might well come down to your office, but who is this?'

'It's Packer,' the voice barked back, 'now get down here.' And then the phone went dead. Dale was left wondering whether it was a hoax call, but decided to go anyway, which was lucky because on this occasion it had been the Big Fella on the line.

439

Packer's rank-and-file journalists rarely saw their fearsome boss, but he was more than capable of leaving a mark on those he met. Several people who used to work at *Australian Business* remember an occasion in the mid 1980s when Packer arrived in their office during the lunch hour, after a hard morning in which they had successfully despatched the final copy for the magazine to the printers. Their boss was in an angry mood. 'Who sits at this desk? Who sits at that desk? Where the hell is everybody?' Packer wanted to know. 'Why aren't they working?' As the few journalists who had remained in the office wondered whether to let the storm blow out, Packer picked on the unfortunate figure of Roger Johnstone who was sitting at his desk eating his lunch. 'What are you doing, eating your lunch in here?' asked Packer, none too quietly. 'I'm eating my lunch,' Johnstone replied. Packer circled the room a couple of times and then came back to the fray. The precise words he used are a matter of debate, but according to those present, he suggested that if Johnstone—whom he addressed as 'son'—had 'a problem', he might like to step outside. The confused Mr Johnstone assured Packer that he had no problem at all, he was just eating his lunch, whereupon Packer stumped out of the room, leaving a handful of startled journalists in his wake.

But despite his frequent rampages, Packer did not exercise the same degree of editorial control over his magazines as Rupert Murdoch did over his newspapers. He was more interested in the ads, the layout and the sales figures than the content. And most of his magazines were non-political anyway, so his intervention in these would hardly have been cause for concern.

The purchase of *Woman's Day*, *People*, *Cosmopolitan*, *Dolly* and other top-selling Fairfax titles in 1987 had made the Packer magazine empire the biggest in Australia with more than 50 per cent of the market and ten of the country's top twenty titles.[2] These were mostly women's magazines, since it was mainly women who bought magazines, and they were glossy, smart and well produced. As a rule, they avoided controversy and shunned investigative journalism, choosing to concentrate almost exclusively on sex, with *Cleo* and *Cosmopolitan* vying to outdo each other in their exploration of G-spots, orgasms, oral sex techniques and sexual fantasies. By the early 1990s, even *Woman's Day* was going down the same route, printing topless pictures of Sarah Ferguson and her lover, and using cover lines such as the one declaring that Rachel Hunter 'strips for Rod', which promoted a picture feature inside the magazine. *Woman's Day* was also offering the confessions and revelations of a man who claimed to have been Elton John's gay lover. And clearly the public loved it, because sales of the magazine rose by 30 per cent in its first five years in Packer's ownership.

The group's two mass-sale men's magazines of the 1980s and early 1990s, *People* and *Picture*, with more than a million buyers between them, were basically soft-porn magazines with a few naughty feature articles thrown in. According to the marketing men they were read by blue-collar workers in their lunch break over a cup of tea and sandwiches, so they bared plenty of breasts and bottoms and went easy on the text. A typical issue of *People* in 1992 featured a pictorial story, 'COVERGIRL TIFFANY BUSTS OUT', an exclusive interview with the 'WORLD'S WORST SEX KILLER' and 'JAPAN GOES BONKERS FOR WEIRD SEX—KINKY PHOTOS'.[3] A more famous issue later in the year featured a cover picture of a naked woman on all fours with a dog collar and lead attached, which brought a host of complaints and caused ACP some problems when demonstrators stormed the company's Park Street offices. *People's* advertising revenue appeared to be derived almost exclusively from ads for phone sex, sex aids and pornographic videos.

It was hard to see press freedom being threatened by Kerry meddling in the editorial policy of publications such as these. And in the case of his news magazines, such as the *Bulletin* and (the now defunct) *Australian Business*, where it would have mattered, he rarely intervened in the way he had in the 1970s and 1980s. The late Jim Hall, editor of the *Bulletin* for eighteen months from mid 1990 to late 1991, said that Packer never interfered once in the running of the magazine while he was in charge and never even had a conversation with him. And Australian Consolidated Press's publisher Richard Walsh confirmed that account in the early 1990s, saying that Packer didn't even ask people about stories *after* they had been printed. He had done so in the past, Walsh admitted, but times had changed. People continued to believe the myth, Walsh told the parliamentary Print Media Inquiry in 1991:

Because it fulfils people's ideas of what a proprietor should be like. Everybody has seen *Citizen Kane* . . . It's a good story to tell; to work as though it's some kind of dinosaur dynasty stuck away there still acting like a combination of Hearst and Beaverbrook at their worst. That is just not the way it is.[4]

Walsh claimed to recall only one occasion on which Packer intervened—by famously sacking the *Bulletin* editor David Dale in March 1990. A year before his departure, Dale had incurred Packer's considerable wrath by publishing a cover story entitled 'AUSTRALIA'S 100 MOST APPALLING PEOPLE' in which a number of Kerry's friends had been featured. The story boosted the magazine's circulation considerably and sold out the individual issue. But Packer hated it, telling the *Bulletin*'s Bruce Stannard in a published interview in November 1989 that he was 'highly offended by it', considered it 'gratuitous impertinence' and thought it 'a mistake to run a stupid thing like that'. Just in case Dale missed this warning, Walsh soon told him that Packer had decreed the 'tasteless' article must not be repeated.

Four months later, a similar story entitled 'AUSTRALIA'S HUMAN BALANCE SHEET' came dangerously close to defying this instruction, classifying a series of famous Australian people as either 'Assets' or 'Liabilities' for the nation, and once again putting some of Kerry's friends in the wrong column. For a week after publication nothing happened and then, just as Dale was telling his *Bulletin* colleagues that he thought he had got away with it, he was summoned to Packer's office and sacked. Dale asked whether he might say something in his defence and was

442

told that he could but that it would do him no good. He was marched back to his office by a security guard and escorted from the building. Dale had been an excellent editor of the *Bulletin* and had boosted the magazine's circulation and staff morale, according to Richard Walsh, who resigned after Dale's sacking— only to change his mind later. But Packer felt he had disobeyed a specific instruction. It was therefore irrelevant that Walsh as ACP publisher had apparently given the article the thumbs up.

Packer's managing director Trevor Kennedy, who ran the *Bulletin* during the 1970s and early 1980s and was editor-in-chief at ACP before becoming Packer's right-hand man in 1986, had a different take on Packer's willingness to intervene. Kennedy told the parliamentary Print Media Inquiry that Packer had some-times ordered articles to be put into the *Bulletin* that he as editor would have preferred did not appear. But this, said Kennedy, was the proprietor's right. Privately, Kennedy admitted that Packer was much the same as Murdoch if he wanted something in the paper, and differed only in that he was less of a journalist, so he was never such a hands-on proprietor. Kerry also had other things on his mind, such as TV, polo and gambling, which made him easier to divert.

Kennedy did not offer examples of articles that Packer had insisted on, but in the 1970s and 1980s the *Bulletin* carried a number that appeared to promote Packer's business ventures. Several argued the case for Packer-style development of the New South Wales ski fields, while the launch of World Series Cricket had produced a classic piece of upbeat, pro-Packer reporting. According to the *Bulletin*'s six-page 'Exclusive' cover story, World Series Cricket was 'one of the most sensational sporting deals ever made . . . probably the most imaginative piece of sporting promotion ever devised', and likely to be 'the greatest boost Australian cricket has ever experienced'. Written by Trevor Kennedy himself, it said that Packer had pulled off a 'staggering coup' in signing up the world's best players, and Australians would be treated to 'some of the most magnificent cricket ever seen'.[5]

443

But it was what did not get into Packer's magazines that was more of a problem, as far as proprietorial influence was concerned. Articles critical of Packer were naturally excluded, as were articles critical of his friends or business partners. So, by a process of osmosis, was almost anything that journalists or editors felt Packer might dislike—such as articles about Aborigines, which Packer was known not to welcome in his magazines. David Marr, who wrote the prize-winning biography of Australian novelist Patrick White and worked as a journalist on the *Bulletin* in the 1970s, says: 'There was only one thing wrong with Packer as a press proprietor, and that was that he terrified people. Instead of sitting around thinking about what the story was or how to get a fresh angle, they sat and worried about what Packer would think. And the fact that he would actually strike only one time in a hundred didn't matter, because when he did it was so devastating.' The same climate of self-censorship and second-guessing existed at Channel Nine, where it would not have been a good career move to investigate the share dealings of Packer's mate Rene Rivkin or probe too deeply into the affairs of political mates such as Graham Richardson. Program makers at Nine knew instinctively what Kerry did and did not like and naturally avoided antagonising him.

One strange aspect of Packer as a media proprietor was that he clearly hated journalists. According to David Dale, he often engaged in tirades about what bastards journalists were, how they always wanted to invade people's privacy and invented stories. It was part of what Packer called the 'kangaroo court' mentality in Australia, where the media was always encouraging exposés of important people and trying to drag them down—the tall poppy syndrome. Somehow, it escaped his attention that his own magazines and Channel Nine's *A Current Affair* often led the pack in this regard. Nor did he appear to see the irony in guarding his own privacy so fiercely while his magazines and TV programs busily invaded other people's.

Packer's own *Bulletin* magazine made his views abundantly clear. 'Kerry Packer loathes the Australian media. And with good reason,' the magazine's Bruce Stannard reported in November 1989 after a long interview with his boss on the subject of the press. 'Few Australians have been subjected to the kind of ordeal by media he endured as a result of allegations thrown up by the Costigan Royal Commission in 1984. Although he was completely exonerated he still maintains a silent rage.' Packer told Stannard that he regarded Australian newspapers in partic-ular as completely irresponsible and was talking to the *Bulletin* only because he felt the press had to put its house in order before the government did it for them. 'Press credibility,' said Packer, 'is getting lower and lower. In fact it's just about at rock bottom . . . it's degenerated into a beat-up. The beat-up is what it's all about. Any story they get, they're looking to embellish so they can boast how they stuck it to someone . . . Unfortunately, many Australians want to pull down anyone who achieves. And journalists are no exception. They have become a law unto themselves.'[6]

To protect people like him, his friends and anyone else from unjustified attack, Packer argued that the defamation laws should be drastically reformed. 'What I think politicians should be doing, if they had any guts,' he told the *Bulletin*, 'is to introduce a libel system which is punitive. If a journalist has the evidence to prove his allegations, then by all means, let them be printed. But if they're wrong, then it should be costing their organisations millions, not tens or hundreds of thousands. Editors have to be made to realise that if they allow some half-baked story to get into print, they may well be placing their entire organisation in jeopardy.'

Packer's personal contribution in this area was to warn jour-nalists they could be hit with the legal equivalent of an Exocet missile if they were unwise enough to write about him. This meant they could be sued personally and, quite possibly, bank-rupted. When ABC TV's *Four Corners* was preparing a profile of him in September 1991, for example, Packer threatened to take legal action against every single person who took part in prepar-ing the program, right down to the film editors and production assistants. He threatened, too, to sue members of the ABC's management and each member of the ABC board, all of whom received letters to this effect *before* the program went out. A similar warning was received from one of Packer's directors at Consolidated Press Holdings in late March 1992 when Kerry Packer was asked whether he would co-operate in the writing of this book. It was another menacing indication of the Packer style:

> Mr Packer does not look upon your project favourably and I am instructed to inform you that should it be completed, your book will be reviewed by our attornies [sic] and, while we reserve all our rights, any false statement, untrue statement, misquotation, innuendo or any other material contained in the book which is misleading, whether deliberately so or not, and which may or is calculated to produce in the mind of the reader, an unfair or biassed view or otherwise derogate in any manner from the good reputation which Mr Packer and the members of his family and the group of companies which he controls enjoy will be prosecuted with the utmost vigour . . .
>
> . . . Any action we may take could comprehend not only yourself and Transworld Publishers but any other person who has any involvement whatsoever in the production of the book and the provision of information to you. You should place such persons on notice of the contents of this letter.

For the record, Packer never did sue me, despite his threats. And, remarkably, my career was in no way blighted by its publication. In fact, Channel Nine eventually hired me, with Kerry's blessing, to work for *60 Minutes* and *A Current Affair* as an investigative journalist. Perhaps less remarkably, my contract was then terminated, suddenly and unceremoniously, after two-and-a-half years, which gave me valuable personal experience of how the Packers deal with people they no longer have time for.

Right to the end of his life, Kerry Packer was convinced that journalists were out to get him and complained that they never bothered to check their facts, which he said they almost always got wrong. Yet his office almost always refused to confirm or deny anything when asked, and kept up a stone wall of no-comments even when presented with quite specific questions. In 1991, for example, I requested an interview for ABC TV's *Four Corners* and sent him a list of nineteen questions that sought to clarify the meaning of his (published) company accounts. I also asked whether it was true that he had more than one hundred polo ponies in the UK and still held gold interests in the Philippines. The sum total of Packer's reply was that Consolidated Press Holdings was operating within the tax laws of Australia and if I suggested otherwise I would be seriously defaming Mr Packer and would have to pay the consequences. That was it. Nor would he appear on the program, despite being offered the chance to have his say at the end of the broadcast, after viewing its contents. Suffice to say, he also refused to co-operate with the production of this book. On several occasions people agreed to talk to me, then changed their minds after ringing his Park Street office. 'Mr Packer is a very private person' was the formula used for keeping intruders like me at bay. But as the 1989 *Bulletin* article admitted, Packer had 'so little respect for the Australian media' (including most of his own employees) that he refused to speak with journalists. Which made his complaints about people never checking facts with him seem rather absurd.

I couldn't help being struck by the difference between him and that other great Australian media proprietor when I went to England in mid-1991 to film a profile of him for *Four Corners*. Kerry's daughter Gretel was getting married at a church in a small Sussex village near his Fyning Hill estate and Rupert Murdoch was one of the guests, along with Neville Wran and various other Australian dignitaries. While Packer did his utmost to avoid our cameras and refused to talk to reporters, Rupert held court in the churchyard in avuncular fashion, beaming, and shooting the breeze with anyone who cared to approach. He even posed for photographs with his then wife Anna. But Murdoch understood journalists and appreciated that they had a job to do.

Kerry Packer, on the other hand, was hostile, paranoid and convinced that the press was out to get him and his friends. And in one respect he was right—some of his racier business partners were deservedly portrayed in a less than favourable light. The Fairfax-owned *National Times*, for example, devoted a lot of space in the mid 1980s to writing about Malcolm Edwards and Neil Ohlsson of Essington, who were both mates of Packer's, and it also wrote extensively about Packer's gold-rush partner Warren Anderson, focussing on his connections to the enforcer Tom Domican and to the Right-wing faction of the New South Wales Labor Party. Neither Packer nor his friends, nor even the Labor Party, liked these articles. But there was no vendetta. They were matters of legitimate public interest that deserved to be given an airing. Packer could not see this.

In the late 1980s, fairly soon after becoming editor of the *Bulletin*, David Dale got a call on the yellow hotline to go and see Packer, and immediately went down to his office to find him in a track suit tossing a football around. With him was another man, who was soon introduced as Warren Anderson. As Dale remembers it, Packer told him that Anderson had a really good story for the *Bulletin* but was reluctant to talk to the media because journalists were all out to get him. The 'good story' that Packer and his friend had in mind was Anderson's plan to save African endangered species by giving them a home at Tipperary, his property in the Northern Territory. Anderson told Dale that journalists always distorted things; Dale therefore suggested that they run an interview unedited, as a question-and-answer session.

And I said, 'But what you have to understand . . .' and I was going to say, 'You have to understand that we will ask a wide range of questions and you can't censor the questions but it's up to you how you answer.' But I didn't get that out because Packer put his hand up. So there was silence. And I looked at him and I said 'What?' And he said, 'He doesn't *have* to do anything, and I don't *have* to do anything. You can't tell us what we have to do. He's a private company. He's a private citizen. He's not an elected politician. He's not a public company. I'm not a politician. I don't have to answer questions from journalists. We don't *have* to do anything.'[7]

Like Packer but more so, Anderson guarded his privacy fiercely, never gave interviews and had a passionate hatred of the press, whom he at times referred to as bloodsuckers and leeches. He also had a deep-seated dislike of having his picture taken. In the late 1980s, Anderson was negotiating with the Northern Territory Government for the contract to run the huge State Square development project in which a parliament house and government office block were being built in the centre of Darwin. Consequently, the picture editor of the *Northern Territory News*, Clive Hyde, decided it was time they had a picture of him.

Having spotted Anderson in the city one day, Hyde followed him to Darwin's airport and asked him whether he would mind having his picture taken. Anderson's reaction was to turn tail and run, ducking behind airline counters in an effort to avoid the photographer, who by this time was giving chase. A bizarre cat-and-mouse game ensued until Hyde finally got the picture, whereupon a furious Anderson came after him, trying to grab the camera, pushing him, throwing punches and sending chairs and tables flying. Hyde escaped from this public melee with his camera intact, but got back to the office fifteen minutes later to find that an angry Anderson had already been on the phone from his private jet, demanding that the managing editor pull the picture. Sure enough, the man's wishes were respected and the picture wasn't used.

Anderson's complaint, like Packer's, was that he was 'a very private person'. The fact that he was dealing with hundreds of millions of dollars of taxpayers' money in the State Square project, for which he was collecting a large management fee, would not have been regarded by him as being of any relevance. Nor, presumably, would the fact that he later donated $200 000 to the NT's ruling Country Liberal Party.[8]

Naturally, Anderson received little critical attention in Packer's magazines or on Channel Nine. And one important story that they ignored altogether was the saga of his property deals with Kerry in Western Australia, where their joint venture came an expensive cropper in the late 1980s. This involved some extraordinary dealings between Packer and Anderson and the Western Australian Government, which made the story far more interesting than Warren and his wild animals. And it was also an intriguing tale because it demonstrated how shallow Kerry's friendships could be when large amounts of money were at stake.

According to Anderson's evidence to the royal commission investigating the mess known as WA Inc, the story began in early 1988 with a phone call from his mate Terry Burke, brother of the then just-retired Western Australian premier. Burke told Anderson, who was a major contributor to the state Labor Party, that the plum Westralia Square development site, on the river side of Perth's business boulevard St George's Terrace, was up for grabs. The Western Australian Government, said Burke, was prepared to do a good deal.[9]

Bids were soon rolling in from the Perth entrepreneurs' club and by March 1988 there were four to be considered, of which Anderson and Packer's was judged to be the most competitive. Their joint venture proposed a huge development, comprising three office towers with a combined floor area of 150 000 square metres, that would add another 15 per cent to the office space in Perth's central business district. The 'landmark' tower in this Westralia Square development was to be fifty-four storeys high, making it easily Perth's tallest building.

In early March, three of Western Australia's key decision makers got on a plane to Sydney to seal the deal. One of them was Kevin Edwards, known to bureaucrats as the de facto premier because he was believed to run the government; another was the new managing director of Rothwells, Tony Lloyd, who had been a powerful public servant prior to his appointment; and the third was Wyvern Rees, chairman of the State Government Insurance Commission (SGIC), which owned the site with the Government Employees Superannuation Board (GESB). The three men had been given their riding instructions by the new premier, Peter Dowding, before their departure and wanted the deal done fast.

The terms they had agreed to offer Anderson and Packer appeared to be generous in the extreme. For while the asking price of $270 million was almost certainly more than the site was worth, a series of sweeteners had been added to make it an attractive proposition. Packer and Anderson would have to fork out only $90 million in cash to buy the property and would need to make no further payments for seven years. Nor would they pay interest on the outstanding balance for the first two years. The Western Australian Government (or strictly speaking, the SGIC and GESB) would also throw in $150 million to help with the cost of development, by contributing money to a new property trust in which Anderson and Packer would be major shareholders. And finally, the SGIC would rent one of the office towers for the first five years after completion at $400 per square metre plus outgoings, which was around $150 a metre above current market rentals.[10]

But there was one small snag to all this, which was that Packer and Anderson were being asked to pay a price for all this benefi-cence. Premier Peter Dowding had insisted the deal could only go ahead if Packer and Anderson lent $50 million to Rothwells to keep Laurie Connell's sinking merchant bank afloat.[11] It was Edwards's job to break the news of this requirement to Anderson and Packer's two representatives, once the sale had been agreed, and his suggestion went down like a lead balloon. Edwards promised the money would be safe, because Rothwells was sound and the Western Australian Government would ensure the $50 million was repaid, but he would not put the guarantee in writing. And Packer's answer—relayed by finance director Don Bourke—was a resounding 'no'. He had already tipped $10 million into the original Rothwells rescue in October 1987 and was not going to hand over any more to Connell's bank. Which left Anderson as the only possible contributor, and he had no money.

As the rest of the people in the meeting listened, Kevin Edwards then rang Perth to seek instructions from Premier

Dowding who, according to Anderson's evidence to the royal commission, screamed down the phone and said the prospective purchasers could get 'whatsisnamed'. Dowding also instructed Edwards and his team to come back to Perth the next morning, because the deal was off.

But this was not the end of the story, because Warren Anderson was still keen to do the deal. That afternoon, he rang Packer in an attempt to change his mind. Then he went round to Sydney's Intercontinental Hotel with his lawyer to see if he could convince Edwards to drop the $50 million condition. Finally, he paid a visit to Packer and persuaded him it would be safe to proceed, as long as the Western Australian Government (and Premier Peter Dowding) would reaffirm Edwards's promise that the $50 million would be safe. On this basis, Packer agreed to lend the $50 million to Anderson, and let *him* take the risk of lending it to Rothwells. Anderson, meanwhile, gave Packer his personal guarantee for the $50 million, so that Kerry could come after him if anything went wrong. Which, of course, it did.

By July 1988, less than four months after the contracts were signed, it was clear the $50 million was at risk, because Rothwells was behind on the interest payments. It was also pretty clear that Kerry was concerned he would end up footing the bill, for as Anderson put it in evidence to the royal commission, Packer was 'sitting on [me] to get his $50 million back' or, even more graphically, 'was about to beat me to death'. Anderson therefore decided to beat up the Western Australian premier in an attempt to save his own skin.

On the evening of Sunday, 16 October 1988, three weeks before Rothwells finally disappeared into a $600 million black hole, Anderson diverted his private Learjet to Derby in north-west Western Australia to confront the premier, who was in town for a Cabinet meeting. Dowding was having dinner and at first refused to meet him, but finally agreed to receive him in his suite, where an angry shouting match took place. According to Anderson's evidence to the royal commission, he threatened Premier Dowding that he would tear his heart out, go for his throat, put Rothwells into liquidation and bring down the Western Australian Government if he didn't get his money back immediately. As he uttered these threats, his lawyers were waiting by the phone in Perth, ready to issue a legal demand for the money that would bring Rothwells crashing down.

The threats struck home, and Dowding agreed to pay Anderson $19.5 million from Rothwells the next day, with the balance of the $50 million to be paid in March 1989. But the money did not materialise, because Rothwells did not have any. Soon afterwards, Dowding made a second agreement to pay Anderson $2 million a day over nine days, but this arrangement also fell through when the first cheque bounced on presentation.

A few days after that, Rothwells collapsed, taking the $50 million with it. Packer then called the personal guarantee, and his old friend Anderson ended up having to sell just about everything he owned. By mid 1991, Packer's people had slapped charges on everything they could find in Anderson's maze of companies and discretionary trusts. By the end of that year, his fabulous properties Fern Hill and Boomerang were both up for sale; soon afterwards his gun collection was also being sold at auction; finally, in late 1992, it was reported that he had sold half his cattle business and half of Tipperary station, his prize property in the Northern Territory, to his Indonesian partners, Bakrie Brothers.[12] Such was the punishment for costing the Big Fella money.

Strangely enough, Packer's magazines had nothing to say about these disastrous deals over Westralia Square, which cost their boss perhaps $200 million, or about Anderson's run-ins with the Western Australian Premier, even though these would have been obvious subject matter for the *Bulletin*. In a 209-line preview of the Western Australian Royal Commission's hearings in *Australian Business* in March 1991, the Westralia Square story managed to rate no more than a four-line mention.

The story was covered, however, in the *Sydney Morning Herald* three months later by Colleen Ryan, who was sued personally by Packer for defamation as a result of her article, and faced the risk of losing her house. Shortly afterwards, a Fairfax magazine, *Business Review Weekly*, analysed Anderson's financial difficulties at some length, with somewhat different consequences.

Two weeks after the article appeared on 27 September 1991, its author Ali Cromie received a furious phone call. Warren Anderson was on the line, calling from Jakarta in Indonesia, and he was not happy. In fact he was spitting blood. Promising to be polite, since she was a 'female', he launched into a tirade of abuse against her, telling her that it was 'a load of shit', that she had wrecked his business, discouraged people from dealing with him and hurt his family into the bargain. 'You criticise Bond and Skase but don't shit on me. I haven't robbed any public companies. It's people like you that are degrading this country.' The phone call lasted for around twenty minutes, with Anderson repeatedly emphasising the same few points: he was a private person, his companies were private, he had a democratic right to privacy, she had no right to write about him. Cromie did not argue the toss with him or point out that his dealings with politicians were the subject of scrutiny by a royal commission. Nor did she suggest that his relationship with Australia's prime minister-to-be Paul Keating made him a legitimate subject of public interest. But she did offer to meet him, listen to his complaints and write about the philanthropy he claimed no one was interested in. Anderson wanted none of it. It was 'beneath' him, he told her, to meet people who wrote for the press.

According to Cromie, Anderson's tone was extremely aggressive. What had upset him most was a cartoon on the magazine's front cover, showing him surrounded by For Sale signs. 'Why would you draw a cartoon like that?' he asked, 'making a bloke look like a clown with For Sale signs all round? Why would you do that about anyone?' And then the bulldozer driver took over: 'If you were a man,' said Anderson, 'I'd give you a hell of a belting.'

Ali Cromie put down the phone, somewhat shattered. She was a tough journalist who was not easily intimidated, but she had already been threatened by one of Anderson's senior executives while researching the story, and Anderson had sounded convincing. It would have crossed her mind, too, that the man abusing her was, or had been, a close friend of Kerry Packer's. And in October 1991, as she listened to the telephone tirade, Packer was lining up with the Tourang consortium to take control of the group that employed her, John Fairfax Ltd. Like a number of other Fairfax journalists, she was not enamoured of the thought that Kerry Packer, who apparently so despised her profession, might soon be her boss.

CHAPTER TWENTY-THREE

FAMILY FEUDS

*For fifty years of my life, Fairfax has been competition to
me and my family. The idea that I can end up buying
15 per cent . . . amuses me.*

Kerry Packer, October 1991[1]

In December 1990, the *Sydney Morning Herald* and the
Melbourne *Age* were put into receivership and offered for sale,
along with the rest of the Fairfax media empire. Since the papers
were crippled by debt, it had been obvious for months that this
was going to happen. And Packer had long been seen as the most
likely buyer. As rumour spread that he might sell his television
network and take control of the newspapers, he told journalists
at Channel Nine that he wasn't interested in buying either the
Herald or the *Age* because print had no future. But those who
had known Kerry and his father over the years were far from
convinced by such denials.

The Packers had fought the Fairfaxes in the Sydney market
one way or another for more than fifty years, with the Packers
almost always coming off second best. They had been seen to be
new money, vulgar and decidedly inferior to their blue-blooded
broadsheet rivals. And the sale offered them the chance of sweet
revenge. It was unthinkable that Kerry would pass up this opportunity to drive the Fairfaxes from the field of battle and fly the
Packer flag over their citadel. His father would have turned in his
grave, he said later, if he had not taken this chance to crush the
old enemy.

But Packer's desire to own the Fairfax papers soon met with quite extraordinary public and political opposition. To the Packer camp, the campaign to stop him getting his hands on Fairfax was quite simply hysteria. To his opponents, it was justifiable concern for the freedom of the press. But whichever way one looked at it, there was no doubting the almost incredible strength of feeling that Kerry Packer aroused. For rightly or wrongly, many politicians and journalists believed that it would be a disaster for Australia if the Fairfax newspapers ended up in his grasp.

The Fall of the House of Fairfax in late 1990 was a tragedy of almost Shakespearean proportions, in which the pathetic figure of young Warwick Fairfax loomed large. The son of old Sir Warwick Fairfax by the press knight's third marriage, he had been neglected by his distant, authoritarian father and smothered by his deeply ambitious mother, Lady Mary, who had paraded him as a genius and thrust him towards his destiny. This, he believed, was to regain the Fairfax throne, from which his father had been removed in 1976 in a family rebellion.

Had young Warwick been prepared to bide his time, he would eventually have inherited the Fairfax kingdom in any case, since his half-brother James's shares were to come to him on the latter's death. But he refused to wait, even though James was thirty years his senior. On the death of old Sir Warwick in January 1987, the young pretender to the Fairfax throne, fresh from Harvard business school and Christian prayer meetings, buckled on his armour to charge into battle. He believed that the kingdom was vulnerable to attack from outside the family and had to be made secure. He was just twenty-six years old.

Young Warwick's strategy, copied from the warriors of 1980s corporate America, was to seize control of John Fairfax & Sons by borrowing huge amounts of money to buy out the rest of his family and the public shareholders. Ignoring clear warnings of disaster from the first adviser he hired, young Warwick persuaded a syndicate led by the ANZ Bank in late 1987 to lend the Fairfax group almost $2 billion so that he and his mother could secure control. It was the biggest takeover the ANZ Bank had ever funded, involving the biggest fees in Australian corporate history along the way, in which the disgraced Western Australian financier Laurie Connell was to be paid $100 million for his advice.[2] And it was doomed to fail.

For young Warwick's plan to succeed, some of the best Fairfax assets needed to be sold at a good price to reduce the $2 billion debt to the banks. Otherwise the company would buckle under the weight of massive interest payments. But just as the deal was about to be signed in mid October 1987, the world's stock markets collapsed. Warwick and his advisers had counted on raising $475 million from the sale of the *Australian Financial Review*, the *Times on Sunday* and the Macquarie radio network to Robert Holmes à Court, but he withdrew when the stock market crashed. They had also counted on $500 million from the public float of 55 per cent of David Syme & Co—the company that owned the *Age*—but the crash made this impossible, too.[3]

Suddenly, a risky strategy had become a suicidal one, yet Warwick was still determined to proceed. As he sat closeted on the twentieth floor of Sydney's Regent Hotel with his gung-ho advisers hammering out the final details of the deal, his mother Lady Mary Fairfax was downstairs in the lobby trying desperately to get in to see him. When Warwick refused to let her come up, she sent him a note begging him to abandon the takeover. Warwick looked at it briefly, said nothing, and threw it in the bin, then went ahead regardless.[4]

Roughly twelve months later, in a desperate effort to get the banks off its back, Fairfax went to the US junk-bond kings Drexel Burnham to borrow $450 million. But just as the company received the money, interest rates rocketed, advertising revenues plummeted, recession hit Australia and disaster became inevitable. By mid 1990 it was clear to almost everyone except Warwick, who had by this time retreated to live in a Christian community in Chicago, that there was no chance of Fairfax surviving. In December 1990 the receivers were called in and on Christmas Eve the newspapers were put up for sale. Given that they were likely to fetch around $1.2 billion while the Fairfax group had debts of $1.7 billion, it was clear that Warwick and his mother, with their respective 75 per cent and 25 per cent shareholdings, would be wiped out. In three years Warwick had brought a proud newspaper dynasty to its knees and spent his inheritance. Had he sat on the street and given the money away he could probably not have got rid of his fortune faster.

The sad demise of the Fairfax newspapers had been watched with interest by the world's media proprietors, since prestigious properties such as the *Sydney Morning Herald* and the *Age* rarely came on the market. And before long three serious bidders attracted the attention of the auctioneers. One was Tony O'Reilly's Irish Independent Newspapers, bringing a touch of the blarney to the battle; another, closer to home, was a cashbox company called Jamison Equity, known as the Vulture Fund because it had raised money on the stock exchange to buy businesses in trouble; the third was Australian Independent Newspapers (AIN), a company backed by Melbourne's financial establishment, which seemed to be keen to preserve the Fairfax papers as supporters of the Liberal Party.

Kerry Packer, meanwhile, was said not to be interested at all. He had never been happy with taking a minority share in a company unless he was guaranteed control. And under the 1986 cross-media laws he could not own more than 15 per cent of the Fairfax group unless he sold Channel Nine, which he had just bought back from Bond. He was also unlikely to sell his television stations again: first, because he had given his word to Nine's bankers and shareholders that he would run the network for two years; second, because putting up For Sale signs would force him to accept a knockdown price, which he was never prepared to do. But for all his hatred of minority shareholdings and pronouncements about how stupid it was to buy newspapers at high prices, he was thinking about doing precisely that. Towards the end of 1990, he ran into Canadian newspaper magnate Conrad Black at a dinner party in London and agreed to talk about a move on Fairfax when the time was right. And by early 1991 it certainly was.

For several months, Packer's former adviser Malcolm Turnbull had been hopping about on the fringe of the Fairfax action, trying to join in the jig. In October 1990 he flew to the United States and persuaded the holders of the $450 million Fairfax junk bonds that they should hire him to look after their interests. Soon afterwards, he was doing the rounds of potential bidders in the hope of getting the bondholders some money back. He went first to Tony O'Reilly with the suggestion that they be cut in on the Independent bid in exchange for a promise not to sue Fairfax for damages. Then, when O'Reilly turned him down flat, he put the same offer to Packer, who scoffed at the idea that he needed anyone.

Faced with a lack of dancing partners, Turnbull opted for legal action against Fairfax to show off the bondholders' steps. By February 1991, they were suing Fairfax and its bankers for $450 million damages, in a case that alleged fraud and breach of fiduciary duty. Given that Fairfax had collapsed eighteen months after promising a glorious future and had been in strife when the $450 million was raised, there was some reason to think this action might succeed.[5] But more immediately, the threat of victory greatly increased the bondholders' nuisance value and gave Turnbull something to sell.

Accordingly, when Turnbull went back to Packer in May 1991 he found him far more interested. He proposed that Packer should be the key player in a consortium to bid for Fairfax, in which the bondholders would also have a share. They could rope in a couple of strong media players from around the world to complete the team and would then have no trouble raising money from the big Australian pension funds and life insurance companies, who would bankroll the deal. Short of selling Channel Nine, such a consortium was of course the only way that Packer could get into the game. One such player, Turnbull suggested, could be the owner of London's *Daily Telegraph*, the Canadian newspaperman Conrad Black, to whom Packer, by coincidence, had spoken three or four times already.

It did not take long to get the team together and reach agreement. On 3 June 1991, Black, Packer, Turnbull and others met in

Packer's suite at London's Savoy Hotel and resolved to join forces for a Fairfax bid. Since Packer was in England for the polo season, they had converged on him for talks. He would have a whisker under 15 per cent of Fairfax if the bid was successful, while Black would get 20 per cent. The US investment fund Hellman & Friedman, which had been invited in by Packer, would have a further 15 per cent, while the rest of the company would be sold to the public. Turnbull's junk-bondholders would get $125 million in debentures in exchange for their promise to drop their legal action.

With the support of Australian institutions, the Black–Packer consortium, officially named Tourang, would easily have the fire-power to see off its opponents if it really wanted to win. And its exclusive agreement with the junk-bondholders would give it an extra edge, or so its members believed.[6] But both of these advantages could be nullified by the political opposition to Packer that was already mounting.

To some extent the battle to stop Packer was one that should have been fought four years earlier against a different enemy. For it was Rupert Murdoch's acquisition of the huge Herald & Weekly Times group in 1987 that had made ownership of the Australian press possibly more concentrated than anywhere else in the Western world. That one transaction had placed some 65 per cent of Australia's newspaper circulation in the hands of one man, who was famous for his willingness to use his papers against governments and to tell his editors what to do. But if the Fairfax papers now fell to Packer, the two powerful men would carve up Australia's press between them. This would certainly be true in Sydney and Melbourne where the six daily papers and four Sunday papers were currently owned by either Murdoch or Fairfax. And in Brisbane and Adelaide, Murdoch already had the field to himself anyway.

In the business press there would be an even greater monopoly if Packer won Fairfax, for the *Australian Business Monthly* was already owned by Consolidated Press, while the other two papers in the market, the *Business Review Weekly* and the *Australian Financial Review*, were both Fairfax-owned. As for the mainstream magazine market, Murdoch and Packer already had a virtual duopoly, while Packer had the country's leading television station, Channel Nine. If Packer owned Fairfax, even as part of a consortium, he and Murdoch would have an iron grip on what Australians did or did not read in the press and did or did not see on their screens—or so it was argued. As a senior journalist at the *Sydney Morning Herald* rhetorically asked, how brave would you be as an editor or a politician if Packer controlled one group of papers and Murdoch the other? How brave would you be to take them on? How sure would you be that you were reading everything you should? Indeed, in such a future, would you ever read about the business activities, tax affairs or close friends of two of the nation's most powerful men?[7]

One certainly never read about Murdoch's tax arrangements in magazines published by Packer, even though News Ltd had paid even less tax than Packer's companies during the late 1980s, thanks to its use of the Cayman Islands tax haven. Nor did one see revelations of the remarkably low tax rate paid by Packer and his companies in papers published by Murdoch's News Ltd. And naturally, one read no critical articles about either of these tycoons in their own publications.

But while Murdoch was arguably the villain as far as concentration of media ownership was concerned, it was unquestionably Packer whom Fairfax journalists regarded as the real demon. Whether he deserved to be the object of such fear and hatred was debatable, but he appeared to hate journalists, had a record of punching cameramen, and was ever ready to sue reporters who wrote about him. He was also believed to be keen to get revenge for the notorious 'Goanna' article in the *National Times* that had made Costigan's allegations public in September 1984. Fairfax journalists believed that Packer had even drawn up a hit list of people to be dismissed. He had supposedly told Robert Holmes à Court in 1990 that he planned to get control of Fairfax and personally sack all those responsible for the Costigan coverage, right down to the sub-editors who had handled the copy. This, at least, was what Holmes à Court told colleagues.

All these fears, however, only made sense if Packer *controlled* Fairfax, and by law he was not allowed to do so unless he sold Channel Nine. Until then, he would be permitted to own only 15 per cent of the shares and would be denied a seat on the board. The Packer camp therefore argued with some logic that he could not possibly call the shots. He would be lucky, they said, to get a free lunch in the canteen, and it was inconceivable that he could wreak revenge on Fairfax journalists by walking through the door and sacking people. These arguments, however, did not convince Packer's opponents. Packer could always sell Channel Nine in the future, they argued, and could control Fairfax in partnership with Conrad Black, even if this was possibly illegal. They were also concerned that Packer's former managing director Trevor Kennedy would run Fairfax if Tourang's bid succeeded. Others simply observed that Packer was so forceful he would be able to get his way whatever his shareholding.

Conrad Black had undoubtedly teamed up with Packer in the belief that the Big Fella would be a major asset in any Fairfax bid. As the richest man in Australia with a formidable record as a media proprietor, Packer was guaranteed to command significant support from Australian financial institutions, while his powerful political contacts seemed to be a virtual passport to success. But when Black flew into Australia on 17 July 1991, the day after Tourang's bid was unveiled, he was soon made to realise that having Packer as a travel companion could turn out to be heavy political baggage.

Black's mission on this flying visit was to sell Tourang's bid to Australia's politicians and financiers, and his inclination was to dismiss concerns about Packer as too ridiculous to bother with. Faced with questions about media concentration and press freedom he replied good-humouredly that he was not going to be part of any conspiracy to muzzle journalists or to subvert the independence of the Australian press. As someone who had built his own newspaper empire and liked to run his own show, Black might well have found it hard to understand that people felt he could be pushed around by anyone—even by Kerry Packer—so he simply did not waste time denying it. But it soon became obvious that it wasn't just a mob of journalists wanting to stop Packer. Powerful members of the government, including the prime minister, were clearly none too keen on his winning Fairfax either.

In the late 1980s, Packer had been able to swing almost any political decision in his favour. But in mid 1991 the tide of Australian politics had turned dramatically against him. On 3 June, after months of speculation in the media, Paul Keating had attempted to mount a coup against Bob Hawke to unseat him as prime minister. Hawke believed that Channel Nine had led the press pack baying for a Keating victory and felt that his 'close personal friend' Kerry Packer had deserted him in his hour of need. Consequently, Hawke had become distinctly cool towards the man he had described three years earlier as a 'very great Australian', and he was now unhappy about the prospect of Packer winning Fairfax. So, too, were backbenchers in the Labor Party's parliamentary Caucus, who were certain to kick up a storm to prevent a Packer victory.

By late June, Hawke's government was already talking tough about its power to intervene, and when the Tourang bid was announced on 16 July 1990, this talk turned to action. On the very day that the Australian press revealed Packer to be a bidder, the papers reported the government's intention to tighten up the cross-media rules in two significant ways. The first important change was to give the Australian Broadcasting Tribunal a new 'tripwire' to bring down any deal that might breach the 1986 cross-media laws until official clearance had been given. The second was to promise a new power that considerably strengthened the actual laws. Both these changes affected Packer and the Tourang consortium but touched none of the other Fairfax bidders.

Packer had complied fully with the law as it stood. His 15 per cent of Fairfax came within the existing limit that banned anyone from owning or controlling a television station and a newspaper in the same city. But the rules were about to be changed. The Australian Broadcasting Tribunal was to be given a power that would allow it to declare the Tourang bid illegal even if Packer were merely 'in a position to control' Fairfax Newspapers through his 'associates'. This obviously raised the threat that the ABT could delve into the details of Packer's relationship with Malcolm Turnbull and Trevor Kennedy, whose long, close association with Packer might well be seen as a problem. It was also likely that it would investigate whether there were any agreements between Packer and Tourang's other shareholders that could deliver Packer more influence than his bare 15 per cent allowed. But even if the ABT found nothing, the mere shadow of a long inquiry might well be enough to knock Tourang out of the contest. It was hardly the sort of political treatment Packer was used to.[8]

The next day Conrad Black received a clear warning of what lay in store when he lunched in Canberra with Communications Minister Kim Beazley. As they sat in the window of the Carousel restaurant, trying to ignore the army of cameramen and journalists who were watching them, Beazley pointed across the table to Trevor Kennedy and indicated his near twenty-year relationship with Packer would be a problem. Black's response was to turn to Kennedy and tell him jokingly that he was sacked. More seriously, when asked on the ABC's *AM* program soon afterwards whether he would consider dumping Packer if he had to, Black replied without hesitation that he would, if it was the only way he could win Fairfax.

Sure enough, when the battle began in earnest, Trevor Kennedy was made to walk the plank. On 16 October 1991, the day that formal bids for Fairfax were to be lodged, he suddenly resigned as Tourang's managing director. An angry public statement blamed his decision on an unwarranted and unjust 'McCarthyist' campaign by Packer's opponents that had made it impossible for him to continue. But this was just spin, for he had in fact been pushed. Kennedy had worked for Packer for almost

465

twenty years and was known to be one of his closest friends, so it was easy for opponents to present him as a stooge who would do his former boss's bidding. This had presented an obvious political problem for Tourang, because the ABT might brand him an 'associate' who could give Packer the potential to control Fairfax.

But he and Kerry had also had a falling out and had been spending less and less time together. As the bid had progressed, Packer had relied more and more on the two men acting for Tourang's other two shareholders. One of these was a Canadian lawyer called Daniel Colson, acting for Conrad Black; the other was an American called Brian Powers who was representing Hellman & Friedman. As these new friends became Packer's best friends, his old mate Trevor Kennedy was left increasingly on the outer. Even though he was Tourang's chief executive, Kennedy was frequently barred from their meetings, dinners and weekend retreats on the grounds that he wasn't a shareholder.

Tensions within Tourang were further increased by a clash of personalities between Turnbull and Kennedy on the one hand and Colson and Powers on the other. From the beginning there were arguments between Colson and Turnbull about who was controlling the deal, and between Turnbull and Powers about the $125 million that was to be paid to the junk-bondholders—which Powers wanted to renegotiate. Both money and ego were at stake; tempers had flared; grudges had grown; Kennedy had been perceived to be on Turnbull's side.

On Saturday 12 October these tensions had come to a head. Kennedy, Turnbull and around a dozen lawyers and accountants kicked their heels for three hours at the Sydney offices of accountants Ernst & Young, waiting for Colson and Powers to arrive for a meeting to settle the final details of Tourang's bid. As an angry Kennedy eventually departed, he bumped into Colson and Powers on the pavement outside. He had been at the offices since 8 a.m. and was absolutely furious at being kept waiting, so he gave them both barrels before roaring off in his BMW to play tennis. The next day, Colson and Powers called him to a meeting at Sydney's

Regent Hotel and told him they felt he wasn't pulling his weight, didn't have command of the numbers or the production side of the business and had performed poorly in public. Then they delivered the punch line: he would be getting only a one-year contract instead of the original three-year deal that all members of Tourang, including Packer, had agreed to give him. Kennedy's three-year contract had even been lying around waiting for Kennedy to sign it; now they were saying they would tear it up.

Kennedy was amazed that they were going back on their word and angry that they dared question his competence. He had run the Packer magazines for ten years and been managing director of Consolidated Press Holdings for five years, during which time the company had been the envy of its competitors and doubled its net worth. He was also one of the few people in the Packer camp who could command respect as a journalist from the staff at Fairfax. And these grey men in suits, who knew little about Australia and even less about journalism, were questioning his ability to do the job.

The following day, the contract offer was effectively reduced further to a guaranteed six months' employment, whereupon there was another row and Kennedy stormed out. He had decided he did not want to work with people who treated him in such cavalier fashion and broke their word in this way. And he was disappointed with Packer.

In his farewell speech at Consolidated Press only three months earlier, in July 1991, Kennedy had said that he regarded Kerry more as a friend than an employer; the sort of friend who would stand by you in any circumstances, who, if you announced you had murdered somebody, would merely ask, 'What are we going to do with the body?' But his loyal mate was now helping to bury him. Packer told Kennedy that the others had severe doubts about him and weren't to be budged. Kennedy replied that he could easily settle the matter if he wanted to. But the Big Fella refused to intervene. He urged Kennedy to stay, but only on Powers's and Colson's revised terms, and told him he was behaving immaturely and being 'difficult'.

For a man who supposedly prided loyalty to his friends above almost everything else in life, it was really quite shocking that Packer should be throwing Kennedy to the wolves. Yet he effectively did the same thing to Malcolm Turnbull in similar circumstances one month later. When Turnbull was ditched by the other members of Tourang in November 1991, Packer refused even to return his telephone calls, thus ending a friendship of seventeen years' standing. It was a guide, perhaps, to how important it was to Packer to win the Fairfax fight, or how little his friendship was worth when money was at stake.

Packer and Kennedy had been chums since 1972 when Trevor had been hired by Kerry's father to edit the *Bulletin* magazine, and they had gambled and caroused together for almost twenty years. But their relationship had started to cool well before Kennedy joined Tourang in June 1991. It was exhausting and sometimes suffocating to be on the Packer payroll and earmarked as a pal, for Kerry paid people handsomely and considered it part of the job to keep him amused. There was constant pressure on Kennedy to go play with the boss, often at a moment's notice, and this did not fit too well with having a family life or time to oneself.

Partly because of this, Kennedy had announced in late 1990 that he wasn't going to stay with Packer after turning fifty in June 1992. And this had given the friendship a further knock, because Kennedy's desire to seek new challenges was interpreted as disloyalty—as the old saying went, you could be sacked by the Packers as many times as they liked, but you could only resign once. Despite arguments and difficulties, they had agreed the terms of Kennedy's departure by early 1991, and Kennedy had received a handsome payoff, rumoured to be up near the $5 million mark.[9] But soon afterwards, he told friends that his relationship with Kerry was falling apart. There had also been reports of at least one major shouting match between them.

Relations had worsened as soon as Kennedy started to think himself into the role of chief executive at Fairfax. Since everyone was accusing him of being a Packer stooge, he was clearly in a difficult position. He would have to convince the journalists at Fairfax that he was his own man, yet he was heading a consortium whose dominant figure undoubtedly saw journalists as the enemy.

Packer had started out with deep feelings of anger towards Fairfax reporters because of the papers' Costigan coverage in 1984, and he became angrier as the bid progressed. The Friends of Fairfax and the Age Independence Committee made no secret of the fact that they regarded him as the bogeyman, and journalists on both newspapers had greeted Tourang's bid with a unanimous public resolution that Packer and Tourang were totally unacceptable as proprietors. A posse of senior journalists had also lobbied Hawke, Beazley and Treasurer John Kerin in Canberra with some success, in an attempt to persuade the government that Packer had to be stopped. On top of all that, as Packer saw it, the *Herald* and the *Age* were reporting the battle for Fairfax unfairly, irresponsibly and untruthfully: in short, they were spreading lies by suggesting that he would be able to control the company.

As Packer became progressively more outraged by what the Fairfax papers were writing—and took legal action against the leading journalists in Friends of Fairfax—Trevor Kennedy's position became increasingly difficult, for Packer was intent on revenge, as many people suspected, and Kennedy would be expected to carry it out. On one occasion, Packer thrust the paper in front of his erstwhile managing director and railed at its contents, saying: 'See what that bastard did today? He's going to go.'

Kennedy had been forced to do his boss's bidding during the twenty years he worked for the Packers' family company but one reason he had resigned was to get away from that. It is not clear whether he told Packer that revenge was out of the question, but he warned him that if journalists at the *Herald* or the *Age* chose to write stories about their new boss, he could do no more than ensure they got their facts right. He could not pull a piece out of the paper just because Kerry didn't like it. It was this assertion of independence that caused the falling out, Kennedy believed.

Despite his public protestations, Packer still intended to run the show.

As Trevor Kennedy signed his letter of resignation, two of Australia's most famous former prime ministers, Gough Whitlam and Malcolm Fraser, were putting their names to an even more important letter to the *Age*, warning of the dangers of greater concentration of Australia's media. It was possibly the first time in their lives that the two men had been on the same side of an argument, and they had hardly even spoken to each other since November 1975 when Prime Minister Gough Whitlam had been sacked by Australia's Governor-General John Kerr in a crisis that Fraser had engineered. 'Kerr's cur', Whitlam had called him then. But so important was this new fight that they had kissed and made up for the cause. The letter they were signing had been drafted by Fraser's former Cabinet minister Peter Nixon, who had been sitting at home on his farm in Victoria's high country worrying about what was happening to Australia and had suddenly decided he could do something about it. Nixon had signed the letter, too, as had the former National Party leader Doug Anthony and a handful of other prominent past politicians. Naturally, there was no mention of the 'P' word or even the 'T' word, but the text of the letter made it abundantly clear that the group saw Packer and Tourang as the enemy. It warned that the Fairfax sale was 'the last chance to arrest the growing concentration of Australian media ownership' and charged Australia's leaders not to shirk their duty to future generations. It went on to say:

> As past senior political figures we have a deep and realistic understanding of the powers and influence of the media. We know of the mechanisms that can be, and have been used to influence policies. We know of circumstances in which such powers have been used.
>
> Parliament must remain supreme, with its integrity and public interest protected at all times. It must not allow a power to be established in Australia which can challenge the supremacy of Parliament ...

> . . . The decision shortly to be taken must not add to media
> concentration and domination. We must not be left with two
> dominant players in newspapers, television and magazines.[10]

It was, of course, in these principled terms that the decision was
presented, but there was no disguising the fact that it was a plea
to stop Packer and Tourang. For none of the other consortia
would increase media domination in the way that the letter
outlined.

As people opened their morning papers to see the
Fraser–Whitlam letter and read of Kennedy's resignation,
Fairfax journalists in Sydney and Melbourne were also stepping
up their campaign to keep Packer out. Once again, they argued
that their fight was about principles, not personalities, but as
journalists from the *Sydney Morning Herald* picketed railway
stations and tramped the streets as part of their day-long protest
strike, they toted placards that made nonsense of this claim.
'APACKERLYPSE NO', said one such banner; 'SAVE US FROM
KERRY PACKER', said another; 'WHAT IF PACKER HOLDS THE
FRONT PAGE?' asked a third. Clearly there was one man whom
the free press brigade had in mind when it came to the risk that
those freedoms would be lost. But just in case passers-by missed
the message, a large group of journalists from the Friends of
Fairfax handed out forms addressed to Will Bailey, head of the
ANZ Bank, which was Fairfax's main banker. These declared
bluntly, 'I believe in a free and independent press and a diversity of ownership of the media. If you sell the Fairfax papers to
Mr Packer, I will close my account with the ANZ Bank.' As
people put their names to this personalised plea, cameras from
the various television networks captured the scene for the
evening news.

Suddenly, everything seemed to be going wrong at once for
Packer and Tourang. Every time they opened a newspaper or
turned on the television there was a new manifestation of the
Stop-Packer push. Colson and Powers had even been waylaid by
one of the *Herald* strikers on their way across town. Later that

morning, a council of war was held, and it was decided that they had to fight back.

Before long, Packer's old friend John Singleton was being asked to spruce up Tourang's image or, as he saw it, to sell Packer to the public. His first suggestion was to run an advertisement in the newspapers that got right to the heart of the problem by displaying a big picture of Packer, accompanied by the slogan: 'I may not be Robert Redford, but that doesn't make me Boris Karloff.' But selling Kerry as soft and lovable, or at least as deserving a fair go, was soon rejected in favour of an even more direct approach. Seven years earlier, Packer had countered Costigan's allegations by standing up in public and tackling them head on. He could do the same with this smear campaign, it was decided, by exposing the lie they claimed was at the heart of it: that with only 15 per cent of Fairfax he could control the company.

Packer's first approach was made to the ABC's *7.30 Report*, but Channel Nine executives reacted in horror to the prospect of their boss being scooped up by the rival channel. So while the ABC still held its breath, agreement was reached with *A Current Affair*, which on 23 October 1991 devoted a whole program to an interview with Packer, followed by a discussion between him and a panel of Fairfax journalists.

Few things unsettled Jana Wendt in her distinguished career at Channel Nine, but this toe-to-toe with her proprietor was clearly one of them. Not only was Packer a ferocious person to interview, but he was also her boss, and he clearly had no intention of giving her special treatment. After the opening titles rolled and the introductions were made, Packer dismissed her first few questions with a series of short, sharp replies that are normally guaranteed to throw interviewers off their rhythm.

Wendt: You are the richest man in Australia with vast commercial interests. How much influence does your money bring with it?
Packer: Not very much.
Wendt: Are you serious?
Packer: I'm very serious.

Wendt: The perception is that you can ring the prime minister and get through in a flash. Is that influence, and do you have it?

Packer: I don't know. I've never tried to dial him.

Wendt: Are you serious?

Packer: Yes.

Perhaps Packer was nervous, although he hardly looked it, or perhaps he thought the questions stupid, but he soon became more expansive, even if some of his answers were no easier to accept than the proposition that he had little influence. Asked whether he saw himself as someone with power, Packer replied that he didn't. Asked whether he exercised power, he countered by saying that stories about him were perversions of the truth and contained enormous inaccuracies. Not 3 per cent of those stories, came the familiar Packer refrain, had been checked with him.

Why then did people fear him and oppose him and harbour all these nasty thoughts? asked Wendt. Packer said he didn't know but he supposed it was because he didn't suffer fools gladly and was prepared to stand up for what he believed in. Asked whether he was a bully, he smiled sweetly and said he thought not.

Minutes later, in the second half of the program, debating with three Fairfax journalists, he gave a perfect demonstration of the bully's art, browbeating his interrogators for the 'lies' they were telling about him. Years earlier, Packer's friend Jimmy Gold-smith had caused a sensation on BBC TV's *Money Programme* in London by repeatedly asking his two interviewers, 'Why did you lie about my company, why did you lie, why did you lie?' His performance had ended the television careers of the two men he faced, one of whom was then business editor of *The Times*, and the video of the program had been a hot property in the City of London for many years afterwards. Packer was not quite so devastating but he was almost as aggressive, for his line of attack against the *Herald*'s journalists was to accuse them and their papers of the 'Big Lie' in suggesting that he would control Fairfax. Tom Burton, one of the three Fairfax journalists facing him, was repeatedly goaded by Packer to read from the Code of Ethics of the Australian Journalists' Association, which Packer said the Fairfax newspapers had broken by pushing the lie that he would control Fairfax.

Few of those watching would have found Packer likeable—he was contemptuous, arrogant and positively frightening—but none could deny that he was tough, quick and formidably smart. And there was also no question that he had won the debate. Only once in the interview did he put a foot wrong. Asked by Jana Wendt why he was interested in owning a stake in the Fairfax papers, he told her that the idea amused him. It was doubtless true, but it seemed an absurd admission to make in the light of the fury that his bid had provoked and the seriousness of the issues it raised.

The audience loved it—after the program, the phones at Channel Nine were jammed with support for Packer, not least because he was giving 'those journalists' a bit of a bashing. But the reaction from Canberra was not so favourable. If the politicians had harboured doubts and fears about Packer beforehand, watching him on *A Current Affair* had increased them tenfold. It was no coincidence that in Canberra the next day John Langmore and David Connolly, two politicians on opposite sides of parliament, decided to gather a petition to present to the prime minister, demanding in effect that Tourang be stopped. Nor was it coincidence that 128 of the Commonwealth Parliament's 224 members had signed it by the end of the afternoon. Five days later, the petition was presented to Prime Minister Bob Hawke, with a further seven signatures, demanding that the government 'oppose the sale of Fairfax to any individual or consortium that would result in a greater concentration of media ownership'. In practical terms, it might just as well have read 'PLEASE STOP PACKER'. As Langmore himself admitted, Tourang and Packer were indeed the target.

There was only one group of politicians that had refused to put their names to the anti-Tourang petition. These were the members of the ALP's New South Wales Right-wing faction, with which Messrs Keating, Richardson, Peter Barron and others were associated. None of the government's thirty ministers was asked to sign, but in a significant demonstration of his personal sympathies, Prime Minister Bob Hawke inquired whether the member for Wills might add his name. His request was refused, on the grounds that it would not be proper for Hawke to petition himself, for Wills was Hawke's own electorate.

As the petition was being gathered and presented, Australia's previous prime minister Malcolm Fraser was also doing his best to prevent a Packer victory. He had already told the parliamentary Print Media Inquiry on 22 October, the day before Packer's appearance on *A Current Affair*, that the big man had applied significant and severe pressure on the Liberal government in the late 1970s over the issue of who should control the new telecommunications satellite. He had warned the inquiry, too, of the threat to democracy if the government allowed Australia's press to be carved up between two immensely powerful groups run by Packer and Murdoch. As a political leader who had experienced pressure from both men and perhaps even buckled to it, Fraser knew well how strong this might be.

Now Fraser took to the public stage with a similar message, addressing a rally organised by the Age Independence Committee in Melbourne's Treasury Gardens. With great passion, Fraser told a cheering crowd of 2000 sympathisers that selling Fairfax to Tourang would be a crime against the Australian people. The next day he was stumping the boards at an even bigger rally at Sydney's Darling Harbour and repeating the warnings, this time joining hands with his old enemy Gough Whitlam in an emotional salute. With the spotlight on these grand old warriors of Australian politics as they stood on stage with their hands held high, it looked as if they were back on the campaign trail together, only now as friends, fighting on the same side.

Once again, there was an almost messianic tone to Fraser's speech. 'If there are two media empires and it's Murdoch and the Black–Packer consortium, there will be a power outside parliament capable of challenging the integrity of parliament,' he warned. Members of parliament, Fraser continued, must pass a resolution blocking the Tourang sale. If they failed to do so, everyone would know how far the rot had spread in Australia. Everyone would know that parliament had been intimidated.

If parliament had not been intimidated already, it was just about to be. For on 4 November 1991 in Canberra, Kerry Packer gave evidence to the parliamentary Print Media Inquiry. So exciting was the possibility of seeing Packer in the flesh again that the ABC decided to televise the hearings and broadcast them live. Thus the Australian public was treated to a second dose of full-strength Kerry Packer, purging his way through the system. For the best part of ten years Packer had refused to appear on television, talk on radio or grant more than the occasional interview to journalists. He was pictured occasionally at dinners, talking to politicians, playing polo or bearing down on unfortunate camera-men. But until now no one had had the chance to judge for themselves what he was really like. What they discovered, as Australia's richest man came out punching for the second time in ten days, was that Packer was not just frightening, he was fright-eningly smart. As a public performer he was quite breathtaking.

Before taking the stand in front of the committee, Packer delivered a written statement on his role in the Fairfax bid that his old friend John Singleton had helped to draft. It was, as one might have expected, blunt and to the point, starting off with the explicit warning that he appeared reluctantly. But it also showed signs of Packer's own dry sense of humour in the way it person-alised the issue.

> Last year I suffered a major heart attack and died. I didn't die for long but it was long enough for me. I didn't come back to control John Fairfax. I didn't come back to break the law. And I certainly didn't intentionally come back to testify before a parliamentary inquiry.

The submission repeated that Packer had complied with all the requirements of the cross-media laws and would continue to do so. He was limited by law to owning less than 15 per cent of Fairfax, so he would have 14.99 per cent. He was prohibited by law from having a seat on the Fairfax board, so he would not have one. He was prohibited by law from controlling Fairfax, so he would not. Nor were there any agreements, arrangements or understandings that would allow him to do so. 'In the Broadcasting Act, there are laws which impose limitations on cross-media ownership,' said Packer. 'I tell you categorically that I intend to abide by these laws.' Packer had not taken the lead in making the bid, he claimed, and had not put the consortium together. In choosing the directors, he had done no more than give the nod to candidates whom others had suggested. He had undertaken what should have been a simple commercial transaction within the law only to find that it had been 'hijacked by a group of self-opinionated and self-interested vigilantes'.

But Packer's real barbs were reserved for a government that was changing the laws in an attempt to catch him out. 'Only a banana republic changes them at the drop of a hat,' said his statement. 'What I can neither understand nor accept is how, as an Australian, I should be the victim of attempted one-minute-to-midnight changes of established and accepted cross-media laws . . . As I understand it, it is against the Constitution to legislate against an individual. An attempt to legislate solely to thwart the legally proper aspirations of an individual just because some people may not like that individual has the same effect. This is what has been suggested here.'

It was a perfectly valid point to make, of course, but Packer had not complained in May 1990 when the government had tightened the television foreign-ownership rules and knocked out his only rival for Channel Nine. Nor would he raise a whisper of criticism in January 1993 when the same Labor government intervened in outrageous fashion by attempting to ban the use of microwave signals for pay TV, with clear benefit to Kerry Packer.[11] The difference, of course, was that those interventions benefited him, whereas on this occasion *he* was the victim.

When the questioning got under way, Packer was perhaps even more formidable and more aggressive than he had been on *A Current Affair*. He had been practising for a couple of days beforehand with Dan Colson and Brian Powers, and the politicians, by comparison, must have seemed easy meat. Was Mr Packer saying, John Langmore asked, that there was no arrangement, formal or informal, with Mr Black to control Fairfax? 'That is exactly what I am saying,' Packer snapped back. 'It is what I have said *ad nauseam* in that document. You are either going to have to believe me or call me a liar . . . I am sick of trying to tell you all, I am not going to run John Fairfax.'[12]

'Are you saying that you do not think Parliament has the right to inquire into the print media?' the same committee member asked a little later.

'Yes, I am saying exactly that,' Packer replied. 'I do not think under the Constitution you have the right to do it.' Not long afterwards, he was sounding off about the absurdity of it all: it was 'crap . . . claptrap . . . a storm in a teacup . . . an intellectual wank'. The public, said Packer, didn't give a damn who owned Fairfax; nor did they think it mattered. They cared about important things, like jobs, which were being 'pissed up against the wall' according to Packer because worthy projects like Tourang's bid were being hindered, and investment discouraged by constant changes of the rules.

As he answered questions, Packer frequently leaned forward and pointed a finger at his accusers; once finished he lolled back in his chair and smiled at the gallery. Meanwhile, his interrogators touched nervous hands to mouths, couched questions as 'your critics would argue' and, for the most part, kept their heads down. The chairman of the inquiry, at least in name, was a young politician named Michael Lee—later elevated to the Keating ministry—but in practice it was Packer who ran the show. Asked about his tax affairs towards the end of the proceedings, Packer called suddenly for a cup of tea. 'Am I the only bloke who doesn't get a cup of tea round here?' he asked. It was brilliant theatre and perfect timing. One could only applaud.

A spoof piece by the comedy writer Patrick Cook in Packer's own *Bulletin* magazine captured the atmosphere perfectly. One might argue that it gave the lie to the charge that Packer refused to allow criticism of him or his friends in his magazines, but in the circumstances it would hardly have been wise for Packer to stop it, even if he had wanted to.

Mr Meek (Chairman ALP): For what we are about to receive, may the Lord make us truly grateful. Call the first witness.

Ground shakes. Hand-turned jarrah doors wrenched from hinges. Eclipse of the sun. Lord Rhino takes his seat.

Mr Meek: State your full name and reason for appearance.

Lord Rhino: You clowns don't know anything do you? Clarence Bullstrode Fenimore Rhino and I appear to be wasting my time.

Mr Mild (Lib): If I may begin . . .

Lord Rhino: On the whole, I'd rather be in Philadelphia.

Mr Mild: If I may . . .

Lord Rhino: Speak up. Stand up. Sit down. Shut up. What's your problem?

Mr Mild: No further questions.

Mr Mouse (ALP): Lord Rhino, this committee understands that you have designs on the former Fairfax conspiracy.

Lord Rhino: Pigs I do.

Mr Mouse: I'm sorry?

Lord Rhino: It's a bit late to apologise now. What a wank!

Mr Milquetoast (Lib): When you say . . .

Lord Rhino: This committee is a wank. A rodwallop. A hands-on experience. A round of the trousers . . .

Ms Karen Allworthy (ALP): Mr Costigan . . .

Volcanic activity. Windows explode. Sound technician staggers from sandbags with bleeding ears. Ms Allworthy peeled off wall, sets to work on written apology. Mr Ian Sinuate (Nat) intercedes.

Mr Ian Sinuate: I'll put it to you straight, Lord Rhino. It's particularly nice weather we're having.

. . . Committee scurries off through hole in skirting board. Lord Rhino leaves and is greeted by vast crowds of viewers, eager to elect him president for life.[13]

At times, Packer's treatment of Australia's elected representatives was so contemptuous as to be embarrassing. One cannot imagine that a similar committee in the United States would have tolerated it for a moment. And his comments about parliament displayed a similar disdain. In Packer's view of the world, governments interfered, changed the rules, made pointless laws and meddled with the rights of people like him to do as they saw fit. If politicians would only leave the field clear to those who had money and were prepared to risk it, then the world would be much improved. 'Since I grew up,' said Packer, 'I would imagine that 10 000 new laws must have been passed through the parliaments of Australia. I do not think it is a much better place . . . This idea of passing a law every time someone blinks is a nonsense . . . Every time you pass a law you take somebody's privileges away from them.' At a stroke, it seemed, Packer would dismiss as worse than useless welfare provisions, Medicare, pollution controls, fair trading laws, and most of the other rules that define our society. It was hard to believe, but it fitted in well with his views on taxes: that the government was not spending his money well enough for Australians like him to want to contribute more. He knew no one, he said, who didn't minimise his taxes.

Packer dismissed his opponents' arguments and the government's new media rules even more contemptuously—as stupid, absurd, or absolute nonsense. Those who disagreed with him were branded directly or indirectly as either fools or knaves. In his version of the world, there was little room for discussion or a point of view that differed from his. He did not appear to be a man who was troubled by doubt. 'I am telling you,' Packer kept saying, 'I am telling you . . . the answer is very clear.'

The day after this stunning performance, the lines to Sydney's talkback radio programs ran hot in Kerry Packer's support. Caller after caller left the message that he should not only be allowed to take over the *Age* and the *Sydney Morning Herald*, but should also be invited to run Australia. He's tough, they said, he's successful, he gets things done. In times of economic gloom, he's just what the country needs. But if the average Australian admired the way in which Packer had pummelled the politicians, there were others who were not very happy with what they saw. Perhaps most of them were politicians or journalists, members of the chattering classes for whom Packer had so little time. But the aggressive dismissal of parliament and its concerns had not served Packer well in the immediate struggle. By demonstrating how powerful he could be, he had merely increased the politicians' desire to stop him. He had told the parliamentary committee that he could not control Fairfax with only 14.99 per cent of the shares. Yet as one correspondent to the *Sydney Morning Herald*'s letters column wittily observed, Packer had easily controlled the parliamentary inquiry, even though he owned no shares at all.

Packer had told the parliamentarians that Tourang's bid was certain to win, adding, 'The only way it can be topped is by political interference.' And, as was so often the case, he was right on target. Five days earlier, Tourang had increased its offer for Fairfax by $300 million to more than $1.4 billion, which was good enough to get Fairfax's bankers off the hook and quite possibly good enough to win the game. It was as much money as Independent was offering and more than AIN, while Tourang was putting up more in cash and still had the bondholders.

But Packer had erred in one respect. He had told the Print Media Inquiry that he didn't believe there would be any 'political interference'. And in this he was wrong.

The Australian Broadcasting Tribunal had long felt pressure for an inquiry, if only to give Messrs Beazley and Hawke some protection from the familiar charge that they were doing the mates a favour. And it had been sniffing around since early September 1991 to see whether there were any grounds for doing so. Its task, of course, was to determine whether there were any agreements or associations between the parties that could put Packer in position to control Fairfax while he also owned Channel Nine. Packer had said fifty times that there were no such arrangements and that he would not break the law even in its new incarnation. But it was the ABT's job to satisfy itself that he was telling the truth.

Since mid September the ABT had called up a raft of documents and statutory declarations from all Tourang's key players to illuminate how the consortium had been put together, how its board members had been chosen and whether agreements existed as to shareholdings or anything else. Trevor Kennedy and Malcolm Turnbull had also been asked in detail about their financial and personal relationships with Packer, past and present. Soon afterwards, the ABT had followed up with a list of forty-one questions that all the major participants in Tourang's bid had been required to answer.

On 25 November 1991, three weeks after Packer's appearance before the Print Media Inquiry, the ABT hit pay dirt. Its lawyers had sent an order to Trevor Kennedy requiring him to surrender all diary notes made since March 1991. They had then been given the hint to redraft this command in a more precise and pedantic fashion. Somehow, it seemed, they had been told the exact formulation that would catch what they were after.

Trevor Kennedy had not in fact kept a diary of his times at Tourang, or not recorded much of interest, but after being bumped from the job in October he had written some angry notes while his memory was still fresh. These were for his memoirs, if he ever wrote them, or for legal action if he decided to take it, and they recorded in detail all sorts of things that would be of interest to the ABT. In particular, they set out the command structure at Tourang and the people to whom Kennedy as chief executive had reported. This went right to the heart of the issue of whether Packer would exercise influence or control if Tourang took over Fairfax. The original ABT notice, sent on a Friday, had asked simply for *diary entries* made during Kennedy's time at Tourang. The new one, drafted on the Monday morning, three days after the first request, specified 'diary entries *or notes made during or after* events relating to the circumstances surrounding your resignation from Tourang'.

The notice demanded delivery of the documents to the ABT that same afternoon, and when they arrived they proved to be sensational. According to Justice Rogers, summing up evidence in a later court case between Tourang and Trevor Kennedy, a letter from Kennedy to the ABT, accompanying the diaries and notes, claimed that he had reported both to Conrad Black and to Kerry Packer while he was chief executive of Tourang, but 'principally to Kerry Packer'. According to Kennedy, Packer had exercised much more influence over Tourang than had ever been publicly admitted.[14]

There was now no question that the ABT would have to go ahead with an inquiry. The next day, the ABT's chairman Peter Westerway announced to a startled Print Media Inquiry in Canberra that, as a result of information it had received, the ABT would begin a hearing into Tourang's bid for Fairfax as soon as possible.

To find against Tourang, the ABT would merely have to establish that there was potential for Packer to control Fairfax, in which the allegations made by Kennedy would be important evidence. But the mere existence of the inquiry could deal a fatal blow to Tourang's chances of winning the auction. For even if the ABT eventually gave Packer and Tourang a clean bill of health, it was likely to take several months to do so, and Fairfax's bankers were unlikely to have the patience to wait. They would almost certainly opt to sell the papers to one of the other bidders, who were offering almost as much money.

Packer was in Argentina playing polo when the ABT's decision to hold an inquiry was announced. Two days later he telephoned Dan Colson and Brian Powers in Sydney to tell them that he had decided to withdraw. He would doubtless have recognised the risk of allowing the inquiry to proceed, even if it could be established that Tourang's bid complied with the law in all respects. But he also told his two new friends 'in his usual colourful language, spiced with plenty of four-letter words' that he had no desire to be grilled in public again.[15] His appearances before Costigan and the Print Media Inquiry had been quite enough for one lifetime, he reckoned.

Packer's anger could only be guessed at, but he had wanted Fairfax dearly and he hated above all to be beaten when he had set his heart on something. Months later, he was telling friends that it was no longer possible for him to do business in Australia because the government didn't dare be seen to give him anything, so politicians would no longer listen to even his most reasonable demands. But the political tide was by this time already turning back again. Six days before Christmas 1991, Prime Minister Hawke was ousted in a coup, and Prime Minister Paul Keating took over. One of his first acts was to install Packer's good friend Senator Graham Richardson, known jokingly in Canberra circles as the Minister for Channel Nine, as the new Minister for Transport and Communications. Some six months later, the man who had killed Packer's hopes of getting Fairfax was dumped as chairman of the Australian Broadcasting Tribunal. Peter Westerway had not only requested the crucial changes in the cross-media laws in July 1991 but had also taken the decision to inquire into Tourang's bid in November. After months of speculation about his future, he was told on 30 June 1992 that his contract would not be renewed; nor would he get the top job at the newly established Australian Broadcasting Authority when it took over from the ABT in October 1992 as industry watchdog.

As for Kerry's old friends Trevor Kennedy and Malcolm Turnbull, they were both cast into outer darkness after Packer's failure to get what he wanted. It seemed their former employer blamed one or other of them for the ABT's good fortune in striking gold. In any case, he accused them both of treason, which the dictionary defines as 'the violation by a subject of his allegiance to his sovereign'. It was an interesting choice of words.

CHAPTER TWENTY-FOUR

TIDYING UP

My interests are playing polo . . . I have absolute trust in Dunlap.

Kerry Packer, April 1992[1]

While the future of Fairfax was being decided in late 1991, Packer was in Argentina for the polo season, staying in the presidential suite of the Alvear Palace Hotel in Buenos Aires. At the end of his sojourn he went into one of the hotel's jewellery shops, a branch of the big H. Stern chain, to buy presents for the wives of his Argentine hosts. A couple of local businessmen had apparently shown him around town and introduced him to important people, and Packer wanted to show his gratitude. Before long, he had selected a $30 000 necklace and asked for the price. When told how much it was, he indicated that he wanted to be told the code price of the item or, in simple terms, the price at which the shop broke even and made no profit. The manager of the shop, incidentally a woman, offered to give him a deal but said that it was not company policy to reveal the code price, so she could not tell him. Packer asked again. The manager stuck to her guns. The following exchange then took place:

> Packer: Do you know who I am?
> Manager: Yes, Mr Packer, I do, you're staying at the hotel.
> Packer: Well, get me the fucking code price.
> Manager: I'm sorry, I can give you a very good deal but I can't tell you the code price. It is not company policy to do so.

At this point, Packer's minder offered the observation that the manager had just made 'a very bad mistake'. The woman now rang her boss to ask what she should do. While she was on the phone, Packer produced a wad of $100 bills from his pocket and started peeling them off to his companion, with instructions to pay them as tips to the various people who had helped out while he was there. The manager then came off the phone to repeat her previous advice that the code price could not be divulged, whereupon a very angry Kerry Packer walked out of the shop. Before doing so, he had one last throw, telling her that if she didn't tell him the 'fucking code price' he would fly to Rio to talk to H. Stern, the owner of the jewellery chain. The young lady, used to the ways of the rich and powerful, was apparently not perturbed by this threat and repeated that it was not company policy to comply with this request. As a result, her shop missed out on Packer's custom. Instead of flying to Rio, the big man went to the jewellery shop next door and bought $100 000 worth of rings.

Since his October 1990 heart attack, Packer had pulled back from the day-to-day running of the company, and he was rarely seen at Consolidated Press's Park Street offices or at Channel Nine any more. Even while he was in Australia, he often spent only two days a week in the office, flying down from Ellerston on Sunday night and flying back again by Tuesday. He was likely to devote only an afternoon during that time to his television station, Channel Nine, and appeared to resent even this limited attention to his businesses, losing his temper more frequently with those who ran the place in his absence. He was more relaxed when he was away from it all, wearing jeans and sneakers and riding round his Ellerston estate or playing snooker in the Ellerston club with his grooms and polo players. He claimed to like being with country people who fought bushfires and drought together, knew nothing about takeovers and didn't spend their days 'cutting some other bastard's throat', as Packer confessed one had to if one wanted to do well in business. But Packer had not so much softened his outlook as discovered that he could get someone even tougher than he was to do the throat-cutting for him.

The new man at Consolidated Press—who had taken over from Trevor Kennedy in mid 1991, was a fifty-five-year-old American called Al Dunlap. A self-made multi-millionaire who had pulled himself up by the straps of his well-polished boots, Dunlap sported a chunky gold ring, an even chunkier gold Rolex watch and big gold cufflinks. He wore signature shirts beneath a high-cornered smile that bared his perfect teeth. The son of a shipyard worker from waterfront New Jersey, he was half Irish and a touch German, with a bit of English thrown in for good measure. Over it all was a tough all-American shell, hardened by several years in the US paratroops and a spell as a nuclear missile site commander.

Like Packer, he had started in business at the bottom, working on the machine lines, on the night shift and loading trucks. Unlike Packer, he had needed to fight every inch of the way. His houses were filled with statues of lions, while his office desk displayed a small metal sculpture depicting four or five sharks in a feeding frenzy, to remind him of how hostile life was in the business world. He had a special love of predators because they had to be smart to survive. Dunlap had a horror of being soft in business, so he wasn't.

Even Packer's friend Jimmy Goldsmith described Dunlap as irascible and dubbed him 'Rambo in pinstripes', which seemed to suit Al just fine. He was proud of being a 'bastard', he told one Australian banker when they came round to discussing the Dunlap business style. Enemies and admirers all agreed he was abrasive and difficult to get along with. But he didn't care about such trivia. What mattered was getting the job done, winning the war against inefficiency, overstaffing, extravagance and waste. In his view, good management left no room for compassion or sentiment.

All of this had given Dunlap the reputation of being the best turnaround man in the business. Jimmy Goldsmith had hired him in March 1986 to sort out the huge American paper and timber group Crown Zellerbach, which was number ninety-nine in *Fortune*'s one hundred worst-managed corporations at the time. In the three years he was there, Dunlap cut the business back to the core, sold assets, sacked staff, closed plants and boosted profits from US$25 million to $130 million. Previously he had worked similar wonders at Lily-Tulip, the US paper cup manufacturer, where a huge leveraged buyout had gone off the rails. Dunlap had got rid of the corporate jet, sacked 20 per cent of the company's salaried employees and put the company back into the black again. This radical surgery had allowed the company's owners, Kohlberg Kravis Roberts, to sell out at a US$131 million profit and had delivered Dunlap a tidy US$6.4 million bonus on his 400 000 shares.

Dunlap had worked briefly for Packer in 1989 as a consultant providing advice on cutting costs at ANI, and had impressed almost everyone he dealt with, including the boss. He was therefore an obvious man to bring in to Consolidated Press when Kennedy resigned as managing director. Packer's empire had severe problems in property, thanks to Warren Anderson, its borrowings had become uncomfortably high and the banks were getting twitchy. Besides, Packer's brief 'death' in October had reminded everyone he would not be around for ever, presenting an obvious opportunity to tidy up the group and make it ready for young James Packer to take over. Dunlap was given instructions to get rid of the dead wood from the business, and promptly set about his task in a manner that looked more like clear felling.

At Consolidated Press, Dunlap soon earned the nickname 'Chainsaw' for the way he went about these cutbacks. Packer had bought all sorts of odd things over the years and allowed the group to grow into a forest of some 400 companies. Dunlap downed all but the tallest trees, piled up some forty businesses to sell and disposed of 300 companies that no longer did anything useful. Except for television, where Dunlap was not allowed to cut, no part of the Packer corporate empire escaped the Chainsaw's attentions. Even 'non-business overheads' were chopped back from $30 million to $5 million, suggesting that Kerry's expenditure was also taking a haircut.

Professional fees to lawyers, barristers and accountants were hacked back from $30 million a year to $12 million a year, with Allen Allen & Hemsley one of the casualties. Once again, old loyalties were no protection. Allens had been doing the Packers' legal work since 1938, but were now just one of several legal firms asked by Dunlap to tender for Consolidated Press's business. Allens was apparently not prepared to engage in a vulgar cost-cutting competition, so it lost the job.

Staff were also cut back drastically. But people in the central company, Consolidated Press Holdings, felt the teeth most sharply. Numbers there were cut from seventy to just thirteen. One accountant was sacked without warning on the day he finished valuing one of the company's corporate assets for imminent sale. He had a new house, a mortgage and a new baby, and suddenly found himself on the streets after fourteen years of loyal service. One long-serving driver was dismissed without notice, handed his money and sent home. All job security had gone. No one knew who was going to go next. 'Everyone is scared they'll get the sack,' said one.

Soon almost all of Packer's old guard was gone. Finance director Donald Bourke was an early departure; his deputy Ray Stone followed soon afterwards; Chris MacKenzie, the man who ran the international companies, also left. Some simply lost their jobs in the reorganisation, others clashed with Dunlap or found they had lost their desire to work for the company. Most would once have done anything for the Packers, but now left with a degree of disillusion.

Dunlap didn't agonise about people losing their jobs. The best decisions in business were the toughest ones and in his view Consolidated Press was wasteful, overstaffed and inefficient. But it was an enormous shock to those who had worked for the Packers that Kerry was letting him behave in this way. For all the talk of being tough in business, the Packer approach had always been softened by a fierce loyalty to their old and trusted employees. It was one of the principles on which the whole Packer enterprise had been built since the 1930s, but Kerry seemed suddenly to have abandoned it. Some of those dismissed felt sure that Kerry was so busy playing polo he couldn't possibly know what was happening. Others observed that he had already fallen out with Chisholm, Kennedy and Turnbull, to whom he had once been so close. And since Packer had given Dunlap his instructions, he clearly did know what was going on, especially since his son James was constantly at Dunlap's elbow, learning how business was done. 'Kerry's been wanting to get rid of staff for years,' said one who had worked close to him since the 1960s. 'He'd prefer to have none at all.'

It was not just the staff that went. Perks were cut back, too. Executives were asked to repay their low-interest mortgages, company cars were taken away and new payment systems were introduced to get more output for Packer's money. The magazine business's advertising salesmen, in particular, were shifted to a new incentive system that cut back their basic salaries and forced them to rely more on commission. This had worked well at Valassis in the USA, where young James Packer had seen it in operation, but ACP's advertising chief Graham Lawrence was not convinced it would work in magazines in Australia, objecting that the salesmen were already poorly paid and hadn't had a pay rise in three years. Lawrence, who had been with the company since the 1970s, was shown the door.

This wholesale cost-cutting naturally made the Packer businesses both more profitable and more valuable. Indeed, this may have been the point of the exercise, because the next stage was to cash in by selling shares in Packer Incorporated to the public. The stock market was in good shape, so it was an opportune time to sell.

The first to go on the block in January 1992 was the ACP magazine business, in a deal that valued the group at $1175 million. In privatising the empire nine years earlier, Packer had bought half these magazines plus the Sydney and Melbourne Channel Nine stations for $110 million. Now he was selling those magazines, plus the ones he had acquired from Fairfax in 1987, for more than ten times the price. The original privatisation deal in 1983 had been quite brilliant for Packer, and this one was looking almost as good. But the Australian public, represented by the big pension funds and insurance companies who managed their money, were not so thrilled. For they were now being asked to shell out ten times as much as they had received in 1983 and getting back a bit more than half of what they had sold.

The clear lesson from this was that Kerry Packer's timing was excellent. But on that basis, it was not a good idea to buy when Packer was selling. The public obviously got this message, for small investors took up only $80 million of the $200 million stock set aside for them, despite a marketing campaign in Packer's magazines to interest the public in the stock. Fund managers also hung back, and in the end more than a quarter of the shares on offer remained unsold, leaving $140 million worth of stock in the hands of the underwriters. When trading began in mid April 1992, ACP's new shares opened almost 50 cents below their $5 issue price. But the disappointing response was not Packer's problem, for the underwriting agreement ensured that the money still came to Consolidated Press. It was the brokers and investment bankers who had taken the risk that the shares wouldn't sell.

By selling just over half the magazine business and shifting debt into the newly floated company, Packer's privately owned flagship, Consolidated Press Holdings, raised $844 million in cash. It also retained 45 per cent of the magazine empire, worth almost $400 million, which ensured that it still controlled the business. (This was remarkably similar to the trick Kerry's son James pulled off in 2007, when roughly half the empire's media assets were hived off to a private equity group, CVC.) Packer's profit on this transaction, amounting to some $400 million for Consolidated Press Holdings, was largely or entirely tax free, because most of the assets had been owned by the Packers since long before 1985, when capital gains tax had been introduced to Australia.

In the same week as the ACP float was announced, the world was also told that half of the American coupon business, Valassis, was for sale. Having bought it in December 1986 for US$363 million, Packer now sold 51 per cent of it to the (mainly American) public for US$375 million. On the face of it, this gave him a cash profit of US$10 million and left him owning half the business for free, which itself was a good enough return. But the real gain was considerably larger, for the sale produced almost US$900 million (A$1270 million) of tax-free dividends for Packer's Netherlands-based company Conpress Investments BV. And on this basis, Packer had more than tripled his money in the space of five years.[2] As with the magazines, he held on to almost half of the coupon business, worth US$375 million (A$530 million), and retained control.

The sale of these two main businesses, along with the other disposals made since mid 1991, showed up dramatically in the 1991–92 accounts of Consolidated Press Holdings. In the space of twelve months, Packer's master company was transformed from a mass of largely unconnected businesses such as ship chandlering, oil exploration, waste management and engineering into an investment company with shares in three key enterprises. Consolidated Press Holdings, which was still privately owned, now held 42 per cent of the Nine Network, 45 per cent of ACP magazines and 49 per cent of Valassis. Other than that, only Packer's vast rural landholdings plus a handful of development properties remained. These hadn't been sold because they would have fetched such a miserable price.

Financially, the transformation was even more dramatic. In the space of twelve months Packer's holding company had repaid $2700 million of borrowings and reduced its debts by more than 90 per cent; it now had borrowings of only $225 million and a remarkable $534 million cash sitting in the bank. The company's net worth, on the accountants' reckoning, was $2400 million, all of which belonged to the Packer family. How much Kerry and his children were worth above that in terms of their holdings in trusts and private companies was a matter of conjecture, but it was certainly several hundred million dollars. *Fortune* magazine in the USA was brave enough to put a figure on it, estimating the entire Packer wealth to be $3200 million, making him the eighty-second richest man in the world. Comparisons with previous guesstimates of his worth showed that he was getting richer fast and outpacing most of the rest of the world's billionaires. Three years earlier the same magazine had clocked him at only $2000 million and ranked him number 108 in the list.[3]

As to what Packer would do with all this money, it was anybody's guess. But there was no rush, he said. 'My interests are playing polo,' he told Trevor Sykes in an April 1992 interview for *Australian Business Monthly.* 'I have management I can trust. I can trust my son. I have absolute trust in Dunlap and I have no doubt whatever he does is for my best interests. And I'm in no hurry at all.'

One of Packer's main reasons for cashing in his chips was that he was convinced everything would be cheaper in two years' time. By 1992, his friend and guru Jimmy Goldsmith had again become deeply pessimistic about the world economy and was forecasting a possible world depression. Packer had also become a convert to the belief that cash is king. In the 1980s it had been possible to get money on easy terms to take over almost anything, so lack of cash had not stopped anyone becoming the owner of a multi-billion-dollar organisation.[4] But in the 1990s, as Packer saw it, there would be a shortage of capital and a lot of cautious bankers. Having no debt and half a billion dollars in one's back pocket would be an enormous advantage in making even more money.

The other reason for tidying up the empire was so it could be handed over to young James, which could happen at any time, given the state of Kerry's health. Even though he had been groomed for the succession and was both bright and tough, it was wise not to leave him too much to do.

Considering how the children of the very rich can turn out, James and his sister Gretel were a credit to their parents. They were polite, friendly and generally unassuming. And those who knew the family said that Kerry and Ros Packer were equally responsible. Kerry had devoted more time to his children than his own father had ever done and was said to adore them. He had also shown them a great deal more love and encouragement. But that would not have been hard. And there was more than a hint of the old-fashioned Packer methods in the way he had gone about it. Like his father, Kerry was a great believer in not spoiling his children, which meant, in James's case, that he rarely praised him. The boy had even been sent to board at Cranbrook School, a stone's throw from the Packer family home, just as Kerry had been thirty years before. James, however, was ten when he was sent away from home, twice the age at which young Kerry had been made to leave. And his father was convinced it was in a good cause, as he told Michael Parkinson in 1979:

> I think boarding school is very important for kids. I think particu-
> larly for kids who have been very lucky and had a lot of privileges.
> I think it's very important for them to learn to get along with other
> people and other kids, some of them not quite as well off as they
> are, and to learn their responsibilities and how to mix with people
> and what to do.

James had found life at Cranbrook difficult for much the same reasons as Kerry had done. The Packers were rich and not exactly popular, and he was no genius academically. Like his father and perhaps also his grandfather before him, James suffered from dyslexia—now known to be a hereditary disorder that is most often passed from father to son—which handicapped him in schoolwork.[5] But as with Kerry, sport had proved to be his saving grace. He was a talented cricketer and had a galaxy of World Series Cricket stars to coach him. One of those who was asked to run his eye over the lad was the dour English Test player Geoff Boycott, who told cricket correspondent Henry Blofeld about going up to the nets in the Packers' back garden to watch him. 'His dad was there, and he has strong views about his son's cricket, with which I disagreed,' said Boycott. 'Dad thought he knew more about cricket than me. I told him that making money was his job, and playing cricket was mine. He was a lovely boy, though, and a nice little cricketer.'[6]

As a child, young James was a gentle boy, according to adults who knew him, and a bit soft, according to some of his school-mates. But on leaving school in 1985 he was given the same toughening-up treatment that the two previous generations of Packers had received and despatched to the bush for a year as a jackeroo, this time at his father's huge Newcastle Waters station in the Northern Territory. When he came back, Kerry set about teaching him the business in a way that his father had never done. Not for James the long years of packing magazines, cleaning the printing presses and working in the bowels of the building. When he did the rounds of the various departments, it was more often to watch than to work. And there were long sessions into the night talking to his father about business.

By early 1987, he was being given a financial training at Consolidated Press. Then, at the suggestion of Neville Wran, who until six months earlier had been premier of New South Wales, he was called into the Whitlam Turnbull merchant bank for a session with Wran's former economic adviser Nigel Stokes. Young James could hardly have asked for better tuition, for Wran and Packer attended as well, and chipped in with a few ideas. When it came to the subject of bankers, Packer Senior's tip was that you should always make them come to your office in order to show them who's boss, then you should knock them round the head a few times to soften them up, and only then would you be ready to get down to business.

By 1992, Kerry was getting Al Dunlap to finish James's training, which was likely to be even more effective than jackerooing in toughening the boy up. James was most obviously impressed by the Chainsaw's ability to sack loyal employees and chop limbs off an organisation without agonising about the pain involved. 'Al is emotionless,' said James admiringly, adding that he meant it as a compliment. 'He has shown me how hard you can push people.'[7] One would have thought he knew this already from watching his father, who before long had decided that he was not going to die after all and might as well get back to business.

The excitement of spending half a billion dollars was bound to draw Kerry back into the game sooner or later, whatever he said about being in no rush. But in the event it was only a few months after the cash came through before he was on the prowl again. The first public hint that he was back on the scene came with a row over Channel Nine's *Naughtiest Home Videos* show on 3 September 1992. Thirty minutes into the hour-long program, presented by the king of Sydney FM radio Doug Mulray, the show went to a commercial break and didn't return. The next morning the papers revealed that an angry Kerry Packer had pulled the program off air. It was a family network, he told Nine's executives, and he wasn't going to tolerate that sort of 'shit'. The program had certainly offended some people with its bare buttocks and copulating cats, but the decision to dump it had apparently offended even more, if the phone calls to Channel Nine and Sydney's newspapers were any guide.

Ironically, Packer himself had played a key part in hiring Doug Mulray in the first place, for Channel Nine had been trying to persuade Mulray to join the network for years and had wined and dined him constantly in their attempts to sign him up. And Packer had then intervened to coax him on board. To Packer's evident surprise, Mulray had been in no hurry to accept an invitation to talks in early 1992, even when he was told that Packer was off to Argentina and wanted to see him before he left. Mulray was on his farm in the Blue Mountains and indicated that he wasn't driving back into Sydney for anyone, even for Kerry Packer. Soon afterwards, a Packer helicopter was sent down to pick him up. Mulray was then flown to Channel Nine and ferried by car to La Strada, an Italian restaurant in Potts Point. There, Packer's opening line was to ask about the size and location of the farm that Mulray obviously loved so much. Mulray told him that it was in the Blue Mountains and covered 10 hectares.

'I've got *gardens* bigger than that,' Packer replied.

During an evening of reasonably good-natured sparring, Packer and Mulray had neither struck a deal nor got down to details, but six months later Channel Nine had come back with a firm proposal, which was for him to introduce a collection of saucy home videos that Nine had already put together from material sent in by viewers.

For the half-hour that the show lasted before being pulled, it 'rated its tits off' in Mulray's colourful description. Then suddenly it gave way to an American sitcom. Some wondered why it had taken Packer half an hour to decide he disliked it, but this puzzle was soon explained. Five minutes after the program began Packer had rung Channel Nine's managing director David Leckie to tell him to take it off air, but Leckie had bravely refused. All of Channel Nine's top management had seen it, the Australian Broadcasting Tribunal had seen it, the censor had seen it, and everyone had decided that it was okay, Leckie supposedly told his boss. What was more, he was paid to make such decisions and wasn't going to be overruled. The argument lasted for some twenty-five minutes until an angry Packer decided to do it himself and rang Channel Nine's Sydney control room.

The next day, Channel Nine's management in Sydney were visited by Packer and given a talking-to. Leckie predictably tendered his resignation. Packer, less predictably, refused to accept it. As Channel Nine insiders told the story, Kerry's attitude was. 'You put up a good fight, son. You're not going anywhere.'

It was not long before Packer's rekindled interest in business was being felt at Park Street, too, and taking more serious shape. For by September 1992, Packer was sizing up a move on the Westpac bank. With the possible exception of the National Australia Bank, Australia's big four lenders had suffered dreadful losses from their involvement in the late 1980s property boom and from shovelling money at Australia's fast-talking entrepreneurs. But there was little doubt that the once-reliable Westpac had fared worst of all. Its exposure to the commercial property markets in Sydney and Melbourne, where prices had plummeted, was far greater than any of the other big Australian banks, and it also faced huge losses in the United States, where it had financed a series of disastrous leveraged buyouts.

Few, however, were prepared for Westpac's rapid descent into chaos during 1992. In February, the bank's chairman Sir Eric Neal told shareholders that he believed the worst was over. Three months later, he came back to announce a record loss of $1.7 billion for the first six months of the financial year. In what was undoubtedly a competitive field, this was up with the biggest losses in Australian corporate history. But shareholders were again assured that the bad news was all behind them and the future was rosy.

With these words of encouragement, Westpac then set about raising $1200 million from its shareholders to replenish the vaults. But rumours and bad news soon sent the share price into free fall again. By September 1992 it became clear that shareholders had given the bank a huge thumbs down. Although Westpac had got its money, the underwriters had been left with $883 million of the $1200 million worth of new shares on offer. What is more, the shares were worth far less than the $3 per share they had agreed to buy them for. The underwriters were thus facing severe losses and there was a chance that some might not survive the disaster. In the bloodletting that followed, five Westpac directors resigned. Meanwhile, a clear opportunity had arisen for Packer to build a stake in the bank.

As Westpac's share price plunged towards $2.50 and the underwriters' potential losses grew even bigger, Packer and his managing director Al Dunlap did the rounds of the institutions to say they would take the shares off people's hands if they could get two seats on Westpac's board and support for a program of drastic cutbacks. One institution above all had the power to deliver the muscle that Packer needed, and this was the Australian Mutual Provident Society (AMP), which had clashed with Packer over his 1983 privatisation deal. The AMP had built up a 15 per cent stake in Westpac at a cost of $1000 million, on which it was now facing a $350 million loss.

The AMP had been appalled by the announcement of Westpac's $1.7 billion loss in May, one month after it took two seats on Westpac's board, and had been getting steadily angrier ever since. The share price had continued to fall and the rights issue had been a fiasco. Then in November 1992 Westpac was forced to cut its dividend, after being hit with a US tax bill for $106 million that it hadn't foreseen. By comparison, the prospect of Packer and the Chainsaw taking charge might have seemed quite attractive. In any case, the AMP pledged its support.

On 26 November 1992, it was announced that Packer had acquired just under 10 per cent of Westpac's capital for close on $500 million, some of which was in shares and some in options.[8] Less than two weeks later, Packer and Dunlap were invited to join the board.

During the raid on the bank's shares, Packer had been in Argentina again playing polo, but no sooner did he return to Sydney than he was into the fray. Just after 8 a.m. on Packer's fifty-fifth birthday, 17 December 1992, his white BMW with his father's FP 222 number plate cruised into the car park beneath Westpac's headquarters in Sydney's Martin Place, with Dunlap and his driver following hard behind. The two men were not yet official board members because Westpac's continuing financial interest in Channel Ten prevented them by law from being so. But they intended to settle what the official board meeting would decide later that day. Taking the lift to the twenty-eighth floor, they were ushered into a meeting with Westpac's non-executive directors for three hours of discussions on the future of the bank and its management. At the end of these talks, Westpac's chief executive Frank Conroy was called into the room. By the time he walked out again, he had resigned as managing director.

Conroy had only been in the top job at Westpac for a year but had been with the bank for more than thirty, and both Packer and Dunlap wanted him out. In Packer's eyes he was too closely associated with the 'old culture' at the bank to implement the cost cuts that Dunlap was planning. What was more, he had proposed a program of reform that would proceed at only half the pace that Packer and Dunlap believed was necessary. Conroy had told the board in November that Westpac should reduce its assets by $10 billion by selling property and realising its problem loans, and that it should cut staff by 10 to 20 per cent. Dunlap had already drawn up detailed plans to reduce assets by $20 billion, pull Westpac out of North America and Europe, and cut staff by nearer 30 per cent, or more than 10 000 people from Westpac's 39 000-strong workforce.

When Packer and Dunlap attended their first formal board meeting on 14 January 1993, they demanded that Dunlap's plan be adopted. They also demanded that Westpac's new chief executive, who had still not been hired, report to a committee that Dunlap would chair. This would arguably make Dunlap the most important man in the bank, superior to both Conroy's replacement and to the existing board. The suggestion did not go down well with Westpac's conservative directors. Nor did the board relish the prospect of giving Dunlap the opportunity to run the chainsaw through Westpac as he had done at Consolidated Press, Crown Zellerbach and Lily-Tulip. It might well bring remarkable results, but recovery could arguably be achieved with less pain and uproar and less long-term damage to the bank.

Few members of the Westpac board would have been used to the blunt confrontational style that Packer and Dunlap employed. But they were the guardians of the oldest bank in Australia, and they did not lack backbone. Westpac's chairman John Uhrig, in particular, had a reputation for stubbornness and a willingness to fight, and he strongly opposed the Packer–Dunlap plan. As a result, it seems, the dispute turned into a vote of confidence in his leadership. In any case, the Westpac board lined up behind him and endorsed Conroy's original program of reform. Packer then flew into one of his rages, banging the table and swearing profusely. He rose to his feet and stumped out of the room with Al Dunlap in his wake.

The lift from Westpac's twenty-eighth floor takes half a minute to get to the ground if it doesn't stop to pick up or drop off passengers, and more like a minute if it does, but even that was clearly too long for Al Dunlap to hold his silence. According to the *Financial Review* the next day, Westpac staff travelling down with the two men witnessed a furious Dunlap turn to Packer and say, 'I couldn't believe the excessive display of stupidity.'[9] There was obvious ambiguity as to whom Dunlap was criticising, but he cleared this up soon afterwards by telling a friendly banker that he couldn't believe Packer had given up when they were so close to success, adding that his boss was like a little child when he couldn't get his way.

The stock market 'experts' immediately predicted that Packer would get his revenge at Westpac's annual general meeting on 19 January, and pronounced that he had planned it all—such was the belief that he could do no wrong. But his supposed plans to persuade thousands of small shareholders to help him overthrow the existing board did not materialise. Nor did he and Dunlap stand for re-election. Doubtless some of the 5000 shareholders who massed at Darling Harbour for the meeting wished he had, for it was an angry gathering with few happy faces, but neither Packer nor his enforcer showed up. The pundits had said that Packer was too smart to walk away from such a huge investment in a fit of pique. But it appeared that he had done just that.

The row between Packer and Dunlap pushed their relationship to breaking point. Rumours had been filtering out of Park Street since mid 1992 that all was not well between them, and now the press got wind of the story, too. Specifically, the fight was said to be about Dunlap's contract, which promised him 5 per cent of any increase he brought in the value of Consolidated Press. But the clash was also about the collision of two huge egos. It had been possible for Dunlap to remain at Consolidated Press while there was a job to do and Packer was playing polo. Now the slashing and burning had been done and Packer was back in business, the town wasn't big enough for both of them.

In mid February 1993, four weeks after the Westpac fiasco, Dunlap joined the list of executives who had left Consolidated Press since his arrival, taking a settlement of perhaps $25 million to ease his departure.[10] He claimed still to be friends with Packer despite the parting of the ways, but there was no denying they had fallen out. To replace him, Packer hired Brian Powers, the American executive who had acted for the US investment fund Hellman & Friedman in Tourang's bid for Fairfax. By the end of April, there was talk that the emollient Mr Powers had smoothed things over with Westpac and they would soon be walking back into the boardroom together.

But that was not to happen. In early May 1993 came the unexpected announcement that Packer was selling his 10 per cent stake in Westpac to the big Australian property company Lend Lease. Packer had done the rounds of the Australian and overseas banks during February and March and failed to interest any of them in buying his shares, so he had been forced to dig in for the longer term. Then Lend Lease had approached Brian Powers with an offer of $3.50 a share, which had been gratefully accepted.

In the space of six months Packer had picked up a profit of around $100 million on his investment in the bank, which wasn't bad for one of his supposed failures. But he would have done far better if he had been patient enough to hold on. Five years later, the shares were selling for $10.50, or three times what Packer sold them for, which would have turned that profit into $1.3 billion. And had he been brave enough to use his 10 per cent stake to mount a takeover of the bank, he would really have minted money, because by 1998 Westpac was capitalised at almost $20 billion.[11]

In the meantime, Packer had a huge pile of cash to invest once more, and the guessing began afresh as to what he would go for next. He had kicked the tyres at MGM early in 1993 with a view to buying its studios and huge film library, which would fit nicely with Channel Nine, but that had come to naught. Closer to home, and closer to his heart, he had built up a 10 per cent stake in Fairfax newspapers again, even though the cross-media laws still prevented him from gaining control. Those who knew Packer well suggested this might be just a bit of fun, designed to put the wind up the journalists at Fairfax, which was now owned by his mates in the Tourang consortium. It would amuse him, they said, to have his old enemies think he could come storming through the door at any time. But one couldn't rule out the possibility that Packer was serious about a takeover. He would need to sell Channel Nine, of course, unless the cross-media rules were scrapped, and then offer enough to dislodge Conrad Black, whose *Daily Telegraph* had been given permission to increase its holding to 25 per cent. But these were probably small concerns if he set his heart on conquering the old enemy.

The key problem was price. Packer hated to buy things unless they were at bargain basement levels, and Fairfax shares in May 1993 were around $2, or twice as expensive as they had been for members of Tourang, when Packer had complained he was being asked to pay too much. Yet, with a $3000 million fortune and no debts to speak of, why shouldn't he indulge himself? In August 1991, he had complained to the merchant bankers at Baring Brothers Burrows who were auctioning Fairfax that the newspapers were overpriced. They had asked him why he was still interested if he felt that way. 'This is not about money,' Packer had told them, 'it's about ego.'

But before he did anything dramatic with Fairfax, there was something more pressing to be sorted out, for after years of dithering, Australia was finally on the point of moving into pay TV. The role that Packer played in this could be crucial to the future of his business empire.

CHAPTER TWENTY-FIVE

PRETTY POLLIES

*I was brought up in a family that exercised a lot of power
. . . I have never exercised it. And that's a deliberate
intention on my part.*

Kerry Packer, October 1991[1]

Augusta, Georgia, in America's deep South, is one of the most
beautiful golf courses in the world. Planted with dogwood and
azaleas and dotted with lakes and creeks, it is home in April each
year to the US Masters championship. It is also one of the world's
most exclusive clubs. Nigh on impossible to join, Augusta automatically bars from membership all those who have the impertinence to apply. And getting in as a casual visitor is no easier,
particularly when the US Masters is only a month away. The
course is certainly not open to the public, nor even to ministers
in the Australian Government. But if you're a friend of Kerry
Packer it's an entirely different story, as Packer's mate Senator
Graham Richardson discovered in March 1992, when he was
permitted to play a round at the famous course during an official
trip to the USA. Understandably, Richardson was so excited by
this rare privilege that he boasted of his luck to ministerial
colleagues in Canberra. His Labor mates naturally asked him
how he had managed this amazing coup. Easy, Richardson
replied, his good friend Kerry had fixed it for him.[2]

Richardson was visiting the USA in his capacity as the
Minister for Transport and Communications, looking at the
workings of pay television in the United States. And as he trod

the hallowed turf, he was already hatching a scheme for the introduction of pay TV in Australia that would give effective control to Packer and the other commercial television networks. Yet he was clearly not troubled by the fact that he was accepting a favour from Packer in such circumstances. Nor did he appear to be embarrassed by his close friendship with Channel Nine's owner or with its key political lobbyist, Peter Barron, who had been Richardson's best mate for almost twenty years. Like the minister, they were powerful, successful people with a strong interest in the media; it was only right that they should all be on such good terms.

By the early 1990s pay TV had been popular in the United States for almost two decades and had proved to be a huge earner for its operators, so much so that the giant Time Warner group was generating 40 per cent of its cash flow from 'cable'. And the future looked even brighter. In 1992, Time Warner was trialling a new pay-per-view service in New York, in which viewers could pick up the phone, dial a current-release movie to watch at home, and be billed automatically. And before long, this pay-per-view system promised to deliver 'a river of gold', or so said Rupert Murdoch, who was already making multi-billion-dollar bets himself on pay TV in the USA and UK with Fox Television and Sky BSB.

The huge success of pay TV was obviously a threat to free-to-air television networks, which in America were already suffering from the onslaught. By the early 1990s, the big three, ABC, CBS and NBC, had seen their share of the prime-time TV audience fall from 93 per cent to 64 per cent, and they were just beginning to lose significant amounts of advertising revenue. In Australia, if pay TV ever arrived, Kerry Packer feared Channel Nine would suffer a similar fate, losing viewers and advertising dollars and ending up in a bidding war for American movies. Consequently, he and the other commercial networks had done their damnedest to stop pay TV coming to Australia, and had managed to keep it at bay for fifteen years, despite a string of government and parliamentary reports recommending its introduction.

Predictably, Packer had found the Labor government to be a willing ally in this enterprise. Hawke and Keating might have been busy deregulating the financial system and introducing competition to telecommunications, the airlines and industrial relations, but they could see clear political advantage in protecting media monopolies. They believed, no doubt, that rich and powerful proprietors such as Packer would want to show their gratitude by giving Labor their support.

Thus, the original Aussat satellites had not been equipped to handle pay TV, because Labor's first Communications Minister, Michael Duffy, had been persuaded by Rupert Murdoch (then owner of Channel Ten in Sydney and Melbourne) that it was undesirable. And thus in 1986 the government actually passed a law to ban pay TV until September 1990 at the earliest—a ban that was extended for another year because the networks were in financial strife.

In practice, of course, pay TV was bound to be introduced to Australia sooner or later. But it was not until the sale of Aussat in late 1991 that the government found a good reason to give it the green light. By this time the government-owned satellite had lost $800 million and desperately needed more customers if taxpayers were to get any money back. Making it the exclusive carrier of a new pay TV service was an obvious way to do that. So, in October 1991 it was decreed that the ban on pay TV would expire twelve months later. There would be six channels in all, to match each of the satellite's six transponders.[3] The first licence would give exclusive use of four channels, with the other two remaining idle until 1997.

But if the networks had at last lost a battle, they had certainly not lost the war, for they had scored two important victories. They had persuaded the government to ban advertising on pay TV for the first five years. And, better still, they had been given the nod that the new pay TV monopoly would be theirs to control. Significantly, neither of these concessions had been granted to the television networks in the UK and USA, where advertising on pay TV was permitted and where participation by

the networks was expressly forbidden. Clearly, this said something about the lobbying power of Packer and his fellow media
moguls, or about the pliability of Australia's politicians.

But changes within the Labor government soon brought even
more comfort to the networks. In December 1991, with less than
ten months to the scheduled start of pay TV, Paul Keating
deposed Bob Hawke as prime minister, and Senator Graham
Richardson was given the communications portfolio. The Minister for Channel Nine as he was jokingly called in Canberra was
well-known as an opponent of pay TV, for he had argued against
it strongly in Cabinet in 1991. And his first meeting with the
networks in February 1992 made it clear he was just as sympathetic on equally important matters.

Channels Seven, Nine and Ten had become deeply concerned
about a separate Labor government plan to throw open the
airwaves in 1997 to anyone who wanted to start a TV station—
a move that would end their statutory oligopoly and tear up their
licence to print money. Richardson told them bluntly not to
worry, and immediately killed the proposal, even though it had
already been spelt out in the draft of the new Broadcasting
Services Bill.[4] Fifteen years later, the TV networks would still
have their privileged position, because no Australian government
had plucked up the courage to take it away from them.

Richardson's first move on pay TV was also reassuring, for
when he came back from his trip to Augusta, he made it clear
he did not want pay TV's introduction to Australia to harm the
existing networks. And he then made a quite remarkable
proposal. Even though there had been one hundred expressions of interest to his department from would-be operators of
pay TV, Richardson's suggestion was that channels Seven, Nine
and Ten should be guaranteed a stake in the winning consortium
ahead of the other ninety-seven applicants. The audacity of this
almost beggared belief. The government was planning to create
a new statutory monopoly in television, and not only were the
networks to be given a share, they were going to be invited to
control it. Richardson told Labor's backbenchers that Seven,

Nine and Ten wanted 45 per cent of this new pay TV monopoly. And without exactly endorsing this demand, he made it clear he thought they should be *guaranteed* a 'significant share'.

If this was accepted, pay TV would arrive in Australia almost risk free. There would be no prospect of the huge losses that had plagued Murdoch's Sky TV and its rival BSB in the UK before amalgamation, because there would be no competition. Nor would anyone steal the networks' customers or bid crazy prices for American films and Australian sport, because channels Seven, Nine and Ten would be running the show.

As one might have expected, Labor's Caucus told the minister that the idea was a complete non-starter. Backbenchers would neither accept the networks being guaranteed a share nor would they countenance their owning 45 per cent. The arrangement would simply hand pay TV to Packer. Richardson was therefore told in no uncertain terms to think again. Two weeks later, he came back to Caucus rubbing his head, to tell backbenchers he had had a 'blazing row' with Kerry, who had phoned to give him an earbashing. Perhaps as a result of this tirade, his new proposal was almost as Packer friendly as before. Even though the *guarantee* of network involvement had been removed, they would still be allowed to own 20 per cent apiece or 35 per cent in total, which could still deliver control of pay TV to the existing commercial stations, and to Packer in particular, since channels Seven and Ten were both in receivership. The new policy did nothing to increase diversity, competition or choice in programming, all of which were dear to Labor backbenchers. Nor did it guarantee a role for the ABC. So a major row seemed inevitable. But before it flared up, Richardson was forced to resign amid allegations in parliament that he had made improper use of his ministerial position to assist a relative charged with fraud in the Marshall Islands.

In a rare moment of candour, a spokesman for the networks admitted they would be lucky to find the new minister, Bob Collins, so sympathetic. He had the reputation of listening to his bureaucrats and had taken a tough line against the airlines in deregulating air transport. It looked as if he would be tough on television, too, for he soon suggested that the networks' aggregate share of pay TV might be cut to only 25 per cent. But the new minister was not going to be allowed to run the show. As the Senate debated whether to censure Graham Richardson, Prime Minister Paul Keating met representatives of the networks. One week later, he went on Channel Nine's *Sunday* program and announced the government's pay TV policy was to be turned on its head.

Even Bob Collins was taken by surprise. Or especially Bob Collins. For Keating had not told his ministerial colleagues what he planned to do and had certainly not cleared the proposals with Cabinet. Nor, it seemed, had he thought them through in detail. Yet he was now proposing that two years of law making be scrapped. It was the sort of vaudeville trick he loved, the old rabbit-out-of-the-hat routine for which he was famous. He had been unhappy, he said, about tying pay TV to one technology when there were so many more exciting ones on the horizon. And he had been unhappy that they were planning to limit the number of players. The answer, said Keating, was to make pay TV truly competitive by opening up the technology to all comers and relaxing the ownership rules so everyone would be allowed to play.

It sounded both new and attractive, but in fact it was already government policy to allow digital signals and fibre optics for pay TV when they were available—which was likely to be about five years down the track.[5] So that wasn't new. And as for the promise of allowing everyone to play, this meant nothing if there were no other technologies on offer. Keating's policy would still allow the networks to have the first four channels on the Optus satellite, which in practice would still be a monopoly. And behind all his fine words, he was pushing for exactly the proposal that Richardson had tried to run through Caucus, which was to allow channels Seven, Nine and Ten 45 per cent of the satellite-delivered pay TV service. As before, there was no doubt who would be the main beneficiary. According to the television industry's most respected analyst, Peter Cox, Keating's proposal 'could effectively deliver control of the pay TV service to Packer'.

Keating's whim was not yet official policy, even though he had announced it on Channel Nine. It still needed the backing of Cabinet and Caucus, and Labor's backbenchers were not going to budge. Forty-eight hours of haggling followed in an attempt to find agreement, with Labor's backbenchers pushing for greater diversity and Labor ministers standing up for their powerful media mates. It was an extraordinary way for laws to be made, especially in an area so vulnerable to influential lobbyists. Keating's behaviour was also extraordinary; he characterised his opponents as 'basketweavers' and repeatedly abused them.

The compromises reached in these marathon negotiating sessions are hardly worth reporting, for they were just another twist and turn on the road to the final outcome, but Keating's hope that the networks could hang on to 45 per cent was rejected by Chris Schacht, John Langmore and the two other backbenchers negotiating on behalf of Caucus. Instead, they agreed to support another Keating proposal, which was to ban the networks from the first four pay TV channels while letting them bid without restrictions for the remaining two channels a year later. Politically this was an inspired solution. It satisfied all who thought Packer had too much power and believed that the media should be opened up to competition. And it knocked out any charge that Keating was delivering pay TV to the networks. Practically, meanwhile, there was a view that it might still do exactly that.

In the *Financial Review* two days later Tom Burton declared the Keating plan to be Packer's worst nightmare because there would now be a powerful pay TV operator with a year's start. But others weren't so sure. The first operator would have to run a family entertainment channel and news on two of its four channels, which would be a financial burden, while Packer would be able to run far more profitable sport and movies if he secured the second or third licence. Meanwhile, the first operator

510

would bear the worst of the start-up costs in the marketing of satellite dishes, while the second and third operators would be able to beam their signals into dishes that had already been erected. Several analysts predicted that it would be a brave outfit that dared take Packer on and a lucky one that could survive the decision. In their view there would be no pay TV unless it was Packer's.

But none of that really mattered, for the pay TV rules would change several more times before the law was made—and a few more times after that. Of greater importance was what the prime minister claimed about the government's aims. It was all classic Keating stuff: he was picking no winners, favouring no technologies and exposing the big boys to the full blast of competition. 'I think everybody is tired of the old faded and jaded players,' he told ABC Radio. Caucus wanted new entrants in the media, said Keating, and he had ensured that they'd be able to get them. From now on, anyone would be allowed to broadcast a pay TV service by any method they chose to use, provided they could interest the public in buying it. 'There's no particular reason why anyone who wants to be in the pay TV business shouldn't be in it,' said Keating.[6] But the question was: did he really mean it?

It took five months of argument in parliamentary committees and on the floor of the Senate before the legislation on pay TV finally emerged in November 1992. And by then it differed in three important respects. The first was that the ABC was to be guaranteed a role in the new satellite service, with two channels reserved for its use. The second was that there would be ten channels on offer rather than the original six, and the networks would be able to bid for four without restrictions. And the third was that pay TV on the satellite would be digital rather than analog. The adoption of a digital standard promised better pictures and far more choice of channels, but it also delayed the arrival of pay TV for at least another 18 months, since digitally compressed signals were not yet available. This would delay satellite-delivered pay TV until 1994 or 1995 or even later, which suited the commercial networks down to the ground, or so they believed.

Unfortunately for them, however, it suited Channel Ten's former boss Steve Cosser even better. Still in his thirties, Cosser was one of the minnows of the Australian media but he was smart, persuasive and reasonably brave. At the age of twenty-two he had been the youngest journalist ever to present ABC Radio's *AM* program; four years later he had anchored Rupert Murdoch's short-lived *Reporters* program at Channel Ten, which had left him with a $200 000 payoff when the program folded. Cosser had then formed his own company, Broadcom, which was soon packaging news for Qantas flights and making *Business Sunday* for Channel Nine. In late 1989, Broadcom had taken over management and program production for the ailing Channel Ten network and Cosser had been installed as Ten's chief executive. By late 1990 he was out again, having been dumped by the banks when they called in the receivers.

Cosser had hit upon pay TV almost by accident, in that he had started what he thought would be a small business and suddenly found it could be turned into a big one. Early in 1992 he had teamed up with a former ABC and Telecom engineer to set up a private encrypted microwave TV service for the Melbourne fire service, which was keen to transmit pictures to local fire stations for training purposes. The system was a success, producing higher-quality pictures than microwave technology had been reputed to deliver, so Cosser decided to broaden out. Soon afterwards, his Newsvision was using microwave television signals to transmit news into businesses and hotels, and Cosser was thinking of expanding further.

In Sydney and Melbourne there were a total of thirty-six microwave transmitting frequencies for which a licence could be bought from the Department of Communications. Almost all were unused because microwave or MDS technology had failed in past attempts during the 1980s to make it work. In mid 1992 a Cosser company called Australis Media started buying up these licences, with the aim of beaming specialised services into Melbourne's numerous ethnic communities. This 'narrowcasting', as it was called, was always going to be allowed under the

Broadcasting Services Bill in which the framework of the new pay TV system was being laid down.

Then in June 1992 came Keating's dramatic intervention, opening up pay TV to any technology that people cared to use and scrapping the satellite's five-year or seven-year monopoly. By November, this concept of 'technological neutrality' was written into the new Broadcasting Services Act. Suddenly the way was clear for Cosser to use microwave to launch a pay TV service in Australia's two biggest cities. The man who had planned to beam kung fu movies into the gambling dens of Melbourne's China-town now found himself with a virtual monopoly of a system that could deliver pay TV to four or five million people. What was more, because the satellite's digital service would not be running before 1995, he would be able to do it two or three years ahead of his rivals and at only a quarter of the cost. European experience with pay TV suggested that if you halved the price of the service, you picked up four times as many viewers.[7] If that held true in Australia, it would be virtually impossible for the satellite to compete.

By late 1992, Cosser had acquired twelve licences in Sydney and twelve in Melbourne, with the potential to deliver a channel of pay TV on each of them—or a twelve-channel service to each city. With only six licences remaining in each of the two capitals, it would be hard for anyone to use microwave to take him on, especially if he bought a couple more channels and closed them off. All he needed in order to start broadcast-ing was a licence from the Australian Broadcasting Authority, which, under the new Broadcasting Services Act, was supposed to be a formality.

Microwave had actually been recommended by the House of Representatives committee in Australia in 1989 as the best delivery system for pay TV, in conjunction with optic fibre. And it was already used widely in the USA. Yet for some strange reason, Cosser's rivals had not taken it seriously. Packer's engi-neers were convinced the technology was a failure and Packer himself appeared to believe that microwave was ruled out by the

Broadcasting Services Act. The ABC also believed that microwave was lousy technology and that it was ruled out for broadcast. Their common mistake seems to have persisted until 6 December 1992, when Bob Collins announced on Channel Ten's *Meet the Press* that the six remaining microwave licences in Sydney and Melbourne would be put up for auction. Each of these licences, Collins made clear, would permit the purchaser to run a pay TV channel.

Soon afterwards, Packer's chief engineer at Channel Nine, Bruce Robertson, was despatched to the USA to re-examine microwave technology; he came back impressed. Then on 7 January, Collins confirmed that the MDS licence auction would go ahead three weeks later. It was now as plain as could be that microwave was good enough for Steve Cosser to offer a pay TV service by mid 1993 to some 70 per cent of Melbourne and Sydney viewers. It was also quite obvious that he would soon have the entire pay TV market in these cities to himself unless something was done.

A procession of pay TV investors now began knocking on Cosser's door to see whether they could do a deal. The big American players such as the Los Angeles Times Mirror group and Time Warner were among them, as were the big cable operators ICI and Continental Cable, Irish Independent's Tony O'Reilly, the New Zealand broadcasters TVNZ, and the ABC, all of whom wanted a share of the action.

But Packer's approach was quite different, for he wanted the whole box and dice. On Wednesday, 27 January, just two days before the auction was due to take place, Packer's executive Lynton Taylor offered Cosser $13 million for his entire pay TV operation and his twenty-four MDS licences.[8] Cosser was given only a matter of hours to make up his mind and to choose, as he described it, 'to get out of the road or get crushed'. Cosser was already negotiating a deal with Times Mirror and O'Reilly to pump in $65 million to the company and yet leave him still owning 44 per cent of it—a far better offer than that made by Packer. He sent back that the answer was 'no'.

All week, rumours had been growing that the auction of MDS licences, which was to take place on Friday, 29 January, would be called off. On Tuesday, 26 January, the day before Packer's 'take it or leave it' offer, the *Financial Review* reported that a meeting had taken place in Los Angeles between Australian TV networks and would-be American pay TV operators to discuss how Cosser could be stopped. Another earlier meeting in Sydney, involving Channel Nine, Channel Seven and someone from Murdoch's News Ltd, had also discussed pay TV strategy in relation to the coming auction. As a consequence Cosser was getting worried. On the day the *Financial Review* article was published he sought and received assurances from Bob Collins's office that nothing had changed; journalists in the press gallery were given similar assurances on both Tuesday and Wednesday. All were told that the law was the law and everything was fine. One hundred and fifty bids had been put in for the microwave licence auction and there would be a lot of angry bidders if it were stopped.

On Thursday, 28 January at 4 p.m., Steve Cosser received a phone call from the head of the new Australian Broadcasting Authority, Brian Johns, to reinforce the message that all was okay. Two hours later the minister himself, Bob Collins, rang to tell Cosser the opposite: the government had decided to cancel the next day's auction and ban microwave delivery of pay TV until after the satellite was ready to go. Moments later, even though the law gave him no power to do so, the minister told the Australian Broadcasting Authority not to give Cosser a licence until the satellite was in a position to operate.[9] This was happening less than twenty-four hours after Kerry Packer had warned Cosser he would be wise to sell him his pay TV business.

Fifteen months earlier, Packer had complained to the parliamentary Print Media Inquiry that it was outrageous for the Australian Government to tighten the cross-media rules at 'one minute to midnight' to prevent him getting his hands on Fairfax. Strangely enough, he now had nothing to say about an even more blatant example of the goalposts being shifted after the ball had been kicked. But on this occasion, he was a major beneficiary of the government's action.

As the recently deposed prime minister, Bob Hawke, pointed out in his column in the *Sun-Herald* a week later, it was interesting that Bob Collins described the backflip as a 'Government' action, since as Hawke put it, 'a decision of principle by the Parliament, Cabinet and Caucus was overturned by the minister and Prime Minister without reference to Cabinet'.[10] According to Hawke, it was Paul Keating who had taken the lead. Public servants and advisers had trekked backwards and forwards to the prime minister's office all week at Keating's command to explain what had gone wrong. They had failed to persuade an angry Keating that the government should not go back on a policy that Cabinet, Caucus and parliament had already made law.

Cosser complained first to the newspapers, then to the Trade Practices Commission, and finally to the Federal Court, where he started legal action in early February 1993 to get Collins's direction to the ABA declared unlawful. Meanwhile, he set about using some of his money to attack the government in a series of full-page advertisements in the Australian press. Bob Collins had said that MDS was a hopeless technology and that only one country in the world was using it, which was Ireland. The Cosser ads pointed out that Collins had omitted to mention the United States of America and some thirty-nine other countries that were already using MDS in addition to another thirty countries on the point of introducing it.[11]

One of Collins's and Keating's professed reasons for dumping MDS was that it was inferior technology. But Graham Richardson put a different gloss on the government's decision a few days later on Channel Ten's current affairs program *Hinch*.[12] Richardson's explanation was that the government hadn't taken microwave seriously in the first place because it had received a lot of advice that 'the microwave proposals weren't bankable ... that you wouldn't get enough money behind them to get them off the ground because they'd only be able to be beamed into a few homes'. Then the policymakers had realised they were wrong, said Richardson: 'It became obvious that most of Melbourne and probably 70 per cent of Sydney could be serviced by it and therefore you'd have microwave into all these homes.' Which presumably meant that it was going to be an extremely popular service.

Cosser reproduced Richardson's explanation in the ads and then added a question of his own: 'Why would a well-funded MDS Pay TV service with wide coverage in Sydney and Melbourne be a problem for the Keating Government?'[13] Why, indeed, especially since Keating's rationale for his first intervention in June 1992 had been to get rid of the 'old faded players' and to put new faces into the game? Cosser didn't know the answer to his question, but suggested that people 'ask the "mates" '.

Even more pungent was the Cosser ad that targeted the prime minister himself.[14] Headed 'FAMOUS LAST WORDS' in mocking anticipation of the Keating government's expected defeat at the imminent federal election, it recalled some of the glib phrases that had tripped off the prime ministerial tongue in mid 1992 when he had turned the pay TV policy upside down. Keating had said then, among other things:

> I have been quite uncomfortable about the fact that we are about to exclusively nominate satellite television as the only vehicle for pay TV, particularly when other technologies are available, like cable, fibre optic and MDS.[15]

> The Government has decided to allow, from the out-set, the widest-possible range of services, using a variety of technologies, including satellite, cable and microwave.[16]

> While the beneficiaries of regulation always say regulation is wise, that would have closed off Australia to the higher technology of fibre optics and MDS in favour of plastic dishes and satellites for a decade. I was never prepared as prime minister to shut that technology off.[17]

Most of all, the pro-competition prime minister had assured everyone: 'There's no particular reason why anyone who wants to be in the pay TV business shouldn't be in it.'

So what had changed in the meantime? Why was the Keating government, in Cosser's words, 'trying to deny Australians immediate, affordable pay TV, destroy 4000 new jobs and reject $200 million worth of investment'? Once again Cosser affected not to know the answer, but suggested that Keating should tell Australians 'the real reasons for killing off MDS pay TV and who the decision benefits', adding for good measure, 'We want a government for all Australians, not a government for mates.'

It was certainly hard for Keating and Collins to argue that they hadn't known about microwave or MDS because both had talked about it in glowing terms since the middle of 1992. And Collins had also appeared to be a great supporter. On the day that the Broadcasting Services Bill had given pay TV the go-ahead, Collins had supposedly rung Cosser in his hotel room at 3 a.m. to say, 'Fantastic, now go and start your service.' He had even suggested he might become a subscriber. But, as Bob Hawke had claimed, it was not Collins who had thrown a spanner in the works. Documents put into evidence in Cosser's Federal Court challenge on 21 April 1993 made it clear that it was the prime minister who had brought things to a halt.

As part of his legal action, Cosser had asked the Department of Trade and Communications (DOTAC), the Department of the Prime Minister, Bob Collins and Paul Keating to surrender diaries, telephone notes, papers and documents relating to the sudden decision to stop MDS from going ahead. In particular, he had sought correspondence and records of meetings between Keating, Collins and Senator Richardson and lobbyists from a number of organisations including the ABC, the Seven Network, the Ten Network, Rupert Murdoch's News Corporation, Optus Communications, the Nine Network and Kerry Packer's lobbyist Peter Barron. These papers now suggested it was the prime minister who had made a reluctant DOTAC go back on the official policy.

Keating's first move had come just four days before the auction with a telephone call from his chief minder Don Russell to the acting head of DOTAC, Roger Beale, in which Russell said he was concerned about 'stories circulating' that MDS would be widely used for pay TV. Russell asked for an urgent paper to be prepared for Keating, setting out the position on MDS licences and stating whether the Australian Broadcasting Authority *had* to issue pay TV licences to MDS licence holders. Two days later, with only forty-eight hours until tenders closed, the prime minister himself phoned Beale to tell him he believed Cabinet had been 'notoriously misled' on the extent to which MDS might be used for pay TV and to indicate his concern 'that Mr Cosser had acquired a large number of MDS licences'. This was an extremely unusual step for Keating to take—to phone the head of a department himself. He demanded to know what attitude DOTAC was taking on MDS in the paper he had asked for. Beale told the prime minister that legislation would be necessary 'to stop the use of MDS for pay TV'. Beale also said that the department would be making a public statement to say that 'current tenders (for the auction) would proceed to finality and that there would be no legislative changes'.

On the following day, Thursday, 28 January, DOTAC was still sticking to its advice that the policy should not be changed. But at 2 p.m. Roger Beale was phoned by Bob Collins's chief of staff Jack Lake. According to Beale's file note, Lake had just had 'a long session with Don Russell in the Prime Minister's office', as a result of which, 'It had been decided and approved by the Prime Minister that the course of action should be to discontinue the MDS tender process.'

Who or what had persuaded the prime minister to intervene to handicap microwave one could only guess, but most people would have put Packer and his lobbyists high on the list.[18] It was practically inconceivable that Kerry Packer, Peter Barron or Lynton Taylor had not argued that Cosser must be stopped; it was just as hard to believe on past performance that Keating would have been unwilling to listen. Press commentators certainly had no doubt that the prime minister had buckled under intense pressure from the industry. It was 'amazing', 'astonishing' or 'quite breathtaking', depending on which newspaper one chose to read. It made Australia look like a 'banana republic' and 'called into question the integrity of the entire government', according to Fred Brenchley in the *Sydney Morning Herald*.[19] It had made Australia 'the laughing stock of the world', said Helen Meredith in the *Australian*.[20] Tom Burton in the *Financial Review* went even further. It was 'a shameful, cowardly decision', he commented, showing 'a weak and desperate government, prostituting its most fundamental policy principles to win favour with the media mates it thinks it needs somehow to cling on to power ... And they used to call Bob Hawke spineless.'[21]

There was perhaps only one thing wrong with this analysis. It was hard to discern any principles that the Labor government had ever had about media policy, except to punish its enemies and reward its powerful friends. This, however, was more blatant and more disgraceful than ever.

Unlike Bob Hawke, Prime Minister Paul Keating was not close to Packer, but he had been friends with Kerry's chief political lobbyist Peter Barron for many years. He had even considered hiring him in early 1992—presumably to run his office—before rejecting the idea on the grounds that it was unwise to have someone at The Lodge who could be seen as Packer's man. And shortly after the pay TV policy was changed he did employ Barron's talents. In fact, when Australia went to the polls in March 1993, six weeks after the pay TV decision, Barron played a leading role in getting Keating re-elected.

On Ash Wednesday, 24 February 1993, according to the *Financial Review*, 'Labor's private polls were showing that the Government faced electoral incineration.'[22] That evening, Paul Keating's advisers met at the prime minister's Sydney residence, Kirribilli House, to search for a strategy that could pull them out of the fire. Three of Keating's personal staff were there, including Don Russell. So were 'Labor's federal secretary Bob Hogg, running his last election campaign, Hogg's predecessor Senator Bob

McMullan, and the rising star of campaign management, NSW secretary John Della Bosca'. Also present was Packer's political lobbyist Peter Barron, whose experience as a veteran of campaigns that put Bob Hawke and Neville Wran in power was clearly of great value.

'Throughout the campaign,' according to the *Financial Review*, 'Barron served as one of Keating's secret sounding boards, passing on tips, coaching him before the first televised debate and keeping in touch with other campaign staff like McMullan.' When Keating opened his campaign at Canberra's National Press Club, both Peter Barron and Kerry Packer watched it on television. After the live broadcast, Packer phoned his adviser, who agreed it had been an excellent performance. Almost immediately afterwards, Paul Keating phoned Barron to ask him what he thought. Barron congratulated the prime minister on his choice of tie and his handling of the occasion, which had been terrific.

Less than two weeks earlier, the prime minister had intervened (to Packer's benefit) to halt the auction of MDS licences and to stop Cosser establishing his cheap pay TV service.

CHAPTER TWENTY-SIX

SECRETS OF THE RICH
AND FAMOUS

*There is more to this story, but I feel loyal to others. So I
will go to my grave with the secrets of the rich and famous
of Good Ole Aussie.*

Carol Lopes

Kerry's father Sir Frank Packer was notorious for his womanising
and whoring, even though his escapades never made it into the
Telegraph. A valued customer of Sydney's infamous brothel queen
Tilly Devine, the tycoon was once forced to climb over the
galvanised roofs of East Sydney to escape a police raid, pulling his
pants up as he went. And he brought up his sons Kerry and
Clyde in the same tradition, taking the elder boy to a Paris
bordello for his twenty-first birthday.

'I am fond of girls and horses,' was Sir Frank's memorable
opening line to the British newspaper magnate Cecil King. And
he devoted much time and money to his favourite pursuits. A
man of many mistresses, he kept a permanent suite at the
Australia Hotel in Sydney for entertaining, and various apartments around town for his extramarital liaisons. The most
notorious of these, which threatened to break up his marriage to
Gretel, was with the Irish fashion designer Sybil Connolly, but
the majority of his flings were with women on the *Telegraph* or
Women's Weekly, where he had a long-running tryst with a senior
writer, Maisie McMahon. Some women clearly found the old
man's charm and power attractive. And no doubt there were
benefits to be had from sleeping with the boss. But he could be

both patronising and predatory. A tremendous flirt, he had a habit of addressing young female journalists as 'Girly' and telling them how pretty they looked. And his managers followed this example, albeit in cruder fashion. Several women who worked on the *Telegraph* in the 1960s and 1970s say they were molested late at night down on the 'stone' (where the type was set), and report there was 'pressure to do it with the bosses' if one wanted to get on.

With Sir Frank in charge, Consolidated Press was a boys' club where women were considered to be fair game. And when Kerry took over the empire in 1974, nothing changed. As one well-known journalist who worked there in the 1980s characterises it, 'It was a nasty macho outfit. They all fucked prostitutes and they all fucked the girls in the office.' Nor was Channel Nine much different. The network's former head of sport, David Hill, tells a story of how he once hired the Australian actress Kate Fitzpatrick as a commentator for World Series Cricket. By all accounts, she was not a great success. At the end of the day's play the phone rang in the commentary box and Hill picked it up. 'Did you fuck her, Hilly?' the voice inquired. 'No, Kerry, I didn't,' Hill replied. 'Well, son,' said Packer, 'you missed out both ways, didn't you?'

As Kerry grew older and his testosterone levels waned, the rutting became less rampant and the boss ceased exercising his *droit du seigneur*. By the 1990s, according to one top executive, 'He no longer stomped through the magazine floor eyeing off all his female staff like a bull in a paddock.'

But Kerry's patronising attitude to women endured. Like his father before him, he would compliment his female editors and senior executives on their choice of outfit, or tell them, 'God, your hair looks lovely today.' The upside was that he always treated them with great courtesy and never subjected them to the sort of bullying that his male rivals received. The downside was that no woman was likely to make it to the top, because none was considered to be good enough—Ita Buttrose being one possible exception. As his long-serving helicopter pilot and drinking buddy Nick Ross admitted, 'Kerry liked the ladies . . . he was always very much a gentleman with [them] . . . He didn't consider most women to be on the same level as a man . . . just slightly underneath.'

Like his father, Kerry was notorious for his love of prostitutes, although no one in the Australian media dared publicise this fact. As one of his most senior journalists described it in the early 1990s, 'Kerry's idea of a night on the town is to go: brothel, casino, brothel,' dragging his companions along behind him. There were regular (and possibly unfounded) rumours that he owned a share in Sydney's most famous establishment, A Touch of Class. On one occasion he certainly hired it for the night, telling the female executive who arranged it for him that a bunch of polo players wanted to have fun with 'some good clean girls'. The young men trashed the place, causing considerable damage, but Packer was happy to pay.

In the mid 1990s, Kerry's exploits with hookers did make it into the newspapers when Hollywood's most famous madam, Heidi Fleiss, went on trial for money laundering. One of Ms Fleiss's high-class call girls, who had a degree in business administration, told a Los Angeles court that she and eight other prostitutes were sent to Las Vegas in 1992 to meet an Australian businessman identified as Kerry Packer. At least three of these women spent the week playing games with the Big Fella at Caesar's Palace on a retainer of US$10 000 a week.

Back home, there were occasional stories of Kerry interrupting important business negotiations to demand that someone find him a girl. And one foreign TV executive will never forget his dinner with the big Australian in Sydney in the early 1990s. As the third member of their party, a music promoter, waxed lyrical about something, a clearly bored Kerry turned to the TV executive and inquired, 'Hey son, do you like fucking?'

'Yes, Kerry, I do,' the young man replied. 'I fuck my wife.'

'Thank God you said that,' the music maestro gushed later. 'Any excuse and he would have had you off whoring all night.'

When it came to extramarital affairs, Kerry was more than a match for his famous father, with a steady stream of mistresses over the years and several private apartments in Sydney in which

Kerry and Ros Packer in England in 1990.

At the Print Media Inquiry in November 1991, Kerry Packer pummelled Australia's politicians. 'Make him PM', said the radio talkback shows the next day.

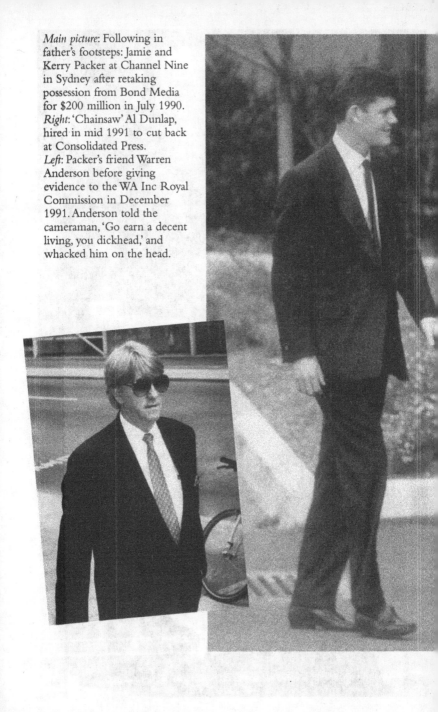

Main picture: Following in father's footsteps: Jamie and Kerry Packer at Channel Nine in Sydney after retaking possession from Bond Media for $200 million in July 1990.
Right: 'Chainsaw' Al Dunlap, hired in mid 1991 to cut back at Consolidated Press.
Left: Packer's friend Warren Anderson before giving evidence to the WA Inc Royal Commission in December 1991. Anderson told the cameraman, 'Go earn a decent living, you dickhead,' and whacked him on the head.

→ WARNING: ALTERATION, ADDITION OR MUTILATION OF ENTRIES IS PROHIBITED. ANY UNOFFICIAL CHANGE WILL RENDER THIS PASSPORT INVALID.

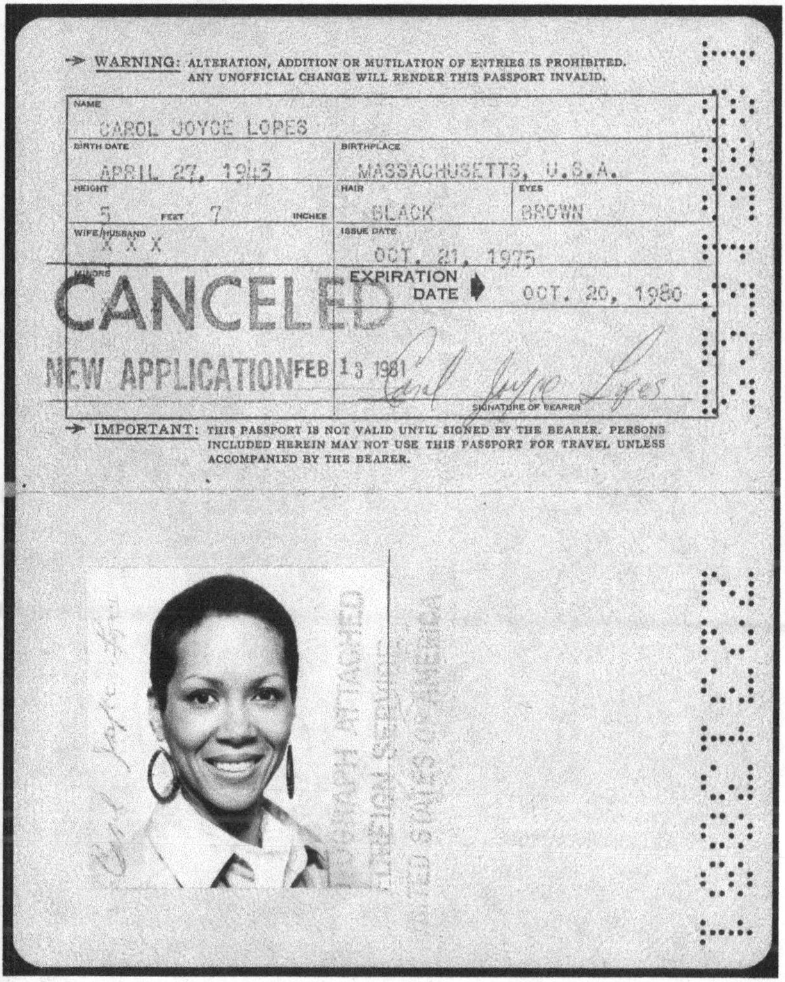

NAME
CAROL JOYCE LOPES

BIRTH DATE
APRIL 27, 1943

BIRTHPLACE
MASSACHUSETTS, U.S.A.

HEIGHT
5 FEET 7 INCHES

HAIR
BLACK

EYES
BROWN

WIFE/HUSBAND
X X X

ISSUE DATE
OCT. 21, 1975

MINORS

EXPIRATION DATE ▶ OCT. 20, 1980

CANCELED

NEW APPLICATION FEB 13 1981

Carol Joyce Lopes

SIGNATURE OF BEARER

→ IMPORTANT: THIS PASSPORT IS NOT VALID UNTIL SIGNED BY THE BEARER. PERSONS INCLUDED HEREIN MAY NOT USE THIS PASSPORT FOR TRAVEL UNLESS ACCOMPANIED BY THE BEARER.

Carol Lopes was a gorgeous black American model who came to Australia in the 1970s. She became Kerry Packer's mistress and then his madam, runing a private bordello for him at Palm Beach in the 1980s. Carol committed suicide in 1991, leaving a note to say she would go to her grave 'with the secrets of the rich and famous of Good Ole Aussie'.

Jamie Packer, $3000 million man. The next generation pondering the future.

he could entertain them. In the late 1970s, he bought three waterfront units in the Toft Monks building at Elizabeth Bay, and knocked two of them into one big home-from-home, which he kept permanently staffed with a cook and a butler. He also bought or rented houses in the eastern suburbs and Palm Beach for women with whom he had more serious, long-term relationships, of which there were at least four over the years. Most of these women were in love with him, wanted to marry him, and apparently expected it to happen. But there was little chance of Kerry divorcing Ros, who stayed at home to bring up the children and manage the households, because it would involve giving up hundreds of millions of dollars. As one of his executives tartly observed, 'Gangsters never leave their wives.' Nor would he have thought there was any need for him to do so, because he carried on these affairs much as he wished. How much Ros knew of them and how she put up with it, God only knows, but she would assure her confidantes from time to time, 'There will only ever be one Mrs Packer.' On top of this, how she put up with his verbal abuse was also a mystery. Some of Kerry's male friends found his habit of shouting at her in front of guests extremely hard to stomach. Perhaps she loved him, in spite of everything. No doubt she was also determined to keep the family together. But whatever her private thoughts, it must have been enormously hard for her, and she bore it with a dignity that impressed her friends.

With the notable exception of Julie Trethowan, who ran the Hyde Park Club in the basement of Packer's Park Street offices from 1983 and was his mistress for almost twenty years until he died, Kerry always tired of these consorts after a time. They became too demanding, too serious, too old or too much like a wife. Or something younger and more attractive came along. But even after dispensing with their services he usually made sure they were taken care of, with a house to live in and an allowance if they needed it. Conceivably, this was out of the kindness of his heart. But it also made sense. It would not have been wise for him to cut his ex-lovers adrift in a small town like Sydney, given the stories they could tell and the distress that a couple of them clearly felt on their dismissal.

Some Kerry even found jobs for, parking them in his magazines (if they weren't already working there) or at Channel Nine, as he did with Kerri Eichhorn, who was his mistress in the early 1980s. And in her case, there was no real pretence about what she was or why he was doing it. According to one trusted executive, Kerry rang out of the blue to 'ask for a favour'. He explained that he had a mistress, that it had been over for many years, but that he had just had another fling with her. She wanted more than money, he said—she needed a job. Could she be taken on in the drama department if he footed the bill? Naturally, the answer was, 'Yes, Mr Packer.' What else could one say to the boss? So Ms Eichhorn was given a job swinging a boom in the studio. Her fellow workers were puzzled as to why she was there and where she had come from. She was very beautiful for a start, had been a well-known TV actress and lacked any experience as a sound-catcher. But the riddle was soon solved. On her first day on the floor, a runner came down to announce that Kerry Packer wanted her on the phone immediately. Not surprisingly, she did not last long in the job. It was just too hard for everyone.

Kerri Eichhorn, who had been voted Miss New South Wales in 1969, told friends that Packer was the love of her life and he was going to divorce Ros and marry her. But it all ended in acrimony. He went off to England, promising to make a decision, and came back to find she had cut her long hair into a bob. According to one close friend's version of events, he walked into the room, took one look at her and said, 'What the fuck have you done with your hair?' then walked straight out again. And that was the end of that. Eichhorn was shocked and upset by Packer's decision to end the affair. Years later, at the end of the 1980s, she was still phoning Kerry's Park Street office and demanding to speak with him. Once or twice, she even turned up there, causing some commotion for the PAs who had to deal with her.

But such ripples were minor compared to the tsunami of trouble that could have been created by another of Packer's long-term mistresses, a strikingly beautiful black fashion model called Carol Lopes. She was Kerry's lover in the late 1970s and early 1980s and procured girls for him for many years after that. In February 1991, after several unsuccessful attempts, Carol took her own life in a rented house in Palm Beach (paid for by Packer), leaving an extremely revealing suicide note addressed to Kerry.

In the mid 1970s, the American-born Ms Lopes had been a darling of the Sydney social scene. Gregarious, glamorous, gorgeous and effervescent, she was a star attraction at fashionable eastern suburbs parties and a regular in the city's gossip columns, which described her as exotic or unique. She was also a wild girl. 'She had a great body which she delighted in showing off,' says one of her oldest and closest friends, who tells the story of her approaching a huge bikie in a Kings Cross bar and suggesting they swap T-shirts. 'She just went up to him and ripped her top off, exposing these fantastic breasts.'

Carol was 'so up front, so special, so out there', according to this friend, that it was no surprise she showed up on Kerry Packer's radar. They met at a party in the late 1970s after she was summoned upstairs for an audience. And thus began an affair that lasted for three or four years, followed by a friendship and professional relationship that endured for almost a decade. It was not hard to see what the tycoon liked about her. She was warm and lovely as well as beautiful. And, for her part, Carol clearly loved him. She had been abused as a child and brought up by foster parents, and she saw Kerry as her guardian and surrogate father. Which is why his ultimate rejection hit her so hard.

Carol was discreet about her connection to Packer, almost to the point of keeping it secret. And on the occasions that she did talk about him to her closest friends, she skimped on the details. She was his SONAP, she said, which stood for 'Sex Only, No Appearances in Public'. To ensure that no one came round when he was visiting, she asked friends to phone ahead and check she was there. If Packer was on the horizon, she would leave a message on her answerphone saying, 'I'm away' or, 'I'm going away in ten minutes. I'll be back soon.' Shortly afterwards, there would be another to say, 'I'm back.'

Thanks to Packer's money, Carol lived in a series of amazing oversize apartments with the best views in Sydney. The first of these, in Fairfax Road, Bellevue Hill, just down the road from Kerry's family home, was absolutely stunning. Coming up the stairs into the living room, guests were confronted by an amazing vista of Sydney Harbour, plus a huge terrace, a vast living area and 'a kitchen you could rollerskate in'. Later apartments in Rose Bay and Billyard Avenue, Elizabeth Bay, were on a par, presumably because Kerry liked to spend time there, but also because Carol had expensive tastes and was hard to say 'no' to.

With dazzling real estate like this and a personality to match, Carol became a magnet for visiting celebrities, who congregated in her apartments on their visits to Sydney. One day it was Bob Dylan sitting on the floor in front of her fire. On other occasions it was Tina Turner, Elvis Costello, Ian Dury or Stevie Wonder. She introduced herself to the blind black singer by taking his hand and telling him, 'If you could see me, you would know how beautiful and sexy I am.' He replied that he had heard as much already.

Carol first came to public attention in 1978, when she was taken on by Packer's Channel Nine to host a late-night movie program with Issy Dye. 'She would lie on a couch in skimpy disco gear and deliver ribald preambles to B-grade movies,' one friend recalls. And she soon attracted a cult following, because she was spectacularly bad. She froze, she stumbled, she looked awkward, she was 'easily the worst thing on Australian TV'. No one could figure out how she had got the job, until people put two and two together and realised she must be having an affair with someone at Channel Nine. Like the boss.

Carol's TV career ended abruptly in the early 1980s when she was charged with possession of marijuana, after police raided her Bellevue Hill apartment. Shortly afterwards, Packer found her a new job as promotions director of *Australian Playboy*, which had been launched a few years earlier by ACP. In 1983, she hosted the Playmate of the Year awards at Sydney's Regent Hotel and appeared in a nude spread in the magazine, at the age of forty. Rather less glamorously, she organised corporate lunches at which scantily clad Playmates served drinks and sandwiches to hungry businessmen.

By this time, Carol was also organising girls for Kerry Packer and his mates to have sex with, both in Australia and overseas. According to another of her close friends, who lived with her in the mid 1980s, she hand-picked girls for Kerry's trips to London, New York and Las Vegas. 'She would know who the women were for and know the men's taste' and select them accordingly, he says. Big dollars were involved, especially for a month in London, and Carol ensured the girls were well looked after. 'She would take them shopping for clothes and jewellery. She would dress them. She would organise hairdressers, manicures, pedicures, and there would be a masseuse there as well.'

By no means all the women were hookers. A couple of Carol's friends say she would pick out strangers on the beach or at parties, assess whether they were suitable, and make them an offer. The money was good and the women often said yes, or so these friends were told.

But even more intriguingly, Carol acted as a madam for Kerry in Australia, providing high-class prostitutes for his mates and clients in business and in politics. Each summer, she ran a big house for him in Palm Beach, which she filled with flowers, rented furniture and half-a-dozen beautiful girls from around the world. This private bordello operated every December and January for most of the 1980s. The venue changed from year to year, but it was always the biggest and best spread she could find. And Packer footed the bill.

One of Carol's close male friends who went along in 1982 and 1983—with strict orders not to touch the merchandise—recalls that there were two houses side by side, one with bedrooms for the girls (and Packer's 'guests') to stay in, the other with a pool and a permanent party atmosphere.

Mark Manion, a close friend of Carol's who helped her find

the houses two or three times in the mid 1980s, says she would decorate them herself, filling them with hired plants, rented art and sculptures. The fridges were always full of Moët or some other high-class French champagne, and there was a chef on call. Always, there was something arriving—food, flowers, laundry, alcohol—because everything had to be perfect for Kerry. There were certain things, too, that the house had to have. A swimming pool and spa were a must, as was a degree of privacy and security. Preferably, there would be walls and a long driveway, so the girls could not be seen by casual passers-by. The rent was paid in cash by Carol, who always had huge wads of notes at her disposal. All the local real estate agents knew her requirements, and knew that discretion was called for. One feared melodramatically that she might get her throat cut if she gossiped about the goings on.

The girls were 'incredibly sexy and beautiful' and 'not your average hooker' according to Manion. And he had ample time to observe them, as they lay round the pool, topless, waiting for custom. The 'extra' who went to parties in 1982 and 1983 also remembers them being 'not like hookers at all'. At that stage, he believes, the girls were all American, hired through Heidi Fleiss and paid $10 000 a week, with a bonus if they were 'used'. They were good company, he recalls. Like the witness in Fleiss's money-laundering trial who spent time with Packer in Las Vegas, they appeared to be intelligent and well educated.

Later in the 1980s, Carol went to South America, New York and London in the search for suitable girls. She was always very specific in what she wanted: two dark South Americans, one blonde Russian, one black girl, or whatever. And they had to be foreign. Local women might recognise Packer's Australian guests.

Carol confided to friends that Kerry ran this private bordello to thank men who had done him a good turn, to pay them back. The beneficiaries were politicians, she told Mark Manion, but also executives and business acquaintances. He names one politician who was set to be the first visitor one year. Another friend of

Carol's confirms the man's identity and claims to have seen him with the girls. Logic also suggests that most of the guests would have been from the country where Packer did most of his business and where politicians were most important to him: Australia. But there is no doubt that businessmen from America also partook.

Carol stopped running the Palm Beach houses in 1987, not long after she met Neil Murray, the white singer in the Aboriginal Warumpi Band, who remained her lover until she died in 1991. They met in a bar called Benny's in Kings Cross, where everyone except Neil was coked off their head and impossibly chic. Shortly afterwards, they drove up to Alice Springs together in his old ute, and slept under the stars. It was then she told him she had been Kerry's mistress for three years. She referred to Packer as His Nibs, Nibbsy or Handsome. Although they were no longer lovers, he was still paying the rent on her apartment and giving her an allowance.

Only later, much later, did she tell Neil about the summer parties at Palm Beach. It was an 'exclusive entertainment' for Kerry and his mates, she told him. Neil asked why they couldn't just go to a normal brothel, and she said, 'They're very important people. They can't be seen in establishments like that because they would be recognised.'

Eventually, after constant pressure from Neil, Carol told Packer she would do it no more. Kerry advised her to find another business in which he would support her. And so began an expensive foray into Aboriginal art, to which Neil had introduced her on their trips to the Northern Territory. In 1988, she set up shop in Sydney, on Foveaux Street in Surry Hills. Soon afterwards, she was using it as a base to conquer America.

The CAZ Gallery ('Caz' being Australian slang for 'Carol') opened on Melrose Avenue in Hollywood in September 1988. A huge, white aircraft hangar of a place with high ceilings, it was probably the biggest private art space in Los Angeles. Launched with a swanky opening party at which Cary Grant, Natalie Cole and Patrick Swayze were among the 600 guests, 'It was a public relations triumph,' according to Packer's own *Bulletin* magazine.

The only mystery was who had put up the money to make it happen. 'She would not say where the $US750 000 came from to start her venture,' the *Bulletin*'s David Hay reported. 'And the reason I won't answer that question,' she told him, 'is because there are so many people who feel they know who our investors are, and they don't.' Those who were curious enough to dig a little deeper would have found some fair-sized clues. Three months later, the public records of CAZ Gallery Pty Ltd in Australia registered a $10 million charge to secure money lent to the venture by Kerry Packer's private company, Consolidated Press Holdings Ltd. But by this time, in the narrow world of Aboriginal art, it was common knowledge where the cash was coming from.

The gallery turned out to be a commercial disaster in double-quick time, burning through some $2 million of Kerry Packer's money, and it closed its doors within a year, apparently without Carol's consent. On the orders of Park Street, bank accounts were shut down, the lease was terminated and the paintings crated up to be shipped back home. Carol's response was to take a drug overdose in an attempt to end her life. Her closest female friend, Shelley, flew over to Los Angeles to sit by her bed for three days, then nurse her back to health. Carol was angry and disappointed she hadn't died.

Back in Australia, over the next fifteen months, she tried everything she could to see Kerry. 'She rang, wrote, turned up at the office, and waited outside his house,' says Mark Manion. 'Then it got worse after his heart attack, and that's when she thought, "Oh, it's impossible, I'll never see him."' She wanted to explain to Packer that the gallery had been a success. She had made a scrapbook with all the pictures and press cuttings, and was desperate to show it to him. She would go down to Park Street and sit in the foyer, dressed up to the nines, hoping to catch him on his way into the building or persuade his drivers to let her see him. Shelley went with her a couple of times, to be turned away on one occasion by Packer's security men and told to leave by his secretary, Pat Wheatley, on another. They also sat outside his house in Palm Beach, to no avail. Carol was convinced that Kerry had no idea she was trying to contact him. But few of her friends believed that. Nor does it seem likely to have been so.

After coming back from Los Angeles in November 1989, Carol made several attempts to commit suicide. The first was after she landed in Sydney, when she ended up in a dirty hotel in Darlinghurst, in a room so small she could hardly turn around. Packer's people in Park Street had ordered her back and promised her a house. Now she felt they were leaving her high and dry, cutting her off. She was rushed to Emergency at St Vincent's Hospital, then rescued by Shelley and Mark and taken to a hotel in North Sydney. As alarm bells started ringing at Park Street about the danger of the story getting out, Pat Wheatley came across town to talk to her. As Shelley remembers it, Wheatley told Carol to stay away from Packer and to sort herself out; there would be no more support. But Shelley had a suicide note mentioning Kerry. When Pat Wheatley demanded it be handed over, Shelley tore it up in front of her.

After a short spell in a private psychiatric hospital, Carol was found a house in Palm Beach and Packer's people were persuaded to pick up the tab, at least for a bit. For the next year, the rent was paid quarterly in advance by an in-house accountant who was used to attending to delicate private matters for his boss. Then Carol was told she would have to find her own place, and the notices to quit started arriving. Throughout this time, Kerry still wouldn't see her or talk to her.

By the end of 1990, Carol was becoming increasingly disturbed. She would walk round the house with no clothes on, the stereo blaring. And she began to drink more heavily. She would go out and not come back for days, says Neil Murray, who would get a call to rescue her from wherever she had ended up. For a short time she was living in a car. Then in October 1990, she went missing. She rang Shelley to say she was going to kill herself, but refused to say where she was. A few days later, she called Neil and asked him if he had seen the TV news. After a frantic search, he found her in a hotel in Darlinghurst, again, surrounded by pills and razor blades. The only thing that had stopped her slashing her wrists was that she had seen Kerry nearly dying on the polo field. She desperately wanted to see him and tried to visit him at St Vincent's Hospital but was kept away by Kerry's minders.

In February 1991, Carol attempted suicide for a fourth time. And on this occasion she left nothing to chance. She was found dead on the sofa in the lounge room of her rented Palm Beach house. On a coffee table beside her were two empty bottles of sleeping tablets and a two-thirds empty bottle of Jack Daniels. The doors and windows were sealed and all four burners of the gas stove had been turned on. She had been dead for approximately three days.

Only one newspaper, Sydney's *Sun-Herald*, was game to report her death in detail, and its report merely hinted at her links to Packer. But the coroner's file on her death contained a statement by film producer James Ricketson, who formally identified the body. He told police that he and his wife had known her well for ten years and were aware of her special relationship with Australia's richest man:

> Kerry Packer had looked after Carol for some 14 years. He was a father figure to her. Packer financed her Aboriginal art gallery in the United States called the CAZ Gallery. He also rented the house for her in Palm Beach.

Near her body, on the kitchen benchtop, Carol had left what the *Sun-Herald* described as 'an exceedingly curious eight-page suicide letter' that referred to 'a series of friends, including Kerry Packer'. Constable Greg Simpson of the Avalon police told the newspaper it was 'a very emotional expression of a very depressed lady. She expressed sorrow about her present standard of living, and her reason for suicide seemed to be that she could not afford to live in Palm Beach for much longer.' As Carol knew well, she was about to be evicted and the money from Park Street had dried up. She had a $20 000 credit card debt that Packer's people were refusing to pay and bills from the CAZ Gallery, which still owed money to its artists. She had no education, no job, no money, no prospects and, as she saw it, no hope.

The suicide note—which is in fact sixteen pages long—remains on file at the New South Wales Coroner's Court, which has ordered that its contents not be published. But it is not the only such letter in existence. Shelley has another that she found in the Palm Beach house when she was clearing up Carol's possessions. Written in biro on cream writing paper in a wild flowing hand, it covers much the same ground as the one found by her body. 'I hope God forgives me for taking my life,' Carol writes. 'I have no reason to be here . . . I have felt alone most of my life.'

In this second letter, Carol mourns the recent death of her sister, who was the only family she had. 'She died a bag lady on the streets with no one, no money, no friends,' she says. 'I fear I will die the same way. How can people be so mean and nasty?'

But the subject that fills most of the pages and is clearly at the front of her mind as she says goodbye is Kerry: 'He is in England now for six months playing polo I presume. I have tried in vain to reach [him] . . . Mr Packer does not know what is really happening.'

'Kerry Packer is the only family I know,' she continues. 'He has taken care of me for twelve years. I have been denied access to this man. For what reason, I don't understand. He is not aware of how distressed I am . . . I have no alternative but to end my life.'

The letter finishes with a teasing farewell that doubtless refers to Carol's long-running affair with Kerry and to the services she performed. 'There is more to this story,' she writes, 'but I feel loyal to others. So I will go to my grave with the secrets of the rich and famous of Good Ole Aussie.'

Carol's funeral was held at the big sandstone church in Sydney's Darlinghurst Road, just 200 metres from the bars of Kings Cross where she had sparkled so much. It was packed to the walls with people who loved her and with flowers, yet there was no wreath from Park Street or Kerry Packer. And the man who had been her lover and surrogate father (as her parting note described him) did not dare to show his face at her farewell. Nonetheless, there were many people whispering about their relationship, which was now common knowledge among her wide circle of friends. And several guessed he was footing the bill for the funeral.

Shelley had promised Carol before she died that she would try to talk to Kerry and set the ledger straight. For the next six years she tried to arrange a meeting with Packer through one of his employees, Michael Karagiannis, who knew Carol well and had access to the boss. But it was to no avail. Finally, in 1997, she wrote a letter to Kerry and asked Karagiannis to deliver it. She still has the rough draft, complete with crossings-out and changes, which talks about how loyal, discreet and secretive Carol had always been about their relationship. 'Carol defended your honour more than any other person she ever spoke to me about,' the letter says. 'She loved you.'

Whether Kerry received the letter, which would have cracked the hardest heart, we will also never know, because Karagiannis is bound by the secrecy agreement that all of Packer's close employees sign, as well as by a further agreement buying his silence when he was dismissed after Kerry's death.

But we do know this: Shelley never got a reply.

CHAPTER TWENTY-SEVEN

MORE

*I don't make friends easily . . . I've had my share of being
attacked . . . when I meet people, I don't expect to like
them.*

Kerry Packer, 1978

Take One: Picture the scene. It is the intensive care ward in the
private wing of St Vincent's Hospital. At one end of the room
a patient is on a respirator. He is in extremis. You can hear him
wheezing, gasping for breath. At the other end, a huge man
naked from the waist up, his legs covered by a single sheet, is
sitting up on a trolley, a drip hanging from his left arm. In his
right hand is a large paper cup of Coke. He is snarling at the
sister in charge. 'I told you I wanted cubes in this, not fucking
crushed ice.' The man is Kerry Packer. It is mid 1983. He has
just been rushed to hospital with a suspected heart attack.
He is already, or will soon become, the hospital's greatest
benefactor.

Take Two: A man and his driver arrive to watch a football
match. There are two dozen children in wheelchairs on the
touchline. The man beckons to the person looking after the
children and asks what is wrong with them. He leaves his card and
suggests they get in touch. A few weeks later, two dozen children
are flying to the United States on an all-expenses-paid trip to
Disneyland. The plane has been specially adapted to cope with
their wheelchairs. It is one of Kerry Packer's unpublicised acts of
generosity.

Take Three: A banker's office. The phone rings and a man picks it up. 'You fucking bastard' are the first words he hears. He thinks it must be a joke but after twenty seconds of blind anger pouring out of the earpiece he realises it is not and puts down the phone. Moments later it rings again. 'No one puts the fucking phone down on me,' says the voice and it all starts again. It is Kerry Packer, upset about a business deal.

Take Four: An elderly Melbourne couple lose their house in a fire. A solicitor approaches several neighbours and suggests they should organise a fund-raising to which his client will make a contribution. The donation is large enough to have the house rebuilt. The one condition is that no one should reveal the identity of the donor. But friends of the Big Fella know that it is Kerry Packer, who has heard of the couple's troubles and wants to help out.

Take Five: A dinner party in Sydney's fashionable Bellevue Hill. There are some eight guests in assorted finery and a big man in shorts and T-shirt. The meal that has been served is not to the big man's liking. He pushes the plate angrily down the table and complains, 'I own more cattle than anyone else in the world; I own more land than any man in Australia; why can't I get a decent fucking steak in my own house?' It is Kerry Packer, back unexpectedly from the country to find that the regular chefs have been given the night off.

Take Six: It is 1991. Ian Kennon hasn't worked for Packer for fifteen years, but he has remained a friend. His son is attacked outside the Pumphouse pub in Sydney's Darling Harbour and needs neurosurgery. The best neurosurgeon is free to do it, but only if the boy is admitted to St Vincent's Hospital, to which Packer has made large donations over the years. Kennon rings Packer's secretary Pat Wheatley to see whether Kerry can get the boy a bed there. He receives a call soon afterwards to say that it is all arranged: the boy is being moved that night and Mr Packer will foot the bill for everything.

Take Seven: A member of staff has used the boss's four-wheel drive because his own car is out of action. The boss is livid and shoots out two of the tyres while the man's wife sits in the vehicle. Apocryphal, perhaps, but quite credible for a man like Kerry Packer.

Take Eight: The public courts at Careel Bay near Palm Beach. A group of young men in fast cars arrive to play tennis, kitted out in the latest Reeboks and flashy gear. They march noisily across the courts without waiting for play to stop. A big man, attired in a cheap Penguin shirt, boxer shorts and $25 Dunlop Volleys, waits patiently for a break before crossing. It is Kerry Packer, who after all these years is still Sir Frank Packer's son.

When I completed the first edition of this book in 1993, Kerry Packer was still only fifty-five years of age but he was already living on borrowed time. He had outlasted his mother and grandfather, and he knew that few of the Packer line survived past the age of sixty. His health was poor and getting worse. He was overweight, smoked heavily, suffered from heart disease and had already survived one cancer scare. He had to diet constantly to keep his weight and blood pressure down, and he complained that he was too old for his greatest love, chasing girls. He had discarded or been deserted by some of his closest friends and was judged to be isolated, lonely and unhappy by those who knew him well.

The ability to have whatever you want is rarely good for people, and there was no reason to think it had been good for him. The stories from Park Street or from visitors to Bellevue Hill suggested that Kerry had cared less and less since his 'death' in 1990 about what people thought of him, and behaved accordingly. But one could hardly be surprised if his wealth, power and upbringing had combined to give him such a bleak view of life, for he had never been encouraged to smile on the world or himself. And even though he was the richest and most powerful man in Australia, he perhaps still remained the sick little boy, mocked at school, branded a dunce, whose father beat him and called him 'boofhead'.

Kerry also had the Packers' sad siege mentality to contend with. He did not expect to like people, he told Michael Parkinson in 1979, because he thought they would try to rip him off or take him for a sucker. Nor did he expect to be liked by others. The Packers had always made enemies, had always been attacked and always expected to be hated. And Kerry's own experience over the years only confirmed the family creed. When his chauffeur drove him around Sydney, he was often jeered at and abused by those who recognised him. Then came the Goanna allegations in 1984 and another wave of hatred and ridicule. Australians deride those who are rich and successful, or so Packer believed, and few came richer or more successful than he.

But Australians also respect aggression, and Kerry was certainly respected. Before his remarkable performances on television in 1991, few had any idea what the man was like, but almost all came away impressed. Some even saw him as a hero, a champion of 'Australian values' and the common man. He was blunt, plain-speaking and unwilling to suffer fools. Journalists and politicians knew nothing about the real world, he seemed to be saying: one group wrote stories they knew to be lies, while the other passed pointless laws they then sought to change.

On the face of it, no one was less suited than Kerry Packer to be the common man's champion, for his life had almost nothing in common with ordinary men and women. He never had to catch a bus, train or even a plane with others. He had servants on call twenty-four hours a day; cars, helicopters and jets were poised to take him wherever he wanted to go; he had a dozen residences to choose from, and the pick of any five-star hotel in the world. And he never had to worry about paying the bills.

Yet in other respects, Kerry Packer was very much an ordinary Australian. He loved football and cricket and lived for sport. He was at home in the locker room with Aussie blokes like himself. He swore like a trooper, loved milkshakes and hamburgers, hated opera and art, and liked to flop in front of the television for hours. He had probably never been to a library in his life and would have had no more desire to build an art collection than James Fairfax would have had to play baseball.

Packer was also a common man in that he was neither an egomaniac nor a visionary. He appeared to dream only of being younger, healthier and better-looking, or of winning at golf, driving faster and getting richer. He didn't crave big buildings with his name on the side, as Alan Bond did, or dream of creating a worldwide communications empire like Rupert Murdoch. Nor did he want to devote his fortune to curing AIDS, or wiping out poverty in Africa.

In 1993, when the first edition of this book was published, Kerry still had a dozen years left to live. And if he did have an ambition, it was a simple one: to make more money. Even with $3 billion in his kick, he could think of no higher calling in life and no greater purpose than to increase his fortune further. Enrichment had not diminished his avarice in any way, nor softened his desire to turn $1 million into $1 billion. Even though he had more money than he could ever possibly spend, Australia's richest man still wanted more. And he would get it. The rise and rise of Kerry Packer was not over yet.

ENDNOTES

ONE: FORTUNE

1. Frank Packer, quoted in Blaikie, George, *Remember Smith's Weekly*, Rigby, 1966, p 40.
2. Dictionary of National Biography Vol II.
3. McKay, Claude, *This is the Life*, Angus & Robertson, 1961, p 174.
4. McKay, op. cit.
5. *Smith's Weekly*, 21 March 1931, p 4.
6. *Daily Telegraph*, 10 December 1931, p 1.
7. *Daily Telegraph*, 16 December 1931, p 1.
8. *Daily Telegraph*, 9 June 1932, p 1.
9. *Daily Telegraph*, 17 September 1931, p 1.
10. *Daily Telegraph*, 19 October 1931, p 6.
11. Australian Archives NSW Series SP141, Item 13; Secret Organisations; secret report to G.S.M.I., Army Headquarters, Melbourne, 26 October 1936.
12. NSW P.D.Vol 132, 8746 *et seq*, 17 March 1932.
13. *Smith's Weekly*, 26 March 1932, p 1.

TWO: WILD MEN OF SYDNEY

1. *Parkinson in Australia*, ABC TV, 1979.
2. For details of the financial plight of the *World* and Theodore's role in its sale, see Australian National University, Archives of Business and Labour (ANU/ABL) AWU, E154/37/6 'The closing of the *World* newspaper'.
3. *Royal Commission into allegations surrounding the seat of Dalley, Sydney*, 2 July 1928

The commission's most important finding concerned the manner in which Theodore had entered the Commonwealth Parliament. W. G. Mahony, the sitting member for Dalley in New South Wales, had resigned in 1927, citing ill-health, on the condition that Theodore be adopted without the normal pre-selection process. The royal commission found that Mahony had been paid 5000 pounds or more to resign. The commission made no finding about the source of the money, apart from identifying 200 pounds paid to Mahoney by Theodore's friend John Wren, the massively wealthy illegal bookmaker, boxing promoter and political fixer, on whom the character John West of Frank Hardy's *Power Without Glory* was based.

The royal commission also found that 8000 pounds had been offered on Theodore's behalf to Federal MP P. E. Coleman, who had turned the money down. It did not accept the evidence of W. H. Lambert, MP, that he, too, had been offered money, because there were no independent witnesses and because Lambert denied the story when it first appeared in 1924.

4. *Royal Commission—Mungana, Chillagoe Mines, etc. Queensland*, 4 July 1930.

The Mungana Royal Commission was set up in February 1930 and reported in July that year. The first matter investigated was whether Theodore had secretly profited from the Queensland Government's purchase of the Mungana mining leases for 40 000 pounds, through a concealed shareholding in Mungana Mines Ltd, and whether he had used his position as Queensland's treasurer to cause the government to pay too much. The royal commission found Theodore guilty on both counts.

The second allegation was that Theodore was secretly a shareholder in the Fluorspar Mining Company, which supplied flux to the state smelters at Chillagoe and received considerable financial support from the Queensland Government. Fluorspar's contract to supply Chillagoe was not only extremely profitable, but there was also considerable doubt about whether the flux had ever been delivered. The commission concluded that Theodore was secretly associated with Fluorspar, and found him 'guilty of the grossest impropriety' in that regard.

Theodore did not give evidence to the royal commission because he was too busy preparing a Federal budget that he hoped would pull Australia out of its economic nosedive. He responded to its verdict by saying, 'As I never had any interest in the Mungana leases or the Mungana company, I naturally feel I am the victim of an atrocious injustice.' He was, nevertheless, forced to resign.

In July 1931 the Queensland Government sued its former premier Theodore, its former home secretary McCormack, and their two alleged partners in Mungana for damages, claiming that the Crown had lost 30 000 pounds through a conspiracy to defraud. The trial did not last long, nor did the Crown succeed. In the course of the trial, it was admitted that McCormack had received some 12 000 pounds as his share of the proceeds from the sale of the Mungana leases. It was also admitted that McCormack had then made out cheques payable to cash totalling almost 6000 pounds, which had been deposited in Theodore's bank account. Theodore admitted that he had received the money.

Theodore's lawyer pointed out that there was no evidence that the 6000 pounds was part of the proceeds of the Mungana sale. But Theodore never denied the allegation on oath. He had previously demanded an opportunity to take the stand in open court so that he might clear his name. Now the opportunity was offered, he declined it. Outside the court, a crowd of 5000 people celebrated Theodore's victory. Messages of congratulation poured in from politicians across Australia. But voters were less impressed. Although Theodore went back into Federal Parliament, he lost his seat at the general election five months later and quit politics.

5. As reported to fellow AWU member Clyde Cameron, and recorded in Cameron's unpublished manuscript.

6. *Newspaper News*, 1 November 1932, p 1.

7. The full text of the agreement is in *The Printer*, 9 December 1932, p 121.

8. Whitington R. S., *Sir Frank: The Frank Packer Story*, Cassell Australia, 1971, pp 117–124.

9. The purchasing power of the pound rose dramatically in the Depression, so that 86 500 pounds in 1932 was worth almost as much as 200 000 pounds had been in 1929.

10. This report is from the *Truth* of 1 May 1938, p 19. The case reference is Sun Newspapers v Taxation Commissioner, High Court of Australia, 1937/16. (Transcript missing, but see in particular the agreement between Associated Newspapers and Sydney Newspapers and correspondence.) Sun Newspapers wanted to claim the payment to Packer as a tax deduction but had been disallowed. They lost the High Court case, too.

11. *Truth*, 20 November 1932, p 1.

12. *Truth*, 20 November 1932, p 1.

13. Cited in O'Brien, Denis, *The Weekly*, Penguin, 1982.

14. NSW Political Debates, 22 June 1933, pp 26–27.

15. Warnecke, George, *Miracle Magazine*, unpublished manuscript. Warnecke is credited with the idea for the *Women's Weekly* by Eric Baume in *I Lived These Years*. He makes the same claim himself in his own book.

16. ABC TV, *Profiles of Power: Sir Frank Packer*, 11 October 1970. The interviewer was Bob Moore.

17. Contemporary press reports make this clear, as does Whitington op. cit. p 125, p 130, and O'Brien, op. cit., p 13, p 14, p 59. Both had access to a Packer corporate history.

18. Associated Newspapers received 160 000 shares in Consolidated Press Limited for the goodwill and plant of the *Telegraph*, while Sydney Newspapers received almost double that, or 265 000 shares for the *Women's Weekly*. In addition Packer and Theodore paid cash for another 100 000 new shares, giving them two-thirds of the new company and ensuring control of the venture. A further 100 000 pounds was raised in preference shares from the public, and it was used to acquire the almost new *Evening News* building at the top of Sydney's Castlereagh Street and to buy new printing equipment.

19. Holt, Edgar, 'Thunder Without Lightning', *Southerly*, No. 4, 1957, p 184.

20. Penton's law: Some remember it as twelve and ten respectively.

21. Souter, Gavin, *Company of Heralds*, Melbourne University Press, 1981, p 179.

22. Associated Newspapers agreed to peg the sale of *Women* at

140 000 for three years. While this competitor was shackled, the *Women's Weekly* increased its sales from 300 000 to 420 000, which gave it an unassailable lead.

23. Gretel Bullmore and Frank Packer were married on Tuesday 24 July 1934. The *Sydney Morning Herald* and the *Telegraph* both reported the wedding.

THREE: THE PACKER PRESS

1. McNicoll, David, *Luck's a Fortune*, Wildcat Press, 1979, p 215, Whitington R. S., *Sir Frank: The Frank Packer Story*, Cassell Australia, 1971, foreword by Sir Robert Menzies p x.

2. *Daily Telegraph*, 14 and 21 September 1951; see also 19 September for editorials.

3. Tom Uren won a record 30 000 pounds damages from Consolidated Press when Packer's *Sunday Telegraph* made this allegation against him in February 1963. Uren says Packer's papers made him out constantly to be a Communist or fellow-traveller. Uren later became a minister in the Whitlam Government; today his views would hardly be regarded as extreme. The extract is from his unpublished memoirs.

4. Fred Daly to author, 1992.

5. Souter, G., *Company of Heralds*, Melbourne University Press, 1981, pp 271–2. The Liberal Party was formed six months later in October 1944, with Bob Menzies as leader.

6. McNicoll, op. cit., p 215; Whitington, op. cit., p xi.

7. Whitington, op. cit., p 270.

8. *Daily Telegraph*, 8 December 1961, p 1. To be fair to the *Telegraph*, there was perhaps some truth in this charge.

9. Freudenberg, G., *A Certain Grandeur*, Sun Books, 1978, p 22.

10. Singleton, John, *True Confessions*, Cassell Australia, 1979, p 97.

11. Mitchell Library, NSW MLK2157, restricted. Horne's private papers show that Jackson Wain earned 3145 pounds' commission on advertisements placed with Consolidated Press, suggesting that more than 30 000 pounds' worth of advertisements was given free. A further 44 000 pounds was spent on buying ad space for Askin from other media organisations. Packer may or may not have paid

all of this himself. But one thing is almost certain: neither Askin nor the Liberal Party footed the bill.

12. Hickie, David, *The Prince and the Premier*, Angus & Robertson, Sydney, 1985.

13. *Daily Telegraph*, 21, 23, 28 and 30 April, 1965.

14. *Daily Telegraph*, 16 April 1965.

15. Gorton to author, 1992.

16. ABC TV, *This Day Tonight*, 12 July 1972.

17. Howson, Peter, *The Howson Diaries—The Life of Politics*, Viking Press, 1984. See entries for 6 to 10 March 1971.

18. House of Representatives, *Hansard*, 15 March 1971, p 832. Bob Baudino, Peter Samuel and Alan Reid were all political journalists in Consolidated Press's Canberra bureau.

19. McNicoll, op. cit., p 130.

20. See Walker, R. B., *Yesterday's News*, Sydney University Press, 1980 pp 201–224; also Souter, op. cit., pp 237–251; also *Sunday Telegraph*, 16 April 1944.

21. ABC TV, *Profiles of Power: Sir Frank Packer*, 11 October 1970.

22. Packer acquired the magazine in 1960.

23. *Bulletin*, 4 February 1967.

24. *Daily Telegraph*, 28 January 1967.

25. *Daily Telegraph*, 7 March 1953, p 1, p 3.

26. Whitington, op. cit., p 8. This version was recounted to Whitington by the *Telegraph*'s editor, King Watson, sixteen years after the event.

27. Souter, op. cit., p 327.

28. *Daily Telegraph*, 27 July 1967, p 1.

29. House of Representatives, *Hansard*, 30 September 1952, p 2320.

30. Australian Archives, ACT. Cabinet Minutes 30 September 1952. Decision No 553. See also Decision No 489.

31. House of Representatives, *Hansard*, 9 October 1952, pp 2882–3.

32. To this point all private companies had been allowed to retain some of their profits, free of 'undistributed profit tax'. Treasurer Fadden was proposing to change this, levying the tax in full on any company income derived from dividends. This had the effect of preventing Packer's companies from ploughing dividends back into the newspaper business tax-free. It was, said the *Telegraph*, 'not

taxation, but confiscation'. And compared with today's taxation arrangements, it certainly was. But the *Telegraph's* parading of small private companies as the impoverished victims was rather more imaginative, since Fadden was in fact reducing the tax rate on the first 5000 pounds of company income from seven shillings in the pound to five shillings in the pound and thus handing money back to most private-company taxpayers. He was also ending the requirement to pay tax in advance, which would do wonders for the cash flow of struggling traders. *Telegraph* editorials failed to mention these benefits.

33. Commonwealth Law Reports 1, (1958); F.C.T. v Newton. The tax scheme Fadden described converted money paid to shareholders from income that was taxable to capital that was not. It worked roughly as follows:

   (a) The company decided how much profit it wanted to distribute, then attached dividend rights to a particular parcel of shares.

   (b) The shareholders sold this parcel of shares to a share-dealing company at a price roughly equal to the face value of the shares, plus the dividend.

   (c) The share-dealing company was then paid the dividend, which it passed back to the shareholders of the original company as a capital payment for the shares. Shareholders thus received a non-taxable capital sum. Meanwhile, the share-dealing company got rid of its tax liability by selling the shares at a loss back to the original shareholders (or, in practice, to a company associated with them).

   The scheme was technically within the law. Fadden would not have been talking about blocking loopholes if it had not been. But Section 260, the anti-avoidance provision, was used by the taxman to defeat it. And severe tax penalties were levied on some, if not all, of the taxpayers whom Ratcliffe put into the scheme.

   The same Section 260 was also used successfully against Lang Hancock and his family, (Hancock v F.C.T. (1961) 108 C.L.R. 258), who engaged in an almost identical dividend-stripping scheme in 1949.

FOUR: PENNY PINCHING

1. Australian Journalists' Association Secretary, H. G. Coleman, to the Commonwealth Conciliation and Arbitration Commission, 15 February 1967.
2. ANU Archives of Business and Labour, N59/400; see also N59/1188 for transcript of the hearing before the Commonwealth Conciliation and Arbitration Commission.
3. Quote from Horne, Donald, *Confessions of a New Boy*, Viking, 1985, p 323.
4. McNicoll, David, *Luck's A Fortune*, Wildcat Press, 1979, p 302.
5. Francis James to author, 1992.
6. McNicoll, David, op. cit., p 298.
7. Whitington R. S., *Sir Frank: The Frank Packer Story*, Cassell Australia, 1971, p 55.
8. Horne, op. cit., p 322.
9. Whitington, op. cit. pp 10–11.
10. ANU Archives of Business and Labour, N59/404, AJA.
11. Whitington, op. cit., pp 14–15.

FIVE: YOUNG KERRY

1. Lane, Terry, ed., *As the Twig is Bent*, Dove Communications, 1979, p 144.
2. Whitington R.S., *Sir Frank: The Frank Packer Story*, Cassell Australia, 1971, p 64.
3. Lane, op. cit., p 148.
4. The *Age*, 19 November 1984, Janet Hawley.
5. Lane, op. cit., p 147.
6. Lane, op. cit., p 146.
7. Lane, op. cit., p 146.
8. Sufferers from dyslexia see letters back to front or in the wrong order. It is now thought to be an inherited condition, much more common in males than females, which passes typically from father to son. Given that Frank Packer was also hopeless at school, he might also have been dyslexic. Kerry's son Jamie also suffers from dyslexia. With modern treatment, it can improve as the sufferer gets older.

9. *Parkinson in Australia*, ABC TV, 1979.
10. Lane, op. cit., p 144.
11. Forsyth, Christopher, *The Great Cricket Hijack*, Widescope, 1978, p 136.
12. Forsyth, op. cit., p 137.
13. *Parkinson in Australia*, ABC TV, 1979.

SIX: THE IDIOT SON

1. 'Bluey' is slang for a speeding ticket or police traffic summons.
2. *Parkinson in Australia*, ABC TV, 1979.
3. *National Times*, 23 May 1977.
4. Coronial inquest into the deaths of Horace Clarke, John Foster, Raymond Phillips at Goulburn, New South Wales, 17 January 1957.
5. Ibid.
6. *Daily Telegraph*, 17 September 1956, p 1.
7. David McNicoll, *Bulletin*, 3 February 1987.
8. *Daily Telegraph*, 17 September 1956, p 5.
9. Australian Broadcasting Control Board, Annual Report, 1955–56, p 62.
10. *Parkinson in Australia*.
11. King, Cecil, *Strictly Personal*, Weidenfeld & Nicolson, 1969, p 180.
12. Horne, Donald, *Portrait of an Optimist*, Penguin, 1988, p 188.

SEVEN: PACKER BUSINESS

1. McNicoll, David, *Luck's A Fortune*, Wildcat Press, 1979, p 261.
2. The row between Frank Packer and Ezra Norton first came to the surface in September 1939 when R. C. Packer's old editor Eric Baume left the *Telegraph* to join Norton's *Truth*. A bitchy article about Baume appeared in the *Telegraph* to celebrate his departure, followed the next day by an even nastier piece in *Truth* about Packer.

   > We herewith publish a posed portrait of Mr Frank Packer, managing director of Consolidated Press. This study is preferred by him to the previous photograph of himself published in Truth and to which he took strong exception.

As a matter of fact, the desired result (from Mr Packer's
point of view) has been achieved only after telephone
communications between himself and Mr Ezra Norton ...
we are only too happy to publish this photograph, which
meets his own approval after obvious labor and execution
of the retouch artists of Consolidated Press. The silhouette
of the features has been carefully touched up. The lips have
been softened. Even the wrinkles on his broad forehead
have been softened.

While the photo is not exactly a Gary Cooper, or shall
we say a Clark Gable study, we agree with Mr Packer that
it will probably meet more with the approval of some of
his friends than the hitherto objected-to photo which we
publish below.

Two weeks later, Packer was taking revenge with a lurid story
about how Ezra Norton had bought a diamond ring and
brooch for 450 pounds cash from a man 'he knew only as
Watson'. The man had offered to sell him the jewellery 'very
cheaply' because he needed the money. Norton had then taken
the ring to a fashionable Sydney jewellers to have it altered,
only to find that it had been stolen. When the thief was subsequently prosecuted, Norton was a star witness. Packer's *Telegraph* published the proceedings in detail, and managed to grab
a picture of an embarrassed Norton scurrying away from the
back entrance of the Central Police Court after giving his
evidence. The very next day, on AJC Derby Day, one of the
social highlights of the Sydney season, the two press proprietors came face to face in the members' enclosure at
Randwick, with Norton accompanied by two professional
boxers dressed in ill-fitting lounge suits. According to a racing
journalist from the Melbourne *Sporting Globe*, Norton sneaked
up behind Packer and threw the first punch, whereupon one of
the heavyweights stepped in and landed a direct hit on Frank
that knocked him to the ground. Somewhat later, as hundreds
of people craned to get a ringside view, 'Packer emerged ...
hatless, breathless and bleeding from a cut over one eye'.

According to *Smith's Weekly*'s man on the spot, he was 'marked on both cheeks, his face puffed, hair tousled, and clothing in disorder'.

Both men were soon hauled up before the AJC committee to explain their unseemly behaviour. Packer was apparently exonerated, while Norton was required to apologise. But this was not the end of the feud, for *Truth* continued to attack Packer in print, while the *Telegraph* responded by publishing unflattering pictures of Norton whenever they could get them. To keep the photographers at bay, Norton surrounded himself with bodyguards. Meanwhile, the *Telegraph* sent its cameramen to chase him, accompanied by ex-pugs or special constables to protect them. Inevitably, another punch-up soon followed, in which one of Norton's bodyguards flattened a *Telegraph* cameraman outside Darlinghurst Court after he had tried to take a picture of Ezra Norton through the witness room window. Norton had instructed his bodyguard to get the cameraman and his camera, and then ripped out the film himself. His actions to some extent foreshadowed Kerry's dust-ups with photographers forty and more years later. But one of Norton's bodyguards was unlucky enough to be prosecuted for common assault and sentenced to three months in jail—a fate Kerry's minders have managed to escape.

3. Francis James to author, 1992. Much of this account of the Anglican Press battle relies on him or on Tom Fitzgerald. Both men are dead, but several other participants or bystanders are still alive. They remain unnamed because they wish to be. There is an account in Munster, George, *Rupert Murdoch, A Paper Prince*, Viking, 1985, pp 59–60, see also *Daily Mirror*, 8 June 1960, p 1, p 3; 9 June 1960, p 2, p 6.

4. Windschuttle, Keith, *The Media*, Penguin, 1984; Souter, Gavin, *Company of Heralds*, Melbourne University Press, 1981, p 512; *Sunday Telegraph*, 25 January 1987. David McNicoll's version in the *Bulletin* of 3 February 1987 is that Warner did not complete the deal with Henderson because he was persuaded by stockbroker Sir Ian Potter that he would destroy his reputation if he

went back on his agreement to sell to Packer. See also contemporary press reports.

5. David Syme also had a right of first refusal when Warner sold his GTV shares, since GTV's Articles of Association required other shareholders to be notified before any block was sold. Warner got round this requirement by selling the shares to a subsidiary of his own Electronic Industries (which he was allowed to do) and then selling that company, Austral Magnus Co Pty Ltd, to Packer. David Syme therefore had two reasons to feel dissatisfied.

6. *TV Times*, 19 June 1963. These paragraphs draw heavily on Munster, George, *Rupert Murdoch, A Paper Prince*, Viking, 1985, pp 44–47 and 65–69.

7. For more on these machinations, see Souter, op. cit., pp 420–424; Munster, op. cit., pp 83–84.

8. *National Times*, 23 May 1977.

9. Horne, Donald, *Money Made Us*, Penguin, 1976, p 53.

10. Munster, op. cit., p 97. *Nation*, 10 June 1972. McMahon told the story to several journalists.

11. *Australian*, 18 May 1977.

12. Horne, Donald, op. cit., p 55.

13. Ibid, p 54.

14. To take one example, Clyde crossed the floor of the NSW Legislative Council in late 1972 to prevent an anti-pornography bill becoming law.

15. *Age*, 19 November 1984.

16 *Pol*, June 1974, pp 6–9.

17. *Age*, 19 November 1984.

18. *Pol*, June 1974, pp 6–9.

19. Ibid.

20. John Cornell was Willesee's producer on Channel Nine's *A Current Affair*, Paul Hogan's manager and later producer of *Crocodile Dundee*.

21. The interview with Bob Hawke went ahead, with Sir Frank Packer watching from the Green Room overlooking the TV studio floor. With him were the chief executives of all the oil companies in Australia. To make sure that Willesee got the message, he was summoned to meet them beforehand. Hawke's 'sensational

evidence' turned out to be a damp squib, and the future Prime Minister eventually requested that the interview be canned.

22. *Bulletin*, 10 November 1973, p 32.

23. *Australian*, 9 November 1973.

24. Channel Nine, 15 November 1972.

25. Channel Nine, 22 November 1972. The rules on TV coverage of elections provided broadly for equal treatment of the parties, but not for equal time. This is still the case in 1993. For more on the incident, see: Oakes and Solomon, *The Making of an Australian Prime Minister*, Cheshire, 1973, pp 283–7.

26. McNicoll, op. cit., pp 286–7.

27. Senate *Hansard*, 13 February 1975, pp 139–140.

28. Records of these companies are held by the Australian Securities Commission. Some are registered in the ACT, others in NSW.

29. ABC TV, *Profiles of Power: Sir Frank Packer*, 11 October 1970.

EIGHT: KERRY TAKES CHARGE

1. *Parkinson in Australia*, ABC TV, 1979.

2. Buttrose, Ita, *Early Edition: My First Forty Years*, Macmillan, 1983, p 107.

3. Sir Frank Packer's will was amended in October 1972 to make Harry Chester, Kerry Packer and Lady Florence Packer joint governing directors of Cairnton Pty Ltd. Chester did not have a major stake in any Packer company.

4. The *Age*, 19 November 1984.

5. *Good Weekend*, 27 October 1984.

6. *Good Weekend*, 27 October 1984.

7. *National Times*, 23 May 1977. See also note 18 in the 1976–77 accounts of Publishing and Broadcasting Ltd.

8. The *Age*, 19 November 1984.

9. The *Age*, 19 November 1984. Clyde was asked by Richard Walsh, now the publisher at Australian Consolidated Press, but then at Angus and Robertson Publishers.

10. Buttrose, Ita, *Early Edition*, p 129.

11. The *Age*, 19 November 1984.

12. *Parkinson in Australia*.

13. *Sunday Mail*, 20 December 1987.

NINE: HOWZAT?

1. Interview with author, August 1992.
2. Trevor Kennedy, 'The Great Cricket Story', *Bulletin*, 14 May 1977.
3. Relations with the Australian Golf Union were never entirely happy. Packer made it clear that he regarded them as amateurs who should not be allowed to interfere with the important business of staging professional sport, and egos were bruised. Meanwhile AGU officials were unhappy about Packer's desire to keep the competition in Sydney every year, and felt strongly that Victoria should be given a chance, for the good of the game. When the deal expired in 1978, Packer's contract was not renewed, even though he was offering far more money than the AGU could muster elsewhere. Packer said at the time that he was fed up with being constantly vilified by those who wanted the Open to be held in Melbourne.

   While still televising the golf, Packer also tried to secure the Australian Tennis Open, which was then a ratings winner for Channel Seven. In return, once again, for the magic $1 million, Packer demanded TV and marketing rights for five years to the Open and other top Australian tennis tournaments. To the Lawn Tennis Association of Australia, this was a seductive offer because it would ensure the tournament's continuing prestige. Packer was guaranteeing huge amounts of prize money, while his partners in the deal, Mark McCormack's International Management Group, were promising the appearance of the world's best tennis players. But it was a dangerous course for the LTAA to take because, with Packer and McCormack calling all the shots, the Australian Open would essentially be controlled by commercial interests. The LTAA split down the middle over the proposal, eventually rejecting Packer's approach by a narrow margin. Had they said yes, the future might have turned out very differently for many people, because the rejection made Kerry Packer much keener to get his hands on cricket, a sport that did not then rate nearly so well on television.
4. There was an argument in London's High Court in October 1977 about precisely what Boycott had said. Packer maintained he had

agreed to join; Boycott denied it. One version offered by the press was that Boycott had agreed to sign, provided that he didn't have to serve under Tony Greig as captain.

5. Both quotes are from *Parkinson in Australia*, ABC TV, 1979.

6. Christopher Forsyth, *The Great Cricket Hijack*, Widescope, 1978, p 30.

7. *The Times*, 10 May 1977.

8. *The Times*, 24 June 1977.

9. *Sunday Press*, 24 July 1977, p 1.

10. Forsyth, op. cit., p 123; previous quotes from p 141.

11. *The Times*, 26 November 1977, p 3. The judge concluded that Tony Greig might not be exempt from criticism, because he had secretly recruited players for Packer while remaining England's captain.

12. *Trinidad Sunday Express*.

13. *Sydney Morning Herald*, 10 May 1977.

14. *Sydney Morning Herald*, 27 July 1977.

15. The NSW Cricket Association argued that it wanted the cricket ground for club matches, yet it had used it for the purpose on only three occasions in the previous thirteen years. (See *NSW Political Debates*, Assembly, p 10346, 28 November, 1977.) While proceedings were before the court in November 1977, the Wran Government attempted to have the law changed in time for World Series Cricket's first season. The Liberal Opposition objected to the new Sydney Cricket and Sports Ground Bill being rushed through with such haste, and delayed its passage through the Legislative Council. But for their opposition, World Series Cricket would have had the Sydney Cricket Ground that first year; instead, the passage of the law was held up until March 1978.

16. Ironically, night cricket might never have been tried if Packer had been allowed to use the traditional cricket grounds from the start, for he and John Cornell decided to experiment with it only after watching floodlit football at VFL Park. At that stage, no cricket ground had lights.

17. *National Times*, 16 December 1978.

18. The team record was not great—they beat India 3–2 in Australia in 1977–78, lost to the West Indies 3–1 in early 1978, which

would have been 3–2 but for the pitch invasion, and then lost to England 5–1 in the summer of 1978–79. But to put it in perspective, the 'first' team, made up almost entirely of Packer players, had lost 3–0 (which could easily have been 4–0) to England on the 1977 tour.

19. *National Times*, 10 March 1979.

20. In the 1980 and 1981 tax years, PBL Marketing Pty Ltd declared a gross income of $4.5 million and $4.6 million respectively for the *sale* of Australian cricket TV rights. It is not clear whether Channel Nine was one of its customers. Even if it were it would appear that Packer's companies more than recouped the money paid to the Australian Cricket Board. See PBL Marketing v Federal Commissioner of Taxation (Yeldham, J.) Supreme Court NSW, 1985, 16 ATR 679.

21. In 1977, when Channel Nine bought television rights from the BBC for the Ashes tour of England, the ABC's general manager Talbot Duckmanton refused to buy the country rights. On this first occasion, the Minister for Posts and Telecommunications was Eric Robinson. He persuaded the ABC's chairman John Norgard into negotiating directly with Packer. ABC management was told by Norgard to buy the rights after all.

On the second occasion, in 1979, the ABC applied to the Trade Practices Commission to have the ten-year exclusive agreement between Packer and the Cricket Board outlawed under the Trade Practices Act. The Trade Practices Commission decided to reject the ABC's application. The ABC then challenged the decision in the Federal Court before reaching an out-of-court settlement in March 1981. According to the Trade Practices Commission, its decision to permit the arrangement 'was very much influenced by the commitment by PBL to truly competitive tendering at the end of the three-year period'. Under this arrangement, PBL agreed to auction the television rights every three years. Theoretically, Channel Nine could therefore lose the right to televise the cricket. In practice, the auction never took place because no one wanted to bid against Channel Nine. Since Packer's PBL Marketing would both conduct the sale and pocket

20 per cent of the fees from the successful bidder as commission, the other television channels did not fancy their chances. When the rights came up in 1982 and 1985, Channel Nine got them unopposed.

22. Costs measured in person-hours per hour of television produced. On this basis, even studio-based game shows, variety shows, magazine programs and news cost five to ten times more than live sport. *Production Personnel Resources*, Sandra Alexander, ABT Paper, November 1987.

23. Forsyth, op. cit., p 143.

TEN: BACKING WINNERS

1. Hawke to author.

2. In 1983 a royal commission under the New South Wales Chief Justice, Sir Laurence Street, investigated an allegation that Premier Wran had interfered in a court case to have the defendant discharged. The defendant was Kevin Humphreys, President of the Australian Rugby League, who was charged with fraud and theft. Wran stood aside as Premier while the royal commission investigated the allegation. In July 1983 the royal commission rejected the allegation as untrue.

3. John Hatton turned the offer down. He supported the government nevertheless.

4. Dale, Brian, *Ascent to Power*, Allen & Unwin, 1985, p 121.

5. Mike Steketee, Milton Cockburn, *Wran, An Unauthorised Biography*, Allen & Unwin, 1986, p 123.

6. Steketee, Cockburn, op. cit., p 164. See also James Fairfax, *My Regards to Broadway*, Angus & Robertson, 1991, p 178. Wran's anger against the *Herald* did not cool, for when Harriott wrote to him three years later suggesting a rapprochement, Wran threw the letter in the bin.

7. Dale, op. cit., p 108.

8. *St George & Sutherland Shire Leader*, 12 July 1978, p 4.

9. Steketee, Cockburn, op. cit., p 165; David Halliday to author, 1992.

10. Fia Cumming, *Mates*, Allen & Unwin, 1991, p 203.

11. *NSW Political Debates*, Assembly, p 3950, 27 February 1985. The matter was raised by the MLA for Pittwater, Max Smith, who was chiefly concerned about Essington and the background of one of its directors, Neil Ohlsson. He told Parliament in 1985 that there were four separate police inquiries at the time into Essington companies or personnel. He highlighted Ohlsson's involvement in attempts to lend large sums of money to the Australian Government in 1975, which had been dismissed in scathing terms by an official Treasury Report in July 1975. He also drew attention to the fact that Ohlsson had been photographed on 17 May 1976 in San Francisco with a 'Mafia leader, Rudy Tham'. Smith was concerned that the New South Wales Government was dealing with Essington. His comments on the group's property dealings focussed on two sites in which a Packer company had become a joint venturer with an Essington company. Smith said, in part:

> What worries me is the remarkable success which Essington has had in obtaining government contracts, in spite of the controversial background of one of its principals. I have mentioned the Joint Coal Board site before, and the Premier sought to avoid responsibility. However, he is responsible for the Joint Coal Board and because of his announcement in Japan of the contract, he must bear criticism for this deal. The outstanding aspect of this contract is the haste with which the tendering was opened and closed. Indeed, I am aware of developers who were told by the Joint Coal Board or its agents not to bother. Without proper tendering, how are honourable members to know that taxpayers received full market value for the property? The people of New South Wales are entitled to a full and open enquiry into the awarding of the Joint Coal Board contract.

12. *Royal Commission into Painters and Dockers*, Transcript p 17922–25, 14 February 1984.

13. PBL Ltd had one of the three shares in Lotto Mangement Services Pty Ltd, which won the NSW Lotto contract. The other two shares were held by News Ltd and the Vernons Organisation—respectively Murdoch and Sangster companies. Even Wran's close

advisers asked what Packer added that wasn't already there. The answer, perhaps, was that he owned a television channel on which the results could be drawn and the game publicised, but Tattslotto in Victoria managed without a television partner, as did Sangster and Murdoch in a similar venture in the USA. And by May 1979 Murdoch had acquired Sydney's Channel Ten in any case.

14. *Bulletin*, 15 November 1975, p 13.
15. ABC TV, *Four Corners*, 5 November 1990 (interviewer, Deborah Snow).
16. Harding, Professor Richard, *Outside Interference*, Sun Books, 1979, p 95.
17. Harding, op. cit., pp 161–2.
18. *Bulletin*, 8 January 1977.
19. This is more fully dealt with in Chapter 16.
20. *Nation Review*, 15 October 1976.
21. The *Bulletin*'s sales had already increased from 35 000 to 50 000 when the campaign started. Three years later they were above 70 000. The campaign coincided with continuing changes to the content supervised by Trevor Kennedy, who had become editor in late 1972. Whether Kennedy or Singleton was responsible was something the two doubtless argued about.
22. Singleton, John, *True Confessions*, Cassell, 1979, p 97.
23. Liberal leader Billy Snedden said afterwards that he believed the Askin/Singleton/Packer campaign had harmed the Liberals' election chances.

ELEVEN: MAKING MILLIONS

1. *Australian*, 18 May 1977.
2. Tess Lawrence, Adelaide *Advertiser*, 1 January 1977.
3. The Australian Broadcasting Tribunal fought a running battle with Channel Nine over the dearth of Australian-produced drama in Nine's schedules, but Channel Nine continued to do much as it thought fit.
4. Kieran Kelly, *Financial Review*, 17 December 1982.
5. Ibid.
6. Coopers & Lybrand, report to the independent directors of Consolidated Press Holdings Ltd on proposal to privatise the group, 28 July 1983.

7. Packer's prediction that there would not be a slump was made to the *Business Review Weekly*, 9 January 1982. Seven months later, preliminary accounts for Consolidated Press Holdings Ltd for 1981–82 showed provisions for property development losses of $8.5 million.

8. This did not happen until the early 1980s.

9. Buttrose, Ita, *Early Edition: My First Forty Years*, Macmillan, 1983, p 164.

10. Ibid, p 165.

11. *Parkinson in Australia*, ABC TV, 1979.

12. Jupiter's Casino in Broadbeach has a turnover of some $150 million a year, of which roughly 10 per cent is profit.

13. Roughly half (47.6 per cent) of the shares in Consolidated Press Holdings were owned by Cairnton Pty Ltd. This company in turn was *controlled* by a Packer company called Cairnton Holdings, which held 51 per cent of Cairnton's shares. (The rest of Cairnton's shares were owned by Consolidated Press Holdings, which therefore owned 23.3 per cent of its own share capital.) This structure gave the Packers absolute control of Consolidated Press, even though they ultimately owned only one-quarter of the shares, because they could vote all of Cairnton's 47.6 per cent shareholding in the group in their favour.

    At the start, ownership of the Packer empire had been divided equally in 1932 between Frank Packer and Ted Theodore, who each owned half of Sydney Newspapers Ltd. In 1936, they had surrendered one-third of the business to Associated Newspapers in exchange for the *Daily Telegraph* and the building that housed the old *Evening News*. They bought the shares back in 1948 and immediately sold them to the public. In 1957, Frank Packer bought out the surviving members of the Theodore family, leaving the Packers with roughly two-thirds of the business. This was diluted through various acquisitions and share issues to take the family share to below 50 per cent by the early 1970s.

14. One of Packer's reasons was that the company would have to pay out less in dividends if it went private. For many years the income tax rules had forced private companies to pay out 50 per cent of

their profits in dividends to avoid paying penalty tax. By 1983 this had been reduced to 20 per cent. As a public company, Consolidated Press Holdings had been paying out between 20 per cent and 40 per cent of its profits to shareholders.

15. Packer's advisers valued the group both on earnings and assets, using the valuation guidelines laid down by the National Companies and Securities Commission for use in takeovers, at around this figure.

    Packer's own words six months earlier confirmed their view, for he told Kieran Kelly of the *Financial Review* on 17 December 1982 that the two Channel Nine television stations alone were worth $4.60 a share, or almost as much as the $220 million price tag he was putting on the entire company. He had suggested that they were probably worth even more than that, for he had said, 'If I put them both up for sale at $200 million between them, I would have a line of buyers out there until the middle of the night—but there is no way in the world I would be selling them.'

16. Packer was in fact able to vote the whole of Cairnton's shareholding, or 47.6 per cent of Consolidated Press's shares (since he controlled the company), even though only half these shares were beneficially owned by him. (See above, note 13.) There were other advantages. Since control of Consolidated Press was transferred without a formal takeover, the deal was not subject to the normal takeover regulations. Nor, for other reasons, was it subject to the Australian Stock Exchange listing rules, the provisions of the Companies' Code or even the scrutiny of the Australian Broadcasting Tribunal. Despite being termed a 'reconstruction of capital', which typically required the approval of a court, the scheme achieved the reconstruction by changing the company's articles, so it bypassed the courts as well.

17. The tax advantages to the institutions were considerable. They had Consolidated Press shares in their books at $2. Packer's company was offering to buy the shares for only 25 cents in 1988, which would deliver the institutions a huge tax loss. In addition, they were guaranteed a dividend on each share of $1.25 a year for four

years. These would be tax-free because they were fully rebatable; income tax would have already been paid by Consolidated Press.

18. It was not just that no other bid was on the horizon; there was no prospect of a hostile bid for Consolidated Press ever succeeding. And all bids were bound to be hostile. Packer had complete control of the group through the family's 51 per cent holding in Cairnton. (See notes 13 and 16.) Consolidated Press could not even dispose of its 49 per cent of Cairnton without Kerry's formal approval. Not even a coup at Consolidated Press could have wrenched the empire from Kerry Packer's control.

19. There was another more magical equation that made the mathematics work in Packer's favour, for he started off with one-quarter of the shares in the company, bought a further half and ended up with all of them. What made this apparently impossible sum add up to 100 per cent was the cross-shareholding between Cairnton and Consolidated Press Holdings that Sir Frank Packer's advisers had put in place in 1972. This had been set up in such a way that no one else had a hope of getting control of the Packer empire. As a result, Kerry's privatisation of the company had been an auction in which there could only ever be one bidder.

20. The Consolidated Press Holdings Group balance sheet for June 1984 showed long-term borrowings of roughly $300 million against shareholders' funds of $214 million. This could have been cause for concern, except that the real value of shareholders' funds was in excess of $330 million.

TWELVE: COSTIGAN INVESTIGATES

1. *National Times*, 14 September 1984. There were references to the cashing of large amounts of money by the Goanna, the delivery of large amounts of cash to him by his partners and a tax-avoidance scheme involving films. Public hearings of the commission or newspaper articles had canvassed all of these details.

2. Freiberg, A., 'Ripples from the bottom of the harbour', *Criminal Law Journal* 136, 158–90, quoted in Cooper, Krever, Vann, *Income Taxation*, Law Book Company 1989, p 1142.

3. *McCabe/Lafranchi Report*, Victorian Government, 1981, Vol 1, p 41.

   With Maher, Beames faced charges in December 1978 of conspiring to prevent the execution of a section of the Queensland Companies Act. These were not proceeded with. His first contact with Maher had been in 1971 when he liquidated Maher's company, Finance & Guidance, a share-tipping outfit. Maher's conduct in this company was attacked in a special investigation report by P. D. Connolly, Inspector of Companies, tabled in the Queensland Parliament in June 1973, which concluded that Maher was guilty of conspiracy to defraud investors. Beames also came under fire in the report over his conduct as liquidator. Connolly said that he had not acted in the interests of creditors. In 1985, Beames pleaded guilty to conspiracy to defraud the revenue and was jailed for two years. Bankrupted by the taxman in 1984 because he owed more than a million dollars in tax, he told his bankruptcy examiner that he had no assets, but lived in a house owned by his wife, worked for a company owned by his family trust, of which he was not a beneficiary, and drove a car owned by that trust without paying anything for it. He died in 1987 of a heart attack aged 43.

4. *Royal Commission on the Activities of the Federated Ship Painters and Dockers Union*, transcript of evidence, p 16310.

5. Ibid, p 16370.

6. Ibid, p 16313.

7. Ibid, p 16317.

8. Ibid, p 17910a.

9. Ibid, p 17911.

10. Ibid, p 16371, p 16375.

11. These criticisms were detailed by Max Smith in the New South Wales Parliament, *NSW Political Debates*, Assembly, p 3950, 27 February 1985. See also note 11 to Chapter 10 and Chapter 15, pp 302–05.

12. *Royal Commission on the Activities of the Federated Ship Painters and Dockers Union*, transcript of evidence, p 17914.

13. For details of the film scheme, see *Australian Broadcasting Tribunal*

Public Inquiry Report 325–327/85R (T) and *353–355/85R (T)*, pp 328–339. This discloses, among other things, that one of the legal opinions was supplied by a leading tax lawyer, Neil Forsyth QC. Forsyth held strong views on the lawyer's right, or even duty, to find ways for his clients to avoid paying tax. 'It seems to me to transcend the proper function of a lawyer,' he told a legal conference in 1981, 'to seek to impose his views of morality . . . on a client who has different views.' Forsyth was committed for trial in Melbourne on 23 June 1986 on two charges of conspiring to defraud the Commonwealth and two more of inciting others to do so. He was alleged (not in relation to the Beames film scheme) to have given his legal blessing to, and participated in, arrangements intended to deprive the taxman of some $30 million in revenue. The charges related to a scheme involving the purchase of twenty-one paintings for $5400 that were inflated in value to $60 million and then 'lodged' in a Norfolk Island art gallery to which investors made large tax-deductible donations. Committing Forsyth for trial, the magistrate Phillip Rodda told the courts he was satisfied that the leading tax barrister had on this occasion been dishonest. The charges of incitement were subsequently dropped by the DPP. Then, after two hearings before the full bench of the Federal Court, the matter came before the Supreme Court of Victoria on 2 February 1990. Mr Justice Hampton ruled that the case had altered so much since the beginning that there was no longer any case to answer.

14. Public statement by Kerry Packer on 28 September 1984, responding to publication of 'the Goanna' allegations in the *National Times*.

15. Packer implied to Costigan that he was $600 000 worse off than if he hadn't invested. It is not clear whether that it is in fact what he meant, but it seems odd, since the ABT was told in 1985 that no penalties were charged by the Tax Office. *Royal Commission on the Activities of the Federated Ship Painters and Dockers Union*, transcript of evidence, p 17915.

16. *Australian Broadcasting Tribunal Public Inquiry Report 325–327/85R (T)* and *353–355/85R (T)*, p 334.

17. *Royal Commission on the Activities of the Federated Ship Painters and Dockers Union*. Final Report, Vol 9, p 15, p 20.

18. *Royal Commission on the Activities of the Federated Ship Painters and Dockers Union*, transcript of evidence, p 16581.

19. The alleged conspiracy involved the film scheme and the alleged evasion of income tax. Robert Redlich QC in summing up to Brian Ray's committal hearing, day 51, 5 August 1985, pp 5006–5009, pp 5039–5041. See also Chapter 15, p 299.

20. *Royal Commission on the Activities of the Federated Ship Painters and Dockers Union*, transcript of evidence, p 16354. Packer had helped put Ray on his feet again in 1978 when he was facing bankruptcy after his property company Donlan Developments had gone bust, by guaranteeing a $4 million loan for a housing development east of Brisbane. This project at Victoria Point had become a joint venture between the two men, with Packer putting up the money and Ray managing the business, and each taking half the profit. Others like it had followed.

21. Ibid, p 16393.

22. Ibid, pp 16396–7.

23. Ian Beames made a statutory declaration that said, among other things, 'As far as I am aware neither Mr Packer nor any other company or entity associated with him had any involvement directly or indirectly in the financing of the film transactions.' This declaration confirmed Ray's and Packer's testimony that Packer had not made up his mind at the August 1979 meeting whether he would fund the film scheme or not, and went on to say that Beames had 'subsequently learned that he [Packer] had declined to provide any financing for the transactions'.

24. Frank Costigan QC was not present on this visit to Touche Ross.

25. *Royal Commission on the Activities of the Federated Ship Painters and Dockers Union*, Final Report, Volume 9, p 90.

26. Affidavit of Patrick Gregory McDonnell, 5 November 1983, Harper and others v Costigan, G342 of 1983, Federal Court of Australia, Sydney.

27. Affidavit of Bruce McWilliam, 8 November 1983, Harper and others v Costigan, G342 of 1983, Federal Court of Australia, Sydney.

28. *Royal Commission on the Activities of the Federated Ship Painters and Dockers Union*, Transcript of evidence 4 November 1983.

29. *Royal Commission on the Activities of the Federated Ship Painters and Dockers Union*, Final Report, Vol 1, p 53. Justice Morling, giving judgment in the Federal Court proceedings on 16 November 1983, said that it was 'not unreasonable for [the Costigan investigators] to suppose that the non-availability of the relevant documents in Singapore and HK was not unconnected with Mr McWilliam's hurried visit to those cities'. (Morling J, Judgment in Harper and others v Costigan, 16 November 1983 p 19.)

30. *Royal Commission on the Activities of the Federated Ship Painters and Dockers Union*, Final Report, Volume 9, p 102.

31. Packer told Costigan that he believed Progress Credit had been set up on the instructions of the International Management Group—the international group that manages golfers, cricketers and other sportsmen, with whom he often did business. The man who had handled its establishment, Alastair Johnson, had had discussions with Jock Harper of Allens in Packer's office, in Packer's presence. Johnson left the country before Costigan could interview him. *Royal Commission on the Activities of the Federated Ship Painters and Dockers Union*, transcript of evidence, pp 17916-7.

32. Police v Lockyer, Beames, Knudsen, Anderson, McTrusty, Ray, magistrate's summing up, p 31, 13 August 1985.

33. Ibid, p 23.

34. Police v Lockyer, Beames, Knudsen, Anderson, McTrusty, Ray, transcript, p 5009, 5 August 1985. See also pp 5006–8.

35. Police v Lockyer, Beames, Knudsen, Anderson, McTrusty, Ray, 13 August 1985, magistrate's summing up, p 25. See also transcript pp 5039–5041, 5 August 1985. According to the evidence, the charge on Halboham's assets and income was secured to Fidel Number 20 Pty Ltd. This company was jointly operated by Savannah Investments Pty Ltd and Molland Pty Ltd.

36. Ibid, magistrate's summing up, p 28, 13 August 1985. According to the magistrate's summing up of the prosecution evidence, Famiti was unable to pay the $175 000. Lockyer and Famiti

agreed instead to provide 100 000 shares in Magnum Exploration to Brian Ray as security on which he could raise money. Ray wrote to Russell Knowles, President of Investments at Consolidated Press Holdings, in October 1980, indicating that he had forwarded 87 150 Magnum shares to him. The letter also said: 'When I spoke with Kerry on Monday, I told him that we had 100 000 shares, that being my understanding from our debtor . . . We would be grateful if you could borrow $200 000 on the scrip.'

THIRTEEN: THE GOANNA

1. Costigan wanted formal references for roughly half the forty matters, because these gave the NCA greater investigative powers. There were rumours (which proved correct) that only a handful of these references would be issued. In fact, the NCA could investigate adequately without a reference.

2. Brian Toohey comments that he never reveals his sources to anyone.

3. Costigan says that he and Meagher were devastated when the *National Times* article was published on 14 September 1984. Whether or not they could have prevented publication, he says that they would have tried to if they had believed that the *National Times* had the case summaries.

4. The commission's confidential *Squirrel Analysis* contains no other drug evidence against Kerry Packer. Since this was prepared in April 1984, it is unlikely that the commission possessed anything else on which to base its case summaries for the NCA.

5. The statement was written by Packer's lawyer Malcolm Turnbull. Unlike the rest of his legal advisers, Turnbull was strongly in favour of Packer making it a public fight. Some of the preliminary remarks, totalling roughly 500 words, have been left out; references to the film scheme were dealt with in Chapter 12. References to the alleged murder of Ian Coote are covered in Chapter 14.

6. *Royal Commission on the Activities of the Federated Ship Painters and Dockers Union.* Final Report, Vol 1, p 274. Costigan says in Vol 1, p 12, that the confidential volumes dealt with:

Some of the activities of Ian Beames, Brian Ray, Phillip Carver and a number of their associates, all of whom have been charged with, and several of whom are committed for trial on serious criminal charges. I am compelled to recommend that they not be published [largely because it would prejudice investigations and trials]. Ultimately, when all investigations are completed and all charges disposed, the public interest may require their publication. These volumes, as it happens, include reports on investigations into the matters disclosed by Mr Packer in his statement of 28 September 1984. My personal preference was to answer his allegations publicly, but I could do so only by the fullest account of each matter. I am prohibited from publishing such an account for the reasons I have given. There are considerations affecting people other than Mr Packer which produce that result.

FOURTEEN: MURDER OR SUICIDE?

1. *Royal Commission on the Activities of the Federated Ship Painters and Dockers Union.* Final Report, Vol 1, p 114.
2. Brisbane *Sun*, 2 November 1984.
3. Costigan could not establish who Richards was. The money had been derived from the Beames–Ray–Packer film scheme. Ian Coote had also arranged for large amounts of cash to be collected by Ray at the Comalco House branch of the Bank of NSW in central Brisbane.
4. This was on the evidence of Phillip Carver, an admittedly unreliable witness.
5. *Squirrel Analysis*, 10.3590, p 255, released to the Coote inquest.
6. Costigan's reasons for rejecting the theory that Coote committed suicide are contained in pp 250–255 of the confidential *Squirrel Analysis*, updated to 10 May 1984, which was released to the Coote inquest.
7. *Royal Commission on the Activities of the Federated Ship Painters and Dockers Union.* Final Report, Vol 1, pp 113–114. The section headed 'Death of Coote' begins: 'As part of my investigation into the connection between Ray and Packer . . .' and goes on to describe Ray and Packer's Victoria Point development and Coote's relations with Ray.

8. Detective Senior Constable Graeme Robert Morgan, NSW Fraud Squad, gave evidence to the Coote inquest of how the alleged Carver note had been obtained, and provided a copy of the note. The fear of Coote and Ray that Carver might harm them was also recorded by Morgan.

9. *National Times*, 14 September 1984.

10. *Royal Commission on the Activities of the Federated Ship Painters and Dockers Union*, transcript p 18994, released to Coote inquest.

11. *Inquest into the Death of Percival Ian Coote*, Brisbane, 4–8 December 1984, transcript, p 328. Meagher denies having said any such thing.

12. Ray gave the following evidence to Costigan:

    I am merely repeating what Mr Coote told me at the time but they had mentioned to him that in relation to a number of loans which had been made against houses that Savannah Investments, the company, in conjunction with one of Mr Packer's companies, had built at Victoria Point, had not been processed properly and they would be proceeding against him for those reasons.

    Q: Did you speak to Mr Packer about it?

    Yes, I think I probably did.

    Royal Commission on the Activities of the Federated Ship Painters and Dockers Union, transcript of evidence p 16367.

13. Scotney and the police agreed that a number of employees of Brian Ray had received 100 per cent finance on houses, outside the bank's guidelines, which had enabled them to make money by renting the houses or selling for capital gain. But the auditor's conclusion was that neither Packer nor Ray was implicated. This evidence was given to the Coote inquest.

14. Statement by Detective Senior Constable Graeme Robert Morgan, NSW Fraud Squad, made to the Coote inquest.

15. Ray said he had helped out because Carver was married to his sister. Packer's motives, one imagines, were purely financial.

16. *Royal Commission on the Activities of the Federated Ship Painters and Dockers Union*, Vol 10, Chapter 10, pp 111–112, released to Coote inquest.

17. Ibid, p 119.

18. *Inquest into the Death of Percival Ian Coote*, p 758.

19. Ibid, pp 760, 764.

20. Ibid, p 764.

21. Ibid, p 765.

22. The *Australian*, 8 December 1984.

FIFTEEN: ENTIRELY INNOCENT

1. Queensland fraud squad report to Costigan interdepartmental committee, 19 December 1984.

2. Queensland fraud squad report, 15 February 1985, p 2.

3. Queensland fraud squad report, 12 July 1985, pp 15–20.

4. On the film tax scheme the ABT accepted the evidence of TCN 9, Malcolm Turnbull and Packer's accountant William Harrington that the scheme had not been shown to be fraudulent because the Australian Tax Office had neither levied penalties nor initiated prosecutions. The ABT also appeared to accept that Packer would not be to blame, even if the scheme had been proven to be fraudulent, because he had acted on advice from experts who had assured him it was legal.

5. *ABT TCN–9 Licence Renewal Hearing Public Inquiry*, Vol 2, Appendix 7 (i), p 9.

   By May 1985 five matters had been officially referred to the NCA. The references were worded in such general terms that it was impossible to be sure which matters they related to. Even the parliamentary committee overseeing the NCA wasn't told, much to its annoyance.

6. The Attorney-General's office in Canberra is unaware of any similar statement having been made.

   Packer's then lawyer, Malcolm Turnbull, says, 'It would have been an act of unutterable bastardry having had Packer go through all this stuff for all these years for the Director of Public Prosecutions to decide not to charge him and the government not to say anything about it. Even if Packer had been charged and convicted on offences relating to the film scheme, that could never ever have justified what had been done to him in respect of all the other allegations.'

Turnbull was by no means alone in this view. It was widely-shared by civil libertarians.

7. Attorney-General Lionel Bowen's statement clearing Packer was received with no enthusiasm by Frank Costigan QC, who promptly started an action for defamation against the *Australian* and the Melbourne *Herald* for the way they reported it. This action soon roped in the attorney-general himself and was still grinding its way towards the courts six years later in mid 1993. Somewhat bizarrely, Frank Costigan had so far been denied access to his own confidential reports, which he was keen to use as evidence.

8. The opinions were given by Robert Alexander QC, Geoffrey Robertson QC and Tom Hughes QC. It is understood that they concluded that neither Packer nor his companies had attempted to conceal anything from the Australian Tax Office when the scheme was challenged. There was therefore no element of dishonesty or intention to deceive in Packer's behaviour that could have made his involvement fraudulent.

9. The 'third principal' who had died, incidentally, was Ian Beames, who suffered a massive heart attack earlier in 1987.

10. *The National Crime Authority—An Initial Evaluation*, Commonwealth Parliament 1988, p 43.

11. *Royal Commission on the Activities of the Federated Ship Painters and Dockers Union,* Vol 1, p 259.

12. *Royal Commission on the Activities of the Federated Ship Painters and Dockers Union*, Vol 9, p 68. Costigan's belief that Packer would fear prosecution was based on his view that the film scheme was fraudulent.

13. *Sydney Morning Herald*, 26 April 1985. Also published in the *Financial Review* and *National Times*.

14. *Geoffrey Robertson's Hypotheticals: A New Collection*, ABC Books, 1991.

15. ADJR Proceedings, Harper and others v Costigan. The order by Justice Morling (16 November 1983, p 22) quotes a letter from the Costigan Royal Commission's solicitor, John Buxton, to Packer's solicitors, Allen, Allen & Hemsley, which informs them

that the Commission wants to question Packer about cash payments to him in relation to its investigation of the financing of drug transactions by painters and dockers in Queensland.

16. Police v Lockyer, Beames, Knudsen, Anderson, McTrusty, Ray, magistrate's summing up, 13 August 1985, p 29.

17. *Canberra Times*, 21 March 1987.

18. Brisbane *Courier Mail*, 15 March 1987.

19. Senate *Hansard*, 25 March 1987, pp 1298–99.

20. According to the company records filed with the Australian Securities Commission, Packer's Consolidated Press Holdings was allotted 3.5 million shares in Essington Ltd on 31 December 1986 for a payment of $10 million. This gave Packer's company 50 per cent of Essington. The shares were sold in 1990.

21. The *Age*, 22 January 1985, p 1.

22. Max Smith MLA Pittwater, *NSW Political Debates*, Assembly, p 3950, 27 February 1985.

23. Jeff Kennett, *Victorian Assembly*, p 54, 24 April 1985.

24. Report by the liquidator, John Walker, into the collapse of Roward Pty Ltd.

25. Ibid.

26. Ohlsson admitted to the *National Times* in August 1985 that he had met Tham and Fratianno about five times in the course of discussing a business deal. See, 'Jaffle King and the Essington Connection', *National Times*, 23 August 1985.

27. *NSW Political Debates*, Assembly, p 3950, 27 February 1985.

28. *NSW Political Debates*, Assembly, p 3950, 27 February 1985. Packer's share in both these New South Wales projects and the Victoria project was held through Toaz Pty Ltd, a company half-owned by his Wentworth Enterprises Pty Ltd. The other half of Toaz was held by Essington. According to ASC records, Toaz's shares in Tilverton, the company that bought the Joint Coal Board site, were allotted in March 1984.

29. *National Times*, 23 August 1985, p 15.

30. Neil Ohlsson ceased to be a director of companies in the Essington group in June 1986. By 1993, three Essington companies connected with Malcolm Edwards were being sued by the Swiss Bank Corporation for recovery of $27 million which was electron-

ically looted from the bank's Zurich office in December 1989. The money ended up in the Sydney bank accounts of Essington Ltd before being flashed to other bank accounts around the world in 60 separate transactions ordered by Malcolm Edwards.

SIXTEEN: MEDIA MATES

1. Hawke speech to *Australian Business* Top 500 Awards dinner, 10 June 1987.

2. The editor of Packer's *Australian Business*, Trevor Sykes, did not. He told the ABC's *AM* program that he thought $1 billion was a lot for anything, and that there was little he would not sell for that price.

3. *Video Age*, February 1983.

4. *The opportunity for television program distribution in Australia using earth satellites*, Donald S. Bond, 15 August 1977, p 26. See also paras S–1, S–5, Introduction, and Foreword by Packer.

5. Commonwealth Government Task Force, *National Communications Satellite System*, Report July 1978, pp xiii–xv, pp 50–54.

6. *Nation Review*, 15 March 1979.

7. *Nation Review*, 15 March 1979. The Packer plan envisaged the new stations transmitting only programs from the Sydney–Melbourne networks. It was likely that these would be supplied already packaged with advertising, which the networks would sell centrally. This would have deprived the existing stations of most of their share of national ad campaigns, which accounted for 75 per cent of their revenue.

8. Malcolm Fraser in evidence to House of Representatives Select Committee on the Print Media, 22 October 1991, *Hansard* report pp 910, 916.

9. This estimate of the satellite's cost and future losses was made in July 1983 by the Australian Telecommunications Employees' Association.

10. In November 1983 the Department of Communications said that it had received no 'viable submission' to use the satellite's broad-cast capability, apart from those made by Channels Nine, Ten and Seven. The *Age*, 16 November 1983, p 15.

11. Hawke told the author in February 1993, 'Peter has always been close to Kerry and has always had a very considerable respect for

him, and I think it's always been the case vice versa, that Kerry has had a considerable respect for Peter, which is not surprising because Peter's a very astute political operator.'

12. Up to this point there had been typically only one operator in each area, who had been able to pick the eyes out of the networks' programs and pay very little for the privilege.

13. The compromise allowed aggregation to be 'triggered' early by any one operator in an area asking for it to happen. In practice, operators were induced by the networks to pull the trigger, so aggregation came in rapidly.

14. The *Australian*, 28 November 1986.

15. When the proposal became law in 1987, the limit was set lower, at 60 per cent, after objections by the ALP Caucus.

16. The Herald & Weekly Times was also handicapped by having newspapers in country towns, which would have made it extremely difficult for the company to build a television network.

17. Interview with author, July 1992.

18. Interview with author, February 1993.

SEVENTEEN: BONDY'S BILLION

1. Whitington R. S., *Sir Frank: The Frank Packer Story*, Cassell Australia, 1971, p 75.

2. Longboat was winner of England's prestigious Ascot Gold Cup, the championship race for stayers. He was rated a stone better than the 1981 Melbourne Cup winner At Talaq, a previous well known English import.

3. Also published in the Sydney *Daily Telegraph*, 12 November 1988.

4. Handicaps are based on the number of goals a player is expected to score in a match. The lowest is minus 2. Tournaments are arranged with a limit on teams' combined handicaps, so that the competition is evenly balanced.

5. *Daily Telegraph*, 12 November 1988.

EIGHTEEN: THE MIDAS TOUCH?

1. House of Representatives Select Committee on the Print Media, official *Hansard* report, 4 November 1991, p 1207.

2. Tom Domican swore a statutory declaration in 1984 that he had been paid by Warren Anderson to work for the then NSW ALP Secretary Graham Richardson, organising numbers for the Right wing of the Labor Party in New South Wales. Group certificates demonstrated that Domican had been paid more than $20 000 between October 1981 and November 1982. Anderson agreed that he had employed Domican, but both he and Richardson denied that Domican had done any work for Richardson. Richardson said Domican's suggestion that he had worked for him was 'a sick joke from a very sick man' (*National Times on Sunday*, 10 August 1988).

3. Packer turned down a bid of around $80 million just for Muswellbrook's coal operations in 1987, so the share price by no means overstated the company's value.

4. For Anderson's WA property losses, see Chapter 22, pp 449–454.

5. Packer in fact bought 48 per cent of the company.

6. Valassis Communications Inc. Registration Statement, form S-1, Securities and Exchange Commission, Washington D.C. 20549, 14 January 1992, p 17.

7. Having bought Valassis in December 1986 for US$365 million, Packer sold 51 per cent of the company in early 1992 for US$375 million. On the face of it, this gave him a cash profit of US$10 million and left him owning half the business for free, which itself was a good enough return. But the real gain was considerably larger, for the sale produced almost US$900 million (A$1270 million) of tax-free dividends for Packer's Netherlands-based company, Conpress Investments BV. This was achieved by allowing Valassis to take on large debts prior to the sale.

NINETEEN: PRINCE OF WHALES

1. A rival version, from someone who claims to have watched Packer lose, is that it was only six million pounds, or a mere $14 million, in two separate sessions.

2. Packer's limit at blackjack in London nowadays is said to be 25 000 pounds a hand, which would allow him, if he played two tables at once, to stake 350 000 pounds a round or more. House

rules at the Ritz allow gamblers to double their stake on any pair except four, five and ten, so it would be possible for him to stake 50 000 or even 100 000 pounds on some individual hands.

3. *Today*, London, 3 May 1990.

4. *Squirrel Analysis*, April 1984, para 1.25. Prepared for the *Royal Commission on the Activities of the Federated Ship Painters and Dockers Union*.

5. *Royal Commission on the Activities of the Federated Ship Painters and Dockers Union*, transcript of evidence, p 17926.

6. Packer's public statement of 3 November 1984 referred to $1 million he had withdrawn in November 1979. There were in fact two million-dollar transactions. The Costigan Royal Commission's information was that only the October 1979 one was in cash.

7. *National Times*, 23 May 1977.

8. Next day the *Telegraph* quoted the Sydney Turf Club Chairman Jim Fleming as saying that Packer had won money off the Rosehill bookies. This did not necessarily mean that he hadn't lost to Bruce McHugh at Randwick, to whom the interstate bets were channelled by Dominic Beirne (the Rosehill bookie taking Packer's bets).

9. Harry Barrett and his wife never moved in. His wife preferred her house in Strathfield, so they sold it again in 1992 at a loss.

TWENTY: KERRY AND THE TAXMAN

1. The *Australian*, 18 May 1977.

2. The *Australian*, 18 May 1977.

3. Companies were arranged in a chain or snake to avoid payment of tax on undistributed profits. Profits could be passed up the chain or along the snake, from one company to another every year, to satisfy the taxman that they had been distributed.

4. Queensland Supreme Court, 339 of 1984. Packer, Ray, Binnu Pty Ltd, Progress Credit Pty Ltd, Molland Pty Ltd, Savannah Investments Pty Ltd, Dealer Holdings Pty Ltd, Cairnton Holdings Pty Ltd, Cairnton Pty Ltd v Deputy Commissioner of Taxation. Judgment, Connolly J, 4.6.1984, p 4.

5. Letter from Deputy Commissioner in Sydney to Commissioner of Australian Taxation Office in Canberra, 18 December 1986, setting out reasons for requesting the help of the US Inland Revenue Service. Exhibit A in C2-87-1285 Ohio court action.

6. Metropolitan Oil Distributors Pty Ltd v Federal Commissioner of Taxation, Federal Court, 1990. 90 ATC 4624.

7. House of Representatives Select Committee on the Print Media, official *Hansard* report, 4 November 1991, p 1208.

8. These figures should reflect the income tax *actually paid* by Consolidated Press Holdings in the financial years 1991–92 and 1992–93.

9. Converted at $A1 = US$0.75 from recorded profit of US$158 million.

10. The ownership structure at mid 1991 was disclosed to the Australian Broadcasting Tribunal. See ABT file IO/91/2, document 46.

Aside from the international holding company and the trusts that owned it, there was a separate ownership structure that went to an Australian trustee, Consolidated Custodians Pty Ltd, as trustee for the Genetout Settlement Number 8 and the K1 Trust. This involved only three shares in Cairnton Holdings (which in turn owned most of Consolidated Press Holdings Ltd), but they were Class C shares. Significantly, the directors of Cairnton Holdings could pay dividends on these Class C shares without paying dividends to any other shares. Theoretically, all the profits of Consolidated Press could therefore be routed this way.

11. To be more precise, the new tax laws sought to define a 'controlled foreign company'. If such a company were owned by a trust whose property had all been transferred by someone now dead, it was impossible to trace control back to a living, taxable Australian. But the fact that Sir Frank Packer had set up the trusts did not guarantee that the new tax laws had not caught Consolidated Press. Nor, to add a further level of complexity, would Consolidated Press necessarily have been caught by the new tax regime even if Kerry Packer (for example) *had* transferred property to these trusts. One could therefore only speculate on whether Packer's legal advisers had found a way through.

12. Consolidated Press Holdings accounts 1991–92, p 37, 1990–91, p 36. These are actual tax payments in the 1991–1992 and 1992–1993 financial years.

13. Although it was almost certainly tax-free, this does not necessarily mean that Consolidated Press had escaped the new Controlled Foreign Company tax regime introduced in July 1990.

14. *House of Representatives Select Committee on the Print Media*, official Hansard report, 4 November 1991, p 1209.

TWENTY-ONE: KING KERRY

1. By 1990 the Nine Network had expanded to include Bond's old Brisbane station QTQ 9 and a 20 per cent share in the North Queensland station QTV 9.

    Packer's opening shot in December 1989 was to make an outright takeover offer for Bond Media, valuing the shares at a paltry $53 million. Since this amounted to 10 cents a share against a current market price of 15 cents, it is hard to believe that Packer expected it to succeed, and indeed it did not. The next move was to wait for the 31 March deadline and make it clear that failure to pay would lead to Bond Media being put into receivership. The deadline came, the $200 million was not produced and legal proceedings to wind up Bond Media were put in train. A date was then set down to hear the case in Perth on 5 June, whereupon Packer's and Bond's lawyers settled into their trenches in Western Australia and prepared for action.

    A deal was finally signed between Packer's and Bond's negotiators at 5 a.m. on 2 June 1990 and legal proceedings were then stayed. Packer was in London for the polo season but had been in touch with his negotiators, finance director Don Bourke and merchant banker Malcolm Turnbull, throughout. The details of the deal were approved by Bond Media shareholders on 19 July 1990.

    The deal turned Consolidated Press's $200 million worth of preference shares into 51.5 per cent of the Nine Network. This was reduced to 38.3 per cent when new shares were issued to Australian institutions to raise $170m. Consolidated Press then increased this share to 41.3 per cent by buying shares in the market in 1992. On 1 June 1993, Consolidated Press Holdings Ltd had 128 million shares in the Nine Network, worth $3.44 each on the stock market. This put a nominal value of $444 million on the Packer stake, but since it was a controlling share in the Nine Network, it was probably worth considerably more.

2. Australian Broadcasting Tribunal, IL 91/30.

3. Nine's demand was later amended by letter to 17.5 per cent of TNQ's gross revenue, rising to 32 per cent after five years. The lower of these was still double what most regional television stations paid the networks in 1991, when stations affiliated to Channel Seven typically paid between 7.5 per cent and 10 per cent of revenue, with an agreement to increase to 20 per cent over five years. The Ten affiliates were typically paying 10 per cent of revenue with no escalation agreement.

4. In October 1986 Bruce Gordon had been the first of the regional television operators to break ranks and trigger aggregation in Australia, and had picked up the Nine Network affiliation in southern New South Wales in the process. This had instantly delivered three customers in that area to the big city networks, to the anger of many of Gordon's regional colleagues.

5. *Sydney Morning Herald*, 12 January 1991.

6. $6 million of Ten's payment to Channel Nine was in cash; the balance was expenditure on production facilities.

7. *Independent Monthly*, June 1991.

8. When asked whether he denied Tilley's version, Packer told the parliamentary Print Media Inquiry in October 1991: 'Mr Tilley was a seller; he came to me to sell the *West Australian*. It was in his interests to turn around and say to me that Rupert Murdoch was a keen seeker of buying the paper. I said, "We all know Rupert Murdoch has no hope of buying the *West Australian* [because of the trade practices laws] ... so don't start telling me about this ... he's not a player because he has absolutely no chance of getting through the necessary regulations to be a player." That is what I said to Mr Tilley. Somehow or other this man—who I believe was getting a commission from someone else to try to sell it—did not want to

sell it and came back with these rather extraordinary statements. Yes, I deny it absolutely.' Packer also denied that there was any game plan between him and Murdoch, telling the inquiry: 'The suggestion that I am conspiring with Murdoch and that I know about his game plan is nonsense. I am saying to you that anyone who has half a wit knows that he is not a player in that game.'

Malcolm Turnbull was also present at the meeting as Kerry Packer's adviser, as was a colleague of Mike Tilley's, Will Jephcott. Turnbull denied that Tilley's version was correct; Jephcott on the other hand supported it. In fact, Murdoch appears to have considered bidding for the *West Australian*. But he would have had to sell his interest in Perth's *Sunday Times* to do so.

TWENTY-TWO: APPALLING PEOPLE

1. ABC TV, *Four Corners, Citizen Packer*, 16 September 1991.
2. One of these ten magazines, *TV Week*, was half owned by ACP and half by Pacific Magazines. ACP's share of the Australian magazine market depended on how you calculated it. ACP's publisher Richard Walsh told the parliamentary Print Media Inquiry in 1991 that ACP had 25 per cent of the market, defined as those magazines audited by the Audit Bureau of Circulation. Trevor Kennedy, the former managing director of Consolidated Press Holdings, told the same inquiry that ACP had 40 per cent plus of the major weekly and monthly magazine market. The prospectus for ACP's public float said that it had 58 per cent of the women's mass market, 81 percent of the young women's market, 46 per cent of the business and news market, 64 per cent of the fashion market, 45 per cent of the homemakers' market, and 75 per cent of the motoring market.
3. *People*, 29 April 1992.
4. Evidence to House of Representatives Select Committee on the Print Media, 5 November 1991.
5. *Bulletin*, 14 May 1977, 'The Great Cricket Story: The Inside Facts'.
6. *Bulletin*, 14 November 1989, 'Why Australia's Media are on the Nose'.

7. ABC TV, *Four Corners*, 16 September 1991.
8. Anderson was awarded the contract to run the building of the State Square project, in which the actual construction was being performed by Multiplex. His fee was originally to be $3.5 million on a $100 million project. When costs rose after design changes to $144 million, Anderson's fee was renegotiated to be 3.75 per cent of construction costs.

    According to another program on ABC TV's *Four Corners*, Anderson made donations in 1990 totalling more than $200 000 to the Northern Territory's Country Liberal Party. Former Chief Minister Ian Tuxworth was quoted in *Business Review Weekly* on 27 September 1991 as saying that a donation of $10 000 to $20 000 would have been 'appropriate' for a man of Anderson's wealth. Evidence was also given to the Western Australian Royal Commission in WA Inc about political donations by Anderson to the Labor Party in Western Australia. This evidence was not made public.
9. WA Royal Commission into WA Inc. Warren Anderson gave evidence on 4 December 1991.
10. This was one of the smaller towers, amounting to roughly one-fifth of the total floor space. The SGIC agreed to make the rent up to $400 plus outgoings if the space were let to someone else in the first five years for less. The $400 figure was for 1990, thereafter it was to increase at 10 per cent a year.
11. This is evidence of Kevin Edwards, given to the Royal Commission on 25 September 1991, p 11 120. Edwards said the government wanted a $50 million deposit with Rothwells so that the government's GESB could get its $50 million out.
12. Packer and Anderson never spoke to each other again. In 2005, Anderson told a court hearing he 'presumed' his one-time buddy was still living on the eastern seaboard but he hadn't seen or heard from him for fifteen years.

TWENTY-THREE: FAMILY FEUDS

1. *A Current Affair*, 23 October 1991.
2. Only $27 million of this fee was in fact ever paid.

3. The public float would have issued new shares in David Syme & Co and sold 55 per cent of the company to the public. In practice the *Age* would still have been controlled by John Fairfax & Sons Ltd.

4. In fact, Lady Mary probably had the option to stop the deal even then. She could have sold her shares to Tryart, the company making the bid for John Fairfax & Sons, which would have rendered the takeover too expensive for the banks to fund. As it was, she took an extra fee for agreeing to pledge her shares at this late stage.

5. The bondholders claimed they had been misled in late 1988 by assurances that Fairfax was financially sound. There might well have been some truth in this, but it was a measure of Malcolm Turnbull's nerve that he dared take the action, for he had been one of Fairfax's advisers only months before the $450 million junk-bond raising. According to Fairfax's bankers, the valuations that the bondholders alleged to be misleading were similar to valuations of Fairfax's assets that Turnbull had done earlier in 1988. Fairfax's bankers put in a cross-claim against Turnbull in April 1991, claiming that they had relied on his valuations in making their representations to the bondholders. The issue never went to court, but the legal action was undoubtedly important in getting the bondholders their money.

6. Legal action by the bondholders would make it very difficult to sell the corporate shell of Fairfax to anyone but Tourang. It would be possible to sell the assets separately, but this would leave out valuable tax losses contained in John Fairfax & Sons Ltd. Turnbull and Tourang therefore reasoned that the banks would have to sell to them.

7. Deborah Light, *Four Corners*, *Citizen Packer*, 16 September 1991.

8. It was argued that Packer and his lawyers were to blame for this change in the cross-media rules. Communications Minister Kim Beazley maintained that the government was simply blocking a loophole that had been exposed eleven months earlier. In buying back Channel 9 in mid 1990, Packer had picked up the Sydney radio station 2UE and inherited a breach of the cross-media laws,

which made it illegal to own a radio station and television station in the same city. Rather than sell 2UE at a rock-bottom price, Packer had instructed his lawyers to find a solution. Allen, Allen & Hemsley had come up with a scheme that hived off ownership of 2UE to a $2 shelf company called Kimshaw, which was 85 per cent owned and supposedly controlled by nominee companies run by Packer's accountants, Ernst & Young. Packer's Nine Network technically owned only 15 per cent of Kimshaw and was supposed to have no control over what the radio station did, but 99 per cent of the dividends from 2UE still flowed to the Packer companies and in practice there was evidence that he still called the shots. When the former Test cricketer Rod Marsh, for example, had been sacked as a 2UE commentator in the middle of a Test match in January 1991, it was Packer he had confronted in his private box at the cricket to complain about it. Packer had also been the one to discuss the potential sale of 2UE with prospective buyers.

The Australian Broadcasting Tribunal had not had a chance to rule whether the Kimshaw structure succeeded in getting round the cross-media laws, because Packer had sold 2UE on the day that the ABT inquiry was due to commence. But it had argued strongly that the law should be changed to knock out similar avoidance schemes in the future. Hence the new definition of being 'in a position to control' through 'associates' was being introduced. The inadequacy of the existing law had been recognised for some time. It was a strange coincidence that the letter from the Australian Broadcasting Tribunal's chairman Peter Westerway to Communications Minister Beazley recommending changes was written on the day after Tourang's bid was announced.

9. Kennedy told the Print Media Inquiry: 'Nothing happens with Kerry without difficulty, but we got through it. There were some aspects of it that he was not happy about, but in the final analysis we parted on good terms.' *House of Representatives Select Committee on the Print Media*, official *Hansard* report, 1 October 1991, pp 24–25.

10. The *Age*, 16 October 1991.

11. See Chapter 25 for coverage of pay TV.
12. *House of Representatives Select Committee on the Print Media*, official Hansard report, 4 November 1991, p 1160.
13. *Bulletin*, 19 November 1991, 'Silence of the lambs'.
14. NSW Supreme Court, Tourang v Kennedy, 21 February 1992.
15. Colleen Ryan and Glen Burge, *Corporate Cannibals: The Taking of Fairfax*, Heinemann, 1992, p 356.

TWENTY-FOUR: TIDYING UP

1. *Australian Business Monthly*, April 1992.
2. The sale of Valassis was accompanied by a note issue in which Valassis took on US$460 million in new debt. This allowed the company to pay large dividends to the Packer company that owned it: Conpress Investments BV. Conpress Investments BV reported an *after-tax* profit in 1991–92 of $1272 million for Packer's Consolidated Press Holdings Group.
3. *Fortune*'s estimates were US$2300 million and US$1400 million respectively. The figures in the text are arrived at after conversion at A$ = US$0.70.
4. In the 1980s the banks were prepared to lend on a non-recourse basis, whereby they effectively assumed a large amount of the risk. One could borrow the best part of $1000 million to take over a $1000-million company, but the banks would have no recourse to one's other assets if the loan couldn't be repaid. Thus the risk could be quarantined from existing businesses.
5. Critchley & Critchley, *Dyslexia Defined*, 1978, pp 10–15, p 149. Dyslexia is five times less common in women than men. It can get better with age and early treatment and is generally agreed to be hereditary.
6. Blofeld, Henry, *The Packer Affair*, 1978.
7. *Australian Business Monthly*, April 1992.
8. 91 million of the 171 million shares were options to purchase at a future date. Packer rolled them over the first time they came due for renewal and then converted them to shares in late April 1993.
9. *Financial Review*, 15 February 1993.
10. Based on the accounts of Consolidated Press 1990–91 and

1990–92, Dunlap was entitled to at least $25 million. Some reports suggested he received nearer $40 million.

11. When Kerry Packer died in December 2005, Wetspac shares had risen even further to $23.50 and the bank was worth around $45 billion.

TWENTY-FIVE: PRETTY POLLIES

1. *A Current Affair*, 23 October 1991.

2. Just how close Graham Richardson was to Packer is a matter of conjecture. Richardson said that they lunched together regularly and talked often on the telephone, and Richardson and Peter Barron were rarely out of touch. Richardson was certainly close enough to Packer to be protective about the man. When I asked him to be interviewed for this book he said that he didn't think he would. When asked why, he said he never talked about his friends without their permission, and he didn't think Kerry would like it. Not long afterwards a message filtered back from Richardson that he had consulted Kerry Packer who did *not* like the idea and Richardson would therefore not be talking to me.

3. This was the new B2 satellite to be launched in late 1992 by Optus. Essentially, Optus had been prepared to pay for the right to carry both pay TV and telephone signals.

4. *Exposure Draft, Broadcasting Services Bill 1992, Section 28 (2)* (published 7 November 1991) prevented the ABA allocating more than three commercial television broadcasting licences in any licence area before 1 July 1997 or such earlier date as the minister specified. The explanatory memorandum said, 'The specification of a date is intended to put the industry on notice that the time frame of the current commercial television oligopoly is finite.'

5. *Exposure Draft, Broadcasting Services Bill 1992, Explanatory Papers*, p 28 says: 'Other technologies for the provision of subscription broadcasting services, such as microwave (MDS) and cable, will be permitted ... Allowing their use will enable other technologies to emerge as delivery mechanisms over time.' It is made clear that they will receive subscription broadcasting licences. This

memorandum was supplied to prospective bidders for the satellite pay TV service in January 1992.

6. Channel Nine, *Sunday*, 31 May 1992.

7. McDonnell Research paper, cited by Fred Brenchley in the *Sydney Morning Herald*, 15 April 1993.

8. The offer was actually made to a businessman who intended to back Cosser, and who then relayed the terms to Cosser.

9. Collins directed the ABA not to issue subscription TV licences to MDS operators until the satellite licences had been awarded and the digital standard for satellite TV set, or until a cable pay TV service was in position to operate, whichever was earlier. Tenders for the two four-channel satellite licences closed at the end of April 1993. It was not clear when a digital standard would be set, but it presumably involved finding technology that would definitely work.

10. *Sun-Herald*, 7 February 1993.

11. *Australian*, 8 February 1993.

12. Channel Ten, *Hinch*, 22 February 1992.

13. *Financial Review*, 1 March 1993.

14. *Financial Review*, 19 February 1993.

15. Channel Nine, *Sunday*, 31 May 1992.

16. Statement from Prime Minister's office, 3 June 1992.

17. ABC Radio, *PM*, 3 June 1992.

18. Neilsen Media Research survey of 1000 households in Sydney and Melbourne, conducted between 1 March and 3 March 1993 found that four out of ten people interviewed knew of the decision to scupper MDS. Seven out of ten of those thought the decision had not been made in the best interests of the Australian people. The same seven out of ten then said they thought it was made in the interests of a particular organisation or individual. The survey was commissioned by Steve Cosser's Australis Media.

19. *Sydney Morning Herald*, 29 January 1993.

20. *Australian*, 29 January 1993.

21. *Financial Review*, 29 January 1993.

22. *Financial Review*, Stephen Mills, Christine Wallace, 19 March 1993.

BIBLIOGRAPHY

Baume, Eric, *I Lived These Years*, George G. Harrap, London, 1941.

Blaikie, George, *Remember Smith's Weekly*, Rigby, Adelaide, 1966.

Blofeld, Henry, *The Packer Affair*, Collins, London, 1978.

Brennan, Niall, *John Wren: Gambler*, Hill of Content, Melbourne, 1971.

Burge, Glenn & Ryan, Colleen, *Corporate Cannibals: The Taking of Fairfax*, Heinemann, Melbourne, 1992.

Buttrose, Ita, *Early Edition: My First Forty Years*, Macmillan, Melbourne, 1983.

Chadwick, Paul, *Media Mates: Carving Up Australia's Media*, Macmillan, Melbourne, 1989.

Critchley, I. & Critchley, M., *Dyslexia Defined*, Heinemann Medical, London, 1978.

Cumming, Fia, *Mates*, Allen & Unwin, Sydney, 1991.

Dale, Brian, *Ascent to Power*, Allen & Unwin, Sydney, 1985.

Fairfax, James, *My Regards to Broadway*, Angus & Robertson, Sydney, 1991.

Forsyth, Christopher, *The Great Cricket Hijack*, Wide-scope, Melbourne, 1978.

Freudenberg, G., *A Certain Grandeur*, Sun Books, Melbourne, 1978.

Harding, Professor Richard, *Outside Interference*, Sun Books, Melbourne, 1979.

Hardy, Frank, *Power Without Glory*, Lloyd O'Neil, Melbourne, 1950.

Hickie, David, *The Prince and the Premier*, Angus & Robertson, Sydney, 1985.

BIBLIOGRAPHY

Horne, Donald, *Confessions of a New Boy*, Viking Press, Melbourne, 1985.

Horne, Donald, *Money Made Us*, Penguin Books, Melbourne, 1976.

Horne, Donald, *Portrait of an Optimist*, Penguin Books, Melbourne, 1988.

Horne, Donald, *The Education of Young Donald*, Angus & Robertson, Sydney, 1967.

Howson, Peter (Don Aitkin *ed*) *The Howson Diaries: The Life of Politics*, Viking Press, Melbourne, 1984.

King, Cecil, *Strictly Personal*, Weidenfeld & Nicolson, London, 1969.

Lane, Terry, *As the Twig is Bent*, Dove Communications, Melbourne, 1979.

Mayer, Henry, *The Press in Australia*, Landsdowne Press, Melbourne, 1964.

McKay, Claude, *This Is the Life*, Angus & Robertson, Sydney, 1961.

McKie, Ronald, *We Have No Dreaming*, Imprint, Sydney, 1988.

McKinlay, Brian, *A Century of Struggle*, Collins Dove, Melbourne, 1988.

McNicoll, David, *Luck's a Fortune*, Wildcat Press, Sydney, 1979.

Munster, George, *Rupert Murdoch: A Paper Prince*, Viking Press, Melbourne, 1985.

Oakes, Laurie & Solomon, David, *The Making of an Australian Prime Minister*, Cheshire, Melbourne, 1973.

O'Brien, Denis, *The Weekly*, Penguin Books, Sydney, 1982.

Robertson, Geoffrey, *Hypotheticals—A New Collection*, ABC Books, Sydney, 1991.

Rolfe, Patricia, *The Journalistic Javelin: An Illustrated History of the Bulletin*, Wildcat Press, Sydney, 1979.

Shawcross, William, *Rupert Murdoch*, Random House, Sydney, 1992.

Singleton, John, *True Confessions*, Cassell Australia, Sydney, 1979.

Souter, Gavin, *Company of Heralds*, Melbourne University Press, Melbourne, 1981.

Steketee, Mike & Cockburn, Milton, *Wran: An Unauthorised Biography*, Allen & Unwin, Sydney, 1986.

Walker, R. B., *Yesterday's News*, Sydney University Press, Sydney, 1980.

Whitington, R. S., *Sir Frank: The Frank Packer Story*, Cassell Australia, Melbourne, 1971.

Windschuttle, Keith, *The Media*, Penguin Books, Melbourne, 1984.

Young, Irwin, *Theodore: His Life and Times*, Alpha Books, Melbourne, 1971.

PHOTOGRAPHIC
ACKNOWLEDGEMENTS

Section 1
Page 1 Fairfax Photos
Page 2 Gilmour/Fairfax Photos
Page 3 ABC TV
Page 4 above: Newspix
    below: ABC TV
Page 5 Newspix
Page 7 above, right: Brannan/Fairfax Photos
    below, right: T. Golding/Fairfax Photos
Page 8 Linsen/Fairfax Photos

Section 2
Page 1 Newspix
Page 2 Newspix
Page 3 Newspix
Page 4 ABC TV
Page 5 ABC TV
Page 6 above: Andrew Taylor/Fairfax Photos
    below: ABC TV
Page 7 Porter/Fairfax Photos
Page 8 Fairfax Photos

Section 3
Page 1 ABC TV
Page 2 above: Renee Nowytarger/Fairfax Photos
    Below: ABC TV
Page 3 above: Fairfax Photos
    below: ABC TV

Page 4 ABC TV
Page 5 ABC TV
Page 6 above: Michele Mossop/Fairfax Photos
  below: ABC TV
Page 7 ABC TV
Page 8 Craig Golding/Fairfax Photos

Section 4

Page 1 A. Davidson/Alpha
Page 2 Peter Morris/Fairfax Photos
Page 3 Peter Morris/Fairfax Photos
Page 4 left: Peter Ramshaw/Newspix
  right: Rick Stevens/Fairfax Photos
Page 5 Fairfax Photos
Page 8 Newspix

ACKNOWLEDGEMENTS

There are several people without whose help this book would never have been written, but the most important is Natalie Young, who left the security of one of Sydney's leading legal firms to be my researcher. For her courage, incredible work rate and general brilliance, I thank her. I also owe special thanks to Kate Owen, Adelaide Beavis and Janet Heywood at the ABC TV Library, who gave me support, encouragement and lemon tea while answering a thousand queries with unfailing good humour. Thanks, also, to Marjorie Wearne at the ABC Reference Library who dug deep into the realms of history on my behalf, to the Archives of Business and Labour at the Australian National University in Canberra and to Rebecca Gorman, who did useful research before joining ABC Radio.

Several hundred people shared their memories of working for the Packers and of meeting or doing business with them over the years. Many were happy to be named, many more helped on the condition that they remained anonymous; they will all know who they are when I say that their contribution was invaluable. Others helped unknowingly by writing books about the Packers and the Australian media over the years. I would particularly like to acknowledge the contributions of Glenn Burge, Ita Buttrose, Paul Chadwick, Milton Cockburn, Chris Forsyth, Donald Horne, Kieran Kelly, Terry Lane, David McNicoll, Colleen Ryan, John Singleton, Gavin Souter, Mike Steketee, R. B. Walker and R. S. Whitington, whose published work I have drawn upon extensively. I am also eternally grateful to Nigel Austin, Wendy Bacon, Fred Brenchley, Tom Burton, Ali Cromie, Janet Hawley,

David Hickie, Tess Lawrence, Adrian McGregor, David Marr, Robert Milliken, Michael Parkinson, Jefferson Penberthy, Max Presnell, Keith Robbins, Bruce Stannard, Trevor Sykes, Rodney Tiffen, Brian Toohey, Bill Whittaker, Marian Wilkinson and any others whose work I have plundered. I hope that I have done them justice in fitting it into a wider picture.

Thanks are due to everybody at *Four Corners*, but particularly to Chris Alderton, Harley, Des Horn, David McKnight, Rosemary Meares, Debra Prince and Debbie Whitmont with whom I made 'Citizen Packer' in September 1991, and to Alec Cullen and Ann Connor who captured some of the pictures from that program for the book. Also to Ian Carroll, Anna Cater, Ross Coulthart, Kate Hodges, Carol Marsh, Chris Masters and Margot Saville who all helped in one way or another. Thanks, too, to Kate Reid and Richard Smart at ABC Books, and everyone at Transworld who made the original version of this book such a success in 1993, but especially to Maggie Hamilton, Jacqueline Kent, Katie Stackhouse and Marie-Louise Taylor. Most of all, I want to thank Judith Curr and Geoff Rumpf for having the courage to publish that edition in the face of considerable legal threats. Thanks, also, to Michael Sexton and Judith Walker for their valuable comments and legal advice which made the aftermath so much easier than it might have been.

I also want to thank everybody at Random House responsible for this updated and expanded edition, *The Rise and Rise of Kerry Packer Uncut*. In particular, I want to thank my wonderful editors Jessica Dettmann and Vanessa Mickan and my longsuffering and cheerful publisher, Fiona Henderson, who nurtured me through this process. Thanks also to Tim Whiting, her successor, and to Margie Seale for her enthusiasm and generous support.

Last but not least, I want to thank my family, who encouraged me, supported me and put up with my literary obsessions for eighteen months back in 1992–1993. I suspect it is harder to live with a writer than to be one. It is scant reward, but this book is dedicated to them.

INDEX

ABOUT THE AUTHOR

Born and educated in England, award-winning investigative reporter and bestselling author Paul Barry studied Politics, Philosophy and Economics at Oxford University. A journalist with the BBC for ten years, he came to Australia in 1987 to work for the ABC's 'Four Corners', where one of his hardest-hitting reports was on multi-millionaire Alan Bond. This led to his first bestseller, *The Rise and Fall of Alan Bond*.

Since then, his books have dominated the bestseller list. His second book, *The Rise and Rise of Kerry Packer*, was the top-selling biography of the 1990s. He followed up with *Going For Broke*, the story of how Alan Bond hid his fortune, and then revealed how the Packers and Murdochs lost $950m in One.Tel in *Rich Kids*. His most recent book was *Spun Out*, an unflinching biography of cricket legend Shane Warne.

Paul Barry's work as a journalist has won numerous awards, including a Walkley in 2001 for an exposé on tax-dodging barristers. He is a former host of the ABC's 'Media Watch' and Channel 7's 'Witness'. He has also reported for Channel 9's 'A Current Affair' and '60 Minutes', written for the *Sydney Morning Herald* and presented Breakfast on Radio National.